INTERCULTURAL JOURNEYS THROUGH READING AND WRITING

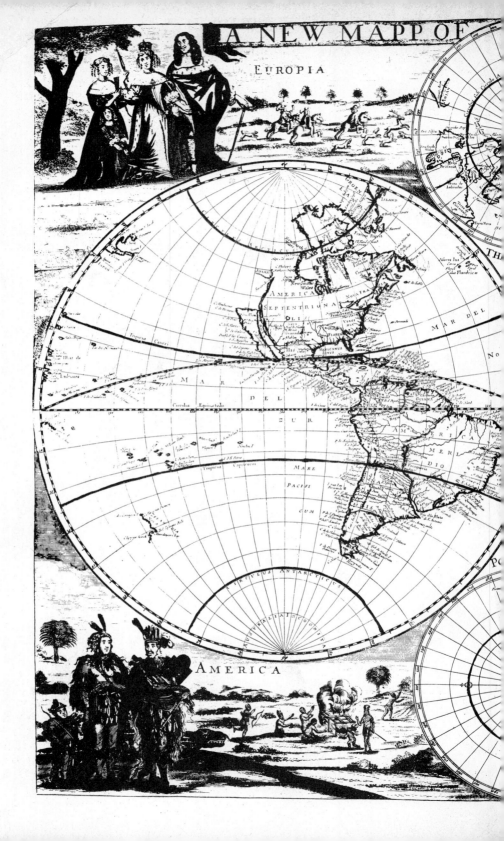

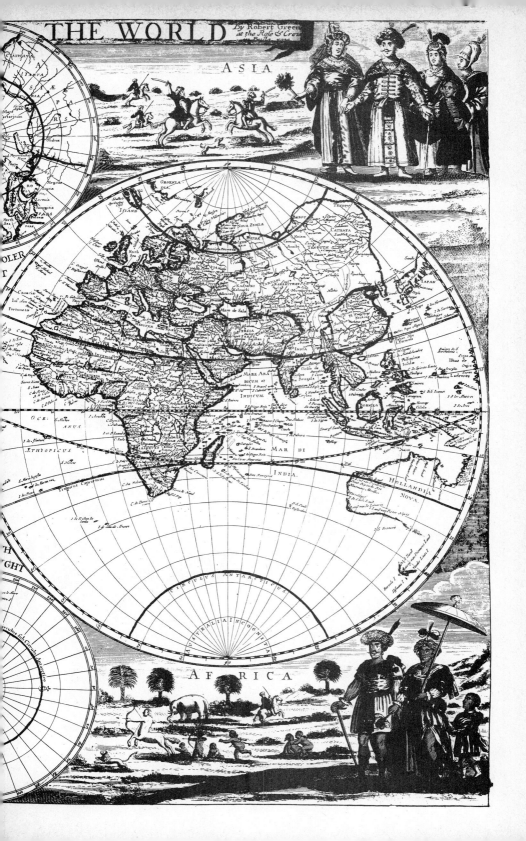

INTERCULTURAL JOURNEYS THROUGH READING AND WRITING

Marilyn Smith Layton

NORTH SEATTLE COMMUNITY COLLEGE

HarperCollins*Publishers*

Sponsoring Editor: Lucy Rosendahl/Patricia Rossi
Project Editor: Karen Trost
Art Direction: Kathie Vaccaro
Text and Cover Design: Levavi & Levavi
Cover Photo: "Discovery at Dal Lake, Kashmir," by Marilyn Smith Layton
Production Administrator: Paula Keller
Compositor: ComCom Division of Haddon Craftsmen, Inc.
Printer and Binder: R. R. Donnelley & Sons Company
Cover Printer: The Lehigh Press, Inc.

Intercultural Journeys Through Reading and Writing

Copyright © 1991 by Marilyn Smith Layton

Frontmatter map: Map of the world c. 1700 from *Thornton's Atlas.* Courtesy of the Map Division, New York Public Library.

Library of Congress Cataloging-in-Publication Data

Smith Layton, Marilyn, 1941–
    Intercultural journeys through reading and writing/Marilyn Smith
Layton.
       p. cm.
    ISBN 0-06-046437-2 (student edition)
    ISBN 0-06-046333-3 (teacher edition)
    1. College readers. 2. English language—Rhetoric. I. Title.
PE1417.L39 1990
808'.0427—dc20   90-31890
                                                   CIP

90 91 92 93 9 8 7 6 5 4 3 2 1

To my students,
fellow travelers
and teachers

F M
16 / 32

CONTENTS

Preface   xix
Acknowledgments   xxi
To Readers   xxiii

**1 THE CHALLENGES OF INTERCULTURAL
EXPERIENCE**   **1**

W. P. Kinsella, "The Moccasin Telegraph"   **3**
*A Canadian Cree Indian murders a white man and is
then killed by the RCMP; a massive response takes
place among the Indians and the whites demand to
know how they communicated so widely and so
quickly.*

Joanne Brown, "Scoshi"   **11**
*A grant creating an exchange between college
teachers from Iowa and Japan has great promise for
both schools until specific intercultural and
interpersonal differences confuse both host and
visitor.*

F
Jap

Solon T. Kimball, "Learning a New Culture"   **25**
*An American anthropologist on his first field work
assignment discovers what it means to become a real
part of the small Irish village in which he is living.*

M

**Paul Bowles, "You Have Left Your Lotus Pods on the
Bus"**   **36**
*An encounter in Thailand between two Americans
and three Buddhist monks shows us how even the
smallest details in a culture can confuse outsiders.*

Thai M

H. Jathar Salij, "A Weekend in Bandung"   44

*An American is spending a fantasy weekend in this
vacation spot in Java, Indonesia; his experiences,
however, impinge on his dreams.*

Ruth Prawer Jhabvala, "Myself in India"   53

*Having married an Indian man and raised her
children in New Delhi, this German-born writer
explains the difficulties she faces in living
permanently in another culture, especially one as
different as India's.*

Zora Neale Hurston, "How It Feels to Be Colored
    Me"   61

*Hurston delivers on the promise of her title in
re-creating her own discovery of being colored, and
concludes by explaining her theory on the "Great
Stuffer of Bags."*

Jawaharlal Nehru, "What Is Culture?"   66

*India's first prime minister probes the problems of
defining culture, showing us that long immersion in
thinking about this question does not produce firm
answers.*

2 PATTERNS, HABITS, AND VALUES OF CULTURE   72

Robert Levine, with Ellen Wolff, "Social Time: The
    Heartbeat of Culture"   75

*Our attitudes toward time are learned and deeply
embedded in the patterns of our lives; when we cross
cultures, we encounter the problems that new
patterns of time can cause if we have no
understanding of them.*

Janette Turner Hospital, "Waiting"   82

*An Indian man and an American woman spend the
same two days waiting to be helped in an Air India
office with vastly divergent responses; the clerk there
responds to them with his own motivations.*

Henry C. Binford, "I Scream, You Scream . . . The
    Cultural Significance of Ice Cream"   91

*Ice cream as a cultural phenomenon can be traced to
the history of industrialization in the United States,
the emerging concept of leisure, and the people's
need for a reputable place to relax.*

Carol Simons, "Kyoiku Mamas"   99   F
*Devoted kyoiku or "education" mamas produce some
of the world's best students, at the same time that the
mothers earn high regard for themselves in carrying
out Japan's demanding cultural expectations of
women.*

William D. Montalbano, "Latin America: A Quixotic
  Land Where the Bizarre Is Routine"   107   M
*For reporter Montalbano, a collection of true reports
from Latin America suddenly added up one day to
this essay, reflecting the surreal nature of real life
there.*

Octavio Paz, "The Day of the Dead"   111   M
*In a land where festivals are vital to the people, the
festival of the Day of the Dead provides an event for
probing the patterns and paradoxes of Mexican
culture and character.*

Nawal el-Saadawi, "Love and Sex in the Life of the
  Arab"   123
*Debunking the sexual intrigues in A Thousand and
One Nights, psychiatrist el-Saadawi traces the
influence of Moslem beliefs and harsh desert life on
love and sex in Arab life over the last several
hundred years.*

3 CULTURE AND LANGUAGE, BODY LANGUAGE, AND PERCEPTION 142

Peter Farb, "Man at the Mercy of Language"   145   M
*The history of thought about the relationship
between language and culture is explored in this
essay through explanations of what some of the
best-known thinkers have discovered in their studies
and work.*

Gordon W. Allport, "Linguistic Factors in Prejudice"   161   M
*In classifying and categorizing people, we risk seeing
them in one category only—what Allport calls a
"label of primary potency"—becoming blind to the
"living, breathing, complex individual."*

Richard Rodriguez, "Memories of a Bilingual
  Childhood"   171 proM
*Rodriguez explores the experiences of his past—what
he lost and what he gained in the trade of one*

language, English, for the other, Spanish—and
builds a case against bilingual education.

Shirley Lauro, "Open Admissions"   185
In this one-act play, an overworked speech teacher
only hears the "mistakes" in the speech of a young
black man from her class, in a late-afternoon
encounter.

Phyllis I. Lyons, "Translating Cultures . . . Or,
What's George Washington Doing in a Sushi Bar?"   196
A story from Japan, "The Garden," illustrates the
complex problems a translator faces, not only in the
language of a story but in its historic, aesthetic, and
psychological values and patterns as well.

Edward T. Hall and Mildred Reed Hall, "The Sounds
of Silence"   207
We are often not conscious of the nonverbal messages
we convey through our bodies and our eyes within
our own culture; when we move across cultures, we
must also learn a new set of nonverbal messages.

Gregory Bateson, "Why Do Frenchmen?"   219
A father listens and responds to his daughter's
queries concerning why Frenchmen use such funny
gestures when they talk to each other.

Sabine Ulibarrí, "The Stuffing of the Lord"   225
Father Benito's mangled pronunciation of Spanish
endears him to the people of Tierra Amarilla in New
Mexico, even as he helps a young boy grow up.

4   ENCOUNTERING AMERICAN PATTERNS OF
CULTURE   232

Horace M. Miner, "Body Ritual Among the
Nacirema"   235
The story of a group of North Americans called the
Nacirema, who fascinate the observer because of their
obsession about certain parts of the body and other
strange patterns in their lives.

Rimma Kazakova, "America of the People"   241
A woman from Moscow describes her first experience
in the United States in a joint Soviet/American cruise
down the Mississippi River.

Tahira Naqvi, "Paths upon Water"   246
*While visiting her son and his friends in the United
States for the first time, a Pakistani mother is
overwhelmed by American patterns of dress at the
beach, particularly by the body-exposing bikini.*

Pak F

Anne Tyler, "Your Place Is Empty"   257   *W F*
*An Iranian mother comes to the United States for the
first time to visit her son and his blonde, American
wife; a son whom she has not seen in more than a
decade and a wife she has not met before.*

Carlos Bulosan, "Be American"   274   *Philip M*
*Bulosan's cousin Consorcio arrives on a boat in San
Francisco, an illiterate peasant from the plains of
Luzon in the Philippines, wanting to be American;
this story recounts the struggle of his
Americanization.*

Bharati Mukherjee, "A Father"   281   *I F*
*A Hindu family from India has worked hard to
adjust to their new lives and culture in the United
States, but no preparation could have helped them
with the problem their daughter brings home.*

Spencer Sherman, "The Hmong in America"   291 *Ch / M*
*The Hmong, tribal mountain dwellers with strong
clan loyalties from Laos, must accommodate their
patterns of life to crowded city conditions as a result
of the devastation of their country during the
Vietnam War.*

Ishmael Reed, "America: The Multinational Society"   301
*Evidence that our society is a "cultural bouillabaisse"
suggests the dangers of thinking and behaving as if
we were a monocultural country.*

B K M

5   **CULTURAL EXCHANGES IN STUDY AND WORK**   **306**

**Raquel Puig Zaldívar, "Nothing in Our Hands but
Age"**   309   *M*
*Two older Cuban immigrants stand out in their class
at a community college in Florida as they prepare
themselves for life in the United States and the time
when their daughter, jailed in Cuba, will join
them.*

Yearn Hong Choi, "Bloomington, Fall 1971"   319
*A Korean student falls in love unexpectedly with
another Korean, but when he writes his devoted
mother in Korea, he is told the match is
unacceptable.*

James R. Corey, "Cultural Shock in Reverse"   329
*Graduate students, returning to Saudi Arabia after
extended study in the United States, reflect the
problems of cultural reentry when their desire to
change their country is treated with contempt.*

William E. Barrett, "Señor Payroll"   334
*Management and Mexican-American workers
complicate each other's lives while the company fails
to understand the motivation behind its employees'
actions.*

Lawrence Stessin, "Culture Shock and the American
   Businessman Overseas"   339
*American businessmen and women encounter
problems overseas when they do not first learn about
the cultural patterns and assumptions of the people
with whom they want to do business.*

Similih M. Cordor, "A Farewell to the Old Order"   350
*A man in Liberia who has risen through connections
to a high government job in Monrovia finds that his
two country wives are unacceptable to the people
with whom he now works.*

David Halberstam, "How Datsun Discovered
   America"   365
*In the style of new journalism, Halberstam tells the
story of Yutaka Katayama, the man from Nissan in
Japan who established Datsun in the United States
and for his success was replaced and recalled to
Japan.*

6 MATTERS OF LOVE AND FAMILY   382

Juanita Platero and Siyowin Miller, "Chee's
   Daughter"   385
*A young Navajo husband who has just lost his wife
discovers that he has also lost his baby daughter to
his wife's parents, who come to claim the child under
Indian custom and law.*

Julio Cortázar, "The Health of the Sick"   396
*A family in Argentina goes to great and amusing
lengths to spare their ill mother the news that her
son has died.*

Aharon Megged, "The Name"   409
*Grandfather Zisskind comes alive at the opportunity
of having his pregnant granddaughter name her
unborn child in Israel by the name of his grandson
Mendele, who perished in the concentration camps.*

Zhang Jie, "Love Must Not Be Forgotten"   421
*Considering marriage to a man she doubts her own
love for, a daughter in China discovers, at the time
of her mother's death, the story of her mother's
unconsummated love for a man she'd known but
couldn't marry.*

Ann Petry, "Solo on the Drums"   432
*His name, flashing on the billboard, has no joy for
Kid Jones the day his wife tells him she is leaving;
he beats his grief out on his drums nonetheless, and
words and music blend together in his pain.*

V. Goryushkin, "Before Sunrise"   437
*A Russian man, limbless and mute as a result of
duty in the war, discovers by accident his wife's real
feelings for him.*

Gabriel García Márquez, "Big Mama's Funeral"   444
*The end of an era and a legend, Big Mama dies
amidst all the wild splendor and crazy celebrations
that her home of Macondo in Colombia can muster
for her passing.*

Linda Hogan, "Making Do"   456
*Her Chickasaw Indian family tries to salve the pain
of Roberta's losing her children, but she has to put
her life together her own way; this is her story of
making do.*

**7 DEPARTURES, JOURNEYS, AND (SOMETIMES)
RETURNS**   464

My Van Vu, "The Village We Left Behind"   467
*Vu re-creates the quiet peace and ancient ways of his
family's village in Vietnam, its jealousies and
triumphs as he lived them before the war brought his
childhood and their life there to an end.*

Doris Lessing, "Sunrise on the Veld" *WF* 471
*A young boy, confident in his ability to control his
life to the last minute, discovers forces at work far
stronger than he on the veld of southern Africa.*

Jamaica Kincaid, "Poor Visitor" *CARF* 479
*Arriving from Antigua in New York, "Poor Visitor"
soon discovers that the home she was so happy to
leave does not look so bad, compared to her life now
as black governess in a blonde-headed family.*

Richard K. Nelson, "Tingiivik Tatqiq: The Moon *M*
   When Birds Fly South (September)" 485
*Kiluk returns to a life of struggle in her Eskimo
village after a long time away at school in an
Alaskan town, where she had learned to enjoy and
accept the English language and creature comforts.*

Graham Sheil, "The Picking Season" *M* 503
*A young Australian boy, fed up with home and
family, begins to reassess the family life he left in
Perth as a result of working with two Germans at a
vineyard during the picking season.*

Milan Kundera, "The Hitchhiking Game" *M* 515
*A young Czechoslovakian couple on a two-week,
tightly scheduled vacation suddenly launch into a
game that takes them on a journey quite different
than the one they had planned.*

Massud Farzan, "The Plane Reservation" *IrM* 530
*A son returns unannounced to see his parents in his
home of Iran after a long time in the United States
and finds that not much has changed except himself.*

N. Scott Momaday, "Grandmother's Country" *NA M* 536
*Momaday returns to the knoll on Rainy Mountain to
see again the place where his grandmother had lived
and died among her Kiowa Indian people.*

8 DEFINING OURSELVES AND OTHERS 542

Shelby Steele, "I'm Black, You're White, Who's
   Innocent?" *BKM* 545
*The elements of race, power, and innocence become
jumbled in an off-hand remark made by a black
engineer at a party that Steele attends; this essay
sorts out the relationship among these elements.*

Feng Jicai, "The Tall Woman and Her Short
  Husband"   558
*The lives of this couple in the People's Republic of
China are shattered by the cruelty of neighbors who
use political ploys to guess at the reason for the
couple's marriage and to disguise their own cruelty.*

Richard Rive, "The Bench"   567
*A black man in South Africa discovers his own
humanity when he listens to speakers at a rally in
Cape Town; he responds immediately to this new
definition of his life by taking action.*

Chinua Achebe, "An Image of Africa"   572
*Nigerian writer Achebe uses a classic of literature,
Heart of Darkness by Joseph Conrad, to argue the
power of Conrad's subtle racism and the damage
such literature can cause in understanding Africa
and its people.*

Norman Mailer, "A Country, Not a Scenario"   584
*Mailer sees beyond his former scenario of the Soviet
Union when he goes there as a visitor, discovering a
country that is in many ways ironically similar to
the United States.*

Premchand, "A Coward"   595
*Meeting at a university, a young man and woman
attempt to override the controls of India's rigid caste
system that would forbid their relationship and
marriage.*

Tewfiq al-Hakim, "Not a Thing Out of Place"   604
*Let the man in European dress beware as he wanders
into this absurd world created by Egyptian
playwright al-Hakim; dangers await him there. The
question is, as always, who is defining what is sane?*

Dean Barnlund, "Communication in a Global Village" 615
*As technological forces reduce our world to a "global
village," where diverse and vastly different cultures
become our neighbors, the need for intercultural
understanding and communication becomes urgent.*

Rhetorical Table of Contents   627
Credits   631
Index of Authors and Titles   637

PREFACE

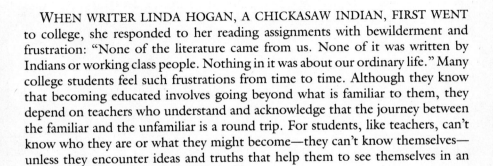

WHEN WRITER LINDA HOGAN, A CHICKASAW INDIAN, FIRST WENT to college, she responded to her reading assignments with bewilderment and frustration: "None of the literature came from us. None of it was written by Indians or working class people. Nothing in it was about our ordinary life." Many college students feel such frustrations from time to time. Although they know that becoming educated involves going beyond what is familiar to them, they depend on teachers who understand and acknowledge that the journey between the familiar and the unfamiliar is a round trip. For students, like teachers, can't know who they are or what they might become—they can't know themselves—unless they encounter ideas and truths that help them to see themselves in an expanding world.

This book accordingly maps many intercultural journeys by moving among nations, regions, times, genders, and classes toward a common destination. My goal has been to enable students to know themselves better by recognizing the possibilities of community that follow from acknowledgment, exploration, and celebration of differences.

The book's 62 reading selections have been chosen for their engaging ideas, their excellence of expression, and the ways in which they might inspire readers from many backgrounds to hear the full range of voices in an intercultural conversation. These selections find their origins and settings in many places. The writers represent 25 nations outside the United States, as well as writers from a wide variety of cultural groups and geographical areas within this country. Selections range from easy but thoughtful to complex and challenging. Essays, short fiction, and two plays explore human experience from a variety of rhetorical perspectives.

Because tomorrow's literature will be written by the students in classes now, I introduce the readings by exploring both the writers' lives and their insights about writing. The assignments in this book can help students reflect upon their own experiences through the perspectives they gain as readers: writing as self-discovery and writing as intellectual or critical discovery. "Before You Read" writing assignments preceding each selection suggest topics and questions that parallel the author's exploration in the reading that follows. These assignments can be used both as fast writing exercises and as the bases for more formal papers. The "Questions for Discussion and Writing" that follow each selection ask readers to interpret, analyze, and evaluate the critical issues and languages of the reading.

An annotated table of contents encourages students to read beyond the selections assigned. An alternate table of contents in the back of the book organizes the selections in the anthology by rhetorical mode. A brief introduction of the theme and an overview of connections among the selections begins each chapter.

The Instructor's Manual provides strategies and resources for teaching reading and writing. A sequence of writing assignments for use over the course of a term proceeds from personal to academic discourse. One section offers assignments that ask students to write about two or more sources from the anthology. Another section on topics for investigation offers instructors ways to use the anthology to guide students in researching subjects that emerge from the reading; and a section on collaborative writing assignments requires small groups to think, explore, and write together.

Many of these assignments have been tested in a variety of reading and writing classes. One student's words typify the responses that students have had to their experiences with some of the reading and writing assignments included in *Intercultural Journeys:* "All the learning this term—about people, about the world, about myself, about writing—it's changed me. I view the world differently than I did before class. I feel a connection now to people I would have rejected because they were different from me. In the process I've discovered my own voice."

Acknowledgments

My gratitude is great to those who, in ways small and large, helped me complete this book:

To Lucy Rosendahl, my former sponsoring editor at HarperCollins, whose clear faith in this project motivated me from the start, and whose clarity and guidance along the way kept me moving; to Karen Trost, project editor, who has seen the book through production with remarkable speed and competence;

To Jeff Parr, former Harper & Row representative in the Pacific Northwest, who appeared like magic in my office in March 1988 to suggest and shepherd the project that Lucy had in mind;

To the reviewers who, along the way of its creation, gave me critical suggestions and helped me to define it ever more clearly: Evelyn Ashton-Jones, University of Tampa; Bonne August, Kingsborough Community College (CUNY); Ian Cruickshank, St. Louis Community College; Toni Empringham, El Camino College; Jeanne Gunner, University of California at Los Angeles; Sharon Hockensmith, University of Texas at San Antonio; Carolina Hospital, Miami Dade Community College; Karen Houch, Bellevue Community College; James King, Hillsdale College; Kate Mangelsdorf, University of Arizona; Bradford Mudge, University of Colorado at Denver; Francis Paz, State University of New York at New Paltz; Betty Jo Hicks Peters, Morehead State University; William Roba, Scott Community College; Carol Schilling, University of Pennsylvania; Barry Seiler, Rutgers University at Newark; David Shimkin, Queensborough Community College (CUNY); Margot Soven, La Salle University; Gary Vaughn, University of Cincinnati; and Ray Wallace, University of Tennessee at Knoxville;

To Allison Phillips and Mark Paluch at HarperCollins, who graciously helped me to pursue the grueling task of permissions for the book;

To Bill Coles, Jr., University of Pittsburgh, who encouraged me to believe I was ready for the challenge, and shared with me a number of helpful ideas toward its approach;

To Professors James Sledd and Dean Barnlund, mentors whose ideas about language and communication have, for over three decades, continued to teach and inspire me;

To my colleagues at North Seattle Community College, whose straight talk and commitment to teaching have kept me motivated for more than twenty years;

To our Humanities Division faculty secretary Betty Gibson and Chair Paul McCarthy, whose constant support kept me at work, both on the book and in the classroom;

To the students at North Seattle who encouraged this project, contributed ideas toward its selections, and were willing to test assignments in their writing; and to the students who, for two decades, have been bringing their worlds into my classroom, enticing me to travel to places, both local and global, I would never have explored without their influence;

To the writers in this book for their contributions, their enthusiasm, and their ideas about the writing process;

To the Kaneta family in Japan and the Ghanchi family in India, wonderful hosts who helped me to learn about their countries;

To Hobart Jarrett, Professor Emeritus of Brooklyn College, New York, and Doris Ginn, Professor of Linguistics, Jackson State University, Jackson, Mississippi, and her family, for sharing their experiences and insights with me;

To friends who have plied me for years with articles and books that they thought I'd find helpful and were;

To my children, Eleanor and Laurence Smith, their new spouses, my three inherited children, and their families—for their love, cheer, and long-distance support;

And to my husband, Richard Layton, also reader and critic, who has shared the work and the worlds in this book with me in uncountable ways.

Marilyn Smith Layton

TO READERS

YOU ARE ABOUT TO TRAVEL THE WORLD. YOU WILL NOT NEED TO fasten your seat belts or suffer long flights to new lands, only to read the pages that follow. Wherever you choose to turn, you will be arriving in the lives of people whose cultures or countries you may know only by name, or not at all. Your contribution to this adventure will be to bring your own life experiences to these pages and the people in them. In that exchange you will discover the pleasures, challenges, and frustrations of intercultural experience.

Even if you have already traveled to the places from which these selections originate, you may not have gotten to know their people as closely as you'll know them through reading. Language barriers, patterns of relationships, indeed your presence itself, often prohibit access or so alter the setting that it changes completely. Through your roles as readers, you become what you often wish in life you could be—invisible—listening not to eavesdrop but to learn.

The goal of this book is to enlarge the circumference of the world you know, and to improve your abilities to read and write about it by experiencing and practicing the relationships between reading and writing in many different contexts and styles. Being able to read and write well are primary requirements for your expanding citizenship in a larger world.

Through the reading selections of this book, you will learn more about other people. Through knowing others we also come to know ourselves more fully. By placing ourselves outside our own culture we begin to learn about our deepest values, expectations, and attitudes. They are so interwoven in our lives that we often cannot acknowledge their presence—like our own faces that we know only through a mirror or a photograph.

These journeys will also support you in your quest to understand, prepare for, and profit from future intercultural experiences in travel, study, and work, both in this country and abroad. Many selections and assignments will also help you discover the diversity of cultures within your own classroom.

Although the selections often take you to new worlds, those worlds will be accessible to you. Expect differences among the patterns of habits and values in the array of cultures you'll step into, but read too for the human experiences that unite us.

As you read, the idea of culture will become clearer to you although, like all abstract words, it will never yield an easy or tidy definition. Culture is not necessarily tied to language, territory, or national boundaries. It has more to do with a mutual history, a shared set of assumptions and values, and a common sense of identity—of routines, rituals, and rules.

As travelers to other cultures, you will experience the stages of being foreign. You'll go from anticipating a destination to arriving there, from those early moments and days when you are an excited spectator to those experiences in which you participate more fully in the new culture. You'll suffer the phase of culture shock, when excitement wears off and you wonder what you're doing as a stranger in strange lands. You'll adapt to the shock, and when it's time to come home, you'll suffer culture reentry, when your familiar world seems strange.

The selections of this book provide all of these intercultural experiences. The word *Intercultural* in the title emphasizes the idea of contact and communication between members of contemporary cultures—interpersonal, informal, day-to-day relationships. Through your reading, discussion, and writing, you become involved with people living in this era.

Marilyn Smith Layton

INTERCULTURAL JOURNEYS THROUGH READING AND WRITING

Chapter **1**

THE CHALLENGES OF INTERCULTURAL EXPERIENCE

*O*ne of the handicaps of the twentieth century is that we still have the vaguest and most biased notions, not only of what makes Japan a nation of Japanese, but of what makes the United States a nation of Americans, France a nation of Frenchmen, and Russia a nation of Russians. Lacking this knowledge, each country misunderstands the other. We fear irreconcilable differences when the trouble is only between Tweedledum and Tweedledee, and we talk about common purposes when one nation by virtue of its whole experience and system of values has in mind a quite different course of action from the one we meant. We do not give ourselves a chance to find out what their habits and values are. If we did, we might discover that a course of action is not necessarily vicious because it is not the one we know.

RUTH BENEDICT from
THE CHRYSANTHEMUM AND THE SWORD

THE GLAMOUR THAT THE TRAVEL BUSINESS ASSOCIATES WITH JOURneys to exotic spots of the world does little to prepare the traveler for the challenges of intercultural experience. Being foreign, wherever and whoever we are, can become hard work. Arrive at a new place and our credentials as human beings can strike us as not much more than a list on paper we left in our life back home. All the old rules and assumptions are back home, too; and no guide can give us a set of new rules for the place at which we've arrived or equip us for knowing when we'll come upon the unwritten rules of culture by which we are expected to abide.

We are vulnerable and we feel it, yet there is also tremendous excitement in us for the potential to see and to learn. Separated from our "home selves," we

1

can look back and see ourselves, as the German poet Rilke said, "whole against the sky." Our senses are tightly tuned and we are ready to learn, to change, to be changed.

What one person or culture expects of another person or culture can be a lens that distorts and changes the object of our focus so that differences become exaggerated or distorted rather than understood. In this chapter, W. P. Kinsella's "The Moccasin Telegraph" and Joanne Brown's "Scoshi" give us insights into the distortions that expectations can create between groups and people from different cultures.

Even if we arrive well trained for observation, as the young anthropologist Solon Kimball was for his first field experience in Ireland in "Learning a New Culture," we realize that culture is only partially visible and conscious. We can't always decide the level at which we will participate in or join another culture. The smallest details about ourselves and others become curiosities. We suddenly become aware of a necktie or eating habits in a whole new way, as Paul Bowles's story, "You Have Left Your Lotus Pods on the Bus," suggests.

In "A Weekend in Bandung," H. Jathar Salij describes how Alan's expectations are foiled too, but in different ways. His eyes, fresh to the sights of Indonesia, have not developed selective blindness for the horrors of the country's poverty. Similarly, Ruth Prawer Jhabvala, a permanent resident of India, draws the shutters of her home, not her eyes, against India's poor. She explains in "Myself in India" the challenges she faces in living permanently in another culture.

In "How It Feels to Be Colored Me," Zora Neale Hurston writes about the very day, at age thirteen, that she became colored; after that she, too, began living in another culture in a school in Jacksonville, Florida, to which she was sent. Her essay suggests that intercultural challenges can take place within a person as well as between people.

India's first prime minister, Jawaharlal Nehru, takes on the challenge of defining the elusive yet omnipresent concept and influence of culture in "What Is Culture?" Although like other important abstract words, *culture* refuses to be neatly caught by definition, Nehru points us in the direction of the most important challenge of all: accepting differences between cultures without wrapping them in the judgments of the culture we know and believe in.

"View us, don't judge us," a guide urged a boatload of foreigners about to witness the throngs of bathers in the holy Ganges River in his city of Benares, India. As we embark on our own tour among cultures spanning the globe, both through the readings in this book and in our lives, these words are ones to remember, the biggest challenge to be met.

W. P. KINSELLA

The Moccasin Telegraph

W. P. Kinsella was born in Edmonton, Alberta, Canada, in 1935. A graduate of the University of Victoria with a B.A. in 1974, and the University of Iowa with an M.F.A. in 1978, he now lives in White Rock, British Columbia. Before becoming a full-time writer in 1983, Kinsella worked for more than two decades in an assortment of jobs: manager of the Retail Credit Company, account executive for the city of Edmonton, owner of Caesar's Italian Village Restaurant, and cabdriver in Victoria. From 1978 to 1983, he was an assistant professor of English at the University of Calgary.

Kinsella is best known for his writings on baseball, the game and its rituals. His two novels, Shoeless Joe *(1982) and* The Iowa Baseball Confederacy *(1986) (on which the 1989 movie "Field of Dreams" is based), both revolve around the sport. Kinsella has also written several volumes of stories about Canadian Indians, including* Scars *(1978),* Born Indian *(1981), and* The Moccasin Telegraph and Other Indian Tales *(1984), from which the following title story is taken. Canadian Indians claim that Kinsella captures their culture so authentically, "it is like he is one of our own."*

Before you read "The Moccasin Telegraph," write about a time in your life when, because you suspected or knew that someone had an attitude toward you that was inaccurate or unfair, you duped that person by playing on his or her expectations and appearing to confirm the judgment about you. Describe the situation, what happened as a result of it, and what the experience taught you.

There was heavy snow on the ground the night Burt Lameman did himself a murder up to Wetaskiwin. He'd been around the reserve in the afternoon and stole Robert Coyote's 22 rifle. They say he looked drunk and stoned when he walked into the 7–11 Store on 49th Ave. and shot the clerk. Clerk's name was Bobby something, a white kid with short hair who went to the high school and was saving his money to buy a fancy pair of skis. At least that's what the newspaper said.

Burt didn't say "This is a holdup," or anything like that. He just walked in and shot the clerk, reached over the counter and took $27 from the till, then staggered out into the dark. There were four or five people who seen him do it. He didn't make much of an attempt to get away, just walked a block or two to a small park, with some people following along, keeping him in sight. He kicked in the door to a skating-rink-shack and went inside. A few minutes later the RCMP come along and Burt take a couple of shots at them as they run up toward the shack. RCMP's don't take kindly to being shot at so they blast through the open door with shotguns, rifles and handguns. Burt he end up with enough bullets in him to kill maybe five or six Indians.

So far that seem like just a story of how a bad dude get blown away by the police, but it don't take long for it to turn into something else altogether.

Even around the reserve nobody like Burt very much. He was a bully, a thief, and a liar. That last day he'd drunk some home-brew and sniffed up some angel dust. "He'd swallow a doorknob if somebody told him it tasted good," is what my friend Frank Fence-post say about him.

When they have the funeral for the store clerk, none of us Indians go. White people are feeling ugly, and they look meaner than usual at us when we walking down the streets in Wetaskiwin.

Burt's funeral get held up 'cause there be no money to pay for it. His mother, Mrs. Bertha Lameman, don't have any, and his father been dead for a lot of years. Ordinarily, we'd take up a collection of some kind, but none of us have much sympathy for what Burt done.

Then the AIM people arrive in town. First I seen a couple of cars and a van with South Dakota license plates, and then I seen Gunner LaFramboise, the Alberta organizer for AIM, sitting with four or five cool looking dudes in the Travelodge cocktail lounge. These guys got shiny braids, hundred dollar black stetsons, and wear plastic Indian jewellery. AIM usually stand for American Indian Movement but most people around here call them Assholes In Moccasins. American Indian Movement act kind of like a religion who say everybody who don't believe in them is gonna go to hell. Gunner, when he see me, motion me over to his table. He introduce me to guys from Montana, Wyoming and someplace else, and say they are Crow, Cheyenne, and Blood.

"Week from today we gonna have a funeral for our murdered brother," say Gunner. "You fellows be sure and come and bring all your friends."

"I think you got it wrong," says Bedelia Coyote. "It was Burt who done a murder."

"Maybe," says Gunner with a sly smile. "It never been proved in court. But the RCMP shot him down in cold blood just because he was an Indian. Maybe Silas here," he say, pointing at me, "could write up a story for the newspaper."

"I don't write for newspapers," I say. "And if I did I'd write the truth."

"Wouldn't want you to write anything but the truth," say Gunner. "Sure somebody shot that guy in the store, but a poor Indian just happened to be walking by and he panicked and run when he seen all them people coming after him and then the RCMP executed him," and Gunner give us all a big, innocent smile.

In a day or two the streets of Wetaskiwin begin filling up with more Indians than I ever seen, even on treaty days. And most of them is strangers. There's about 4,000 Indians in the four bands that make up the Ermineskin Reserve, so there's lots of people from Hobbema that I don't know, but I can tell just by looking that most of the Indians walking the sidewalks and darkening the doorways of businesses is strangers. The weather has warmed up, which ain't usual for this part of Alberta in the winter. The air get soft and the streets and sidewalks covered in a black slush. And everywhere is strange and calm just like when the wind dies for a few seconds before a thunderstorm hits.

When I go into the Gold Nugget Cafe, where I work some Saturdays, Miss Goldie, the owner, put me right to work, say she is busier than a weekend even though it only Tuesday.

"People are so quiet," she say. "I know how to handle drunks and troublemakers, but all this silence frightens me."

If it scares Goldie, it scare the TV and radio guys too.

The murder get good play in the *Wetaskiwin Times* and on CFCW, the Camrose radio station, but hardly get a paragraph in the *Edmonton Journal*.

TV, radio, and newspapers always listen to people who yell loudest, so Gunner LaFramboise and his friends get a lot of time and space. Gunner take credit for all the people coming to town, but those arriving sure don't look like militants. They is just ordinary folks and lot of them bring along their kids and their campers.

The next night about 11 o'clock, everybody is in bed when I hear a car stop outside the cabin and lights blaze bright as the sun shine through the windows. When I open the door, with Ma, Sadie, and my brothers and sisters peeking out behind me, it is like the Northern Lights been squeezed together and pointed at the cabin.

"Are you Silas Ermineskin, the assistant medicine man?" a white voice say.

I tell them that I am.

"What's going on up in Wetaskiwin? Where are all the people coming from?" the voice say.

I shield my eyes from the light and by squinting real hard can see a guy with a camera on his shoulder, and two or three more people behind him aiming the lights at me. They've opened up the doors of a white van that say Canadian Broadcasting Corporation on the side.

"What is it you want to know?" I say. I'm sleepy and ain't thinking so good.

The voice says something about them coming here because I had some books printed up, and that somebody told them I'd make a good spokesman for my people. Then it repeats the question again.

"Bunch of folks come to a funeral," I say. I've learned by listening to Chief Tom how to not really answer a question.

"But there are more people arriving every hour. There are Indians from as far away as Sioux Lookout in Northern Ontario, some have come from the North-west Territories, Arizona, New Mexico, and Colorado, and from all over the Prairie Provinces too."

"No law against folks coming to a funeral," I say. I wish Mad Etta was here.

About this time my friend Frank Fence-post push through the crowd and stand beside me. Frank he ain't afraid of nobody and likes to talk about things he don't know nothing about. He would make a good reporter but a better politician.

"I'm his manager," Frank says, pointing at me. And pretty soon I hear him saying to the TV people, while he smile as if a pretty girl just asked him to her hotel room. "On a bad weekend the bear will eat its own young." I don't know what that means and I know Frank don't, but the TV film it, the Radio people who followed the TV out here, record it, and a couple of newspaper ladies who followed the radio car, write it down like it coming out of a minister.

Frank, he sure is happy to get to talk. "Just call me Chief Frank," he says. He tell one story about how us Indians get our names by being called after the first thing our fathers seen after we was born. It is a pretty good story but end with some four-letter words that catch a radio lady by surprise. I can hear a man's voice, must be all the way back at her radio station, yelling at her.

"Chief Frank, how do all these people know to come here?" ask one TV man who got slick yellow hair, and headphones big as frying pans cover his ears.

"You never heard of the moccasin telegraph?" say Frank, get a surprised look on his face.

"No," say the TV man.

"Well," says Frank, and take a deep breath, and I bet if I listen close I could hear the wheels turning inside Frank's head. "The moccasin telegraph is how white men say us Indians get messages to Indians a long ways away. I let you in on the secret. You know how prairie chickens drum in the underbrush in the fall, and how that sound travel for miles? Well, a wise old medicine man name of Buffalo-who-walks-like-a-man, long time ago mix up some herbs and roots in a porcupine bladder, and use it to tan prairie chicken hides. When them hides is stretched over a special drum why the sound travel for maybe a hundred miles. And it don't make a bump-bump-bump sound like a regular drum, but a quiet hum like the telegraph wires do way out in the country on a quiet night."

All these press peoples look at Frank like they was three years old and he was this Big Bird off the television.

"Messages just hum across the country—go from medicine man to medicine man; tells all the Indians when they are to gather for a pow-wow, or celebration, or in this case Burt Lameman's funeral," and Frank he fold his arms across his chest, look real solemn.

"How many people do you think have arrived so far and how many do you expect by the day of the funeral?" ask a girl with silver hair, so stiff it look like it got glue mixed with it.

Frank screw up his face. "Hey, us Indians is just like the Government. We got different departments. Numbers ain't my department. You ask my friend Silas here about that. Hell, I know so little about numbers I keep my fly open in case I have to count to eleven," and he grin at that radio lady, make sure her eyes get down to see the bulge in his jeans.

The next day Frank's picture on the front page of the *Edmonton Journal* along with the story about thousands of people converging on Wetaskiwin for a murderer's funeral, and they say he was on the CBC Evening News too.

"That was a pretty good story," I say to Frank later. "You're getting almost as good as me at making them up."

"What do you mean making up?" says Frank. "That was all true. Would I lie to the CBC?"

Actually, Buffalo-who-walks-like-a-man was the father of our medicine lady, Mad Etta. And next day Frank he send a television crew up to interview her. My girl, Sadie One-wound was there and say that Etta, who weigh close to 400 lbs., look at the TV crew mean as a bear been got out of her den in February and toss one of the cameramen about 50 feet into the willows. Then she rock that white van back and forth, and if Sadie hadn't talked soft to her and got one of the TV crew to promise her two dozen of Lethbridge Pale Ale, she would of tipped that van right over on its side.

Gunner LaFramboise from AIM follow the radio and TV people around like he was puppy and they got pork chops tied to their ankles.

"You can call it anything you want, but I call it an execution. If it had been a white man in that shack they would have just surrounded it and would have brought in ten social workers, a couple of priests, his parents, aunts and uncles, and his favorite hockey player to talk him into giving himself up."

"Why are you here?"

"Me and my red brothers are here to try and see that justice is done," and he smile real friendly for the camera.

By next afternoon the press people are so desperate for news they now go around interviewing each other.

Frank get to tell his stories over and over and people keep asking me questions. Chief Tom put in an appearance 'cause he can smell a reporter from five miles away, but they get tired of him quick 'cause he don't even know who Burt Lameman was, and all he want to talk about is the Alberta Government oil pricing policies. He don't know nothing about that either but he read off a letter sent to him personal by Peter Lougheed.

Frank he get tired of telling stories and interrupt a guy who got a silver microphone pushed right up into his face. "Hey," says Frank, "I want to show you guys my guitar," and shove under the reporter's nose a little transistor radio which ain't much bigger than a deck of cards, and what he carry in the pocket of his jean jacket most of the time.

"This is a radio," say the reporter, who wearing a top coat over a yellow blazer, toe rubbers and a red wool scarf about ten feet long. "And turn it off or we'll get feedback," he say in a cross voice.

"You guys too proud to look at a poor Indian's guitar?" say Frank. "I mean it ain't as fancy as what Johnny Cash or Roy Clark play on, but it's the best I can afford."

That announcer quick look over at his assistant who carrying something like a parachute full of batteries on his back. There be black wires connecting the two of them together like they be divers or maybe that special kind of twins.

"It's a radio," the assistant man says.

"Pretend it's a guitar," I say, doing as good as I can to keep a straight face. "He's likely to get mean if you don't."

"That's a really nice guitar, man," says the announcer.

"That's better," says Frank.

David One-wound, my girlfriend's brother, make his living by several kinds of creative borrowing. He carry on his back, all year round, a red nylon back-pack, which hold a car jack, a lug-wrench, and six different kinds of screwdriver. David claim he can take all four wheels off a car or truck in less than four minutes.

While these interviews been going on David One-wound and his friends took off the two far-side tires of the white CBC van, did it so careful even the engineer man inside didn't notice. They carried off the wheels and left blocks of wood under the axles.

Them guys get really mad when they try to drive away and the blocks tip over. They want somebody to call the RCMP.

"What good would that do?" we say. RCMP don't carry no spare wheels. But I bet somebody from around here have spare parts. Chief Frank, why don't you whistle up the One-wound Car Part Company."

Frank he make a face like he whistling but no sound come out. The reporters is real surprised when David One-wound, and Eddie Powder come from behind the hall, each carrying a tire and wheel.

"Those are our tires," say the reporters.

"Oh, no, those are spare parts we keep around in case of emergency," says Frank, and everyone laugh. "We sell them to you for only a hundred dollars each."

"But they're our wheels."

"You guys don't catch on very quick," says Frank. "Look, to be fair we even take a vote on it. How many say those are Indian wheels, and how many say they are white man wheels?"

Everybody vote for them being Indian wheels, even some of the other reporters.

The funeral: First it was gonna be from the little church on the reserve with Father Alphonse doing the service. Ordinarily, there wouldn't have been 20 people there. Just a few relatives and one or two friends—if Burt had that many. Even militant people like Bedelia Coyote was mad at Burt for giving all us Indians a bad name.

"Who do you figure gonna get remembered and used as an example every time Indians get mentioned?" say Bedelia. "It ain't guys like Mark Antelope, who run in the Commonwealth Games, or Sandra Bitternose, who getting to be a lawyer, or any of the people who got good jobs and stay out of trouble. Burt Lameman's name get thrown up for the next ten years," and Bedelia bang her fist on the table in the Gold Nugget Cafe, make the coffee cups jump.

Next, they move the funeral to the big Sacred Heart Catholic Church in Wetaskiwin, then it get moved over to the Canadian Legion Hall which hold more than 500 people, but as the town get fuller and fuller until it bulge like a gunny-sack filled with hay, the funeral get sent over to the hockey arena. At the arena they put boards down to cover the ice and the church have to hire a carpenter to build an altar. I hear that he build it too wide and tall and they have a hard time gather up enough of their religious rugs and scarves to cover it up.

The night before, all the cafes, stores, and bars was full with Indians; they say motels from Lacombe to Edmonton is full up. But it like the streets full of shadow people who walk quiet as if the slushy sidewalks was made of moss. Nobody get in trouble and the only noise is Gunner LaFramboise and his friends from AIM who set up a card table on the corner of 51st Ave. across from the Alice Hotel and try to sell memberships in AIM. But I don't see nobody buying.

The funeral set for ten o'clock but the arena start to fill up about eight. It got real cold overnight, and the mud of the parking lot, froze solid, look like fancy chocolate, and there be little puddles of water turned to ice and they crack loud as breaking glass when cars and campers crunch across the lot. The cars covered deep with frost and I can see the marks where windows been scraped off.

The TV and radio men have faces red with cold and they slap their arms against their sides while they take pictures of everybody filing in for the service. It funny to see people walking slow into an arena, looking like they just come off a hard day's work, instead of having expectant faces like hockey crowds usually do.

There don't be no hearse. Instead, Gunner hired old Pete Crookedneck, one of the only Indians who still know how, to build a travois. An old white horse, got a big black bow tied to his bridle, drag the travois carrying the coffin, from the funeral home to the hockey rink. Then eight guys, who I guess is all from AIM, 'cause they headed by Gunner LaFramboise, lift the coffin up shoulder high and carry it slow into the arena.

Toward the end of the service, somebody give a signal, I don't see who, but a couple of hundred men stand up in all different parts of the arena and file outside real quiet.

Father Alphonse from Hobbema, do the Catholic burial service, but nothing more, with the priest from Sacred Heart in Wetaskiwin helping out. I heard that Father Alphonse tell Gunner LaFramboise he have him carted away by the RCMP if he try to speak at the funeral. There be a half-dozen or so RCMP's back behind the altar but they stay mainly out of sight.

All Father Alphonse say about Burt is that it a shame he died so young, and about that time his microphone stop working so if he planned more he couldn't say it anyway.

There had to be close to 6,000 people at that funeral. Seeing that many quiet people send a shiver down my back. But what get to me even more is when we walk outside—right from the front of the arena, clear down to 51st Ave. there be, about every six feet, on both sides of the road, an Indian, stand with his feet at attention and his arms folded across his chest. The old white horse drag the travois and coffin past that honour guard and on to the funeral home where they say Burt going to be cremated.

Bertha Lameman, Burt's mother, and four of her other kids walk along behind the coffin. I hear that AIM bought her a new coat for the funeral.

After the funeral I hear just the end of a interview a radio man doing with Burt's mother.

"Tell me about your other children, Mrs. Lameman?" say the interviewer. She talk a long time but what it amounts to is three of her kids turn out good and three don't. That don't impress the reporter but it impress me; it's a lot better than the average around here.

Later on the bars and cafes fill up again, but people stay quiet. Somebody tell me that for all their trouble AIM only signed up three new members. Pretty soon the cars, pickups and vans head out to Highway 2A and turn either north or south. Some of those people look kind of puzzled on the outside, like I feel on the inside.

Questions for Discussion and Writing

1. Silas's style as narrator grabs the reader from his first line in the story. Make a list of the narrator's descriptions that especially caught your attention. What elements make his style and descriptions effective, and why?

2. In what ways do Silas and other Indians fall prey to the reporters' attitudes and expectations? In what ways do they delude the reporters? What are the underlying implications of the symbol of the moccasin telegraph?

3. What role do the "AIM people" play in Kinsella's story? How do the Indians feel about AIM?

4. Why do the people at the end of the story "look kind of puzzled on the outside, like [Silas feels] on the inside"? Describe a time in your life when this line could have described your own feelings of confusion.

5. What questions of justice and injustice does Kinsella address in "The Moccasin Telegraph"?

JOANNE BROWN

Scoshi

*For many years, Joanne Brown hung her undergraduate and gradu-
ate degrees over her washing machine. "Education is the housewife's
curse," she'd say as her three children were growing up. In those
years, writing and part-time teaching were her links to the world
beyond her home.*

*When Brown began working full time at Des Moines Area Com-
munity College, she taught speech, drama, and composition. She
later took on administrative responsibilities as dean of Humanities
and Public Services at the college, through which she became involved with a number of international programs. The exchange
with Japan that she writes about in "Scoshi" grew out of the college's commitment to bring other cultures closer to its students and
faculty.*

*Today Joanne Brown is on the faculty of the English Department
at Drake University in Des Moines, where she teaches composition,
creative writing, and business writing. She is also a writing consultant for various business communications.*

**Before you read "Scoshi," write about a time in your life when a friendship
with someone started out well but then seemed to disintegrate. Describe the
situation as your friendship began, the reasons for its promise, and the
subsequent decline. As you think back to it now, how can you explain what
happened? (You might also write about a friendship that evolved in the other
direction—that is, in which you expected gaps with the other person but
instead discovered a real friend.)**

The noodle shop was small and dimly lit. Behind the counter, a man stirred
liquid into an enormous steel bowl, closing his eyes as he sniffed the rising
steam, like a wine connoisseur about to sip from a rare vintage. A group of men
at the back of the room rose from their table. As they filed past the booth where

Yoshiko Sajima and I sat, they turned briefly to stare. I was the only Caucasian in the room.

Ignoring them, Yoshiko Sajima took another sip of tea and leaned forward. She was slender and graceful, her face framed by thick black hair that curved into a pageboy and brushed her cheek when she moved. "Are you tired?" she asked.

We had been sitting at our low table for nearly two hours, and I was trying to conceal a severe case of jet lag. Back home in Iowa it was midnight. "Scoshi," I said, using the Japanese word I had learned for "a little." It was an answer I had already found handy when people asked if I spoke Japanese or wanted more sake.

"Would you like to leave?" she asked. I shook my head no. She would be spending three months at the community college where I worked as dean of a liberal arts division, and I was glad for this chance to know her better. We were discovering that we had much in common. Like me, she had earned graduate degrees in English with an emphasis in American literature, and we enjoyed the same authors, respected the same critics. She was the first and only woman faculty member in her division, I the first and only woman dean at my college. We had both suffered miscarriages, liked museums, and avoided housework.

She told me that she once visited the United States briefly, and now that we had met, she was looking forward "with great thrill" to a longer stay. But she was worried about her English. Was it satisfactory?

She spoke English very well, I said, addressing her as *Sajima-sensei*, meaning teacher, a title of great respect.

She smiled broadly, then ducked her head as if the smile might have revealed too much. "Please, call me Yoshiko," she said.

I smiled back, pleased at the friendship her request implied.

She explained that her special interest was American drama and that she hoped to do some research on Eugene O'Neill and Tennessee Williams while she was in the States.

"Do you approve, Dr. Brown?" she asked.

An undergraduate drama major myself with more than a passing interest in both O'Neill and Williams, I nodded—with great thrill.

"Please, call me Joanne," I said in Japanese. I wanted to say more to her in her language, but the unfamiliar words filled my mouth like marbles, awkward and slippery, almost as if I had wandered by accident into a play for which I hadn't rehearsed.

In fact, this trip *was* an accident of sorts. Until the previous year, when I had helped to write a federal grant for a faculty exchange between a Japanese university and my own college, I had known little about Japan. Then the grant was approved, and plans evolved for me to spend a week in Japan getting acquainted with the exchange faculty.

Despite my sense of being unrehearsed, my preparations for the trip had been intense. I had read slender paperbacks on Japanese religion and weighty tomes on Japanese history, enrolled in a crash course in Japanese taught from a text called *Japanese for Busy People,* sat through a five-hour *kabuki* performance, attended lectures on Japanese flower arranging, and learned enough about Japanese social customs so that I could eat with chopsticks and bow with poise.

But having read of the celebrated Japanese politeness, of their unwillingness to criticize and their high regard for harmonious relations, I harbored some concerns about the exchange. What if our guests found some arrangement unsatisfactory—but were reluctant to speak out? I hoped that this visit to Japan would provide me not only with the opportunity to meet our guests prior to their arrival in Iowa, but to assure them that they should feel free while there to speak openly to me about anything.

My conversation with Yoshiko was reassuring. If her easy informality was at all representative, I had worried needlessly. She told stories about friends who had visited the United States, one of whom refused to sleep in a bed for fear of falling out, and another who was so busy taking photographs that he complained at the end of his stay that he hadn't had a chance to see anything. Her amusement implied that nothing would arise that a sense of humor couldn't overcome. In my mind, I was already composing the quarterly report to Washington: "The Japanese faculty members have approached their exchange visits in a spirit of marked cooperation and flexibility . . ."

Yoshiko gathered up her purse and wrap, indicating that it was time to leave. But we continued to sit while she spoke of her plans. Because she would be the first of her faculty to come, she wanted "to make a thriving start." She hoped to speak to our students and faculty about the contrasting roles of women in Japan and America. Did I approve? Of course. She would come for the spring semester. Did I approve? She would arrive on April 1.

Her arrival date coincided with the start of her spring term, a time convenient for her, but—as I had already explained in an earlier letter—so many weeks into our semester that she would be coming just as the term was winding down. No longer buoyed by the great thrill, I explained again that our academic calendars differed, that American schools did not observe the long winter break between January and March common to Japanese universities, and that if she didn't come until April, much of her visit would coincide with the vacation between spring and summer terms when neither students nor teachers would be on campus. Could she come earlier, in February perhaps? Or even March?

She nodded (assent or politeness?), but made no other response except to rise. I rose too, but persisted: A local Eugene O'Neill festival was scheduled the last week in February. Should I reserve tickets? Again, she said nothing, only touched my arm and led me from the restaurant.

The week at the university passed rapidly. Everyone was unfailingly cordial, eager to answer my questions about Japanese culture and to talk with me about American culture. A professor of law divulged that his hobby was tap dancing to American music of the 1940s, and a professor of anthropology showed me his collection of American presidential campaign buttons. The exchange faculty seemed well prepared for their visits; the advance arrangements they wanted me to make for their research kindled my own interests in their subjects, which ranged from the AIDS epidemic to criminal court proceedings. Yoshiko asked for help in obtaining some recent essays by American feminists. When my visit ended, I felt sad to leave the friends I had made.

They lined up beside the car that was to take me to Tokyo, waving and smiling. *"Sayonara,"* they called as I climbed into the back seat, "goodbye. Take care of yourself. *Ogenki de.* We hope to see you soon."

I rolled down the window and leaned out for a final farewell. "Yes," I said. "Soon." I smiled meaningfully at Yoshiko as I repeated with deliberate emphasis, "Soon."

She nodded back. "Very soon," she said.

Soon. I was to discover that it was a flexible word.

Upon my return to Iowa, I again sent letters to Yoshiko suggesting arrival dates in January or February. To each of my letters, she responded warmly ("Speak of angels and you shall hear their wings"), but ignored the question of when she would come. As January moved toward February, I hoped for March. In late February, she called to explain that she had encountered a delay in obtaining a visa. I began to wonder if she would make it to Iowa before summer.

Then I received a letter saying that she would leave Japan on March 19 and spend ten days in New York with a friend who was studying drama at New York University. "I would like to warm up," she wrote, "before I begin the true American life with you." She would arrive on April 1.

Late on the afternoon of April 1, the phone rang as I was arranging flowers for Yoshiko's room. She had accepted my offer to stay with my husband and me for a week or two until she felt comfortable enough with American culture to move into her own place, a one-bedroom furnished apartment that the college had outfitted with dishes, linens, cleaning supplies, and grocery staples.

"Joanne? It is Yoshiko, your friend." I tensed, afraid she had arrived early at the airport with no one to meet her. Her voice sounded subdued and muffled, barely audible.

"Yoshiko? Where are you?" Perhaps she was calling from Chicago to say her plane had been delayed.

"I have been thinking of you." The crackle of static nearly drowned out her voice. "I am in London. I will arrive in Iowa in a few days."

"London?" I set down the irises I had been holding and switched the receiver to my other ear, as if changing ears would change what I was hearing. "What are you doing in London?"

"To see theatre, of course."

"Theatre?"

"Les Misérables. Glenda Jackson in *Strange Interlude."* Through the static, I could detect an undercurrent of polite amusement: Didn't I know what was

playing in London? She went on to explain that she was able to get a "very excellent" rate from New York to London via Air India. As long as she was in London, she had gone on to Paris and Venice. However, when it was time for her return to the States, her scheduled plane had some mechanical difficulties, and its departure had been postponed for "a while." She promised to call when she arrived in New York.

Nothing that I had read about Japanese women had prepared me for this development, and I stood, mute, trying to take it in. Then she was saying goodbye (what sounded like "Toot, toot"), there was a click on the line, and the dial tone hummed over the wires. I thought wryly—and with a surge of anger—that perhaps I had not learned as much about intercultural matters while abroad as I was going to learn at home.

I was also alarmed. Yoshiko's behavior seemed not only irresponsible, but rude and manipulative. *You can't trust the Japanese.* Growing up in post-World War II years, I had heard that warning many times without paying much heed, but now it stung me with the force of truth. I had a quick mental image of the grant—each of its 60 pages, plus subsequent letters and memos—being swept away into a giant maelstrom of suspicion.

Then I replaced the receiver and took a deep breath, remembering the friends I had made in Japan and ashamed of my facile judgment. After all, this was only one incident with one person, and that person was the same Yoshiko with whom I had sat so long in the noodle shop while we explored all that we shared, both as women and as scholars.

As I arranged the irises one by one in a slender vase, I tried to understand. Perhaps after years of abiding by the constraints that dictated how a proper Japanese woman was to behave, Yoshiko was finding freedom headier than she had anticipated, more than she could handle. Temporarily beyond her control.

Although I had known something of the role of women in Japan, about the docility and obedience that their culture insisted upon, even my brief stay there had dramatized the difficulty and uneasiness of that role as no amount of reading could. Women were so often excluded. (One professor had sent his young wife home on the bus after an evening reception at the university, then had stayed on with us to eat and drink at a local restaurant.) Women such as Yoshiko— intelligent and well-educated—had few outlets for their ambitions. (When I had asked the dean of the law college about the number of women deans in Japan, he answered, "None," a terse reply clearly intended to reflect a status quo well worth preserving.) And gender seemed to be the main principle by which women—all women—were defined. (During lunch in the school cafeteria, when Yoshiko had poured water for everyone at our table, one of the men had toasted this domestic gesture with his brimming glass and joked, "Ah, Yoshiko, now we know that you are not so much teacher as woman.")

So perhaps when Yoshiko wrote about "warming up" and "the true American life," she was telling me about her need for flight—not a means of travel, but escape—an impulse to cut loose before settling down to serious work. If that were the case, and by now I had convinced myself that it was, then her behavior was as inevitable and as temporary as adolescence.

By the time Yoshiko actually landed in Iowa, I took some pride in what she had done, prompting her in those first days to "tell where you went after you left Japan," like a mother whose righteous indignation over a misbehaving child is dimmed by the daring of his exploits.

Still, I was wary. On the one hand, Yoshiko seemed delighted with everything: "full of happy," she said. She made charming speeches at a reception in her honor and to the board of directors, praising New York cabdrivers, the college faculty, Ronald Reagan (then president) and me, who together, she implied, had made her trip possible.

On the other hand, once she rented a car, learned to drive on the right side of the street, and moved into her own apartment, we saw her less and less. She seemed uninterested in getting to know our students or faculty, instead seeking out other Japanese living in the community. During her time on campus, she secluded herself in her office with the door closed. There were days when she didn't appear at all. She promised several instructors that she would address their classes at specified times—and never showed up. A month into her visit, I received a call from Northwestern Bell asking me if I were aware that Yoshiko Sajima had already incurred long-distance charges of over $500.

There were also troubling rumbles from Japan. An exchange faculty member from our college now in Japan wrote, "Perhaps Yoshiko has not been able to adjust to our country. She has taken a hostile attitude toward many things, and her criticisms have put our college in an unfavorable light." The comment, jotted in careful script at the end of a typewritten letter, offered no further explanation.

Was Yoshiko calling her colleagues long-distance with $500 worth of criticism? Had she written unhappy letters, like a homesick child at camp? And what could she have said?

Yoshiko had expressed no criticisms to me over anything other than the refrigerator in her apartment, which she said was noisy and kept her awake at night. I had called the landlord, a cooperative man who responded promptly to all our requests. He called back so quickly to report the problem solved that I had forgotten about it.

Had the complaint about the refrigerator masked more serious matters? Perhaps an incident at the college had upset her so much that, restrained by her sense of Japanese propriety, she could not bring herself to discuss it. Had she resorted to reporting "criticisms" as a ploy to gain our attention, knowing that we were likely to learn of what she had written or said?

Or were domestic tensions back home clouding her experiences here? Although she was married, she never spoke of her family except to say that her husband was a city official and that she had left her nine-year-old son in the care of her mother.

To resolve the problem—or at least to define it—I stopped by Yoshiko's office several times, dropping casually into a chair to ask about her research or some event I knew she had attended. Her answers were always guarded, but reassuring: everything was "coming along excellent."

I teetered between irritation and worry. Was she unhappy or wasn't she? She could hardly expect me to read her mind. But of course, coming from a culture that encourages ambiguity over candor, she could.

Remembering that the grant materials had included some information about making cultural adjustments, I retrieved the packet from my files and found what I was looking for on a page titled "Common Symptoms of Culture Shock." The list, directed at Americans studying in Japan, described feelings of isolation, frustration, hostility, and "deep doubts about the wisdom" of being involved in an international project. Whether or not the list applied to Yoshiko, it depicted exactly my own state of mind.

To compound my anxiety, several major administrative problems had surfaced in the last few weeks. None was related to the grant, but all were requiring considerable time and energy, leaving me little of either to deal with Yoshiko. I reread the postscript several times during the next few days and hoped, without doing much else, that everything would work itself out.

The next week there was a dinner in Yoshiko's honor, and I made arrangements to drive her there, thinking that our ride might provide her with an opportunity to talk frankly. Uncertain of how to introduce the subject, I rehearsed and discarded several openings on the way to pick her up.

She had hardly settled herself in the passenger seat when she unceremoniously introduced her own subject and what seemed to be the source of the problem: a profound dissatisfaction with her apartment. The building was too old, the furniture too worn, the refrigerator still noisy. She preferred an electric range to the gas one she had, and she wanted a color television, not the small black-and-white set that we had lent. And she needed a microwave.

When she had first seen the apartment, she had thrown her arms around me and professed "large joy." She was delighted with the pictures we had hung, the rolltop desk we had provided, the bookshelf and the night light above the bed.

But now as I swung the car into the freeway traffic, Yoshiko was complaining bitterly about that same apartment. She could get along in less space, she said, but she demanded the microwave and a different refrigerator: "We Japanese don't like anything old. We have to have good equipment." And, she added, the new apartment must be in a different neighborhood.

She had been living near the campus of a private university, within walking distance of the university library. Originally, she had been enthusiastic about the location of the apartment and the library privileges she had been granted, but now she complained about seeing men (students?) walking about on warm days without shirts. One sported a tattoo. Some were black men. Why had I put her in a neighborhood with black people?

I knew that Japan was a homogeneous, exclusive society, but I was offended by her remarks and overwhelmed at the thought of moving her. The search for Yoshiko's apartment had been intense and frantic. We had agreed to provide housing for the Japanese professors when the president of their university, aware that the weakening dollar threatened to make housing prohibitively expensive for our teachers, suggested a housing exchange. Although our college owned no housing, not even student dormitories, a local landlord had offered a free apartment for the duration of the grant.

Then, just before Yoshiko left Japan, the landlord suddenly sold his building, leaving us to scurry around for another place. To complicate the situation, the college was in the middle of a funding crisis, with a budget too tight to cover even modest rental fees. After inspecting a dozen or so possibilities, we had been fortunate, we thought, to find one so reasonably priced, so clean and nicely furnished and roomy, with so much free parking space.

But tonight Yoshiko wondered aloud why we had chosen that apartment, repeating her criticism of the television set and black men as if the two had some relationship to each other and insisting again on new equipment for the kitchen: "It is the Japanese way."

Weaving furiously in and out of traffic lanes, I swallowed hard against what I dare not say—that she was not in Japan but in Iowa, that she had come to learn about another culture instead of clinging to her own, and that it was time she tried making compromises instead of demands. "It is the American way," I wanted to say.

Only later did I learn that in Japan, men with bare chests, especially those with tattoos, are perceived as menacing. At the time, I brushed aside what was probably an honest fear for her own safety by curtly explaining about American warm-weather attire. But Yoshiko was firm: to remain in that apartment was "impossible."

I had signed a six-month lease, thinking to use the apartment at least through the summer for the next exchange professor. Finally, wondering how to break the lease, I said that we would make other arrangements for an apartment, but that she would have to remain where she was a little longer while we found another place.

She agreed, and we drove in silence. Then, "Perhaps you are upset," she said.

"Scoshi," I said, gripping the steering wheel and refusing to look at her.

During the next week, I scanned the want ads and made some phone calls without results. Yoshiko had gone on her own search and presented me with a list of possibilities, all of them at least double what we could afford. Meanwhile, I received another letter from our instructor in Japan. Continuing word of Yoshiko's dissatisfaction was threatening the affiliation between the two institutions.

Then came an unexpected offer from the widowed mother of one of the faculty. Her house had many spare bedrooms, and she invited Yoshiko to move into one. She herself would be spending the summer in Maine, but Yoshiko was welcome to remain in the house for as long as she liked.

Wondering how a liking for Eugene O'Neill's plays had involved me in this international complication, I tagged along with Yoshiko while she inspected the house and asked questions about the washing machine and piano. Finally she accepted the offer and moved in the next week. When a third letter arrived from Japan that said, "You have finally succeeded in making Yoshiko happy," I rejoiced.

The end of the semester coincided with my own professional crisis. I was finding my dean's job increasingly difficult, rocked by constant turmoil in the top administration. There had been an exodus of deans from the college that year, and at the end of May, I became the sixth to resign. My new job, at the university near where Yoshiko had lived, would start in September.

Yoshiko was upset and baffled by my resignation. "But why? But why?" she asked again and again.

I could only imagine what she thought. Even had she known of the politics behind my decision, she could hardly have understood it. In Japan, I knew, there is very little moving about from one job to another; employment is usually life-long. People are expected to stay put, to adapt their individual concerns to the common good. How much adapting Yoshiko had done seemed problematic. She had told me that she considered the president of her university a "tyrant" and that she had disagreed with him "in loud voice" on several occasions. But a resignation was another matter entirely.

I tried to explain, without divulging confidential information, what had motivated me, but she seemed not to comprehend. Aloud, she speculated about who had forced my resignation. Did the teachers no longer want to work with me? Was the president angry with me? There seemed little point in trying to set her right.

She had begun to write her final report, a comparison of Japanese and American women, to be presented at an open meeting in late June. She had been sporadic in her preparation, delaying for so long that she felt great pressure at the end. On several occasions, she told me, she had trouble sleeping.

When I read what she had written, it hardly seemed the capstone of a three-month visit to another country. Yoshiko had limited most of her discussion to Japanese women, to what she surely knew before coming to Iowa; her comparisons to American women drew conclusions so obvious that I could have written them myself. (Married women, both Japanese and American, spend more time doing household chores than married men or unmarried women.)

Although she was concerned about her presentation, she worried more about the form than the substance, about "saying the correct English." Partly to ease her mind and partly to encourage her to broaden her approach, I offered to help her edit the paper. As we sat working side by side at a table in my office, I would look up to find her watching me. "Why do you resign?" she asked if my gaze caught hers. "Why?"

In mid-June Yoshiko was joined by Tadaharu Shibata, a sociology professor. There had been some question over whether he would come, as his wife was expecting their first child, and the president of his university had urged him to postpone his trip. But he was not to be dissuaded. Yoshiko worried about Tadaharu's reaction to her report. "Will he approve?" she sometimes wondered aloud as together we bent over her paper. Then, reassuring herself, she would murmur, "My English is better than his."

She was right. Tadaharu spoke ponderously, with many pauses while he searched for words, stroking his chin and gazing into the distance. But he adjusted quickly to American culture; from the very beginning he made himself at home with an easy confidence that had eluded Yoshiko. I attributed the contrast partly to the different gender roles they played, he assured and out-spoken, very much in charge, she trying to conceal her own strong will beneath a carefully docile manner that must have been as uncomfortable as clothing worn a size too small.

Also, Tadaharu benefitted from our earlier rental experiences. For him we had rented an efficiency apartment in a new downtown complex that boasted an electric range and microwave in every unit. The rent was far beyond what we could afford, with no free parking for the used car that he promptly purchased, but Tadaharu—unmindful, of course, of our budget problems—loved everything about his new home except the hide-a-bed; he didn't want to make it up each day.

Unlike Yoshiko, he quickly made contacts among the faculty and emulated things American. "Call me Tad," he urged new acquaintances and sprinkled his conversation with a mixture of slang and bureaucratese, shaking his head, for example, over the "red tape" that his research had engendered, over the "up tight" officials he had encountered, over the delays that interfered with his "implementation of a strategic plan."

Shortly after his arrival, his wife, who remained in Japan, prematurely delivered a son by Caesarean section. There were complications, both baby and mother developed an infection, and Tad worried a lot. He did not, however, return home, despite pleas from his wife to do so. We assured him that we would understand if he cut short his visit, but he refused to consider such an alternative: "I am an urban prince now," he said, shutting off further discussion. I wondered what Yoshiko, with her feminist leanings, thought about the urban prince, but she seemed pleased that he had come, less withdrawn and more responsive when he was around.

"I think Yoshiko is happy to see you," I said to him one day.

"Yoshiko," he said and smiled, indulgent but patronizing. "At my university we call her a small tornado."

I said nothing.

"It is too bad," he continued, "how it works out."

There was a silence, then, "What is too bad?" I asked.

"Yoshiko did not have a good stay." He stroked his chin in the familiar manner, but his voice went strangely flat. "Her apartment troubled her very much."

"Yes, I know," I said. "I'm sorry about the apartment, but at least now she has a nice place."

Tad shook his head. "She does not like it. It is not her home." His voice grew sharper. "She must worry all the time about breaking things and who pays. It was the same at your house. Not good." I tried to keep my face impassive, but he responded to something he saw there. "Perhaps you do not understand. We Japanese need privacy." He stared at me, his eyes stern. "There have been many problems with her visit."

For once we were in total agreement. "You're right," I said and changed the subject.

We videotaped Yoshiko's presentation. The tape, filmed by the college's media department, captures the scene in careful detail, zooming in for a closeup of Yoshiko's face at just the right moment, panning across the audience to catch someone nodding in agreement, frowning in concentration. Watching it, I am there again.

The auditorium is full, packed with both teachers and students. Yoshiko walks to the podium, hesitant and demure, very much the Yoshiko I remember from our first meeting. She expresses her appreciation to the American women she has met, those who have assisted her during her stay. "It is entirely thanks to their help that I can stand here." Her voice is soft, and she leans toward the microphone. She is so tiny that the lectern hides all but her shoulders and head.

"In ancient times," she begins, "we women were like the sun, shining with glory. It is said that Japanese history begins with the goddess of the sun. She was angry with the males because of their lesser behavior, so she hid herself in a dark cave and closed the entrance with a heavy rock so that her light could not escape. People could not be without the sun, so they asked the god of power—a male god—to put the goddess out. He opened the door and begged her to leave the cave. Being begged, she finally appeared again and gave her sunlight to the world. This was the beginning of Japan."

She looks up from her notes, uncertain. Is she saying the words right? Does the audience approve of what they are hearing? Somewhere among all those faces, she finds the encouragement she needs and resumes again: "Today women in Japan are trying to be liberated from their burden, to be like the sun, as they once were." Her voice gains power. "When I was in college, I was strongly influenced by the American women's liberation movement. I believed that I could build a successful career, get married, have a child, and lead a happy life." She has added this material since I last read her report, and I am moved by her words, by her intensity.

"My parents worried when I decided to attend graduate school to study American literature. They believed if a woman was highly educated, she couldn't find a good husband because in those days men disliked highly educated women." She looks up from her notes and searches the auditorium until she finds Tad. "Most people still think like that."

There is a long pause while she scans her notes, the forefinger of her right hand skimming down the page to find her place, the fingers of her other hand to her lips. She shifts her weight slightly, picks up her manuscript with both hands, and taps it smartly on the lectern, as if to align the pages. Without setting it down again, she begins speaking. I am not sure if she is reading or improvising. "After I had my son, I realized how difficult it is to have it as I thought. Every woman who has had a baby in mid-career can understand. Both my home life and my professional life demanded much time, and I was always tired. After I gave birth to my son, I tried to have a second child, but the result was miserable. I got pregnant three times, but I miscarried twice, and then I had a stillborn. After those sad experiences, I finally gave up giving my son a brother or sister, and now I feel a kind of guilt for him."

Her voice falters. There is an uneasy silence, she again consults her notes, then looks up to finish her story. "When I had a stillborn baby, my doctor said, 'You have to choose whether to quit your job and have a baby or to work and give up having another baby.'" She tells how her teaching position at a girls' junior college in Tokyo required her to commute two hours, and she is explaining that her doctor felt that the demands were too much for her when she interrupts herself. "Two hours each way." She spreads her hands, as if indicating a huge distance. "People would ask me why I didn't quit my career, but—" Her tempo slows, and she pauses between phrases, her voice striking each word like a hammer: "I knew that if I quit that full-time job, I could never get a full-time position again." She knows where I am sitting, far to her left in the front row, and she turns in my direction, thin-lipped and reproving. I smile encouragingly, neutrally, as if she is discussing Japanese recipes or geography.

"I was staying at home," she says, "feeling sad for two months after that birth, and I would look around at my neighbors, all full-time housewives. They spent their time chatting with each other outside their house until their husbands and children came home. They spent their daily lives doing nothing. They now have two or three children, each without problems. Their husbands are supported by a tax credit for dependents while I pay expensive taxes without tax exemption."

There is another silence, this one very long, while she alternately shuffles through her papers and looks up at the waiting audience. She drops a page and retrieves it. Then she resumes, reading from a section already familiar to me. It traces the history of women in Japan, their decline from the days of the emperors, through the period of the shoguns. "They became men's possessions. They could have never their own houses. When they were young, they lived in their father's houses, and they obeyed their fathers. After marriage, they lived in their husband's houses and obeyed their husbands. Then, when they grew old, they lived with their sons and obeyed their sons. Women had no place where they could rest their soul. They only had to obey men. So obedience was a life-long duty."

She is reading in a sing-song rhythm, hurrying along. "Also, they were considered child-bearing machines. If they could not give birth within the first three years of marriage, the husband could divorce his wife at will by writing a letter that stated in three and one-half lines that he wanted her to leave."

Things improved, she tells us, after World War II, when a new constitution was imposed by the United States occupational forces. "So sometimes we Japanese women feel that we have been saved by the United States, because this constitution gives us fundamental rights. Fundamental rights." She leans forward, as if confiding in the audience.

"My father often said to me, 'You are a girl, so you should behave in a feminine way. Don't put on pants and sit like a man. Help your mother and learn how to cook.' Sometimes I would quarrel with my brothers and then my father would blame me: 'You are a girl. Don't talk back to your brothers.' I would feel that he was not fair, so I talked back to Father. 'Why do I have to obey my brothers when they are not right?' I did not understand. Then my father would get angry.

"When I decided to go to the university in Tokyo, Father wanted me to go to a women's college. He was afraid I would lose my femininity if I went to the university where male students were in the majority. But I had already lost my femininity. I knew that femininity was obedience to men and being coquettish. I disagreed with my father's demands and was disgusted with my father.

"Fortunately, Mother was always on my side. She thought I should have the same opportunities as my brothers and always persuaded Father to agree with my decisions. Because of this, I could always have my own way. But when I decided to study at a large school, Mother could not agree at first. Then we discussed what was a truly happy life for women. Finally she encouraged me to do what I wanted." She smiles a very small, private smile, her fingers gently tracing the edges of the lectern. When she speaks again, it is with such a strange blend of tenderness and scorn that I am glad we have preserved the moment on tape.

"Why did she allow me to do so? I think it was because she had a bitter experience when she was young. She wanted to take higher education, but her parents did not allow it even though they could afford the tuition. She had to obey her father's decision and was forced into a marriage he arranged. In those times an arranged marriage was very common and a love marriage was considered without prestige, but she could not understand to get married with an unknown man. She ran away from her husband's house on the first night of her marriage. After that, she met my father and she married him by her own will."

The camera swings across the auditorium, row after row. Everyone sits motionless, absorbed by the story, their eyes fixed on the stage, on Yoshiko. She looks up at them, lifting her chin in a defiant gesture that I do not understand. Surely, she must feel the bond of their approval. But her glance is aloof, even fierce. Then her features relax; she looks down at her manuscript and reads the flat facts and figures comparing American and Japanese women. Gone is the tenderness, the passion. The audience becomes restless, listening politely, but shifting occasionally, turning at the sound of the auditorium door opening, twisting to see the clock in the back of the room. Yoshiko reads faster and faster, then stops. Her manner softens again, and she takes a deep breath. "I thought often of my mother when I worked on this paper," she says. "I think she was a brave woman. I have learned through these bitter conflicts in my family that I am very lucky to have such a brave mother. I am proud of her from the bottom of my heart. This is my mother's story."

Yoshiko left for Japan the next day. I drove her to the airport, making chitchat about the weather and her return trip, but thinking of her office, its walls stripped of her posters, the shelves emptied of her books. During the preceding weeks, I had often looked toward this moment with anticipated relief, but when I waved her off at the boarding gate and watched her plane lift into the clear sky, I felt hollow and disappointed.

Months later, she sent me a Christmas card, signed "with fondness." I sent her a review of a Tennessee Williams revival and jotted a brief note. We have not corresponded since.

Early in her stay, Yoshiko had confided that she would like to buy a house in Iowa and return every summer. Does she still harbor that dream? Would we be friends if she returned? Politics, as Sam Rayburn once said, is always local. I hoped to learn about a people, but understanding even one individual—a woman much like myself—had stymied me.

Not long ago, I said as much to a friend. "But surely," she responded, "you learned a lot. Didn't you? All those books you read. You must have learned something."

I thought back to Yoshiko and smiled at my friend's certainty. "Maybe," I said. "Scoshi. I don't know."

Questions for Discussion and Writing

1. At the beginning of the international exchange, what are the expectations held by both Brown and Yoshiko? On what bases does each person build her expectations? Use brief passages from the story to support your response.

2. In what ways do you think each woman is responsible for the outcome of their relationship, and why? What cultural assumptions and values influenced their relationship? What cultural assumptions and values have influenced your assessment of their roles?

3. Why does Brown tell us so little about her own reactions to Yoshiko's final speech? What effect do you think the speech had on the author, and why? In what ways does Yoshiko's speech alter your understanding of who she is?

4. Near the end of the story, Brown quotes Sam Rayburn: "Politics are always local." What does this passage mean to you? What does it explain about Brown's story?

5. What narrative techniques does Brown use to tell her story? In what ways do they or do they not keep you interested in the narrative?

SOLON T. KIMBALL

Learning a New Culture

Born in 1909 in Manhattan, Kansas, Solon T. Kimball earned his Ph.D. from Harvard University. As an avid anthropologist, he studied many cultures. In "Learning a New Culture," Kimball details his first experience in anthropological field work, in Ireland in the 1930s. The essay was first published in 1972, in a book he edited with James B. Watson, Crossing Cultural Boundaries: The Anthropological Experience. *Kimball's experiences in Ireland reflect the phases of being foreign long before the concept of culture shock had been delineated.*

Prior to his death, Kimball taught in the Department of Anthropology at the University of Florida in Gainesville. Long interested in the relationship between culture and education, Kimball wrote a number of books on the subject: Education and the New America *(1962),* Learning and Culture *(1973), and* Culture and the Educative Process *(1974).*

In "Learning a New Culture," Kimball reflects on the idea that taking on the characteristics of another culture occurs, most significantly, at the subconscious level.

Before you read "Learning a New Culture," write about a time in your life when, through prolonged experience with another person, place, or culture, you surprised yourself by taking on qualities you hadn't been consciously aware of in your surroundings. Describe what happened, and how you responded to this surprise in yourself.

S oon after the beginning of my graduate-student days, I began to collect a set of guiding principles about the behavior which I would follow if I ever became a field worker. It is now no longer possible nor would it be of very great significance if I were able to pinpoint the source and situation in which these principles were accumulated. There can be no question, however, that their apprehension was by bits and pieces and not by any orderly transmission and acquisition.

Surely the most inclusive of these prescriptions was the insistence that the successful field worker must adjust to the way of life of the people he studies. Modification of behavior toward native style should be as near total as possible. This process would include, for example, changes in dress, food habits, eating patterns, speech, greetings, gesture pattern, and walking. These were counted as the more obvious culture traits which, if acquired, would reduce the differences setting the ethnographer-stranger apart from his group and hence would facilitate the collection of the data he sought.

Immersion in the cultural life of the natives beyond that necessary for collecting information required adjustments of a more fundamental sort. The rationale for such an objective is clearer today than it was then, but the purpose to be served remains the same. It was believed that only as the field worker became able to view objects and happenings from the same perspective as that of the natives would it be possible for him to understand the cultural context which gave them meaning. This dictum bears the unmistakable stamp of Malinowski.

Exactly how far one should go in adopting the native way of life was never made clear. The danger of "going native" was an unlikely possibility. What was more probable was that some unwitting violation of a religious or social taboo would place one in jeopardy. If the field worker observed the suggested limitations on his behavior, such dangers would not arise. These cautions were not urged as much to protect him from the threats to his physical or mental health as they were to ensure his effectiveness in gathering data and the success of the project. Some behavioral guides contradicted each other, particularly those which set limitations on the degree of involvement. Opinions contrary to local views or that might identify one with a local controversy, for example, were not to be expressed. Partisan alignments with religious, political, or familial factions were to be avoided although the existing divisions were to be investigated. Sexual or romantic involvement with native women was to be strictly avoided. As Lloyd Warner once explained it to me, a sexual linkage with a female of one moiety of the Murngin immediately involved you in a whole set of obligations with her kinsmen as well as in their quarrels with the opposing moiety. An angry tribesman of the opposite moiety who was seeking to avenge some insult to him by a newly acquired distant kin of yours might throw spears at you. Such a powerful joining of anxiety, fear, and pragmatism should restrain all but the most lubricious male.

That these directives should be heeded I quickly learned in my baptism to field work in Ireland. At a late-evening gathering of supporters of the political party which favored close ties with Great Britain—a fact I had not yet discerned—I called for a free Ireland, bringing my innocence to a sudden and unhappy end when I found that I was in the wrong crowd for such a sentiment. I attempted to recover the lost neutrality by reciting Lincoln's Gettysburg address. Near-mute wariness was the watchword from then on although I made other mistakes from which I also learned.

Through strict neutrality it was presumably possible to avoid the status identification that would limit access to all segments of a population. Although it didn't occur to me until much later, such status anonymity must create confusion among members of a society who have been trained to identify and respond to others primarily upon the cues of status. I also learned quickly enough in the field that the preservation of neutrality created an ambiguous and ambivalent position for me, with resultant social and psychic tensions from which there was no release. Even the intimacy of friendship did not engender full freedom of expression. The unwitting report of your private view might do great harm.

It had been drilled into me that neutrality and success were inextricably linked. Success would be evident in fat piles of field notes. But I recall nothing being said about the effect on the novice enthnographer of long-term isolation from his own kind combined with a restricted involvement in the affairs of a host culture. For me, the acquisition of a native perspective was slow, erratic, and often traumatic, but I was driven by the near-compulsive conviction that the costs of transformation were the inescapable price paid for success in one's research. Whatever comfort contemporary students may derive from knowing that such suffering is normal and can be labeled "culture shock" was not then available. Certainly I was unprepared for the recurrent attempts to incorporate me in the lifeways of a West Ireland county where I conducted my first major field research in 1933–1934. The process of induction was both subtle and direct and I must also admit, effective. Although at the time I believed that control of my cultural destiny resided in my hands, hindsight suggests that the reality was something quite different. The guiding principle which prescribed no overt entanglements became increasingly pro forma as I became more deeply enmeshed in Irish culture. In fact, the transformation at the psychic level seemed to have moved quite beyond any conscious control. At least, no other explanation seems as valid for interpreting the event which I shall describe here.

My introduction to Ireland came on a cold, gray morning in April 1933 at the small, West Irish port of Galway. A handful of steerage Irish and I disembarked from a North German Lloyd steamship to a small lighter which deposited us at a nearby quay where a dozen or so hackney drivers solicited customers for their hotels. My destination was the Queen's Hotel, Ennis, County Clare, about forty miles away, where I was to be met by my co-worker, Conrad Arensberg. After some minor misadventures caused primarily by my ignorance of local custom and my inability to comprehend the thick Irish brogue of western Ireland, I employed the driver of an ancient Ford to carry me to my destination. By late afternoon we managed to get within sight of the Queen's Hotel when the last of several blowouts occurred and the driver, his helper, and I trudged the final two blocks laden with my luggage. Arensberg, who had failed to receive word of my coming, had gone off to visit friends in England and did not appear until several days later. But the hotel personnel and guests were friendly, and the bar sold drinks on tick. Thus began my stay in Ireland which was to end some thirteen months later.

The process of my transformation and incorporation into Irish life was affected by experiences both in the town of Ennis, where the Queen's Hotel was the base of operation, and in the countryside. I lived with two farm families on four different occasions, each for periods of several weeks. Arensberg returned to Harvard about two months after my arrival, so that the companionship which had been so valuable during the early, stressful period of adjustment to a strange way of life ended. Although the townspeople were friendly and helpful and I entered into many of the summer activities, I knew that I could never understand the Irish people until I became directly involved with the seemingly remote and different life-style of the small farmers. A direct approach seemed utterly impossible. This feeling may have been the result of the townsmen's appraisal of rural folk. To them the country fellow was "deep," "cute," "untrustworthy," enmeshed in kinship obligations which excluded outsiders, and suspicious if not hostile to strangers. Furthermore, their ways were considered to be uncouth and at times even barbarous. However typical these attitudes may have been as an urban stereotype of the countryman, they were just that and nothing more. Later I was to discover that the country people reciprocated with equally uncomplimentary ideas when they warned me about the evil ways of the townsmen.

During the early fall, arrangements were made for me to take up residence with a family of the small-farmer class in the townland of Rynamona near the village of Corofin in North Clare. This move was accomplished in a manner which the Irish understand so well and which they phrase as "Everything goes by friends and friendship." The local district health officer, Donough McNamara, a man much interested in the history of the county and a friend, secured the help of the local schoolmaster, who found a suitable location for me. Thus it was that with a bicycle for transportation and wearing a black suit that was appropriately respectable for Sunday Mass, a country-style wool hat, and farmer-type brogans, my other belongings stowed in a pack on my back, I left Ennis one midmorning on a new venture. Two hours later in time, but what for me was a century in cultural difference, I wheeled down the narrow borheen toward the modest thatched cottage where John and Mary Quin lived with Mary's older widowed sister, whom I came to know only by the respectful title of "the old lady."

The Quins were middle-aged and childless, as was "the old lady." After her husband's death she had brought her younger sister to live with her, and in due course, John Quinn married into the house and farm as husband of the younger sister. A dowry always accompanies the in-marrying individual, but it is usually somewhat larger with a male since the name on the land has been changed in the process.

In layout the house displayed a pattern distinctive of West Ireland, with a central kitchen and small bedrooms on both east and west ends. At the western end of the rectangular kitchen was an open hearth where food for both humans and animals was prepared and around which evening visitors gathered for warmth and conversation. There the family concluded the day with its recitation of the rosary. Furnishings were few and simple, including a dresser with its display of seldom-used delftware, a benchlike settle bed along the north wall, and a deal table and sugon (caned straw seat) chairs by the one small window on the south. On the wall was a small shrine displaying a brightly colored lithograph of the Sacred Heart of Jesus.

John Quin was a stalwart man. Big-boned, he stood better than six feet. He moved with the easy, deliberate pace common to the countryman. He paid serious attention to his farm duties and had learned to perform the tasks required of the small farmer with skill and despatch. But he was also full of lightheartedness and wit and took part in the country dances or turkey-gambles with zest. Quin responded well to the happenings of the moment, but he was a poor informant on past customs. When I attempted to get him to tell me about country matchmaking, his response was to condemn the practice as a bad old custom. My probings into other ways of life of the past met with similarly brief replies.

At first I thought that my inability to collect information from John Quin might be due to a defensive reluctance to talk about matters which he felt were no proper concern of the stranger. Later on, after the bonds of friendship had developed between us and he still showed no inclination to talk at length about the past, I concluded that for him the natural flow of life was the present. From the vantage of time and distance, however, I now appreciate that John Quin led me to a deeper understanding of Irish life than I could ever have obtained through direct and full replies to my queries. I was not at the time aware of his effect on my behavior and thinking. Nor do I believe that Quin's course of action was consciously planned, although I later learned he had a genuine concern about my welfare. Quin became my tutor of the proper ways of behavior, though I never thought of myself as pupil. He became my guide to the small farmer's world.

His own position was somewhat marginal since he had not been born in the townland but had come to it through marriage. He did not have a solid place among the elders, nor could he be counted as one of the young men because of his position as head of a household. But he was fully welcome in both groups, and I came to know their members as we made the almost nightly visits to the locale of their gatherings. Round the hearth of old man O'Donoghue's house gathered the responsible small farmers whose deliberations rendered the decisions and set the policy for Rynamona. Occasionally the young men and women gathered at Moroney's house for a songfest and dance, a country form of entertainment condemned by the stricter clergy who believed these gatherings might threaten the moral virtues of the young. It was there that I learned the Irish country dances and heard for the first time the poignant laments of the Irish soloist. To Oscar's, a genial country laborer of great physical prowess, came another category of men, those whose marginality excluded them from easy association with other small farmers. In these diversities there was a rich spread of the variety of Irish country life.

I took part in many of the activities connected with Quin's daily work, tending animals, crops, and field. But there were less-frequent events to which I was also introduced. For example, Quinn and I gathered with the other men when the sheaves of wheat were brought to the steam-powered threshing machine. We took our stand at the winter sheep fair in Corofin and, after our animals were sold, joined in a communal drink with other men in the local pub. From the peat bog several miles away we hauled a creel of dried turf for the household hearth. And on Sundays we walked the mile or so to the parish church and waited outside with the other men until the pealing bell announced the beginning of Mass, when with the others we entered and took our seats.

Meanings were conveyed much more fully by the doing than by explanation. I learned to return the country greeting with an appropriate reply, to praise no human, animal, or object without appending the proper "God bless" to remove any suspicion of envy or evil intent, and to call out "God bless all here" as I crossed the threshold of a house.

My gradual acquisition of the small farmer's behavior pattern moved along smoothly enough. Once I had recognized some piece of behavior, I could then practice it. But in the early phases of learning, it was sometimes difficult to remember the appropriate behavior for each situation. Sometimes focus on one item obscured its connection with others. Style of walking can serve as an example. I was aware that the townsman walked differently from the countryman and that my American style was still another variation. My goal was to pick up the gait of the countryman and drop whatever I had learned about town walking. I thought that all I need do was observe the style of walking and then consciously imitate what I saw. What I didn't perceive at first, however, was that walking and talking were sequential rather than simultaneous. If you have something important to say, you come to a halt until the subject has been covered. When talking started and walking stopped, I would at first stand with the others only because I wanted to remain with the group, but not because I recognized the obligatory nature of this practice. After the insight came to me, I practiced the behavior. Returning one night from the men's gathering, I brought my two companions to a halt to initiate a topic for discussion. A few moments later we resumed our homeward course. The incident had not been momentous, but I felt a glow of triumph.

I should mention some of the difficulties, real or imagined, that accompanied the gradual acquisition of Irish thought and manners. A degree of anxiety always seemed to be present. There was the ever-present danger that an unforgivable offense might bring acceptance to an abrupt end. Warnings of this possibility had been given in graduate-school days, and there was sufficient distrust and insecurity among the Irish themselves that the belief had support in reality.

There was widespread acceptance of supernatural causes as explanations for even ordinary events, and this belief could work either to one's advantage or to one's disadvantage. I was always fortunate in this regard. For example, the first night after my arrival at Quin's house, one of his cows was ready to calve, and I was fully aware that a stillbirth might mean the end of my welcome. Luckily, the new calf was a healthy little animal, and I was told that I had brought good luck.

Identification of psychological states such as paranoia, depression, or hysteria is more difficult to make. We know that individuals do suffer stress in cross-cultural situations, but the separation of cultural factors from the idiosyncratic is not easy. I experienced the most severe stress at my second visit to the Quinn household during the Christmas–New Year holiday season. There were clearly marked periods of inertia, and it became increasingly difficult for me to seek out others or to plan a departure. At the end of five weeks the unexpected arrival of an American colleague rescued me from the situation. I have some-times wondered if this period was basically one of accelerated absorption into Irish culture.

Departure was always difficult. Somehow I had failed to learn the behavior which permitted one to disengage himself with a minimum of stress to his hosts and himself. But ignorance of the ritual of leavetaking was only part of the problem. Weeks of close association had forged emotional links of some strength, and these were not easy to break. Departures tended to be abrupt, unsatisfying, even touched with anger. There were elements of sadness, but the joy that came with escape and freedom was more powerful. Escape and freedom were only momentary realities, however, because the Queen's Hotel at Ennis was at the other end of the line.

Reentry into the life of the town was never easy. There was the need to reestablish relationships and to exchange the outlook and manner of the country-man for those of the townsman. The immediate transition was helped immensely by a hot bath, a change of costume, and a few stiff drinks.

During the late winter I made two additional excursions of several weeks each to another small farmer's household in a different part of the county. My objec-tive was to gather comparative material and to extend my knowledge of the countryman's way of life. The contrast in life-style with Rynamona was not great, but I was made much more aware of the deep connections between life's happen-ings and supernatural powers. These periods of living in the country must also have affected my attitude toward the town, for the Queen's Hotel became home and refuge.

By early spring my entire effort was concentrated on research in the town. In addition to the usual pursuit of information, there were a number of affairs in which I was invited to participate. One of the more dramatic of these events was the week-long mission, or religious revival, which a local physician invited me to attend with him. I viewed the invitation as a friendly act on his part, but it might also have been interpreted as an interest in my conversion and later I learned that the good sisters of a nearby convent had offered prayers toward that end. These gestures toward me I took to be evidence of an increasing acceptance and under-standing of my purposes, and my broadened activities also contributed to my progressive acquisition of an Irish perspective. These experiences might also be viewed as prologue to another event that spring which took place without warning and with unexpected consequences.

One midweek night I had talked late with one of the town's doctors about his family history, and it was past 1:00 A.M. when I returned to my hotel. The

Queen's Hotel was situated on a corner where a narrow side street joined Abbey Street, which was barely wide enough for two cars to squeeze by each other. It was, however, a main artery lined on both sides with two- and three-story buildings and ended at the height of the street where the monument to Daniel O'Connell stood. The main door of the hotel faced up the street. On the side-street side there was a utility pole which also held a street light. It was a dark night with an overcast sky, and all the street lights had been off for more than an hour. If a guest of the hotel arrived after the main door had been locked, he rang the outside bell and in a few minutes the porter appeared and let him in.

This night was no different from the others and I had rung the bell and was waiting for the sound of footsteps in the hall to announce the coming of the porter. Suddenly a figure appeared from the side street and stopped about three feet away. My first thought was that this was a member of the Civic Guard who patrol the streets at night and take the names of those who are out after midnight. I greeted the presumed guard with a "Hello," but there was no reply and I thought the figure began to move toward me. My sense of danger and my reaction were almost simultaneous. I kicked with all my force at the midsection of the approaching threat. But there was no connection with anything solid. Instead my foot went through the air and I was nearly thrown off balance. The figure moved backward a foot or two, and I had the sense that I had repelled what was intended to be a friendly advance. The figure then disappeared. In the meantime I had reconnected with the bell and was pushing with all my might. In a few moments the porter arrived and opened the door. As I stepped quickly inside, somewhat shaken, I said in what I tried to make an off-hand manner, "I have just seen a ghost outside the hotel door."

The news of my adventure preceded me to the breakfast table, via the porter and his fellow hotel employees, I presume. I repeated the story several times to interested residents of the hotel, but the reaction was something for which I was not prepared. Several of the more permanent guests of the hotel began to relate supernatural experiences they had had. I learned that the hotel possessed quite a collection of ethereal inhabitants. One ghostly monk was such a persistent visitor to the room of a schoolteacher that she finally sought the assistance of the Franciscan fathers, whose spiritual powers relieved her of his nightly presence. One of the land commissioners kept a light burning throughout the night since the occasion when he had awakened to find a figure standing at the foot of his bed. More otherworldly but apparently harmless presences were recounted. It was presumed that the husband of the widow who ran the hotel, a man who had hanged himself some years earlier, was another of the nightly wanderers, but he was never specifically identified.

Word of my experience also passed into the town. I have no idea how extensive was the network of communication that carried the story. But a few days later a man, then unknown to me, sought me out in the hotel and confirmed for some, at least, the identity of the ghostly creature I had met. He said that some years previously a Tim Malloy had been kicked to death by a drunk along that side street. He himself had seen Malloy's apparition on a number of occasions in the vicinity of that street, so that undoubtedly it was Tim Malloy's spirit I had encountered.

Some of the aftereffects of the ghostly encounter should be mentioned. I found myself the center of favorable attention, for now I had had a legitimate Irish experience. Moreover, I needed to have no hesitancy in reporting all the details since the experience was wholly mine. Nor did I need to fear adverse repercussions about the legitimacy of the story, for I have never met any Irishman who scoffed at the possibility of supernatural occurrences. On subsequent occasions I asked questions about supernatural experiences with none of the constraints about invasion of privacy or broaching sensitive subjects that I had felt earlier. Now that I had been through this serious, even dangerous experience, I seemed to acquire a new status which entitled me to considerations not previously granted. Perhaps as a consequence or even because of other reasons less explicit, extensive changes in my relationships appeared along a broad spectrum of activity. Barriers no longer seemed formidable.

The ghostly incident raises two interesting questions, and I have puzzled over both. Many people asked, and so did I initially, a question which assumed an answer based on a certain premise of reality. Was there in fact a disembodied figure at the door of the Queen's Hotel on this particular night, or was I subject to an hallucination? If you are a transcendentalist, you can argue that possibly there was a spirit there, perhaps the lonely soul of Tim Malloy. If you are a materialist, your conclusion might well be that I was hallucinating, or that it would be possible to explain in quite another manner why it was that I thought I had seen a ghost. Neither transcendentalists nor materialists can ever provide that solid proof that would clinch the argument for their side. They can engage in the game of speculation, but after a while that too loses its novelty. Since no answer about the reality of the existence of the ghost can be given, the question is unanswerable. But there is a question that can be framed within the context of behavior and meaning that is worthy of our consideration.

I did not clearly formulate this second question until long after I had returned from Ireland. In fact, its explicit statement was delayed until I began to share, along with other colleagues, an interest in the cultural transformation which an anthropologist in the field undergoes. The phrasing of the problem has now been expanded to include his impact on and sequential modification of his relationships with members of the host culture as he comes increasingly to resemble them. The specific problem is how far my ghostly encounter may be considered as some index or measure of the extent to which I had absorbed the Irish perspective and been incorporated in Irish culture.

As we know, the capacity for supernatural experience as well as its form and content is culturally learned. The visions which the Sioux youth receives, including prayers, songs, and sacred designs, all fall within culturally known limits. The same statement can be made about ghostly and spiritual doings for other cultures. From this perspective it is quite irrelevant whether I actually did see a ghost or whether it was pure hallucination. The point is that I thought I saw one, and the Irish also believed so. Some months later, upon my return to the United States, I told my colleague, Arensberg, of this experience. His immediate reply was that the Irish had made me one of them. For a variety of reasons I disliked this idea, although I now realize I was responding to my biases. In fact, I might have been more willing to accept some mystic genetic linkage with Celtic ancestors as valid explanation. But anthropologists have long known that culture is learned and transmitted, not inherited.

But there is no known device that measures the degree of penetration into an alien culture. It is relatively easy to observe and conform to many items of behavior, but outward appearances may be largely superficial. Change would not be significant until it began to appear at the psychic level in the patterns of cognitive and emotional response and in the unconscious manifestations through dreams and visions.

We must also take account of the incorporative processes associated with interaction and group identification. Among the country people it was much easier to place an individual if you knew his kin connections, and on one occasion a whole set of these was invented for me. But when a half-serious effort was made to find me a suitable country girl as wife in the pre-Lenten matchmaking period, it was time to remember the principle about avoiding entangling sexual alliances and to take evasive action. The invitation to take part in the mission services might also be viewed as an incorporative act. The proselytizing was never insistent or offensive, so that polite joking about the matter could prevent any hard feelings. In these and other areas I maintained a polite aloofness which announced my intended separateness.

The direct participation in the supernatural world was, however, a quite different matter. I became the central character of an event in which my involvement was outside my conscious control. But if one were to choose an identification with powerful and positive overtones of acceptance, it would be difficult to find an area that was more deeply embedded in the Irish past and present than belief in the supernatural. Is it possible that unwittingly in this precipitous and dramatic fashion I had declared a fully Irish cultural perspective?

The question was asked more to evoke interest in a line of inquiry than to solicit a reply. Is it not likely that there is a regular course, a natural history, which each anthropologist experiences during his initial and perhaps even subsequent episodes of field work? Orderliness is further confirmed by some striking parallels between the *schema* of *rites de passage* and the introduction, involvement, and eventual withdrawal of a researcher in a culturally different environment. The time may have arrived when we are ready to undertake systematic observations of the processes of induction and involvement in another culture. We are far more sophisticated today about research in the field than we were in the early 1930's; and with the continuing increase of our self-conscious concern with what we do and its effects on ourselves and others, it should not be too long before such a venture is attempted.

Reference

Arensberg, Conrad M., and Solon T. Kimball. 1968. *Family and Community in Ireland.* 2nd ed.; Cambridge: Harvard University Press. Ch. 10.

Questions for Discussion and Writing

1. Kimball tells us that he could "never understand the Irish people until [he] became directly involved with the seemingly remote and different life-style of the small farmers" (p. 28). What does the author mean by "involved"? Why or why not was his conviction confirmed by his experiences?
2. What did the author learn about the patterns of verbal and nonverbal communication in Irish culture? How did what he learned influence his reporting on it?
3. What does Kimball's experience in moving from an outsider to an insider in the town teach us about the challenges of intercultural experience?
4. In what ways does "Learning a New Culture" reflect the difficulties of avoiding "overt entanglements" in a prolonged stay in another culture?
5. How can you describe Kimball's writing style in the essay? In what ways does his style contribute to or detract from your ability to understand his experiences and insights?

PAUL BOWLES

You Have Left Your Lotus Pods on the Bus

To learn something about the life of Paul Bowles is to get the impression that three or four people got accidentally mixed into his biography. There is Paul Bowles the musician who studied music and composition with Aaron Copland in New York and Berlin, and who composed scores for operas, films, ballets, songs, and chamber music. There is Paul Bowles the translator—from French, Spanish, Italian, Arabic, and Moghrebi (an Arabic dialect in North Africa on the Mediterranean coast). There is Paul Bowles the writer—of short stories, novels, and poetry—who wrote all over the world about the world. And there is Paul Bowles the husband, of writer Jan Auer (his second wife), who gave up writing fiction himself when his wife's long-failing health demanded his constant care and time.

Bowles's best-known novel, The Sheltering Sky *(1949, reprinted 1978) probes the lives of two sophisticated American drifters, Port and Kit Moresby. In one startling line from that book, we feel the emptiness in their lives: "We've never managed, either of us," Port tells his wife Kit, "to get all the way into life." Yet Bowles appears to have succeeded where his characters failed. Born in 1910 in New York, he has lived most of his adult life in Morocco. In 1931 in Paris, he met Gertrude Stein and her companion, Alice B. Toklas. Stein critiqued his writing and suggested that some time away from Western culture would help Bowles discover his own style. Toklas suggested Morocco, and thus introduced Bowles to the place he would live for most of his life, as well as the setting for the greater part of his fiction.*

In the story "You Have Left Your Lotus Pods on the Bus," two Americans spend a confusing day exploring Thailand with three Thai monks.

Before you read "You Have Left Your Lotus Pods on the Bus," write about an experience in which you did not understand the meaning of what you were seeing and experiencing, especially if you were in a new place or with a person you did not know well. Describe the things that confused you, your misinterpretation of them, and how you finally discovered (or didn't discover) what was really going on.

I soon learned not to go near the windows or to draw aside the double curtains in order to look at the river below. The view was wide and lively, with factories and warehouses on the far side of the Chao Phraya, and strings of barges being towed up and down through the dirty water. The new wing of the hotel had been built in the shape of an upright slab, so that the room was high and had no trees to shade it from the poisonous onslaught of the afternoon sun. The end of the day, rather than bringing respite, intensified the heat, for then the entire river was made of sunlight. With the redness of dusk everything out there became melodramatic and forbidding, and still the oven heat from outside leaked through the windows.

Brooks, teaching at Chulalongkorn University, was required as a Fulbright Fellow to attend regular classes in Thai; as an adjunct to this he arranged to spend much of his leisure time with Thais. One day he brought along with him three young men wearing the bright orange-yellow robes of Buddhist monks. They filed into the hotel room in silence and stood in a row as they were presented to me, each one responding by joining his palms together, thumbs touching his chest.

As we talked, Yamyong, the eldest, in his late twenties, explained that he was an ordained monk, while the other two were novices. Brooks then asked Prasert and Vichai if they would be ordained soon, but the monk answered for them.

"I do not think they are expecting to be ordained," he said quietly, looking at the floor, as if it were a sore subject all too often discussed among them. He glanced up at me and went on talking. "Your room is beautiful. We are not accustomed to such luxury." His voice was flat; he was trying to conceal his disapproval. The three conferred briefly in undertones. "My friends say they have never seen such a luxurious room," he reported, watching me closely through his steel-rimmed spectacles to see my reaction. I failed to hear.

They put down their brown paper parasols and their reticules that bulged with books and fruit. Then they got themselves into position in a row along the couch among the cushions. For a while they were busy adjusting the folds of their robes around their shoulders and legs.

"They make their own clothes," volunteered Brooks. "All the monks do."

I spoke of Ceylon; there the monks bought the robes all cut and ready to sew together. Yamyong smiled appreciatively and said: "We use the same system here."

The air-conditioning roared at one end of the room and the noise of boat motors on the river seeped through the windows at the other. I looked at the three sitting in front of me. They were very calm and self-possessed, but they seemed lacking in physical health. I was aware of the facial bones beneath their skin. Was the impression of sallowness partly due to the shaved eyebrows and hair?

Yamyong was speaking. "We appreciate the opportunity to use English. For this reason we are liking to have foreign friends. English, American; it doesn't matter. We can understand." Prasert and Vichai nodded.

Time went on, and we sat there, extending but not altering the subject of conversation. Occasionally I looked around the room. Before they had come in, it had been only a hotel room whose curtains must be kept drawn. Their presence and their comments on it had managed to invest it with a vaguely disturbing quality; I felt that they considered it a great mistake on my part to have chosen such a place in which to stay.

"Look at his tattoo," said Brooks. "Show him."

Yamyong pulled back his robe a bit from the shoulder, and I saw the two indigo lines of finely written Thai characters. "That is for good health," he said, glancing up at me. His smile seemed odd, but then, his facial expression did not complement his words at any point.

"Don't the Buddhists disapprove of tattooing?" I said.

"Some people say it is backwardness." Again he smiled. "Words for good health are said to be superstition. This was done by my abbot when I was a boy studying in the *wat*. Perhaps he did not know it was a superstition."

We were about to go with them to visit the *wat* where they lived. I pulled a tie from the closet and stood before the mirror arranging it.

"Sir," Yamyong began. "Will you please explain something? What is the significance of the necktie?"

"The significance of the necktie?" I turned to face him. "You mean, why do men wear neckties?"

"No. I know that. The purpose is to look like a gentleman."

I laughed. Yamyong was not put off. "I have noticed that some men wear the two ends equal, and some wear the wide end longer than the narrow, or the narrow longer than the wide. And the neckties themselves, they are not all the same length, are they? Some even with both ends equal reach below the waist. What are the different meanings?"

"There is no meaning," I said. "Absolutely none."

He looked to Brooks for confirmation, but Brooks was trying out his Thai on Prasert and Vichai, and so he was silent and thoughtful for a moment. "I believe you, of course," he said graciously. "But we all thought each way had a different significance attached."

As we went out of the hotel, the doorman bowed respectfully. Until now he had never given a sign that he was aware of my existence. The wearers of the yellow robe carry weight in Thailand.

A few Sundays later I agreed to go with Brooks and our friends to Ayudhaya. The idea of a Sunday outing is so repellent to me that deciding to take part in this one was to a certain extent a compulsive act. Ayudhaya lies less than fifty miles up the Chao Phraya from Bangkok. For historians and art collectors it is more than just a provincial town; it is a period and a style—having been the Thai capital for more than four centuries. Very likely it still would be, had the Burmese not laid it waste in the eighteenth century.

Brooks came early to fetch me. Downstairs in the street stood the three bhikkus with their book bags and parasols. They hailed a cab, and without any previous price arrangements (the ordinary citizen tries to fix a sum beforehand) we got in and drove for twenty minutes or a half-hour, until we got to a bus terminal on the northern outskirts of the city.

It was a nice, old-fashioned, open bus. Every part of it rattled, and the air from the rice fields blew across us as we pieced together our bits of synthetic conversation. Brooks, in high spirits, kept calling across to me: "Look! Water buffaloes!" As we went further away from Bangkok there were more of the beasts, and his cries became more frequent. Yamyong, sitting next to me, whispered: "Professor Brooks is fond of buffaloes?" I laughed and said I didn't think so.

"Then?"

I said that in America there were no buffaloes in the fields, and that was why Brooks was interested in seeing them. There were no temples in the landscape, either, I told him, and added, perhaps unwisely: "He looks at buffaloes. I look at temples." This struck Yamyong as hilarious, and he made allusions to it now and then all during the day.

The road stretched ahead, straight as a line in geometry, across the verdant, level land. Paralleling it on its eastern side was a fairly wide canal, here and there choked with patches of enormous pink lotuses. In places the flowers were gone and only the pods remained, thick green disks with the circular seeds embedded in their flesh. At the first stop the bhikkus got out. They came aboard again with mangosteens and lotus pods and insisted on giving us large numbers of each. The huge seeds popped out of the fibrous lotus cakes as though from a punchboard; they tasted almost like green almonds. "Something new for you today, I think," Yamyong said with a satisfied air.

Ayudhaya was hot, dusty, spread-out, its surrounding terrain strewn with ruins that scarcely showed through the vegetation. At some distance from the town there began a wide boulevard sparingly lined with important-looking buildings. It continued for a way and then came to an end as abrupt as its beginning. Growing up out of the scrub, and built of small russet-colored bricks, the ruined temples looked still unfinished rather than damaged by time. Repairs, done in smeared cement, veined their facades.

The bus's last stop was still two or three miles from the center of Ayudhaya. We got down into the dust, and Brooks declared: "The first thing we must do is find food. They can't eat anything solid, you know, after midday."

"Not noon exactly," Yamyong said. "Maybe one o'clock or a little later."

"Even so, that doesn't leave much time," I told him. "It's quarter to twelve now."

But the bhikkus were not hungry. None of them had visited Ayudhaya before, and so they had compiled a list of things they most wanted to see. They spoke with a man who had a station wagon parked nearby, and we set off for a ruined *stupa* that lay some miles to the southwest. It had been built atop a high mound, which we climbed with some difficulty, so that Brooks could take pictures of us standing within a fissure in the decayed outer wall. The air stank of the bats that lived inside.

When we got back to the bus stop, the subject of food arose once again, but the excursion had put the bhikkus into such a state of excitement that they could not bear to allot time for anything but looking. We went to the museum. It was quiet; there were Khmer heads and documents inscribed in Pali. The day had begun to be painful. I told myself I had known beforehand that it would.

Then we went to a temple. I was impressed, not so much by the gigantic Buddha which all but filled the interior, as by the fact that not far from the entrance a man sat on the floor playing a *ranad* (pronounced *lanat*). Although I was familiar with the sound of it from listening to recordings of Siamese music, I had never before seen the instrument. There was a graduated series of wooden blocks strung together, the whole slung like a hammock over a boat-shaped resonating stand. The tones hurried after one another like drops of water falling very fast. After the painful heat outside, everything in the temple suddenly seemed a symbol of the concept of coolness—the stone floor under my bare feet, the breeze that moved through the shadowy interior, the bamboo fortune sticks being rattled in their long box by those praying at the altar, and the succession of insubstantial, glassy sounds that came from the *ranad*. I thought: If only I could get something to eat, I wouldn't mind the heat so much.

We got into the center of Ayudhaya a little after three o'clock. It was hot and noisy; the bhikkus had no idea of where to look for a restaurant, and the prospect of asking did not appeal to them. The five of us walked aimlessly. I had come to the conclusion that neither Prasert nor Vichai understood spoken English, and I addressed myself earnestly to Yamyong. "We've got to eat." He stared at me with severity. "We are searching," he told me.

Eventually we found a Chinese restaurant on a corner of the principal street. There was a table full of boisterous Thais drinking *mekong* (categorized as whiskey, but with the taste of cheap rum) and another table occupied by an entire Chinese family. These people were doing some serious eating, their faces buried in their rice bowls. It cheered me to see them: I was faint, and had half expected to be told that there was no hot food available.

The large menu in English which was brought us must have been typed several decades ago and wiped with a damp rag once a week ever since. Under the heading SPECIALTIES were some dishes that caught my eye, and as I went through the list I began to laugh. Then I read it aloud to Brooks.

"Fried Sharks Fins and Bean Sprout
Chicken Chins Stuffed with Shrimp
Fried Rice Birds
Shrimps Balls and Green Marrow
Pigs Lights with Pickles
Braked Rice Bird in Port Wine
Fish Head and Bean Curd"

Although it was natural for our friends not to join in the laughter, I felt that their silence was not merely failure to respond; it was heavy, positive.

A moment later three Pepsi-Cola bottles were brought and placed on the table. "What are you going to have?" Brooks asked Yamyong.

"Nothing, thank you," he said lightly. "This will be enough for us today."

"But this is terrible! You mean no one is going to eat *anything?*"

"You and your friend will eat your food," said Yamyong. (He might as well have said "fodder.") Then he, Prasert, and Vichai stood up, and carrying their Pepsi-Cola bottles with them, went to sit at a table on the other side of the room. Now and then Yamyong smiled sternly across at us.

"I wish they'd stop watching us," Brooks said under his breath.

"They were the ones who kept putting it off," I reminded him. But I felt guilty, and I was annoyed at finding myself placed in the position of the self-indulgent unbeliever. It was almost as bad as eating in front of Moslems during Ramadan.

We finished our meal and set out immediately, following Yamyong's decision to visit a certain temple he wanted to see. The taxi drive led us through a region of thorny scrub. Here and there, in the shade of spreading flat-topped trees, were great round pits, full of dark water and crowded with buffaloes; only their wet snouts and horns were visible. Brooks was already crying: "Buffaloes! Hundreds of them!" He asked the taxi driver to stop so that he could photograph the animals.

"You will have buffaloes at the temple," said Yamyong. He was right; there was a muddy pit filled with them only a few hundred feet from the building. Brooks went and took his pictures while the bhikkus paid their routine visit to the shrine. I wandered into a courtyard where there was a long row of stone Buddhas. It is the custom of temple-goers to plaster little squares of gold leaf into the religious statues in the *wats*. When thousands of them have been stuck onto the same surface, tiny scraps of the gold come unstuck. Then they tremble in the breeze, and the figure shimmers with a small, vibrant life of its own. I stood in the courtyard watching this quivering along the arms and torsos of the Buddhas, and I was reminded of the motion of the bô-tree's leaves. When I mentioned it to Yamyong in the taxi, I think he failed to understand, for he replied: "The bô-tree is a very great tree for Buddhists."

Brooks sat beside me on the bus going back to Bangkok. We spoke only now and then. After so many hours of resisting the heat, it was relaxing to sit and feel the relatively cool air that blew in from the rice fields. The driver of the bus was not a believer in cause and effect. He passed trucks with oncoming traffic in full view. I felt better with my eyes shut, and I might even have dozed off, had there not been in the back of the bus a man, obviously not in control, who was intent on making as much noise as possible. He began to shout, scream, and howl almost as soon as we had left Ayudhaya, and he did this consistently throughout the journey. Brooks and I laughed about it, conjecturing whether he was crazy or only drunk. The aisle was too crowded for me to be able to see him from where I sat. Occasionally I glanced at the other passengers. It was as though they were entirely unaware of the commotion behind them. As we drew closer to the city, the screams became louder and almost constant.

"God, why don't they throw him off?" Brooks was beginning to be annoyed.

"They don't even hear him," I said bitterly. People who can tolerate noise inspire me with envy and rage. Finally I leaned over and said to Yamyong: "That poor man back there! It's incredible!"

"Yes," he said over his shoulder. "He's very busy." This set me thinking what a civilized and tolerant people they were, and I marvelled at the sophistication of the word "busy" to describe what was going on in the back of the bus.

Finally we were in a taxi driving across Bangkok. I would be dropped at my hotel and Brooks would take the three bhikkus on to their *wat.* In my head I was still hearing the heartrending cries. What had the repeated word patterns meant?

I had not been able to give an acceptable answer to Yamyong in his bewilderment about the significance of the necktie, but perhaps he could satisfy my curiosity here.

"That man in the back of the bus, you know?"

Yamyong nodded. "He was working very hard, poor fellow. Sunday is a bad day."

I disregarded the nonsense. "What was he saying?"

"Oh, he was saying: 'Go into second gear,' or 'We are coming to a bridge,' or 'Be careful, people in the road.' What he saw."

Since neither Brooks nor I appeared to have understood, he went on. "All the buses must have a driver's assistant. He watches the road and tells the driver how to drive. It is hard work because he must shout loud enough for the driver to hear him."

"But why doesn't he sit up in front with the driver?"

"No, no. There must be one in front and one in the back. That way two men are responsible for the bus."

It was an unconvincing explanation for the grueling sounds we had heard, but to show him that I believed him I said: "Aha! I see."

The taxi drew up in front of the hotel and I got out. When I said good-by to Yamyong, he replied, I think with a shade of aggrievement: "Good-by. You have left your lotus pods on the bus."

Questions for Discussion and Writing

1. What elements of setting are conveyed in the first paragraph? In what ways does this sense of place become an important part of the story as the narrative unfolds?
2. In what ways and why do the two Americans and three Thais repeatedly misunderstand each other? Why or why not could their misunderstandings have been averted in some way?
3. Which elements in the story, if any, made you smile or laugh? Explain why you found them funny as well as how they contribute to the whole story. Why or why not might the men in the story also find these same elements funny?
4. Explain the meaning of the last line of the story, spoken by Yamyong: "Good-by. You have left your lotus pods on the bus." Ask some Asian friends about the meanings of the lotus flower and lotus pods. Look up the word *lotus* in a dictionary or an encyclopedia for additional information on the meaning of this line, which is also the title of the story.
5. What did the American men learn from their day with the Thai monks? What did the monks learn? Explain your responses.
6. In what ways does the author's use of dialogue reflect the character and situation of each man in the story? Why does Bowles use a lot of dialogue to tell his story?
7. Why do you think Bowles wrote this story? For whom do you think he wrote it?

H. JATHAR SALIJ

A Weekend in Bandung

In the frenzy of growing up on three continents, H. Jathar Salij has managed to keep most of the details of his life from biographers. Aside from writing, Salij teaches at universities in the East and West. He completed his doctoral dissertation in comparative literature at the University of Washington in 1971.

One of Salij's main concerns in his writing is the way people go about their daily, often precarious lives in a rapidly changing world. "A Weekend in Bandung" comes from Shadow Play and Other Stories *(1982), a collection of stories set in Malaysia, Indonesia, and Singapore. This story's primary locale is the village of Bandung, on the island of Java in western Indonesia.*

Before you read "A Weekend in Bandung," write about a time in your life when, in attempting to realize a fantasy or dream of travel, you encountered elements in the experience for which you were not prepared or that conflicted with your original fantasies. Describe your fantasies, what happened to surprise and upset you as you sought to experience them, and what you did as a result.

H e woke deliberately slowly and somewhat unwillingly from a confused dream and listened to the sounds on the other side of the thin hotel room door: rapid men's voices, a car that refused to start, a sweeping broom, the dragging feet of someone going from one end of the hotel courtyard to the other.

Waking up in the tropics had a deceptive sort of near-harmony to it. You were never sure where the sleeping ended and the waking began. The humid bright heat, the sounds and noises in many tonal varieties, the myriads of colours became part of your dreams: you woke up with them, hardly ever because of them.

In Solo, the week before, it had been the same: after half-sleepless nights, transpierced by the stings of mosquitoes, the gap between the dream he was emerging from and the one he was about to enter was filled with the sounds of subdued voices, a softly strummed guitar, a low-tuned radio playing an Indonesian folk-song. He squinted through sleep-heavy lashes at the dusty window panes, grey enough to filter out some of the bright sun, and saw the emerald contours of slowly waving banana trees. That had been in a hardboard-walled room in one of the buildings of the *Kraton,* where the days were somnambulant and filled with *gamelan* music, dance, and monophonic songs.

But outside the heavy grey walls of the *Kraton,* in the humid midday heat of the dusty streets, were the many hands of the hungry reaching out toward him, and the cry *"Kasihan!"* echoed in his ears from everywhere. The word meant 'pity' and it hung unerasable in the hot air.

In the vagueness of the room he became aware of the figure on the other bed, closer to the soft-red curtains covering the windows. Lying on her side, Ratih was looking at him. When she saw him awake, she got up and came over and lay beside him. A faint scent of perfume spread. A tear slowly furrowed down from her left eye and fell on the bedsheet.

"Don't cry," he mumbled and put his arm under her head in a gesture of consolation.

"But what else can I do when I think that this is the last week and then you'll be gone." She rose halfway, leaned on an elbow. "Don't leave me, darling," she whispered. "Don't leave me." She pressed a small, white embroidered handkerchief against her eyes.

"Oh Ratih, you know I can't stay."

She nodded and pressed a sad kiss on his mouth. "Yes, I know," she mumbled mournfully, "but what am I going to do when you're gone? What am I going to do? I just don't know. I'll be so alone." She shook her head in dejection. Her long black hair fell forward in waves. With a sigh she got up and walked over to the cracked mirror above the basin with its superfluous faucets.

He felt guilty and was slightly annoyed and could not justify either feeling.

"We must eat and get our train tickets," she said, looking in the mirror. She began to put on her make-up.

The weekend in Bandung had begun with feelings of nostalgia on Alan's part because of a girl named Ambar who had been born there. Ambar was the first girl he had ever taken an interest in. He had loved her with adolescent ease and had imagined her birthplace amidst the green density of equatorial forests, an abundance of brilliant, exotic flowers, and inhabited by kind, healthy, golden-brown people. After a year in Java, he still felt that Bandung was going to be different from all other cities.

They caught a train in Jakarta, got off in Bandung, and stood in the tepid late afternoon warmth, looking at the vaguely lit rectangle that quivered with activity: on the right an endless and beginningless flow of people moving into one shop and out of another. On the left, exhaust-spewing buses and taxicabs, and beggars shuffling about, holding up their hands to invisible people behind the windows. Alan was lost. He recognized nothing of what had been so clear in his mind and suddenly wished he could trade places with the unassuming librarian with whom Ambar lived on in prosaic wedlock in the suburbs of some Western city. Have a steady job, raise children and think of the world as a perfect place. The last time he had seen Ambar, she had told him she didn't want to go back to Indonesia, because "I couldn't live with all that poverty surrounding me." He had shrugged it off.

Ratih and Alan silently watched and tried to ignore the pedicab drivers encircling them, their shrill voices tearing through the fast falling dark: *"Becak, tuan! Becak!"* A small man outside the circle of pedicab drivers came forward slowly and limpingly, leaning on a walking stick, eyes fixed on the couple. In front of Alan he stopped and held out his hand. *"Kasihan,"* he lisped hoarsely.

Alan turned to Ratih. "Let's go. Quick," he said a bit nervously. Hurriedly they got into one of the pedicabs. In the uncertain dark the man's face had resembled that of his father, but where the nose had been was a large dark hole with frayed edges.

Ratih told the driver to stop at a hotel in the centre of town, near a drawbridge at an intersection. It was fairly close to Jalan Braga, the famed shopping street of Bandung, featured in all tourist brochures. They registered, put their things in a room semi-lit by the glow of a forty-watt bulb and without running water. Then they took a walk through silent streets, where oil lamps spread a yellow glow: electricity had been rationed on account of the drought, which had nearly emptied the reservoirs of the hydro-electric plants.

The streets were lined with pedicabs in which drivers lay curled up like foetuses. Others were still awake and hoping for a customer. They hailed Ratih and Alan. Again others sat quietly gambling by oil lamps on the pavement, smoking clove cigarettes. Now and then they uttered a word or two about a won game and laughed in low-key. A man passed, silently sweeping rubbish into the monsoon drain.

They came to Jalan Braga. It was dark; only here and there an oil lamp in a shop window spread some light. A shout ripped stridently through the dark from beyond the cars parked on both sides of the street: *"Kasihan!"* A boy, little girl and an old blind woman, all three in rags, moved behind one another like ducks, the boy first. The old woman and the girl held on to the shoulder in front with one hand, thrust out the other toward Ratih and Alan, and cried, *"Kasihan! Kasi wang!* Money! Money!"* The words reverberated through the street on two tone levels and with a terrifying rhythm, to which the boy added his own. He pulled the old woman and the little girl forward so that they often stumbled. *"Kasihan!"* he yelled. Passing through the weak light of the sporadic oil lamps, they looked like phantoms chased by the wind.

Ratih and Alan walked on, trying not to pay attention. But an opening between two cars allowed the three to cross the street. *"Kasihan! Kasi wang!"* Ratih and Alan went as fast as they could. So did the three beggars. Like a slithering serpent, the rag-clad figures followed, their heads bobbing up and down. The boy went too fast for the little girl and the old woman, and they lost contact. Yelling, he went on alone: *"Kasihan!"* then slowed down. The others linked up with him again, all the while screaming in chorus: *"Kasihan!"* The boy cried that they were poor and hungry. They hadn't eaten all day. It sounded like an accusation.

Alan looked back and saw three hands coming in his direction, becoming bigger and bigger. The three heads bobbed and wagged, and the mouths were wide dark holes. The three beggars ran as fast as they could to catch up with the couple, but the little girl and the old woman were beginning to show signs of fatigue and lagged behind. The boy went on alone for a while, but finally gave up, too.

Ratih laughed. "What an absurd race," she said. "You're funny, you know." She hugged Alan. "The way you were running away with those beggars at your heels." She hugged him again. "I love you," she added, and took his hand.

"Don't you think you were a bit funny yourself, running along like that?" he asked. He stopped short before a grinning demon's mask with sharp, pointed teeth that stuck through a harelip. The canines were fangs. The yellow light of an oil lamp, hanging in a shop entrance, shone weirdly on the mask. Or was it a face? It was, and it belonged to a boy. *"Kasihan,"* he whispered hoarsely. Ratih gave him a coin. *"Terima kasih,"* he lisped and retreated into a dark corner of the shop entrance.

The same here as in Solo: people whispering or yelling, sometimes cursing you if you didn't give them anything. The blind, the paralysed, the syphilitics, the lepers, the deformed. Old people and children. Men and women. People on their way out of their world of misery and people just coming into it. They all asked for pity, and hardly anyone paid attention.

One afternoon the skeletal hand of an old woman, held up by a girl of about six, interrupted him during his rice-and-fish meal in a market place. He put a ten-rupiah note in the bony hand. The girl closed the old woman's fingers around it and whispered something into her ear. The woman turned her face toward Alan. He looked at two glaucous bulbs that stared bluish and stiff back at him. *"Terima kasih, tuan,"* she mumbled. The little girl led the woman away. They disappeared in the crowd between two rows of *batik* shops. Somebody tapped him on the arm from the other side, stopping the spoonful of rice on its way to his mouth. A woman in dirty grey rags held up a rusty tin can, pointed at the food on his plate. He filled her tin can with the remainder of his meal. Scraping the food out hurriedly with dirty fingers, she went away.

Ratih and Alan walked on. At the end of the street a dark figure suddenly stepped forward and lisped *"Kasihan!"* in a rasping voice. A hand appeared before Alan's eyes. It was the man with the hole in his face. Alan felt in his pocket and found a coin. He dropped it in the man's hand with a strange feeling that it was falling into the hollow face. *"Terima kasih, tuan,"* rasped the man. Alan ran off as fast as he could and only stopped near the drawbridge a hundred or so yards away. There he waited for Ratih, who joined him silently. They walked back to the hotel.

He spent the rest of the night with begging men, women, and children. Some had fanged masks that whispered and cursed. He tried to tear them off and only held rapidly decaying faces in his hands. The faces got inflamed and swelled up and stared back at him out of dark holes. Others had heads like snakes that danced up and down in a dark street and hit him with mad laughter: *"Kasihan! Kasihan!"* With the rotting faces in his hands, he ran into ever-narrowing streets, yelling: "Go away! Go away! There's not enough money for everybody!" but they sneered and snorted and hissed and came closer and closer, until there was no way out, and he threw the faces at them, which they caught, ripped to pieces, screaming and cursing that they were too poor to go on living but couldn't die either.

There was no end to their suffering nor to Alan's dreams, and restlessly he slept on, walking through Bandung, the birthplace of Ambar, who couldn't live with the poor because she knew what it meant. Buzzing mosquitoes circled through the room, and Ratih's slender form was near.

At last daylight broke. The sun climbed and heat enveloped the world. Through sunlit streets Alan and Ratih went in search of a restaurant. At the lowest levels of the sunlight were the vendors of fruits, vegetables, scrap metal, old and new clothes, and junk. Pedicab drivers and all sorts of people sat, stood, or crouched against buildings and away from them. Not far from the hotel, on the other side of the intersection, they found a Chinese restaurant. They went in and sat down near the window. Alan looked at the hundreds of people trying to sell their wares, some buying, always in motion, yet seemingly standing still. Traffic moved in all directions under the constantly and predictably changing traffic lights. A man with a kind, round face sold a yellow blouse to a small woman with oily blue hair after much gesturing and moving of lips. He turned excitedly to his neighbour, who was selling old shoes, and showed him the money he had just made.

Amidst the geometrically placed tables and chairs in the dark-brown interior of the restaurant ambulated a short-skirted, half-smiling waitress with the beginnings of wrinkles around her almond-shaped eyes. She came to their table and, whispering into Alan's right ear, she asked, while looking at Ratih, if he wanted anything else. They had nearly finished their meal, and he was eager to join the crowd and the sunlight beyond the window. He looked at Ratih, who shook her head slightly. "Thank you, no," he said to the waitress, also whispering, and ate the rest of his rice.

Afterwards they went to the mountain called Tangkuban Prahu because of its resemblance to an upturned boat—an active volcano and a sight for tourists. A taxi driver, willing to take them for a reasonable fare, drove them to the top, and soon they stood at the edge of the crater sniffing the sulphurous smells rising from the boiling pool below. The air was invigorating and quite different from the oppressive heat in the swampy lowlands of Jakarta. Even high-altitude Bandung was suffocating at this time of day, but here, on the mountain top, was the peaceful steaming and bubbling of the pool. The sounds of softly exploding gas, released from somewhere deep below. The twittering of a bird.

"Ratih, come, let's follow the path," he cried, and pointed to the left. His lungs were filled with power. After the heat of the valley, the thin, cold air was a treat he had not enjoyed for months. He ran up the uneven mountain path. But Ratih couldn't move as fast as he in her flimsy sandals, and the high altitude left her breathless.

They came to a grassy spot, sat down, and kissed. Furtively. There was always somebody somewhere, and Javanese women don't kiss. "Oh Alan," she sighed, "I love you so. Why must you go away?"

He gave her a sombre look. "Must we always think about my going away? Come on. Let's enjoy these moments now." He took her hands in his.

"Yes, yes," she said quickly. She did not want to spoil this togetherness with her worries, but there was sorrow in her voice.

Ratih was an attractive, somewhat melancholy woman, and the daughter of a wealthy, high-ranking Javanese. He had died on one of the usual hot and humid Jakarta afternoons, during a nap beside his second wife, who had demanded too much of his heart. Ratih languished and suffered in her amorous somnolence from which Alan's departure would wake her up temporarily. But soon after, she would sink back into dreaming that the separation would not be forever and that things would remain as they used to be. Meanwhile she nourished her forthcoming loneliness with many tears and somewhat languorous depressions.

Sometimes he was convinced that he loved her. In this steaming, hot universe she was his only real comfort, and as a destitute English teacher with below-subsistence wages he could appreciate, but not afford, a good meal and a cool drink. Ratih provided him with everything that her love for him inspired her with.

But outside the family compound sat men and women in rags. At times they had old shoes or other old things for sale, which they had collected from the garbage bins in the districts of the wealthy. They washed in the filthy water of the monsoon drain, and many of them were sick. Almost all were underfed. On the rubbish piles that lay here and there in the streets you saw old people scrounging for something to eat. The difference between their hardships and Ratih's privileged life gave him a morose sense of guilt, which made him scowl at her seeming indifference.

"But darling," she objected, aggrieved and with tears in her eyes, "you can't go on living if you take these things too seriously. You can't do a thing about them and you can't just stop because of that."

"That's probably true," he said, regretting his harshness. "Maybe you're right, but you see, the difference between them and you is what virtually makes the difference between you and me." Sometimes he wondered how he would feel if he had enough money to have the benefit of nutritious food and the comfort of an air-conditioned bedroom.

At first he had avoided her at all cost. But she was in love, which made her persistent. She'd come over to his room in her chauffeured Mercedes and surround him with her subtly perfumed presence, pretending she was bringing him some food from her kitchen. Soon, however, she'd take off her jewellery and her clothes, in that order, and stand brown and slender before him. In the dizzying afternoon heat of his room she was too beautiful to ignore. But Ratih's dream was nearly over, and the nightmares in anticipation of a terrible loneliness became more and more frequent.

They got up from their grassy spot and walked back to the road. On the summit, tourism was feverishly being developed: men were busily building lodges and eating places for hungry and thirsty tourists, who would surely flock to the place under the government's new promotion programme. They bought an ice-cream cone in one of the restaurants that smelled of half-finished newness. Soon beggars would find their way up the mountain road and try to make it through the day on the coins thrown in their direction by tourists.

Ratih was divorced from a man who had been forced on her by her parents. She was not considering remarrying unless she loved the man. "But my relatives keep on bugging me about it. My elder sister even suggested I become the mistress of some high-ranking fifty-year-old army man. It makes me sick." Alan felt slightly embarrassed whenever he ran into these relatives in the compound that Ratih shared with her mother, her little daughter, and a number of servants.

Ratih had finished putting on her make-up. "You'd better get ready if we want to be back in Jakarta in time," she said, looking at him in the cracked mirror.

Alan nodded and got up.

"And we also want to eat something before getting on the train."

He nodded again and began to put on his clothes.

They had their meal in a small eating place near the railway station. In the rectangle of the door-frame he saw worn-out taxi cabs and buses in the hazy yellow glare of the mid-morning sun. An emaciated man with empty sockets and wrinkles like furrows in a freshly plowed field felt his way around, using a dead tree branch to guide him from vehicle to vehicle. Moving his lips, incessantly praying or cursing, he held a hand up toward each open window, always going on without receiving anything.

The dark form of a small man appeared in the door opening, hiding the blind man from Alan's view. The man came in, tapping his stick on the floor as he, dragging one foot, moved toward the table where Ratih and Alan were having their meal. The man stopped near Alan and leaned on his stick, clasping it with force. His right hand came forward slowly and, it seemed, a little reluctantly. With a rasping lisp he said, *"Kasihan, tuan. Kasi wang. Saya sakit sekali."*

Alan wanted to ignore the man and stirred his rice with his spoon. But the man's hand and voice were very near, and he raised his head. He looked directly into the hole in the middle of the man's face. The man had spoken the truth: he was very ill indeed. Repulsed and fascinated Alan stared into its frayed darkness, unable to take his eyes off and wondering how anyone could go on living with a hole in his face, functioning, thinking. The man had to eat, and in order to eat, he approached people in the midst of their meal, attacking them in one of their most vulnerable moments, with his horrible disease as a weapon.

The man's red-rimmed eyes stared at Alan, and from between inflamed gums the lisped words came again and again: he wanted money and he was very sick. There was something in those wet, inflamed eyes that reminded Alan of better times, when his father was still alive and the family together. The man did look like his father, and the thought gave him a slightly nauseous feeling.

The beggar stood with his hand out, softly and persistently mumbling. Ratih stared past the hand through the open door, as if in a trance. Alan put down his spoon and searched in his trouser pockets. He found a hundred-rupiah note and dropped it into the cupped, deformed hand. With something like fright in his voice and staring at the dark hole, Alan said, *"Pergilah! Sila pergi!"* The man's short, nailless fingers clutched the bank note. With down-cast eyes he lisped, *"Terima kasih, tuan,"* through his toothless jaws, turned, and painfully shuffled outdoors. In an instant he had merged with the yellow and the grey of sun and dust and the noise of idling bus engines. Neither Alan nor Ratih wanted food anymore. They picked up their bags from the floor and went to the railway station.

At last the train rolled through mountainous areas and green sawahs, away from the chaos of Bandung and into the lowlands, sluggishly sliding back into the incoherence of Jakarta. The sun was setting in streaks of red and grey. It was time for evening baths and prayers. In some of the shacks, sprawling in massive numbers on both sides of the railroad tracks, people were pouring water over themselves. A little girl with a Coca-Cola can filled with water, a toothbrush in her white-smeared mouth, was watching the passing train from a pile of rubble.

It stopped in ripples of sudden shocks and spasms. Ratih and Alan stepped down onto the platform of Gambir Station. He took her slim dancer's hand in his, and they walked slowly into the Jakarta evening, which smelled fresh as after a downpour. It was dark now, and the sky was full of stars. Alan looked at the sky and said, "The hour of prayer. You think God will take care of all these people?"

She said that she didn't know what he meant. "I didn't see anything. What do you mean?"

"But . . ."

She squeezed his hand a little as if to comfort him and leaned her head on his shoulder. In an affectionately low voice she said, "I love you, darling, isn't that the important thing right now?" He could smell her delicate perfume. And a little louder, but still with affection, she added, "Besides, I can't let all that spoil my life. There's nothing one can do about it, my love."

"Really," he said thoughtfully. "Really. Forget what I asked you. It was a stupid question anyway."

She already had.

Love? Perhaps she was right and perhaps it was the only important thing. But you couldn't forget about everything else just because you were in love! The hole in that leper's face was real. So was the glare in the eyes of that old woman in Solo. Seeing all those hands reaching out to you, you could at the most say that love was a precarious urge at best, harmful to those produced by it, and at worst the source of unspeakable suffering, at least for a large majority.

In a way, love meant suffering for Ratih too. But it was suffering of the romantic kind, caused by her uncertainty about Alan's feelings for her and the fear that another would take her place. It was Ratih's only hardship and her major challenge. She was as persistent in the pursuit of her dream as the poor who were trying to survive on the charity of others. It filled her life in which servants made her existence problemless.

In another week it would seem that all this had merely existed in a dream. Just like it had been a dream to believe that the place where he had just spent the weekend would be different because of an adolescent love he could not forget. Everything with which this past year had confronted him would gradually evaporate in the computerized world to which he was returning. It might be, however, that the dream was where he was going back to and that his only waking hours had been here.

He would take her to her room in the family compound and, if she did not hold him back with insistence on love and tears, he'd catch the bus right away and go home.

Questions for Discussion and Writing

1. The chorus of *"Kasihan"* begins slowly and builds quickly in the story. In what contexts do Alan and Ratih encounter it, and how do their responses foreshadow the story's end? In what ways does the refrain work as a narrative device?

2. What does Alan mean when he says to Ratih about her response to the beggars, "the difference between them and you is what virtually makes the difference between you and me" (p. 49)?

3. Near the end of the story, when Alan says, "The hour of prayer," (p. 51) he is referring to the time of the Muslim prayers that will engulf the city. What is the significance of his asking Ratih, "You think God will take care of all these people?" and of her response?

4. What does Salij mean when he says this about Alan: "It might be, however, that the dream was where he was going back to and that his only waking hours had been here" (p. 52)?

5. What does Salij's story say about love, and especially about love between people from such different cultures?

RUTH PRAWER JHABVALA

Myself in India

Born in 1927 in Cologne, Germany, Ruth Prawer Jhabvala emigrated with her family to England in 1948. After receiving her M.A. from Queen Mary College in 1951, Jhabvala moved to New Delhi, India, where she still lives and writes today. In that same year, she married C. S. H. Jhabvala, an Indian architect, and began her career as a full-time writer of short stories, screenplays, and novels.

Jhabvala's first two novels, Amrita *(1956) and* The Nature of Passion *(1956), deal with the "absurdities arising from the juxtaposition of Eastern and Western ideals," in critic Patricia Hodgart's words. Jhabvala has been described as the best Anglo-Indian novelist writing today. She writes from within the extended Indian family structure and, as the following essay reflects, of her personal struggle between traditional Indian passivity and the Western need to act.*

The essay "Myself in India" introduces a collection of short stories entitled How I Became a Holy Mother and Other Stories *(1976). In it we see the long-term intercultural encounters and collisions of the author who, through marriage and choice, permanently trades her European past for a world as stunningly different as India.*

Before you read "Myself in India," write about a time in your life, if there was one, when you lived a long time in another culture or place. What stages do you recall in your adjustment to your new surroundings? What differences between your old patterns and assumptions and those of the new setting were most difficult to handle? In what ways were you able to adapt? In what ways did you fail to adapt? What do you remember most fondly about the experience now?

I have lived in India for most of my adult life. My husband is Indian and so are my children. I am not, and less so every year.

India reacts very strongly on people. Some loathe it, some love it, most do both. There is a special problem of adjustment for the sort of people who come today, who tend to be liberal in outlook and have been educated to be sensitive and receptive to other cultures. But it is not always easy to be sensitive and receptive to India: there comes a point where you have to close up in order to protect yourself. The place is very strong and often proves too strong for European nerves. There is a cycle that Europeans—by Europeans I mean all Westerners, including Americans—tend to pass through. It goes like this: first stage, tremendous enthusiasm—everything Indian is marvellous; second stage, everything Indian not so marvellous; third stage, everything Indian abominable. For some people it ends there, for others the cycle renews itself and goes on. I have been through it so many times that now I think of myself as strapped to a wheel that goes round and round and sometimes I'm up and sometimes I'm down. When I meet other Europeans, I can usually tell after a few moments' conversation at what stage of the cycle they happen to be. Everyone likes to talk about India, whether they happen to be loving or loathing it. It is a topic on which a lot of things can be said, and on a variety of aspects—social, economic, political, philosophical: it makes fascinating viewing from every side.

However, I must admit that I am no longer interested in India. What I am interested in now is myself in India—which sometimes, in moments of despondency, I tend to think of as my survival in India. I had better say straightaway that the reason why I live in India is because my strongest human ties are here. If I hadn't married an Indian, I don't think I would ever have come here for I am not attracted—or used not to be attracted—to the things that usually bring people to India. I know I am the wrong type of person to live here. To stay and endure, one should have a mission and a cause, to be patient, cheerful, unselfish, strong. I am a central European with an English education and a deplorable tendency to constant self-analysis. I am irritable and have weak nerves.

The most salient fact about India is that it is very poor and very backward. There are so many other things to be said about it but this must remain the basis of all of them. We may praise Indian democracy, go into raptures over Indian music, admire Indian intellectuals—but whatever we say, not for one moment should we lose sight of the fact that a very great number of Indians never get enough to eat. Literally that: from birth to death they never for one day cease to suffer from hunger. *Can* one lose sight of that fact? God knows, I've tried. But after seeing what one has to see here every day, it is not really possible to go on living one's life the way one is used to. People dying of starvation in the streets, children kidnapped and maimed to be sent out as beggars—but there is no point in making a catalogue of the horrors with which one lives, *on* which one lives, as on the back of an animal. Obviously, there has to be some adjustment.

There are several ways. The first and best is to be a strong person who plunges in and does what he can as a doctor or social worker. I often think that perhaps this is the only condition under which Europeans have any right to be here. I know several people like that. They are usually attached to some mission. They work very hard and stay very cheerful. Every few years they are sent on home leave. Once I met such a person—a woman doctor—who had just returned from her first home leave after being out here for twelve years. I asked her: but what does it feel like to go back after such a long time? How do you manage to adapt yourself? She didn't understand. This question which was of such tremendous import to me—how to adapt oneself to the differences between Europe and India—didn't mean a thing to her. It simply didn't matter. And she was right, for in view of the things she sees and does every day, the delicate nuances of one's own sensibilities are best forgotten.

Another approach to India's basic conditions is to accept them. This seems to be the approach favoured by most Indians. Perhaps it has something to do with their belief in reincarnation. If things are not to your liking in this life, there is always the chance that in your next life everything will be different. It appears to be a consoling thought for both rich and poor. The rich man stuffing himself on pilao can do so with an easy conscience because he knows he has earned this privilege by his good conduct in previous lives; and the poor man can watch him with some degree of equanimity for he knows that next time round it may well be *he* who will be digging into that pilao while the other will be crouching outside the door with an empty stomach. However, this path of acceptance is not open to you if you don't have a belief in reincarnation ingrained within you. And if you don't accept, then what can you do? Sometimes one wants just to run away and go to a place where everyone has enough to eat and clothes to wear and a home fit to live in. But even when you get there, can you ever forget? Having once seen the sights in India, and the way it has been ordained that people must live out their lives, nowhere in the world can ever be all that good to be in again.

None of this is what I wanted to say. I wanted to concentrate only on myself in India. But I could not do so before indicating the basis on which everyone who comes here has to live. I have a nice house, I do my best to live in an agreeable way. I shut all my windows, I let down the blinds, I turn on the air-conditioner; I read a lot of books, with a special preference for the great masters of the novel. All the time I know myself to be on the back of this great animal of poverty and backwardness. It is not possible to pretend otherwise. Or rather, one does pretend, but retribution follows. Even if one never rolls up the blinds and never turns off the air-conditioner, something is bound to go wrong. People are not meant to shut themselves up in rooms and pretend there is nothing outside.

Now I think I am drawing nearer to what I want to be my subject. Yes, something is wrong: I am not happy this way. I feel lonely, shut in, shut off. It is my own fault. I should go out more and meet people and learn what is going on. All right, so I am not a doctor nor a social worker nor a saint nor at all a good person; then the only thing to do is to try and push that aspect of India out of sight and turn to others. There are many others. I live in the capital where so much is going on. The winter is one round of parties, art exhibitions, plays, music and dance recitals, visiting European artistes: there need never be a dull moment. Yet all my moments are dull. Why? It is my own fault, I know. I can't quite explain it to myself but somehow I have no heart for these things here. Is it because all the time underneath I feel the animal moving? But I have decided to ignore the animal. I wish to concentrate only on modern, Westernized India, and on modern, well-off, cultured Westernized Indians.

Let me try and describe a Westernized Indian woman with whom I ought to have a lot in common and whose company I ought to enjoy. She has been to Oxford or Cambridge or some smart American college. She speaks flawless, easy, colloquial English with a charming lilt of an accent. She has a degree in economics or political science or English literature. She comes from a good family. Her father may have been an ICS officer or some other high-ranking government official; he too was at Oxford or Cambridge, and he and her mother travelled in Europe in pre-war days. They have always lived a Western-style life, with Western food and an admiration for Western culture. The daughter now tends rather to frown on this. She feels one should be more deeply Indian, and with this end in view, she wears handloom saris and traditional jewellery and has painted an abnormally large vermilion mark on her forehead. She is interested in Indian classical music and dance. If she is rich enough—she may have married into one of the big Indian business houses—she will become a patroness of the arts and hold delicious parties on her lawn on summer nights. All her friends are there—and she has so many, both Indian and European, all interesting people—and trays of iced drinks are carried round by servants in uniform and there is intelligent conversation and then there is a superbly arranged buffet supper and more intelligent conversation, and then the crown of the evening: a famous Indian maestro performing on the sitar. The guests recline on carpets and cushions on the lawn. The sky sparkles with stars and the languid summer air is fragrant with jasmine. There are many pretty girls reclining against bolsters; their faces are melancholy for the music is stirring their hearts, and sometimes they sigh with yearning and happiness and look down at their pretty toes (adorned with a tiny silver toe-ring) peeping out from under the sari. Here is Indian life and culture at its highest and best. Yet, with all that, it need not be thought that our hostess has forgotten her Western education. Not at all. In her one may see the best of East and West combined. She is interested in a great variety of topics and can hold her own in any discussion. She loves to exercise her emancipated mind, and whatever the subject of conversation—economics, or politics, or literature, or film—she has a well-formulated opinion on it and knows how to express herself. How lucky for me if I could have such a person for a friend! What enjoyable, lively times we two could have together!

In fact, my teeth are set on edge if I have to listen to her for more than five minutes—yes, even though everything she says is so true and in line with the most advanced opinions of today. But when she says it, somehow, even though I know the words to be true, they ring completely false. It is merely lips moving and sounds coming out: it doesn't mean anything, nothing of what she says (though she says it with such conviction, skill, and charm) is of the least importance to her. She is only making conversation in the way she knows educated women have to make conversation. And so it is with all of them. Everything they say, all that lively conversation round the buffet table, is not prompted by anything they really feel strongly about but by what they think they ought to feel strongly about. This applies not only to subjects which are naturally alien to them—for instance, when they talk oh so solemnly! and with such profound intelligence! of Godard and Beckett and ecology—but when they talk about themselves too. They know Modern India to be an important subject and they have a lot to say about it: but though they themselves *are* Modern India, they don't look at themselves, they are not conditioned to look at themselves except with the eyes of foreign experts whom they have been taught to respect. And while they are fully aware of India's problems and are up on all the statistics and all the arguments for and against nationalization and a socialistic pattern of society, all the time it is as if they were talking about some *other* place—as if it were a subject for debate—an abstract subject—and not a live animal actually moving under their feet.

But if I have no taste for the company of these Westernized Indians, then what else is there? Other Indians don't really have a social life, not in our terms; the whole conception of such a life is imported. It is true that Indians are gregarious in so far as they hate to be alone and always like to sit together in groups; but these groups are clan-units—it is the family, or clan-members, who gather together and enjoy each other's company. And again, their conception of enjoying each other's company is different from ours. For them it is enough just to *be* together; there are long stretches of silence in which everyone stares into space. From time to time there is a little spurt of conversation, usually on some commonplace everyday subject such as rising prices, a forthcoming marriage, or a troublesome neighbour. There is no attempt at exercising the mind or testing one's wits against those of others: the pleasure lies only in having other familiar people around and enjoying the air together and looking forward to the next meal. There is actually something very restful about this mode of social intercourse and certainly holds more pleasure than the synthetic social life led by Westernized Indians. It is also more adapted to the Indian climate which invites one to be absolutely relaxed in mind and body, to do nothing, to think nothing, just to feel, to *be*. I have in fact enjoyed sitting around like that for hours on end. But there is something in me that after some time revolts against such lassitude. I can't just *be!* Suddenly I jump up and rush away out of that contented circle. I want to do something terribly difficult like climbing a mountain or reading the *Critique of Pure Reason*. I feel tempted to bang my head against the wall as if to wake myself up. Anything to prevent myself from being sucked down into that bog of passive, intuitive being. I feel I cannot, I must not allow myself to live this way.

Of course there are other Europeans more or less in the same situation as myself. For instance, other women married to Indians. But I hesitate to seek them out. People suffering from the same disease do not usually make good company for one another. Who is to listen to whose complaints? On the other hand, with what enthusiasm I welcome visitors from abroad. Their physical presence alone is a pleasure to me. I love to see their fresh complexions, their red cheeks that speak of wind and rain; and I like to see their clothes and their shoes, to admire the texture of these solid European materials and the industrial skills that have gone into making them. I also like to hear the way in which these people speak. In some strange way their accents, their intonations are redolent to me of the places from which they have come, so that as voices rise and fall I hear in them the wind stirring in English trees or a mild brook murmuring through a summer wood. And apart from these sensuous pleasures, there is also the pleasure of hearing what they have to say. I listen avidly to what is said about people I know or have heard of and about new plays and restaurants and changes and fashions. However, neither the subject nor my interest in it is inexhaustible; and after that, it is my turn. What about India? Now they want to hear, but I don't want to say. I feel myself growing sullen. I don't want to talk about India. There is nothing I can tell them. There is nothing they would understand. However, I do begin to talk, and after a time even to talk with passion. But everything I say is wrong. I listen to myself with horror; they too listen with horror. I want to stop and reverse, but I can't. I want to cry out, this is not what I mean! You are listening to me in entirely the wrong context! But there is no way of explaining the context. It would take too long, and anyway what is the point? It's such a small, personal thing. I fall silent. I have nothing more to say. I turn my face and want them to go away.

So I am back again alone in my room with the blinds drawn and the air-conditioner on. Sometimes, when I think of my life, it seems to have contracted to this one point and to be concentrated in this one room, and it is always a very hot, very long afternoon when the air-conditioner has failed. I cannot describe the *oppression* of such afternoons. It is a physical oppression—heat pressing down on me and pressing in the walls and the ceiling and congealing together with time which has stood still and will never move again. And it is not only those two— heat and time—that are laying their weight on me but behind them, or held within them, there is something more which I can only describe as the whole of India. This is hyperbole, but I need hyperbole to express my feelings about those countless afternoons spent over what now seem to me countless years in a country for which I was not born. India swallows me up and now it seems to me that I am no longer in my room but in the white-hot city streets under a white-hot sky; people cannot live in such heat so everything is deserted—no, not quite, for here comes a smiling leper in a cart being pushed by another leper; there is also the carcase of a dog and vultures have swooped down on it. The river has dried up and stretches in miles of flat cracked earth; it is not possible to make out where the river ceases and the land begins for this too is as flat, as cracked, as dry as the river-bed and stretches on for ever. Until we come to a jungle in which wild beasts live, and then there are ravines and here live outlaws with the hearts of wild beasts. Sometimes they make raids into the villages and they rob and burn and mutilate and kill for sport. More mountains and these are very, very high and now it is no longer hot but terribly cold, we are in snow and ice and here is Mount Kailash on which sits Siva the Destroyer wearing a necklace of human skulls. Down in the plains they are worshipping him. I can see them from here—they are doing something strange—what is it? I draw nearer. Now I can see. They are killing a boy. They hack him to pieces and now they bury the pieces into the foundations dug for a new bridge. There is a priest with them who is quite naked except for ash smeared all over him; he is reciting some holy verses over the foundations, to bless and propitiate.

I am using these exaggerated images in order to give some idea of how intolerable India—the idea, the sensation of it—can become. A point is reached where one must escape, and if one can't do so physically, then some other way must be found. And I think it is not only Europeans but Indians too who feel themselves compelled to seek refuge from their often unbearable environment. Here perhaps less than anywhere else is it possible to believe that this world, this life, is all there is for us, and the temptation to write it off and substitute something more satisfying becomes overwhelming. This brings up the question whether religion is such a potent force in India because life is so terrible, or is it the other way round—is life so terrible because, with the eyes of the spirit turned elsewhere, there is no incentive to improve its quality? Whichever it is, the fact remains that the eyes of the spirit *are* turned elsewhere, and it really is true that God seems more present in India than in other places. Every morning I wake up at 3 A.M. to the sound of someone pouring out his spirit in devotional song; and then at dawn the temple bells ring, and again at dusk, and conch-shells are blown, and there is the smell of incense and of the slightly overblown flowers that are placed at the feet of smiling, pink-cheeked idols. I read in the papers that the Lord Krishna has been reborn as the son of a weaver woman in a village somewhere in Madhya Pradesh. On the banks of the river there are figures in meditation and one of them may turn out to be the teller in your bank who cashed your cheque just a few days ago; now he is in the lotus pose and his eyes are turned up and he is in ecstasy. There are ashrams full of little old half-starved widows who skip and dance about, they giggle and play hide and seek because they are Krishna's milkmaids. And over all this there is a sky of enormous proportions—so much larger than the earth on which you live, and often so incredibly beautiful, an unflawed unearthly blue by day, all shining with stars at night, that it is difficult to believe that something grand and wonderful beyond the bounds of human comprehension does not emanate from there.

I love listening to Indian devotional songs. They seem pure like water drawn from a well; and the emotions they express are both beautiful and easy to understand because the imagery employed is so human. The soul crying out for God is always shown as the beloved yearning for the lover in an easily recognizable way ("I wait for Him. Do you hear His step? He has come"). I feel soothed when I hear such songs and all my discontentment falls away. I see that everything I have been fretting about is of no importance at all because all that matters is this promise of eternal bliss in the Lover's arms. I become patient and good and feel that everything is good. Unfortunately this tranquil state does not last for long, and after a time it again seems to me that nothing is good and neither am I. Once somebody said to me: "Just see, how sweet is the Indian soul that can see God in a cow!" But when I try to assume this sweetness, it turns sour: for, however much I may try and fool myself, whatever veils I may try, for the sake of peace of mind, to draw over my eyes, it is soon enough clear to me that the cow *is* a cow, and a very scrawny, underfed, diseased one at that. And then I feel that I want to keep this knowledge, however painful it is, and not exchange it for some other that may be true for an Indian but can never quite become that for me.

And here, it seems to me, I come to the heart of my problem. To live in India and be at peace one must to a very considerable extent become Indian and adopt Indian attitudes, habits, beliefs, assume if possible an Indian personality. But how is this possible? And even if it were possible—without cheating oneself—would it be desirable? Should one want to try and become something other than what one is? I don't always say no to this question. Sometimes it seems to me how pleasant it would be to say yes and give in and wear a sari and be meek and accepting and see God in a cow. Other times it seems worth while to be defiant and European and—all right, be crushed by one's environment, but all the same have made some attempt to remain standing. Of course, this can't go on indefinitely and in the end I'm bound to lose—if only at the point where my ashes are immersed in the Ganges to the accompaniment of Vedic hymns, and then who will say that I have not truly merged with India?

I do sometimes go back to Europe. But after a time I get bored there and want to come back here. I also find it hard now to stand the European climate. I have got used to intense heat and seem to need it.

Questions for Discussion and Writing

1. Why does Jhabvala say that all of her moments are dull? What is the relationship between her dull moments and the adjustment she makes to the horrors of India? What does this dullness have to do with the retribution she writes about for those who shade their windows against misery?
2. Why do the words of the emancipated, Western-educated Indian woman ring "completely false" (p. 56) in Jhabvala's ears? What does the author's response have to do with her European background?
3. Explain the "something" within Jhabvala that prevents her for very long from just sitting around, from just *being* (p. 57).
4. What cultural differences and dilemmas permanently separate Jhabvala from India? Why does India forever threaten to swallow her up? What is it about India that draws her back when she leaves?
5. What paradoxes does the essay teach us about being a permanent resident from the West in a land like India?
6. In what ways does Jhabvala's essay convey the difficulties and challenges of being honest as a writer?

ZORA NEALE HURSTON

How It Feels to Be Colored Me

Born in Eatonville, Florida, Zora Neale Hurston was educated first at Howard University and then at Barnard College and Columbia University. She once claimed she was arrested for crossing against a red light, but escaped punishment by arguing, "I had seen white folks pass on green and therefore assumed the red light was for me." In this same way, Hurston evaded her biographers about many details of her life, even the year of her birth (1891?, 1901?, 1903?).

Contemporary writer Alice Walker discovered in Hurston's books—especially the novel Their Eyes Were Watching God *(1937, reprinted 1978) and her autobiography* Dust Tracks on a Road *(1937, reprinted 1978)—her own models for becoming a writer. Walker's words about Hurston capture the highlights of Hurston's life:*

> *Folklorist, novelist, anthropologist, serious student of voo-doo, also all-around black woman. . . .*
>
> *Zora Hurston, who went to Barnard to learn how to study what she really wanted to learn: the ways of her own people, and what ancient rituals, customs, and beliefs had made them unique.*
>
> *Zora, of the sandy-colored hair and the daredevil eyes, a girl who escaped poverty and parental neglect by hard work and a sharp eye for the main chance.*
>
> *Zora, who left the South only to return to look at it again. Who went to root doctors from Florida to Louisiana and said, "Here I am. I want to learn your trade."*
>
> *Zora, who had collected all the black folklore I could ever use. That Zora.*
>
> *And having found that Zora (like a golden key to a storehouse of varied treasure), I was hooked.**

Hurston's study of anthropology led her to her own notions of race and racial groups: "Light came to me when I realized that I did not

*Walker, Alice 1983. "Saving the Life That is Your Own." In Search of Our Mothers' Gardens. Orlando, Fla.: Harcourt Brace Jovanovich Inc., pp. 11–12.

have to consider any racial group as a whole. God made them duck by duck and that was the only way I could see them," she writes in Dust Tracks. *"Nothing that God ever made is the same thing to more than one person. That is natural. There is no single face in nature, because every eye that looks upon it, sees it from its own angle. So every man's spicebox seasons his own food."*

The essay that follows was first published on May 11, 1928, in a journal entitled The World Tomorrow. *It has been reprinted in a collection of Hurston's works edited by Alice Walker,* I Love Myself When I Am Laughing *(1979).*

Zora Neale Hurston died in Fort Pierce, Florida, on January 28, 1960.

Before you read "How It Feels to Be Colored Me," write your own essay by this same title, filling in your own choice for the word *colored* and developing your ideas in whatever ways they come to mind.

I am colored but I offer nothing in the way of extenuating circumstances except the fact that I am the only Negro in the United States whose grandfather on the mother's side was *not* an Indian chief.

I remember the very day that I became colored. Up to my thirteenth year I lived in the little Negro town of Eatonville, Florida. It is exclusively a colored town. The only white people I knew passed through the town going to or coming from Orlando. The native whites rode dusty horses, the Northern tourists chugged down the sandy village road in automobiles. The town knew the Southerners and never stopped cane chewing when they passed. But the Northerners were something else again. They were peered at cautiously from behind curtains by the timid. The more venturesome would come out on the porch to watch them go past and got just as much pleasure out of the tourists as the tourists got out of the village.

The front porch might seem a daring place for the rest of the town, but it was a gallery seat to me. My favorite place was atop the gate-post. Proscenium box for a born first-nighter. Not only did I enjoy the show, but I didn't mind the actors knowing that I liked it. I usually spoke to them in passing. I'd wave at them and when they returned my salute, I would say something like this: "Howdy-do-well-I-thank-you-where-you-goin'?" Usually the automobile or the horse paused at this, and after a queer exchange of compliments, I would probably "go a piece of the way" with them, as we say in farthest Florida. If one of my family happened to come to the front in time to see me, of course negotiations would be rudely broken off. But even so, it is clear that I was the first "welcome-to-our-state" Floridian, and I hope the Miami Chamber of Commerce will please take notice.

During this period, white people differed from colored to me only in that they rode through town and never lived there. They liked to hear me "speak pieces" and sing and wanted to see me dance the parse-me-la, and gave me generously of their small silver for doing these things, which seemed strange to me for I wanted to do them so much that I needed bribing to stop. Only they didn't know it. The colored people gave no dimes. They deplored any joyful tendencies in me, but I was their Zora nevertheless. I belonged to them, to the nearby hotels, to the county—everybody's Zora.

But changes came in the family when I was thirteen, and I was sent to school in Jacksonville. I left Eatonville, the town of the oleanders, as Zora. When I disembarked from the river-boat at Jacksonville, she was no more. It seemed that I had suffered a sea change. I was not Zora of Orange County any more, I was now a little colored girl. I found it out in certain ways. In my heart as well as in the mirror, I became a fast brown—warranted not to rub nor run.

But I am not tragically colored. There is no great sorrow dammed up in my soul, nor lurking behind my eyes. I do not mind at all. I do not belong to the sobbing school of Negrohood who hold that nature somehow has given them a lowdown dirty deal and whose feelings are all hurt about it. Even in the helter-skelter skirmish that is my life, I have seen that the world is to the strong regardless of a little pigmentation more or less. No, I do not weep at the world—I am too busy sharpening my oyster knife.

Someone is always at my elbow reminding me that I am the granddaughter of slaves. It fails to register depression with me. Slavery is sixty years in the past. The operation was successful and the patient is doing well, thank you. The terrible struggle that made me an American out of a potential slave said "On the line!" The Reconstruction said "Get set!"; and the generation before said "Go!" I am off to a flying start and I must not halt in the stretch to look behind and weep. Slavery is the price I paid for civilization, and the choice was not with me. It is a bully adventure and worth all that I have paid through my ancestors for it. No one on earth ever had a greater chance for glory. The world to be won and nothing to be lost. It is thrilling to think—to know that for any act of mine, I shall get twice as much praise or twice as much blame. It is quite exciting to hold the center of the national stage, with the spectators not knowing whether to laugh or to weep.

The position of my white neighbor is much more difficult. No brown specter pulls up a chair beside me when I sit down to eat. No dark ghost thrusts its leg against mine in bed. The game of keeping what one has is never so exciting as the game of getting.

I do not always feel colored. Even now I often achieve the unconscious Zora of Eatonville before the Hegira. I feel most colored when I am thrown against a sharp white background.

For instance at Barnard. "Beside the waters of the Hudson" I feel my race. Among the thousand white persons, I am a dark rock surged upon, overswept by a creamy sea. I am surged upon and overswept, but through it all, I remain myself. When covered by the waters, I am; and the ebb but reveals me again.

Sometimes it is the other way around. A white person is set down in our midst, but the contrast is just as sharp for me. For instance, when I sit in the drafty basement that is The New World Cabaret with a white person, my color comes. We enter chatting about any little nothing that we have in common and are seated by the jazz waiters. In the abrupt way that jazz orchestras have, this one plunges into a number. It loses no time in circumlocutions, but gets right down to business. It constricts the thorax and splits the heart with its tempo and narcotic harmonies. This orchestra grows rambunctious, rears on its hind legs and attacks the tonal veil with primitive fury, rending it, clawing it until it breaks through to the jungle beyond. I follow those heathen—follow them exultingly. I dance wildly inside myself; I yell within, I whoop; I shake my assegai above my head, I hurl it true to the mark *yeeeeooww!* I am in the jungle and living in the jungle way. My face is painted red and yellow and my body is painted blue. My pulse is throbbing like a war drum. I want to slaughter something—give pain, give death to what, I do not know. But the piece ends. The men of the orchestra wipe their lips and rest their fingers. I creep back slowly to the veneer we call civilization with the last tone and find the white friend sitting motionless in his seat, smoking calmly.

"Good music they have here," he remarks, drumming the table with his fingertips.

Music! The great blobs of purple and red emotion have not touched him. He has only heard what I felt. He is far away and I see him but dimly across the ocean and the continent that have fallen between us. He is so pale with his whiteness then and I am *so* colored.

At certain times I have no race, I am *me*. When I set my hat at a certain angle and saunter down Seventh Avenue, Harlem City, feeling as snooty as the lions in front of the Forty-Second Street Library, for instance. So far as my feelings are concerned, Peggy Hopkins Joyce on the Boule Mich with her gorgeous raiment, stately carriage, knees knocking together in a most aristocratic manner, has nothing on me. The cosmic Zora emerges. I belong to no race nor time. I am the eternal feminine with its string of beads.

I have no separate feeling about being an American citizen and colored. I am merely a fragment of the Great Soul that surges within the boundaries. My country, right or wrong.

Sometimes, I feel discriminated against, but it does not make me angry. It merely astonishes me. How *can* any deny themselves the pleasure of my company! It's beyond me.

But in the main, I feel like a brown bag of miscellany propped against a wall. Against a wall in company with other bags, white, red and yellow. Pour out the contents, and there is discovered a jumble of small things priceless and worthless. A first-water diamond, an empty spool, bits of broken glass, lengths of string, a key to a door long since crumbled away, a rusty knife-blade, old shoes saved for a road that never was and never will be, a nail bent under the weight of things too heavy for any nail, a dried flower or two, still a little fragrant. In your hand is the brown bag. On the ground before you is the jumble it held—so much like the jumble in the bags, could they be emptied, that all might be dumped in a single heap and the bags refilled without altering the content of any greatly. A bit of colored glass more or less would not matter. Perhaps that is how the Great Stuffer of Bags filled them in the first place—who knows?

Questions for Discussion and Writing

1. What intercultural journeys of her own did Hurston make, and why?
2. If you were attempting to date this essay without knowing when it was written, what clues does it contain that would help you to know?
3. What do you think the author means by her statement, "But I am not tragically colored" (p. 63)? How does this statement relate to Hurston's attitudes toward her family's history as slaves? What are your own responses to the word *colored*?
4. What observations can you make about the author's encounter with the white man she sits next to in the New World Cabaret?
5. What metaphors in the essay work well and why?
6. Why do you think Hurston divides her essay into four sections? In what ways does each section of the essay connect to the others and contribute meaning to the whole? (Consider how you might use a similar technique in the writing you've begun on how it feels to be some aspect of yourself.)

JAWAHARLAL NEHRU

What Is Culture?

India's first prime minister following independence from Britain in 1947, Jawaharlal Nehru led his country until his death from a heart attack in 1964. In 1966, his daughter, Indira Nehru Gandhi, followed her father as India's leader. Although Nehru lived his adult years in New Delhi, he was born in Allahabad, India, in 1889, and received his education at Trinity College in Cambridge, England. From 1920 to his death, he was a member of Mahatma Gandhi's nonviolence movement. A principal protégé of Gandhi, Nehru was in the forefront of India's nationalist movement.

Nehru "envisioned a world of equal opportunity, education, and living standards for all mankind, made safe and just by an enlightened government operating on socialistic principles," his sister, Krishna Nehru Hutheesing, wrote of him. In his commitment to developing India into a self-sufficient world power, Nehru ardently supported research in science and technology to study a wide range of subjects, including agriculture, medicine, the causes of cancer, nutrition, fuel, and textiles. He personally headed the ministry of atomic energy.

A Hindu Brahman, Nehru nevertheless fought the iniquities of the Hindu caste system by promulgating the Untouchability Act of 1955, forbidding the practice of untouchability. For his commitment to Gandhi's philosophy of civil disobedience, Nehru was sentenced to jail many times throughout his life—serving a total of nine years in confinement. While in jail, he became immersed in study and writing. A prolific writer on many topics, Nehru accomplished most of his writing behind bars. In his autobiography Toward Freedom *(1941) he wrote: "The primary object in writing these pages was to occupy myself with a definite task, so necessary in the long solitudes of jail life, as well as to review past events in India, with which I had been connected, to enable myself to think clearly about them."*

In "What Is Culture?" Nehru struggles with the complexities of defining the elusive characteristics of culture, showing us that even decades of contemplation on the subject does not produce clear answers.

Before you read "What Is Culture?" describe your own definition of the word *culture*. Approach the idea of culture not only with an abstract definition but with some of the concrete manifestations that you associate with the word. After you've defined culture, write about the problems you encountered, if any, while trying to pinpoint a meaningful definition.

What exactly is the "culture" that people talk so much about? When I was younger in years, I remember reading about German "kultur" and of the attempts of the German people to spread it by conquest and other means. There was a big war to spread this "kultur" and to resist it. Every country and every individual seems to have its peculiar idea of culture. When there is talk about cultural relations—although it is very good in theory—what actually happens is that those peculiar ideas come into conflict and instead of leading to friendship they lead to more estrangement. It is a basic question—what is culture? And I am certainly not competent to give you a definition of it because I have not found one.

One can see each nation and each separate civilisation developing its own culture that had its roots in generations hundreds and thousands of years ago. One sees these nations being intimately moulded by the impulse that initially starts a civilisation going on its long path. That conception is affected by other conceptions and one sees action and interaction between these varying conceptions. There is I suppose, no culture in the world which is absolutely pristine, pure and unaffected by any other culture. It simply cannot be, just as nobody can say that he belongs one hundred per cent, to a particular racial type, because in the course of hundreds and thousands of years unmistakable changes and mixtures have occurred.

So culture is bound to get a little mixed up, even though the basic element of a particular national culture remains dominant. If that kind of thing goes on peacefully, there is no harm in it. But it often leads to conflicts. It sometimes leads a group to fear that their culture is being overwhelmed by what they consider to be an outside or alien influence. Then they draw themselves into a shell which isolates them and prevents their thoughts and ideas going out. That is an unhealthy situation because in any matter and much more so in what might be called a cultural matter stagnation is the worst possible thing.

My own view of India's history is that we can almost measure the growth and the advance of India and the decline of India by relating them to periods when India had her mind open to the outside world and when she wanted to close it up. The more she closed it up, the more static she became. Life, whether of the individual, group, nation or society, is essentially a dynamic, changing, growing thing. Whatever stops that dynamic growth also injures it and undermines it.

We have had great religions and they have had an enormous effect on humanity. Yet, if I may say so with all respect and without meaning any ill to any person, those very religions, in the measure that they made the mind of man static, dogmatic and bigoted, have had, to my mind, an evil effect. The things they said may be good but when it is claimed that the last word has been said, society becomes static.

The individual human being or race or nation must necessarily have a certain depth and certain roots somewhere. They do not count for much unless they have roots in the past, which past is after all the accumulation of generations of experience and some type of wisdom. It is essential that you have that. Otherwise you become just pale copies of something which has no real meaning to you as an individual or as a group.

On the other hand, one cannot live in roots alone. Even roots wither unless they come out in the sun and the free air. Only then can the roots give you sustenance. Only then can there be a branching out and a flowering. How, then, are you to balance these two essential factors? It is very difficult, because some people think a great deal about the flowers and the leaves on the branches, forgetting that they only flourish because there is a stout root to sustain them. Others think so much of the roots that no flowers or leaves or branches are left: there is only a thick stem somewhere. So, the question is how one is to achieve a balance.

Does culture mean some inner growth in the man? Of course, it must. Does it mean the way he behaves to others? Certainly it must. Does it mean the capacity to understand the other person? I suppose so. Does it mean the capacity to make yourself understood by the other person? I suppose so. It means all that. A person who cannot understand another's viewpoint is to that extent limited in mind and culture, because nobody, perhaps, barring some very extraordinary human beings, can presume to have the fullest knowledge and wisdom. The other party or the other group may also have some inkling of knowledge or wisdom or truth and if we shut our minds to that then we not only deprive [ourselves] of it but we cultivate an attitude of mind which, I would say, is opposed to that of a cultured man.

The cultured mind, rooted in itself, should have its doors and windows open. It should have the capacity to understand the other's viewpoint fully even though it cannot always agree with it. The question of agreement or disagreement only arises when you understand a thing. Otherwise, it is blind negation which is not a cultural approach to any question.

I should like to use another word—science. What is a scientific approach to life's problems? I suppose it is one of examining everything, of seeking truth by trial and error and by experiment, of never saying that this must be so but trying to understand why it is so and, if one is convinced of it, of accepting it, of having the capacity to change one's notions the moment some other proof is forthcoming, of having an open mind, which tries to imbibe the truth wherever it is found. If that is culture, how far is it represented in the modern world and in the nations of today? Obviously, if it was represented more than it is, many of our problems, national and international, would be far easier to solve.

Almost every country in the world believes that it has some special dispensation from Providence, that it is of the chosen people or race and that others, whether they are good or bad, are somewhat inferior creatures. It is extraordinary how this kind of feeling persists in all nations of the East as well as of the West without exception. The nations of the East are strongly entrenched in their own ideas and convictions and sometimes in their own sense of superiority about certain matters.

Anyhow, in the course of the last two or three hundred years, they have received many knocks on the head and they have been humiliated; they have been debased and they have been exploited. And so, in spite of their feeling that they were superior in many ways, they were forced to admit that they could be knocked about and exploited. To some extent, this brought a sense of realism to them.

There was also an attempt to escape from reality by saying that it was sad that we were not so advanced in material and technical things but that these were after all superficial things. Nevertheless, we were superior in essential things, in spiritual things, in moral values. I have no doubt that spiritual things and moral values are ultimately more important than other things but the way one finds escape in the thought that one is spiritually superior simply because one is inferior in a material and physical sense, is surprising. It does not follow by any means. It is an escape from facing up to the causes of one's degradation.

Nationalism, of course, is a curious phenomenon which at a certain stage in a country's history gives life, growth, strength, and unity but at the same time, it has a tendency to limit one because one thinks of one's country as something different from the rest of the world. The perspective changes and one is continuously thinking of one's own struggles and virtues and failings to the exclusion of other thoughts. The result is that the same nationalism, which is the symbol of growth for a people, becomes a symbol of the cessation of that growth in the mind. Nationalism, when it becomes successful sometimes goes on spreading in an aggressive way and [becomes] a danger internationally. Whatever line of thought you follow, you arrive at the conclusion that some kind of balance must be found. Otherwise something that was good can turn into evil.

Culture, which is essentially good, becomes not only static but aggressive and something that breeds conflict and hatred when looked at from a wrong point of view. How you are to find a balance, I do not know. Apart from the political and economic problems of the age, perhaps, that is the greatest problem today, because behind it there is a tremendous conflict in the spirit of man and a tremendous search for something which it cannot find. We turn to economic theories because they have an undoubted importance. It is folly to talk of culture or even of God when human beings starve and die. Before one can talk about anything else one must provide the normal essential of life to human beings. That is where economics comes in. Human beings today are not in the mood to tolerate this suffering and starvation and inequality when they see that the burden is not equally shared. Others profit while they only bear the burden.

I have not the shadow of a doubt that it is a fundamental rule of human life that if the approach is good the response is good. If the approach is bad, the response is likely to be bad too. So, if we approach our fellow human beings or countries in a friendly way, with our minds and hearts open and prepared to accept whatever good comes to them—and that does not mean surrendering something that we consider of essential value to truth or to our genius—then we shall be led not only towards understanding, but the right type of understanding.

So, I shall leave you to determine what culture and wisdom really are. We grow in learning, in knowledge and in experience. Till we have such an enormous accumulation of them that it becomes impossible to know exactly where we stand. We are overwhelmed by all this and at the same time, somehow or other we have a feeling that all these put together do not necessarily represent a growth in the wisdom of the human race. I have a feeling that perhaps some people who did not have all the advantages of modern life and modern science were essentially wiser than most of us are. Whether or not we shall be able in later times to combine all this knowledge, scientific growth and betterment of the human species with true wisdom, I do not know. It is a race between various forces. I am reminded of the saying of a very wise man who was a famous Greek poet:

What else is wisdom?
What of man's endeavour or
God's high grace, so lovely and so great?
To stand from fear set free,
to breathe and wait,
To hold a hand uplifted over hate.
And shall not loveliness be loved for ever?

Questions for Discussion and Writing

1. Why, according to Nehru, is a culture "bound to get a little mixed up" (p. 67)? What happens to a culture when it fears being overwhelmed by an "outside or alien influence" (p. 67)?
2. The author uses the metaphor of roots to suggest both their necessity and their danger. Why are they at once necessary and dangerous?
3. Nehru asserts, "The question of agreement or disagreement [with another's viewpoint] only arises when you understand a thing. Otherwise, it is blind negation which is not a cultural approach to any question" (p. 68). Paraphrase these ideas and explain their implications.

4. Nehru occasionally departs from the general truths he is exploring about the meaning of culture to address his own country's attitudes specifically. What messages about culture does he have for India?
5. At the close of his essay, Nehru questions not only the meaning of culture but also the challenge of combining "all this knowledge, scientific growth and betterment of the human species with true wisdom." What do you think Nehru has in mind when he writes of wisdom? Why is wisdom an essential ingredient in his responding to the question "What is culture?"
6. Why or why not do you think Nehru answers his own question about the meaning of culture in the essay?

Chapter 2

PATTERNS, HABITS, AND VALUES OF CULTURE

It is very difficult to know people and I don't think one can ever really know any but one's own countrymen. For men and women are not only themselves; they are also the region in which they were born, the city apartment or the farm in which they learnt to walk, the games they played as children, the old wives' tales they overheard, the food they ate, the schools they attended, the sports they followed, the poets they read, and the God they believed in. It is all these things that have made them what they are and these are things that you can't come to know by hearsay, you can only know them if you have lived them. You can only know them if you are *them.*

W. SOMERSET MAUGHAM, from
THE RAZOR'S EDGE

"THE THING A FISH IS LEAST LIKELY TO UNDERSTAND," SOMEONE quipped, "is the water in which it swims." Culture, we could say, is our water. As you will come to understand more fully through reading the stories, essays, and plays in this anthology, culture is learned. Intricate systems of patterns, habits, and values of culture are embedded so thoroughly in our lives that we often do not realize they even exist. We are also unaware of how deeply these cultural systems influence the choices we make each moment and each day.

When we talk about culture, we are talking about shared patterns of assumptions and values, and a common sense of identity, of history, of routines, rituals, and rules. Two of the most important patterns in every culture concern assumptions about time and space in relationships among people. In "Social Time: The Heartbeat of Culture," Robert Levine explains how deeply our attitudes about time are based in our lives. (The Halls's essay, "The Sounds of Silence," in

Chapter Three, addresses values of space.) In Janette Turner Hospital's story "Waiting," an Indian man and an American woman reflect vast differences in attitudes toward the two days they both wait to be helped in an Air India office in India.

Like time, food in all its dimensions is always tied to cultural patterns and values. A food as apparently simple as ice cream has a long and complex relationship to American culture. In "I Scream, You Scream . . . The Cultural Significance of Ice Cream," Henry C. Binford explains how ice cream parlors became tied to the changing patterns of industrialization, an emerging concept called "leisure," and respectability, American style.

The ways in which a culture envisions women's roles provide another source of insight into its values and patterns. Carol Simons describes the lives of "Kyoiku [or education] Mamas," showing how and why mothers in Japan spend nearly every minute of the day helping their children to excel academically.

In "Latin America: A Quixotic Land Where the Bizarre Is Routine," reporter William D. Montalbano shows us how our American ideas of what is bizarre have little to do with Latin American assumptions. Octavio Paz explains what appears to be the bizarre frenzy of "The Day of the Dead," showing the need for the outlet of such festivals in the Mexican character, and this festival's relationship to Mexican attitudes about life and death.

Egyptian psychiatrist Nawal el-Saadawi closes the chapter with "Love and Sex in the Life of the Arab," in which she traces the effects of Muslim influence and the harsh desert life on cultural assumptions, values, and practices in love and sex among Arabs.

It's hard to see water when we're in it, but we'll try.

ROBERT LEVINE, WITH ELLEN WOLFF

Social Time: The Heartbeat of Culture

Robert Levine is a social psychologist who has been on the faculty at California State University at Fresno for over fifteen years. He changed directions in focus along the way of his graduate studies, when, after completing his master's degree in clinical psychology, he decided he was more interested in people research.

Levine is also interested in the process of writing, in the need he perceives of balancing academic rigor with writing that has both vigor and life. "How hard it is to push out a simple sentence," he says, especially when the words of a field like psychology seem to trip over each other in the name of science, "like intervening variables convoluting on one another."

Levine first became interested in the idea of social time during the year he spent teaching in Niterói, Brazil, as a Latin American Teaching Fellow. His interests developed further in a year-long trip he made around the world in 1980, but it took him time to digest the data he had gathered. Although letters and tales of his travels to friends created lively interest, as soon as he hit the typewriter "the words came out wrong." This is when Levine contacted Ellen Wolff, a free-lance writer living in Los Angeles and a former student who had dropped out of his doctoral program at New York University to do something more creative. As Levine says, "I needed Ellen for confidence. She knew how to ask the right questions. Writing was a strange land for me after my academic training."

Robert Levine still does the technical writing required of academics, but as background, in tandem with, the articles he likes to write—"science-based articles in English." He goes from one to the other to express the same material for two audiences, and, as he points out, "in two versions of English."

Published in Psychology Today *in March 1985, "Social Time: The Heartbeat of Culture" reflects his success in writing a science-based article in English for a popular audience.*

Before you read "Social Time: The Heartbeat of Culture," write about a recent experience in which you had a problem with time; the problem can involve another person or just yourself. Explain the problem, what attitudes of your own underlie the problem, and the ways in which the problem might be the result or influence of the culture in which you live.

"*I**f a man does not keep pace with his companions, perhaps it is because he hears a different drummer.*" This thought by Thoreau strikes a chord in so many people that it has become part of our language. We use the phrase "the beat of a different drummer" to explain any pace of life unlike our own. Such colorful vagueness reveals how informal our rules of time really are. The world over, children simply "pick up" their society's time concepts as they mature. No dictionary clearly defines the meaning of "early" or "late" for them or for strangers who stumble over the maddening incongruities between the time sense they bring with them and the one they face in a new land.

I learned this firsthand, a few years ago, and the resulting culture shock led me halfway around the world to find answers. It seemed clear that time "talks." But what is it telling us?

My journey started shortly after I accepted an appointment as visiting professor of psychology at the federal university in Niteroi, Brazil, a midsized city across the bay from Rio de Janeiro. As I left home for my first day of class, I asked someone the time. It was 9:05 A.M., which allowed me time to relax and look around the campus before my 10 o'clock lecture. After what I judged to be half an hour, I glanced at a clock I was passing. It said 10:20! In panic, I broke for the classroom, followed by gentle calls of "Hola, professor" and "Tudo bem, professor?" from unhurried students, many of whom, I later realized, were my own. I arrived breathless to find an empty room.

Frantically, I asked a passerby the time. "Nine forty-five" was the answer. No, that couldn't be. I asked someone else. "Nine fifty-five." Another said: "Exactly 9:43." The clock in a nearby office read 3:15. I had learned my first lesson about Brazilians: Their time pieces are consistently inaccurate. And nobody minds.

My class was scheduled from 10 until noon. Many students came late, some very late. Several arrived after 10:30. A few showed up closer to 11. Two came after that. All of the latecomers wore the relaxed smiles that I came, later, to enjoy. Each one said hello, and although a few apologized briefly, none seemed terribly concerned about lateness. They assumed that I understood.

The idea of Brazilians arriving late was not a great shock. I had heard about "mãnha," the Portuguese equivalent of "mañana" in Spanish. This term, meaning "tomorrow" or, "the morning," stereotypes the Brazilian who puts off the business of today until tomorrow. The real surprise came at noon that first day, when the end of class arrived.

Back home in California, I never need to look at a clock to know when the class hour is ending. The shuffling of books is accompanied by strained expressions that say plaintively, "I'm starving. . . . I've got to go to the bathroom. . . . I'm going to suffocate if you keep us one more second." (The pain usually becomes unbearable at two minutes to the hour in undergraduate classes and five minutes before the close of graduate classes.)

When noon arrived in my first Brazilian class, only a few students left immediately. Others slowly drifted out during the next 15 minutes, and some continued asking me questions long after that. When several remaining students kicked off their shoes at 12:30, I went into my own "starving/bathroom/suffocation" routine.

I could not, in all honesty, attribute their lingering to my superb teaching style. I had just spent two hours lecturing on statistics in halting Portuguese. Apparently, for many of my students, staying late was simply of no more importance than arriving late in the first place. As I observed this casual approach in infinite variations during the year, I learned that the "mãnha" stereotype oversimplified the real Anglo/Brazilian differences in conceptions of time. Research revealed a more complex picture.

With the assistance of colleagues Laurie West and Harry Reis, I compared the time sense of 91 male and female students in Niterói with that of 107 similar students at California State University in Fresno. The universities are similar in academic quality and size, and the cities are both secondary metropolitan centers with populations of about 350,000.

We asked students about their perceptions of time in several situations, such as what they would consider late or early for a hypothetical lunch appointment with a friend. The average Brazilian student defined lateness for lunch as 33½ minutes after the scheduled time, compared to only 19 minutes for the Fresno students. But Brazilians also allowed an average of about 54 minutes before they'd consider someone early, while the Fresno students drew the line at 24.

Are Brazilians simply more flexible in their concepts of time and punctuality? And how does this relate to the stereotype of the apathetic, fatalistic and irresponsible Latin temperament? When we asked students to give typical reasons for lateness, the Brazilians were less likely to attribute it to a lack of caring than the North Americans were. Instead, they pointed to unforeseen circumstances that the person couldn't control. Because they seemed less inclined to feel personally responsible for being late, they also expressed less regret for their own lateness and blamed others less when they were late.

We found similar differences in how students from the two countries characterized people who were late for appointments. Unlike their North American counterparts, the Brazilian students believed that a person who is consistently late is probably more successful than one who is consistently on time. They seemed to accept the idea that someone of status is expected to arrive late. Lack of punctuality is a badge of success.

Even within our own country, of course, ideas of time and punctuality vary considerably from place to place. Different regions and even cities have their own distinct rhythms and rules. Seemingly simple words like "now," snapped out by an impatient New Yorker, and "later," said by a relaxed Californian, suggest a world of difference. Despite our familiarity with these homegrown differences in tempo, problems with time present a major stumbling block to Americans abroad. Peace Corps volunteers told researchers James Spradley of Macalester College and Mark Phillips of the University of Washington that their greatest difficulties with other people, after language problems, were the general pace of life and the punctuality of others. Formal "clock time" may be a standard on which the world agrees, but "social time," the heartbeat of society, is something else again.

How a country paces its social life is a mystery to most outsiders, one that we're just beginning to unravel. Twenty-six years ago, anthropologist Edward Hall noted in *The Silent Language* that informal patterns of time "are seldom, if ever, made explicit. They exist in the air around us. They are either familiar and comfortable, or unfamiliar and wrong." When we realize we are out of step, we often blame the people around us to make ourselves feel better.

Appreciating cultural differences in time sense becomes increasingly important as modern communications put more and more people in daily contact. If we are to avoid misreading issues that involve time perceptions, we need to understand better our own cultural biases and those of others.

When people of different cultures interact, the potential for misunderstanding exists on many levels. For example, members of Arab and Latin cultures usually stand much closer when they are speaking to people than we usually do in the United States, a fact we frequently misinterpret as aggression or disrespect. Similarly, we assign personality traits to groups with a pace of life that is markedly faster or slower than our own. We build ideas of national character, for example, around the traditional Swiss and German ability to "make the trains run on time." Westerners like ourselves define punctuality using precise measures of time: 5 minutes, 15 minutes, an hour. But according to Hall, in many Mediterranean Arab cultures there are only three sets of time: no time at all, now (which is of varying duration) and forever (too long). Because of this, Americans often find difficulty in getting Arabs to distinguish between waiting a long time and a very long time.

According to historian Will Durant, "No man in a hurry is quite civilized." What do our time judgments say about our attitude toward life? How can a North American, coming from a land of digital precision, relate to a North African who may consider a clock "the devil's mill"?

Each language has a vocabulary of time that does not always survive translation. When we translated our questionnaires into Portuguese for my Brazilian students, we found that English distinctions of time were not readily articulated in their language. Several of our questions concerned how long the respondent would wait for someone to arrive, as compared with when they hoped for arrival or actually expected the person would come. In Portuguese, the verbs "to wait for," "to hope for" and "to expect" are all translated as "esperar." We had to add further words of explanation to make the distinction clear to the Brazilian students.

To avoid these language problems, my Fresno colleague Kathy Bartlett and I decided to clock the pace of life in other countries by using as little language as possible. We looked directly at three basic indicators of time: the accuracy of a country's bank clocks, the speed at which pedestrians walked and the average time it took a postal clerk to sell us a single stamp. In six countries on three continents, we made observations in both the nation's largest urban area and a medium-sized city: Japan (Tokyo and Sendai), Taiwan (Taipei and Tainan), Indonesia (Jakarta and Solo), Italy (Rome and Florence), England (London and Bristol) and the United States (New York City and Rochester).

What we wanted to know was: Can we speak of a unitary concept called "pace of life"? What we've learned suggests that we can. There appears to be a very strong relationship (see chart below) between the accuracy of clock time, walking speed and postal efficiency across the countries we studied.

We checked 15 clocks in each city, selecting them at random in downtown banks and comparing the time they showed with that reported by the local telephone company. In Japan, which leads the way in accuracy, the clocks averaged just over half a minute early or late. Indonesian clocks, the least accurate, were more than three minutes off the mark.

I will be interested to see how the digital-information age will affect our perceptions of time. In the United States today, we are reminded of the exact hour of the day more than ever, through little symphonies of beeps emanating

The Pace of Life in Six Countries

	Accuracy of Bank Clocks	Walking Speed	Post Office Speed
Japan	1	1	1
United States	2	3	2
England	4	2	3
Italy	5	4	6
Taiwan	3	5	4
Indonesia	6	6	5

Numbers (1 is the top value) indicate the comparative rankings of each country for each indicator of time sense.

from people's digital watches. As they become the norm, I fear our sense of precision may take an absurd twist. The other day, when I asked for the time, a student looked at his watch and replied, "Three twelve and eighteen seconds."

" 'Will you walk a little faster?' said a whiting to a snail. 'There's a porpoise close behind us, and he's treading on my tail.' "

So goes the rhyme from *Alice in Wonderland,* which also gave us that famous symbol of haste, the White Rabbit. He came to mind often as we measured the walking speeds in our experimental cities. We clocked how long it took pedestrians to walk 100 feet along a main downtown street during business hours on clear days. To eliminate the effects of socializing, we observed only people walking alone, timing at least 100 in each city. We found, once again, that the Japanese led the way, averaging just 20.7 seconds to cover the distance. The English nosed out the Americans for second place—21.6 to 22.5 seconds—and the Indonesians again trailed the pack, sauntering along at 27.2 seconds. As you might guess, speed was greater in the larger city of each nation than in its smaller one.

Our final measurement, the average time it took postal clerks to sell one stamp, turned out to be less straight-forward than we expected. In each city, including those in the United States, we presented clerks with a note in the native language requesting a common-priced stamp—a 20-center in the United States, for example. They were also handed paper money, equivalent of a $5 bill. In Indonesia, this procedure led to more than we bargained for.

At the large central post office in Jakarta, I asked for the line to buy stamps and was directed to a group of private vendors sitting outside. Each of them hustled for my business: "Hey, good stamps, mister!" "Best stamps here!" In the smaller city of Solo, I found a volleyball game in progress when I arrived at the main post office on Friday afternoon. Business hours, I was told, were over. When I finally did get there during business hours, the clerk was more interested in discussing relatives in America. Would I like to meet his uncle in Cincinnati? Which did I like better: California or the United States? Five people behind me in line waited patiently. Instead of complaining, they began paying attention to our conversation.

When it came to efficiency of service, however, the Indonesians were not the slowest, although they did place far behind the Japanese postal clerks, who averaged 25 seconds. That distinction went to the Italians, whose infamous postal service took 47 seconds on the average.

"A man who wastes one hour of time has not discovered the meaning of life. . . ."

That was Charles Darwin's belief, and many share it, perhaps at the cost of their health. My colleagues and I have recently begun studying the relationship between pace of life and well-being. Other researchers have demonstrated that a chronic sense of urgency is a basic component of the Type A, coronary-prone personality. We expect that future research will demonstrate that pace of life is related to rate of heart disease, hypertension, ulcers, suicide, alcoholism, divorce and other indicators of general psychological and physical well-being.

As you envision tomorrow's international society, do you wonder who will set the pace? Americans eye Japan carefully, because the Japanese are obviously "ahead of us" in measurable ways. In both countries, speed is frequently confused with progress. Perhaps looking carefully at the different paces of life around the world will help us distinguish more accurately between the two qualities. Clues are everywhere but sometimes hard to distinguish. You have to listen carefully to hear the beat of even your own drummer.

Questions for Discussion and Writing

1. In what ways are attitudes about time tied to larger cultural patterns and values?
2. What are the differences between formal "clock time" and "social time"? In what ways can you imagine using these two concepts of time in future intercultural travel, study, and work?
3. Why do we tend to make judgments about people whose pace of life is markedly faster or slower than our own?
4. What discoveries did Levine and Bartlett make in their research on whether "we [can] speak of a unitary concept called 'pace of life'" (p. 79)?
5. In the concluding paragraph of the essay, Levine asserts and fears that in both the United States and Japan, "speed is frequently confused with progress." What does he mean here, especially in regard to patterns of social time?
6. Why or why not has Levine succeeded here in writing a "science-based article in English" for a popular audience rather than a technical article for academics? What elements in his writing engage your interest, and why?

JANETTE TURNER HOSPITAL

Waiting

Janette Turner Hospital was born in Melbourne, Australia, in 1942. After she graduated from the University of Queensland and before she left Australia, Hospital taught high school English in Brisbane. From 1967 to 1971, she was a librarian at Harvard University. She has also taught on the university level.

The story "Waiting" was first published in 1978, in the Atlantic Monthly, *from which it won a citation. It since has become part of a collection of short stories entitled* Dislocations *(1987), in which Hospital probes the intercultural perspective in various settings. The author's comments on her own life further explain her interest in the lives of people who move across cultures: "I have lived for extended periods in Australia, the United States, Canada, England, and India, and I am very conscious of being at ease in many countries but belonging nowhere," she says. "All my writing reflects this. My characters are always caught between worlds or between cultures or between subcultures."*

In "Waiting" we see the same world three times, through the eyes of each of its principal characters.

Before you read "Waiting," write about a time in your life when you shared the same experience with someone but later discovered that each of you perceived it in entirely different ways. Describe the experience, your responses to it, the person with whom you shared it, how you discovered that your perceptions differed, and the result of those differences.

M r. Matthew Thomas owed his name and faith, as well as his lands, to those ancestors of lowly caste who had seen the salvation of the Lord. (It had been brought to South India by St. Thomas the Apostle, and by later waves of Portuguese Jesuits, Dutch Protestants, and British missionaries.) Now, heir of both East and West, Matthew Thomas sat quietly in one of the chairs at the crowded Air India office, waiting for his turn. It was necessary to make inquiries on behalf of a cousin of his wife, and although his wife had died ten years ago, these family obligations continued. The cousin, whose son was to be sent overseas for a brief period of foreign education, lived in the village of Parassala and could not get down to Trivandrum during the rice harvest. Mr. Matthew Thomas did not mind. He had much to think about on the subject of sons and daughters and foreign travel, and he was glad of this opportunity for quiet contemplation away from the noisy happiness of his son's house.

It was true that he had been waiting since nine o'clock that morning and it was now half past three in the afternoon. It was also true that things would have been more pleasant if the ceiling fan had been turning, for it was that steamy season when the monsoon is petering out, and the air hangs as still and hot and heavy as a mosquito net over a sick-bed. But the fan had limped to a halt over an hour ago, stricken by the almost daily power failure, and one simply accepted such little inconveniences.

Besides, Mr. Thomas could look from the comfortable vantage point of today back toward yesterday, which had also been spent at the Air India office, but since he had arrived too late to find a chair it had been necessary to stand all day. At the end of the day, someone had told him that he was supposed to sign his name in the book at the desk and that he would be called when his turn came. Wiser now, he had arrived early in the morning, signed his name, and found a chair. He was confident that his turn would come today, and until it did he could sit and think in comfort. Mr. Thomas was often conscious of God's goodness to him in such matters. All the gods were the same, he reflected, thinking fondly of the auspicious match which had just been arranged for the daughter of his neighbour Mr. Balakrishnan Pillai. Lord Vishnu; Lord Shiva; the Allah of his friend Mr. Karim, the baker; the One True God of his own church: all protected their faithful. He did not dwell on paradox.

God was merciful. It was sufficient.

The problem which demanded attention, and which Mr. Thomas turned over and over in his mind, peacefully and appraisingly as he might examine one of his coconuts, concerned both his married daughter in Burlington, Vermont, and the white woman waiting in another chair in the Air India office.

Burlingtonvermont. Burlingtonvermont. What a strange word it was. This was how his son-in-law had pronounced it. His daughter had explained in a letter that it was like saying Trivandrum, Kerala. But who would ever say Trivandrum, Kerala? Why would they say it? He had been deeply startled yesterday morning to hear the word suddenly spoken aloud, just when he was thinking of his daughter. Burlingtonvermont. The white woman had said it to the clerk at the counter, and she had been told to write her name in the book and wait for her turn.

This is a strange and wonderful thing, he had thought. And now he understood why God had arranged these two days of waiting. It was ordained so that he would see this woman who came, it seemed, from the place where his daughter was; so that he might have time to study her at leisure and consider what he should do.

He thought of Kumari, his youngest and favourite child. What did she do in Burlingtonvermont? He tried to picture her now that she was in her confinement, her silk sari swelling slightly over his grandchild. A terrible thought suddenly presented itself to him. If she had no servants, who was marketing for her at this time when she should not leave the house? Surely she herself was not . . . ? No. His mind turned from the idea, yet the bothersome riddles accumulated.

She was in her third month now, so he knew from the four child-bearings of his own wife that she would be craving for sweet mango pickle. He had written to say he would send a package of this delicacy. *Dear daddy,* she had written back, *please do not send the sweet pickle. I have no need of anything. I am perfectly happy.*

How could this be? It was true that her parents-in-law lived only five kilometres distant in the same city, and her brother-in-law and his wife also lived close by, and of course they would do her marketing and bring her the foods she craved. Of course, they were her true family now that she was married. Even so, when a woman was in the family way, it was a time when she might return to the house of her father, when she would want to eat the delicacies of the house of her birth.

He could not complain of the marriage. He was very happy with the marriages of all four of his children. They had all made alliances with Christian families of high caste. He had been able to provide handsome dowries for his daughters, and the wives of his sons had brought both wealth and beauty with them. God had been good. It was just a little sad that his elder daughter's husband was chief government engineer for Tamil Nadu instead of Kerala, and was therefore living in Madras. But at least he saw them and his grandchildren at the annual festival of Onam.

It was four years since he had seen Kumari. The week after her wedding her husband and his family had returned to America, where they had been living for many years. Only to arrange the marriages of their sons had they come back to Kerala. The arrangements had been made through the mail. Mr. Thomas had been content because the family was distantly related on his wife's side and he had known them many years ago, before they had left for America. Also the son was a professor of chemistry at the university in Burlingtonvermont, which was fitting for his daughter who had her B.A. in English literature. So they had come, the wedding had taken place, and they had gone.

For four years Mr. Matthew Thomas had waited with increasing anxiety. What is a father to think when his daughter does not bear a child in all this time? Now, as God was merciful, a child was coming. Yet she had written: *Dear daddy, please do not send the sweet pickle. I am perfectly happy.*

It had been the same when he had expressed his shock at her not having servants. *Dear daddy,* she had written, *you do not understand. Here we are not needing servants. The machines are doing everything. Your daughter and your son-in-law are very happy.* Of course this was most reassuring, if only he could really believe it. He worried about the snow and the cold. How was it possible to live with such cold? He worried about the food. The food in America is terrible, some businessmen at the Secretariat had told him. It is having no flavour. In America, they are not using any chili peppers. And yet, even at such a time as this, she did not want the sweet pickle. Could it mean that she had changed, that she had become like a Western woman?

He looked steadily and intently at the white woman in the room. Certainly, he thought, my daughter will be one of the most beautiful women in America. White women were so unattractive. It was not just their wheat-coloured hair, which did indeed look strange, but they seemed to have no understanding of the proper methods of beauty. They let their hair fly as dry and fluffy as rice chaff at threshing time instead of combing it with coconut oil so that it hung wet and glossy.

The woman was wearing a sari, which was, without question, better than the other Western women he had sometimes seen at the Mascot Hotel; those women had worn trousers as if they were men. It was amazing that American men allowed their women to appear so ugly. True, he had heard it said that women in the north of India wore trousers, but Mr. Thomas did not believe it. An Indian woman would not do such a thing. Once he had seen a white woman in a short dress, of the kind worn by little girls, with half her legs brazenly showing. He had turned away in embarrassment.

Mr. Thomas was pleased that the woman from Burlingtonvermont was wearing a sari. Still, it did not look right with pale skin and pale hair. It is the best she can do, he concluded to himself. It is simply not possible for them to look beautiful, no matter what they do.

The thing that was important, and must now be considered, was what to do with this manifestation sent by God. The woman from Burlingtonvermont perhaps had all the answers to his questions. Perhaps she could even explain the matter of the sweet pickle. But what to do? One did not speak to a woman outside of the family. And yet why else would it have been arranged that he should have two days to observe this very woman? God would also arrange the solution, he thought simply. He had only to wait.

As he continued to study that strange pale face an amazing thing happened. A tear rolled slowly down one cheek and fell into the soft folds of the sari. Mr. Thomas was shocked and looked away. After a little while, he looked back again. The woman seemed to be holding herself very tightly, as still as death, he thought. Her hands were clasped together in her lap so rigidly that the knuckles showed white. Her eyes were lowered, but the lashes glistened wetly. It must be a matter of love, he thought. Tragic love. Her parents have forbidden the match. For what other reason could a young woman, scarcely more than a girl, be weeping? Then his name was called and he went to the counter.

◄ ►

At the counter, Mr. Chandrashekharan Nair consulted the timetables and folders which would answer the queries of Mr. Matthew Thomas. He handled his sheaves of printed information reverently, occasionally pausing to make a small notation in ink in one of the margins, or to dignify a page with one of his rubber stamps. It always gave him a sense of pleasurable power. It was so fitting that the Nairs, who had from ancient times guarded the Maharajah of Travancore and defended his lands, should be as it were the guardians of Kerala in this modern age, watchmen over all the means of entry and egress.

It had given him particular pleasure to announce the name of Mr. Matthew Thomas. It was like the pleasure which comes after a summer's day of torpid discomfort, when the air is as damp and still as funeral bindings, until the monsoon bursts in a torrent of cool blessing. Just such a salvific release from several days of tension had come when he passed over the name of Miss Jennifer Harper to announce instead that of Mr. Matthew Thomas.

Life was distressingly complicated at the moment for Chandrashekharan Nair, who was twenty-six years old, and who owed his present position to his master's degree in economics as well as to his uncle who was a regional manager for Air India. The trouble was that two years ago, when he was still a student at the University of Kerala, he had joined one of the Marxist student groups. Well, in a sense joined. They had been an interesting bunch, livelier than other students. Mostly low-caste of course, even Harijans, not the sort of people one usually associated with, and this gave a risqué sense of exhilaration. But the leaders had all been decent fellows from the right families—Nairs, Pillais, Iyers. They read a bit too much for his liking, but the demonstrations had been rather fun, milling along Mahatma Gandhi Road in front of the Secretariat, confusing the traffic, making the withered old buffalo-cart drivers curse, jeering at the occasional American tourist. It was a student sort of thing to do. He had not expected that they would hang on to him in this way. It was beginning to become very embarrassing.

Of course he was all for progress. He agreed that more had to be done for the poor people. He felt that when he had his own household he would not expect so much from the *peon* as his father did. They really should not make the boy walk five kilometres each noontime to take young Hari's lunch to him at college, he thought. It was too much for a twelve-year-old boy.

In theory, he also agreed with the Marxists about dowry. Nevertheless, when he had studied so hard for his master's degree, he felt he could expect a *lakh* of rupees from his bride's family. That was simple justice. He would be providing her with security and prestige. He had *earned* the money. Strictly speaking, it was not dowry. Dowries were illegal anyway. It was simply that a girl's family would be embarrassed not to provide well for her, and a bridegroom from a good family, with a master's degree into the bargain, had every right to expect that they provide for her in a manner suited to his status.

Chandrashekharan Nair's marriage, and his *lakh* of rupees, was all but arranged. There was one slight problem. The girl's family was raising questions about his associations with the Marxists. His father had assured them that this had been the passing fancy of a student, wild oats only, but they wanted something more, a public statement or action.

Chandrashekharan Nair was nervous. One of his cousins, who had held an influential position in the Congress party of Kerala, was now under attack in the newspapers. It was possible that he would have to stand trial for obscure things, and his career would be ruined. It did not seem likely that the Marxists would regain total power in Kerala, but they were becoming stronger all the time and one should not take chances. It was not wise to be on record for any political opinion, for or against anything. One should always appear knowing but vague, erudite but equivocal.

Chandrashekharan Nair leafed through the problems in his mind day after day as he leafed through the papers on his desk. The girl's family was waiting. His own family was waiting. His father was becoming annoyed. It was simply not fair that he should be forced into such a dangerous position. Three days ago some of his former Marxist friends had come to the office. They were jubilant about the Coca-Cola business, and had just erected near the Secretariat a huge billboard showing Coca-Cola bottles toppling onto lots of little American businessmen who were scattering like ants. There was to be a major demonstration and they wanted him to take part.

All of Chandrashekharan Nair's anxiety became focused on the American girl who had walked into his office yesterday. It was her fault, the fault of Americans and their Coca-Cola and their independent women, that all these problems had come to plague his life. And then the glimmer of a solution appeared to him. He would make a public statement about Coca-Cola. He would praise the new Indian drink and the name chosen for it. He would mention Gandhi, he would say that this nonviolent method, following in Gandhiji's footsteps, was the correct political way for India. All this was quite safe. Morarji Desai and Raj Narain were saying it in the newspapers every day. The girl's family would be satisfied. But he would also say a few carefully ambiguous words about American businessmen that would please the Marxists. And as he slid easily over Miss Jennifer Harper's name, he thought with a surge of delight of how he would tell his Marxist friends in private of his personal triumphant struggle with an imperialist in the Air India office.

He saw the tear run down Miss Jennifer Harper's cheek and frowned with disgust. He felt vindicated. Integrated. Both Hindu and Marxist teachings agreed: compassion and sentiment were signs of weakness. The West was indeed decadent.

◄►

Jennifer Harper concentrated all her energy on waiting. There is just this one last ordeal, she promised herself, and even if I have to wait all tomorrow too, it must come to an end. I will not let the staring upset me. There is just this last time.

After months of conspicuous isolation as the only Western student at the University of Kerala, she was leaving. She wondered how long it would be before her sleep was free of hundreds of eyes staring the endless incurious stare of spectators at a circus. Or at a traffic accident. If one saw the bloodied remains of a total stranger spread across a road, one watched in just that way—with a fascinated absorption, yet removed, essentially unaffected.

She looked up at the counter with mute resignation. Surely her turn would come today. Inadvertently, she became aware of the intent gaze of the gentleman who had arrived next after her that morning. He also had waited all yesterday, but it did not seem to ruffle him. Nor did he show any sign of the exhausted dejection she had felt. Time means nothing to them, she thought with irritation. She decided to meet his gaze evenly, to stare him into submission.

He did not seem to notice. Her eyes bounced back off a stare as impenetrable as the packed red clay beneath the coconut palms. She felt as stupid and insignificant as a coconut, a stray green coconut that falls before its time, thuds onto the unyielding earth, and lies ignored, merely something for the scavenger dogs. It was intolerable. She could feel tears pricking her eyes.

Damn, damn, damn, she thought, pressing her hands together with all the force of her desire not to fall apart from the heat, the exhaustion, the dysentery, the inefficiency, the interminable waiting. Just this one last little thing, she pleaded with her self-respect. Then a name was called, and the impertinent staring gentleman went to the counter. They had missed her name by accident. But what would be the good of attempting to protest? Communication would be a shambles. The clerk would be confident that he was speaking English but would be virtually unintelligible. He would understand almost nothing she was trying to explain. Then she would try her halting Malayalam, but all her velar and palatal *r*s and *l*s, and all those impossible *d*s and *t*s, would get mixed up, and the people in the room would stare and giggle. Better to wait. He would soon notice that he had omitted a name.

◄►

There was a blare of loudspeakers passing the office. No one paid any attention to it. Every day some demonstration or other muddled the already chaotic traffic of Trivandrum's main road. If it was not the Marxists, it would be the student unions of the Congress party or the Janata party marching to protest each other's corruptions. Or it would be the bus drivers on strike, or the teachers picketing the Secretariat, or the rubber workers clamouring for attention, or perhaps just a flower-strewn palanquin bearing the image of some guru or deity.

The blast from the loudspeaker was so close that those at the counter could not hear one another speak. There was a milling crowd at the Air India doors, which gave way suddenly to the pressure of bodies. Mr. Chandrashekharan Nair blanched to see several Marxist leaders. He was going to have to make some snap decision that might have frightening repercussions for the rest of his life. He breathed a prayer to Lord Vishnu.

Mr. Matthew Thomas, who knew that the ways of God were inscrutable but wise, felt that something important was about to happen and waited calmly for it.

Jennifer Harper thought with despair that the office would now be closed and she would have to come back again the next day.

The student leader made an impassioned speech in Malayalam, which culminated in a sweeping accusatory gesture toward Jennifer. She rose to her feet as if in the dock. The student advanced threateningly, glared, and said in heavily accented English: "Imperialists out of India!" In equally amateur Malayalam, and in a voice from which she was unable to keep a slight quiver, Jennifer replied, "But I am not an imperialist."

There was a wave of laughter, but whether it was directed at her accent or her politics she could not say. Several things happened so quickly that she could never quite remember the order afterward. First, she thought, the gentleman who had stared so hard stepped between herself and the student, protective.

At the same time, the clerk at the desk had said, with a rather puzzling sense of importance, that he was especially arranging for the American woman to leave the country as quickly as possible. At any rate, she was now in a taxi on her way to the airport with nothing but her return ticket and her pocket-book. Next to the driver in the front seat was the gentleman who had defended her. She was thinking how sweet and easy and simple it was to sacrifice the few clothes and books, the purchased batiks and brasses, left back at the hostel. But the gentleman was saying something.

"My name is Matthew Thomas and I am having a daughter in Burlingtonvermont. I am hearing you say this place yesterday, and I am thinking perhaps you know my daughter?"

She shook her head and smiled.

"My daughter . . . I am missing her very much. . . . She is having a child. . . . There are many things I am not understanding. . . ."

They talked then, waiting at the airport where the fans were not working and the plane was late. When the boarding call finally came, Jennifer promised: "I will visit your daughter, and I will write. I understand all the things you want to know."

Mr. Matthew Thomas put his hands on her shoulders in a courteous formal embrace. She was startled and moved. "It is because you are the age of my daughter," he said, "and because you go to where she is."

Mr. Chandrashekharan Nair watched the plane circle overhead. He was on his way to the temple of Sree Padmanabhaswamy to receive prasadam and to give thanks to Lord Vishnu. He had just made a most satisfactory report of the incident to the newspaper reporter, and had been able to link it rather nicely to the Coca-Cola issue. It was a most auspicious day.

The ways of God are truly remarkable, thought Mr. Matthew Thomas as he left the airport. To think that the whole purpose behind the education of his wife's cousin's son had been the answer to his prayers about Kumari.

Jennifer Harper watched the red-tiled flat roofs and the coconut plantations and the rice paddies dwindle into her past. "Oh yes," she would say casually in Burlington, Vermont. "India. A remarkable country."

Questions for Discussion and Writing

1. What is significant about Mr. Matthew Thomas's belief that "God had arranged these two days of waiting" (p. 84)?
2. In what ways do Mr. Matthew Thomas's thoughts on life in America and the woman in the sari from Burlingtonvermont relate to the concerns he has for his daughter?
3. What does Hospital accomplish by telling this story from three different points of view?
4. What patterns of social time does "Waiting" reflect through each of its characters?
5. How does each of the story's characters interpret Jennifer Harper's leaving India, including Jennifer herself? In what ways is each person's interpretation tied to cultural values and attitudes?
6. Why do you think Hospital wrote this story? What audience do you think she had in mind as she wrote it?

HENRY C. BINFORD

I Scream, You Scream . . .
The Cultural Significance of Ice Cream

A member of the faculty of History and American Culture at Northwestern University, Henry C. Binford teaches, writes, and does research. His own education includes undergraduate and doctoral degrees from Harvard University in 1966 and 1973, respectively, as well as a master's degree from the University of Sussex in England.

Binford's major research has been on the history of American cities and suburbs. On these topics he has written numerous articles and one book, The First Suburbs: Residential Communities on the Boston Periphery, 1815–1860 *(1985). In the essay that follows, published in 1987 in* Arts & Sciences *magazine, Binford addresses the significance of ice cream in American culture.*

The author's favorite flavor is chocolate, in almost any version.

Before you read "I Scream, You Scream . . . The Cultural Significance of Ice Cream," write about the meaning of ice cream (or some other food) in your life: when you eat it and with whom, where you go to buy it, which brands and flavors you like and dislike, and the ways in which it is tied to memories of family, childhood, or other categories of your life. If you substituted another food for ice cream, write about why you made that choice, or why you don't eat ice cream at all, if that's the case.

Ice cream is one of the essential features of American culture. Most of us would not even question this proposition, but for doubters there is plenty of evidence, both in the testimony of outsiders and in international statistics. Consider the words of Fidel Castro, who loves to twit the United States by insisting that Cuba can outdo us even in those pursuits we hold most sacred—playing baseball, for example. Castro's multi-hour televised speeches, a hallmark of his regime from the beginning, offer useful texts in determining what is quintessentially American. In 1967, after several years of boasting about Cuba's

91

rising glory and the fading star of the United States, Castro decided he would go for the jugular. He proudly announced one day in the midst of a long harangue that Cuba would soon surpass capitalism, yet again, by producing 42 flavors of ice cream. But Fidel had picked the wrong target. That very afternoon the Cuban minister of information got a long distance phone call from Irv Robbins in California. Robbins, president of the Baskin-Robbins ice cream company, notified the Cubans that they had a long way to go, because at that point Baskin-Robbins was producing 290 flavors of ice cream (they have now passed the 400 mark).

Other numbers tell the same story of our cultural obsession. The American people consumed more than 1.2 billion gallons of ice cream last year, as they have every year for over a decade. That works out to about 6 gallons for every man, woman, and child in the United States. Considering that for one reason or another there are many Americans who don't eat ice cream, either because they are allergic to it, or are too young, or too old, or because for some unimaginable reason they don't like it, the rest of us must be consuming with gusto. And we are well in advance of the rest of the world. France, a country known for its esteem of things culinary, consumes a measly 4 gallons of ice cream per capita per year. The Soviet Union, which produces wonderful delicacies, and whose citizens also have a voracious appetite for things American, consumes only 3 gallons per capita per year. Japan, the great power of the Orient, beating the pants off of us in making computer chips and automobiles, cannot manage more than about 2½ gallons per capita per year.

In addition to these bits of evidence from the modern world, there is all sorts of evidence from history that we have been identified for a long time by our peculiar obsession with ice cream, and in general by our devotion to what is now called fast food. Fast food may be defined as relatively simple cuisine, meant to be eaten in a hurry, aimed at a mass market, and often associated with outdoor activity, excursions, and mass entertainment. Ice cream, one of the original fast foods, may be considered the direct ancestor of many all-American forms of recreational gluttony.

Clearly, Americans have a patriotic duty not only to eat ice cream but to understand its place in our heritage. In these times, when our schools are widely condemned for neglecting the content of history and the values of democracy, it is all the more important to probe the central beliefs and rituals of our culture.

Why is ice cream such an essential and distinctive feature of American culture? And more generally, why are we so obsessed with fast food? It seems to me that the answers to these questions lie in history. (If you ask a historian, the answers to any question lie in history.) They lie in a series of developments connected with what is now loosely called the Industrial Revolution, and especially with the way industrialization affected cities in the nineteenth-century United States.

Many scholars have noted that the rise of industrial society radically changed the nature of leisure throughout the Western world. In the pre-industrial era there was no sharp distinction between work and play—between the time and activity devoted to productive ends and governed by someone else's rules, and the time and activity devoted to recreation and not governed by obligations or rules. It was common for people to eat, drink, sing, and amuse themselves while they were, by our standards, on the job—that is, in workshops, engaged in farm labor, weaving at looms, and so forth. And by the same token, what we would regard as work, as productive labor, often took place in periods of time that we would now call leisure—in evenings, in off seasons, at the discretion of the individual. Moreover, in the pre-industrial era, activities that were clearly recreational or celebratory (such as harvest rituals, carnivals, and pageants) were generally undertaken in family or small community settings, and governed by long-standing customs.

Industrialization reared its ugly head and changed all the rules of the game. Industrialization, first of all, sharpened that distinction between work and leisure, in fact made it quite rigid, especially in the early stages of the process. Beginning in the late eighteenth century, employers put their workers on tighter schedules and defined tasks more precisely. Now there would be work time and play time, and the things one did at work were different from the things one did while playing. No more drinking and carousing, having a good time while on the job. Nope. From now on, get there, punch the clock, engage in productive labor for X hours, then go home. This change was, of course, most obvious for those in the early factories, but the custom of dividing sharply the time for work from the time for play spread throughout the whole society. Some historians have argued that the hallmark of industrialization was not the factory, but the clock. In the nineteenth century, clocks proliferated, especially in the cities and towns. Think of your image of the nineteenth-century American community—with people in carriages, and streets lined with shops. Almost invariably that image includes clocks, often a clock in a tower, a clock on a pedestal on the sidewalk, clocks in windows or hanging from storefronts.

Another part of the change in leisure came, inevitably, with the urbanization of the population. As the urban population grew at phenomenal rates, large numbers of people were uprooted from the family and community settings their ancestors had known. In the United States the growth of cities involved the merging of migrants not only from one country but from a host of foreign countries. Often young, single, and transient, these new city dwellers found themselves cut off from traditional recreation and thrust among people from very different backgrounds.

These two changes together created what might be called The Problem of Leisure. Especially in the cities, a great number of people lived lives in which relaxation was steadily purged from the realm of work, and consigned to whatever precious time remained between labor and sleep. Many of these city dwellers also lived among strangers, in an environment that did not offer all of the familiar supports and pastimes available in pre-industrial communities. What would so many people in such unprecedented circumstances do with this new piece of life called leisure?

In the nineteenth-century city a number of institutions sprang up to resolve that problem of leisure, to meet the set of difficulties that accompanied urban industrialization. Many of these institutions involved mass eating and drinking. The restaurant, for example, was largely a nineteenth-century invention. In eighteenth-century America there were taverns and inns but no restaurants as we know them. By and large, people did not go out to eat as a means of recreation, unless invited by other people to their homes. In the United States, restaurants began to appear roughly in the 1820s, in the big cities, for affluent people. Probably the most famous restaurant in America in the nineteenth century was Delmonico's in New York. Delmonico's strove to make eating in a restaurant attractive and different from the run-of-the-mill eating one did at home. It was one of the first places in the United States to offer people fresh vegetables and seafood, making early use of the railroad to supply these items out of season from distant places. It offered all sorts of rare concoctions that you could not find or could not easily make in the home. Delicacies and treats, often requiring ice shipped by the railroad, made this and other restaurants appealing places in which to spend leisure time.

For less well-to-do Americans, the bar, or the saloon as it was called in the nineteenth century, was also a solution to the problem of leisure. Saloons, augmented in the 1840s by German beer gardens, were characteristically city institutions. They offered good fellowship, drink, and usually food. Sausages, cheese, bread, and eventually sandwiches were common in nineteenth-century American bars. The Germans introduced large, often outdoor, family kinds of places where men, women, and children would go for an evening. There was usually music and dancing and lights and beer—lots of beer. German lager beer quickly gained a following in the United States, and, partly because of the shrewdness of a few entrepreneurs, Americans learned to drink it cold. Ice salesmen, who had already found a market for their wares in chilling perishables for the restaurants, now worked to convince leisure-time drinkers that cold beer was both healthy and tasty. Indeed the rise of leisure institutions like the restaurant and saloon both depended on and encouraged an expansion of the American ice industry. By the middle of the nineteenth century, merchants like Frederick Tudor of Boston were growing wealthy by harvesting ice from New England ponds, storing it in underground bunkers, and shipping it in insulated rail cars and sailing vessels to markets not only in the United States but in South America and India. Back home, Americans were hooked: cold drinks and chilled food became essential to the new urban leisure.

Restaurants and bars are still with us, but the nineteenth century also spawned another institution, now practically defunct, that must be considered as part of the history of recreational eating—the oyster bar. Oyster bars served city dwellers at the lowest end of the economic spectrum. Railroads and cheap ice touched off a positive craze for fresh oysters in the nineteenth century. Some of the establishments that sprang up to meet this demand offered all you could eat for five cents. In these bars, which resembled British fish-and-chips houses, we can see embryonic characteristics of the fast food joints that would appear decades later.

All of these institutions—the restaurant, the saloon, and the oyster bar—had some things in common: they made use of new technology, they provided a public means of occupying leisure time for people in the city, and they "democratized" various kinds of perishable delicacies.

But all these institutions had their defects. The restaurants were too expensive for all but a small segment of the population. The saloons and the beer gardens began to seem disreputable as the temperance movement increasingly persuaded native-born Americans that drinking was a bad idea, especially drinking in public with unwashed immigrants in places where you might catch who-knows-what disease, and, more important, where you might get visibly drunk. The oyster bars, while they were not expensive, and while they did not have that disreputable overtone, were often unhealthy because, despite the railroad and despite the fresh ice, oysters spoiled in a hurry and at the all-you-can-eat rate it was quite likely that you were going to come across a bad oyster or two pretty frequently. In fact there were rumors that the proprietors threw in the bad oysters along with the good ones just to make sure people didn't eat too much.

After the Civil War, urban Americans turned to a wondrous new institution that had many of the advantages and none of the drawbacks of restaurants, saloons, and oyster bars—the ice cream parlor. The ice cream parlor solved the problem of urban leisure in a new and wholly acceptable way. Not as expensive as restaurants, not disreputable like saloons, not unhealthy like oyster bars, the ice cream parlor brought together several of the achievements of industrial technology to provide a superb respite from the pressures of industrial schedules. Thanks to mass-produced ice, rail-transported cream and fruit, and improved knowledge of insulation, millions of Americans could enjoy what had once been a rare and fragile treat.

There was, of course, nothing new about ice cream itself. Historians have traced ice cream back at least to Elizabethan England, whence it came to the American colonies. There is some evidence that it existed before that, perhaps even as far back as the Roman Empire. We have descriptions of confections that Roman nobles served at banquets for very important people, and they include items that seem to have been frozen desserts, ices of one kind or another, and perhaps ice cream. But since neither the Romans nor anybody else before the Renaissance made much use of recipes, we don't really know what was in these antique confections. All we know is that by the time of the Tudors, ice cream was popular in England, and when Elizabethan Englishmen and women came to the new world, they brought with them recipes for ice cream. We also know that it was popular among elite Americans all through the eighteenth and nineteenth centuries. George Washington, for example, proved himself a noteworthy father of our country when in the summer of 1790 he spent $200 (a truly enormous amount of money at the time) for ice cream for various notables in New York. Until the nineteenth century, however, ice cream remained something for the wealthy.

In the mid-nineteenth century, a series of innovations prepared Americans for the rapid spread of ice cream parlors. The first of these was the hand-cranked ice cream maker, essentially the kind of thing we used when we were kids: you add a little rock salt, a little ice, a little flavoring, a little cream—good. The ice cream makers were patented in the 1840s and gave people the idea for starting small-scale retail outlets. Then in the 1860s and '70s machines were invented which allowed large-scale production. These inventions, combined with the explosive growth of the cities, spurred the opening of ice cream parlors.

Then in the late nineteenth century, a series of other developments, all connected with urbanization and industrialization, increased the popularity of ice cream and made it the ancestor of a host of other fast foods. First, Americans began to gather in large places in large numbers for public entertainment of a new kind: professional sports. Starting in the 1870s and '80s, baseball, football, and a variety of other sports began attracting thousands of people at a time to arenas specifically built to house major competitions between professional teams. In addition, the colleges began building their own arenas and stadiums for the same purpose. But what do you do in a stadium besides watch a game, especially if the game is boring? You eat and drink. Now we're still in the nineteenth century, so the consumption of beer and alcohol in these stadiums is generally frowned upon. It happens, but only on an on-again-off-again basis. Fancy foods are difficult to prepare and to sell in stadiums. Sausages are one answer. But remember that many of these sporting events take place in the summer and it's hot and you want something cold. And that druggist in Atlanta has not yet conceived of the mass distribution of Coca Cola. The perfect answer of course is ice cream.

A second change in the environment came with the great nineteenth-century fairs. Americans took to having great fairs to celebrate their industrial triumphs, to celebrate themselves, to celebrate almost anything. After the Centennial Exposition in Philadelphia in 1876 (which saw the first large soda fountain), a number of major cities organized such huge events. We had, among others, the famous World's Columbian Exposition in Chicago in 1893 and the fairs in St. Louis and San Francisco at the turn of the century. The fairs were an ideal marketing ground for things portable and edible, and ice cream was a central feature. The fertile minds of American inventors, confronted with so many new events, came up with new ways to package the product to make it more portable and attractive. At the St. Louis World's Fair of 1904, for example, an ice cream vendor who sold his product in little dishes, and a vendor of waffles (another new fast food), combined to invent the cone. At some time the ice cream vendor ran out of the dishes at his stand, and he complained to his neighbor the waffle vendor, and the waffle vendor had a bright idea. He took one of his waffles and wrapped it into a cone shape, stuck it in the oven, and baked it hard. Eureka! Ice cream cone.

Later entrepreneurs started making ice cream and derivative products in fancy forms and fancy flavors, adapting the product through marketing innovations, in an effort to capture a larger share of those big audiences out there for fancy frozen concoctions. The Eskimo Pie, for example, ice cream on a stick, was patented in 1921. In 1923 a maker of lemonade powder in New Jersey accidentally left a glass of lemonade on his windowsill with a spoon in it overnight. It froze solid. In the morning, he grabbed the spoon, yanked it out of the glass, and bing—the popsicle was born. Street vendors had sold cheap ice cream and ices since the nineteenth century. In the early 1920s the Good Humor Corporation not only patented its own product but systematized and motorized the summer evening neighborhood trade as well.

But the crowning achievement in the saga of ice cream came with the innovations of Howard Johnson, a druggist in Wollaston, Massachusetts. Like many others, Johnson's drug store included a soda fountain that sold homemade ice cream. During the 1920s Johnson gained a marketing advantage by expanding his range of flavors to 28, and then gained immortality by franchising others to make and sell ice cream from his recipe and under his name at locations across the nation.

Howard Johnson's innovations were crucial not only in opening the way for flavor titans like Baskin-Robbins, but in setting the pattern for the mass sales networks of post-World War II fast food moguls. When Ray Kroc bought out a California hamburger stand owned by the McDonald brothers in the late 1940s, he began an empire which, with its imitators, now shapes the lives, tastes, and physical surroundings of nearly every American. But he was only building on an established set of habits and institutions, long embedded in American culture by the rise of ice cream.

Questions for Discussion and Writing

1. What relationships does Binford create among the industrialization of the last century, the emerging concept of leisure, and the idea of "recreational eating"?
2. According to the author, what is the relationship between the phenomenon of ice cream and its cultural significance, and emerging technologies in the late nineteenth century?
3. For whom do you think Binford wrote this analysis of the cultural significance of ice cream? In what ways and for what reasons does he or does he not succeed in capturing your interest?
4. If you were writing a similar kind of analysis on a different American phenomenon—such as blue jeans or sweatshirts—which elements of Bin-

ford's writing approach would you want to imitate, and why? Which elements would you prefer to avoid, and why?

5. Reevaluate the writing you did about the meaning of ice cream or some other food in your life. In what ways might you argue that the cultural significance of ice cream (or the food of your choice) is continuing to evolve, if your use of it can be taken as an example of its present history?

CAROL SIMONS

Kyoiku Mamas

A former associate editor at the Smithsonian *magazine, Carol Simons has lived in many parts of Asia with her children and her husband, a foreign correspondent—including Vietnam, Malaysia, Hong Kong, Thailand, India, Japan (for six years), and most recently, Beijing, China. She continues to write for the* Smithsonian *and other publications on such issues as education, horticulture, nature, and popular technology. "One of the advantages of journalism," she writes, "is that it is transportable and adaptable; not only have I been able to work in many countries, but I have been able to learn about them as well."*

"Kyoiku Mamas," published in the Smithsonian *in 1987, grew out of Simons's interest in what mothers in Japan do on a day-to-day basis to help their children achieve academically. "While my small son played in the afternoons," she explains, "theirs were going to music classes, gymnastics, math. At one point, I even suggested to my son, then seven, that he go to after-school math classes to speed up his computation, but he looked at me like I was crazy." The author wrote this essay over a period of two years, finding it difficult to reach a conclusion. "At first, the advantages were more obvious than the disadvantages," she says. "But after interviewing many women, and observing the pressures as we became friends, I decided theirs was a plight, forced by competition in the system, that I was fortunate to escape. Most Japanese mothers, though proud of their roles, felt burdened by them and wished their children could have more of a childhood."*

Before you read "Kyoiku Mamas," reflect on and then write about the ideas of duty and responsibility and the cultural dictates or standards that influenced your mother or the person who cared for you as a child. What were her major convictions as a parent—as you know them directly and in-

directly—and why and where do you suppose she found them? If you are now a mother, you might prefer to examine the cultural dictates or standards influencing you.

T wo-year-old Hiromasa Itoh doesn't know it yet, but he's preparing for one of the most important milestones of his life, the examination for entry into first grade. Already he has learned to march correctly around the classroom in time with the piano and follow the green tape stuck to the floor—ignoring the red, blue and yellow tapes that lead in different directions. With the other 14 children in his class at a central Tokyo nursery school, he obeys the "cleaning-up music" and sings the good-bye song. His mother, observing through a one-way glass window, says that it's all in preparation for an entrance examination in two or three years, when Hiromasa will try for admission to one of Tokyo's prestigious private schools.

Forty-five minutes south of the capital city by train, in the small suburb of Myorenji, near Yokohama, 13-year-old Naoko Masuo returns from school, slips quietly into her family's two-story house and settles into her homework. She is wearing a plaid skirt and blue blazer, the uniform of the Shoe-ei Girls School, where she is a seventh-grader. "I made it," her smile seems to say. For three years, when she was in fourth through sixth grades in public school, Naoko's schedule was high-pressure: she would rush home from school, study for a short time and then leave again to attend *juku,* or cram school, three hours a day three times a week. Her goal was to enter a good private school, and the exam would be tough.

Her brother, Toshihiro, passed a similar exam with flying colors several years ago and entered one of the elite national schools in Tokyo. The summer before the exam, he went to *juku* eight hours a day. Now, as a high school graduate, he is attending prep school—preparing for university entrance exams that he will take in March.

Little Hiromasa, Naoko and Toshihiro are all on the Japanese road to success. And alongside them, in what must surely be one of the world's greatest traffic jams, are thousands of the nation's children, each one trying to pass exams, enter good schools and attain the good jobs that mark the end of a race well run.

But such children are by no means running as independents. They are guided and coached, trained and fed every step of the way by their mothers, who have had sharp eyes on the finish line right from the start.

No one doubts that behind every high-scoring Japanese student—and they are among the highest scoring in the world—there stands a mother, supportive, aggressive and completely involved in her child's education. She studies, she packs lunches, she waits for hours in lines to register her child for exams and waits again in the hallways for hours while he takes them. She denies herself TV so her child can study in quiet and she stirs noodles at 11 P.M. for the scholar's snack. She shuttles youngsters from exercise class to rhythm class to calligraphy and piano, to swimming and martial arts. She helps every day with homework, hires tutors and works part-time to pay for *juku*. Sometimes she enrolls in "mother's class" so she can help with the drills at home.

So accepted is this role that it has spawned its own label, *kyoiku mama* (education mother). This title is not worn openly. Many Japanese mothers are embarrassed, or modest, and simply say, "I do my best." But that best is a lot, because to Japanese women, motherhood is a profession, demanding and prestigious, with education of the child the number-one responsibility. Cutthroat competition in postwar Japan has made her job harder than ever. And while many critics tend to play down the idea of the perpetually pushy mother, there are those who say that a good proportion of the credit for Japan's economic miracle can be laid at her feet.

"Much of a mother's sense of personal accomplishment is tied to the educational achievements of her children, and she expends great effort helping them," states *Japanese Education Today,* a major report issued in January by the U.S. Department of Education. "In addition, there is considerable peer pressure on the mother. The community's perception of a woman's success as a mother depends in large part on how well her children do in school."

Naoko's and Toshihiro's mother, Mieko Masuo, fully fills the role of the education mother, although she'd be the last to take credit for her children's accomplishments. This 46-year-old homemaker with a B.A. in psychology is a whiz at making her family tick. She's the last one to go to bed at night ("I wait until my son has finished his homework. Then I check the gas and also for fire. My mother stayed up and my husband's mother, and it's the custom for me, too") and the first one up in the morning, at 6. She prepares a traditional breakfast for the family, including *miso* soup, rice, egg, vegetable and fish. At the same time, she cooks lunch for her husband and Naoko, which she packs up in a lunch box, or *o-bento.* She displays the *o-bento* that Naoko will carry to school. In the pink plastic box, looking like a culinary jigsaw puzzle, are fried chicken, boiled eggs, rice, lotus roots, mint leaves, tomatoes, carrots, fruit salad and chopsticks. No pb&j sandwiches in brown bags for this family.

"Every morning, every week, every year, I cook rice and make *o-bento.*" Mrs. Masuo says with a laugh, winking at Naoko. "I wouldn't want to give her a *tenuki o-bento.*" Naturally. Everyone knows that a "sloppy lunch box" indicates an uncaring mother.

But Mrs. Masuo doesn't live in the kitchen. She never misses a school mother's meeting. She knows all the teachers well, has researched their backgrounds and how successful their previous students have been in passing exams. She carefully chose her children's schools and *juku,* and has spent hours accompanying them to classes. "It's a pity our children have to study so much," she apologizes. "But it's necessary." She says that someday she'd like to get a part-time job—perhaps when exams are over. "But at the moment I must help my children. So I provide psychological help and *o-bento* help." Then she laughs.

Toshihiro says that it was his mother who drilled him in elementary school and instilled in him his good work habits. And he says it was she who "forced" him to go to *juku* from fifth grade on, even though he hated it and "missed being able to play after school." And it was she who made sure the money was set aside to pay for his many lessons—up to $12,000 for two years before he took the junior high exam. Mrs. Masuo explains that her husband, who works for an oil company, didn't feel *juku* was necessary "because he didn't go when he was young." But, like most Japanese husbands, he works late and doesn't get involved in the children's activities. "So what happened was that Toshihiro just started to go, and afterward the subject was raised. Naoko, being the second, was no problem."

Some evenings she went with Naoko to *juku*. Mother and daughter walked the 15 minutes down the hill to the train station and took the Tokyo line four stops to Yokohama, then walked past the brightly lit shops and kiosks and along the glittering lanes that make so much of Japan's shopping streets look like Coney Island. They passed *sake* shops and bakeries, Kentucky Fried Chicken and a clanging pachinko parlor, and turned in at the modern high-rise where the *juku* occupies two floors.

Naoko studied Japanese, math and science. Today, in her former math class, the *juku* teacher rapidly explains algebra problems to 50 fifth-graders. He lectures; they listen. In a science class down the hall, a young teacher explains photosynthesis and pretends to be a drooping plant. Seated at long tables, the children listen attentively, occasionally giggling at his antics. It is almost 8:30 P.M. and many of them haven't been home since breakfast.

"Yes, it's difficult," says Masato Nichido, assistant director of the *juku*. "But most of these children like *juku* better than public school. These children want to study more. And whether they want to or not is beside the point. They must, in order to pass exams."

It is this prospect of exams, known in Japan as "examination hell," that has prompted Yukiko Itoh to expose little Hiromasa to early training in the hope that he will get into a prestigious private school. Just over ten percent of Tokyo's children attend private schools, some of which run from first grade through high school and even through university. Assuming there are no major mishaps, a child who enters one of these schools can pass the rest of his academic career without the fierce examinations children such as the Masuos must face.

Like most Japanese mothers, Mrs. Itoh spends most of her time with her son and her six-month-old daughter, Emi. Babysitters and play groups are not part of her life. She has dinner with the children well before her husband comes home from work. She takes them to the park, to swimming lessons and music, much of the time carrying her baby in a pack on her back. Indeed, a young mother with an infant in a sling and a toddler by the hand walking along a subway platform or a city street is a sight that evokes the very essence of motherhood to most Japanese.

This physical tie between mother and child is only a small part of the strong social relationship that binds members of the family together in mutual dependency and obligation. It's the mother's job to foster this relationship. From the beginning, the child is rarely left alone, sleeps with the parents, is governed with affectionate permissiveness and learns through low-key signals what is expected and what to expect in return.

Many American children are also raised with affection and physical contact, but the idea is to create independent youngsters. Discipline begins early. Children have bedrooms separate from their parents. They spend time playing alone or staying with strangers and learn early that the individual is responsible for his own actions. An American mother, in disciplining, is more likely to scold or demand; a Japanese mother is apt to show displeasure with a mild rebuke, an approach that prompted one American six-year-old to tell his own mother: "If I had to be gotten mad at by someone, I wish it would be by a Japanese."

Even a casual observer is struck by the strong yet tender mother-child connection. A Japanese senior high school teacher said that many wives, including his own, sleep in a room with their children and not their husbands. "Is it the same in America?" he asked. At a dinner party, a businessman made his wife's excuses: "I'm sorry she couldn't come tonight. My son has an exam tomorrow." Even if the excuse was not true, the use of it says a lot.

You Must Do Well or People Will Laugh

The relationship of dependency and obligation fostered in the child by the mother extends to family, school, company and country, and is the essence of Japanese society. The child is taught early that he must do well or people will laugh at him—and laugh at his mother as well. "Most Japanese mothers feel ashamed if their children do not do well at school," said one mother. "It is our responsibility to see that the child fulfills his responsibility." Bad behavior may bring shame, but good behavior has its own rewards. One woman described a friend by saying: "Her son studied very hard in order to get into a good high school and he got in. She is very clever."

This attitude is precisely what gives education mothers such as Mrs. Masuo and her *o-bento* philosophy such esteem and why they take such pride in their role, even if they don't admit it. Their goal is clear: success in entrance exams, good school, a good college and a good job. (For daughters the goal has a twist: good schools lead to good husbands.)

For the majority of students who go the public school route, test scores become key and it is this fact that motivates many of the 11- and 12-year-olds traveling home from *juku* on evening trains. Many try out for the elite national junior high schools which, because of the demand, grant entrance on a combination of scores and lottery. Three years later they test again, for placement in high schools which, unlike the egalitarian lower grades, are organized according to ability. And three years after that, they test for college.

Passing the final obstacle isn't easy; only about half get into college on their first try. Many try again, for a year or two, attending prep schools and *juku*, memorizing facts for exams to come. Such students are called *ronin*, literally "masterless samurai," and even are referred to in government statistics by this term.

A $5 Billion-a-year Industry

But "exam hell" doesn't stop with college. Companies and government ministries administer highly competitive tests to prospective employees, sometimes only to graduates of the prestigious universities—a system that increases the pressure even more.

This competition at all levels has generated the *"juku* boom," a $5 billion-a-year industry of prep schools for *ronin,* cram schools, tutors and special courses. Over the past ten years, the number of children attending *juku* has increased by half—now more than 16 percent of the primary school children and 45 percent of junior high students. Attending *juku* can cost well over $200 a month.

Even the *juku* compete with each other—there are now 36,000 of them in Japan. One Tokyo *juku* administers practice exams to 20,000 youngsters on Sundays. Some of the more famous cram schools give their own admission tests, promoting jokes about going to *juku* for *juku.* Can a student get into a prestigious high school or college with just the information learned in public school? "Highly unlikely," said one local public high school teacher. "The exams are very severe."

So, in the evenings and on Saturdays and Sundays, subway platforms are crowded with students of all ages. Dressed in casual clothes or sober midnight blue school uniforms and lugging heavy black leather book bags, they are traveling to the thousands of cram schools tucked into office buildings, down side lanes and in every corner of every neighborhood.

Sometimes, children are launched into the system when they are barely old enough to walk, some of them starting "school" when they are still in diapers. They learn to obey such commands as how to clench and open their fists. "The future of a child here begins with conception," said one Tokyo mother. "Schools, after-school schools, calligraphy, piano, exercises—Japanese mothers don't waste any time." A documentary film on nursery schools by the Japan Broadcasting Company followed a five-year-old named Yasukata and his mother around on their weekly activities. Every morning he went to kindergarten. Three afternoons a week he attended "special strengthening class" ($500 a month), which included rhythm exercises, simple academics and etiquette. His mother waited two and a half hours while he took the class. On another afternoon, she took him to athletics, and on another to drawing. Such preparations, the mother said, would help her son "jump the puddles" ahead of him. By the program's end, Yasukata was one of 1,066 to "challenge" the prestigious Keio private school—which continues through university—and one of the 132 first-graders to gain entrance. On the same program, a mother of twin girls who had also been accepted to a famous private school said, "It's as though I have received a long-distance ticket to life."

Hoping for the same ticket are many of the mothers sitting on the benches in the large gymnasium at a branch of the ponderously named Japan Athletic Club Institute for Education of Infants (JAC for short), the school that Hiromasa attends. They are watching an afternoon class of about 50 four-year-olds in their regulation red-and-blue shorts and T-shirts. The children have finished exercising and are beginning a "voice obedience" session. Abreast in a straight line, the group is told to "hop forward to the beat of the tambourine, jump in place to the tweet of the whistle." It sounds easy but not everyone arrives at the finish line at the same time, indicating a slipup in obeying the tweets and beats. Some private primary schools might use such exercises in their entrance exams, so practice is considered practical.

Watching the mothers watch their children, JAC Director Naomi Ooka says he is dismayed by the pressure of the exams on the mothers and their children. In his view, modern Japanese mothers and children spend too much time together. "It's not good," he says.

Today, more and more educators and parents are questioning the high-pressure system that gives rise to such popular sayings as "Sleep four hours, pass; sleep five hours, fail." Educationists speak of lost childhoods, kids never getting a chance to play, "eating facts" to pass exams, and the production of students who memorize answers but can't create ideas. They cite the cruelty of students who take pleasure when their classmates fail, increasing delinquency, and high incidence of bullying in the schools.

Not surprisingly, Japanese mothers have been among the major critics, perhaps because they bear much of the brunt and witness the effects of the pressure on their children. "My son kept getting headaches and then he didn't want to go to school," said one mother. "So I stopped the *juku.*" Recently, such mothers have gained an ally in Prime Minister Yasuhiro Nakasone, whose government has been seeking ways to depressurize the education system. Nevertheless, many doubt that his efforts will have any effect in a society dedicated to hard work and competition.

For on a measuring stick, the competition has surely paid off. In math and science, Japanese children rank highest in the world. They do long division before American children, take more years of a foreign language (English), learn chemistry earlier, and are overflowing with factual knowledge about history, geography, scientific formulas and other bits of information that to many Americans would seem encyclopedic.

And the accomplishments don't stop there. A stunning 94 percent of Japanese youth go to high school. Some 90 percent graduate (compared with 76 percent in the United States) and are well qualified to take their place in the work force. At the college level, the comparison shifts: only 29 percent of Japanese high school graduates go on to college (compared with 58 percent of American graduates). It is here, at the highest level, that Japanese education is considered inferior to that in the United States. The Japanese college years are often referred to as a "four-year vacation," although a well-earned vacation since the years through high school produce students who shine.

Among Japanese who are beginning to fight the system are the increasing numbers who have lived abroad. Quite simply, they want their children to have more time to play; they want them to learn more and memorize less; they want them to be more creative and independent. Critics say that small families, small houses and modern conveniences lead to children being babied by mothers who don't have enough to do; and that mothers themselves are stifled at an age when women should have more freedom.

Chikako Ishii claims to know a better life. She spent several years in New York City with her family and is an outspoken opponent of the education mother and the highly competitive education system. "I don't think women like this role," she says, "but the competition is pushing them into it."

Mrs. Ishii teaches Parent Effectiveness Training, an approach to learning that emphasizes the individuality of the child. It's an idea long accepted in the West but anathema in group-oriented Japan, where one of the most repeated proverbs is the "nail that protrudes will be hammered down." Her two sons go to neighborhood schools. Masahiro, 12, is in the sixth grade and Hideaki, 14, is in the eighth, where he is ranked number one in his class. They do not attend *juku* and do not have tutors. "So far they're both doing well," remarks their mother. "I am watching to see how they develop."

Like those around them, the Ishiis have high expectations for their children, but their wait-and-see approach is baffling to many. "She's brave," said one young mother. "It's fine, I suppose," allowed another. "But what if she fails?"

Questions for Discussion and Writing

1. By what cultural patterns of values and expectations is the mother–child relationship governed in Japan? In what ways are the achievements of both mother and child intertwined?
2. What contrasting cultural patterns of values and expectations underlie the mother–child relationship in the United States?
3. In what ways might "one of the world's greatest traffic jams [of people]" (p. 100) influence the patterns of values explored in this essay?
4. What are your responses to Simon's descriptions of the demands placed on Japanese mothers? What elements in your background influence your responses?
5. Why or why not do you agree with the author's assertion that "theirs [Japan's mothers'] was a plight forced by competition in the system" (p. 99)?

WILLIAM D. MONTALBANO

Latin America: A Quixotic Land Where the Bizarre Is Routine

Born in 1940, William D. Montalbano is a writer and reporter. He is currently working as a foreign correspondent in Rome, where he writes news and feature stories on Italy and the Vatican and travels with the Pope. He also reports on Greece, Turkey, Spain, and Portugal. The recipient of numerous journalism awards, Montalbano sometimes finds time to write novels, too—"flighty airplane books," as he calls them.

In his work as a foreign correspondent, information is his trade. "To be able to write a story about anything—a person, an issue, a country, a continent or a state of mind, I assemble a welter of data, much more than I could ever get into the paper," Montalbano explains. "Then I hone, trying to build a word picture that will make people read, and learn, about things for which they have no innate interest. When reporter becomes writer, he can bob and weave, he can back and fill. One thing he can't do is write good copy with bad information."

The essay that follows—"that surrealism piece," as Montalbano describes it and one of his all-time favorites—was first published in the Los Angeles Times *in 1986. "After covering Latin America for a long time, it finally dawned on me that the two halves of the hemisphere are cursed into examining one another through opposite ends of the same telescope. The* latinos *see us bigger than life. We see pygmies. Not true. Not true. The incomprehension is fueled by a skewered mindset. We think that if we only got to know them, why, they'd be just like us. Baloney. They're different, man; different products of a different, whacky, magical kind of place. . . . So the story is about incomprehension, or it's an aide to understanding misunderstanding."*

According to Montalbano, the essay was created as a result of a "feet-on-the desk review of snippets of anecdotal string" he'd been storing in his back pocket for six months or a year. Nobel Prize-winner Gabriel García-Márquez's acceptance speech gave him the framework with which to stitch all his collected improbabilities together.

Before you read "Latin America: A Quixotic Land Where the Bizarre Is Routine," ask some of your classmates who are not originally from your area or maybe even your country to describe the surprises and strange experiences they had in adjusting to their new surroundings. What appeared bizarre, and why? Take notes on what they describe, and then write a story from the viewpoint of a reporter. You could title your piece "_____ (Fill in the name of your city, town, or country): An Exotic Spot Where the Bizarre Is Routine."

H earing that a former provincial governor named Luis Cruz had died, the Argentine Senate rose to praise him.

Senator followed senator in flowery procession until all the major parties had paid tribute to Cruz. A steadfast "workman of democracy," one grieving legislator called him.

Two hours later, a message arrived from Cruz. Thanks for the memories, he told the senators from a hospital bed, but it might be best to wait a bit.

Doubtless there are places on this inconstant earth where death and taxes may be counted as certainties. Latin America is not one of them. Only the flat-footed pay up, and even death can be a relative thing through the Latin American looking glass.

As successive generations of North Americans learn, to their amazement and often to their chagrin, reality south of the Rio Grande rarely matches an outsider's conception of what is real.

Reality and fiction, fact and fantasy whirl in kaleidoscopic tumult until at times they become indistinguishable. The startling is commonplace; the bizarre is routine.

Latin America seems to be trapped in a quixotic dimension, a wonderland where the skies are filled with planes that do not fly, the air shrieks with the ringing of phones that do not work and everybody understands but the gringos.

In the past two years, four Latin American countries—Peru, Argentina, Brazil and Bolivia—have changed their currencies. One—Haiti—has changed its flag. Argentina and Peru say they will move their capital cities to provincial backwaters.

In Bolivia one night last July, dinner for three cost 43,050,000 pesos, including tax and tip—about $22. In Ecuador, where a bygone dictator wore a bemedaled uniform to his own wake, at which he was seated on the presidential throne, the incumbent president calls his pistol "my best friend" and never leaves home without it.

In Argentina, a few months after being sentenced to life in prison for human-rights abuses, a former member of a governing junta was pictured in a magazine nattily dressed in gym shorts on his way to the squash court at the military garrison where he was being held.

While American critics applaud the "magical realism" that so distinguishes modern Latin American literature, some of its practitioners argue that surrealism is not just an important facet of Latin America, but its underpinning.

Accepting the 1982 Nobel Prize for literature with a lecture entitled "The Solitude of Latin America," Colombian novelist Gabriel Garcia-Marquez noted the impact on foreigners of "the unearthly tidings of Latin America, that boundless realm of haunted men and historic women whose unending obstinacy blurs into legend."

Colombia's master of fantastical fiction was only saying what Latin Americans are born knowing: that anything is believable, that life is one big surprise, unsurprisingly.

In Peru, for example, where beating is the historic means of extracting criminal confessions, the Lima police unexpectedly turned over a suspected serial murderer to a psychologist who had lectured on the criminal mind at the police academy. The psychologist examined the suspect, became convinced of his guilt and strangled him in an interrogation room at police headquarters.

The story is told in Argentina of a company pilot, preoccupied with plans for his wife's birthday party, who forgot to lower his landing gear and totaled the plane. He walked away without a scratch, but on his way to the party his car was hit by a train. The pilot escaped with minor cuts and bruises, but friends took him to a hospital anyway. There the staff marveled at his good luck and gave him a precautionary tetanus shot. He died a few minutes later in reaction to the shot.

In Latin America, the eerie is everyday. Seers, healers, witch doctors, fortune tellers, mediums, soothsayers, witches, and warlocks far outnumber Catholic priests.

Latin America abounds with questions that should not be asked:

Why is the cow painted on the roof of a chapel at the Metropolitan Cathedral in Buenos Aires reading a Bible? Why must the passports of dogs leaving Uruguay include a noseprint?

And it abounds with truths that must not be told:

After the armed forces used heavy explosives to quell a riot by Maoist guerrilla prisoners in a Lima prison, the state television showed the resulting devastation to the strains of Anton Dvorak's "New World Symphony."

Latin America echoes with the impact of events that have not occurred:

In its coverage of municipal elections last month, a Peruvian television station announced that Enrique Zileri, a prominent magazine editor, was en route to the studio to analyze the results.

"It's amazing how many people called this morning to say they agreed with what I said on TV," Zileri marveled the next day.

"Sorry I missed it," a friend murmured politely.

"You didn't. I never went," Zileri replied.

Questions for Discussion and Writing

1. Using examples from the essay, explain what Montalbano means when he says that for some Latin American writers "surrealism is not just an important facet of Latin America, but its underpinning" (p. 109).
2. What North American assumptions about what is "real" are refuted by the behaviors in the sampling of Latin American countries mentioned in this essay?
3. Montalbano says that he created this essay from "snippets of anecdotal string." What do you suppose are those individual snippets? What transitional devices does the author use to stitch them together?

OCTAVIO PAZ

The Day of the Dead

Octavio Paz began his literary career in 1931, at the age of seventeen. Today he is a well-known Mexican poet and essayist and considered a major figure in contemporary Latin American literature. Describing himself as a "disillusioned leftist," Paz does not confine himself to the typewriter. He has worked in the Mexican Embassy in Paris (1945) and Japan (1951), and has represented Mexico as its ambassador to India (1962–1968). In the early 1970s, he spent time on the faculties of the University of Texas and Harvard University.

Paz is also a critic and social philosopher, concerned about his country and its patterns, especially as they contrast with those of the United States—what he calls the "extremes within Western civilization." The essay that follows comes from his book The Labyrinth of Solitude, Life and Thought in Mexico *(1961), in which he explores ideas of Mexican time, life, and death through the phenomenon of the Mexican fiesta—in this particular case, "The Day of the Dead." "Acceleration in time is very dangerous," Paz argues. "Established societies that develop very slowly . . . can preserve themselves better than societies which have the idolatry of change. We shouldn't forget that primitive societies have endured millennia, but developed societies, after two or three centuries, explode."*

Before you read "The Day of the Dead," write about a time in your life when you celebrated without restraint—when you really "let loose." Describe the occasion, the ways in which you abandoned control, why you decided to do so, the results of the experience, and what you thought about it after it was over.

T he solitary Mexican loves fiestas and public gatherings. Any occasion for getting together will serve, any pretext to stop the flow of time and commemorate men and events with festivals and ceremonies. We are a ritual people, and this characteristic enriches both our imaginations and our sensibilities, which are equally sharp and alert. The art of the fiesta has been debased almost everywhere else, but not in Mexico. There are few places in the world where it is possible to take part in a spectacle like our great religious fiestas with their violent primary colors, their bizarre costumes and dances, their fireworks and ceremonies, and their inexhaustible welter of surprises: the fruit, candy, toys and other objects sold on these days in the plazas and open-air markets.

Our calendar is crowded with fiestas. There are certain days when the whole country, from the most remote villages to the largest cities, prays, shouts, feasts, gets drunk and kills, in honor of the Virgin of Guadalupe or Benito Juárez. Each year on the fifteenth of September, at eleven o'clock at night, we celebrate the fiesta of the *Grito** in all the plazas of the Republic, and the excited crowds actually shout for a whole hour . . . the better, perhaps, to remain silent for the rest of the year. During the days before and after the twelfth of December,† time comes to a full stop, and instead of pushing us toward a deceptive tomorrow that is always beyond our reach, offers us a complete and perfect today of dancing and revelry, of communion with the most ancient and secret Mexico. Time is no longer succession, and becomes what it originally was and is: the present, in which past and future are reconciled.

But the fiestas which the Church and State provide for the country as a whole are not enough. The life of every city and village is ruled by a patron saint whose blessing is celebrated with devout regularity. Neighborhoods and trades also have their annual fiestas, their ceremonies and fairs. And each one of us—atheist, Catholic, or merely indifferent—has his own saint's day, which he observes every year. It is impossible to calculate how many fiestas we have and how much time and money we spend on them. I remember asking the mayor of a village near Mitla, several years ago, "What is the income of the village government?" "About 3,000 pesos a year. We are very poor. But the Governor and the Federal Government always help us to meet our expenses." "And how are the 3,000 pesos spent?" "Mostly on fiestas, señor. We are a small village, but we have two patron saints."

This reply is not surprising. Our poverty can be measured by the frequency and luxuriousness of our holidays. Wealthy countries have very few: there is neither the time nor the desire for them, and they are not necessary. The people have other things to do, and when they amuse themselves they do so in small groups. The modern masses are agglomerations of solitary individuals. On great occasions in Paris or New York, when the populace gathers in the squares or stadiums, the absence of people, in the sense of *a* people, is remarkable: there are couples and small groups, but they never form a living community in which the individual is at once dissolved and redeemed. But how could a poor Mexican live without the two or three annual fiestas that make up for his poverty and misery? Fiestas are our only luxury. They replace, and are perhaps better than, the theater and vacations, Anglo-Saxon weekends and cocktail parties, the bourgeois reception, the Mediterranean café.

---

*Padre Hidalgo's call-to-arms against Spain, 1810.—*T.*:
†Fiesta of the Virgin of Guadalupe.—*Tr.*

In all of these ceremonies—national or local, trade or family—the Mexican opens out. They all give him a chance to reveal himself and to converse with God, country, friends or relations. During these days the silent Mexican whistles, shouts, sings, shoots off fireworks, discharges his pistol into the air. He discharges his soul. And his shout, like the rockets we love so much, ascends to the heavens, explodes into green, red, blue, and white lights, and falls dizzily to earth with a trail of golden sparks. This is the night when friends who have not exchanged more than the prescribed courtesies for months get drunk together, trade confidences, weep over the same troubles, discover that they are brothers, and sometimes, to prove it, kill each other. The night is full of songs and loud cries. The lover wakes up his sweetheart with an orchestra. There are jokes and conversations from balcony to balcony, sidewalk to sidewalk. Nobody talks quietly. Hats fly in the air. Laughter and curses ring like silver pesos. Guitars are brought out. Now and then, it is true, the happiness ends badly, in quarrels, insults, pistol shots, stabbings. But these too are part of the fiesta, for the Mexican does not seek amusement: he seeks to escape from himself, to leap over the wall of solitude that confines him during the rest of the year. All are possessed by violence and frenzy. Their souls explode like the colors and voices and emotions. Do they forget themselves and show their true faces? Nobody knows. The important thing is to go out, open a way, get drunk on noise, people, colors. Mexico is celebrating a fiesta. And this fiesta, shot through with lightning and delirium, is the brilliant reverse to our silence and apathy, our reticence and gloom.

According to the interpretation of French sociologists, the fiesta is an excess, an expense. By means of this squandering the community protects itself against the envy of the gods or of men. Sacrifices and offerings placate or buy off the gods and the patron saints. Wasting money and expending energy affirms the community's wealth in both. This luxury is a proof of health, a show of abundance and power. Or a magic trap. For squandering is an effort to attract abundance by contagion. Money calls to money. When life is thrown away it increases; the orgy, which is sexual expenditure, is also a ceremony of regeneration; waste gives strength. New Year celebrations, in every culture, signify something beyond the mere observance of a date on the calendar. The day is a pause: time is stopped, is actually annihilated. The rites that celebrate its death are intended to provoke its rebirth, because they mark not only the end of an old year but also the beginning of a new. Everything attracts its opposite. The fiesta's function, then, is more utilitarian than we think: waste attracts or promotes wealth, and is an investment like any other, except that the returns on it cannot be measured or counted. What is sought is potency, life, health. In this sense the fiesta, like the gift and the offering, is one of the most ancient of economic forms.

This interpretation has always seemed to me to be incomplete. The fiesta is by nature sacred, literally or figuratively, and above all it is the advent of the unusual. It is governed by its own special rules, that set it apart from other days, and it has a logic, an ethic and even an economy that are often in conflict with everyday norms. It all occurs in an enchanted world: time is transformed to a mythical past or a total present; space, the scene of the fiesta, is turned into a gaily decorated world of its own; and the persons taking part cast off all human or social rank and become, for the moment, living images. And everything takes place as if it were not so, as if it were a dream. But whatever happens, our actions have a greater lightness, a different gravity. They take on other meanings and with them we contract new obligations. We throw down our burdens of time and reason.

In certain fiestas the very notion of order disappears. Chaos comes back and license rules. Anything is permitted: the customary hierarchies vanish, along with all social, sex, caste, and trade distinctions. Men disguise themselves as women, gentlemen as slaves, the poor as the rich. The army, the clergy, and the law are ridiculed. Obligatory sacrilege, ritual profanation is committed. Love becomes promiscuity. Sometimes the fiesta becomes a Black Mass. Regulations, habits and customs are violated. Respectable people put away the dignified expressions and conservative clothes that isolate them, dress up in gaudy colors, hide behind a mask, and escape from themselves.

Therefore the fiesta is not only an excess, a ritual squandering of the goods painfully accumulated during the rest of the year; it is also a revolt, a sudden immersion in the formless, in pure being. By means of the fiesta society frees itself from the norms it has established. It ridicules its gods, its principles, and its laws: it denies its own self.

The fiesta is a revolution in the most literal sense of the word. In the confusion that it generates, society is dissolved, is drowned, insofar as it is an organism ruled according to certain laws and principles. But it drowns in itself, in its own original chaos or liberty. Everything is united: good and evil, day and night, the sacred and the profane. Everything merges, loses shape and individuality and returns to the primordial mass. The fiesta is a cosmic experiment, an experiment in disorder, reuniting contradictory elements and principles in order to bring about a renascence of life. Ritual death promotes a rebirth; vomiting increases the appetite; the orgy, sterile in itself, renews the fertility of the mother or of the earth. The fiesta is a return to a remote and undifferentiated state, prenatal or presocial. It is a return that is also a beginning, in accordance with the dialectic that is inherent in social processes.

The group emerges purified and strengthened from this plunge into chaos. It has immersed itself in its own origins, in the womb from which it came. To express it in another way, the fiesta denies society as an organic system of differentiated forms and principles, but affirms it as a source of creative energy. it is a true "re-creation," the opposite of the "recreation" characterizing modern vacations, which do not entail any rites or ceremonies whatever and are as individualistic and sterile as the world that invented them.

Society communes with itself during the fiesta. Its members return to original chaos and freedom. Social structures break down and new relationships, unexpected rules, capricious hierarchies are created. In the general disorder everybody forgets himself and enters into otherwise forbidden situations and places. The bounds between audience and actors, officials and servants, are erased. Everybody takes part in the fiesta, everybody is caught up in its whirlwind. Whatever its mood, its character, its meaning, the fiesta is participation, and this trait distinguishes it from all other ceremonies and social phenomena. Lay or religious, orgy or saturnalia, the fiesta is a social act based on the full participation of all its celebrants.

Thanks to the fiesta the Mexican opens out, participates, communes with his fellows and with the values that give meaning to his religious or political existence. And it is significant that a country as sorrowful as ours should have so many and such joyous fiestas. Their frequency, their brilliance and excitement, the enthusiasm with which we take part, all suggest that without them we would explode. They free us, if only momentarily, from the thwarted impulses, the inflammable desires that we carry within us. But the Mexican fiesta is not merely a return to an original state of formless and normless liberty: the Mexican is not seeking to return, but to escape from himself, to exceed himself. Our fiestas are explosions. Life and death, joy and sorrow, music and mere noise are united, not to re-create or recognize themselves, but to swallow each other up. There is nothing so joyous as a Mexican fiesta, but there is also nothing so sorrowful. Fiesta night is also a night of mourning.

If we hide within ourselves in our daily lives, we discharge ourselves in the whirlwind of the fiesta. It is more than an opening out: we rend ourselves open. Everything—music, love, friendship—ends in tumult and violence. The frenzy of our festivals shows the extent to which our solitude closes us off from communication with the world. We are familiar with delirium, with songs and shouts, with the monologue . . . but not with the dialogue. Our fiestas, like our confidences, our loves, our attempts to reorder our society, are violent breaks with the old or the established. Each time we try to express ourselves we have to break with ourselves. And the fiesta is only one example, perhaps the most typical, of this violent break. It is not difficult to name others, equally revealing: our games, which are always a going to extremes, often mortal; our profligate spending, the reverse of our timid investments and business enterprises; our confessions. The somber Mexican, closed up in himself, suddenly explodes, tears open his breast and reveals himself, though not without a certain complacency, and not without a stopping place in the shameful or terrible mazes of his intimacy. We are not frank, but our sincerity can reach extremes that horrify a European. The explosive, dramatic, sometimes even suicidal manner in which we strip ourselves, surrender ourselves, is evidence that something inhibits and suffocates us. Something impedes us from being. And since we cannot or dare not confront our own selves, we resort to the fiesta. It fires us into the void; it is a drunken rapture that burns itself out, a pistol shot in the air, a skyrocket.

Death is a mirror which reflects the vain gesticulations of the living. The whole motley confusion of acts, omissions, regrets and hopes which is the life of each one of us finds in death, not meaning or explanation, but an end. Death defines life; a death depicts a life in immutable forms; we do not change except to disappear. Our deaths illuminate our lives. If our deaths lack meaning, our lives also lacked it. Therefore we are apt to say, when somebody has died a violent death, "He got what he was looking for." Each of us dies the death he is looking for, the death he has made for himself. A Christian death or a dog's death are ways of dying that reflect ways of living. If death betrays us and we die badly, everyone laments the fact, because we should die as we have lived. Death, like life, is not transferable. If we do not die as we lived, it is because the life we lived was not really ours: it did not belong to us, just as the bad death that kills us does not belong to us. Tell me how you die and I will tell you who you are.

The opposition between life and death was not so absolute to the ancient Mexicans as it is to us. Life extended into death, and vice versa. Death was not the natural end of life but one phase of an infinite cycle. Life, death and resurrection were stages of a cosmic process which repeated itself continuously. Life had no higher function than to flow into death, its opposite and complement; and death, in turn, was not an end in itself: man fed the insatiable hunger of life with his death. Sacrifices had a double purpose: on the one hand man participated in the creative process, at the same time paying back to the gods the debt contracted by his species; on the other hand he nourished cosmic life and also social life, which was nurtured by the former.

Perhaps the most characteristic aspect of this conception is the impersonal nature of the sacrifice. Since their lives did not belong to them, their deaths lacked any personal meaning. The dead—including warriors killed in battle and women dying in childbirth, companions of Huitzilopochtli the sun god—disappeared at the end of a certain period, to return to the undifferentiated country of the shadows, to be melted into the air, the earth, the fire, the animating substance of the universe. Our indigenous ancestors did not believe that their deaths belonged to them, just as they never thought that their lives were really theirs in the Christian sense. Everything was examined to determine, from birth, the life and death of each man: his social class, the year, the place, the day, the hour. The Aztec was as little responsible for his actions as for his death.

Space and time were bound together and formed an inseparable whole. There was a particular "time" for each place, each of the cardinal points and the center in which they were immobilized. And this complex of space-time possessed its own virtues and powers, which profoundly influenced and determined human life. To be born on a certain day was to pertain to a place, a time, a color and a destiny. All was traced out in advance. Where we dissociate space and time, mere stage sets for the actions of our lives, there were as many "space-times" for the Aztecs as there were combinations in the priestly calendar, each one endowed with a particular qualitative significance, superior to human will.

Religion and destiny ruled their lives, as morality and freedom rule ours. We live under the sign of liberty, and everything—even Greek fatality and the grace of the theologians—is election and struggle, but for the Aztecs the problem reduced itself to investigating the never-clear will of the gods. Only the gods were free, and only they had the power to choose—and therefore, in a profound sense, to sin. The Aztec religion is full of great sinful gods—Quetzalcóatl is the major example—who grow weak and abandon their believers, in the same way that Christians sometimes deny God. The conquest of Mexico would be inexplicable without the treachery of the gods, who denied their own people.

The advent of Catholicism radically modified this situation. Sacrifice and the idea of salvation, formerly collective, became personal. Freedom was humanized, embodied in man. To the ancient Aztecs the essential thing was to assure the continuity of creation; sacrifice did not bring about salvation in another world, but cosmic health; the universe, and not the individual, was given life by the blood and death of human beings. For Christians it is the individual who counts. The world—history, society—is condemned beforehand. The death of Christ saved each man in particular. Each one of us is Man, and represents the hopes and possibilities of the species. Redemption is a personal task.

Both attitudes, opposed as they may seem, have a common note: life, collective or individual, looks forward to a death that in its way is a new life. Life only justifies and transcends itself when it is realized in death, and death is also a transcendence, in that it is a new life. To Christians death is a transition, a somersault between two lives, the temporal and the otherworldly; to the Aztecs it was the profoundest way of participating in the continuous regeneration of the creative forces, which were always in danger of being extinguished if they were not provided with blood, the sacred food. In both systems life and death lack autonomy, are the two sides of a single reality. They are references to the invisible realities.

Modern death does not have any significance that transcends it or that refers to other values. It is rarely anything more than the inevitable conclusion of a natural process. In a world of facts, death is merely one more fact. But since it is such a disagreeable fact, contrary to all our concepts and to the very meaning of our lives, the philosophy of progress ("Progress toward what, and from what?" Scheler asked) pretends to make it disappear, like a magician palming a coin. Everything in the modern world functions as if death did not exist. Nobody takes it into account, it is suppressed everywhere: in political pronouncements, commercial advertising, public morality and popular customs; in the promise of cut-rate health and happiness offered to all of us by hospitals, drugstores and playing fields. But death enters into everything we undertake, and it is no longer a transition but a great gaping mouth that nothing can satisfy. The century of health, hygiene and contraceptives, miracle drugs and synthetic foods, is also the century of the concentration camp and the police state, Hiroshima and the murder story. Nobody thinks about death, about his own death, as Rilke asked us to do, because nobody lives a personal life. Collective slaughter is the fruit of a collectivized way of life.

Death also lacks meaning for the modern Mexican. It is no longer a transition, an access to another life more alive than our own. But although we do not view death as a transcendence, we have not eliminated it from our daily lives. The word death is not pronounced in New York, in Paris, in London, because it burns the lips. The Mexican, in contrast, is familiar with death, jokes about it, caresses it, sleeps with it, celebrates it; it is one of his favorite toys and his most steadfast love. True, there is perhaps as much fear in his attitude as in that of others, but at least death is not hidden away: he looks at it face to face, with impatience, disdain or irony. "If they are going to kill me tomorrow, let them kill me right away."*

The Mexican's indifference toward death is fostered by his indifference toward life. He views not only death but also life as nontranscendent. Our songs, proverbs, fiestas and popular beliefs show very clearly that the reason death cannot frighten us is that "life has cured us of fear." It is natural, even desirable, to die, and the sooner the better. We kill because life—our own or another's—is of no value. Life and death are inseparable, and when the former lacks meaning, the latter becomes equally meaningless. Mexican death is the mirror of Mexican life. And the Mexican shuts himself away and ignores both of them.

Our contempt for death is not at odds with the cult we have made of it. Death is present in our fiestas, our games, our loves and our thoughts. To die and to kill are ideas that rarely leave us. We are seduced by death. The fascination it exerts over us is the result, perhaps, of our hermit-like solitude and of the fury with which we break out of it. The pressure of our vitality, which can only express itself in forms that betray it, explains the deadly nature, aggressive or suicidal, of our explosions. When we explode we touch against the highest point of that tension, we graze the very zenith of life. And there, at the height of our frenzy, suddenly we feel dizzy: it is then that death attracts us.

Another factor is that death revenges us against life, strips it of all its vanities and pretensions and converts it into what it really is: a few neat bones and a dreadful grimace. In a closed world where everything is death, only death has value. But our affirmation is negative. Sugar-candy skulls, and tissue-paper skulls and skeletons strung with fireworks . . . our popular images always poke fun at life, affirming the nothingness and insignificance of human existence. We decorate our houses with death's heads, we eat bread in the shape of bones on the Day of the Dead, we love the songs and stories in which death laughs and cracks jokes, but all this boastful familiarity does not rid us of the question we all ask: What is death? We have not thought up a new answer. And each time we ask, we shrug our shoulders: Why should I care about death if I have never cared about life?

Does the Mexican open out in the presence of death? He praises it, celebrates it, cultivates it, embraces it, but he never surrenders himself to it. Everything is remote and strange to him, and nothing more so than death. He does not surrender himself to it because surrender entails a sacrifice. And a sacrifice, in turn, demands that someone must give and someone receive. That is, someone must open out and face a reality that transcends him. In a closed, nontranscend-

---

*From the popular folk song *La Valentina.—Tr.*

ent world, death neither gives nor receives: it consumes itself and is self-gratify-ing. Therefore our relations with death are intimate—more intimate, perhaps, than those of any other people—but empty of meaning and devoid of erotic emotion. Death in Mexico is sterile, not fecund like that of the Aztecs and the Christians.

Nothing is more opposed to this attitude than that of the Europeans and North Americans. Their laws, customs and public and private ethics all tend to preserve human life. This protection does not prevent the number of ingenious and refined murders, of perfect crimes and crime-waves, from increasing. The professional criminals who plot their murders with a precision impossible to a Mexican, the delight they take in describing their experiences and methods, the fascination with which the press and public follow their confessions, and the recognized inefficiency of the systems of prevention, show that the respect for life of which Western civilization is so proud is either incomplete or hypocritical.

The cult of life, if it is truly profound and total, is also the cult of death, because the two are inseparable. A civilization that denies death ends by denying life. The perfection of modern crime is not merely a consequence of modern technical progress and the vogue of the murder story: it derives from the con-tempt for life which is inevitably implicit in any attempt to hide death away and pretend it does not exist. It might be added that modern technical skills and the popularity of crime stories are, like concentration camps and collective extermina-tion, the results of an optimistic and unilateral conception of existence. It is useless to exclude death from our images, our words, our ideas, because death will obliterate all of us, beginning with those who ignore it or pretend to ignore it.

When the Mexican kills—for revenge, pleasure or caprice—he kills a person, a human being. Modern criminals and statesmen do not kill: they abolish. They experiment with beings who have lost their human qualities. Prisoners in the concentration camps are first degraded, changed into mere objects; then they are exterminated en masse. The typical criminal in the large cities—beyond the specific motives for his crimes—realizes on a small scale what the modern leader realizes on a grand scale. He too experiments, in his own way: he poisons, destroys corpses with acids, dismembers them, converts them into objects. The ancient relationship between victim and murderer, which is the only thing that humanizes murder, that makes it even thinkable, has disappeared. As in the novels of Sade, there is no longer anything except torturers and objects, instru-ments of pleasure and destruction. And the nonexistence of the victim makes the infinite solitude of the murderer even more intolerable. Murder is still a relation-ship in Mexico, and in this sense it has the same liberating significance as the fiesta or the confession. Hence its drama, its poetry and—why not say it?—its gran-deur. Through murder we achieve a momentary transcendence.

At the beginning of his eighth Duino Elegy, Rilke says that the "creature," in his condition of animal innocence, "beholds the open" . . . unlike ourselves, who never look forward, toward the absolute. Fear makes us turn our backs on death, and by refusing to contemplate it we shut ourselves off from life, which is a totality that includes it. The "open" is where contraries are reconciled, where light and shadow are fused. This conception restores death's original meaning: death and life are opposites that complement each other. Both are halves of a sphere that we, subjects of time and space, can only glimpse. In the prenatal world, life and death are merged; in ours, opposed; in the world beyond, re-united again, not in the animal innocence that precedes sin and the knowledge of sin, but as in innocence regained. Man can transcend the temporal opposition separating them (and residing not in them but in his own consciousness) and perceive them as a superior whole. This recognition can take place only through detachment: he must renounce his temporal life and his nostalgia for limbo, for the animal world. He must open himself out to death if he wishes to open himself out to life. Then he will be "like the angels."

Thus there are two attitudes toward death: one, pointing forward, that conceives of it as creation; the other, pointing backward, that expresses itself as a fascination with nothingness or as a nostalgia for limbo. No Mexican or Spanish-American poet, with the possible exception of César Vallejo, approaches the first of these two concepts. The absence of a mystic—and only a mystic is capable of offering insights like those of Rilke—indicates the extent to which modern Mexican culture is insensible to religion. But two Mexican poets, José Gorostiza and Xavier Villaurrutia, represent the second of these two attitudes. For Gorostiza life is a "death without end," a perpetual falling into nothingness; for Villaurrutia it is no more than a "nostalgia for death."

The phrase that Villaurrutia chose for his book, *Nostalgia de la Muerte,* is not merely a lucky hit. The author has used it in order to tell us the ultimate meaning of his poetry. Death as nostalgia, rather than as the fruition or end of life, is death as origin. The ancient, original source is a bone, not a womb. This statement runs the risk of seeming either an empty paradox or an old commonplace: "For thou art dust, and unto dust shalt thou return." I believe that the poet hopes to find in death (which is, in effect, our origin) a revelation that his temporal life has denied him: the true meaning of life. When we die,

> The second hand
> will race around its dial,
> all will be contained in an instant . . .
> and perhaps it will be possible
> to live, even after death.

A return to original death would be a return to the life before life, the life before death: to limbo, to the maternal source.

Muerte sin Fin, the poem by José Gorostiza, is perhaps the best evidence we have in Latin America of a truly modern consciousness, one that is turned in upon itself, imprisoned in its own blinding clarity. The poet, in a sort of lucid fury, wants to rip the mask off existence in order to see it as it is. The dialogue between man and the world, which is as old as poetry and love, is transformed into a dialogue between the water and the glass that contains it, between the thought and the form into which it is poured and which it eventually corrodes. The poet warns us from his prison of appearances—trees and thoughts, stones and emotions, days and nights and twilights are all simply metaphors, mere colored ribbons—that the breath which informs matter, shaping it and giving it form, is the same breath that corrodes and withers and defeats it. It is a drama without personae, since all are merely reflections, the various disguises of a suicide who talks to himself in a language of mirrors and echoes, and the mind also is nothing more than a reflection of death, of death in love with itself. Everything is immersed in its own clarity and brilliance, everything is directed toward this transparent death: life is only a metaphor, an invention with which death—death too!—wants to deceive itself. The poem is a variation on the old theme of Narcissus, although there is no allusion to it in the text: And it is not only the consciousness that contemplates itself in its empty, transparent water (both mirror and eye at the same time, as in the Valéry poem): nothingness, which imitates form and life, which feigns corruption and death, strips itself naked and turns in upon itself, loves itself, falls into itself: a tireless death without end.

If we open out during fiestas, then, or when we are drunk or exchanging confidences, we do it so violently that we wound ourselves. And we shrug our shoulders at death, as at life, confronting it in silence or with a contemptuous smile. The fiesta, the crime of passion and the gratuitous crime reveal that the equilibrium of which we are so proud is only a mask, always in danger of being ripped off by a sudden explosion of our intimacy.

All of these attitudes indicate that the Mexican senses the presence of a stigma both on himself and on the flesh of his country. It is diffused but none the less living, original, and ineradicable. Our gestures and expressions all attempt to hide this wound, which is always open, always ready to catch fire and burn under the rays of a stranger's glance.

Now, every separation causes a wound. Without stopping to investigate how and when the separation is brought about, I want to point out that any break (with ourselves or those around us, with the past or the present) creates a feeling of solitude. In extreme cases—separation from one's parents, matrix or native land, the death of the gods or a painful self-consciousness—solitude is identified with orphanhood. And both of them generally manifest themselves as a sense of sin. The penalties and guilty feelings inflicted by a state of separation can be considered, thanks to the ideas of expiation and redemption, as necessary sacrifices, as pledges or promises of a future communion that will put an end to the long exile. The guilt can vanish, the wound heal over, the separation resolve itself in communion. Solitude thus assumes a purgative, purifying character. The solitary or isolated individual transcends his solitude, accepting it as a proof or promise of communion.

The Mexican does not transcend his solitude. On the contrary, he locks himself up in it. We live in our solitude like Philoctetes on his island, fearing rather than hoping to return to the world. We cannot bear the presence of our companions. We hide within ourselves—except when we rend ourselves open in our frenzy—and the solitude in which we suffer has no reference either to a redeemer or a creator. We oscillate between intimacy and withdrawal, between a shout and a silence, between a fiesta and a wake, without ever truly surrendering ourselves. Our indifference hides life behind a death mask; our wild shout rips off this mask and shoots into the sky, where it swells, explodes, and falls back in silence and defeat. Either way, the Mexican shuts himself off from the world: from life and from death.

Translated by Lysander Kemp

Questions for Discussion and Writing

1. What major elements in Mexican culture account for and underlie the fiestas? In what ways does the Mexican attitude toward time play a role in the fiestas?
2. What does Paz mean when he talks about the solitude of the Mexican? How does the Mexican love of fiestas relate to this solitude? What paradoxes does the author establish about Mexican character, and in what ways do they relate to that solitude?
3. Paz explores the meaning of the Mexican fiesta in general and the "Day of the Dead" in particular. He explains the meaning of death for Mexicans as it has evolved throughout their history. Why is it important to understand this history of attitudes about death if we are to understand this particular fiesta? In what ways are the Mexican ideas about death tied to how they celebrate this fiesta?
4. Throughout the essay, Paz compares the Mexican's attitudes toward time, life, and death to those of the European and North American. In what major ways do their attitudes differ, and with what results? Why are these comparisons necessary to our understanding of the Mexican fiesta?
5. What audience do you think Paz had in mind as he wrote this essay, and why?

NAWAL EL-SAADAWI

Love and Sex in the Life of the Arab

A psychiatrist, feminist, novelist, and nonfiction writer, Nawal el-Saadawi was born in 1931 in Kafr, Egypt. She has suffered for her outspoken support of political and sexual rights for women, and has been arrested and imprisoned more than once for her views. After the publication of her book Women and Sex *in 1972, el-Saadawi was dismissed from her positions as director of education in Egypt's Ministry of Health and as editor of* Health *magazine. Subsequently, her books were banned in Egypt and some other Arab countries.*

The essay that follows was first published in Arabic in Beirut in 1977. It is now included in a collection of el-Saadawi's works entitled The Hidden Face of Eve: Women in the Arab World, *published in 1980 and translated by her husband Sherif Hetata. This book was the author's first to be translated into English.*

Although el-Saadawi has also written several novels and numerous short stories, it is as a physician and advocate of women's rights that she continues to be best known. "Writing to me is like breathing," she has said. "I cannot live without it. Expression of one's self is an essential part of a process of knowing and fighting for liberation." She points out that "the oppression of women is not characteristic of Arab or Moslem societies or countries of the so-called Third World alone. It constitutes an integral part of the political, economic, and cultural system preponderant in most of the world . . . that made one class rule over another and men dominate women."

Before you read "Love and Sex in the Life of the Arab," reflect on and then write about the forces that influence and even create patterns of sexual habits, expectations, and values in American society. Consider what you believe about sexuality, and attempt to trace the influences of your own beliefs through family, religion, and culture. A big order, of course, but at least get some thoughts started about these questions.

A famous work of art, *A Thousand and One Nights,* has been used by many Western researchers and authors, who describe themselves as "orientalists," as a source of material and information for studying the life of the Arab. They consider that these stories especially those dealing with love and sexual intrigues, afford an insight into the understanding of the Arab character, seeing them as keys with which to open the doors to the "Arab Soul," and as valuable means towards penetrating the depths, or rather the shallow waters, of the Arab mind and heart.

Yet anyone with the slightest knowledge of Arab literature knows that the stories related in *A Thousand and One Nights* are only a partial and one-sided reflection of a very narrow section of Arab society, as it lived and dreamed, loved and fornicated, intrigued and plundered, more than ten centuries ago. I do not know very much about the level reached by European civilization at the time, the state of human affairs in society there, in the sciences and in the arts, but I at least know enough to be able to say that Arab society had undoubtedly advanced much further. Many are the scholars, writers and researchers who have made comparisons between the West and the Arab World, only drawing their examples from a period in our history, now more than a thousand years old. One would have to have a very bad memory to forget, in one gigantic leap, what is in terms of time half the number of years which have elapsed since the birth of Christ. How can we depict the contrasts between the Arab character at the time when the people of *A Thousand and One Nights* flew on their magic carpets, and the Western mind of the Victorian era when purity floated like a thick veil over the corrupt and bloated features of a hypocritical society. [1] How much more true and scientific would a comparative study have been of the lifestyles of Arab and European men from the same period, or at least from the Middles Ages when the clergy, who were the male intelligentsia of the time, were busy prompting women accused of sorcery to utter the most obscene sexual epithets, and, under insufferable torture, forcing them to admit to the very crimes which they had been taught to describe? [2]

This picture of the sex-mad Arab fawning on an extensive harem is maintained with dubious insistence even today. Without exception the films, magazines and newspapers that roll out from the reels of Western producers and the dark-rooms of Western monopolies, depict Arab men as trotting behind the skirts of women, ogling the ample bosoms of seductive blondes, and squandering their money, or quenching their thirst for alcohol or sex. Arab women, in their turn, are depicted as twisting and turning in snake-like dances, flaunting their naked bellies and quivering hips, seducing men with the promise of dark passion, playful, secretive and intriguing, a picture drawn from the palaces of *A Thousand and One Nights* and the slave women of the Caliph, Haroun El Rachid.

Is it possible to believe that this distorted image of Arab men and women is representative of their true life and character in the Arab world of today? Personally, I am sure that it is not even representative of men and women living at the time of Haroun El Raschid. Perhaps it has some authenticity as a reflection of certain aspects of the life led by palace rulers and their concubines in those bygone days, but these were only an infinitesimal minority compared to the vast mass of Arabs, who led a harsh and difficult existence with no room for, nor possibility of ever experiencing, the silken cushions, soft flesh and fiery liquids of dissipation. The sexual life of kings and princely rulers, whether in the past or present, in the modern West or more archaic East, to the South of the Earth's equator or to the North, has maintained the same essential pattern, embroidered with a greater or lesser degree of sophistication or refinement, sadism or depravity.

Sweeping judgments, which depict the nature of Arabs in general, and the men of the Arab world in particular, as being obsessed with sex and more inclined to pursue the pleasures of the body than men from other regions or countries, are therefore unfounded and incorrect. Their aim is to contribute to and maintain a distorted image of the Arabs in the minds of people all over the world, to falsify the true colours of their struggle for independence, progress and control over their destinies, and to facilitate the task of conservative, reactionary and imperialist forces that continue to survive and prosper by such means.

I believe that freedom in all its forms, whether sexual, intellectual, social or economic, is a necessity for every man and woman, and for all societies. Nevertheless, I feel that the sexual freedom that has accompanied the evolution of modern capitalist society has been developed very much in a unilateral direction and has not been linked with, or been related to, a parallel development of social and economic freedoms. This sheds some doubt on the real motives behind the consistent and ever increasing campaign calling upon men and women to throw their sexual inhibitions and beliefs overboard. It also jeopardizes the chances of human progress and fulfilment, since a one-sided development that does not take into consideration the totality of life can only lead to new distortions and monstrosities.

This is why there is a growing realization that sexual freedom, as it is preached today in modern capitalist society, has no valid answers or solutions to many of the problems of personal life and human happiness, and that it is only another and perhaps more ingenuous way of making people pay the price of ever expanding consumption, of accumulating profits and of feeding the appetites of monopolistic giants. Another opium to be inhaled and imbibed so that mobilized energies may be dissipated rather than built up into a force of resistance and revolt against all forms of exploitation.

In this respect, Eastern and Arab societies have not differed from the West. Here again it is mainly economic necessity which governs the direction in which values, human morals and norms of sexual behaviour move. The economic imperatives of Arab society required a wide degree of sexual freedom to ensure the provision of large numbers of offspring. Polygamy, as against polyandry, tends to be more prolific as far as children are concerned. Arab society, still primitive and badly equipped to face the vicissitudes and harshness of desert life, suffered from a very high mortality rate, especially among infants and children, which had to be compensated for by correspondingly high birth rates. The economic and military strength of tribes and clans in a society which possessed neither modern tools or machines, nor modern weapons, depended very much on their numbers. In addition, the simple crude existence of desert life and the extreme poverty of nomadic tribes meant that, while the cost of maintaining a child was minimal, the child could play useful roles in meeting the productive needs of the time, being capable of running errands or looking after the camels and sheep.

Wars and battles were an integral part of tribal life and flared up at frequent intervals, and death took a heavy toll of the men. This was particularly the case after Islam started to establish itself and expand. It was natural that this new threat should meet with the resistance of the neighbouring rulers and the older religions entrenched in the surrounding regions, and that the Muslims should be obliged to fight numerous battles before they could succeed in establishing and stabilizing their new State. The result was heavy losses in men and a marked imbalance characterized by a much higher number of women, accentuated by the throngs of women slave prisoners brought back from victorious battles.

The easiest and most natural solution to such a situation was to allow men to marry more than one woman, and in addition to choose from among the women brought back from the wars, or sold in the markets, those whom they considered suitable to be wives, concubines or slaves in their households. Each man did so according to his means, and these means of course varied widely from one man to another. With a superfluity of women, a man would take pride in the number of women he could maintain, and the bigger this number, the more occasion for him to boast about the extensiveness of his female retinue, and about his powers over women, whether in marriage or in love. On the other hand, women would compete for the favours of men and excel in subtle allurements to attract men towards marriage, love and sex.

This was perhaps an additional factor which tended to make Arab women more forward and positive in love and sex, characteristics in clear contrast to the passive attitudes assumed by the vast majority of women living in our modern era. The other factors, mentioned previously, were the matriarchal vestiges which at the time were still strong in Arab society, and the naturalistic attitudes of Islamic teachings which prevented love and sex from being considered sinful as they were by Christianity. On the contrary, Islam described sexual pleasure as one of the attractions of life, one of the delights for those who go to Paradise after death. As a result, Arab women had no hesitation in being positive towards sex, in expressing their desire for men, in exercising their charms, and weaving their net around whoever might be the object of their attentions. Perhaps they were following in the footsteps of their mother, Eve, who had so ably enticed Adam to comply with her wishes and fall victim to *fitna,* [3] with the result that he dropped from the high heavens in which he was confined and landed with his two feet on the solid, rough, but warm and living earth.

For the Arabs the word "woman" invariably evokes the word *fitna*. Arab women combined the qualities of a positive personality and *fitna,* or seductiveness, to such an extent that they became an integral part of the Islamic ethos which has, as one of its cornerstones, the sexual powers of women, and which maintains that their seductiveness can lead to a *fitna* within society. Here the word is used in a related but different sense to mean an uprising, rebellion, conspiracy or anarchy which would upset the existing order of things established by Allah (and which, therefore, is not to be changed). From this arose the conception that life could only follow its normal steady and uninterrupted course, and society could only avoid any potential menace to its stability and structure, or any disruption of the social order, if men continued to satisfy the sexual needs of their women, kept them happy, and protected their honour. If this was not ensured a *fitna* could easily be let loose, since the honour of women would be in doubt, and as a result uneasiness and trouble could erupt at any moment. The virtue of women had to be ensured if peace was to reign among men, not an easy task in view of the *fitna* (seductiveness) of women.

Islam's contribution to the understanding of love, sex and the relations between the sexes has never to my knowledge been correctly assessed and given the consideration it deserves. However, the contradictory aspects inherent in Islamic society are reflected in another dramatically opposed tendency which runs through the body of Islamic teaching, and is a continuation of the rigid, reactionary and conservative reasoning that dominated the concepts and practices of Judaism and Christianity in matters related to sex.

Islam inherited the old image of Eve and of women that depicts them as the close followers and instruments of Satan, the body of women being his abode. A well-known Arab saying maintains that: "Whenever a man and a woman meet together, their third is always Satan." Mahomet the Prophet, despite his love for and understanding of women, warns that: "After I have gone, there will be no greater danger menacing my nation and more liable to create anarchy and trouble than women."[4]

This attitude towards woman was prominent throughout Islamic thought and she always remained a source of danger to man and to society on account of her power of attraction or *fitna*. Man in the face of such seduction was portrayed as helpless, drained of all his capacities to be positive or to resist. Although this was not a new idea, it assumed big proportions in Islamic theology and was buttressed by many *Ahadith* (proverbs and sayings).

Woman was therefore considered by the Arabs as a menace to man and society, and the only way to avoid the harm she could do was to isolate her in the home, where she could have no contact with either one or the other. If for any reason she had to move outside the walls of her prison, all necessary precautions had to be taken so that no one could get a glimpse of her seductiveness. She was therefore enveloped in veils and flowing robes like explosive material which has to be well packed. In some Arab societies, this concern to conceal the body of women went so far that the split-second uncovering of a finger or a toe was considered a potential source of *fitna* in society which might therefore lead to anarchy, uprisings, rebellions and the total destruction of the established order!

Thus it is that Islam confronted its philosophers and theologians with two contradictory, and in terms of logic, mutually exclusive conceptions: (1) Sex is one of the pleasures and attractions of life; (2) To succumb to sex will lead to *fitna* in society—that is crisis, disruption and anarchy.

The only way out of this dilemma, the only path that could reconcile these two conflicting views, was to lay down a system or framework for sex which on the one hand had to avoid *fitna* while on the other would permit abundant reproduction and a good deal of pleasure within the limits of Allah's prescriptions.

The Imam, El Ghazali, explains how the will of Allah and his wisdom are manifested in the fact that he created sexual desire in both men and women. This is expressed in the words of his Prophet when he said: "Marry and multiply." "Since Allah has revealed his secret to us, and has instructed us clearly what to do, refraining from marriage is like refusing to plough the earth, and wasting the seed. It means leaving the useful tools which Allah has created for us idle, and is a crime against the self-evident reasons and obvious aims of the phenomenon of creation, aims written on the sexual organs in Divine handwriting."[5]

For El Ghazali, apart from reproduction, marriage aims at immunity from the Devil, breaking the sharp point of desire, avoiding the dangers of passion, keeping our eyes away from what they should not see, safeguarding the female sexual organs, and following the directives of our Prophet when he said: "He who marries has ensured for himself the fulfilment of half his religion. Let him therefore fear Allah for the other half."[6]

Islamic thought admits the strength and power of sexual desire in women, and in men also. Fayad Ibn Nageeh said that, "if the sexual organ of the man rises up, a third of his religion is lost." One of the rare explanations given to the Prophets' words by Ibn Abbas, Allah's blessing be upon both of them, is that "he who enters into a woman is lost in a twilight" and that "if the male organ rises up, it is an overwhelming catastrophe for once provoked it cannot be resisted by either reason or religion. For this organ is more powerful than all the instruments used by Satan against man." That is why the Prophet, Allah's peace be upon him, said, "I have not seen creatures lacking in mind and religion more capable of overcoming men of reason and wisdom than you [women]."[7] He also warned men: "Do not enter the house of those who have absent ones"—meaning those women whose husbands are away—"for Satan will run out from one of you, like hot blood." And we said, "From you also, O Prophet!" He answered, "And from me also, but Allah has given me his support and so Satan has been subdued."[8]

From the above, it is clear that the Arabs were accustomed to discuss freely with Mahomet and treated him as an ordinary human being like themselves. If he said that Satan ran in their blood, they would riposte that Satan also ran in his blood. Upon which, Mahomet admitted that he was no different from them except in the fact that Allah has come to his rescue and subdued Satan within him. The Arabic word which has been translated into "subdued" is *aslam,* which means "to become a Muslim" (to know peace, to be saved). The meaning of Mahomet's words, therefore, is that his Satan has become a Muslim. Mahomet emphasized the same point when he said: "I have been preferred to Adam in two ways. His wife incited him to disobedience, whereas my wives have helped me to obey. His Satan was a heretic, whereas mine was a Muslim inviting me always to do good."[9]

Islam, therefore, inherited the attitude of Judaism towards Eve, the sinful woman who disobeyed God, and towards sex as related essentially to women, and to Satan. Man, on the other hand, though endowed with an overpowering sexual passion, does not commit sin except if incited to do so by the seductiveness and devilry of woman. He is therefore enjoined to marry and thereby is able to beat back the evils of Satan and the bewitching temptations of women.

Islam encourages men to marry. Mahomet the Prophet of the Muslims, says to them: "Marriage is my law. He who loves my way of life, let him therefore follow my law."[10]

Despite the fact that Islam recognized the existence of sexual passion in both women and men, it placed all its constraints on women, thus forgetting that their sexual desire also was extremely strong. Islam never ignored the deep-seated sexual passion that lies in men, and therefore suggested the solutions that would ensure its satisfaction.

Islamic history, therefore, witnessed men who married hundreds of women. In this connection we may once more quote El Ghazali: "And it was said of Hassan Ibn Ali that he was a great marrier of women, and that he had more than two hundred wives. Sometimes he would marry four at a time, or divorce four at a time and replace them by others." The Prophet Mahomet, Allah's blessings and peace be upon him, said of Hassan Ibn Ali: "You resemble me, and my creativity."[11] The Prophet had once said of himself that he had been given the power of forty men in sex."[12] Ghazali admits that sexual desire in men is very strong and that: "Some natures are overwhelmed by passion and cannot be protected by only one woman. Such men should therefore preferably marry more than one woman and may go up to four."[13]

Some of the close followers of Mahomet (El Sahaba) who led an ascetic life would break their fast by having sexual intercourse before food. At other times they would share a woman's bed before the evening prayer, then do their ablutions and pray. This was in order to empty the heart of everything and so concentrate on the worship of Allah. Thus it was that the secretions of Satan were expelled from the body.

Ghazali carries his thoughts further and says: "Since among Arabs passion is an overpowering aspect of their nature, they have been allowed to marry women slaves if at some time they should fear that this passion will become too heavy a burden for their belief and lead to its destruction. Though it is true that such a marriage could lead to the birth of a child that will be a slave, yet enslaving the child is a lighter offence than the destruction of religious belief." Ghazali evidently believes that religion cannot be preserved from destruction unless men are allowed to marry as many women as they wish, even though in so doing they would be harming the interests of the children.

It is clear that Islam has been very lenient with men in so far as the satisfaction of their sexual desires is concerned. This was true even if it led to the enslavement of children and injustice to innocent creatures or if sought at the expense of a woman slave completely deprived of a wife's normal rights and whose children were destined never to enjoy the rights of a free child born of a free mother.

The inevitable question which arises in the face of these facts is: Why has religion been so lenient towards man? Why did it not demand that he control his sexual passions and limit himself to one wife, just as it demanded of the woman that she limit herself to one husband, even though it had recognized that women's sexual desire was just as powerful, if not more so, as that of men? Why is it that religion was so understanding and helpful where men were concerned, to the extent of sacrificing the interests of the family, the women and even the children, in order to satisfy their desires? Why, in contrast, was it so severe with woman that death could be her penalty if she so much as looked at a man other than her husband?

Islam made marriage the only institution within which sexual intercourse could be morally practised between men and women. Sexual relations, if practised outside this framework, were immediately transformed into an act of sin and corruption. A young man whom society had not endowed with the possibilities of getting married, or buying a woman slave from the market, or providing himself with a concubine, had no way of expending or releasing his pent-up sexual energies. Not even masturbation was permissible.

Ibn Abbas was once asked what he thought of masturbation? He exclaimed: "Ouph, it is indeed bad. I spit on it. To marry a slave woman is better. And to marry a slave woman is preferable to committing adultery." Thus it is that an unmarried youth is torn between three evils. The least of them is to marry a slave woman and have a slave child. The next is masturbation, and the most sinful of all is adultery.[14]

Of these three evils, only the first two were considered permissible. However, the institution of marriage remained very different for men to what it was for women, and the rights accorded to husbands were distinct from those accorded to wives. In fact, it is probably not accurate to use the term "rights of the woman" since a woman under the Islamic system of marriage has no human rights unless we consider that a slave has rights under a slave system. Marriage, in so far as women are concerned, is just like slavery to the slave, or the chains of serfdom to the serf. Ghazali expressed this fact clearly and succinctly when speaking of the rights enjoyed by a husband over his wife: "Perhaps the real answer is that marriage is a form of serfdom. The woman is man's serf and her duty therefore is absolute obedience to the husband in all that he asks of her person."[15] Mahomet himself said: "A woman, who at the moment of death enjoys the full approval of her husband, will find her place in Paradise."[16]

The right enjoyed by a wife in Islam is to receive the same treatment as her husband's other wives. Yet such "justice" is impossible, as the Koran itself has stated: "You will not be able to treat your women equally even if you exert much effort."[17] The Prophet himself preferred some of his wives to others. Some Muslim thinkers opposed polygamous marriage for this reason, and maintained that marriage to more than one woman in Islam was tied to a condition which itself was impossible to fulfil, namely to treat the different wives in exactly the same way and avoid any injustice to one or other of them. A man obviously desires his new wife more than the preceding one(s), otherwise he would not seek to marry her. Justice in this context should mean equality in love, or at least the absence of any tendency to like one wife more and so prefer her to the other(s).[18]

Some Muslim thinkers interpret the two relevant verses of the Koran differently: "Marry as many women as you like, two, three, or four. If you fear not to treat them equally, then marry only one" and "You will not succeed in being just with your women, no matter how careful you are."[19] They consider that justice in this context simply implies providing the women with an equal share of material means for the satisfaction of their needs and that it does not refer to equality in the love and affection borne by the husband for his women.[20]

The question, however, is: What is more important to a woman, or to any human being who respects her dignity and her human qualities, justice in the apportioning of a few piastres,[21] or justice in true love and human treatment? Is marriage a mere commercial transaction by which a woman obtains some money from her husband, or is it a profound exchange of feelings and emotions between a man and a woman?

Even if we were to assume the impossible, and arrive at a situation where the man treats his wives equally, it would not be possible to call this a "right," since the first and foremost criterion of any right is that it should be enjoyed equally by all individuals without distinction or discrimination. If a man marries four wives, even if he treats them equally, it still means that each woman among them has only a quarter of a man, whereas the man has four women. The women here are only equal in the sense that they suffer an equal injustice, just as in bygone days all slaves were "equal" in that sense under the system of slavery. This can in no way be considered equality or justice or rights for women.

The slave and feudal systems came into being in order to serve the interests of the slave and feudal landowners. In the same way, the system of marriage was created to serve the interests of the man against those of the woman and the children.

El Ghazali when speaking of the benefits of marriage for men expresses himself in these words:

Marriage relieves the mind and heart of the man from the burden of looking after the home, and of being occupied with cooking, sweeping, cleaning utensils and arranging for the necessities of life. If the human being did not possess a passion for living with a mate, he would find it very difficult to have a home to himself, since if obliged to undertake all the tasks of looking after the home, he would find most of his time wasted and would not be able to devote himself to work and to knowledge. A good woman, capable of setting things to rights in the home, is an invaluable aid to religious holiness. If however things go wrong in this area, the heart becomes the seat of anxieties and disturbances, and life is seized with things that chase away its calm. For these reasons Soleiman El Darani has said: "A good wife is not a creation of this world, for in fact she permits you to be occupied with the life of the hereafter, and this is so because she looks after the affairs of your home and in addition assuages your passions."[22]

Thus it is that a man cannot devote himself to his religious life, or to knowledge, unless he has a wife who is completely preoccupied with the affairs of his home, with serving him, and feeding him, cleaning his clothes and looking after all his needs. But are we not justified in asking: What about the wife? How can she in turn devote herself to her religious life and the search for knowledge? It is clear that no one has ever thought of the problem from this angle, as if it were a foregone conclusion that women have nothing to do with either religion or knowledge. That their sole function in life is sweeping, cooking, washing clothes and cleaning utensils, and undertaking those tasks that Ghazali has described as a source of trouble and disturbance to the heart, and that chase away the calm of life.

How clear it is that the mind of women and their ambitions, whether in science or in culture, have been completely dropped from all consideration, so that man can consecrate himself completely to such fields of human activity. He further-more imposes on woman the troubles and disturbances of the heart and mind that result from being occupied with such domestic tasks, after which she is accused of being stupid and lacking in religious conviction. Woman shoulders all these burdens without receiving any remuneration except the food, clothing and shelter required to keep her alive. Man not only exploits her mind for his own ends by abolishing it, or at least preventing it from developing any potential through science, culture and knowledge, not only does he plunge her whole life into working for him without reward, but he also uses her to satisfy his sexual desires to the extent required by him. It is considered one of her duties, and she must respond to his desires at any time. If she fails to do so, falls ill, refuses, or is prevented by her parents, it is his right to divorce her, and in addition deprive her of alimony.

Among the sacred duties of the wife is complete obedience to the husband. She is not allowed to differ with him, to ask questions, or even to argue certain points. The man on the other hand is not expected to obey his wife. On the contrary, it is considered unworthy of a man to do what his wife suggests or asks of him. Omar Ibn El Khattab once said: "Differ with your women and do not do what they ask. Thus you will be blessed. For it is said: Consult them and then act differently." The Prophet advises: "Do not live a slave to your wife." The Muslim religious leader, El Hassan, goes even further when he maintains that: "Whenever a man has started to obey the desires and wishes of his woman, it has ended by Allah throwing him into the fires of Purgatory."[23]

One of the rights of a woman is to be paid a sum of money in the form of a dowry when she is married, and to receive another sum of money as alimony if her husband divorces her. In addition, he is supposed to feed and clothe her, to give her shelter in a home. However, the woman cannot specify any conditions as far as the home she is expected to live in is concerned. It might be a hut made of wood or mud, or a beautiful brick house, depending on the means of the husband. She cannot determine the size of the dowry, or the sum paid to her as alimony, or the food which she is supposed to eat and the clothes she will wear. All these things are decided by the husband according to his assessment of the financial means at his disposal, and how he should spend them.

According to Islamic rules, a woman can ask to be paid for breastfeeding her child. [24] The husband is obliged to pay her for this from his earnings, if the child itself has not some financial resources laid aside for it. If these exist, the payment is made to the mother out of them. The mother is not forced to breastfeed the child if she does not want to, even if pay is offered to her. She can ask to be paid as long as there is no other woman who has voluntarily agreed to breastfeed the child, and to whom the father has no objection. However, if such a woman does exist, the wife no longer has the right to ask for any nursing payment.

Here again it is the husband's will that is crucial, since he can prevent the mother from being paid for nursing her child by finding another woman for this purpose, either on a voluntary basis or for a lower wage.

The mother is also eligible for payment for the rearing of her children, but here again it is the father's prerogative to choose another woman who can offer her services either on a voluntary basis or for less pay.

Such limited rights are almost insignificant, surrounded as they are by impossible conditions and cannot be considered of any real value. On the contrary, they afford the man a possibility of dispensing with the services of the children's mother [as soon as] she makes a request to be paid, thereby in fact obliging her to forego her right to payment for nursing or child-rearing. The vast majority of women, unable to be immune to the tendency for society and families to exaggerate and sanctify the functions of motherhood, cannot but sacrifice themselves for their children and give them everything, including their lives. To sacrifice some minor sum of money is therefore a matter of no consequence.

The exploitation to which a wife and a mother is exposed is evident from the fact that she carries out a number of vital functions without being paid. She is cook, sweeper, cleaner, washerwoman, domestic servant, nurse, governess and teacher to the children, in addition to being an instrument of sexual satisfaction and pleasure to her husband. All this she does free of charge, except for the expenses of her upkeep, in the form of food, clothing and shelter. She is therefore the lowest paid labourer in existence.

The exploitation of woman is built upon the fact that man pays her the lowest wage known for any category of human beasts of burden. It is he who decides what she is paid, be it in the form of a few piastres, some food, a dress, or simply a roof over her head. With this meagre compensation, he can justify the authority he exercises over her. Men exercise their tutelage over women because, as stated in the Koran, they provide them with the means of livelihood.

Man's lordship over woman is therefore enforced through the meagre piastres he pays her and also through imposing a single husband upon her to ensure that the piastres he owns are not inherited by the child of another man. Preserving this inheritance is the motive force behind the severe and rigid laws which seek to maintain a woman's loyalty to her husband so that no confusion can affect the line of descent. It is not love between husband and wife which is sought to be nurtured and cherished by these rules. If it were love between the couple that was the basis of this search for loyalty between husband and wife, such loyalty would be required equally from both the woman and the man. However, since loyalty is sought in the woman alone, by imposing monogamy on her, whereas the man is permitted to multiply and diversify his sexual relations, it becomes self-evident that conjugal devotion is not a human moral value, but one of the instruments of social oppression exercised against the woman to make sure that the succession and inheritance is kept intact. The line of descent which is sought to be preserved is, of course, that of the man. Thus adultery on the part of the woman, her betrayal of the nuptial vows sworn to on the day of marriage, means the immediate destruction of patrilineal descent and inheritance.

Money is therefore the foundation of morals, or at least of the morals prevalent where property, exploitation and inheritance are the essence of the economic system. Yet in religion it is assumed that true morals are dependent rather on human values. The Koran clearly says: "Neither your wealth, nor your children can, even if you tread the path of humiliation, bring you close to me." "The highest esteem is given by Allah to those who are the purest."[25]

We have mentioned before that society realized early on the powerful biological and sexual nature of women, which power it compared to that of Satan. It was therefore inevitable that her loyalty and chastity could only be ensured by preventing her from having relations with any males apart from her husband and the men with whom she was forbidden to have sex such as the father, brother, and paternal or maternal uncles. This is the reason behind the segregation that arose between men and women, and the outlawing of free intermixing between them, a segregation put into effect by imprisoning the women within the four walls of the home. This confinement of women to the home permits the attainment of three inter-related aims: (1) It ensures the loyalty of the woman and prevents her from mixing with strange men; (2) It permits her to devote herself entirely to the care of her home, husband and children and the aged members of the family; and (3) It protects men from the dangers inherent in women and their powers of seduction, which are so potent that when faced by them "men lose two-thirds of their reason and become incapable of thinking about Allah, science and knowledge."

The Muslim philosophers who so oft proclaim such opinions borrow most of their ideas from the myth of Adam and Eve, seeing woman as a replica of Eve, endowed with powers that are dangerous and destructive to society, to man, and to religion. They believe that civilization has been gradually built up in the struggle against these "female powers," in an attempt to control and suppress them, so as to protect the man and to avoid their minds from being preoccupied with women to the detriment of their duties towards Allah and society.

In order to preserve society and religion from such evils, it was essential to segregate the sexes, and subjugate women by fire and steel when necessary for fire and steel alone can force slaves to submit to unjust laws and systems built on exploitation. Woman's status within marriage is even worse than that of the slave, for woman is exploited both economically and sexually. This apart from the moral, religious and social oppression exercised over her to ensure the maintenance of her double exploitation. Slaves, at least, are partially compensated for the efforts they make in the form of some material reward. But a woman is an unpaid servant to the husband, children and elderly people within the home. And a slave may be liberated by his master to become a free man, and thus enjoy the rights of free men, foremost amongst which is the recognition that he has a brain and religious conviction. But a woman, as long as she remains a woman, has no chance or hope of ever possessing the brain and religious conviction of a man. For women are "lacking in their minds and in their religious faith."

Since men possess more reason and wisdom than women it has become their right, and not that of women, to occupy the positions of ruler, legislator, governor etc. One of the primary conditions in Islam to become a religious or political leader (Imam) or governor (Wali) is to be a "male."[26] Then follow piety, knowledge and competence.

The major ideas on which Islam has based itself in dealing with the question of women and sex can thus be listed as follows:

1. Men should exercise their tutelage over women because they provide for them economically. They are also superior to women as far as reason, wisdom, piety, knowledge and religious conviction are concerned. Authority is the right of men, and obedience the duty of women.
2. Men's energies should be expended in worship, religious activities and in the search for knowledge. This is to be attained by making women devote themselves to serving their men in the home, preparing food and drink, washing, cleaning and caring for the children and elderly.
3. The sexual desires of men should be duly satisfied so that they can concentrate with a clear mind and heart on religious activities, the worship of Allah, the search for knowledge, and the service of society. This also aims to ensure that religion is safeguarded and society preserved from being undermined, or even collapsing. Sexual desire is to be satisfied through marriage, the aims of which are reproduction and also experience of one of the pleasures promised in Paradise, so that men may be motivated to do good and so be rewarded in the after-life. It is men's uncontested right to

fully satisfy their sexual needs by marrying several women, or by taking unto themselves women slaves and concubines. Masturbation however is an evil, and adultery an even greater sin. "Let those who cannot marry remain chaste so that Allah may bestow upon them of His riches. Let he who can marry a woman, who has matured without marriage, take her as a wife. If he cannot, then abstinence is the path."[27]

4. The seduction of women and their powers of temptation are a danger and a source of destruction. Men must be protected from their seductive powers, and this is ensured by confining them to the home. Man is exposed to annihilation if he succumbs to the temptations of women. In the words of Ibrahim Ebn Adham, "he who is accustomed to the thighs of women will never be a source of anything."[28]

5. Women are forbidden to leave the home and enter the outside world of men except if an urgent necessity to do this arises, as in illness or death. If a woman goes outside her home she must cover her body completely and not expose her attractions or anything that is liable to seduce a man. Her ornaments should be hidden and her external genital organs preserved intact.

Islam encouraged men to marry and went as far as considering it a religious duty. A familiar Arab saying goes as follows: "Marriage is half of religion." Men were not only asked to marry, but permitted to take several wives, and to have extramarital sexual relations almost at will, by living with concubines or women slaves. They were thus led to boast of the number of women they owned, and to speak with pride of their sexual powers.

The sexual powers of man became a part of the Arab ethos, and within this ethos, were related to manliness and virility. It became a matter for shame if a man was known to be impotent or sexually weak. Obviously, it could only be a woman who would be able to know, and therefore judge, if a man was sexually deficient, and in this resided another source of woman's hidden strength enhancing the dangers she represented. Men therefore had to be protected from her, and society did this by ensuring that her eyes were prevented from seeing anything outside the home—like an animal that becomes blind from being kept in the dark—by covering her face with the thickest of veils, and by obscuring her mind so she would become incapable of discerning the weak from the strong. This is the origin of the greater value attached to a virgin as compared with a woman, when the time comes for her to marry. The virgin knows little or nothing about men and sex, whereas a woman has experience drawn from her past relations with men and from her knowledge of the arts of sex. She can easily discern where lie the weaknesses of a man and where lies his strength. Hence the reduced value attached to a widow or a divorced woman.

Mahomet the Prophet, however, did not comply with these general rules of male conduct in Arab society. He was married fourteen times to women who had been divorced or widowed. The only virgin he married was Aisha. In this respect he was also much more progressive, and much more open-minded than most of the men of today, who still prefer to marry a virgin and look for the usual bloodstains on the nuptial sheet or cloth. That is why, especially in rural areas, the custom of defloration by the husband's or *daya's* finger is still widespread, and is meant to demonstrate the red evidence of virginity on a white cloth symbolic of purity and an intact family honour.

As we have seen, the status of women and the attitudes towards them changed rapidly after the death of Mahomet. In the very essence of Islam, and in its teachings as practised in the life of the Prophet, women occupied a comparatively high position. But once they were segregated from men and made to live within the precincts of the home, the values of honour, self-respect and pride characteristic of Arab tribal society became closely and almost indissolubly linked to virginity, and to preventing the womenfolk of the family from moving into the outside world. A popular saying among the Palestinians, very common until the middle of the 20th century, goes: "My woman never left our home until the day she was carried out."[29] I remember my mother describing my grandmother and saying that she had only ever moved through the streets on two occasions. The first was when she left her father's house and went to her husband after marriage. And the second when she was carried out of her husband's house to be buried. Both times no part of her body remained uncovered.[30]

Segregation between the world of men and that of women was so strict that a woman who dared to go outside the door of her home was liable to be maltreated at the hands of men. They might limit themselves to a few rude and insolent glances, or resort to coarse sexual remarks and insults, but very often things would go even further. A man or a boy might stretch out his hand and seize her by the arm or the breast. Sometimes young boys would throw stones at her in the lanes and by-roads of cities and towns, and follow in her footsteps with jeering remarks or sexual insults, in which the organs of her body would be villified in a chorus of loud voices. As a girl I used to be scared of going out into the streets in some of the districts of Cairo during my secondary school days (1943–48). I remember how boys sometimes threw stones at me, or shouted out crude insults as I passed by, such as "Accursed be the cunt of your mother" or "Daughter of the bitch fucked by men." In some Arab countries women have been exposed to physical or moral aggression in the streets simply because their fingers were seen protruding from the sleeves of their dress.[31]

This tendency among males to harm any woman caught crossing the boundaries of her home, and therefore the outer limits of the world prescribed for her by men, or who dares break into and walk through domains reserved for men, proves that they cannot consider her as merely weak and passive. On the contrary, they look upon her as a dangerous aggressor the moment she steps over the frontiers, an aggressor to be punished and made to return immediately to the restrictions of her abode. This attitude bears within itself the proof of woman's strength, a strength from which man seeks to protect himself by all possible means. Not only does he imprison woman within the house, but he also surrounds the male world with all sorts of barricades, stretches of barbed wire, fortifications and even heavy guns.

The female world, on the other hand, is looked upon by men as an area surrounded by, and peopled with, obscure and puzzling secrets, filled with all the dark mystery of sorcery, devilry and the works of Satan. It is a world that a man may only enter with the greatest caution, and a prayer for Allah's help, Allah who alone can give us strength and show us the way. Thus it is that the Arab man in the rural areas of Egypt mutters a string of Allah's names through pursed, fast moving lips, on entering a house in which there are women: *"Ya Hafez, ya Hafes, ya Lateef, ya Sattar, ya Rab, ya Satir, ya Karim."* ("O great preserver, almighty one, God the compassionate, who art alone shielder from all harm, protector from evil, bountiful and generous.") In some Arab societies the man might add *destour*, which is the same word used by peasants to chase away evil spirits or devils. [32]

Here again we can observe the commonly held idea of a close link between women and devils or evil spirits. It goes back to the story of Eve, and the belief that she was positive and active where evil is concerned, an instrument of Satan's machinations. The development of a Sufi theology in Islam, characterized by renunciation of the world, and meditation and love for Allah—which became a cult of love in general—allowed women to rise to the level of saints. However, the number of women saints remained extremely small as compared with men. On the other hand, where it came to evil spirits 80% of them were popularly considered to be female. [33]

The history of the Arabs shows that the women were undoubtedly much less afraid of the men than the men were of the women. The tragedy of Arab men however, or rather of most men all over the world, is that they fear woman and yet desire her. But I think it can be said that Arab men in some periods, especially in the pre-Islamic and early Islamic eras, were able to overcome their fear of women to a much greater degree than men in the West. Or perhaps, more precisely, the men's desire for their women was stronger than the inhibitions built from fear. This is due to the difference in the objective conditions prevailing in Arab societies as compared to the West, and to the fact, discussed earlier, that Islam (contrary to Christianity) recognized the validity and legitimacy of sexual desire.

As a result, sex and love occupied a much more important place in the life of the Arabs, and in their literature and arts. But parallel to this flowering in the passions which bind men and women together, there was an opposite and almost equally strong tendency in the teachings of philosophers and men of wisdom, and in the literary works of writers and poets, that warned against indulging in the pleasures of sex. Men were abjured not to become "impassioned" with women or to fall victims to their seductions. One of the famous injunctions of the prominent Arab thinker, Ibn El Mokafa, says: "Know well that one of the things that can cause the worst of disasters in religion, the greatest exhaustion to the body, the heaviest strain on the purse, the highest harm to the mind and reason, the deepest fall in man's chivalry, and the fastest dissipation of his majesty and poise, is a passion for women." [34]

Ibn Mokafa was no doubt directing his remarks exclusively to those men who possessed "majesty," "poise," and a well garnished purse, since only those who possessed these trappings could possibly lose them through love of women. Other men, those that constituted the vast majority among the people and who possessed neither majesty, nor poise, nor purse of any kind could not benefit from his advice, or even be in the least concerned with it. They were completely, or almost completely, stripped of all worldly possessions and therefore sometimes even of the means to have just one lawful wife, pay her dowry and keep her children. Such men could not be expected to strut back and forth on the scenes of love and passion.

In Arab society, as in all societies governed by a patriarchal class system where enormous differences exist between various social levels, sex and love, sexual freedom and licence and a life of pleasure were only the lot of a very small minority. The vast majority of men and women were destined to toss and turn on a bed of nails, to be consumed by the flames of sacrifice and to be subjugated by a load of traditions, laws and codes which forbid sex to all except those who can pay its price.

The Arabs, exposed as they were to the shortages and harshness of desert life, to the difficulties and perils of obtaining the bare necessities in a backward and rather savage society, and to the burden of exploitation by their own and surrounding ruling classes, were known for their fortitude, patience, and capacity to stand all kinds of deprivation, whether from food, sex or even water. Yet they were capable, like people in all lands, and at all stages in human development, of finding compensation in other things. This might explain to us why the Arab people were so fond of listening to the stories of *A Thousand and One Nights,* pulsating as they were with the passions of beautiful women and the seductions of sex. This eagerness to listen to, and repeat, what had been told over a thousand nights, aroused a fiery imagination and substituted illusions for what life could not give them in fact.

References

1. P. H. Newby, *A Selection from the Arabian Nights,* translated by Sir Richard Burton, Introduction from pp. vii–xvii (Pocket Books, N.T., 1954).
2. Franz G. Alexander and Sheldon T. Selesnick, *The History of Psychiatry,* p. 68.
3. *Fitna,* in Arabic means woman's overpowering seductiveness. It combines the qualities of attraction and mischievousness.
4. Abou Abdallah Mohammed Ismail El Bokhary, *Kitab El Gami El Sahib,* (1868), p. 419.
5. Abou Hamid El Ghazali, *Ihya Ouloum El Dine,* Dar El Shaab Publishers (Cairo, 1970), p. 689.
6. *Ibid.,* p. 693.
7. *Ibid.,* p. 695.
8. *Ibid.,* p. 696.
9. *Ibid.,* p. 700.
10. *Ibid.,* p. 683.
11. *Ibid.,* p. 697.
12. Mohammed Ibn Saad, *El Tabakat El Kobra,* Vol. 8, Dar El Tahrir (Cairo, 1970), p. 139.

13. *Ibid.*
14. Abou Hamid, El Ghazali, *Ihy'a Ouloum El Dine,* Dar El Shaab Publishers (Cairo, 1970), p. 697.
15. *Ibid.,* p. 746.
16. *The Koran: Sourat El Nissa'a,* Verse 129.
17. *Ibid.*
18. *El Zamakhshari,* Vol. I, p. 143 and *El Kourtoubi,* Vol. 5, pp. 407–8.
19. *The Koran: Sourat El Nissa'a,* Verses 3 and 129.
20. *El Kourtoubi,* Vol. 5, pp. 20–2; *El Galadine,* Vol. I, p. 27; El Hassas, *Ahkam El Koran.*
21. Egyptian unit of money. One hundred piastres equal one Egyptian pound.
22. Abou Hamid El Ghazali, *Ihya Ouloum El Dine,* p. 699.
23. *Ibid.,* p. 706.
24. Sheikh Mohammed Mahdi Shams El Dine, *Al Islam wa Tanzeem El Waledeya,* Al Ittihad El Aalami Litanzeem El Waledeya. El Maktab El Iklimi Lilshark El Awsat wa Shamal Afrikia 1974, Vol. 2, p. 84.
25. *The Koran: Sourat Sab'a,* Verse 37.
26. *Al Imam Abou Hamid El Ghazali,* Dar El Shaab Publishers (Cairo, 1970), Chapter 3, p. 202.
27. *The Koran: Sourat El Nour,* Verse 33.
28. Abou Hamid El Ghazali, *Ihy'a Ouloum El Dine,* Dar El Shaab Publishers (Cairo, 1970), p. 706.
29. Tewfih Canaan, *Kawaneen Gheir Maktouba Tatahakam fi Makanat El Mara'a El Filistineya (Magalat El Torath, Wal Mogtam'a)* El Takadoum Publishers Al Kouds (Jerusalem), No. 2, 1974, p. 39.
30. My maternal grandmother lived in Cairo (1898–1948). She spent her whole life doing the chores at home and looking after her husband and children. She belonged to a middle class or rather higher middle class family. On the other hand, my paternal grandmother who lived during almost the same period in our village, Kafr Tahla, never knew what it was to wear a veil and used to go out to work in the fields or to buy and sell in the market every day, just as other poor peasant women did.
31. Tewfik Canaan, *Kawaneen Gheir Maktouba Tatahakam fi Makanat El Mara'a,* p. 40.
32. I very often heard the word *destour* repeated by villagers, whether men or women, in gatherings for *zar* (exhortational sessions) when mention was made of evil spirits or devils. One of those present would shout *destour* which means "O God, chase away the evil spirits from our way." The same word is used to clear the way for a man, especially when women are present, and are required to withdraw or to be warned by him that he is about to come in. The word also means the established order, constitution, or constitutional laws.
33. Tewfik Canaan, *El Yanabi'i El Maskouna Wa Shayatin El Ma'a (fi filistine) Magalat El Torath Wal Mogtama,* El Takadam Press, (Jerusalem), No. 2, July 1974, p. 38.
34. Ibn El Mokafa, *El Adab El Saghir, Wal Adab El Kebir,* Maktabat El Bayan (Beirut, 1960), p. 127.

Translated by Sherif Hetata

Questions for Discussion and Writing

1. According to el-Saadawi, in what ways has *A Thousand and One Nights* created images of love and sex in Arab life? For what reasons does the author explain that they are not valid?
2. What, according to el-Saadawi, are the major premises in Arab life today about sexuality? What are the major attitudes toward women's sexuality? Toward men's sexuality?

3. In what ways has the Muslim religion influenced current convictions and practices? In developing your response, use brief passages from the Koran—the holy book of Islam—in support where appropriate.
4. In what ways have their surroundings influenced those convictions and practices?
5. How would you characterize el-Saadawi's presentation of her material? What audience do you think she had in mind while writing the essay? What elements in her writing suggest her own feelings about her exploration of history, religion, and culture? Use brief passages from the text to support your analysis.

Chapter 3

CULTURE AND LANGUAGE, BODY LANGUAGE, AND PERCEPTION

I'll try to give the story in your language. It's hard to express the way I feel in it but I don't feel the pain so much when I talk about it in your language. My own words carry too much weight. But I always worry when I finish a part, did I say enough? Did I really connect by those words? You see, your language is set for your way of thinking. It's like a different current. The situation I want to explain is set for another current, and that current carries the strong feelings from a different way of thinking. So it's like plugging a lamp into the wrong current. The energy I put into it takes more than it gives out.

MOHM PHAT, a young victim of Cambodia's Khmer Rouge, recounting her story to adoptive mother, Gail Sheehy, in *SPIRIT OF SURVIVAL*

CULTURE AND LANGUAGE ARE TIGHTLY CONNECTED. NOT KNOWing the language of a people keeps a newcomer forever outside their culture. Language systems determine what we see when we open our eyes, and they give us templates for organizing and shaping our lives.

Communication, however, involves much more than language. We communicate meaning every minute of our lives, though we cannot control what we communicate as fully as we like to think we do. A message from a Chinese fortune cookie captures this idea: "You think that it's a secret, but it never has been."

We cannot always control what we communicate because much of what we convey is nonverbal—in our eyes, the way we walk, the tone in our voice, the gestures we make—of which we are both conscious and unconscious. When we travel to other cultures, we can no longer depend on language, and what we take in by our senses may mislead us. Language and nonverbal communication are culturally learned and based.

The essays, play, and story in this chapter will help us to understand some of the issues involved in the relationships among language, culture, nonverbal communication, and perception. In "Man at the Mercy of Language," Peter Farb introduces important concepts that scholars such as Edward Sapir and Benjamin Whorf have defined in their studies. Gordon W. Allport explains the relationship between categorizing people and prejudice in "Linguistic Factors in Prejudice."

Richard Rodriguez builds a case against bilingual education as a result of his own experiences in learning English—in "Memories of a Bilingual Childhood." Teaching students in their own language, Rodriguez argues, "reinforces feelings [in them] of public separateness." In Shirley Lauro's one-act play "Open Admissions," feelings of separateness make Calvin, a young black man, desperate as he confronts his overworked speech teacher. Although both speak English, teacher and student cannot understand each other.

In communication in which one written language must be translated into another, the complexities involve not only the words but also the history, psychology, and aesthetic dimensions of the culture from which the piece comes. In "Translating Cultures," Phyllis I. Lyons takes us through the translator's tasks in helping us to grasp a short story by a Japanese writer.

In "The Sounds of Silence," Edward T. Hall and Mildred Reed Hall explore the idea that we are often not consciously aware of messages we convey nonverbally. The next selection, "Why Do Frenchmen?" by Gregory Bateson, further supports the Halls's essay. Through a brief dialogue between a father and his inquiring daughter, Bateson takes a look at nonverbal communication among Frenchmen: "The point is that *no* mere words exist," the father claims. In the last selection of this chapter, "The Stuffing of the Lord," Sabine Ulibarrí reminds us that there are exceptions to every rule of language and culture.

It is not possible to consider language in isolation from the contexts of a culture or its patterns of nonverbal communication. *"No* mere words exist," the father tells his daughter. We need to remember that, too.

PETER FARB

Man at the Mercy of Language

From 1953 to his death from leukemia in 1980 at age fifty-one, Peter Farb was a prolific free-lance writer and researcher interested in the science and natural history of North America. His books reflect the large range of his interest and study—from insect life and the story of dams for the young scientist to ambitious histories of North American Indians. His last book, coauthored with George Armelagos and completed just before Farb's death, Consuming Passions: The Anthropology of Eating *(1980), addresses the ways in which eating affects cultural patterns as varied as rites of passage, sex, religion, and gift-giving.*

"Man at the Mercy of Language" is taken from Word Play: What Happens When People Talk *(1973). As Farb explains in that book, because writing about language demands exploration of many disciplines, he was thus exposed to "the hazards of interdisciplinary points of view." He notes further that "in writing about language, I had no alternative but to use the medium of language itself—which is nearly as difficult as lifting oneself by one's bootstraps." As readers, we need to remember that we too face these same demands as we build our understanding of the concepts in this essay.*

Before you read "Man at the Mercy of Language," write about what the title of the essay means to you, explaining the reasons for your interpretation. Then describe the colors you see in the room you're in by using only three color names of your choice. Finally, think about how your reader would see the room differently because of these descriptive limitations.

E very human being is creative both in putting together novel statements and in employing them in various speech situations. Yet no one is free to employ his innate capacity in any way he wishes. Indeed, freedom of speech does not exist anywhere, for every community on earth forbids the use of certain sounds, words, and sentences in various speech situations. In the American speech community, for example, the habitual liar faces social sanctions—and criminal punishment should he lie under oath. Speakers are not allowed to misrepresent what they are selling, to defame other people in public, to maliciously shout "Fire!" in a crowded movie theater, or to utter obscenities on the telephone. In addition, less obvious constraints upon freedom of speech may exist. They may be the structures of languages themselves—and they may restrict the speaker as rigidly as do the community's social sanctions.

Every moment of the day the world bombards the human speaker with information and experiences. It clamors for his attention, claws at his senses, intrudes into his thoughts. Only a very small portion of this total experience is language—yet the speaker must use this small portion to report on all the experiences that exist or ever existed in the totality of the world since time began. Try to think about the stars, a grasshopper, love or hate, pain, anything at all—and it must be done in terms of language. There is no other way; thinking is language spoken to oneself. Until language has made sense of experience, that experience is meaningless.

This inseparableness of everything in the world from language has intrigued modern thinkers, most notably Ludwig Wittgenstein, of Cambridge University, who was possibly this century's most influential philosopher. He stated the problem very directly: "The limits of my language mean the limits of my world." Wittgenstein offered pessimistic answers to questions about the ability of language to reveal the world. He claimed that language limited his capacity to express certain ideas and opinions; nevertheless, he did manage to say a great deal about topics he felt were inexpressible. By the time of his death in 1951, Wittgenstein had arrived at a more positive view of language. If its limits—that is, the precise point at which sense becomes nonsense—could somehow be defined, then speakers would not attempt to express the inexpressible. Therefore, said Wittgenstein, do not put too great a burden upon language. Learn its limitations and try to accommodate yourself to them, for language offers all the reality you can ever hope to know.

For tens, and perhaps hundreds, of thousands of years, people regarded language as a holy instrument that let them look out upon the world in wonder and fear and joy. "In the beginning was the Word" is the reassuring first line of the Gospel According to St. John. Only in the last few decades have people suspected that their window on the world has a glass that gives a distorted view. Language no longer is certain to open up new sights to the imagination; rather, it is thought by some to obscure the vision of reality. The French philosopher Jean-Paul Sartre, who has often written about what he calls today's "crisis of language," has stated: "Things are divorced from their names. They are there, grotesque, headstrong, gigantic, and it seems ridiculous to . . . say anything at all about them: I am in the midst of things, nameless things." Indeed, in this century many of the foundation "things" of civilization—God, truth, fact, humanity, freedom, good and evil—have become nameless and have lost their traditional reference points. An entire generation has grown up that distrusts language's ability to express a true picture of reality and that relies upon the empty intercalations of *like, you know, I mean.* The world has grown inarticulate at the very time that an unprecedented number of words flood the media. The output has burgeoned, but speakers have retreated into the worn paths of stock phrases. A statistical study of telephone speech showed that a vocabulary of only 737 words was used in 96 per cent of such conversations. Apparently people speak more, yet say less.

Exaggerated anxieties about language's ability to express reality result in the pathology of "logophobia" (literally, "fear of words"). Logophobia has found popular expression in recent decades in the movement known as General Semantics. Two books with this point of view have had a wide readership—Stuart Chase's *Tyranny of Words* and S. I. Hayakawa's *Language in Action*— and both derive their ideas largely from the writings of a Polish count. Alfred Korzybski (1879–1950) was an engineer, an officer in the Russian army, an official at the League of Nations, and a researcher into mental illness after he migrated to the United States. The key element in his theory about language was: "The map does not represent all of the territory." That is, no matter how much detail a cartographer puts into a drawing of a map, it can never represent all of the ridges, slopes, valleys, and hillocks in a territory. Korzybski similarly believed that language can no more say everything about an event than the map can show everything in a territory. *The grass is green* cannot be a true utterance because it is incomplete. What kind of grass? Where is it growing? What shade of green is meant?

Korzybski felt that speakers could nevertheless emancipate themselves from the tyranny of language by changing their orientation. They must imitate mathematics as a way to state precise relationships between things; they must avoid abstractions; they must be wary of the troublesome word *is* because it often implies an identification that does not exist in reality. Freedom from language's distortions would be achieved by rigorously rating all statements to determine whether speakers could back them up. And no longer would general words that expressed categories be acceptable. A *cow* would not be just a cow, but a particular kind of animal, with certain characteristics, named "Elsie" or "Bossie."

Almost all linguists reject Korzybski's theories on the basis of their logophobia and their inadequate solutions. Nevertheless, he did isolate a logical contradiction: Language is supposed to communicate experience, yet by its very nature it is incapable of doing so. A moment's thought reveals how ill-equipped language is to render a true account of an experience. Picture an autumn scene with a single leaf close up: its color scarlet and edged with burnished gold, the spaces between the veins eaten out by insects in a filigree pattern, the edges gracefully curled, the different textures of the upper and lower surfaces, the intense light of Indian summer falling on the leaf. And this leaf which I have scarcely begun to describe is only one out of the countless millions that surround a stroller in the autumn woods, each unique in its color and shape, the way it catches the light and flutters in the breeze.

How can language possibly render such an experience? The obvious fact is that it cannot—and few people would want it to, for such detail would bog down language in a morass of trivial observations. People do not demand that language describe an entire experience, even if it could. No one confuses speech about a leaf with a real leaf any more than people confuse a painting of a leaf with a leaf. The function of language is not to duplicate reality, but to recall it, comment upon it, and make predictions about it. A much more significant limitation upon language is that each language can comment upon experience only in its own way. Some languages of interior New Guinea, for example, are severely hampered in conveying even leaf color because they lack a convenient terminology to describe colors other than black and white.

Since human beings are born with the same senses and approximately the same degree of intelligence, they should be able to report equally well whatever they experience. But different languages make such equality difficult to achieve. Imagine two forest rangers, one a white speaker of Standard English and the other an Indian speaker of Navaho, riding together on inspection in Arizona. They notice a broken wire fence. When they return to their station, the English-speaking ranger reports *A fence is broken.* He is satisfied that he has perceived the situation well and has reported it conscientiously. The Navaho, though, would consider such a report vague and perhaps even meaningless. His report of the same experience would be much different in Navaho—simply because his language demands it of him.

First of all, a Navaho speaker must clarify whether the "fence" is animate or inanimate; after all, the "fence" might refer to the slang for a receiver of stolen goods or to a fence lizard. The verb the Navaho speaker selects from several alternatives will indicate that the fence was long, thin, and constructed of many strands, thereby presumably wire (the English-speaking ranger's report failed to mention whether the fence was wood, wire, or chain link). The Navaho language then demands that a speaker report with precision upon the act of breaking; the Indian ranger must choose between two different verbs that tell whether the fence was broken by a human act or by some nonhuman agency such as a windstorm. Finally, the verb must indicate the present status of the fence, whether it is stationary or is, perhaps, being whipped by the wind. The Navaho's report would translate something like this: "A fence (which belongs to a particular category of inanimate things, constructed of long and thin material composed of many strands) is (moved to a position, after which it is now at rest) broken (by nonhumans, in a certain way)." The Navaho's report takes about as long to utter as the English-speaking ranger's, but it makes numerous distinctions that it never occurred to the white ranger to make, simply because the English language does not oblige him to make them.

Each language encourages its speakers to tell certain things and to ignore other things. *The women bake a cake* is an acceptable English sentence. Speakers of many other languages, though, would regard it as inadequate and would demand more specific information, such as whether exactly two women or more than two women did the baking, and whether the women are nearby or distant. Some languages would force their speakers to select a word for "cake" that tells whether the cake is round or rectangular and whether or not the cake is visible to the listener at the time of speaking. Many languages are not as concerned as English that the tense of the verb tell whether the cake was baked in the past, is being baked now, or will be baked in the future—although some languages make even finer distinctions of tense than English does. Several American Indian languages of the Pacific Northwest divide the English past tense into recent past, remote past, and mythological past.

The way people talk about the color spectrum, and even perceive it, varies from one speech community to another, although all human eyes see the same colors because colors have their own reality in the physical world. Color consists of visible wavelengths which blend imperceptibly into one another. No sharp breaks in the spectrum separate one color from another, such as orange from red. But when speakers in most European communities look at a rainbow, they imagine they see six sharp bands of color: red, orange, yellow, green, blue, and purple. Chopping the continuous spectrum of the rainbow into color categories in this way is an arbitrary division made by European speech communities. People elsewhere in the world, who speak languages unrelated to European ones, have their own ways of partitioning the color spectrum. The Shona of Rhodesia and the Bassa of Liberia, for example, have fewer color categories than speakers of European languages, and they also break up the spectrum at different points, as the diagrams show:

ENGLISH

red	orange	yellow	green	blue	purple

SHONA

cipsuka	cicena	citema	cipsuka

BASSA

ziza	hui

The Shona speaker divides the spectrum into three portions, which he pronounces approximately as *cipsuka, cicena,* and *citema* (*cipsuka* appears twice because it refers to colors at both the red end and the purple end of the spectrum). Of course, the Shona speaker is able to perceive and to describe other colors—in the same way that a speaker of English knows that *light orangish yellow* is a variant of yellow—but the Shona's basic divisions represent the portions of the spectrum for which his language has convenient labels.

Charts obtainable at paint stores provide samples of hundreds of colors to help homeowners select the exact ones they want. An English speaker who glances quickly at one of these charts recognizes certain colors and can name them immediately as *yellow, green,* and so forth. Other colors require a moment of hesitation before the speaker finally decides that a particular hue falls into the category of, let us say, *green* rather than *yellow.* Still other colors demand not only considerable thought but also a hyphenated compromise, such as *greenish-yellow.* Finally, the English speaker finds himself totally unable to name many colors by any of the categories available to him; he is forced to make up his own term or to use a comparison, such as *It looks like the color of swamp water.* The ease with which verbal labels can be attached to colors is known as "codability." The color that a speaker of English unhesitatingly describes as *green* has high codability for him, and it also evokes a quick response from speakers of his language, who immediately know what hues fall into that category. Similarly, when a Shona says *citema,* a high-codability color, other members of his speech community immediately know that he refers to "greenish-blue." In contrast, the color that a speaker describes as *like swamp water* has low codability, which means that other speakers cannot be certain exactly what color is intended.

Some linguists have found in color codability a fruitful way to experiment with the relationships between thought and language. In one such experiment, people who served as test subjects were shown a large selection of plastic squares, each colored differently. Usually, when someone sees a color, his mind stores it for a mere few moments and he can identify the color again only if he sees it almost immediately. If a delay occurs, the stored image is no longer a reliable guide because it has become faint and distorted. Yet when the squares were hidden from sight even for several minutes, the test subjects could pick out again certain colors—the high-codability ones for which the English language has convenient labels like *red, blue, yellow,* and so on. Subjects were able to remember the high-codability colors because they had simply attached common English-language words to them. In other words, they stored colors in their minds not as colors but as verbal labels for them. Even though the images had completely faded from their memories after a few moments, the subjects still remembered the verbal labels they had given the colors—and they were therefore able to identify the plastic squares again. The human being's ability to encode experience in this way is not limited to color. Similar experiments have been performed with other experiences, such as the recognition of facial expressions, and the results have been the same.

Experiments like these have shown that at least one aspect of human thought—memory—is strongly influenced by language. That is not the same thing, however, as proving that man is at the mercy of his language. The convenient labels that a speech community gives to certain colors are a great aid in remembering them, but the absence of such labels does not prohibit a community from talking about the low-codability colors. When people develop a need for an expanded color vocabulary—as have artists, decorators, and fashion designers—they simply invent one. Witness the recent plethora of colors for decorating the home: *riviera blue, alpine green, lime frost, birch gray,* and so forth.

Nevertheless, the colors that a speaker "sees" often depend very much upon the language he speaks, because each language offers its own high-codability color terms. Recently, two anthropologists at the University of California, Brent Berlin and Paul Kay, have attempted to show that speech communities follow an evolutionary path in the basic color terms they offer their speakers. For example, several New Guinea tribes have in their vocabularies only two basic color words, which translate roughly as "black" (or "dark") and "white" (or "light"). A greater number of languages in widely separated areas of the world possess three color terms—and the startling fact is that they usually retain words for "black" and "white" and add the same third color, "red." The languages that have four color terms retain "black," "white," and "red"—and almost always add either "green" or "yellow." Languages with five color terms add the "green" or the "yellow" that was missed at the fourth level, with the result that nearly all such languages have words for "black" (or "dark"), "white" (or "light"), "red," "green," and "yellow," and for no other colors. Languages with six terms add a word for "blue," and those with seven terms add a word for "brown."

The completely unanticipated inference of this study is that the languages of the world, regardless of their grammars, follow an evolutionary sequence, at least so far as color terms go. A language usually does not have a word that means "brown" unless it already has the six earlier color words. A language rarely has "blue" in its vocabulary unless it already has words for both "green" and "yellow." (English, and most western European languages, Russian, Japanese, and several others add four additional color terms—"gray," "pink," "orange," and "purple"—but these languages do not do so until they already offer the seven previous color terms.) Berlin and Kay believe that a language, at any given point in time, can be assigned to only one stage of basic color terms and apparently must have passed through the prior stages in the appropriate sequence. Such regularity on the part of unrelated languages in adding color terms is astonishing, and no one has as yet offered a suitable explanation for it.

Berlin and Kay have also correlated this sequence with the general complexity of the cultures in which the languages are spoken. Languages with only the two color terms "black" and "white" are spoken in cultures at a very simple level of technology—and the only languages known to have all eleven terms are spoken in cultures with a long history of complexity. Between these two extremes are the languages of such peoples as the Tiv of Africa with three terms, the Homeric Greeks and Ibo of Africa with four terms, the Bushmen of Africa and the Eskimos of North America with five, and the Mandarin Chinese as well as the Hausa and Nupe of Africa with six. Of course, it is understandable that cultures have more need to talk about different colors as they grow more complex. Small bands of

New Guinea hunters need to evaluate the darkness of shadows which might conceal enemies or animal prey; complex European cultures need additional terms to talk about color-coded electrical circuits. Ever since Berlin and Kay put forth in 1969 their startling analysis of the basic color terms in ninety-eight languages, their findings have been under attack, primarily on the basis of questioned methodology and ethnocentric bias. But their general conclusions have also been defended by other researchers. Apparently Berlin and Kay have isolated some general truths about how people around the world talk about color and the possible evolutionary implications of language—even though neither they nor anyone else has been able to offer a suitable explanation for why languages seem to add words for colors to their vocabularies in such an orderly sequence.

Nor is the way in which a speech community rounds off its numbers haphazard; rather it is explainable as an interplay between language and culture. Americans and Englishmen have traditionally expressed excellence in sports by certain round numbers—the 4-minute mile, the 7-foot high jump, the 70-foot shot put, the .300 baseball batting average. Once a speech community has established a general range of goals of excellence that are within the realm of possibility, the exact number chosen has little to do with the objective reality of measurable goals. Instead, the community chooses an exact goal that makes sense to it linguistically in terms of the measure it uses and the way it rounds off numbers. That is why Americans and Englishmen never talk about the 3⅞-minute mile or the 69-foot shot put.

The American-British target for the 100-yard dash is 9 seconds, but the French speech community, which uses the metric system, expresses the target as 100 meters in 10 seconds. Simple arithmetic shows that the two goals do not refer to equal distances covered in comparable amounts of time. Allowing for 10 seconds of running time, the metric race would mean covering 109.36 yards and the American-British race would mean covering 111.1 yards. Obviously, the French goal for excellence speaks about a different real distance than the American or English—simply because a Frenchman rounds off his numbers for distances and for time in a different way than English-speaking peoples do. When speakers thus round off numbers to make them manageable, they give preference to those numbers that their speech community regards as significant. Americans see nothing wrong with rounding off numbers to 4 because they are familiar with that number for measurement, as in 4 ounces in a quarter pound or 4 quarts in a gallon. A Frenchman, however, would not regard such a number as round at all; because of his familiarity with the decimal system, he would round off to 5.

A speech community's method of rounding off its numbers often bears no relation to the real situation, and it may actually work against the best interests of the community. Fishing laws in some states specify, for example, that half a dozen trout larger than 10 inches may be caught in a day. Research by fish-management specialists might instead indicate that trout would thrive better if fishermen took 7 (not half a dozen) trout larger than 10½ (not 10) inches—but

Americans round off to 6 and 10, not to 7 and 10½. The ideal speed for a stretch of highway, as scientifically determined by engineers, might be 57 miles per hour—but that number will be rounded off to a too-slow 55 or a too-fast 60 because it is customary for highway speeds to be based on the decimal system. Only one justification exists for the use of imprecise rounded numbers: The speech community has decreed that the linguistic ease of inexact combinations is preferable to the linguistic complexity of precise numbers.

That the way speakers round off numbers is often a linguistic convenience is clearly seen by comparing English with other languages. The ancient Greeks rounded off to 60 and 360 for their high numbers; and the old Germanic languages of northern Europe used 120 to mean "many." Most of the Indian tribes in primeval California based their numbers on multiples of 5 and 10. However, at least half a dozen tribes found great significance in the number 4, no doubt because it expressed the cardinal directions. Others emphasized the number 6, which probably represented the four directions plus the above-ground and below-ground worlds. The Yuki of northern California were unique in counting in multiples of 8 and in rounding off high numbers at 64.

A misunderstanding about the way Chinese speakers round off their numbers has led many Europeans to state glibly that "in China you're a year old when you're born." That is because most European systems of stating one's age are different from the Chinese. In English, a speaker usually states his age as his most recent birthday followed by the measure *years old.* Exceptions are young children who often place their age between birthdays, as in *I'm three and a half years old,* and parents who usually express the age of infants in months and weeks. Chinese also use a round number followed by the measure *swei* in place of the English measure *years old.* Confusion has resulted because *swei* is not exactly equivalent to the English measure but rather is closer in meaning to "the number of years during all or part of which one has been alive." In the case of newborn infants, they have, according to the *swei* measure, already lived for "part" of a year—and therefore their age is *yi swei,* which English translators usually render erroneously as "one year old" instead of as "part of one year."

Each language also encourages certain kinds of place names and makes difficult the formation of others. *Golden Gate* is a typical English place name, a noun *(Gate)* modified by an adjective *(Golden)*—but *Gately Gold* is an improbable construction in English and no place is likely to bear such a name. The importance of a language's structure in determining place names was pointed out by the anthropologist Franz Boas when he compared terms used by the Kwakiutl Indians and the Eskimos. The Kwakiutl are a seafaring people of British Columbia, Canada, whose survival is based almost solely on what they can wrest from the Pacific Ocean and the nearby rivers. So it is no wonder that their place names rarely celebrate history or myth but instead are descriptive in order to give practical benefits in navigation and in food-gathering, such as Island at the Foot of the Mountains, Mouth of the River, Having Wind, Place for Stopping, and so on. The Kwakiutl language makes it easy to form descriptive names because suffixes can be conveniently added to stem words. For example, a Kwakiutl speaker can discriminate among a great number of different kinds of islands—Island at the Point, Island in the Middle, and so on—simply by adding the suffixes for "at the point" and "in the middle" to the stem word for "island."

The nearby Eskimos also base their culture on the sea, and so they might be expected to name places in a similar way. But they do not—because the structure of their language makes it very difficult to do so. What are suffixes in Kwakiutl are in Eskimo the very words to which suffixes are added. Eskimos cannot create the name Island at the Point because in their language "at the point" is not a suffix but a stem word to which other words are added. To describe a place as Island at the Point, the Eskimo speaker would have to put together a circumlocution much too complicated for everyday use. Furthermore, the Eskimo language offers its speakers only a limited number of suffixes to attach to stem words, whereas Kwakiutl offers a great many. The result is that Kwakiutl possesses an extraordinarily rich and poetic catalogue of place names—such as Birch Trees at the Mouth of the River and Receptacle of the North Wind, names that make one's heart yearn to visit the places they identify—whereas the Eskimo list is considerably shorter and much less metaphorical.

Eskimos do not differ significantly from Kwakiutls in intelligence, imagination, the ability to abstract, or other mental capacities. Solely because of the structure of his language, the Eskimo fisherman is unable to talk easily about a place the Kwakiutl names Birch Trees at the Mouth of the River. If an Eskimo has no easy way to talk about a clump of birches at the mouth of a river, will he therefore be less alert to perceive that kind of a place? And is it possible that language, instead of clarifying reality, forces the Eskimo to think about the world in ways different from speakers of Kwakiutl or other languages?

Such a connection between language and thought is rooted in common-sense beliefs, but no one gave much attention to the matter before Wilhelm von Humboldt, the nineteenth-century German philologist and diplomat. He stated that the structure of a language expresses the inner life of its speakers: "Man lives with the world about him, principally, indeed exclusively, as language presents it." In this century, the case for a close relationship between language and reality was stated by Edward Sapir:

> Human beings do not live in the objective world alone, nor alone in the world of social activity as ordinarily understood, but are very much at the mercy of the particular language which has become the medium for their society. . . . The fact of the matter is that the "real world" is to a large extent built up on the language habits of the group. No two languages are ever sufficiently similar to be considered as representing the same social reality. The worlds in which different societies live are distinct worlds, not merely the same world with different labels attached.

About 1932 one of Sapir's students at Yale, Benjamin Lee Whorf, drew on Sapir's ideas and began an intensive study of the language of the Hopi Indians of Arizona. Whorf's brilliant analysis of Hopi placed common-sense beliefs about language and thought on a scientific basis—and it also seemed to support the view that man is a prisoner of his language. Whorf concluded that language "is not merely a reproducing instrument for voicing ideas but rather is itself the shaper of ideas. . . . We dissect nature along lines laid down by our native languages."

Whorf emphasized grammar—rather than vocabulary, which had previously intrigued scholars—as an indicator of the way a language can direct a speaker into certain habits of thought. The Eskimo speaker, for example, possesses a large and precise vocabulary to make exacting distinctions between the kinds and conditions of seals, such as "young spotted seal," "swimming male ribbon seal," and so on. But such an extensive vocabulary has less to do with the structure of the Eskimo language than with the fact that seals are important for the survival of its speakers. The Eskimo would find equally strange the distinctions that the English vocabulary makes about horses—*mare, stallion, pony, bay, paint, appaloosa,* and so forth. And both Eskimos and Americans would be bewildered by the seventeen terms for cattle among the Masai of Africa, the twenty terms for rice among the Ifugeo of the Philippines, or the thousands of Arabic words associated with camels.

Instead of vocabulary, Whorf concentrated on the differences in structure between Hopi and the European languages—and also on what he believed were associated differences in the ways speakers of these languages viewed the world. In his analysis of plurality, for example, he noted that English uses a plural form for both *five men* and *five days. Men* and *days* are both nouns, but they are otherwise quite different. A speaker can see with his own eyes a group of five men, but he cannot perceive five days through any of his senses. To visualize what a day looks like, the speaker of English has to conjure up some sort of abstract picture, such as a circle, and then imagine a group of five such circles. The Hopi has no such problem. He does not rely on his imagination to provide him with plurals that cannot be detected by his senses. He would never use a cyclic noun—one that refers to "days," "years," or other units of time—in the same way that he would use an aggregate noun ("men"). His language is more precise, and he has a separate category altogether for cycles. For him, cycles do not have plurals but rather duration, and so the Hopi equivalent for the English *He stayed five days* is "He stayed until the sixth day."

Nor does the Hopi language possess tenses, which in most European languages stand time in a row as distinct units of past, present, and future. A speaker of English expresses an event that is happening in the present as *He runs* or *He is running,* but the speaker of Hopi can select from a much wider choice of present tenses, depending upon his knowledge, or lack of it, about the validity of the statement he is making: "I know that he is running at this very moment." "I know that he is running at this moment even though I cannot see him." "I remember that I saw him running and I presume he is still running." "I am told that he is running."

A further contrast between the two languages concerns duration and intensity. English employs such words as *long, short,* and *slow* for duration and *much, large,* and *high* for intensity. Speakers of English, accustomed to this usage, overlook the fact that these words refer to size, shape, number, or motion—that is, they are really metaphors for space. Such a situation is quite ridiculous because duration and intensity are not spatial. Yet speakers of English unconsciously use these metaphors for space in even the simplest utterances—such as *He* SLOWLY *grasped the* POINT *of the* LONG *story* or *The* LEVEL *of the assignment was* TOO HIGH *and so the student considered it* A LOT OF *nonsense.* The Hopi language is equally striking in its avoidance of metaphors of imaginary space for qualities that are nonspatial.

After his painstaking analysis of such differences between Hopi and European languages, Whorf asked the question that was central to his research. Do the Hopi and European cultures confirm the fact that their languages conceptualize reality in different ways? And his answer was that they do. Whereas European cultures are organized in terms of space and time, the Hopi culture, Whorf believed, emphasizes events. To speakers of European languages, time is a commodity that occurs between fixed points and can be measured. Time is said to be *wasted* or *saved;* an army fighting a rear-guard action tries to *buy* time; a television station *sells* time to an advertiser. People in the European tradition keep diaries, records, accounts, and histories; their economic systems emphasize wages paid for the amount of time worked, rent for the time a dwelling is occupied, interest for the time money is loaned.

Hopi culture has none of these beliefs about time, but instead thinks of it in terms of events. Plant a seed—and it will grow. The span of time the growing takes is not the important thing, but rather the way in which the event of growth follows the event of planting. The Hopi is concerned that the sequence of events in the construction of a building be in the correct order, not that it takes a certain amount of time to complete the job. That is why the building of a Hopi house, adobe brick by adobe brick, may go on for years. Whorf's comparison of Hopi and European languages and cultures—considerably more involved than the summary I have presented—convinced him that the contrasting world views of their speakers resulted from contrasts in their languages. He concluded that, linguistically speaking, no human being is born free; his mind was made up for him from the day he was born by the language of his speech community. Whorf questioned people's ability to be objective, and he threw into doubt the rationality of everyday utterances. He suggested that all their lives English speakers have been tricked by their language into thinking along certain channels—and it is small consolation to know that the Hopi has also been tricked, but in a different way.

Whorf's theories about the relationship between culture and language have been greeted enthusiastically by some scholars and attacked or treated warily by others. The weakness of the Sapir–Whorf Hypothesis, as it has come to be known, is the impossibility of generalizing about entire cultures and then attributing these generalizations to the languages spoken. The absence of clocks, calendars, and written histories obviously gave the Hopis a different view of time than that found among speakers of European languages. But such an observation is not the same thing as proving that these cultural differences were caused by the differences between Hopi and European grammars. In fact, an interest in time-reckoning is not characteristic solely of European cultures but can be found among speakers of languages as different as Egyptian, Chinese, and Maya. And, on the other hand, thousands of unrelated speech communities share with the Hopis a lack of concern about keeping track of time. To attempt to explain cultural differences and similarities as a significant result of the languages spoken is to leave numerous facts about culture unexplained. The great religions of the world—Judaism, Christianity, Hinduism, and Mohammedanism—have flourished among diverse peoples who speak languages with sharply different grammars. Mohammedanism, for example, has been accepted by speakers of languages with grammars as completely different as those of the Hamito-Semitic, Turkish, Indo-Iranian, Tibeto-Burman, and Malayo-Polynesian families. And the reverse is true as well. Cultures as diverse as the Aztec Empire of Mexico and the Ute hunting bands of the Great Basin spoke very closely related tongues.

Nevertheless, attempts have been made to prove the Sapir–Whorf Hypothesis, such as one experiment which used as test subjects bilingual Japanese women, living in San Francisco, who had married American servicemen. The women spoke English to their husbands, children, and neighbors, and in most everyday speech situations; they spoke Japanese whenever they came together to gossip, reminisce, and discuss the news from home. Each Japanese woman thus inhabited two language worlds—and according to the predictions of the hypothesis, the women should think differently in each of these worlds. The experiment consisted of two visits to each woman by a bilingual Japanese interviewer. During the first interview he chatted with them only in Japanese; during the second he carried on the same discussion and asked the same questions in English. The results were quite remarkable; they showed that the attitudes of each woman differed markedly, depending upon whether she spoke Japanese or English. Here, for example, is the way the same woman completed the same sentences at the two interviews:

> "When my wishes conflict with my family's . . .
> . . . it is a time of great unhappiness." (Japanese)
> . . . I do what I want." (English)

> "Real friends should . . .
> . . . help each other." (Japanese)
> . . . be very frank." (English)

Clearly, major variables in the experiment had been eliminated—since the women were interviewed twice by the same person in the same location of their homes, and they discussed the same topics—with but one exception. And that sole exception was language. The drastic differences in attitudes of the women could be accounted for only by the language world each inhabited when she spoke.

The Sapir–Whorf Hypothesis also predicts that language makes its speakers intellectually lazy. They will categorize new experiences in the well-worn channels they have been used to since birth, even though these channels might appear foolish to an outsider. The language spoken by the Western Apaches of Arizona, for example, has long had its own channels for classifying the parts of the human body, a system which ignores certain distinctions made in other languages and which makes different ones of its own. Then, about 1930, a new cultural item, the automobile, was introduced into the Apache reservation. An automobile, surely, is different from a human body, yet the Apaches simply applied their existing classification for the human body to the automobile. The chart below lists approximate pronunciations of the Apache words for the parts of the human body, the way they are categorized—and the way their meanings were extended to classify that new cultural item, the automobile.

Many linguists nowadays are wary of the Sapir–Whorf Hypothesis. Research that has attempted to confirm the hypothesis, such as the experiment with the Japanese women or the study of Apache terms for the automobile, is usually

Apache Words for Parts of the Human Body and the Automobile

Human Anatomical Terms		Extended Auto Meanings
EXTERNAL ANATOMY:		
daw	"chin and jaw"	"front bumper"
wos	"shoulder"	"front fender"
gun	"hand and arm"	"front wheel"
kai	"thigh and buttocks"	"rear fender"
ze	"mouth"	"gas-pipe opening"
ke	"foot"	"rear wheel"
chun	"back"	"chassis"
inda	"eye"	"headlight"
FACE:		
chee	"nose"	"hood"
ta	"forehead"	"auto top"
ENTRAILS:		
tsaws	"vein"	"electrical wiring"
zik	"liver"	"battery"
pit	"stomach"	"gas tank"
chih	"intestine"	"radiator hose"
jih	"heart"	"distributor"
jisoleh	"lung"	"radiator"

regarded as fascinating examples rather than as universal truths about the way speech communities view the world. Neither Whorf nor any of his followers has proven to everyone's satisfaction that differences between two speech communities in their capacity to understand external reality are based entirely or even overwhelmingly on differences in their languages. Whorf overemphasized one point (that languages differ in what *can* be said in them) at the expense of a greater truth (that they differ as to what is *relatively easy* to express in them). Languages, rather than causing cultural differences between speech communities, seem instead to reflect the different cultural concerns of their speakers. The history of language is not so much the story of people misled by their languages as it is the story of a successful struggle against the limitations built into all language systems. The Western Apache system for classifying the human body did not lock them into certain habitual patterns of thought that prevented them from understanding the automobile. In fact, the existence of these patterns may have aided the Apaches in making sense out of that new cultural item.

The true value of Whorf's theories is not the one he worked so painstakingly to demonstrate—that language tyrannizes speakers by forcing them to think in certain ways. Rather, his work emphasized something of even greater importance: the close alliance between language and the total culture of the speech community. No linguist today doubts that language and culture interpenetrate one another; nor does any linguist fail to pay due respect to Whorf for emphasizing this fact.

References

Basso, Keith H. 1967. "Semantic Aspects of Linguistic Acculturation." *American Anthropologist*, vol. 69, pp. 471–477.

Berlin, Brent, and Kay, Paul. 1969. *Basic Color Terms: Their Universality and Evolution.* University of California Press.

Brown, Roger, and Lenneberg, Eric H. 1954. "A Study in Language and Cognition." *Journal of Abnormal and Social Psychology*, vol. 49, pp. 454–462.

Ervin-Tripp, Susan. 1964. "Interaction of Language, Topic and Listener." *American Anthropologist*, vol. 66, pp. 86–102.

Ferguson, Charles A. 1968. "Language Development." In Fishman, Ferguson, C.A., and Das Gupta, J., editors. 1968. *Language Problems of Developing Nations.* Wiley.

Fridja, N.H., and Van de Geer, J.P. 1961. "Codeability and Facial Expressions." *Acta Psychologica*, vol. 18, pp. 360–367.

Gleason, Henry A., Jr. 1961. *An Introduction to Descriptive Linguistics.* Holt, Rinehart & Winston, revised edition.

Hays, David G., *et al.* 1972. "Color Term Salience." *American Anthropologist*, vol. 74, pp. 1107–1121.

Heider, Eleanor R. 1972 A. "Universals in Color Naming and Memory." *Journal of Experimental Psychology*, vol. 93, pp. 10–20.

———. 1972 B. "The Structure of the Color Space in Naming and Memory for Two Languages." *Cognitive Psychology*, vol. 3, pp. 337–354.

Heizer, R.F., and Whipple, M.A. 1951. *The California Indians.* University of California Press.

Hoijer, Harry, editor. 1954. *Language in Culture.* University of Chicago Press.

Hymes, Dell H., editor. 1964. *Language in Culture and Society: A Reader in Linguistics and Anthropology.* Harper & Row.
———. 1961. "Functions of Speech: An Evolutionary Approach." In *Anthropology and Education,* edited by Frederick C. Gruber (1961), pp. 55–83. University of Pennsylvania Press.
Lotz, John. "On Language and Culture." In Hymes (1964), pp. 182–183.
Menninger, Karl. 1969. *Number Words and Number Symbols.* M.I.T. Press.
Nickerson, Nancy P. 1971. "Review of Basic Color Terms." *International Journal of American Linguistics,* vol. 37, pp. 257–270.
Sapir, Edward. 1929. "The Status of Linguistics as a Science." *Language,* vol. 5, pp. 207–214.
Sartre, Jean-Paul. 1959. *Nausea.* New Directions.
Swadesh, Morris. 1971. *The Origin and Diversification of Language,* edited by Joel Sherzer, Aldine-Atherton.
Whorf, Benjamin L. 1956. *Language, Thought and Reality.* M.I.T. Press.
Wittgenstein, Ludwig. 1963. *Tractatus Logico-Philosophicus.* Humanities Press, second edition.

Questions for Discussion and Writing

1. Farb quotes Ludwig Wittgenstein's thinking about language: "The limits of my language mean the limits of my world" (p. 146). Wittgenstein argued that if the limits of language could somehow be defined, speakers would not attempt to express the inexpressible. What do you think the philosopher meant when he said not to put too great a burden on language?
2. Farb refers to our long history of regarding language as a "holy instrument," a "window on the world" (p. 146). How are these attitudes about language changing today, and why?
3. What examples does Farb use in the essay to help us understand that "each language can comment upon experience only in its own way" (p. 148)?
4. Farb uses the color spectrum to explain the variations in perception that result from the naming of colors in different cultures. What ideas about these variations in perception did you gain from the comparison he makes among the English, the Shona, and the Bassa?
5. Explain your understanding of the weaknesses and strengths of the Sapir–Whorf hypothesis. Use examples of cultures from the essay to support your response.
6. Keeping in mind that this essay was published in 1973 as part of the book *Word Play,* in what ways can you argue that its title—"Man at the Mercy of Language"—reflects the relationship of language to culture and history?

GORDON W. ALLPORT

Linguistic Factors in Prejudice

Personality theory, social ethics, religion, and prejudice were pri-
mary among the lifelong interests of psychologist Gordon W. All-
port. After a one-year stint as instructor in English at Robert College
in Istanbul, Turkey (1919–1920), Allport began his career in teach-
ing and studying psychology. Following completion of his Ph.D.
from Harvard University in 1922, Allport taught psychology at
Dartmouth College for four years and then at Harvard until his
death at the age of seventy in 1967.

In addition to more than two hundred journal articles, Allport also
found time to write a long list of books on a strikingly diverse range
of subjects—from The Psychology of Radio *(1935) to* Waiting for the
Lord: 33 Meditations on God and Man *(published posthumously in*
1978).

"Linguistic Factors in Prejudice" is taken from one of Allport's
most important contributions, The Nature of Prejudice *(1954). In*
this essay, the author helps us to understand why the role of lan-
guage is central to the formation and perpetuation of prejudice.

Before you read "Linguistic Factors in Prejudice," write about a time in
your life when someone used a label to describe you—a label that hurt
you and maybe even changed the way you saw yourself. Looking back to
the experience now, why do you think that label had such a powerful effect on you? How does your experience deny the truth of that old childhood ditty, "Sticks and stones may break my bones, but words will never
hurt me"?

W ithout words we should scarcely be able to form categories at all. A dog
    perhaps forms rudimentary generalizations, such as small-boys-are-to-
be-avoided—but this concept runs its course on the conditioned reflex level, and
does not become the object of thought as such. In order to hold a generalization

161

in mind for reflection and recall, for identification and for action, we need to fix it in words. Without words our world would be, as William James said, an "empirical sand-heap."

Nouns That Cut Slices

In the empirical world of human beings there are some two and a half billion grains of sand corresponding to our category "the human race." We cannot possibly deal with so many separate entities in our thought, nor can we individualize even among the hundreds whom we encounter in our daily round. We must group them, form clusters. We welcome, therefore, the names that help us to perform the clustering.

The most important property of a noun is that it brings many grains of sand into a single pail, disregarding the fact that the same grains might have fitted just as appropriately into another pail. To state the matter technically, a noun *abstracts* from a concrete reality some one feature and assembles different concrete realities only with respect to this one feature. The very act of classifying forces us to overlook all other features, many of which might offer a sounder basis than the rubric we select. Irving Lee gives the following example:

> I knew a man who had lost the use of both eyes. He was called a "blind man." He could also be called an expert typist, a conscientious worker, a good student, a careful listener, a man who wanted a job. But he couldn't get a job in the department store order room where employees sat and typed orders which came over the telephone. The personnel man was impatient to get the interview over. "But you're a blind man," he kept saying, and one could almost feel his silent assumption that somehow the incapacity in one aspect made the man incapable in every other. So blinded by the label was the interviewer that he could not be persuaded to look beyond it. [1]

Some labels, such as "blind man," are exceedingly salient and powerful. They tend to prevent alternative classification, or even cross-classification. Ethnic labels are often of this type, particularly if they refer to some highly visible feature, e.g., Negro, Oriental. They resemble the labels that point to some outstanding incapacity—*feeble-minded, cripple, blind man*. Let us call such symbols "labels of primary potency." These symbols act like shrieking sirens, deafening us to all finer discriminations that we might otherwise perceive. Even though the blindness of one man and the darkness of pigmentation of another may be defining attributes for some purposes, they are irrelevant and "noisy" for others.

Most people are unaware of this basic law of language—that every label applied to a given person refers properly only to one aspect of his nature. You may correctly say that a certain man is *human, a philanthropist, a Chinese, a physician, an athlete*. A given person may be all of these; but the chances are that *Chinese* stands out in your mind as the symbol of primary potency. Yet neither this nor

Labels of Primary Potency

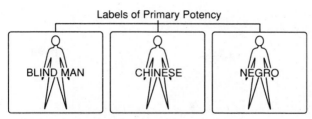

The effect of linguistic symbols upon perception and thinking about individuals.

any other classificatory label can refer to the whole of a man's nature. (Only his proper name can do so.)

Thus each label we use, especially those of primary potency, distracts our attention from concrete reality. The living, breathing, complex individual—the ultimate unit of human nature—is lost to sight. As in the figure, the label magnifies one attribute out of all proportion to its true significance, and masks other important attributes of the individual.

. . . [A] category, once formed with the aid of a symbol of primary potency, tends to attract more attributes than it should. The category labeled *Chinese* comes to signify not only ethnic membership but also reticence, impassivity, poverty, treachery. To be sure, . . . there may be genuine ethnic-linked traits, making for a certain *probability* that the member of an ethnic stock may have these attributes. But our cognitive process is not cautious. The labeled category, as we have seen, includes indiscriminately the defining attribute, probable attributes, and wholly fanciful, nonexistent attributes.

Even proper names—which ought to invite us to look at the individual person—may act like symbols of primary potency, especially if they arouse ethnic associations. Mr. Greenberg is a person, but since his name is Jewish, it activates in the hearer his entire category of Jews-as-a-whole. An ingenious experiment performed by Razran shows this point clearly, and at the same time demonstrates how a proper name, acting like an ethnic symbol, may bring with it an avalanche of stereotypes. [2]

Thirty photographs of college girls were shown on a screen to 150 students. The subjects rated the girls on a scale from one to five for *beauty, intelligence, character, ambition, general likability.* Two months later the same subjects were asked to rate the same photographs and fifteen additional ones (introduced to complicate the memory factor). This time five of the original photographs were given Jewish surnames (Cohen, Kantor, etc.), five Italian (Valenti, etc.), and five Irish (O'Brien, etc.); and the remaining girls were given names chosen from the signers of the Declaration of Independence and from the Social Register (Davis, Adams, Clark, etc.).

When Jewish names were attached to photographs there occurred the following changes in ratings:

decrease in liking
decrease in character
decrease in beauty
increase in intelligence
increase in ambition

For those photographs given Italian names there occurred:

decrease in liking
decrease in character
decrease in beauty
decrease in intelligence

Thus a mere proper name leads to prejudgments of personal attributes. The individual is fitted to the prejudiced ethnic category, and not judged in his own right.

While the Irish names also brought about depreciated judgment, the depreciation was not as great as in the case of the Jews and Italians. The falling of likability of the "Jewish girls" was twice as great as for "Italians" and five times as great as for "Irish." We note, however, that the "Jewish" photographs caused higher ratings in *intelligence* and in *ambition*. Not all stereotypes of out-groups are unfavorable.

The anthropologist, Margaret Mead, has suggested that labels of primary potency lose some of their force when they are changed from nouns into adjectives. To speak of a Negro soldier, a Catholic teacher, or a Jewish artist calls attention to the fact that some other group classifications are just as legitimate as the racial or religious. If George Johnson is spoken of not only as a Negro but also as a *soldier,* we have at least two attributes to know him by, and two are more accurate than one. To depict him truly as an individual, of course, we should have to name many more attributes. It is a useful suggestion that we designate ethnic and religious membership where possible with *adjectives* rather than with *nouns.*

Emotionally Toned Labels

Many categories have two kinds of labels—one less emotional and one more emotional. Ask yourself how you feel, and what thoughts you have, when you read the words *school teacher,* and then *school marm.* Certainly the second phrase calls up something more strict, more ridiculous, more disagreeable than the former. Here are four innocent letters: m-a-r-m. But they make us shudder a bit, laugh a bit, and scorn a bit. They call up an image of a spare, humorless, irritable old maid. They do not tell us that she is an individual human being with sorrows and troubles of her own. They force her instantly into a rejective category.

In the ethnic sphere even plain labels such as Negro, Italian, Jew, Catholic, Irish-American, French-Canadian may have emotional tone for a reason that we shall soon explain. But they all have their higher key equivalents: nigger, wop, kike, papist, harp, cannuck. When these labels are employed we can be almost certain that the speaker *intends* not only to characterize the person's membership, but also to disparage and reject him.

Quite apart from the insulting intent that lies behind the use of certain labels, there is also an inherent ("physiognomic") handicap in many terms designating ethnic membership. For example, the proper names characteristic of certain ethnic memberships strike us as absurd. (We compare them, of course, with what is familiar and therefore "right.") Chinese names are short and silly; Polish names intrinsically difficult and outlandish. Unfamiliar dialects strike us as ludicrous. Foreign dress (which, of course, is a visual ethnic symbol) seems unnecessarily queer.

But of all these "physiognomic" handicaps the reference to color, clearly implied in certain symbols, is the greatest. The word Negro comes from the Latin *niger,* meaning black. In point of fact, no Negro has a black complexion, but by comparison with other blonder stocks, he has come to be known as a "black man." Unfortunately *black* in the English language is a word having a preponderance of sinister connotations: the outlook is black, blackball, blackguard, black-hearted, black death, blacklist, blackmail, Black Hand. In his novel *Moby Dick,* Herman Melville considers at length the remarkably morbid connotations of black and the remarkably virtuous connotations of white.

Nor is the ominous flavor of black confined to the English language. A cross-cultural study reveals that the semantic significance of black is more or less universally the same. Among certain Siberian tribes, members of a privileged clan call themselves "white bones," and refer to all others as "black bones." Even among Uganda Negroes there is some evidence for a white god at the apex of the theocratic hierarchy; certain it is that a white cloth, signifying purity, is used to ward off evil spirits and disease.[3]

There is thus an implied value-judgment in the very concept of *white race* and *black race.* One might also study the numerous unpleasant connotations of *yellow,* and their possible bearing on our conception of the people of the Orient.

Such reasoning should not be carried too far, since there are undoubtedly, in various contexts, pleasant associations with both black and yellow. Black velvet is agreeable, so too are chocolate and coffee. Yellow tulips are well liked; the sun and moon are radiantly yellow. Yet it is true that "color" words are used with chauvinistic overtones more than most people realize. There is certainly conde-scension indicated in many familiar phrases: dark as a nigger's pocket, darktown strutters, white hope (a term originated when a white contender was sought against the Negro heavyweight champion, Jack Johnson), the white man's burden, the yellow peril, black boy. Scores of everyday phrases are stamped with the flavor of prejudice, whether the user knows it or not.[4]

We spoke of the fact that even the most proper and sedate labels for minority groups sometimes seem to exude a negative flavor. In many contexts and situations the very terms *French-Canadian, Mexican,* or *Jew,* correct and nonmalicious though they are, sound a bit opprobrious. The reason is that they are labels of social deviants. Especially in a culture where uniformity is prized, the name of *any* deviant carries with it *ipso facto* a negative value-judgment. Words like *insane, alcoholic, pervert* are presumably neutral designations of a human condition, but they are more: they are finger-pointings at deviance. Minority groups are deviants, and for this reason, from the very outset, the most innocent labels in many situations imply a shading of disrepute. When we wish to highlight the deviance and denigrate it still further we use words of a higher emotional key: crackpot, soak, pansy, greaser, Okie, nigger, harp, kike.

Members of minority groups are often understandably sensitive to names given them. Not only do they object to deliberately insulting epithets, but sometimes see evil intent where none exists. Often the word Negro is spelled with a small *n,* occasionally as a studied insult, more often from ignorance. (The term is not cognate with white, which is not capitalized, but rather with Caucasian, which is.) Terms like "mulatto" or "octoroon" cause hard feeling because of the condescension with which they have often been used in the past. Sex differentiations are objectionable, since they seem doubly to emphasize ethnic difference: why speak of Jewess and not of Protestantess, or of Negress and not of whitess? Similar overemphasis is implied in terms like Chinaman or Scotchman; why not American man? Grounds for misunderstanding lie in the fact that minority group members are sensitive to such shadings, while majority members may employ them unthinkingly.

The Communist Label

Until we label an out-group it does not clearly exist in our minds. Take the curiously vague situation that we often meet when a person wishes to locate responsibility on the shoulders of some out-group whose nature he cannot specify. In such a case he usually employs the pronoun "they" without an antecedent. "Why don't they make these sidewalks wider?" "I hear they are going to build a factory in this town and hire a lot of foreigners." "I won't pay this tax bill; they can just whistle for their money." If asked "who?" the speaker is likely to grow confused and embarrassed. The common use of the orphaned pronoun *they* teaches us that people often want and need to designate out-groups (usually for the purpose of venting hostility) even when they have no clear conception of the out-group in question. And so long as the target of wrath remains vague and ill-defined specific prejudice cannot crystallize around it. To have enemies we need labels.

Until relatively recently—strange as it may seem—there was no agreed-upon symbol for *communist*. The word, of course, existed but it had no special emotional connotation, and did not designate a public enemy. Even when, after World War I, there was a growing feeling of economic and social menace in this country, there was no agreement as to the actual source of the menace.

A content analysis of the *Boston Herald* for the year 1920 turned up the following list of labels. Each was used in a context implying some threat. Hysteria had overspread the country, as it did after World War II. Someone must be responsible for the postwar malaise, rising prices, uncertainty. There must be a villain. But in 1920 the villain was impartially designated by reporters and editorial writers with the following symbols:

> alien, agitator, anarchist, apostle of bomb and torch, Bolshevik, communist, communist laborite, conspirator, emissary of false promise, extremist, foreigner, hyphenated-American, incendiary, IWW, parlor anarchist, parlor pink, parlor socialist, plotter, radical, red, revolutionary, Russian agitator, socialist, Soviet, syndicalist, traitor, undesirable.

From this excited array we note that the *need* for an enemy (someone to serve as a focus for discontent and jitters) was considerably more apparent than the precise *identity* of the enemy. At any rate, there was no clearly agreed upon label. Perhaps partly for this reason the hysteria abated. Since no clear category of "communism" existed there was no true focus for the hostility.

But following World War II this collection of vaguely interchangeable labels became fewer in number and more commonly agreed upon. The out-group menace came to be designated almost always as *communist* or *red*. In 1920 the threat, lacking a clear label, was vague; after 1945 both symbol and thing became more definite. Not that people knew precisely what they meant when they said "communist," but with the aid of the term they were at least able to point consistently to *something* that inspired fear. The term developed the power of signifying menace and led to various repressive measures against anyone to whom the label was rightly or wrongly attached.

Logically, the label should apply to specifiable defining attributes, such as members of the Communist Party, or people whose allegiance is with the Russian system, or followers, historically, of Karl Marx. But the label came in for far more extensive use.

What seems to have happened is approximately as follows. Having suffered through a period of war and being acutely aware of devastating revolutions abroad, it is natural that most people should be upset, dreading to lose their possessions, annoyed by high taxes, seeing customary moral and religious values threatened, and dreading worse disasters to come. Seeking an explanation for this unrest, a single identifiable enemy is wanted. It is not enough to designate "Russia" or some other distant land. Nor is it satisfactory to fix blame on "changing social conditions." What is needed is a human agent . . . near at hand: someone in Washington, someone in our schools, in our factories, in our neighborhood. If we *feel* an immediate threat, we reason, there must be a near-lying danger. It is, we conclude, communism, not only in Russia but also in America, at our doorstep, in our government, in our churches, in our colleges, in our neighborhood.

Are we saying that hostility toward communism is prejudice? Not necessarily. There are certainly phases of the dispute wherein realistic social conflict is involved. American values (e.g., respect for the person) and totalitarian values as represented in Soviet practice are intrinsically at odds. A realistic opposition in some form will occur. Prejudice enters only when the defining attributes of "communist" grow imprecise, when anyone who favors any form of social change is called a communist. People who fear social change are the ones most likely to affix the label to any persons or practices that seem to them threatening.

For them the category is undifferentiated. It includes books, movies, preachers, teachers who utter what for them are uncongenial thoughts. If evil befalls— perhaps forest fires or a factory explosion—it is due to communist saboteurs. The category becomes monopolistic, covering almost anything that is uncongenial. On the floor of the House of Representatives in 1946, Representative Rankin called James Roosevelt a communist. Congressman Outland replied with psychological acumen, "Apparently everyone who disagrees with Mr. Rankin is a communist."

When differentiated thinking is at a low ebb—as it is in times of social crises— there is a magnification of two-valued logic. Things are perceived as either inside or outside a moral order. What is outside is likely to be called "communist." Correspondingly—and here is where damage is done—whatever is called communist (however erroneously) is immediately cast outside the moral order.

This associative mechanism places enormous power in the hands of a demagogue. For several years Senator McCarthy managed to discredit many citizens who thought differently from himself by the simple device of calling them communists. Few people were able to see through this trick and many reputations were ruined. But the famous senator has no monopoly on the device. As reported in the *Boston Herald* on November 1, 1946, Representative Joseph Martin, Republican leader in the House, ended his election campaign against his Democratic opponent by saying, "The people will vote tomorrow between chaos, confusion, bankruptcy, state socialism or communism, and the preservation of our American life, with all its freedom and its opportunities." Such an array of emotional labels placed his opponent outside the accepted moral order. Martin was re-elected.

◄►

Not everyone, of course, is taken in. Demagogy, when it goes too far, meets with ridicule. Elizabeth Dilling's book, *The Red Network,* was so exaggerated in its two-valued logic that it was shrugged off by many people with a smile. One reader remarked, "Apparently if you step off the sidewalk with your left foot you're a communist." But it is not easy in times of social strain and hysteria to keep one's balance, and to resist the tendency of a verbal symbol to manufacture large and fanciful categories of prejudiced thinking.

Verbal Realism and Symbol Phobia

Most individuals rebel at being labeled, especially if the label is uncomplimentary. Very few are willing to be called *fascistic, socialistic,* or *anti-Semitic.* Unsavory labels may apply to others; but not to us.

An illustration of the craving that people have to attach favorable symbols to themselves is seen in the community where white people banded together to force out a Negro family that had moved in. They called themselves "Neighborly Endeavor" and chose as their motto the Golden Rule. One of the first acts of this symbol-sanctified band was to sue the man who sold property to Negroes. They then flooded the house which another Negro couple planned to occupy. Such were the acts performed under the banner of the Golden Rule.

Studies made by Stagner[5] and by Hartmann[6] show that a person's political attitudes may in fact entitle him to be called a fascist or a socialist, and yet he will emphatically repudiate the unsavory label, and fail to endorse any movement or candidate that overtly accepts them. In short, there is a *symbol phobia* that corresponds to *symbol realism.* We are more inclined to the former when we ourselves are concerned, though we are much less critical when epithets of "fascist," "communist," "blind man," "school marm" are applied to others.

When symbols provoke strong emotions they are sometimes regarded no longer as symbols, but as actual things. The expressions "son of a bitch" and "liar" are in our culture frequently regarded as "fighting words." Softer and more subtle expressions of contempt may be accepted. But in these particular cases, the epithet itself must be "taken back." We certainly do not change our opponent's attitude by making him take back a word, but it seems somehow important that the word itself be eradicated.

Such verbal realism may reach extreme lengths.

> The City Council of Cambridge, Massachusetts, unanimously passed a resolution (December, 1939) making it illegal "to possess, harbor, sequester, introduce or transport, within the city limits, any book, map, magazine, newspaper, pamphlet, handbill or circular containing the words Lenin or Leningrad."[7]

Such naiveté in confusing language with reality is hard to comprehend unless we recall that word-magic plays an appreciable part in human thinking. The following examples, like the one preceding, are taken from Hayakawa.

> The Malagasy soldier must eschew kidneys, because in the Malagasy language the word for kidney is the same as that for "shot"; so shot he would certainly be if he ate a kidney.
>
> In May, 1937, a state senator of New York bitterly opposed a bill for the control of syphilis because "the innocence of children might be corrupted by a widespread use of the term. . . . This particular word creates a shudder in every decent woman and decent man."

This tendency to reify words underscores the close cohesion that exists between category and symbol. Just the mention of "communist," "Negro," "Jew," "England," "Democrats," will send some people into a panic of fear or a frenzy of anger. Who can say whether it is the word or the thing that annoys them? The label is an intrinsic part of any monopolistic category. Hence to liberate a person from ethnic or political prejudice it is necessary at the same time to liberate him from word fetishism. This fact is well known to students of general semantics who tell us that prejudice is due in large part to verbal realism and to symbol phobia. Therefore any program for the reduction of prejudice must include a large measure of semantic therapy.

Notes and References

1. I. J. Lee. How do you talk about people? *Freedom Pamphlet.* New York: Anti-Defamation League, 1950, 15.
2. G. Razran. Ethnic dislikes and stereotypes: A laboratory study. *Journal of Abnormal and Social Psychology,* 1950, *45,* 7–27.
3. C. E. Osgood. The nature and measurement of meaning. *Psychological Bulletin,* 1952, *49,* 226.
4. L. L. Brown. Words and white chauvinism. *Masses and Mainstream,* 1950, *3,* 3–11. See also: *Prejudice Won't Hide! A Guide for Developing a Language of Equality.* San Francisco: California Federation for Civic Unity, 1950.
5. R. Stagner. Fascist attitudes: An exploratory study. *Journal of Social Psychology,* 1936, *7,* 309–319; Fascist attitudes: their determining conditions, *ibid.,* 438–454.
6. G. Hartmann. The contradiction between the feeling-tone of political party names and public response to their platforms. *Journal of Social Psychology,* 1936, *7,* 336–357.
7. S. I. Hayakawa. *Language in Action.* New York: Harcourt, Brace, 1941, 29.

Questions for Discussion and Writing

1. According to Allport, what is the problem with the act of classifying? What does he mean by "labels of primary potency" (p. 162)? What happens to the "living, breathing, complex individual" (p. 163) when such labels are used?
2. "Until we label an out-group," Allport asserts, "it does not clearly exist in our minds" (p. 166). In what ways does the history of the word *Communist* support this statement?
3. What is the relationship between labels of primary potency and prejudice?
4. What is "semantic therapy" (p. 170), and why is it necessary for people who want to be liberated from ethnic or political prejudice?
5. In what ways can you argue that Allport's essay itself offers semantic therapy? Use concrete examples and brief passages from the text to support your response.

RICHARD RODRIGUEZ

Memories of a Bilingual Childhood

Richard Rodriguez was born in San Francisco in 1944. His parents had both come from Mexico to San Francisco, where they met. Determined that her child would never join the ranks of los pobres—*poor, non-English-speaking workers who were badly exploited—Rodriguez's mother made certain that her son had the advantages of an excellent education. Rodriguez used his early education well, later graduating from Stanford University (1967), receiving his master's degree from Columbia University (1969), and continuing his graduate study at the University of California at Berkeley (1969–1972 and 1974–1975). Since 1981, he has been a full-time writer.*

Rodriguez turned down invitations to teach at several prominent universities because he knew the offers were made under the pressures of affirmative action. He could not withstand the irony of being counted a minority when in fact "the irreversibly successful effort of [his] life had been to become a fully assimilated member of the majority."

"It takes me a very long time to write," Rodriguez has said. His autobiography, Hunger of Memory: The Education of Richard Rodriguez *(1982), took him six years to write. Guided by his own experiences, Rodriguez insists that public educators have an obligation to teach "the language of public society, the language that people outside that public sector resist. . . . My argument has always been that the imperative is to get children away from those languages that increase their sense of alienation from the public society." In the essay that follows, published in 1981 in* American Educator, *Rodriguez argues against bilingual education.*

Before you read "Memories of a Bilingual Childhood," write about the experiences you may have had in bridging the language spoken at home with the language learned in school. Describe the situation in your family, the

problems you encountered at school, and what you learned as a result. If you haven't had this experience, write instead about a time in your life when the language you usually spoke didn't feel right to you in a particular situation. Describe the situation, how you knew your language wasn't "right," how you handled the problem, and what happened as a result. What lasting effects, if any, did this experience have on you?

I remember, to start with, that day in Sacramento, in a California now nearly thirty years past, when I first entered a classroom—able to understand about fifty stray English words. The third of four children, I had been preceded by my older brother and sister to a neighborhood Roman Catholic school. But neither of them had revealed very much about their classroom experiences. They left each morning and returned each afternoon, always together, speaking Spanish as they climbed the five steps to the porch. And their mysterious books, wrapped in brown shopping-bag paper, remained on the table next to the door, closed firmly behind them.

An accident of geography sent me to a school where all my classmates were white, and many were the children of doctors and lawyers and business executives. On that first day of school, my classmates must certainly have been uneasy to find themselves apart from their families, in the first institution of their lives. But I was astonished. I was fated to be the "problem student" in class.

The nun said, in a friendly but oddly impersonal voice: "Boys and girls, this is Richard Rodriguez." (I heard her sound it out: *Rich-heard Road-ree-guess.*) It was the first time I had heard anyone say my name in English. "Richard," the nun repeated more slowly, writing my name down in her book. Quickly I turned to see my mother's face dissolve in a watery blur behind the pebbled-glass door.

Now, many years later, I hear of something called "bilingual education"—a scheme proposed in the late 1960s by Hispanic-American social activists, later endorsed by a congressional vote. It is a program that seeks to permit non-English-speaking children (many from lower-class homes) to use their "family language" as the language of school. Such, at least, is the aim its supporters announce. I hear them and am forced to say no: It is not possible for a child, any child, ever to use his family's language in school. Not to understand this is to misunderstand the public uses of schooling and to trivialize the nature of intimate life.

Memory teaches me what I know of these matters. The boy reminds the adult. I was a bilingual child, but of a certain kind: "socially disadvantaged," the son of working-class parents, both Mexican immigrants.

In the early years of my boyhood, my parents coped very well in America. My father had steady work. My mother managed at home. They were nobody's victims. When we moved to a house many blocks from the Mexican-American section of town, they were not intimidated by those two or three neighbors who initially tried to make us unwelcome. ("Keep your brats away from my sidewalk!") But despite all they achieved, or perhaps because they had so much to achieve, they lacked any deep feeling of ease, of belonging in public. They regarded the people at work or in crowds as being very distant from us. Those were the others, *los gringos.* That term was interchangeable in their speech with another, even more telling: *los americanos.*

I grew up in a house where the only regular guests were my relations. On a certain day, enormous families of relatives would visit us, and there would be so many people that the noise and the bodies would spill out to the back yard and onto the front porch. Then for weeks no one would come. (If the doorbell rang, it was usually a salesman.) Our house stood apart—gaudy yellow in a row of white bungalows. We were the people with the noisy dog, the people who raised chickens. We were the foreigners on the block. A few neighbors would smile and wave at us. We waved back. But until I was seven years old, I did not know the name of the old couple living next door or the names of the kids living across the street.

In public, my father and mother spoke a hesitant, accented, and not always grammatical English. And then they would have to strain, their bodies tense, to catch the sense of what was rapidly said by *los gringos.* At home, they returned to Spanish. The language of their Mexican past sounded in counterpoint to the English spoken in public. The words would come quickly, with ease. Conveyed through those sounds was the pleasing, soothing, consoling reminder that one was at home.

During those years when I was first learning to speak, my mother and father addressed me only in Spanish; in Spanish I learned to reply. By contrast, English *(inglés)* was the language I came to associate with gringos, rarely heard in the house. I learned my first words of English overhearing my parents speaking to strangers. At six years of age, I knew just enough words for my mother to trust me on errands to stores one block away—but no more.

I was then a listening child, careful to hear the very different sounds of Spanish and English. Wide-eyed with hearing, I'd listen to sounds more than to words. First, there were English (gringo) sounds. So many words still were unknown to me that when the butcher or the lady at the drugstore said something, exotic polysyllabic sounds would bloom in the midst of their sentences. Often the speech of people in public seemed to me very loud, booming with confidence. The man behind the counter would literally ask, "What can I do for you?" But by being so firm and clear, the sound of his voice said that he was a gringo; he belonged in public society. There were also the high nasal notes of middle-class American speech—which I rarely am conscious of hearing today because I hear them so often, but could not stop hearing when I was a boy. Crowds at Safeway or at bus stops were noisy with the birdlike sounds of *los gringos.* I'd move away from them all—all the chirping chatter above me.

But then there was Spanish: *español,* the language rarely heard away from the house; *español,* the language that seemed to me, therefore, a private language, my family's language. To hear its sounds was to feel myself specially recognized as one of the family, apart from *los otros.* A simple remark, an inconsequential comment could convey that assurance. My parents would say something to me, and I would feel embraced by the sounds of their words. Those sounds said: *I am speaking with ease in Spanish. I am addressing you in words I never use with* los gringos. *I recognize you as someone special, close, like no one outside. You belong with us. In the family. Ricardo.*

At the age of six, well past the time when most middle-class children no longer notice the difference between sounds uttered at home and words spoken in public, I had a different experience. I lived in a world compounded of sounds. I was a child longer than most. I lived in a magical world, surrounded by sounds both pleasing and fearful. I shared with my family a language enchantingly private—different from that used in the city around us.

Supporters of bilingual education imply today that students like me miss a great deal by not being taught in their family's language. What they seem not to recognize is that, as a socially disadvantaged child, I regarded Spanish as a private language. It was a ghetto language that deepened and strengthened my feeling of public separateness. What I needed to learn in school was that I had the right, and the obligation, to speak the public language. The odd truth is that my first-grade classmates could become bilingual, in the conventional sense of the word, more easily than I. Had they been taught early (as upper-middle-class children often are taught) a "second language" like Spanish or French, they could have regarded it simply as another public language. In my case, such bilingualism could not have been so quickly achieved. What I did not believe was that I could speak a single public language.

Without question, it would have pleased me to have heard my teachers address me in Spanish when I entered the classroom. I would have felt much less afraid. I would have imagined that my instructors were somehow "related" to me; I would indeed have heard their Spanish as my family's language. I would have trusted them and responded with ease. But I would have delayed—postponed for how long?—having to learn the language of public society. I would have evaded—and for how long?—learning the great lesson of school: that I had a public identity.

Fortunately, my teachers were unsentimental about their responsibility. What they understood was that I needed to speak public English. So their voices would search me out, asking me questions. Each time I heard them I'd look up in surprise to see a nun's face frowning at me. I'd mumble, not really meaning to answer. The nun would persist. "Richard, stand up. Don't look at the floor. Speak up. Speak to the entire class, not just to me!" But I couldn't believe English could be my language to use. (In part, I did not want to believe it.) I continued to mumble. I resisted the teacher's demands. (Did I somehow suspect that once I learned this public language my family life would be changed?) Silent, waiting for the bell to sound, I remained dazed, diffident, afraid.

Three months passed. Five. A half year. Unsmiling, ever watchful, my teachers noted my silence. They began to connect my behavior with the slow progress my brother and sisters were making. Until, one Saturday morning, three nuns arrived at the house to talk to our parents. Stiffly they sat on the blue living-room sofa. From the doorway of another room, spying on the visitors, I noted the incongruity, the clash of two worlds, the faces and voices of school intruding upon the familiar setting of home. I overheard one voice gently wondering, "Do your children speak only Spanish at home, Mrs. Rodriguez?" While another voice added, "That Richard especially seems so timid and shy."

That Rich-heard!

With great tact, the visitors continued, "Is it possible for you and your husband to encourage your children to practice their English when they are home?" Of course my parents complied. What would they not do for their children's well-being? And how could they question the church's authority, which those women represented? In an instant they agreed to give up the language (the sounds) that had revealed and accentuated our family's closeness. The moment after the visitors left, the change was observed. *"Ahora,* speak to us only *en inglés,"* my father and mother told us.

At first, it seemed a kind of game. After dinner each night, the family gathered together to practice "our" English. It was still then *inglés,* a language foreign to us, so we felt drawn to it as strangers. Laughing, we would try to define words we could not pronounce. We played with strange English sounds, often over-anglicizing our pronunciations. And we filled the smiling gaps of our sentences with familiar Spanish sounds. But that was cheating, somebody shouted, and everyone laughed.

In school, meanwhile, like my brother and sisters, I was required to attend a daily tutoring session. I needed a full year of this special work. I also needed my teachers to keep my attention from straying in class by calling out, *"Rich-heard!"*—their English voices slowly loosening the ties to my other name, with its three notes, *Ri-car-do.* Most of all, I needed to hear my mother and father speak to me in a moment of seriousness in "broken"—suddenly heartbreaking—English. This scene was inevitable. One Saturday morning I entered the kitchen where my parents were talking, but I did not realize that they were talking Spanish until, the moment they saw me, their voices changed and they began speaking English. The gringo sounds they uttered startled me. Pushed me away. In that moment of trivial misunderstanding and profound insight, I felt my throat twisted by unsounded grief. I simply turned and left the room. But I had no place to escape to where I could grieve in Spanish. My brother and sisters were speaking English in another part of the house.

Again and again in the days following, as I grew increasingly angry, I was obliged to hear my mother and father encouraging me: "Speak to us *en inglés."* Only then did I determine to learn classroom English. Thus, sometime afterward it happened: One day in school, I raised my hand to volunteer an answer to a question. I spoke out in a loud voice, and I did not think it remarkable when the entire class understood. That day I moved very far from being the disadvantaged child I had been only days earlier. Taken hold at last was the belief, the calming assurance, that I *belonged* in public.

Shortly after, I stopped hearing the high, troubling sounds of *los gringos*. A more and more confident speaker of English, I didn't listen to how strangers sounded when they talked to me. With so many English-speaking people around me, I no longer heard American accents. Conversations quickened. Listening to persons whose voices sounded eccentrically pitched, I might note their sounds for a few seconds, but then I'd concentrate on what they were saying. Now when I heard someone's tone of voice—angry or questioning or sarcastic or happy or sad—I didn't distinguish it from the words it expressed. Sound and word were thus tightly wedded. At the end of each day, I was often bemused, and always relieved, to realize how "soundless," though crowded with words, my day in public had been. An eight-year-old boy, I finally came to accept what had been technically true since my birth: I was an American citizen.

But diminished by then was the special feeling of closeness at home. Gone was the desperate, urgent, intense feeling of being at home among those with whom I felt intimate. Our family remained a loving family, but one greatly changed. We were no longer so close, no longer bound tightly together by the knowledge of our separateness from *los gringos*. Neither my older brother nor my sisters rushed home after school any more. Nor did I. When I arrived home, often there would be neighborhood kids in the house. Or the house would be empty of sounds.

Following the dramatic Americanization of their children, even my parents grew more publicly confident—especially my mother. First she learned the names of all the people on the block. Then she decided we needed to have a telephone in our house. My father, for his part, continued to use the word gringo, but it was no longer charged with bitterness or distrust. Stripped of any emotional content, the word simply became a name for those Americans not of Hispanic descent. Hearing him, sometimes, I wasn't sure if he was pronouncing the Spanish word *gringo,* or saying gringo in English.

There was a new silence at home. As we children learned more and more English, we shared fewer and fewer words with our parents. Sentences needed to be spoken slowly when one of us addressed our mother or father. Often the parent wouldn't understand. The child would need to repeat himself. Still the parent misunderstood. The young voice, frustrated, would end up saying, "Never mind"—the subject was closed. Dinners would be noisy with the clinking of knives and forks against dishes. My mother would smile softly between her remarks; my father, at the other end of the table, would chew and chew his food while he stared over the heads of his children.

My mother! My father! After English became my primary language, I no longer knew what words to use in addressing my parents. The old Spanish words (those tender accents of sound) I had earlier used—*mamá* and *papá*—I couldn't use any more. They would have been all-too-painful reminders of how much had changed in my life. On the other hand, the words I heard neighborhood kids call their parents seemed unsatisfactory. "Mother" and "father," "ma," "papa," "pa," "dad," "pop" (how I hated the all-American sound of that last word)—all these I felt were unsuitable terms of address for *my* parents. As a result, I never used them at home. Whenever I'd speak to my parents, I would try to get their attention by looking at them. In public conversations, I'd refer to them as my "parents" or my "mother" and "father."

My mother and father, for their part, responded differently as their children spoke to them less. My mother grew restless, seemed troubled and anxious at the scareness of words exchanged in the house. She would question me about my day when I came home from school. She smiled at my small talk. She pried at the edges of my sentences to get me to say something more. ("What . . . ?") She'd join conversations she overheard, but her intrusions often stopped her children's talking. By contrast, my father seemed to grow reconciled to the new quiet. Though his English somewhat improved, he tended more and more to retire into silence. At dinner he spoke very little. One night his children and even his wife helplessly giggled at his garbled English pronunciation of the Catholic "Grace Before Meals." Thereafter he made his wife recite the prayer at the start of each meal, even on formal occasions when there were guests in the house.

Hers became the public voice of the family. On official business it was she, not my father, who would usually talk to strangers on the phone or in stores. We children grew so accustomed to his silence that years later we would routinely refer to his "shyness." (My mother often tried to explain: both of his parents died when he was eight. He was raised by an uncle who treated him as little more than a menial servant. He was never encouraged to speak. He grew up alone—a man of few words.) But I realized my father was not shy whenever I'd watch him speaking Spanish with relatives. Using Spanish, he was quickly effusive. Especially when talking with other men, his voice would spark, flicker, flare alive with varied sounds. In Spanish he expressed ideas and feelings he rarely revealed when speaking English. With firm Spanish sounds he conveyed a confidence and authority that English would never allow him.

The silence at home, however, was not simply the result of fewer words passing between parents and children. More profound for me was the silence created by my inattention to sounds. At about the time I no longer bothered to listen with care to the sounds of English in public, I grew careless about listening to the sounds made by the family when they spoke. Most of the time I would hear someone speaking at home and didn't distinguish his sounds from the words people uttered in public. I didn't even pay much attention to my parents' accented and ungrammatical speech—at least not at home. Only when I was with them in public would I become alert to their accents. But even then, their sounds caused me less and less concern. For I was growing increasingly confident of my own public identity.

I would have been happier about my public success had I not recalled, sometimes, what it had been like earlier, when my family conveyed its intimacy through a set of conveniently private sounds. Sometimes in public, hearing a stranger, I'd hark back to my lost past. A Mexican farm worker approached me one day downtown. He wanted directions to some place. *"Hijito, . . ."* he said. And his voice stirred old longings. Another time I was standing beside my mother in the visiting room of a Carmelite convent, before the dense screen that rendered the nuns shadowy figures. I heard several of them speaking Spanish in their busy, singsong, overlapping voices, assuring my mother that, yes, yes, we were remembered, all our family were remembered in their prayers. Those voices echoed faraway family sounds. Another day, a dark-faced old woman touched my shoulder lightly to steady herself as she boarded a bus. She murmured something to me I couldn't quite comprehend. Her Spanish voice came near, like the face of a never-before-seen relative in the instant before I was kissed. That voice, like so many of the Spanish voices I'd hear in public, recalled the golden age of my childhood.

Bilingual educators say today that children lose a degree of "individuality" by becoming assimilated into public society. (Bilingual schooling is a program popularized in the seventies, that decade when middle-class "ethnics" began to resist the process of assimilation—the "American melting pot.") But the bilingualists oversimplify when they scorn the value and necessity of assimilation. They do not seem to realize that a person is individualized in two ways. So they do not realize that, while one suffers a diminished sense of *private* individuality by being assimilated into public society, such assimilation makes possible the achievement of *public* individuality.

Simplistically again, the bilingualists insist that a student should be reminded of his difference from others in mass society, of his "heritage." But they equate mere separateness with individuality. The fact is that only in private—with intimates—is separateness from the crowd a prerequisite for individuality; an intimate "tells" me that I am unique, unlike all others, apart from the crowd. In public, by contrast, full individuality is achieved, paradoxically, by those who are able to consider themselves members of the crowd. Thus it happened for me. Only when I was able to think of myself as an American, no longer an alien in gringo society, could I seek the rights and opportunities necessary for full public individuality. The social and political advantages I enjoy as a man began on the day I came to believe that my name is indeed *Rich-heard Road-ree-guess.* It is true that my public society today is often impersonal; in fact, my public society is usually mass society. But despite the anonymity of the crowd, and despite the fact that the individuality I achieve in public is often tenuous—because it depends on my being one in a crowd—I celebrate the day I acquired my new name. Those middle-class ethnics who scorn assimilation seem to me filled with decadent self-pity, obsessed by the burden of public life. Dangerously, they romanticize public separateness and trivialize the dilemma of those who are truly socially disadvantaged.

I grew up the victim of a disconcerting confusion. As I became fluent in

English, I could no longer speak Spanish with confidence. I continued to understand spoken Spanish, and in high school I learned how to read and write
Spanish. But for many years I could not pronounce it. A powerful guilt blocked
my spoken words; an essential glue was missing whenever I would try to connect
words to form sentences. I would be unable to break a barrier of sound, to speak
freely. I would speak, or try to speak, Spanish, and I would manage to utter
halting, hiccupping sounds that betrayed my unease. (Even today, I speak Spanish very slowly, at best.)

When relatives and Spanish-speaking friends of my parents came to the house,
my brother and sisters would usually manage to say a few words before being
excused. I never managed so gracefully. Each time I'd hear myself addressed in
Spanish, I couldn't respond with any success. I'd know the words I wanted to
say, but I couldn't say them. I would try to speak, but everything I said seemed
to me horribly anglicized. My mouth wouldn't form the sounds right. My jaw
would tremble. After a phrase or two, I'd stutter, cough up a warm, silvery
sound, and stop.

My listeners were surprised to hear me. They'd lower their heads to grasp
better what I was trying to say. They would repeat their questions in gentle,
affectionate voices. But then I would answer in English. No, no, they would say,
we want you to speak to us in Spanish (*"en español"*). But I couldn't do it. Then
they would call me *Pocho*. Sometimes playfully, teasing, using the tender diminu-
tive—*mi pochito*. Sometimes not so playfully but mockingly, *pocho*. (A Spanish
dictionary defines that word as an adjective meaning "colorless" or "bland." But
I heard it as a noun, naming the Mexican-American who, in becoming an
American, forgets his native society.) *"¡Pocho!"* my mother's best friend mut-
tered, shaking her head. And my mother laughed, somewhere behind me. She
said that her children didn't want to practice "our Spanish" after they started
going to school. My mother's smiling voice made me suspect that the lady who
faced me was not really angry at me. But searching her face, I couldn't find the
hint of a smile.

Yet, even during those years of guilt, I was coming to grasp certain consoling
truths about language and intimacy—truths that I learned gradually. Once, I
remember playing with a friend in the back yard when my grandmother appeared
at the window. Her face was stern with suspicion when she saw the boy (the
gringo boy) I was with. She called out to me in Spanish, sounding the whistle
of her ancient breath. My companion looked up and watched her intently as she
lowered the window and moved (still visible) behind the light curtain, watching
us both. He wanted to know what she had said. I started to tell him, to translate
her Spanish words into English. The problem was, however, that though I knew
how to translate exactly what she had told me, I realized that any translation
would distort the deepest meaning of her message: it had been directed only to
me. This message of intimacy could never be translated because it did not lie in
the actual words she had used but passed through them. So any translation would
have seemed wrong; the words would have been stripped of an essential meaning.

Finally, I decided not to tell my friend anything—just that I didn't hear all she had said.

This insight was unfolded in time. As I made more and more friends outside my house, I began to recognize intimate messages spoken in English in a close friend's confidential tone or secretive whisper. Even more remarkable were those instances when, apparently for no special reason, I'd become conscious of the fact that my companion was speaking *only to me*. I'd marvel then, just hearing his voice. It was a stunning event to be able to break through the barrier of public silence, to be able to hear the voice of the other, to realize that it was directed just to me. After such moments of intimacy outside the house, I began to trust what I heard intimately conveyed through my family's English. Voices at home at last punctured sad confusion. I'd hear myself addressed as an intimate—in English. Such moments were never as raucous with sound as in past times, when we had used our "private" Spanish. (Our English-sounding house was never to be as noisy as our Spanish-sounding house had been.) Intimate moments were usually moments of soft sound. My mother would be ironing in the dining room while I did my homework nearby. She would look over at me, smile, and her voice sounded to tell me that I was her son. *Richard*.

Intimacy thus continued at home; intimacy was not stilled by English. Though there were fewer occasions for it—a change in my life that I would never forget— there were also times when I sensed the deep truth about language and intimacy: *Intimacy is not created by a particular language; it is created by intimates.* Thus the great change in my life was not linguistic but social. If, after becoming a success- ful student, I no longer heard intimate voices as often as I had earlier, it was not because I spoke English instead of Spanish. It was because I spoke a public language for most of my day. I moved easily at last, a citizen in a crowded city of words.

As a man I spend most of my day in public, in a world largely devoid of speech sounds. So I am quickly attracted by the glamorous quality of certain alien voices. I still am gripped with excitement when someone passes me on the street speaking in Spanish. I have not moved beyond the range of the nostalgic pull of those sounds. And there is something very compelling about the sounds of lower-class blacks. Of all the accented versions of English that I hear in public, I hear theirs most intently. The Japanese tourist stops me downtown to ask me a question, and I inch my way past his accent to concentrate on what he is saying. The Eastern European immigrant in the neighborhood delicatessen speaks to me, and, again, I do not pay much attention to his sounds, nor to the Texas accent of one of my neighbors or the Chicago accent of the woman who lives in the apartment below me. But when the ghetto black teenagers get on the city bus, I hear them. Their sounds in my society are the sounds of the outsider. Their voices annoy me for being so loud—so self-sufficient and unconcerned by my presence, but for the same reason they are glamorous: a romantic gesture against public acceptance. And as I listen to their shouted laughter, I realize my own quietness. I feel envious of them—envious of their brazen intimacy.

I warn myself away from such envy, however. Overhearing those teenagers, I think of the black political activists who lately have argued in favor of using black English in public schools—an argument that varies only slightly from that of foreign-language bilingualists. I have heard "radical" linguists make the point that black English is a complex and intricate version of English. And I do not doubt it. But neither do I think that black English should be a language of public instruction. What makes it inappropriate in classrooms is not something in the language itself but, rather, what lower-class speakers make of it. Just as Spanish would have been a dangerous language for me to have used at the start of my education, so black English would be a dangerous language to use in the schooling of teenagers for whom it reinforces feelings of public separateness.

This seems to me an obvious point to make, and yet it must be said. In recent years, there have been many attempts to make the language of the alien a public language. "Bilingual education, two ways to understand . . ." television and radio commercials glibly announce. Proponents of bilingual education are careful to say that above all they want every student to acquire a good education. Their argument goes something like this: Children permitted to use their family language will not be so alienated and will be better able to match the progress of English-speaking students in the crucial first months of schooling. Increasingly confident of their ability, such children will be more inclined to apply themselves to their studies in the future. But then the bilingualists also claim another very different goal. They say that children who use their family language in school will retain a sense of their ethnic heritage and their family ties. Thus the supporters of bilingual education want it both ways. They propose bilingual schooling as a way of helping students acquire the classroom skills crucial for public success. But they likewise insist that bilingual instruction will give students a sense of their identity apart from the English-speaking public.

Behind this scheme gleams a bright promise for the alien child: One can become a public person while still remaining a private person. Who would not want to believe such an appealing idea? Who can be surprised that the scheme has the support of so many middle-class ethnic Americans? If the barrio or ghetto child can retain his separateness even while being publicly educated, then it is almost possible to believe that no private cost need be paid for public success. This is the consolation offered by any of the number of current bilingual programs. Consider, for example, the bilingual voter's ballot. In some American cities, one can cast a ballot printed in several languages. Such a document implies that it is possible for one to exercise that most public of rights—the right to vote—while still keeping oneself apart, unassimilated in public life.

It is not enough to say that such schemes are foolish and certainly doomed. Middle-class supporters of public bilingualism toy with the confusion of those Americans who cannot speak standard English as well as they do. Moreover, bilingual enthusiasts sin against intimacy. A Hispanic-American tells me, "I will never give up my family language," and he clutches a group of words as though they were the source of his family ties. He credits to language what he should credit to family members. This is a convenient mistake, for as long as he holds on to certain familiar words, he can ignore how much else has actually changed in his life.

It has happened before. In earlier decades, persons ambitious for social mobility, and newly successful, similarly seized upon certain "family words." Workingmen attempting to gain political power, for example, took to calling one another "brother." The word as they used it, however, could never resemble the word (the sound) "brother" exchanged by two people in intimate greeting. The context of its public delivery made it at best a metaphor; with repetition it was only a vague echo of the intimate sound. Context forced the change. Context could not be overruled. Context will always protect the realm of the intimate from public misuse. Today middle-class white Americans continue to prove the importance of context as they try to ignore it. They seize upon idioms of the black ghetto, but their attempt to appropriate such expressions invariably changes the meaning. As it becomes a public expression, the ghetto idiom loses its sound, its message of public separateness and strident intimacy. With public repetition it becomes a series of words, increasingly lifeless.

The mystery of intimate utterance remains. The communication of intimacy passes through the word and enlivens its sound, but it cannot be held by the word. It cannot be retained or ever quoted because it is too fluid. It depends not on words but on persons.

My grandmother! She stood among my other relations mocking me when I no longer spoke Spanish. *Pocho,* she said. But then it made no difference. She'd laugh, and our relationship continued because language was never its source. She was a woman in her eighties during the first decade of my life—a mysterious woman to me, my only living grandparent, a woman of Mexico in a long black dress that reached down to her shoes. She was the one relative of mine who spoke no word of English. She had no interest in gringo society and remained completely aloof from the public. She was protected by her daughters, protected even by me when we went to Safeway together and I needed to act as her translator. An eccentric woman. Hard. Soft.

When my family visited my aunt's house in San Francisco, my grandmother would search for me among my many cousins. When she found me, she'd chase them away. Pinching her granddaughters, she would warn them away from me. Then she'd take me to her room, where she had prepared for my coming. There would be a chair next to the bed, a dusty jellied candy nearby, and a copy of *Life en Español* for me to examine. "There," she'd say. And I'd sit content, a boy of eight. *Pocho,* her favorite. I'd sift through the pictures of earthquake-destroyed Latin-American cities and blonde-wigged Mexican movie stars. And all the while

I'd listen to the sound of my grandmother's voice. She'd pace around the room, telling me stories of her life, her past. They were stories so familiar that I couldn't remember when I'd heard them for the first time. I'd look up sometimes to listen. Other times she'd look over at me, but she never expected a response. Sometimes I'd smile or nod. (I understood exactly what she was saying.) But it never seemed to matter to her one way or the other. It was enough that I was there. The words she spoke were almost irrelevant to that fact. We were content. And the great mystery remained: intimate utterance.

The child reminds the adult: to seek intimate sounds is to seek the company of intimates. I do not expect to hear those sounds in public. I would dishonor those I have loved, and those I love now, to claim anything else. I would dishonor our intimacy by holding on to a particular language and calling it my family language. Intimacy cannot be trapped within words; it passes through words. It passes. Intimates leave the room. Doors close. Faces move away from the window. Time passes, and voices recede into the dark. Death finally quiets the voice. There is no way to deny it, no way to stand in the crowd claiming to utter one's family language.

The last time I saw my grandmother I was nine years old. I can tell you some of the things she said to me as I stood by her bed, but I cannot quote the message of intimacy she conveyed with her voice. She laughed, holding my hand. Her voice illumined disjointed memories as it passed them again. She remembered her husband—his green eyes, his magic name of Narcissio, his early death. She remembered the farm in Mexico, the eucalyptus trees nearby (their scent, she remembered, like incense). She remembered the family cow, the bell around its neck heard miles away. A dog. She remembered working as a seamstress, how she'd leave her daughters and son for long hours to go into Guadalajara to work. And how my mother would come running toward her in the sun—in her bright yellow dress—on her return. "MMMMAAAAMMMMÁÁÁÁ," the old lady mimicked her daughter (my mother) to her daughter's son. She laughed. There was the snap of a cough. An aunt came into the room and told me it was time I should leave. "You can see her tomorrow," she promised. So I kissed my grandmother's cracked face. And the last thing I saw was her thin, oddly youthful thigh, as my aunt rearranged the sheet on the bed.

At the funeral parlor a few days after, I remember kneeling with my relatives during the rosary. Among their voices I traced, then lost, the sounds of individual aunts in the surge of the common prayer. And I heard at that moment what since I have heard very often—the sound the women in my family make when they are praying in sadness. When I went up to look at my grandmother, I saw her through the haze of a veil draped over the open lid of the casket. Her face looked calm—but distant and unyielding to love. It was not the face I remembered seeing most often. It was the face she made in public when the clerk at Safeway asked her some question and I would need to respond. It was her public face that the mortician had designed with his dubious art.

Questions for Discussion and Writing

1. What does Rodriguez mean by his claim that "It is not possible for a child, any child, ever to use his family's language in school" (p. 172)?
2. What does Rodriguez mean when he writes of "Learning the great lesson of school: that I had a public identity" (p. 174)?
3. What factors finally convinced eight-year-old Rodriguez that he was an American citizen? What had he and his family lost by that time? Why or why not do you agree with Rodriguez about these matters?
4. What insights does Rodriguez gain about the messages of intimacy carried through language? In this connection, what does he mean by breaking through "the barrier of public silence" (p. 180)?
5. Rodriguez presents the advocates' argument about bilingual education and his own argument against it. What is your position on this issue after reading his essay?
6. Why do you think Rodriguez writes about his grandmother at the end of the essay?
7. What audience do you think Rodriguez had in mind when he wrote this essay, and why?

SHIRLEY LAURO

Open Admissions

Being on Broadway was part of playwright Shirley Lauro's dreams even as she graduated from high school in Des Moines, Iowa. In the Roosevelt High School Class of 1951 yearbook, she promised to "hit Broadway and not bounce back." She has, but as a playwright, not an actress.

As a student at Northwestern University, Lauro sold a short story for $25 to New Idea *magazine and her writing career took root. The original one-act play of "Open Admissions" that follows was later expanded to a full-length script that had a short run on Broadway and after that was made into a CBS-television special. With rare exceptions, Lauro points out, Broadway has sexist barriers: "Playwrights were* men; *that was a given." Women were told they could act, get into makeup or costuming, or teach. She likes to think her plays have helped change that attitude.*

"Almost everything I write has a Midwest character," Lauro says. "I'm an Iowa girl and always will be. It's one of my strongest selling points in New York."

Lauro has also been a college speech instructor in New York. "Open Admissions" refers to programs enacted during the last few decades across the United States by many colleges and universities to admit disadvantaged minority students to their schools so that they might gain the opportunities of a college education. The play was published in 1983 in Off-Off Broadway Festival Plays.

Before you read "Open Admissions," write about a time in your life when a teacher could not hear the meaning in your words or see you for the person you are. Describe the situation, what you were asking for, why you thought the teacher was incapable of hearing or seeing you, and what influence the experience has had on you.

The Characters

PROFESSOR ALICE MILLER—	Professor of Speech Communications. Started out to be a Shakespearean scholar. Has been teaching Speech at a city college in New York for 12 years. She is overloaded with work and exhausted. Late thirties. Wears skirt, blouse, sweater, coat, gloves. Carries briefcases.
CALVIN JEFFERSON—	18, a Freshman in Open Admissions Program at the College. Black, powerfully built, handsome, big. At first glance a streetperson, but belied by his intensity. Wears jacket, jeans, cap, sneakers. Has been at the College 3 months, hoping it will work out.

The Place

A cubicle Speech Office at a city college in New York.

The Time

The Present. Late fall. 6 o'clock in the evening.

The play begins on a very high level of tension and intensity and builds from there. The level of intensity is set by CALVIN who enters the play with a desperate urgency, as though he had arrived at the Emergency Room of a Hospital, needing immediate help for a serious problem. He also enters in a state of rage and frustration but is containing these feelings at first. The high level of tension is set by both ALICE and CALVIN and occurs from the moment CALVIN enters. ALICE wants to leave. She does not want the scene to take place. The audience's experience from the start should be as if they had suddenly turned in on the critical round of a boxing match.

CALVIN's speech is "Street Speech" jargon. Run-on sentences and misspellings in the text are for the purpose of helping the actor with the pronunciations and rhythms of the language.

The Speech office of Professor Alice Miller in a city college in New York. A small cubicle with partitions going ¾ of the way up. Windowless, airless, with a cold antiseptic quality and a strong sense of impersonalness and transience. The cubicle has the contradictory feelings of claustrophobia and alienation at the same time. It is a space used by many teachers during every day of the week.

On the glass-windowed door it says:

SPEECH COMMUNICATIONS DEPT.
Prof. Alice Miller, B.A., M.A., Ph.D.

There are other names beneath that.

In the cubicle there is a desk with nothing on it except a phone, a chair with a rain coat on it, a swivel chair and a portable black board on which has been tacked a diagram of the "Speech Mechanism." Room is bare except for these things.

At Rise: Cubicle is in darkness. Muted light filters through glass window on door from hallway. Eerie feeling. A shadow appears outside door. Someone enters, snapping on light.

It is ALICE. She carries a loose stack of essays, a book sack loaded with books and a grade book, one Shakespeare book, two speech books, and a portable cassette recorder. She closes the door, crosses to the desk, puts the keys in her purse, puts purse and booksack down and dials "O."

ALICE: Outside please. (*Waits for this, then dials a number.*) Debbie? Mommy, honey . . . A "93"? Terrific! Listen, I just got through. I had to keep the class late to finish . . . So, I can't stop home for dinner. I'm going right to the meeting . . . no, I'll be safe . . . don't worry. But you go put the double lock on, ok? And eat the cold meatloaf. (*She puts essays in book sack.*) See you later. Love you too. (*She kisses the receiver.*) Bye.

(*She hangs up, puts on coat, picks up purse and book sack, crosses to door and snaps off light. Then opens door to go. CALVIN looms in doorway.*)

ALICE: OOHH! You scared me!

CALVIN: Yes ma'am, I can see I scared you okay. I'm sorry.

ALICE: Calvin Washington? 10:30 section?

CALVIN: Calvin Jefferson. 9:30 section.

ALICE: Oh, right. Of course. Well, I was just leaving. Something you wanted?

CALVIN: Yes, Professor Miller. I came to talk to you about my grades. My grade on that Shakespeare project especially.

ALICE: Oh. Yes. Well. What did you get, Calvin? A "B" wasn't it? Something like that?

CALVIN: Umhmm. Thass right. Somethin like that . . .

ALICE: Yes. Well, look, I don't have office hours today at all. It's very dark already. I just stopped to make a call. But if you'd like to make an appointment for a conference, I'm not booked yet next month. Up 'till then, I'm just jammed.

CALVIN: Thass two weeks! I need to talk to you right now!

ALICE: Well what exactly is it about? I mean the grade is self-explanatory— "Good"—"B" work. And I gave you criticism in class the day of the project, didn't I? So what's the problem?

CALVIN: I wanna sit down and talk about *why* I got that grade! And all my grades in point of fact.

ALICE: But I don't have office hours today. It's very late and I have another commitment. Maybe tomorrow—(*She tries to leave.*)

CALVIN: (*voice rising*) I have to talk to you *now!*

ALICE: Look, tomorrow there's a Faculty Meeting. I can meet you here after-wards . . . around 12:30. Providing Professor Roth's not scheduled to use the desk.

CALVIN: I got a job tomorrow! Can't you talk to me right now?

ALICE: But what's it about? I don't see the emergen—

CALVIN: (*voice rising loudly*) I jiss *tole* you what it's about! My project and my *grades* is what it's about!

ALICE: (*glancing down the hall, not wanting a commotion overheard*) All right! Just stop shouting out here, will you? (*She snaps on light and crosses to desk.*) Come on in. I'll give you a few minutes now.

(*He comes in.*)

ALICE: (*She puts purse and book sack down and sits at desk.*) Okay. Now then. What?

CALVIN: (*Closes door and crosses UC. Silent for a moment, looking at her. Then:*) How come all I ever git from you is "B"?

ALICE: (*stunned*) What?

CALVIN: This is the third project I did for you. An all I ever git is "B."

ALICE: Are you joking? This is what you wanted to talk about? "B" is an excellent grade!

CALVIN: No it's not! "A" is "excellent." "B" is "good."

ALICE: You don't think you deserved an "A" on those projects, do you?

CALVIN: No. But I got to know how to improve myself somehow, so maybe sometime I can try for a "A." I wouldn't even mind on one of those projects if I got a "C." Thass average—if you know what I mean? Or a "D." But all I ever git from you is "B." It don't matter what I do in that Speech Communications Class, seems like. I come in the beginnin a it three months ago? On the Open Admissions? Shoot, I didn't know which end was up. I stood up there and give this speech you assigned on "My Hobby." You remember that?

ALICE: (*Reads note on desk.*) About basketball?

CALVIN: Huh-uh. That was Franklin Perkins give that speech. Sits in the back row?

ALICE: (*Tosses note in wastebasket.*) Oh. Yes. Right. Franklin.

CALVIN: Umhmm. I give some dumb speech about "The Hobby a Makin Wooden Trays."

ALICE: Oh, yes. Right. I remember that.

CALVIN: Except I didn't have no hobby makin wooden trays, man. I made one in high school one time, thass all.

ALICE: (*Leafs through pages of speech books.*) Oh, well, that didn't matter. It was the speech that counted.

CALVIN: Umhmm? Well, that was the sorriest speech anybody ever heard in their lives! I was scared to death and couldn't put one word in front a the other any way I tried. Supposed to be 5 minutes. Lasted 2! And you give me a "B"!

ALICE: (*Rises, crosses to DR table and puts speech books down.*) Well, it was your first time up in class, and you showed a lot of enthusiasm and effort. I remember that speech.

CALVIN: Everybody's firss time up in class, ain't it?

ALICE: Yes. Of course.

CALVIN: (*Crosses DR to ALICE.*) That girl sits nex to me, that Judy Horowitz— firss time she was up in class too. She give that speech about "How to Play the Guitar?" And man, she brought in charts and taught us to read chords and played a piece herself an had memorized the whole speech by heart. An you give *her* a "B."

ALICE: (*Crosses to desk, picks up book sack and puts it on desk.*) Well, Judy's organiza- tion on her outline was a little shaky as I recall.

CALVIN: (*Crosses end of desk.*) I didn't even turn no outline in.

ALICE: (*Picks up purse and puts it on desk.*) You didn't?

CALVIN: (*Leans in.*) Huh-uh. Didn't you notice?

ALICE: Of course! It's—just—well, it's been sometime—(*She quickly takes the grade book from the book sack and looks up his name.*) Let me see, oh, yes. Right. Here, I see. You didn't hand it in . . .

CALVIN: Thass right, I didn'.

ALICE: You better do that before the end of the term.

CALVIN: I can't. Because I don't know which way to do no outline!

ALICE: (*Looks up name in grade book and marks it with red pencil.*) Oh. Well . . . that's all right. Don't worry about it, okay? (*She puts grade book away.*) Just work on improving yourself in other ways.

CALVIN: What other ways? Only thing you ever say about anything I ever done in there is how I have got to get rid of my "Substandard Urban Speech!"

ALICE: (*Picks up 2 files from desk and crosses to UCR file cabinet.*) Well, yes, you do! You see, that's your real problem, Calvin! "Substandard Speech." It under- cuts your "Positive Communicator's Image!" Remember how I gave a lecture about that? About how all of you here have Substandard Urban Speech because this is a Sub—an *Urban* College. (*She puts on gloves.*) Remember? But that's perfectly okay! It's okay! Just like I used to have Substandard Midwestern Speech when I was a student. Remember my explaining about that? How I used to say "crik" for "creek," and "kin" for "can" and "tin" for "ten?" (*She crosses in back of desk and chuckles at herself.*) Oh, and my breathiness! (*She picks up purse.*) That was just my biggest problem of all: Breathiness. I just about worked myself to death up at Northwestern U. getting it right straight out of my speech. Now, that's what you have to do too, Calvin. (*She picks up book sack and keys.*) Nothing to be ashamed of—but get it right straight out! (*She is ready to leave. She pats CALVIN on the shoulder and crosses UC.*)

CALVIN: (*Pause. Looks at her.*) Thass how come I keep on gittin "B"?

ALICE: "That's."

CALVIN: (*Steps in to ALICE.*) Huh?

ALICE: "That's." Not "Thass." Can't you hear the difference? "That's" one of the words in the Substandard Black Urban Pattern. No final "T's." Undermining your Positive Image . . . labeling you. It's "Street Speech." Harlemese. Don't you remember? I called everyone's attention to your particular syndrome in class the minute you started talking?

(*He looks at her, not speaking.*)

ALICE: It's "last," not "lass;" "first," not "firss." That's your friend, that good old "Final T!" Hear *it* when I talk?

CALVIN: Sometimes. When you say *it*, hit*t*in i*t* like tha*t*!

ALICE: Well, you should be going over the exercises on it in the speech book all the time, and recording yourself on your tape recorder. (*She pats book sack.*)

CALVIN: I don't got no tape recorder.

ALICE: Well, borrow one! (*She turns away.*)

CALVIN: (*Crosses in back of ALICE to her right.*) On that Shakespeare scene I jiss did? Thass why I got a "B"? Because of the "Final T's?"

ALICE: (*Backs DS a step.*) Well, you haven't improved your syndrome, have you?

CALVIN: How come you keep on answerin me by axin me somethin else?

ALICE: And that's the other one.

CALVIN: What "other one"?

ALICE: Other most prevalent deviation. You said: "ax-ing" me somethin else.

CALVIN: Thass right. How come you keep axin me somethin else?

ALICE: "Asking me," Calvin, "asking me!"

CALVIN: I jiss did!

ALICE: No, no. Look. That's classic Substandard Black! Text book case. (*She puts purse and book sack down and crosses to diagram on blackboard.*) See, the jaw and teeth are in two different positions for the two sounds, and they make two completely different words! (*She writes "ass-king," and "ax-ing" on the blackboard, pronouncing them in an exaggerated way for him to see.*) "ass-king" and "ax-ing." I am "ass-king" you the question. But, the woodcutter is "ax-ing" down the tree. Can't you hear the difference? (*She picks up his speech book from desk.*) Here.

(*CALVIN follows her to desk.*)

ALICE: Go over to page 105. It's called a "Sharp S" problem with a medial position "sk" substitution. See? "skin, screw, scream"—those are "sk" sounds in the Primary Position. "Asking, risking, frisking,—that's medial position. And "flask, task, mask"—that's final position. Now you should be working on those, Calvin. Reading those exercises over and over again. I mean the way you did the Othello scene was just ludicrous: "Good gentlemen, I *ax* thee—" (*She crosses to the board and points to "ax-ing". She chuckles.*) That meant Othello was chopping the gentlemen down!

CALVIN: How come I had to do the Othello scene anyhow? Didn git any choice. An Franklin Perkins an Sam Brown an Lester Washington they had to too.

ALICE: What do you mean?

CALVIN: An Claudette Jackson an Doreen Simpson an Melba Jones got themselves assigned to Cleopatra on the Nile?

ALICE: Everyone was assigned!

CALVIN: Uh-huh. But everybody else had a choice, you know what I mean? That Judy Horowitz, she said you told her she could pick outa five, six different characters. And that boy did his yesterday? That Nick Rizoli? Did the Gravedigger? He said he got three, four to choose off of too.

ALICE: (*Crosses to Calvin.*) Well some of the students were "right" for several characters. And you know, Calvin, how we talked in class about Stanislavsky and the importance of "identifying" and "feeling" the part?

CALVIN: Well how Doreen Simpson "identify" herself some Queen sittin on a barge? How I supposed to "identify" some Othello? I don't!

ALICE: (*Crosses to blackboard, picks up fallen chalk.*) Oh, Calvin, don't be silly.

CALVIN: (*Crosses center.*) Well, I don'! I'm not no kind a jealous husband. I haven' got no wife. I don' even got no girlfriend, hardly! And thass what it's all about ain't it? So what's it I'm supposed to "identify" with anyhow?

ALICE: (*Turns to CALVIN.*) Oh, Calvin, what are you arguing about? You did a good job!

CALVIN: "B" job, right?

ALICE: Yes.

CALVIN: (*Crosses to ALICE.*) Well, what's that "B" standin for? Cause I'll tell you somethin you wanna know the truth: I stood up there didn' hardly know the sense a anythin I read, couldn't hardly even read it at all. Only you didn't notice. Wasn't even listenin, sittin there back a the room jiss thumbin through your book.

   (*ALICE crosses to desk.*)

CALVIN: So you know what I done? Skip one whole paragraph, tess you out— you jiss kep thumbin through your book! An then you give me a "B"! (*He has followed Alice to desk.*)

ALICE: (*Puts papers in box and throws out old coffee cup.*) Well that just shows how well you did the part!

CALVIN: You wanna give me somethin I could "identify" with, how come you ain' let me do that other dude in the play . . .

ALICE: Iago?

CALVIN: Yeah. What is it they calls him? Othello's . . .

ALICE: Subordinate.

CALVIN: Go right along there with my speech syndrome, wouldn' it now? See, Iago has to work for the Man. I identifies with him! He gits jealous man. Know what I mean? Or that Gravedigger? Shovelin dirt for his day's work! How come you wouldn't let me do him? Thass the question I wanna ax you!

ALICE: (*Turns to CALVIN.*) "Ask me," Calvin, "Ask me!"

CALVIN: (*Steps SR.*) "Ax you?" Okay, man. (*Turns to ALICE.*) Miss Shakespeare, Speech Communications 1! (*Crosses US of ALICE.*) Know what I'll "ax" you right here in this room, this day, at this here desk right now? I'll "ax" you how come I have been in this here college 3 months on this here Open Admissions an I don't know nothin more than when I came in here? You know what I mean? This supposed to be some big break for me. This here is where all them smart Jewish boys has gone from the Bronx Science and went an become some Big Time Doctors at Bellvue. An some Big Time Judges in the Family Court an like that there. And now it's supposed to be my turn.

(*ALICE looks away and CALVIN crosses R of ALICE.*)

CALVIN: You know what I mean? (*He crosses UR.*) An my sister Jonelle took me out of foster care where I been in 6 homes and 5 schools to give me my chance. (*He crosses DR.*) Livin with her an she workin 3 shifts in some "Ladies Restroom" give me my opportunity. An she say she gonna buss her ass git me this education I don't end up on the streets! (*Crosses on a diagonal to ALICE.*) Cause I have got *brains!*

(*ALICE sits in student chair. CALVIN crosses in back, to her left.*)

CALVIN: You understand what I am Communicatin to you? My high school has tole me I got brains an can make somethin outta my life if I gits me the chance! And now this here's supposed to be my chance! High school says you folks gonna bring me up to date on my education and git me even. Only nothin is happenin to me in my head except I am getting more and more confused about what I knows and what I don't know! (*He sits in swivel chair.*) So what I wanna "ax" you is: How come you don't sit down with me and teach me which way to git my ideas down instead of givin me a "B."

(*ALICE rises and crosses UR.*)

CALVIN: I don't even turn no outline in? Jiss give me a "B." (*He rises and crosses R of ALICE.*) An Lester a "B"! An Melba a "B"! An Sam a "B"! What's that "B" standin for anyhow? Cause it surely ain't standin for no piece of work!

ALICE: Calvin don't blame me!

(*CALVIN crosses DR.*)

ALICE: I'm trying! God knows I'm trying! The times are rough for everyone. I'm a Shakespearean scholar, and they have me teaching beginning Speech. I was supposed to have 12 graduate students a class, 9 classes a week, and they gave me 35 Freshmen a class, 20 classes a week. I hear 157 speeches a week! You know what that's like? And I go home late on the subway scared to death! In Graduate School they told me I'd have a first rate career. Then I started here and they said: "Hang on! Things will improve!" But they only got worse . . . and worse! Now I've been here for 12 years and I haven't written one word in my field! I haven't read 5 research books! I'm exhausted . . . and I'm finished! We all have to bend. I'm just hanging on now . . . supporting my little girl . . . earning a living . . . and that's all . . . (*She crosses to desk.*)

CALVIN: (*Faces ALICE.*) What I'm supposed to do, feel sorry for you? Least you can *earn* a livin! Clean office, private phone, name on the door with all them B.A.'s, M.A.'s, Ph.D.'s.

ALICE: You can have those too. (*She crosses DR to CALVIN.*) Look, last year we got 10 black students into Ivy League Graduate Programs. And they were no better than you. They were just *perceived* (*Points to blackboard.*) as better. Now that's the whole key for you . . . to be perceived as better! So you can get good recommendations and do well on interviews. You're good looking and ambitious and you have a fine native intelligence. You can make it, Calvin. All we have to do is work on improving your Positive Communicator's Image . . . by getting rid of that Street Speech. Don't you see?

CALVIN: See what? What you axin *me* to see?

ALICE: *"Asking"* me to see, Calvin. *"Asking"* me to see!

CALVIN: (*Starts out of control at this, enraged, crosses UC and bangs on file cabinet.*) Ooooeee! Ooooeee! You wanna *see?* You wanna *see?* Ooooeee!

ALICE: Calvin stop it! STOP IT!

CALVIN: "Calvin stop it"? "Stop it"? (*Picks up school books from desk.*) There any black professors here?

ALICE: (*Crosses UR.*) No! They got cut . . . the budget's low . . . they got . . .

CALVIN: (*interrupting*) Cut? *They* got CUT? (*Crosses to ALICE and backs her to the DS edge of desk.*) Gonna *cut you,* lady! Gonna cut you, throw you out the fuckin window, throw the fuckin books out the fuckin window, burn it all mother fuckin down. FUCKIN DOWN!!!

ALICE: Calvin! Stop it! STOP IT! YOU HEAR ME?

CALVIN: (*Turns away, center stage.*) I CAN'T!! *YOU* HEAR *ME?* I CAN'T! *YOU* HEAR *ME!* I CAN'T! YOU GOTTA GIVE ME MY EDUCATION! GOTTA TEACH ME! GIVE ME SOMETHING NOW! GIVE ME NOW! NOW! NOW! NOW! NOW! NOW!

(*CALVIN tears up text book. He starts to pick up torn pages and drops them. He bursts into a wailing, bellowing cry in his anguish and despair, doubled over in pain and grief. It is a while before his sobs subside. Finally, ALICE speaks.*)

ALICE: Calvin . . . from the bottom of my heart . . . I want to help you . . .

CALVIN: (*barely able to speak*) By changin my words? Thass nothin . . . nothin! I got to know them big ideas . . . and which way to git em down . . .

ALICE: But how can I teach you that? You can't write a paragraph, Calvin . . . or a sentence . . . you can't spell past 4th grade . . . the essay you wrote showed that . . .

CALVIN: (*rises*) What essay?

ALICE: (*Crosses to UL files, gets essay and hands it to CALVIN.*) The autobiographical one . . . you did it the first day . . .

CALVIN: You said that was for *your* reference . . . didn't count . . .

ALICE: Here . . .

CALVIN: (*Opens it up. Stunned.*) "F"? Why didn't you tell me I failed?

ALICE: (*Crosses to desk, puts essay down.*) For what?

CALVIN: (*Still stunned.*) So you could teach me how to write.

ALICE: (*Crosses DL.*) In 16 weeks?

CALVIN: (*Still can't believe this.*) You my teacher!

ALICE: That would take years! And speech is my job. You need a tutor.

CALVIN: I'm your job. They outa tutors!

ALICE: (*Turns to him.*) I can't do it, Calvin. And that's the real truth. I'm one person, in one job. And I can't. Do you understand? And even if I could, it wouldn't matter. All that matters is the budget . . . and the curriculum . . . and the grades . . . and how you look . . . and how you talk!

CALVIN: (*Pause. Absorbing this.*) Then I'm finished, man.

(*There is a long pause. Finally:*)

ALICE: (*Gets essay from desk, refiles it and returns to desk.*) No, you're not. If you'll bend and take what I can give you, things will work out for you . . . Trust me . . . Let me help you Calvin . . . Please . . . I can teach you speech . . .

CALVIN: (*Crosses to UC file cabinet. Long pause.*) Okay . . . all right, man . . . (*Crosses to student chair and sits.*)

ALICE: (*Crosses to desk, takes off rain coat and sits in swivel chair.*) Now, then, we'll go through the exercise once then you do it at home . . . please, repeat after me, slowly . . . "asking" . . . "asking" . . . "asking" . . .

CALVIN: (*long pause*) Ax-ing . . .

ALICE: Ass-king . . .

CALVIN: (*During the following, he now turns from ALICE, faces front, and gazes out beyond the audience; on his fourth word, lights begin to fade to black:*) Ax-ing . . . Aks-ing . . . ass-king . . . asking . . . asking . . . asking . . .

Blackout

End of Play

Questions For Discussion and Writing

1. What important information does Alice's opening telephone conversation with her daughter convey about the character? For what reasons do you think Alice cannot hear Calvin?
2. What are the implications of the college's "Open Admissions" program for both Alice and Calvin?
3. What does Calvin really want from Alice, and why?
4. When Alice tells Calvin that the ten black students who went to Ivy League graduate programs were no better than he is, "just perceived as better" (p. 193), pointing to the blackboard, what is she implying?
5. What does Alice mean when she says Calvin must improve his "Positive Communicator's Image" (p. 193)? What value, if any, could her conviction about this image have for Calvin?
6. What does Calvin mean when he says, "I got to know them big ideas . . . and which way to git em down . . ." (p. 194)? What is the significance of Calvin's last line in the play?

PHYLLIS I. LYONS

Translating Cultures . . .
Or, What's George Washington Doing in a
Sushi Bar?

Since 1978, Phyllis I. Lyons has been on the faculty of Northwestern University in the Department of Japanese Languages and Literature. In 1983, she won the Japan–United States Friendship Commission Prize for Japanese Literary Translation, for her translation of Saga of Dazai Osamu, *the author of the story she uses as an example in the selection that follows.*

Lyons studied at the University of Rochester before earning her Ph.D. at the University of Chicago. During her graduate years, she also attended the Inter-University Center for Japanese Language Studies and Keio University in Japan. Although she had lived in Japan for several years as a child, she had not learned the language. In those three years as a graduate student in Japan, however, Lyons not only learned the Japanese language but also experienced for the first time being an adult member of a minority—a Caucasian, American woman in an Asian society. This experience caused her to inquire more consciously into her own culture. Lyons came to understand more fully that the metaphor translation *points not only to translating one language and culture to another but more importantly to translating the perceptions and judgments of her own culture into language that conveys accurate meanings.*

The challenges of translating literary works involve many issues. "Before I myself translated," Professor Lyons writes, "I used to think that an awkward translation was justifiable: at least it made a work available to an audience that couldn't read the original. Now that I translate—and teach translations—I know that if a translation is awkward, readers think of the culture it represents as awkward and incomprehensible. In the case of Japan, readers tend to give transla-

196

tions a 'free pass,' as representing an intrinsically incomprehensible culture. That's not fair to Japan. On the other hand, to rewrite a text because it 'sounds better in English' that way, oversteps the bounds of poetic license. The translator walks the thin line between these two extremes."

The essay and story that follow will challenge the reader in a number of ways. While trying to keep track of the Japanese names, concepts, and history that Lyons gives us, which we need to grasp the meaning of the story she translates entitled "The Garden," we experience a kind of culture shock. Keep in mind that the confusion you may feel about understanding what you're reading is part of the lesson to be learned about the difficulties inherent in translating cultures.

"Translating Cultures" was published in 1985 in Arts & Sciences *magazine.*

Before you read "Translating Cultures," think of an object that is special to you (such as a painting, a gift you received, or something you made) but that someone else—perhaps someone from another culture—is not likely to appreciate at first or at all. Describe the object's history, the psychological significance it has for you, and any other details that might help another person appreciate it as you do. Then write about the problems you would encounter in convincing the person you've chosen of the object's value.

The class might approach this selection by first reading the story of "The Garden" together and then discussing the meanings of it before reading the background information given in Lyons's essay.

I n a *New Yorker* cartoon, a middle-aged, middle-brow husband leans across the restaurant table and asks his wife anxiously, "Which one is it I can't stand—sushi or sashimi?" The cultural and social history of Japan, we know, differs sharply from our own. But we also know that Japan is becoming much less alien and impenetrable. Even Americans who have not visited that country are now comfortably acquainted with Japanese food, theater, and garden design.

This fact points to a paradox faced by translators: The less alien a culture is, the heavier small increments in popular knowledge of that culture weigh. Our confidence in the universality and translatability of human experience grows with other forms of inflation. Yet, to change metaphors, the broader the plains that are domesticated, the higher and more taxing are the peaks of what remains to be explained.

When the average response to Japanese cuisine is, "Raw fish? Seaweed? Yuck!", the specialist may easily enlighten. But when young American executives routinely come to know the difference between *maguro* (tuna) and *toro* (the prized cut of the tuna), and may even ask for *gari* (prepared ginger) and *murasaki* (soy sauce), what is left to the translator? Only to try to illuminate the whole complex ethos of Edo popular culture evoked by the world of sushi, in which much of what we think of as traditional Japan—samurai, geisha, flower arranging, tea ceremony, haiku, woodblock prints, and so forth—originated. The Edo or Tokugawa period, *c.* 1600–1868, got its name from the city of Edo, now Tokyo, where the shoguns of the Tokugawa family ruled in the name of the emperors, and a vigorous middle-class culture flourished within a bureaucratized, feudalistic system of government. It is this Edo culture to which the heartstrings of the Japanese themselves, no matter how internationalized, continue to vibrate. To the Japanese, the Edo nineteenth century is sometimes realer than the industrialized twentieth.

And the specialist, faced with getting all that across while translating a short, lively story from Japanese into English, may simply sigh and drink another cup of tea, or *sake*.

Translation is, obviously, more than a matter of linguistic competence. The problem is sometimes not whether two idioms are compatible, but whether situations simply require too much explaining, are too much a part of another national culture to be happily translated. I don't mean explaining exoticisms like strange apparel or curious customs. In fact, stories about samurai-spirit terrorists, lesbian princesses, or insane monks who burn down temples—all of these actually appear in novels by Mishima Yukio—may be relatively easy to export. Their very exoticism promotes a comfortable suspension of disbelief.

I would not have chosen to translate the story that follows except for the special circumstance that I can present it here with an introduction, conferring (I hope) instant cultural citizenship on its readers. Really, the story is not very complex. It is a good example of the almost minimalist art that characterizes one kind of largely untranslated Japanese literature, a kind to which the Japanese themselves are extremely responsive. But such stories can be like a joke whose punchline has to be explained: the joke risks becoming only a cultural artifact, and not a joke. This is a funny story, and one that Japanese readers can enjoy even while sharing the discomfort of the story's narrator.

Three knots, historical, aesthetic, and psychological, must be untied before we too can enter the intimate garden of the title. First, who are "the Taikō" and "Rikyū"? The historian breathes a sigh of relief: That's easy. But the translator-critic's heart sinks: If it's necessary to explain Abraham Lincoln and Frank Lloyd Wright to get to the point of this story, maybe I'd better find another story.

"Taikō" was an honorary title given to a retired imperial office-holder. It has become synonymous with its most famous bearer, Toyotomi Hideyoshi (1537–1598), the next-to-last unifier of Japan after centuries of bloodshed when great warlords jockeyed to rule in the name of the emperor. Hideyoshi was, as "The Garden" tells us, an ugly man; his lord, Oda Nobunaga, called him "Monkey." He rose from the lowest ranks of the soldiery, was therefore little more than a peasant, but was a gifted military and political strategist. When his lord,

Nobunaga, was maneuvered by a rival into having to commit suicide in 1582, Hideyoshi the loyal retainer, after avenging Nobunaga, went on eventually to become the Great Minister of State and regent to the emperor.

Hideyoshi often demonstrated the strategic wisdom of magnanimity toward defeated enemies, but late in his life he grew erratic. Grandiose dreams of pan-Asian empire led him to two unsuccessful attempts to invade Korea, in 1592 and 1597. After the death of his infant son in 1591, he named his adult nephew Hidetsugu heir; when another son was born two years later, the nephew was disinherited, forced to commit suicide, and his family executed.

Hideyoshi's relationship with Rikyū dated from the 1570s, when they were both retainers of Oda Nobunaga, one as military deputy, the other as tea master. Sen no Rikyū (1522–1591) came from generations of tea masters. Nominally he belonged to the merchant class; temperamentally, as a student of tea and Zen, he was an aristocrat. After Nobunaga's death, he moved to Hideyoshi's court, where he officiated at tea ceremonies for the emperor and at Hideyoshi's famous Great Tea Party at Kitano Shrine in 1587, a scene that seems to have been a cross between Woodstock and Ravinia. (Invitations were issued by placards set up in town squares around the country. Thousands came. It was to have lasted ten days, but was closed down after the first day, when Hideyoshi had to leave to suppress a revolt in Kyushu.)

Such excess was typical of Hideyoshi's taste; and the art of the castle-building eras of Nobunaga and Hideyoshi is characterized by massive structures with large open spaces, and by brilliant gold leaf and bold primary-color washes on the screens used to adorn the large spaces.

Rikyū's personal style, in contrast, was characterized by *wabi:* restraint and austerity, a detached and tranquil frame of mind, rusticity, many of those features we now associate with the Japanese aesthetic: "richness in poverty, beauty in simplicity," in one formulation. For tea implements, Rikyū chose unpolished textures, dark hues, and "natural" materials—bamboo where it could replace lacquer, rough Raku ware rather than Chinese porcelains. He decreased the size of the already small tearoom to promote even greater spiritual intimacy among participants in the tea ceremony.

In 1591, for motives that are unclear and endlessly debated, Hideyoshi ordered Rikyū to commit suicide. Among possible causes are a life-sized statue of himself that Rikyū donated to the temple where he had studied Zen, a statue placed in a niche above the gate so that anyone entering, including Hideyoshi, passed under its feet; Rikyū's refusal to give his daughter, who had caught Hideyoshi's eye, to his master; Hideyoshi's irritation at the prices Rikyū charged for tea implements; Hideyoshi's jealousy over Rikyū's closeness to other great lords; simply the tension between two very strong and increasingly inflexible wills. Suffice it to say that, at least in aesthetic matters, their tastes were sometimes less than compatible.

Hideyoshi regretted his impetuous command almost immediately (as despots are wont to do), and a year later he ordered a garden to be built in the style of Rikyū—whose influence has endured. The Sen school (or schools) of tea still flourishes. *Wabi* has become our idea of the Japanese aesthetic.

This historical account partly unties the second knot in the story as well—but only partly. Without going into the aesthetic of the tea ceremony, an exoticism we will take on faith, we can see that the relationship between these two historical figures is important to the meaning of "The Garden." If the love-hate struggle between Hideyoshi and Rikyū symbolizes in some way the relationship between the two brothers in the story, which one is Hideyoshi, which Rikyū? Certainly the elegant, educated, aristocratic—and pompous and self-important—older brother must be Rikyū, while the ex-delinquent, "parasitic" younger brother, who resists the usual definitions of landscape beauty, and also tells the tale, must be Hideyoshi.

In this connection, it is important to realize that the practice of Rikyū's aesthetic of humble naturalness is itself a marvel of artificiality. Anyone who has been to a formal garden in Japan knows that luxuriant grass is out of the question, bare ground the surface of choice. Little, old men shape tiny patches of green with manicure scissors, mist the moss thrice a day, and catch each autumn leaf as it falls—unless that patch of the garden is meant to represent "Autumn," in which case the tender red and yellow leaves may lie as they fall, "naturally," but brown and wrinkled casualties are whisked away instantly.

Yet at the same time, of course, Rikyū was truly the aesthete and Hideyoshi the man of affairs—and the bully. And the younger brother is trying to make a claim for himself as the artist and suggesting that the older brother is a philistine. The relationship between the two historical figures and the two characters in the story presents a richly involved puzzle. Ambiguities and tensions vibrate below the surface.

The third knot, the psychological knot, is tight indeed. On the one hand, sibling rivalry may well be universal. On the other, consider the Japanese family in general and the author's family in particular. Especially before the Second World War, the Japanese family played a major part in the country's social structure. It was a dense legal entity which exerted kinds of power over its members that were not purely emotional but produced their own emotional supports and vulnerabilities.

The autobiographical narrator of "The Garden" refers to several unspecified "things" he had done in his twenties which had "brought shame" on his relatives. In the life of Dazai Osamu, the story's author (as distinct from the tale's teller), those "things" had included three suicide attempts (during one of which a female companion died); marriage to a geisha (in a family for whom such dalliance was fine, but not marriage); involvement in leftist politics during Japan's ultra-rightist police-state prewar years; months of drug addiction following an emergency appendectomy, cured when Dazai was incarcerated by his friends in a mental institution; and, along the way, expulsion from Tokyo Imperial University!

All the while, Dazai's older brother was one of the largest landowners in northern Japan, president of the family bank, mayor of his town, and representative in the prefectural legislature—as well as financial supporter of his messed-up younger brother. In later years, after "The Garden" had appeared, he was elected to the national legislature and became governor of the prefecture.

When the narrator says that the family house was in his brother's care, the resonances in Japanese are heavy. "House" means family, and the entire family was that brother's responsibility. Dazai's problems in the 1930s were not just awkward for his family; they were politically dangerous. In the story, in a sense, the narrator had been a kind of malignant tumor in the body of the family and by extension, in the body politic. Yet he was irrevocably a part of the family, and he never ceased relying on its support. Nor did the family ever totally cease to provide that support.

Hence the story's contradictory tones of wistful dependency and prickly standoffishness. The older brother, as portrayed in Dazai's fifteen years of autobiographical writing, never understood how sensitive and gifted his black-sheep younger brother was, and in fact insulted and thwarted him. Yet the older brother never ceased being a protective head of the family, almost a father—with all the ambivalences that *that* relationship implies.

When "The Garden" was written, Dazai was in his mid-thirties and already well known. With publication of his novel, *The Setting Sun,* the next year, he became the most famous writer of his day, and today he holds a prominent position in the literary pantheon and is as known to the general public as his brother has been forgotten. But however successful he was as a writer, he felt he was a failure as a human being (and committed suicide in 1948). That tension in "The Garden" is transformed into gentle self-mockery and a yearning for self-validation.

Dazai Osamu wrote in the genre of what the Japanese call the "I-novel," autobiographical stories in which personal experience is much more than background; the author's experience is translated whole-cloth into the realm of art. "The Garden" is in a way Dazai speaking to himself. We, the readers, are invited to erase our separateness and enter into his personal, emotional world—to know not just what he's doing, but how he feels as he's doing it. On the one hand, this is a dangerous project for the writer: by and large, the portrait of the older brother is distinctly unflattering, despite moments of sympathy, as if the younger brother were inviting a blow he has braced for. But it is also an act of love, a gesture toward reconciliation couched in terms of a plea for understanding, but one made awkwardly, like an accident victim learning to walk again.

Much of Dazai's work is about the costs of emotional estrangement and a yearning for reunion. In the nonfiction novel *Tsugaru,* Dazai's narrator, really Dazai himself, says: "Being an adult is lonely. Even if you love one another, you must be cautious and treat each other with propriety, like strangers. Why, do you suppose, must we be so cautious? The answer is simple: because we've been greatly betrayed and humiliated too many times. The first lesson that turns a youth into an adult is that you cannot trust other people. An adult is a youth betrayed." "The Garden" speaks in the tones of a joke, but it is also serious about the pain beneath the surface of so many human relationships.

Earlier I mentioned cultural exoticisms, and some of those remain to be cleared up. "The Garden" was written in 1946; the destruction of war is a sustained undertone. Kōfu is a couple of hours northwest of Tokyo by train, Tsugaru about five hundred miles to the northeast, but by mid-1945 bombing had destroyed much of the train system, which is why the trip took four days. In Japan only one broadcast is referred to as *The* Radio Broadcast: the Emperor's announcement on August 15, 1945, of his empire's capitulation.

"Snowsheds," works of art in themselves, are protections for prized flora in the winter garden. The language of the samurai swordsman is still part of Japan's vocabulary in a way that the language of fencing is no longer part of ours, so I have translated a metaphorical swordstroke in the Japanese into a modern American gunshot, but have thus forfeited a nuance: in Japanese, sword-play is ceremonial and formal; contestants do not merely hack at each other, but also parry and stand en garde.

Matsuo Bashō (1644–1694), the greatest haiku poet of them all, wrote in a long tradition of monkish poet-recluses. The narrator updates Bashō's Zen-tinged wanderlust and retreat from society; it becomes a sort of nihilism-of-art depression and alienation. *Shinnai* is a form of traditional ballad-singing performed to *samisen* accompaniment, deriving from the *bunraku,* Japan's puppet theater. The *shinnai* selections in the story are from the eighteenth and nineteenth centuries.

Two living novelists are cited as the older brother's favorites—the younger brother's disappointment that he is not one of them is palpable: Kafū is Nagai Kafū (1879–1959); Jun'ichirō is Tanizaki Jun'ichirō (1886–1965). Wu Ch'ing-yüan is a Chinese chess expert who has lived much of his life in Japan and may still be alive today.

Last but not least, a matter of dimly remembered myths and their meanings. Remember the story of George Washington and the cherry tree? As everybody knows, it has a moral. It shows that you're not supposed to tell lies. Remember also the story about George throwing a silver dollar across the Potomac? Remember what *that* shows? You don't really—though it sort of rings a bell? Well, in "The Garden" there is a reference to a bean paste made with citron fruit. I didn't know the story that was alluded to. Nor did East Asian librarians I went to—although they said it sort of rang a bell. Nor did any of my Japanese-national colleagues.

Thanks to cooperative scholarship in the person of Professor Robert Kramer of Northwestern's History Department, himself a scholar of the tea ceremony, here it is. It is said that one snowy night, as Hideyoshi was wandering the streets of Kyoto in disguise, looking for a tea gathering that he had heard about, he came upon a singular teahouse. The tea master invited him in and prepared a simple meal for his guest (who, he sensed, was someone important): rice gruel and bean-paste soup seasoned with the juice of the two citrons *(yuzu)* that he had just knocked down from the snow-covered tree. In all his life, Hideyoshi said, he had never experienced a tea gathering as interesting as that one.

THE GARDEN
by Dazai Osamu

Our house in Tokyo was destroyed in the bombing so we moved to my wife's family's home in Kōfu, but then their house was burnt to the ground in the fire-bombing, and so the four of us, myself, my wife, our five-year-old daughter and two-year-old son, had no choice but to head for the house of my birth in Tsugaru. My father and mother were dead, and my oldest brother, some ten years or so older than I, was guardian of the homestead. Now some of you might well argue that before getting wiped out twice, we should have gone straight to my hometown; but, you see, several things I'd done in my twenties had brought shame on my relatives and now I found myself simply not in any position to go barging in on my brother. On the other hand, here I was, two catastrophes, two babes in arms, and nowhere else to go; so I figured what the hell, and sent him a telegram telling him he was our last resort. We left Kōfu at the end of July and had quite a time of it along the way—it took four full days and nights—but at last we arrived at my family home in Tsugaru. They all greeted us with smiles. At dinner, there was even *sake* at my place.

But the carrier-based planes had reached here too, the northernmost end of Honshū, and were bombing our towns at will. From the day after we arrived, I was helping build bomb shelters out in the fields.

And then, before long, there came The Radio Broadcast.

The following day, my brother began fixing up the garden. I was his helper. "When I was young," my brother opined as he pulled weeds, "I thought clumps of grass growing all over the garden gave it a special tone, but as I've gotten older, it bothers me to see even a single blade of grass."

Well then, did that mean I still young? I didn't find the overgrown garden unattractive.

"Even in a garden of this size," he continued in an undertone, as if to himself, "If you want to keep it in order, you've got to have a gardener work at it every single day. And there are all those snowsheds you have to build for the trees."

"It *is* quite a job," timidly chimed in yours truly, the younger brother, the sponger.

My brother went on with great seriousness: "In the past we could do it, but nowadays there just aren't any extra hands, and what with all that commotion from the bombing, it was hardly the time for landscape gardeners. This won't be a bad garden when we get it back together."

"You're quite right." Younger brother wasn't much of a connoisseur of gardens. He was a barbarian who could look out at an overgrown garden rank with weeds and find it beautiful.

My brother then went on at length to explain what landscape school the garden belonged to, how the school's practices had come about, how they were transmitted, and how they had come all the way to Tsugaru. And the subject naturally shifted to Rikyū.

"Why don't you fellows ever write about Rikyū? I should think that'd make a fine story."

"Um," I answered ambiguously. Whenever conversation turned to literature, younger brother, the parasite, exhibited something of the defensiveness of the specialist himself.

"He was quite a man," continued my brother obliviously. "Even the Taikō, great as he was, was always getting shot down. I suppose you know the story of the citron *miso?*"

"Um," the younger brother responded, more ambiguously.

"A teacher who never studies!" he said with a grimace, apparently deciding that I didn't know anything. His scowling face always struck terror into my heart. He'd clearly decided I was an ignoramus who'd never read a book, and he was distinctly displeased.

Now I've done it, I thought. The parasite squirmed and tried to get out of it with a laugh: "The thing is, I just somehow don't like Rikyū much."

"That's because he's complex."

"Precisely. There are things about it that are hard to figure. He seemed to have contempt for the Taikō, and yet he still couldn't bring himself to leave him. I find that a bit murky."

"That's because the Taikō was so fascinating," my brother said, his good humor restored. "You can't say which one was the superior, as a human being. The two were locked in mortal combat. They were diametrically opposed in every possible way. One rose from humble origins, a small, shriveled man with no air of quality about him, and that monkey face, not a bit of education or culture; all the same, he brought about the splendor of the Momoyama period, with all that gorgeous, extravagant architectural art. The other came from a fairly affluent family, and he was a substantial, dignified, fine-looking man with a good education. And he countered with the *wabi* of his world of the grass hut—that's what's so interesting about it."

"But all the same, Rikyū was Hideyoshi's retainer—his tea man, right? So wasn't the outcome inevitable from the start?" I of course laughed as I said this.

My brother, however, was not laughing at all. "That's not what the relationship between the Taikō and Rikyū was. Rikyū had almost more influence than the great lords, and the—well, let's call them the 'intelligentsia' among the lords, they were drawn far more to the elegant Rikyū than to the ignorant Taikō. That's why the Taikō couldn't help being so nervous about it."

What strange creatures men are, I thought as I silently continued pulling weeds. Here's Hideyoshi, the great political leader—wouldn't you think he'd be able to cede at least stylishness to Rikyū and just laugh it off? Does a man have to feel compelled to win in absolutely everything? And Rikyū—couldn't he have let the master he served get in at least one shot? I mean, after all, there's no chance that someone like the Taikō would ever be likely to understand something like the nihility of stylishness, so how could he possibly have suddenly dropped everything and gone off wandering for the rest of his life like Bashō? There was just something opaque to me in the picture of the two of them trading shots, locked in mortal combat—with Rikyū not breaking away from the Taikō and, more to the point, not even seeming much to dislike his political power, so that he was always hanging around the Taikō. I found myself thinking that if the Taikō was indeed such a charismatic figure, Rikyū might much better have demonstrated the purity of his love by sharing the rest of his life with him.

"It doesn't have any of those beautiful scenes that arouse the readers' emotions." Maybe it was that I was still young—to write a story without a scene like that would be more trouble than it was worth.

My brother laughed. Sentimental as usual, he seemed to imply. "That's not it. You probably just can't write something like that. It's time for you to start spending some more time studying the big world out there. What an uneducated teacher you are!"

He stood up, as if giving up on me, and gazed at the garden. I stood up too, and gazed at the garden.

"It looks good, doesn't it."

"Um."

Sorry, Rikyū. I just don't want to be sniping at my brother, especially since I'm living off him. That kind of rivalry is shameful. Even if I weren't sponging— never once have I ever thought of competing with him. The outcome was set from the moment we were born.

My brother's gotten horribly thin these days. He's not been well. All the same, rumors are afield that he will run for the national legislature, or governor, or something like that. The family worry about his health.

Guests of all kinds come. My brother takes each one up to the parlor on the second floor to talk, and never admits he's tired. Yesterday a lady came, a master of *shinnai,* apparently the best of Fujidayu's disciples. She spoke to my brother about *shinnai* in the second-floor room with the golden screen. They let me join them to listen in. They talked about "Akegarasu" and "The Selling of Kasane." As I listened, my legs started to go to sleep and I was in quite a bit of pain; besides, I felt I was getting a cold. But my brother, for all that he was not well, seemed perfectly comfortable, and he asked her himself to go on about "Nochi no Masayume" and "Ranchō."

After that, we all moved to the parlor, and my brother said to her, "These are terrible times we live in. It must have been awful for you to have had to evacuate to the countryside and work in the fields yourself. But then, the thing about art is that as long as you keep your spirit firmly fixed on it, even if you have to set aside your *samisen* for a year or two, your art will not suffer. I think your best is ahead of you, the best is yet to come." Here was this artist, famous even in Tokyo, and yet he actually told her this—straight out, unabashed—and he, a total amateur. It was as if someone had shouted out, "Great job!" from the peanut gallery.

The Japanese writers my brother apparently respects these days are Kafū and Jun'ichirō. And he reads the work of Chinese essayists with great pleasure. Tomorrow Wu Ch'ing-yüan will be visiting him. Not to talk about chess, apparently, but for a leisurely exploration of world affairs.

My brother's gotten up early today and he's out weeding the garden. Yours truly, his barbarian younger brother, seems indeed to have caught a cold at yesterday's *shinnai* discussion, and is currently sitting over the charcoal brazier in the back room of the house annex, debating with myself whether or not to help him weed the garden. While letting my mind wander at will, thinking self-serving thoughts: Mightn't it be remotely possible that this Wu Ch'ing-yüan would be the kind of man to find a wild and overgrown garden not all that bad?

Questions for Discussion and Writing

"Translating Cultures"

1. What are some of the major problems faced by a translator of a story such as "The Garden"? According to Lyons, what are the "knots" with which stories are tied together?
2. What ideas do we need to understand about the third knot, the psychological one, especially in regard to Japanese ideas about family and the relationship of Osamu to his story?

"The Garden"

1. In what ways does the garden have literal and symbolic importance to the brothers?
2. Why is the history we learn about the Taikō and Rikyū so important to our understanding of the brothers' dialogue about them? In what ways does the relationship between these historic figures parallel the brothers' own relationship?
3. Younger brother claims that he has never "thought of competing" with older brother: "The outcome," he says, "was set from the moment we were born" (p. 205). Why or why not do you agree with his statement?
4. What elements of the story do you think are experienced by people of many cultures? Explain.
5. What is your answer to the question posed in the last line of the story?

EDWARD T. HALL AND MILDRED REED HALL

The Sounds of Silence

*Edward T. Hall and Mildred Reed Hall, married in 1946, have writ-
ten a number of articles and books together. Their first collaborative
book, published in 1975, is entitled* The Fourth Dimension in Architecture: The Impact of Building on Man's Behavior. *Their most recent collaboration,* Hidden Differences: Doing Business with the Japanese, *was published in 1988.*

*Like many of the writers in this anthology who share an interest
in intercultural matters, Edward Hall pursued a diversity of careers
and study—from working for the U.S. Department of State and
being a professor at several universities to conducting anthropological field research in Micronesia, the southwestern United States, and
Europe. His best-known books include* The Silent Language *(1959),*
The Hidden Dimension *(1966), and* Beyond Culture *(1976)—considered landmarks of thought in the field of intercultural communication. Hall's writings help us to understand the essential idea that,
from the largest to the smallest patterns of our lives, culture is
learned.*

*In "The Sounds of Silence," first published in 1971, the Halls
address the importance of nonverbal language in our lives.*

**Before you read "The Sounds of Silence," write about a time when some-
one's body language communicated messages different than that person's
words. Describe the situation and how you interpreted the language of the
person's eyes or body. Did you talk with that person about the unintended
communication, and if so, what was the result? If not, why did you ignore
it? What made you certain that you had read the nonverbal language correctly?**

B ob leaves his apartment at 8:15 A.M. and stops at the corner drugstore for breakfast. Before he can speak, the counterman says, "The usual?" Bob nods yes. While he savors his Danish, a fat man pushes onto the adjoining stool and overflows into his space. Bob scowls and the man pulls himself in as much as he can. Bob has sent two messages without speaking a syllable.

Henry has an appointment to meet Arthur at 11 o'clock; he arrives at 11:30. Their conversation is friendly, but Arthur retains a lingering hostility. Henry has unconsciously communicated that he doesn't think the appointment is very important or that Arthur is a person who needs to be treated with respect.

George is talking to Charley's wife at a party. Their conversation is entirely trivial, yet Charley glares at them suspiciously. Their physical proximity and the movements of their eyes reveal that they are powerfully attracted to each other.

José Ybarra and Sir Edmund Jones are at the same party and it is important for them to establish a cordial relationship for business reasons. Each is trying to be warm and friendly, yet they will part with mutual distrust and their business transaction will probably fall through. José, in Latin fashion, moved closer and closer to Sir Edmund as they spoke, and this movement was miscommunicated as pushiness to Sir Edmund, who kept backing away from this intimacy, and this was miscommunicated to José as coldness. The silent languages of Latin and English cultures are more difficult to learn than their spoken languages.

In each of these cases, we see the subtle power of nonverbal communication. The only language used throughout most of the history of humanity (in evolutionary terms, vocal communication is relatively recent), it is the first form of communication you learn. You use this preverbal language, consciously and unconsciously, every day to tell other people how you feel about yourself and them. This language includes your posture, gestures, facial expressions, costume, the way you walk, even your treatment of time and space and material things. All people communicate on several different levels at the same time but are usually aware of only the verbal dialog and don't realize that they respond to nonverbal messages. But when a person says one thing and really believes something else, the discrepancy between the two can usually be sensed. Nonverbal-communication systems are much less subject to the conscious deception that often occurs in verbal systems. When we find ourselves thinking, "I don't know what it is about him, but he doesn't seem sincere," it's usually this lack of congruity between a person's words and his behavior that makes us anxious and uncomfortable.

Few of us realize how much we all depend on body movement in our conversation or are aware of the hidden rules that govern listening behavior. But we know instantly whether or not the person we're talking to is "tuned in" and we're very sensitive to any breach in listening etiquette. In white middle-class American culture, when someone wants to show he is listening to someone else, he looks either at the other person's face or, specifically, at his eyes, shifting his gaze from one eye to the other.

If you observe a person conversing, you'll notice that he indicates he's listening by nodding his head. He also makes little "Hmm" noises. If he agrees with what's being said, he may give a vigorous nod. To show pleasure or affirmation, he smiles; if he has some reservations, he looks skeptical by raising an eyebrow or pulling down the corners of his mouth. If a participant wants to terminate the conversation, he may start shifting his body position, stretching his legs, crossing or uncrossing them, bobbing his foot or diverting his gaze from the speaker. The more he fidgets, the more the speaker becomes aware that he has lost his audience. As a last measure, the listener may look at his watch to indicate the imminent end of the conversation.

Talking and listening are so intricately intertwined that a person cannot do one without the other. Even when one is alone and talking to oneself, there is part of the brain that speaks while another part listens. In all conversations, the listener is positively or negatively reinforcing the speaker all the time. He may even guide the conversation without knowing it, by laughing or frowning or dismissing the argument with a wave of his hand.

The language of the eyes—another age-old way of exchanging feelings—is both subtle and complex. Not only do men and women use their eyes differently but there are class, generation, regional, ethnic and national cultural differences. Americans often complain about the way foreigners stare at people or hold a glance too long. Most Americans look away from someone who is using his eyes in an unfamiliar way because it makes them self-conscious. If a man looks at another man's wife in a certain way, he's asking for trouble, as indicated earlier. But he might not be ill mannered or seeking to challenge the husband. He might be a European in this country who hasn't learned our visual mores. Many American women visiting France or Italy are acutely embarrassed because, for the first time in their lives, men really look at them—their eyes, hair, nose, lips, breasts, hips, legs, thighs, knees, ankles, feet, clothes, hairdo, even their walk. These same women, once they have become used to being looked at, often return to the United States and are overcome with the feeling that "No one ever really looks at me anymore."

Analyzing the mass of data on the eyes, it is possible to sort out at least three ways in which the eyes are used to communicate: dominance *vs.* submission, involvement *vs.* detachment and positive *vs.* negative attitude. In addition, there are three levels of consciousness and control, which can be categorized as follows: (1) conscious use of the eyes to communicate, such as the flirting blink and the intimate nose-wrinkling squint; (2) the very extensive category of unconscious but learned behavior governing where the eyes are directed and when (this unwritten set of rules dictates how and under what circumstances the sexes, as well as people of all status categories, look at each other); and (3) the response of the eye itself, which is completely outside both awareness and control— changes in the cast (the sparkle) of the eye and the pupillary reflex.

The eye is unlike any other organ of the body, for it is an extension of the brain. The unconscious pupillary reflex and the cast of the eye have been known by people of Middle Eastern origin for years—although most are unaware of their knowledge. Depending on the context, Arabs and others look either directly at the eyes or deeply *into* the eyes of their interlocutor. We became aware of this in the Middle East several years ago while looking at jewelry. The merchant suddenly started to push a particular bracelet at a customer and said, "You buy this one." What interested us was that the bracelet was not the one that had been consciously selected by the purchaser. But the merchant, watching the pupils of the eyes, knew what the purchaser really wanted to buy. Whether he specifically knew *how* he knew is debatable.

A psychologist at the University of Chicago, Eckhard Hess, was the first to conduct systematic studies of the pupillary reflex. His wife remarked one evening, while watching him reading in bed, that he must be very interested in the text because his pupils were dilated. Following up on this, Hess slipped some pictures of nudes into a stack of photographs that he gave to his male assistant. Not looking at the photographs but watching his assistant's pupils, Hess was able to tell precisely when the assistant came to the nudes. In further experiments, Hess retouched the eyes in a photograph of a woman. In one print, he made the pupils small, in another, large; nothing else was changed. Subjects who were given the photographs found the woman with the dilated pupils much more attractive. Any man who has had the experience of seeing a woman look at him as her pupils widen with reflex speed knows that she's flashing him a message.

The eye-sparkle phenomenon frequently turns up in our interviews of couples in love. It's apparently one of the first reliable clues in the other person that love is genuine. To date, there is no scientific data to explain eye sparkle; no investigation of the pupil, the cornea or even the white sclera of the eye shows how the sparkle originates. Yet we all know it when we see it.

One common situation for most people involves the use of the eyes in the street and in public. Although eye behavior follows a definite set of rules, the rules vary according to the place, the needs and feelings of the people, and their ethnic background. For urban whites, once they're within definite recognition distance (16–32 feet for people with average eyesight), there is mutual avoidance of eye contact—unless they want something specific: a pickup, a handout or information of some kind. In the West and in small towns generally, however, people are much more likely to look at and greet one another, even if they're strangers.

It's permissible to look at people if they're beyond recognition distance; but once inside this sacred zone, you can only steal a glance at strangers. You *must* greet friends, however; to fail to do so is insulting. Yet, to stare too fixedly even at them is considered rude and hostile. Of course, all of these rules are variable.

A great many blacks, for example, greet each other in public even if they don't know each other. To blacks, most eye behavior of whites has the effect of giving the impression that they aren't there, but this is due to white avoidance of eye contact with *anyone* in the street.

Another very basic difference between people of different ethnic backgrounds is their sense of territoriality and how they handle space. This is the silent communication, or miscommunication, that caused friction between Mr. Ybarra and Sir Edmund Jones in our earlier example. We know from research that everyone has around himself an invisible bubble of space that contracts and expands depending on several factors: his emotional state, the activity he's performing at the time and his cultural background. This bubble is a kind of mobile territory that he will defend against intrusion. If he is accustomed to close personal distance between himself and others, his bubble will be smaller than that of someone who's accustomed to greater personal distance. People of North European heritage—English, Scandinavian, Swiss and German—tend to avoid contact. Those whose heritage is Italian, French, Spanish, Russian, Latin American or Middle Eastern like close personal contact.

People are very sensitive to any intrusion into their spatial bubble. If someone stands too close to you, your first instinct is to back up. If that's not possible, you lean away and pull yourself in, tensing your muscles. If the intruder doesn't respond to these body signals, you may then try to protect yourself, using a briefcase, umbrella or raincoat. Women—especially when traveling alone—often plant their pocketbook in such a way that no one can get very close to them. As a last resort, you may move to another spot and position yourself behind a desk or a chair that provides screening. Everyone tries to adjust the space around himself in a way that's comfortable for him; most often, he does this unconsciously.

Emotions also have a direct effect on the size of a person's territory. When you're angry or under stress, your bubble expands and you require more space. New York psychiatrist Augustus Kinzel found a difference in what he calls Body-Buffer Zones between violent and nonviolent prison inmates. Dr. Kinzel conducted experiments in which each prisoner was placed in the center of a small room and then Dr. Kinzel slowly walked toward him. Nonviolent prisoners allowed him to come quite close, while prisoners with a history of violent behavior couldn't tolerate his proximity and reacted with some vehemence.

Apparently people under stress experience other people as looming larger and closer than they actually are. Studies of schizophrenic patients have indicated that they sometimes have a distorted perception of space, and several psychiatrists have reported patients who experience their body boundaries as filling up an entire room. For these patients, anyone who comes into the room is actually inside their body, and such an intrusion may trigger a violent outburst.

Unfortunately, there is little detailed information about normal people who live in highly congested urban areas. We do know, of course, that the noise, pollution, dirt, crowding and confusion of our cities induce feelings of stress in most of us, and stress leads to a need for greater space. The man who's packed into a subway, jostled in the street, crowded into an elevator and forced to work all day in a bull pen or in a small office without auditory or visual privacy is going to be very stressed at the end of his day. He needs places that provide relief from constant overstimulation of his nervous system. Stress from overcrowding is cumulative and people can tolerate more crowding early in the day than later;

note the increased bad temper during the evening rush hour as compared with the morning melee. Certainly one factor in people's desire to commute by car is the need for privacy and relief from crowding (except, often, from other cars); it may be the only time of the day when nobody can intrude.

In crowded public places, we tense our muscles and hold ourselves stiff, and thereby communicate to others our desire not to intrude on their space and, above all, not to touch them. We also avoid eye contact, and the total effect is that of someone who has "tuned out." Walking along the street, our bubble expands slightly as we move in a stream of strangers, taking care not to bump into them. In the office, at meetings, in restaurants, our bubble keeps changing as it adjusts to the activity at hand.

Most white middle-class Americans use four main distances in their business and social relations: intimate, personal, social and public. Each of these distances has a near and a far phase and is accompanied by changes in the volume of the voice. Intimate distance varies from direct physical contact with another person to a distance of six to eighteen inches and is used for our most private activities— caressing another person or making love. At this distance, you are overwhelmed by sensory inputs from the other person—heat from the body, tactile stimulation from the skin, the fragrance of perfume, even the sound of breathing—all of which literally envelop you. Even at the far phase, you're still within easy touching distance. In general, the use of intimate distance in public between adults is frowned on. It's also much too close for strangers, except under conditions of extreme crowding.

In the second zone—personal distance—the close phase is one and a half to two and a half feet; it's at this distance that wives usually stand from their husbands in public. If another woman moves into this zone, the wife will most likely be disturbed. The far phase—two and a half to four feet—is the distance used to "keep someone at arm's length" and is the most common spacing used by people in conversation.

The third zone—social distance—is employed during business transactions or exchanges with a clerk or repairman. People who work together tend to use close social distance—four to seven feet. This is also the distance for conversations at social gatherings. To stand at this distance from someone who is seated has a dominating effect (e.g., teacher to pupil, boss to secretary). The far phase of the third zone—seven to twelve feet—is where people stand when someone says, "Stand back so I can look at you." This distance lends a formal tone to business or social discourse. In an executive office, the desk serves to keep people at this distance.

The fourth zone—public distance—is used by teachers in classrooms or speakers at public gatherings. At its farthest phase—25 feet and beyond—it is used for important public figures. Violations of this distance can lead to serious complications. During his 1970 U.S. visit, the president of France, Georges Pompidou, was harassed by pickets in Chicago, who were permitted to get within touching distance. Since pickets in France are kept behind barricades a block or more away, the president was outraged by this insult to his person, and President Nixon was obliged to communicate his concern as well as offer his personal apologies.

It is interesting to note how American pitchmen and panhandlers exploit the unwritten, unspoken conventions of eye and distance. Both take advantage of the fact that once explicit eye contact is established, it is rude to look away, because to do so means to brusquely dismiss the other person and his needs. Once having caught the eye of his mark, the panhandler then locks on, not letting go until he moves through the public zone, the social zone, the personal zone and, finally, into the intimate sphere, where people are most vulnerable.

Touch also is an important part of the constant stream of communication that takes place between people. A light touch, a firm touch, a blow, a caress are all communications. In an effort to break down barriers among people, there's been a recent upsurge in group-encounter activities, in which strangers are encouraged to touch one another. In special situations such as these, the rules for not touching are broken with group approval and people gradually lose some of their inhibitions.

Although most people don't realize it, space is perceived and distances are set not by vision alone but with all the senses. Auditory space is perceived with the ears, thermal space with the skin, kinesthetic space with the muscles of the body and olfactory space with the nose. And, once again, it's one's culture that determines how his senses are programmed—which sensory information ranks highest and lowest. The important thing to remember is that culture is very persistent. In this country, we've noted the existence of culture patterns that determine distance between people in the third and fourth generations of some families, despite their prolonged contact with people of very different cultural heritages.

Whenever there is great cultural distance between two people, there are bound to be problems arising from differences in behavior and expectations. An example is the American couple who consulted a psychiatrist about their marital problems. The husband was from New England and had been brought up by reserved parents who taught him to control his emotions and to respect the need for privacy. His wife was from an Italian family and had been brought up in close contact with all the members of her large family, who were extremely warm, volatile and demonstrative.

When the husband came home after a hard day at the office, dragging his feet and longing for peace and quiet, his wife would rush to him and smother him. Clasping his hands, rubbing his brow, crooning over his weary head, she never left him alone. But when the wife was upset or anxious about her day, the husband's response was to withdraw completely and leave her alone. No comforting, no affectionate embrace, no attention—just solitude. The woman became convinced her husband didn't love her and, in desperation, she consulted a psychiatrist. Their problem wasn't basically psychological but cultural.

Why has man developed all these different ways of communicating messages without words? One reason is that people don't like to spell out certain kinds of messages. We prefer to find other ways of showing our feelings. This is especially true in relationships as sensitive as courtship. Men don't like to be rejected and most women don't want to turn a man down bluntly. Instead, we work out subtle ways of encouraging or discouraging each other that save face and avoid confrontations.

How a person handles space in dating others is an obvious and very sensitive indicator of how he or she feels about the other person. On a first date, if a woman sits or stands so close to a man that he is acutely conscious of her physical presence—inside the intimate-distance zone—the man usually construes it to mean that she is encouraging him. However, before the man starts moving in on the woman, he should be sure what message she's really sending; otherwise, he risks bruising his ego. What is close to someone of North European background may be neutral or distant to someone of Italian heritage. Also, women sometimes use space as a way of misleading a man and there are few things that put men off more than women who communicate contradictory messages—such as women who cuddle up and then act insulted when a man takes the next step.

How does a woman communicate interest in a man? In addition to such familiar gambits as smiling at him, she may glance shyly at him, blush and then look away. Or she may give him a real come-on look and move in very close when he approaches. She may touch his arm and ask for a light. As she leans forward to light her cigarette, she may brush him lightly, enveloping him in her perfume. She'll probably continue to smile at him and she may use what ethologists call preening gestures—touching the back of her hair, thrusting her breasts forward, tilting her hips as she stands or crossing her legs if she's seated, perhaps even exposing one thigh or putting a hand on her thigh and stroking it. She may also stroke her wrists as she converses or show the palm of her hand as a way of gaining his attention. Her skin may be unusually flushed or quite pale, her eyes brighter, the pupils larger.

If a man sees a woman whom he wants to attract, he tries to present himself by his posture and stance as someone who is self-assured. He moves briskly and confidently. When he catches the eye of the woman, he may hold her glance a little longer than normal. If he gets an encouraging smile, he'll move in close and engage her in small talk. As they converse, his glance shifts over her face and body. He, too, may make preening gestures—straightening his tie, smoothing his hair or shooting his cuffs.

How do people learn body language? The same way they learn spoken language—by observing and imitating people around them as they're growing up. Little girls imitate their mothers or an older female. Little boys imitate their fathers or a respected uncle or a character on television. In this way, they learn the gender signals appropriate for their sex. Regional, class and ethnic patterns of body behavior are also learned in childhood and persist throughout life.

Such patterns of masculine and feminine body behavior vary widely from one culture to another. In America, for example, women stand with their thighs together. Many walk with their pelvis tipped slightly forward and their upper arms close to their body. When they sit, they cross their legs at the knee or, if they are well past middle age, they may cross their ankles. American men hold their arms away from their body, often swinging them as they walk. They stand with their legs apart (an extreme example is the cowboy, with legs apart and thumbs tucked into his belt). When they sit, they put their feet on the floor with legs apart and, in some parts of the country, they cross their legs by putting one ankle on the other knee.

Leg behavior indicates sex, status and personality. It also indicates whether or not one is at ease or is showing respect or disrespect for the other person. Young Latin-American males avoid crossing their legs. In their world of *machismo,* the preferred position for young males when with one another (if there is no older dominant male present to whom they must show respect) is to sit on the base of their spine with their leg muscles relaxed and their feet wide apart. Their respect position is our military equivalent; spine straight, heels and ankles together—almost identical to that displayed by properly brought up young women in New England in the early part of this century.

American women who sit with their legs spread apart in the presence of males are *not* normally signaling a come-on—they are simply (and often unconsciously) sitting like men. Middle-class women in the presence of other women to whom they are very close may on occasion throw themselves down on a soft chair or sofa and let themselves go. This is a signal that nothing serious will be taken up. Males, on the other hand, lean back and prop their legs up on the nearest object.

The way we walk, similarly, indicates status, respect, mood and ethnic or cultural affiliation. The many variants of the female walk are too well known to go into here, except to say that a man would have to be blind not to be turned on by the way some women walk—a fact that made Mae West rich before scientists ever studied these matters. To white Americans, some French middle-class males walk in a way that is both humorous and suspect. There is a bounce and looseness to the French walk, as though the parts of the body were somehow unrelated. Jacques Tati, the French movie actor, walks this way; so does the great mime, Marcel Marceau.

Blacks and whites in America—with the exception of middle- and upper-middle-class professionals of both groups—move and walk very differently from each other. To the blacks, whites often seem incredibly stiff, almost mechanical in their movements. Black males, on the other hand, have a looseness and coordination that frequently makes whites a little uneasy; it's too different, too integrated, too alive, too male. Norman Mailer has said that squares walk from the shoulders, like bears, but blacks and hippies walk from the hips, like cats.

All over the world, people walk not only in their own characteristic way but have walks that communicate the nature of their involvement with whatever it is they're doing. The purposeful walk of North Europeans is an important component of proper behavior on the job. Any male who has been in the military knows how essential it is to walk properly (which makes for a continuing source of tension between blacks and whites in the Service). The quick shuffle of servants in the Far East in the old days was a show of respect. On the island of Truk, when we last visited, the inhabitants even had a name for the respectful walk that one used when in the presence of a chief or when walking past a chief's house. The term was *sufan,* which meant to be humble and respectful.

The notion that people communicate volumes by their gestures, facial expressions, posture and walk is not new; actors, dancers, writers and psychiatrists have long been aware of it. Only in recent years, however, have scientists begun to make systematic observations of body motions. Ray L. Birdwhistell of the University of Pennsylvania is one of the pioneers in body-motion research and coined the term kinesics to describe this field. He developed an elaborate notation system to record both facial and body movements, using an approach similar to that of the linguist, who studies the basic elements of speech. Birdwhistell and other kinesicists such as Albert Sheflen, Adam Kendon and William Condon take movies of people interacting. They run the film over and over again, often at reduced speed for frame-by-frame analysis, so that they can observe even the slightest body movements not perceptible at normal interaction speeds. These movements are then recorded in notebooks for later analysis.

To appreciate the importance of nonverbal-communication systems, consider the unskilled inner-city black looking for a job. His handling of time and space alone is sufficiently different from the white middle-class pattern to create great misunderstandings on both sides. The black is told to appear for a job interview at a certain time. He arrives late. The white interviewer concludes from his tardy arrival that the black is irresponsible and not really interested in the job. What the interviewer doesn't know is that the black time system (often referred to by blacks as C.P.T.—colored people's time) isn't the same as that of whites. In the words of a black student who had been told to make an appointment to see his professor: "Man, you *must* be putting me on. I never had an appointment in my life."

The black job applicant, having arrived late for his interview, may further antagonize the white interviewer by his posture and his eye behavior. Perhaps he slouches and avoids looking at the interviewer; to him, this is playing it cool. To the interviewer, however, he may well look shifty and sound uninterested. The interviewer has failed to notice the actual signs of interest and eagerness in the black's behavior, such as the subtle shift in the quality of the voice—a gentle and tentative excitement—an almost imperceptible change in the cast of the eyes and a relaxing of the jaw muscles.

Moreover, correct reading of black-white behavior is continually complicated by the fact that both groups are comprised of individuals—some of whom try to accommodate and some of whom make it a point of pride *not* to accommodate. At present, this means that many Americans, when thrown into contact with one another, are in the precarious position of not knowing which pattern applies. Once identified and analyzed, nonverbal-communication systems can be taught, like a foreign language. Without this training, we respond to nonverbal communications in terms of our own culture; we read everyone's behavior as if it were our own, and thus we often misunderstand it.

Several years ago in New York City, there was a program for sending children from predominantly black and Puerto Rican low-income neighborhoods to summer school in a white upper-class neighborhood on the East Side. One morning, a group of young black and Puerto Rican boys raced down the street, shouting and screaming and overturning garbage cans on their way to school. A doorman from an apartment building nearby chased them and cornered one of them inside a building. The boy drew a knife and attacked the doorman. This tragedy would not have occurred if the doorman had been familiar with the behavior of boys from low-income neighborhoods, where such antics are routine and socially acceptable and where pursuit would be expected to invite a violent response.

The language of behavior is extremely complex. Most of us are lucky to have under control one subcultural system—the one that reflects our sex, class, generation and geographic region within the United States. Because of its complexity, efforts to isolate bits of nonverbal communication and generalize from them are in vain; you don't become an instant expert on people's behavior by watching them at cocktail parties. Body language isn't something that's independent of the person, something that can be donned and doffed like a suit of clothes.

Our research and that of our colleagues has shown that, far from being a superficial form of communication that can be consciously manipulated, nonverbal-communication systems are interwoven into the fabric of the personality and, as sociologist Erving Goffman has demonstrated, into society itself. They are the warp and woof of daily interactions with others and they influence how one expresses oneself, how one experiences oneself as a man or a woman.

Nonverbal communications signal to members of your own group what kind of person you are, how you feel about others, how you'll fit into and work in a group, whether you're assured or anxious, the degree to which you feel comfortable with the standards of your own culture, as well as deeply significant feelings about the self, including the state of your own psyche. For most of us, it's difficult to accept the reality of another's behavioral system. And, of course, none of us will ever become fully knowledgeable of the importance of every nonverbal signal. But as long as each of us realizes the power of these signals, this society's diversity can be a source of great strength rather than a further—and subtly powerful—source of division.

Questions for Discussion and Writing

1. Through what kinds of expressions is nonverbal language communicated? Why are we often not consciously aware of the messages conveyed nonverbally?
2. In what ways do we recognize a lack of congruity between a person's words and behavior? Why is the role of listener important?
3. How can understanding that nonverbal messages differ among different groups of people help people to communicate more accurately? Use examples and brief quotes from the essay to support your analysis.

4. The Halls conclude their essay by asserting that "as long as each of us realizes the power of these [nonverbal] signals, this society's diversity can be a source of great strength rather than a further—and subtly powerful— source of division" (p. 217). In what specific ways do the ideas presented in the essay support this assertion?

5. For what audience do you think the Halls wrote this essay, and why?

6. At which points in the essay, if any, did your interest as a reader lag, and why? At which points were you most interested, and why? Use brief quotes from the essay to support your responses.

GREGORY BATESON

Why Do Frenchmen?

Born in 1904 in Cambridge, England, Gregory Bateson can claim a long and diverse career—teaching, traveling, studying, and lecturing in distant places. He's been a professor at several universities, an anthropological field worker in New Guinea and Bali, an ethnologist for the Veterans Administration Hospital in Palo Alto, California, chief of the Biological Relations Division in Waimanalo, Hawaii, and a regent of the University of California. In that position, Newsweek *wrote of him: the "brilliant, peevish Gregory Bateson . . . has let fly with stinging opinions on every aspect of university life, from the quality of students to the competence of the regents themselves. . . ."*

    Bateson has two daughters, from his first and third marriages (his first wife was Margaret Mead). The child in the script that follows may or may not be fictional, but Bateson uses her in this dialogue, with a child's innocence, to probe the questions she raises about the significance of gestures and nonverbal language in communication, especially the gestures of other cultures. "Why Do Frenchmen?" is taken from the book Language, Meaning and Maturity *(1954).*

Before you read "Why Do Frenchmen?", write a dialogue or script in which you raise a question about the mannerisms of a person or group with someone who you think might know a little more than you do about the topic. Let that person attempt to answer your question. Before you begin to write the script, make a list of questions related to the main question you've chosen.

DAUGHTER: Daddy, why do Frenchmen wave their arms about?

FATHER: What do you mean?

D: I mean when they talk. Why do they wave their arms and all that?

F: Well, why do you smile? Or why do you stamp your foot sometimes?

D: But that's not the same thing, Daddy. I don't wave my arms about like a Frenchman does. I don't believe they can stop doing it, Daddy. Can they?

F: I don't know. They might find it hard to stop. Can you stop smiling?

D: But, Daddy, I don't smile *all* the time. It's hard to stop when I feel like smiling. But I don't feel like it all the time. And then I stop.

F: That's true—but then a Frenchman doesn't wave his arms in the same way all the time. Sometimes he waves them in one way and sometimes in another— and sometimes, I think, he stops waving them.

◄►

F: What do you think? I mean, what does it make you think when a Frenchman waves his arms?

D: I think it looks silly, Daddy. But I don't suppose it looks like that to another Frenchman. They cannot all look silly to each other. Because if they did they would stop it, wouldn't they?

F: Perhaps—but that is not a very simple question. What else do they make you think?

D: Well—they look all excited . . .

F: All right—"silly" and "excited."

D: But are they *really* as excited as they look? If I were as excited as that, I would want to dance or sing or hit somebody on the nose . . . but they just go on waving their arms. They can't be really excited.

F: Well, are they really as silly as they look to you? And anyhow, why do you sometimes want to dance and sing and punch somebody on the nose?

D: Oh, sometimes I just feel like that.

F: Perhaps a Frenchman just feels "like that" when he waves his arms about.

D: But he couldn't feel like that *all* the time, Daddy, he just couldn't.

F: You mean—the Frenchman surely does not feel when he waves his arms exactly as you would feel if you waved yours. And surely you are right.

D: But, then, how *does* he feel?

F: Well, let us suppose you are talking to a Frenchman and he is waving his arms about, and then in the middle of the conversation, after something that you have said, he suddenly stops waving his arms, and just talks. What would you think then? That he had just stopped being silly and excited?

D: No . . . I'd be frightened. I'd think I had said something that hurt his feelings and perhaps he might be really angry.

F: Yes, and you might be right.

◄►

D: All right—so they stop waving their arms when they start being angry.

F: Wait a minute. The question, after all, is what does one Frenchman tell another Frenchman by waving his arms? And we have part of an answer—he tells him something about how he feels about the other guy. He tells him he is not seriously angry—that he is willing and able to be what you call "silly."

D: But, no—that's not sensible. He cannot do all that work so that *later* he will be able to tell the other guy that he *is* angry by just keeping his own arms still. How does he know he is going to be angry later on?

F: He doesn't know. But, just in case . . .

D: No, Daddy, it doesn't make sense. I don't smile so as to be able to tell you I am angry by not smiling later on.

F: Yes, I think that that *is* part of the reason for smiling. And there are lots of people who smile in order to tell you that they are *not angry*—when they really are.

D: But that's different, Daddy. That's a sort of telling lies with one's face. Like playing poker.

F: Yes.

◄►

F: Now where are we? You don't think it sensible for Frenchmen to work so hard to tell each other that they are not angry or hurt. But after all, what is most conversation about? I mean, among Americans?

D: But, Daddy, it's about all sorts of things—baseball and ice cream and gardens and games. And people talk about other people and about themselves and about what they got for Christmas.

F: Yes, yes—but who listens? I mean—all right, so they talk about baseball and gardens. But are they exchanging information? And, if so, *what* information?

D: Sure—when you come in from fishing, and I ask you, "Did you catch anything?" and you say, "Nothing," I didn't *know* that you wouldn't catch anything till you told me.

F: Hmm.

◄►

F: All right—so you mention my fishing, a matter about which I am sensitive—and then there is a gap, a silence in the conversation—and that silence tells you that I don't like cracks about how many fish I didn't catch. It's just like the Frenchman who stops waving his arms about when he is hurt.

D: I'm sorry, Daddy, but you *did* say . . .

F: No, wait a minute—let's not get confused by being sorry. I shall go out fishing again tomorrow and I shall still know that I am unlikely to catch a fish . . .

D: But, Daddy, you said all conversation is only telling other people that you are not angry with them.

F: Did I? No—not *all* conversation but much of it. Sometimes if both people are willing to listen carefully it is possible to do more than exchange greetings and good wishes. Even to do more than exchange information. The two people may even find out something which neither of them knew before.

F: Anyhow, most conversations are only about whether people are angry or something. They are busy telling each other that they are friendly—which is sometimes a lie. After all, what happens when they cannot think of anything to say? They all feel uncomfortable.

D: But wouldn't that be information, Daddy? I mean—information that they are not cross?

F: Surely yes. But it's a different sort of information from "the cat is on the mat."

D: Daddy, why cannot people just *say,* "I am not cross at you" and let it go at that?

F: Ah, now we are getting to the real problem. The point is that the messages which we exchange in gestures are really not the same as any translation of those gestures into words.

D: I don't understand.

F: I mean—that no amount of telling somebody in mere words that one is or is not angry is the same as what one might tell them by gesture or tone of voice.

D: But, Daddy, you cannot have words without some tone of voice, can you? Even if somebody uses as little tone as he can, the other people will hear that he is holding himself back—and that will be a sort of tone, won't it?

F: Yes, I suppose so. After all, that's what I said just now about gestures—that the Frenchman can say something special by *stopping* his gestures.

F: But then, what do I mean by saying that "mere words" can never convey the same message as gestures—if there are no "mere words"?

D: Well, the words might be written.

F: No—that won't let me out of the difficulty. Because written words still have some sort of rhythm and they still have overtones. The point is that *no* mere words exist. There are *only* words with either gesture or tone of voice or something of the sort. But, of course, gestures without words are common enough.

D: Daddy, when they teach us French at school, why don't they teach us to wave our hands?

F: I don't know. I'm sure I don't know. That is probably one of the reasons why people find learning languages so difficult.

F: Anyhow, it is all nonsense. I mean, the notion that language is made of words is all nonsense—and when I said that gestures could not be translated into "mere words," I was talking nonsense, because there is no such thing as "mere words." And all the syntax and grammar and all that stuff is nonsense. It's all based on the idea that "mere words" exist—and there are none.

D: But, Daddy . . .

F: I tell you—we have to start all over again from the beginning and assume that language is first and foremost a system of gestures. Animals after all have *only* gestures and tones of voice—and words were invented later. Much later. And after that they invented school-masters.

D: Daddy?

F: Yes.

D: Would it be a good thing if people gave up words and went back to only using gestures?

F: Hmm. I don't know. Of course we would not be able to have any conversations like this. We could only bark, or mew, and wave our arms about, and laugh and grunt and weep. But it might be fun—it would make life into a sort of ballet—with the dancers making their own music.

Questions for Discussion and Writing

1. In what ways does the daughter's interpretation of the Frenchmen's waving their arms give us insight into our own perceptions of the body language of others?
2. What does it take for people "to do more than exchange greetings and good wishes," or to do more than exchange information (p. 222)?
3. What does the father mean when he says, "The point is that *no* mere words

exist"? What does he mean when he says that we have to assume that "language is first and foremost a system of gestures" (p. 223)?

4. What unstated truths about other languages and cultures might we infer from this dialogue?

5. Why do you think Bateson chose to write this piece as a script? What does he gain and lose in this choice? How might you have written this piece, given the ideas the author is attempting to communicate?

SABINE ULIBARRÍ

The Stuffing of the Lord

Sabine Ulibarrí grew up in the Spanish-American village of Tierra Amarilla in New Mexico's high northern mountains, where he was born in 1919. The story that follows is taken from a book of stories entitled Tierra Amarilla: Stories of New Mexico *(1971), in which Ulibarrí writes about the people from his youth, whose ancestors had settled in the area before either Jamestown or Plymouth Colony was established. In this area of New Mexico, still steeped in its traditions and the spirit of its isolation, the descendants of the first colonists remain more Spanish than American, with Spanish the universal speech. Because the area has been isolated from the normal development of the mother tongue, its Spanish has retained certain sixteenth-century forms now obsolete in other parts of the world.*

Eventually, Ulibarrí left behind a childhood of riding the ranges on his father's ranch to study and travel in far places, from Europe to Latin America. Since 1947, he has been teaching at the University of New Mexico, where he became a professor of Spanish in 1968. He first told these stories of his youth in Tierra Amarilla, and later, encouraged by his listeners, wrote them in Spanish, after which they were translated into English by Thelma Campbell Nason. As she writes in the Introduction to Tierra Amarilla, *the stories "focus on a facet of American life that is passing with no hope of return." They also represent "the profound Hispanicity of this part of the country."*

In "The Stuffing of the Lord," Ulibarrí tells us of a priest whose lack of facility in a language endears people ever more fully to him, even as his mispronunciation—especially of reino *(kingdom, "rey-ee-no") versus* relleno *(stuffing, "rey-yey-no")—threatens to make them explode from containing their laughter.*

Before you read "The Stuffing of the Lord," write about a time in your life when you were changed for the better by a person not directly attempting

to influence you. Describe that person, how you changed under his or her influence, and why, looking back, you believe the influence was so great. An alternative approach is to write about a time when, in some solemn place, you nearly exploded from laughter. Describe the situation, what caused your response, and in what ways, if any, you suffered for it.

Father Benito almost saved my soul. Certainly he put me on the road to salvation, a feat which shocked and surprised my parents and elicited admiring exclamations from all the townsfolk. And wherever he may now be, Father Benito probably still regards me as saved.

The truth is that up to the age of twelve I had never shown the least interest in religion, much less any inclination to the priesthood or any other hood, priestly or otherwise. I had, in fact, given many indications of traveling in the opposite direction.

That is the way things were going when Father Benito came to Tierra Amarilla for the first time. Tierra Amarilla has never been the same since that day, nor have any of us who used to live there. The good father brought us light and life, tenderness and joy. He filled the town with talk and gaiety. He drew us to the Kingdom of Heaven by the strangest method ever used in the history of religion. If dying of laughter is a good thing, Father Benito brought us to a good death many, many times.

He had a round, bald head like a pale pumpkin. In the center of the tremendous hood of the Franciscan habit, it seemed to be loose, placed there without reason. Its position looked so precarious that one expected to see it roll from its place at any moment. On his saintly, round, slightly foolish face there was always a fixed smile—a truly beatific expression. He wore rimless glasses, out of style even then, on the end of his nose. I don't know why. Certainly it was not for seeing. Perhaps they were the transparent vestments for an extremely naked face. It was a nudity, stemming from innocence, turned virtue and purity. His small paunch, round as the loaves of San Roque,* was supported by a white cord. Biblical sandals completed the angelic image of the priest who filled the entire valley of Tierra Amarilla with affection and harmony.

He was like the sun. When he passed along the street, he scattered smiles and good humor about him, banishing shadows, warming the dying, animating the conversation, provoking an occasional burst of laughter. Mirth was his constant companion.

He spoke terrible Spanish, fluent but mutilated. He could not pronounce the word reino in his favorite expression, el reino de Dios (the Kingdom of God), but he repeated it so often that it acquired a strange, fatal importance. Saying mass, he used to chant in magisterial tones, "In order to enter into the relleno of God. . . ." Relleno, dear readers, sounds a little like reino, but it means

---

San Roque: saint who, when stricken with the plague, was brought bread each day by a faithful hound "stuffing"! While the words and the ascending intonation seemed to build a stairway to heavenly places, the faithful were in misery. They were broken up. They squirmed, they hunched their shoulders and lowered their heads. Spasms. Contortions. Agony. Fierce and fatal laughter, unbearable because it had to be contained.

The Father's ignorance of the language forced him to inquire about words when he was preparing his sermons. On one occasion, he asked a waggish character the word for "foundation," since he planned to preach a sermon about the poor condition of the substructure of the church.

Nobody ever stayed away from mass while Father Benito was in Tierra Amarilla. As usual, the church was full. The good priest began to scold us with his usual sincerity and fervor.

"You neglect your church. You are a disgrace to your religion. Today there will be a special collection to provide fundaments for this church. The fundaments we have now are filthy, they have a bad odor. . . ." Nobody heard another word.

I doubt that in the history of Catholicism any priest ever had as unusual and eccentric an audience as Father Benito—without his ever knowing it. It was a congregation of convulsed faces, puffed cheeks, trembling chins, and bulging eyes. Noses were blown. Arms and legs twitched. Ears turned purple. Groans, moans, stifled cries—strange noises. The parishioners lowered their heads, bit their lips, held their stomachs, shuddered and shook. They were in agony.

The saintly priest from his pulpit, blind and deaf to what was going on, looked over his glasses at the bowed heads of the faithful. He saw them overcome by religious fervor. Virtuous and sincere, he gave us his best, he became more and more eloquent, he soared to the heights of passionate feeling.

All of us left the church exhausted. Pale, spent, with tears still in our eyes. We went home in silence. Without speaking. Without laughing. Without strength for anything else. Later, some other day, we would laugh. Then we would talk it over. Not now. Suppressed laughter is a savage beast in a cage.

Of course, nobody talked about anything else. The acolytes* talked, too. They said that our beloved priest had one other peculiarity that they alone knew about. He did not like wine! The nuns always filled the little jar for communion, and he left it almost full. I had heard my father and other men say that priests had the best wine in the world. For that reason and no other, I entered on the path of salvation.

For the first time I began to pay attention at catechism. I stopped asking the impertinent questions that had brought me so many catholic, apostolic, and Roman† lumps on the head. I learned to lower my eyes properly and humbly at the least pretext and also to roll them piously upward toward the electric light

---

acolytes: altar boys, who assist the priest at mass.
†*catholic, apostolic, and Roman:* probably a humorous reference to a phrase in the creed that members of the catechism class would have learned.

bulb among the cracks and spider webs of the ceiling. I answered the questions of the priests and the nuns correctly, without creating the least disturbance. In short, I became so extremely sanctimonious that I surpassed the oldest and ugliest female fanatics of the area.

My parents did not know about all this, since it happened at school. Occasionally an aunt or a friend would remark to my mother that I was behaving myself very well and that it was high time. Once, when this happened in my presence, my mother looked at me suspiciously. The conversation continued, however, and she forgot about it. I never knew whether my father found out.

But in the convent school the word certainly got around. The happiness of the sisters was almost more than they could bear. It was a miracle. I had been a student of theirs for six years, and those six years had been purgatory for them—and for me, too. For a long time I carried a body full of welts as holy testimony to my suffering.

No one can possibly know the joy—I mean delirium—I should say ecstasy—of a devoted sister who carries an unregenerate, submissive sinner and lays him in the lap of the Lord. I saw their rhapsodic glances and trembled, but not with pleasure. There is something frenzied and frightening about a woman in ecstasy. When I saw them, my hair stood on end, or as one could say, reached toward heaven. The latter seemed to be their interpretation.

They became gentle, sweet, and kindly toward me. In my new role of lamb, or little suckling pig, I accepted their kindnesses. The most generous of all was Sister Generosa.

The nuns had charge of the altar and of dressing the saints. One day, when I felt that my campaign had achieved its purpose, I presented myself to be dressed—as an altar boy, of course. That day there was rejoicing in the fields of the Lord, at least in one of them.

Thus began my religious career. It soon became evident that there was great promise in the new acolyte. During the Mea Culpa* my chest-pounding resounded throughout the tiny temple. My amens were the most amenable that had ever been heard in that region. All the way to the Ite Missa Est† I was the most attentive and zealous of the crowd.

There were two altar boys. Completely organized. The priest fawned upon by the good ladies of the town. The sisters lining up the children. We tidying up, folding, arranging, in the sacristy.‡ One swallow for me. One for you. Another for me. First we drank the wine and then we sniffed the jar dry. When Sister Generosa came in, the heavenly jar was empty, completely clean. Neither she nor any of the sisters ever knew that Father Benito did not like wine.

I accompanied Father Benito to many a wedding and many a funeral. He with

---

Mea Culpa: part of the Latin mass in which there was a confession of fault. The words mean "through my fault."
†*Ite Missa Est:* "Go; the mass is ended."
‡*sacristy:* room in a church building where clerical robes, altar linen, etc., are kept.

his hyssop and I with the censer.* The odor of sanctity must be something like the smell of that smoke. At all these festivities they served the priest first from the best they had, then his assistant, naturally. For the intelligent assistant there is a good swig behind each blessing and a blessing in each swig. I always returned from these expeditions spiritually enriched. That life was becoming more and more fascinating to me.

My mother always accompanied me to high mass, the one read by Father Benito. I was now beginning to give her something to be proud of, whereas formerly I had given her only trouble. At least that is what I thought, although I frequently suspected that she was not really convinced of my conversion. But at any rate, the women of the town who used to have so many complaints about me now heaped me with praises. It was a well-deserved rest for my mother.

My father never saw me or heard me at the altar, except for my baptism and first communion. Due to a series of unexpected incidents he had to go on trips most weekends when I was displaying my chest-beating and my amenable amens. Some Sundays he had to go to six o'clock mass because of pressing duties. And unfortunately he contracted a mysterious illness which struck him on five successive Sundays and prevented his attending mass. His friends were much concerned, for they said he had not been seen for months. This troubled me a great deal. How I wanted to impress him—for the first time! Wasn't I now a real personality?

The usual thing happened to us. They took our good Father Benito away from us. I did not know what to do. My whole new life was abruptly ended. We said good-bye. I, with deeply sincere tears. He, with a sad smile. There are priests who inspire heartfelt love, others who are loved from a sense of duty, and—one must confess—some who are never loved at all. Father Benito belonged to the first group.

The day he left, the whole town came out to bid him good-bye. I do not think there was a dry eye in the crowd. That innocent spirit went away without knowing what he had brought us, without knowing what had happened. Without knowing what he was taking away with him. He carried with him much of the day's brightness, much laughter, and much happiness. He left us only the knowledge that we would never again know the same measure of those qualities. I believe that I felt his departure more than anyone else.

I returned to my post the next Sunday with the new priest. It was not the same. My chest-pounding sounded dull and hollow. My amens lacked the old resonance. When the moment of communion arrived, I poured the accustomed amount of the sacramental wine. The priest shook the divine vessel impatiently. Reluctantly I poured a little more. He insisted. Finally I poured it all.

How indecent that seemed to me! What bad taste! I was—well, not raging, because that would have been a sacrilege at the altar—but something very much

*hyssop, censer: references to sprinkling with holy water and using incense.

like it until the Ite Missa Est, which rang down the final curtain on my religious career.

I returned to my old ways and my old pranks. I acted almost as I had before—almost but not quite. Something new, something unforeseen, had come to me in Father Benito's wine. I could not forget the good priest. My parents were surprised once more, but I think they were relieved and secretly thanked God. One thing is sure: my father no longer had to go away on Sundays, and his mysterious illness disappeared. Once again we went to mass as a family. My mother between us giving a pinch to my father and another to me in moments when they were needed.

The years passed. My parents had died by this time. My siblings and I were now living in Santa Fe. We saw in the newspaper that a friend of ours, Flavio Hernández, had died. The rosary would be in the Salazar Funeral Home, and Father Benito would conduct the service!

I don't know which of our two motives was more powerful. We wanted to pay our respects to the dead, but we were also very eager to see Father Benito again. When we reached the mortuary, which was unfamiliar to us, we followed some people who were entering and found ourselves in a chapel where the deceased lay.

My sister, my brother, and I entered respectfully, our heads bowed. We threaded our way through the crowd, approached the coffin, knelt, and began to pray. I tried to think about my prayers, but my thoughts kept going back to Tierra Amarilla and Father Benito. I remembered that at that time I had a very vague idea of what the Kingdom of God might be, but that I had a very clear and grotesque image of what the relleno de Dios might be. The revival of that memory started in me the silent tickling of a mad mirth. There is no laughter so wicked as that which strikes in a serious or sacred place.

I was trying to control myself when my brother nudged me. I heard a frightened whisper, "That isn't Flavio!" I raise my eyes and look. Not only is it not Flavio, but is a woman! I nudge my sister. She looks. We all stare. We turn our heads. We are surrounded by people we don't know.

Suddenly, without any warning, wild laughter swirls inside us. The absurdity of that situation is too much. We do everything possible to control ourselves, but to no avail. We bite our lips. Our abdomens ache. Our faces become livid, congested. The suffering is indescribable. One of the others breaks out in a snort. We have to hide this, cover it up. I begin to weep noisily. My brother and sister follow my lead. Our tears flow freely. Our cries become more and more despairing. Hastily we stumble out, blind with tears and suffering. The real mourners have nothing to complain about. Our lamentations were certainly the hit of the year and the pride of the mortuary.

We reached home exhausted, literally sick. We should laugh and talk about it another day, but now it was impossible, as in the days of Father Benito and his masses. That night Father Benito made us laugh as he had in the old days.

Without even seeing him. His physical presence was not needed. His trademark is laughter.

Always, when someone laughs deeply and helplessly, I think about the good father and laugh, too. And wonder how many souls may have reached heaven, having died laughing, saved that way by Saint Benito. I don't know what has become of him, but I am sure that he is still living. Certainly the day he enters the relleno de Dios, we will hear the peals of laughter, the cries, the guffaws, and the moans of the saints and the little angels—all this followed by long silences.

Translated by Thelma Campbell Nason

Questions for Discussion and Writing

1. Why did Father Benito engender in his congregation the agony of suppressed laughter? What are the other sources of humor in this story?
2. What effect has Father Benito had on the narrator, and why? What changes has Father Benito created in other people of Tierra Amarilla, usually unintentionally, and why?
3. In what ways is Father Benito's Spanish the key to this story? Would the people have loved him as much had he been fluent in their language? Use brief quotes from the story to support your analysis.
4. In what ways does the scene in the funeral home tie the story together?
5. What truths about the people of Tierra Amarilla is Ulibarrí trying to convey in "The Stuffing of the Lord"?

Chapter 4

ENCOUNTERING AMERICAN PATTERNS OF CULTURE

What is always needed in the appreciation of art, or life, is the larger perspective. Connections made, or at least attempted, where none existed before, the straining to encompass at one's glance at the varied world the common thread, the unifying theme through immense diversity, a fearlessness of growth, of search, of looking, that enlarges the private and the public world.

ALICE WALKER, in
"SEEING THE LIFE THAT IS YOUR OWN"

PATTERNS OF CULTURE WITHIN THE UNITED STATES CAN BE AS NU-merous as the people who live here, and yet in spite of our diversity as a nation, common habits, assumptions, and values often unite us without our being aware of them. The smallest details to the largest ones reflect these patterns and common assumptions: how many ice cubes fill your glass of water at a restaurant, the way you greet a friend, the meaning of independence from family, how you schedule your day, the ways you drive a car, the kind of books available—like this one, for example.

The selections in this chapter help us discover these common assumptions through the eyes and experiences of people who come to the United States from other places. The first person on the scene is an anthropologist who—reported by Horace M. Miner in "Body Ritual Among the Nacirema"—has discovered and observed the body and mind rituals of a peculiar group in North America called the Nacirema.

Cruising down the Mississippi River, a Russian guest, Rimma Kazakova, encounters the United States from a Soviet/American meeting on a boat in "America of the People." Through her experience, we can perhaps understand how small a slice of a culture we experience when we travel, even though when we return, we speak about a place as if we have seen the whole of it.

In the next two stories, two mothers—one from Pakistan, the other from Iran—come to the United States to visit their sons. In Tahira Naqvi's "Paths upon Water," a mother encounters American bathing practices at the beach. In "Your Place Is Empty" by Anne Tyler, a mother faces the strange forces of the culture to which her son now belongs.

Cousin Consorcio arrives alone in San Francisco, an immigrant wanting to "Be American." Carlos Bulosan reflects the difficulties this illiterate peasant from the Philippines encounters as Consorcio attempts to fit his life to his dream. The whole family has immigrated here from India in the story "A Father," but their unexpected encounter with America's technological possibilities pushes them well beyond the small symbolic adjustments that, until that time, they had chosen to make.

The Hmong, mountain people from Laos, did not choose to change their lives in the ways they have been required to adapt to the crowded, urban California setting into which they were plunked. In "The Hmong in America," Spencer Sherman analyzes not only their present conditions but also the history of their culture, their habits, and their values, so that readers can more fully understand their difficulties now.

The chapter closes with Ishmael Reed's "America: The Multinational Society." His irrefutable images from the sources he's gathered show that we are indeed a multinational society, in which cultural patterns that once distinctly represented foreign groups have threaded their way into the tapestry of this country.

HORACE M. MINER

Body Ritual Among the Nacirema

Born in 1912, Horace M. Miner has spent his professional life as an observer of people. Until his retirement in 1978, he was professor of sociology and anthropology at the University of Michigan. Both in his work and his writing, Miner concentrates on the African continent; The City in Modern Africa *(1967) and* The Primitive City of Timbuctoo *(1953) are two of his best-known books. On a Rockefeller Foundation Grant (1970–1971), he did research on the ecology of change among the Hausa of the Anchau Corridor in Nigeria.*

In "Body Ritual Among the Nacirema," written in 1956, Miner reflects his intimate knowledge of a group of people who inhabit a large tract of land in North America. The essay has captured the interest of readers all over the world, even though Miner dashed it off in a few hours. To the field of anthropology Miner brought his own brand of satire, helping us to see this culture from the distance we need to feel comfortable having a look at its rituals and foibles.

Before you read "Body Ritual Among the Nacirema," write about a ritual or rituals you have in your family or the place that you live. Write about it as if you were viewing your family from the eyes of an anthropologist who has suddenly appeared on the scene but knows nothing of your background or the rituals. Describe the rituals so that the familiar becomes strange to uninitiated eyes.

T he anthropologist has become so familiar with the diversity of ways in which different peoples behave in similar situations that he is not apt to be surprised by even the most exotic customs. In fact, if all of the logically possible combinations of behavior have not been found somewhere in the world, he is apt to suspect that they must be present in some yet undescribed tribe. The point has, in fact, been expressed with respect to clan organization by Murdock (1949:71). In this light, the magical beliefs and practices of the Nacirema present such unusual aspects that it seems desirable to describe them as an example of the extremes to which human behavior can go.

Professor Linton first brought the ritual of the Nacirema to the attention of anthropologists twenty years ago (1936:326), but the culture of this people is still very poorly understood. They are a North American group living in the territory between the Canadian Cree, the Yaqui and Tarahumare of Mexico, and the Carib and Arawak of the Antilles. Little is known of their origin, although tradition states that they came from the east. According to Nacirema mythology, their nation was originated by a culture hero, Notgnihsaw, who is otherwise known for two great feats of strength—the throwing of a piece of wampum across the river Pa-To-Mac and the chopping down of a cherry tree in which the Spirit of Truth resided.

Nacirema culture is characterized by a highly developed market economy which has evolved in a rich natural habitat. While much of the people's time is devoted to economic pursuits, a large part of the fruits of these labors and a considerable portion of the day are spent in ritual activity. The focus of this activity is the human body, the appearance and health of which loom as a dominant concern in the ethos of the people. While such a concern is certainly not unusual, its ceremonial aspects and associated philosophy are unique.

The fundamental belief underlying the whole system appears to be that the human body is ugly and that its natural tendency is to debility and disease. Incarcerated in such a body, man's only hope is to avert these characteristics through the use of the powerful influences of ritual and ceremony. Every household has one or more shrines devoted to this purpose. The more powerful individuals in the society have several shrines in their houses and, in fact, the opulence of a house is often referred to in terms of the number of such ritual centers it possesses. Most houses are of wattle and daub construction, but the shrine rooms of the more wealthy are walled with stone. Poorer families imitate the rich by applying pottery plaques to their shrine walls.

While each family has at least one such shrine, the rituals associated with it are not family ceremonies but are private and secret. The rites are normally only discussed with children, and then only during the period when they are being initiated into these mysteries. I was able, however, to establish sufficient rapport with the natives to examine these shrines and to have the rituals described to me.

The focal point of the shrine is a box or chest which is built into the wall. In this chest are kept the many charms and magical potions without which no native believes he could live. These preparations are secured from a variety of specialized practitioners. The most powerful of these are the medicine men, whose assistance must be rewarded with substantial gifts. However, the medicine men do not provide the curative potions for their clients, but decide what the ingredients should be and then write them down in an ancient and secret language. This writing is understood only by the medicine men and by the herbalists who, for another gift, provide the required charm.

The charm is not disposed of after it has served its purpose, but is placed in the charm-box of the household shrine. As these magical materials are specific for certain ills, and the real or imagined maladies of the people are many, the charm-box is usually full to overflowing. The magical packets are so numerous that people forget what their purposes were and fear to use them again. While the natives are very vague on this point, we can only assume that the idea in retaining all the old magical materials is that their presence in the charm-box, before which the body rituals are conducted, will in some way protect the worshipper.

Beneath the charm-box is a small font. Each day every member of the family, in succession, enters the shrine room, bows his head before the charm-box, mingles different sorts of holy water in the font, and proceeds with a brief rite of ablution. The holy waters are secured from the Water Temple of the community, where the priests conduct elaborate ceremonies to make the liquid ritually pure.

In the hierarchy of magical practitioners, and below the medicine men in prestige, are specialists whose designation is best translated "holy-mouth-men." The Nacirema have an almost pathological horror of and fascination with the mouth, the condition of which is believed to have a supernatural influence on all social relationships. Were it not for the rituals of the mouth, they believe that their teeth would fall out, their gums bleed, their jaws shrink, their friends desert them, and their lovers reject them. They also believe that a strong relationship exists between oral and moral characteristics. For example, there is a ritual ablution of the mouth for children which is supposed to improve their moral fiber.

The daily body ritual performed by everyone includes a mouth-rite. Despite the fact that these people are so punctilious about care of the mouth, this rite involves a practice which strikes the uninitiated stranger as revolting. It was reported to me that the ritual consists of inserting a small bundle of hog hairs into the mouth, along with certain magical powders, and then moving the bundle in a highly formalized series of gestures.

In addition to the private mouth-rite, the people seek out a holy-mouth-man once or twice a year. These practitioners have an impressive set of paraphernalia, consisting of a variety of augers, awls, probes, and prods. The use of these objects in the exorcism of the evils of the mouth involves almost unbelievable ritual torture of the client. The holy-mouth-man opens the client's mouth and, using the above mentioned tools, enlarges any holes which decay may have created in the teeth. Magical materials are put into these holes. If there are no naturally occurring holes in the teeth, large sections of one or more teeth are gouged out so that the supernatural substance can be applied. In the client's view, the purpose of these ministrations is to arrest decay and to draw friends. The extremely sacred and traditional character of the rite is evident in the fact that the natives return to the holy-mouth-men year after year, despite the fact that their teeth continue to decay.

It is to be hoped that, when a thorough study of the Nacirema is made, there will be careful inquiry into the personality structure of these people. One has but to watch the gleam in the eye of a holy-mouth-man, as he jabs an awl into an exposed nerve, to suspect that a certain amount of sadism is involved. If this can be established, a very interesting pattern emerges, for most of the population shows definite masochistic tendencies. It was to these that Professor Linton referred in discussing a distinctive part of the daily body ritual which is performed only by men. This part of the rite involves scraping and lacerating the surface of the face with a sharp instrument. Special women's rites are performed only four times during each lunar month, but what they lack in frequency is made up in barbarity. As part of this ceremony, women bake their heads in small ovens for about an hour. The theoretically interesting point is that what seems to be a preponderantly masochistic people have developed sadistic specialists.

The medicine men have an imposing temple, or *latipso,* in every community of any size. The more elaborate ceremonies required to treat very sick patients can only be performed at this temple. These ceremonies involve not only the thaumaturge but a permanent group of vestal maidens who move sedately about the temple chambers in distinctive costume and headdress.

The *latipso* ceremonies are so harsh that it is phenomenal that a fair proportion of the really sick natives who enter the temple ever recover. Small children whose indoctrination is still incomplete have been known to resist attempts to take them to the temple because "that is where you go to die." Despite this fact, sick adults are not only willing but eager to undergo the protracted ritual purification, if they can afford to do so. No matter how ill the supplicant or how grave the emergency, the guardians of many temples will not admit a client if he cannot give a rich gift to the custodian. Even after one has gained admission and survived the ceremonies, the guardians will not permit the neophyte to leave until he makes still another gift.

The supplicant entering the temple is first stripped of all his or her clothes. In everyday life the Nacirema avoids exposure of his body and its natural functions. Bathing and excretory acts are performed only in the secrecy of the household shrine, where they are ritualized as part of the body-rites. Psychological shock results from the fact that body secrecy is suddenly lost upon entry into the *latipso.* A man, whose own wife has never seen him in an excretory act, suddenly finds himself naked and assisted by a vestal maiden while he performs his natural functions into a sacred vessel. This sort of ceremonial treatment is necessitated by the fact that the excreta are used by a diviner to ascertain the course and nature of the client's sickness. Female clients, on the other hand, find their naked bodies are subjected to the scrutiny, manipulation, and prodding of the medicine men.

Few supplicants in the temple are well enough to do anything but lie on their hard beds. The daily ceremonies, like the rites of the holy-mouth-men, involve discomfort and torture. With ritual precision, the vestals awaken their miserable charges each dawn and roll them about on their beds of pain while performing ablutions, in the formal movements of which the maidens are highly trained. At other times they insert magic wands in the supplicant's mouth or force him to eat substances which are supposed to be healing. From time to time the medicine men come to their clients and jab magically treated needles into their flesh. The fact that these temple ceremonies may not cure, and may even kill the neophyte, in no way decreases the people's faith in the medicine men.

There remains one other kind of practitioner, known as a "listener." This witch-doctor has the power to exorcise the devils that lodge in the heads of people who have been bewitched. The Nacirema believe that parents bewitch their own children. Mothers are particularly suspected of putting a curse on children while teaching them the secret body rituals. The counter-magic of the witch-doctor is unusual in its lack of ritual. The patient simply tells the "listener" all his troubles and fears, beginning with the earliest difficulties he can remember. The memory displayed by the Nacirema in these exorcism sessions is truly remarkable. It is not uncommon for the patient to bemoan the rejection he felt upon being weaned as a babe, and a few individuals even see their troubles going back to the traumatic effects of their own birth.

In conclusion, mention must be made of certain practices which have their base in native aesthetics but which depend upon the pervasive aversion to the natural body and its functions. There are ritual fasts to make fat people thin and ceremonial feasts to make thin people fat. Still other rites are used to make women's breasts larger if they are small, and smaller if they are large. General dissatisfaction with breast shape is symbolized in the fact that the ideal form is virtually outside the range of human variation. A few women afflicted with almost inhuman hypermammary development are so idolized that they make a handsome living by simply going from village to village and permitting the natives to stare at them for a fee.

Reference has already been made to the fact that excretory functions are ritualized, routinized, and relegated to secrecy. Natural reproductive functions are similarly distorted. Intercourse is taboo as a topic and scheduled as an act. Efforts are made to avoid pregnancy by the use of magical materials or by limiting intercourse to certain phases of the moon. Conception is actually very infrequent. When pregnant, women dress so as to hide their condition. Parturition takes place in secret, without friends or relatives to assist, and the majority of women do not nurse their infants.

Our review of the ritual life of the Nacirema has certainly shown them to be a magic-ridden people. It is hard to understand how they have managed to exist so long under the burdens which they have imposed upon themselves. But even such exotic customs as these take on real meaning when they are viewed with the insight provided by Malinowski when he wrote (1948:70):

> Looking from far and above, from our high places of safety in the developed civilization, it is easy to see all the crudity and irrelevance of magic. But without its power and guidance early man could not have mastered his practical difficulties as he has done, nor could man have advanced to the higher stages of civilization.

References Cited

Ralph Linton, *The Study of Man,* D. Appleton-Century Co., New York, 1936.
Bronislaw Malinowski, *Magic, Science, and Religion,* The Free Press, Glencoe, 1948.
George P. Murdock, *Social Structure,* The Macmillan Co., New York, 1949.

Questions for Discussion and Writing

1. What, claims the anthropologist, do the "magical beliefs and practices of the Nacirema" (p. 235) represent for the anthropologist? In what ways does the anthropologist characterize Nacireman culture?
2. Why is their focus on the human body central to their ritual activity? What evidence of "sadism" does the writer find among the Nacirema?
3. In what ways is the anthropologist's claim that the ritual life of the Nacirema shows them to be a "magic-ridden people" (p. 239) valid according to the evidence of this analysis?
4. What is the anthropologist/narrator's attitude toward the Nacirema, and why does he so name them? What goals do you think the author had in mind when he wrote this essay? Why or why not do you think he has accomplished them?
5. What observations and details in Miner's essay (written in 1956) are now outdated? What changes would you make to the essay so to reflect the present practices of the Nacirema?

RIMMA KAZAKOVA

America of the People

The following essay was published in 1987 in Soviet Literature, *an English-language periodical from the Soviet Union, under a section called "Topics of the Day." No information is given about its author, Rimma Kazakova, and all we learn about her in the essay is that she writes songs, lives in Moscow, has a four-year-old grandson by the name of Alyosha, and had the good fortune to be part of the cruise she writes about here.*

In "America of the People," Kazakova relates a fanciful, warm encounter with America, an experience in which she and the assembled celebrators glide over the waters of the Mississippi in nearly perfect peace.

Before you read "America of the People," record some notes for yourself about the great rivers of the world and the associations you have in your mind or experience with them. Describe how these famous rivers are central to the people and cultures of the countries through which they run. In the United States, what rivers are best known, and what do they represent in the history and culture through which they flow?

I t was an event which needs to be thought over, and not only by those who took part in it. After several joint Soviet-American cruises on the Volga, 13 American anti-war and trade-union organisations decided to organise a "reciprocal" cruise on America's great river.

The Volga . . . The Mississippi . . . They can be seen as "the Elbe" of our time. How often the Elbe was recalled in the postwar years as an almost unique example of a mass meeting of two peoples imbued with a feeling of uplift for the victory won for mankind. This river has been a symbol of unity—and also a bitter reminder of the discord that started immediately afterwards. The consequences for the world of that discord have proved to be very grave indeed. If only it were possible to direct the flow of time into the natural channel of good will and peace!

. . . And so here we are, gliding along the Mississippi and looking at the luxuriant foliage of the trees on the banks and at the quiet, greenish water. One feels like pinching oneself and asking: isn't this all just a dream? We are sailing on the beautiful *Delta Queen* with its red paddle wheel reminiscent of the times of Mark Twain, passing big and small towns, to the accompaniment of exalted tunes, simple as a shepherd's horn, played by a small, steam-powered organ. We go through 27 locks, farther and farther downstream. "We" constitute 46 Soviet and 130 American passengers who are to live together on one ship as if it were one earth, which we have to share. We have to live in the manner that people close to one another live—sharing meals, talking, having a good time, and arguing. Included among us on the American side are such well-known people as Admiral La Rocque, Director of the Washington Centre of Defence Information, Douglas Mattern, General Secretary of the peace organisation "The World Citizens Registry", film-producer Edward Levis, who made such films as *Spartak, The Blue Bird* and *The Missing,* the couple Alice and Howard Frazier representing the organisation "The Coalition for Promoting Enduring Peace" and the initiators and co-ordinators of the cruise—the life and soul of all its events.

Among the Soviet passengers are the cosmonaut Georgi Grechko, Professor Mikhail Milstein of the USSR Institute for USA and Canada Studies, the "opposite number" of Admiral La Rocque, the actress Vija Artmane, Anna Sivolap of Poltava Region, a diary worker and a Deputy of the Supreme Soviet of the USSR, Stanislav Kondrashov, an observer of the newspaper *Izvestia,* who worked for a long time in the USA as a correspondent, and Talyat Kasumov, Minister of Public Health of Azerbaijan. But what is of primary importance, both among the American and the Soviet passengers there are ordinary people, active members of peace organisations, teachers, doctors, writers, journalists, scientists and priests. It is impossible to name all of them. We ordinary people are sailing along the Mississippi, ever more fully understanding one another, sharing our thoughts, singing together Soviet and American songs, reciting poetry, and dancing to music played by a small American jazz band, or to Larry's guitar, or to Nikolai Tishchenko's accordion. We are under the close scrutiny of three American TV crews and one Soviet, and we are "tortured" by the press—there are numerous press conferences and interviews. We discover that we know very little about one another. An old lady confesses that she is afraid of Russians. Cooky Anderson, who is very nice, and who made two thousand small paper cranes as a present to the participants in the cruise, interrupts her: "I'm more scared of Americans!" Everyone laughs, feeling at home. The artist Rad Dike is always up on the deck drawing something. Bud Salk, a bearded, sly and merry man, a banker from Chicago, limps with one foot in a plaster cast. He is very active in trying to improve and widen Soviet-American relations. There is among us our common favourite, Jannet Kern, who met us with the TV crews in Washington. Every day she strikes us with her extravagant clothes: breeches, bright orange shoes, a fanciful T-shirt—all this makes her an American version of the beloved personage of our children's fairy-tale—Buratino. She has a very pleasant personality, and is extremely active and attentive.

The Americans say: "You love children, just as we do; you want to live in peace; your concerns are similar to ours." A poster of ours hanging up on the deck attracts everyone's attention. In America there was a film called *The Russians Are Coming.* Our poster says, "The Russians are coming with peace and friendship." In the lounge where we usually drink coffee and talk, hangs an American poster, "I've never met a Russian whom I didn't like."

Our life on board the ship, short on sleep, packed with events, full of smiles and inquisitive stares, runs on swiftly and tirelessly. We celebrate "Ukraine Day" by treating the Americans to a Ukrainian delicacy, singing Ukrainian songs and dancing together with them the Ukrainian *hopak.* We organise a "talent evening", sing together with Tanya Petrova the song *Katyusha,* and with Larry Long, *Study War No More,* present the Americans with books, badges, placards and photographs, and receive similar presents from them. We work out and sign collectively an appeal for peace addressed to all the peoples of the world; we denounce the Reagan administration for rejecting the Soviet government's peace proposals. We look at each other with understanding, we simply live, believing in the brotherhood of men, to use the words of the famous American song. This cruise, the songs of unity and the mutual fellow-feeling will forever remain in our hearts. Everything that helped Nikolai Tishchenko and me to compose a song, *Volga-Mississippi* about our cruise on the *Delta Queen,* will also remain in our memory. The song contains the following lines: "The *Delta Queen* is similar to the globe, Above its stern shines Mark Twain's smile."

The main events, however, took place not on board the ship but on the banks of the river. Hundreds of people came to meet us, both in the daytime and in the middle of the night, with music, flowers and words of greetings and friendship. This started from the very beginning, from the moment of our embarkation. We did not expect such a happy crowd displaying good will and also curiosity. Children in T-shirts with the inscription: "I like Russian", who had come from a camp, "Forest Lake", where they learn the Russian language, sang Russian and American songs and immediately got acquainted with us. There reigned a joyous atmosphere that was just like meetings of close friends.

In Davenport we met a 600-strong march of peace, whose participants were confident that their march, which lasted for many months and took them from California to Washington, and in which their children also took part, would draw the attention of the whole country to the global problem of disarmament and the prevention of a nuclear catastrophe.

Sometimes we did encounter on the piers pathetic, lonely figures carrying anti-Soviet placards. Our American friends put them to shame and apologised on their behalf as though these people were not their countrymen but some disagreeable aliens. But what significance could those lonely figures have against the background of the crowds of animated people who were hurrying to express to those on board the departing ship their warm goodbyes and their hope for peace and friendship!

Two episodes have stuck in my memory with especial clarity. It was night. The river was wider in that place, and we saw before us a boundless expanse of water.

Judging by vague silhouettes and rustling noises on the bank crowds of people were there. Here and there lights glimmered, and by these lights we could see hands waving to us in welcome. The people on the bank and the Americans on board our ship were singing—softly, solemnly and trustingly the patriotic song of the United States, *America, America*. One couldn't but feel deep sympathy towards this America, an America of people with open hearts, of people concerned for the future of their children and of the whole world.

Another episode took place later, in the town of Dubuque, where the local authorities organised a gala concert to commemorate our visit. After the concert, all the Soviet guests were invited up on the stage, and there, together with the Americans, we rapturously sang our Soviet song, *"You are boundlessly wide, my dear country."*

Our cruise was nearing its end and we felt that we had not managed to say everything there was to say to one another . . . We reached St. Louis, and there by the magnificent steel monument symbolising man's amazing capabilities, a final rally was held. Vladimir Chernov, from Volgograd, carefully poured into a glass vessel some water he had brought from the Volga in a flask, and it was ceremonially blended with water from the Mississippi.

However, even the happiest moments of mutual understanding were at times clouded by the thought of the sharp contrast between all this and the political course steered by the ruling circles of America, the madness of the "star wars" programme, the immorality and inhumanity of quite a number of American actions on the international scene. If it had not been for all that, how quickly the striving of human hearts to meet one another could have developed, to the immense benefit of the whole world!

The words of the song Nikolai Tishchenko and I have written—*"Visit the Volga any time you wish, as to the Mississippi, our friends will meet us on its banks"*—these words denote something desirable, hypothetical rather than something that really exists. But that is how it is going to be. After all, we, the people inhabiting our Earth, all, with the exception of madmen and criminals, so passionately want peace!

. . . Our cruise is finished. I take leave of the Americans, many of whom, I am sure, have become my friends for years to come. I say goodbye to little Alex, the only child among the passengers of our ship, and tell his father Martin, and his mother, Laura, that in Moscow I also have an Alex—in Russian he is called Alyosha—a four-year-old son of my own son. I tell them how, as we walked along Prospekt Mira (Peace), my grandson Alyosha asked me, "Is this street called this way because there has never been a war here?"

"No," I answered, "not because of that, but because there never will be a war here!"

Alex's parents smile, and the fair American boy laughs. A generous sun beats down, scorching the Earth. The unforgettable *Delta Queen* bids us farewell with a long hoot. . . .

Translated by Valeria Isakovich

Questions for Discussion and Writing

1. What is the significance of Kazakova's invoking of the "mass meeting" (p. 241) on the Elbe? What are her purposes in naming some of the participants, both American and Soviet?
2. What are the images Kazakova retains of America, and how do you evaluate their validity? On what criteria do you base your evaluation? What is the significance of the similarities that underlie the two episodes that have "stuck in [her] memory with especial clarity" (p. 243)?
3. In what ways are the writer's complaints about America similar to the things she comes to treasure?
4. How effective do you think an experience like Kazakova's might be for intercultural understanding? Explain your response.

TAHIRA NAQVI

Paths upon Water

When Tahira Naqvi and her husband, a physician, arrived in the United States in 1971 from Pakistan with their two-month-old son, their plan was for Dr. Naqvi to practice medicine here for a short time and return after that to their country. Instead they stayed on, had two more sons, and Mrs. Naqvi devoted the following decade to caring for their children.

Although Naqvi came to the United States with a masters degree in psychology from Pakistan, she returned to school at Western Connecticut State University for further study. The program she entered, a masters of science in education, required she take a number of courses in writing and literature. In 1983, in response to an assignment in a course in advanced composition to write about a place she knew well as a child, Naqvi wrote about her ancestral home in Lahore, Pakistan, and thus began her career as a writer.

Central to her life today is the challenge of living in two cultures, of trying to raise children according to Pakistani values and at the same time adjusting to the culture of the United States. Her family has created a world within a world, and it is the tension of this duality that gives her the impetus to write. "When I write, I'm whole again," she says. She is also a translator of Urdu fiction, work in which she has found another connection to her culture—"something so essential I'm drawn to it like a child to a treasured toy. Perhaps," she explains, "that is because I am a translation myself, a work in progress."

Both English and Urdu, the national language of Pakistan, are spoken in the Naqvi home here, even as they were in Pakistan. Tahira Naqvi concentrates on writing about the experiences that Pakistanis have in adjusting to this country. She also teaches composition at Western Connecticut State University. The son who was a small baby

*in 1971 is today one of his mother's most helpful critics; she relies
on him for his American cultural point of view.*
   "Paths upon Water" first appeared in The Forbidden Stitch, an
Asian American Women's Anthology *(1989).*

**Before you read "Paths upon Water," write about an adjustment you had
to make when you came to the United States, if you are not originally from
this country. If you are from the United States, write about a time in your
life when you were in another culture and encountered a practice there that
seemed strange to you. Describe the situation, what appeared so strange to
you, and how you adapted to its strangeness.**

T here had been little warning, actually none at all to prepare her for her
first encounter with the sea. At breakfast that morning, her son Raza said,
"Ama, we're going to the seaside today. Jamil and Hameeda are coming with
us." She had been turning a *paratha** in the frying pan, an onerous task since
she had always fried *parathas* on a flat pan with open sides, and as the familiar
aroma of dough cooking in butter filled the air around her, she smiled happily
and thought, I've only been here a week and already he wants to show me the
sea.
   Sakina Bano had never seen the sea. Having lived practically all her life in a
town which was a good thousand miles from the nearest shoreline, her experience
of the sea was limited to what she had chanced to observe in pictures. One
picture, in which greenish-blue waves heaved toward a gray sky, she could recol-
lect clearly; it was from a calendar Raza brought home the year he started college
in Lahore. The calendar had hung on a wall of her room for many years only
to be removed when the interior of the house was whitewashed for her daughter's
wedding, and in the ensuing confusion it was misplaced and never found. The
nail on which the calendar hung had stayed in the wall since the painter, too lazy
to bother with detailed preparation, had simply painted around the nail and over
it; whenever Sakina Bano happened to glance at the forgotten nail she remembered the picture. Also distinct in her memory was a scene from a silly Urdu film
she had seen with her cousin's wife Zohra and her nieces Zenab and Amina
during a rare visit to Lahore several years ago. For some reason she hadn't been
able to put it out of her mind. On a brown and white beach, the actor Waheed
Murad, now dead but then affectedly handsome and boyish, pursued the actress
Zeba, who skipped awkwardly before him—it isn't at all proper for a woman to
be skipping in a public place. Small foam-crested waves lapped up to her, making
her *shalwar*† stick to her skinny legs, exposing the outline of her thin calves.

paratha: thin, round, flat bread cooked with butter.
†*shalwar:* trousers worn in India and Pakistan.

Why, it was just as bad as baring her legs, for what cover could the wet, gossamer-like fabric of the *shalwar* provide?

The two frolicked by an expanse of water that extended to the horizon and which, even though it was only in a film, had seemed to Sakina Bano frightening in its immensity.

"Will Jamal and his wife have lunch here?" she asked, depositing the dark, glistening *paratha* gently on Raza's plate. She would have to take out a packet of meat from the freezer if she was to give them lunch, she told herself while she poured tea in her son's cup.

"No, I don't think so. I think we'll leave before lunch. We can stop somewhere along the way and have a bite to eat."

"They'll have tea then." She was glad Raza had remembered to pick up a cake at the store the night before (she didn't know why he called it a pound cake), and she would make some rice *kheer.* *

If she had anything to do with it, she would avoid long trips and spend most of her time in Raza's apartment cooking his meals and watching him eat. The apartment pleased her. The most she would want to do would be to go out on the lawn once in a while and examine her surroundings.

Bordering each window on the outside, were narrow white shutters; these had reminded her of the stiffened icing on a cake served at her niece Amina's birthday once. And on the face of the building the white paint seemed impervious to the effects of the elements. Discolorations or cracks were visible, and she had indeed craned her neck until it hurt while she scrutinized it.

The apartment building was set against a lawn edged with freshly green, sculptured bushes, evenly thick with grass that looked more like a thick carpet than just grass. Located in a quiet section of town, the apartments overlooked a dark, thickly wooded area, a park, Raza had told her. Although tired and groggy on the evening of her arrival from Pakistan, she had not failed to take note of the surroundings into which she found herself. Her first thought was, 'Where is everybody?' while to her son she said, "How nice everything is."

Looking out the window of his sitting room the next morning, she was gladdened at the thought of her son's good fortune. The morning sky was clear like a pale blue, unwrinkled *dupatta* † that has been strung out on a line to dry. Everything looked clean, so clean. Was it not as if an unseen hand had polished the sidewalks and swept the road? They now glistened like new metal. 'Where do people throw their trash?' she wondered when she went down to the lawn again, this time with Raza, and gazed out at the shiny road, the rows and rows of neat houses hedged in by such neat white wooden fences. In hasty answer to her own query, she told herself not to be foolish; this was *Amreeka*. Here trash was in its proper place, hidden from view and no doubt disposed of in an appropriate manner. No blackened banana peels redolent with the odor of neglect here, or

---

*kheer: rice pudding.
†*dupatta:* head covering, somewhat like a large shawl.

rotting orange skins, or worse, excrement and refuse to pollute the surroundings and endanger human habitation.

She had sighed in contentment. Happiness descended upon her tangibly like a heavy blanket affording warmth on a chilly morning. Once again, she thanked her Maker. Was He not good to her son?

"Is the sea far from here?" she asked casually, brushing imaginary crumbs from the edges of her plate. Raza must never feel she didn't value his eagerness to show off his new environment. This was his new world after all. If he wanted to take her to the seaside, then seaside it would be. Certainly she was not about to be fussy and upset him.

"No, *Ama,* not too far. An hour-and-a-half's drive, that's all. Do you feel well?" His eyes crinkled in concern as he put aside the newspaper he had been reading to look at her.

She impatiently waved a hand in the air, secretly pleased at his solicitude. "Yes, yes, I'm fine son. Just a little cough, that's all. Now finish your tea and I'll make you another cup." She knew how much he liked tea. Before she came, he must have had to make it for himself. Such a chore for a man if he must make his own tea.

The subject of the sea didn't come up again until Jamil and his new bride arrived. Jamil, an old college friend of Raza's, angular like him, affable and solicitous, was no stranger to Sakina Bano. But she was meeting his wife Hameeda for the first time. Like herself, the girl was also a newcomer to this country.

"*Khalaji,* the sea's so pretty here, the beaches are so-o-o-o large, nothing like the beaches in Karachi," Hameeda informed Sakina Bano over tea, her young, shrill voice rising and falling excitedly, her lips, dark and fleshy with lipstick, wide open in a little girl's grin. There's wanderlust in her eyes already, Sakina Bano mused, trying to guess her age. Twenty-one or twenty-two. She thought of the girl in Sialkot she and her daughter had been considering for Raza. Was there really a resemblance? Perhaps it was only the youth.

"Well child, for me it will be all the same. I've never been to Karachi. Here, have another slice of cake, you too Jamil, and try the *kheer.*"

For some reason Sakina Bano couldn't fathom, sitting next to the young girl whose excitement at the prospect of a visit to the seaside was as undisguised as a child's preoccupation with a new toy, she was suddenly reminded of the actress Zeba. The image of waves lapping on her legs and swishing about her nearly bare calves rose in Sakina Bano's mind again. Like the arrival of an unexpected visitor, a strange question crossed her mind: were Hameeda's legs also skinny like Zeba's?

Drowned in the clamor for the *kheer* which had proven to be a great hit and had been consumed with such rapidity she wished she had made more, the question lost itself.

"*Khalaji,* you must tell Hameeda how you make this," Jamil was saying, and Hameeda hastily interjected, "I think you used a lot of milk."

"Have more," Sakina Bano said.

Tea didn't last long. Within an hour they were on their way to the sea, all of them in Raza's car. Jamil sat in the front with his friend, and Sakina Bano and Hameeda sat in the back, an unfortunate arrangement, Sakina Bano discovered after they had driven for what seemed to her like an hour. It wasn't Hameeda's persistent prattle that vexed her, she realized, it was her perfume. So pungent she could feel it wafting into her nostrils, it irritated the insides of her nose, and then traveled down her throat like the sour after-taste of an overripe orange. But her discomfort was short-lived; soon she became drowsy and idled into sleep.

◄►

To be sure she had heard stories of people who swam in the ocean. She wasn't so foolish as to presume that swimming was undertaken fully clothed. After all, many times as a child she had seen young boys and men from her village swim, dressed in nothing but loincloths as they jumped into the muddy waters of the canal that irrigated their fields. But what was this?

As soon as Raza parked the car in a large, compound-like area fenced in by tall walls of wire mesh, and when her dizziness subsided, Sakina Bano glanced out of the window on her left. Her attention was snagged by what she thought was a naked woman. Certain that she was still a little dazed from the long drive, her vision subsequently befogged, Sakina Bano thought nothing of what she had seen. Then the naked figure moved closer. Disbelief gave way to the sudden, awful realization that the figure was indeed real and if not altogether naked, very nearly so.

A thin strip of colored cloth shaped like a flimsy brassiere loosely held the woman's breasts, or rather a part of her breasts; and below, beneath the level of her belly button, no, even lower than that, Sakina Bano observed in horror, was something that reminded her of the loincloths the men and youths in her village wore when they swam or worked on a construction site in the summer.

The girl was pretty, such fine features, hair that shone like a handful of gold thread, and she was young too, not much older than Hameeda perhaps. But the paleness of her skin was marred by irregular red blotches that seemed in dire need of a cooling balm. No one with such redness should be without a covering in the sun, Sakina Bano offered in silent rebuke.

The woman opened the door of her car, which was parked alongside Raza's, and as she leaned over to retrieve something from the interior of her car, Sakina Bano gasped. When the young female lowered her body, her breasts were not only nearly all bared, but stood in imminent danger of spilling out of their meager coverage. O God! Is there no shame here? Sakina Bano's cheeks burned. Hastily she glanced away. In the very next instant she stole a glimpse at her son from the corners of her eyes, anxiously wondering if he too were experiencing something of what she was going through; no, she noted with a mixture of surprise and relief, he and Jamil were taking things out from the trunk of their car. They did not show any signs of discomfort. Did she see a fleeting look of curiosity on Hameeda's face? There was something else, too, she couldn't quite decipher.

Relieved that her male companions were oblivious to the disturbing view of the woman's breasts, Sakina Bano sighed sadly. She shook her head, adjusted her white, chiffon *dupatta* over her head, and slowly eased her person out of her son's car.

The taste of the sea was upon her lips in an instant. Mingled with an occasional but strong whiff of Hameeda's perfume, the smell of fish filled her nostrils and quickly settled in her nose as if to stay there forever.

Milling around were countless groups of scantily clad people, men, women, and children, coming and going in all directions. Is all of *Amreeka* here? she asked herself uneasily. Feeling guilty for having judged Zeba's contrived imprudence on film a little too harshly, she tightened her *dupatta* about her and wondered why her son had chosen to bring her to this place. Did he not know his mother? She was an old woman, and the mother of a son, but she would not surrender to anger or derision and make her son uncomfortable. His poise and confidence were hers too, were they not? Certainly he had brought her to the sea for a purpose. She must not appear ungrateful or intolerant.

While Raza and Jamil walked on casually and without any show of awkwardness, laughing and talking as though they might be in their sitting room rather than a place crowded with people in a state of disconcerting undress, she and Hameeda followed closely behind. Her head swam as she turned her eyes from the glare of the sun and attempted to examine the perturbing nakedness around her.

Sakina Bano's memories of nakedness were short and limited, extending to the time when she bathed her younger brother and sister under the water pump in the courtyard of her father's house, followed by the period in which she bathed her own three children until they were old enough to do it themselves. Of her own nakedness she carried an incomplete image; she had always bathed sitting down, on a low wooden stool.

Once, and that too shortly before his stroke, she came upon her husband getting out of his *dhoti*** in their bedroom. Standing absently near the foot of his bed as if waiting for something or someone, the *dhoti* a crumpled heap about his ankles, he lifted his face to look at her blankly when she entered, but made no attempt to move or cover himself. Not only did she have to hand him his pajamas, she also had to assist him as he struggled to pull up first one leg and then the other. A week later he suffered a stroke, in another week he was gone. It had been nearly ten years since he died. But for some reason the image of a naked disoriented man in the middle of a room clung to her mind like permanent discolorations on a well-worn copper pot.

And there was the unforgettable sharp and unsullied picture of her mother's

---

*dhoti: special length of fabric worn around the waist, like a sarong, by men.

body laid out on a rectangular slab of cracked, yellowed wood for a pre-burial bath, her skin, ash-brown, laced with a thousand wrinkles, soft, like wet, rained-on mud.

But nothing could have prepared her for this. Nakedness, like all things in nature, has a purpose, she firmly told herself as the four of them trudged toward the water.

The July sun on this day was not as hot as the July sun in Sialkot, but a certain oily humidity had begun to attach itself to her face and hands. Lifting a corner of her white *dupatta,* she wiped her face with it. Poor Hameeda, no doubt she too longed to divest herself of the *shalwar* and *qamis** she was wearing and don a swimming suit so she could join the rest of the women on the beach, be more like them. But could she swim?

They continued onward, and after some initial plodding through hot, moist sand, Sakina Bano became sure-footed; instead of having to drag her feet through the weighty volume of over-heated sand, she was now able to tread over it with relative ease. They were receiving stares already, a few vaguely curious, others unguardedly inquisitive.

Where the bodies ended she saw the ocean began, stretching to the horizon in the distance. The picture she had carried in her head of the boyish actor Waheed Murad running after Zeba on a sandy Karachi beach quickly diminished and faded away. The immensity of the sea on film was reduced to a mere blue splash of color, its place usurped by a vastness she could scarce hold within the frame of her vision; a window opened in her head, she drew in the wonder of the sea as it touched the hem of the heavens and, despite the heat, Sakina Bano shivered involuntarily. God's touch is upon the world, she silently whispered to herself.

Again and again, as she had made preparations for the journey across what she liked to refer to as the 'seven seas,' she had been told *Amreeka* was so large that many Pakistans could fit into it. The very idea of Pakistan fitting into anything else was cause for bewilderment, and the analogy left her at once befuddled and awed. But had she expected this?

The bodies sprawled before her on the sand and exposed to the sun's unyielding rays seemed unmindful of what the ocean might have to say about God's touch upon the world. Assuming supine positions, flat either on their backs or their bellies, the people on the beach reminded Sakina Bano of whole red chilies spread on a rag discolored from overuse, and left in the sun to dry and crackle. As sweat began to form in tiny droplets across her forehead and around her mouth, the unhappy thought presented itself to her that she was among people who had indeed lost their sanity.

In summer, one's first thought is to put as much distance as possible between oneself and the sun. Every effort is made to stay indoors; curtains are drawn and

qamis: a tunic worn over the *shalwar.*

jalousies unfurled in order to shut out the fire the sun exudes. In the uneasy silence of a torrid June or July afternoon, even stray dogs seek shade under a tree or behind a bush, curling up into fitful slumber as the sun beats its fervid path across the sky.

Sakina Bano couldn't understand why these men and women wished to scorch their bodies, and why, if they were here by the shore of an ocean which seemed to reach up to God, they didn't at least gaze wide-eyed at the wonder which lay at their feet. Why did they choose instead to shut their eyes and merely wallow in the heat. Their skins had rebelled, the red and darkly-pink blotches spoke for themselves. Perhaps this is a ritual they must, of necessity, follow, she mused. Perhaps they yearn to be brown as we yearn to be white.

She felt an ache insidiously putter behind her eyes. The sun always gave her a headache, even in winter, the only season when sunshine evoked pleasing sensations, when one could look forward to its briskness, its sharp touch. The heat from the sand under the *dari* on which she and Hameeda now sat seeped through the coarse fabric after a while and hugged her thighs; as people in varying shades of pink, white and red skin ran or walked past them, particles of sand flew in the air and landed on her clothes, her hands, her face. Soon she felt sand in her mouth, scraping between her teeth like the remains of *chalia* * heavy on her tongue.

Ignoring the sand in her mouth and the hot-water-bottle effect of the sand beneath her thighs, Sakina Bano shifted her attention first toward a woman on her left, and then to the man on her right whose stomach fell broadly in loose folds (like dough left out overnight); he lay supine and still, his face shielded by a straw hat. Puzzled by the glitter on their nakedness, she peered closely and with intense concentration—she had to observe if she were to learn anything. The truth came to her like a flash of sudden light in a dark room: both the man and the woman had smeared their bodies with some kind of oil! Just then she remembered the oversized cucumbers she had encountered on her first trip to the Stop and Shop; shiny and slippery, one fell from her hands as she handled them, and she exclaimed in disbelief, "They've been greased!" How amused Raza had been at her reaction.

It's really very simple, Sakina Bano finally decided, sighing again, these people wish to be fried in the sun. But why? Not wishing to appear ignorant, she kept her mouth shut, although if she had addressed the query to Hameeda, she was sure she would not have received a satisfactory reply. The girl was a newcomer like herself. In addition, she was too young to know the answers to questions which warranted profound thought preceded by profound scrutiny. She didn't look very comfortable either; perhaps the heat was getting to her, too.

Raza and Jamil, both in swimming trunks, appeared totally at ease as they ran to the water and back, occasionally wading in a wave that gently slapped the

chalia: betel nut.

beach and sometimes disappearing altogether for a second or two under a high wave. Then Sakina Bano couldn't tell where they were. They certainly seemed to be having a good time.

She and Hameeda must be the only women on the beach fully clothed, she reflected, quite a ridiculous sight if one were being viewed from the vantage point of those who were stretched out on the sand. And while Sakina Bano grappled with this disturbing thought, she saw the other woman approaching.

Attired in a *sari* and accompanied by a short, dark man (who had to be her son for he undoubtedly had her nose and her forehead) and an equally short, dark woman, both of whom wore swimming suits (the girl's as brief as that of the woman Sakina Bano had seen earlier in the parking lot), she looked no older than herself. Clutching the front folds of her *sari* as if afraid a sudden wind from the ocean might pull them out unfurling the *sari,* leaving her exposed, she tread upon the sand with a fiercely precarious step, looking only ahead, her eyes shielded with one small, flat palm.

This is how I must appear to the others, Sakina Bano ruminated. Suddenly, she felt a great sadness clutching at her chest and rising into her throat like a sigh as she watched the woman in the *sari* begin to make herself comfortable on a large, multi-colored towel thrown on the sand by her son and his wife; those two hurriedly dashed off in the direction of the water. Why are they in such haste? Sakina Bano wondered.

Her knees drawn up, one arm tensely wrapped around them, the woman appeared to be watching her son and her daughter-in-law. But could Sakina Bano really be sure? The woman's hand against her forehead concealed her eyes. As she continued to observe the woman's slight figure around which the green and orange cotton *sari* had been carelessly draped, she wondered what part of India she might be from. Perhaps the south, which meant she spoke no Hindi, which also meant a conversation would not be at all possible.

Sakina Bano's attention returned to Hameeda who had not said a word all this time. Like a break-through during muddled thought, it suddenly occurred to Sakina Bano that there was a distinct possibility Hameeda would be swimming if it weren't for her. In deference to her older companion she was probably foregoing the chance to swim. Will Raza's wife also wear a scant swimming suit and bare her body in the presence of strange men? The question disturbed her; she tried to shrug it aside. But it wouldn't go away. Stubbornly it returned, not alone this time but accompanied by the picture of a young woman who vaguely resembled the actress Zeba and who was clothed, partially, in a swimming suit much like the ones Sakina Bano saw about her. Running behind her was a man, not Waheed Murad, but alas, her own son, her Raza. Was she dreaming, had the sun weakened her brain? Such foolishness. Sakina Bano saw that Hameeda was staring ahead, like the woman on the towel, her eyes squinted because of the glare. Frozen on her full, red lips was a hesitant smile.

Once again Sakina Bano sought her son's figure among the throng near the water's edge. At first the brightness of the sun blinded her and she couldn't see where he was. She strained her eyes, shielding them from the sun with a hand on her forehead. And finally she spotted him. He and Jamil were talking to some people. A dark man and a dark girl. The son and daughter-in-law of the woman in the *sari*. Were they acquaintances then, perhaps friends? The four of them laughed like old friends, the girl standing so close to Raza he must surely be able to see her half-naked breasts. The poor boy!

They had begun to walk toward where she and Hameeda were seated. Raza was going to introduce his friends to his mother. How was she to conceal her discomfort at the woman's mode of dress?

"Ama, I want you to meet Ajit and Kamla. Ajit works at Ethan Allen with me. Kamla wants you to come to their house for dinner next Sunday."

Both Ajit and Kamla lifted their hands and said *"Namaste,"** and she nodded and smiled. What does one say in answer to *namaste,* anyway?

Hameeda was also introduced. Kamla made a joke about "the shy new bride," Hameeda showed her pretty teeth in a smile, and then Kamla said, "You have to come, Auntie." Sakina Bano wondered why Raza appeared so comfortable in the presence of a woman who was nearly all naked. Even her loincloth was flimsy. Granted it wasn't as bad as some of the others she had been seeing around her, but it was flimsy nonetheless.

"Yes, it's very nice of you to invite us. It's up to Raza. He's usually so busy. But if he is free . . ."

"Of course I'm free next Sunday. We'd love to come, Kamla."

Kamla said, "Good! I'll introduce you and Auntie to my mother-in-law after a swim. Coming?" She laid a hand on Raza's arm and Sakina Bano glanced away, just in time to catch Hameeda's smile of surprise. Well, one's son can become a stranger too, even a good son like Raza.

"Sure. *Yar,* Ajit, are you and Kamla planning to go to the late show?"

"Yes we are. You? Do you have tickets?" Ajit wasn't a bad looking boy. But he didn't measure up to Raza. No, Raza's nose was straight and to the point, his forehead wide and his eyes well-illuminated. But he had changed somehow; she felt she was distanced from him. A son is always a son, she thought and smiled and nodded again as Ajit and Kamla uttered their *Namaste's* and returned to the water with Raza and Jamil.

"Khalaji, why don't we wet our feet before we go?" Hameeda suddenly asked her.

"Wet our feet?"

"Yes, *Khala.* Just dip our feet in sea water. Come on. You're not afraid of the water, are you?"

"No, child." She wasn't afraid. Her mind was playing tricks with her, filling her head with thoughts that had no place there. A change was welcome. "Yes, why not?" she said, as if speaking to herself. When she attempted to get up she found that her joints had stiffened painfully. "Here, girl, give me your hand."

*Namaste: Hindu form of greeting.

She extended an arm toward Hameeda. Why not, especially since they had come so far and she had suffered the heat for what had seemed like a very long time.

Hameeda had rolled up her *shalwar* almost to the level of her knees. How pretty her legs are, the skin hairless and shiny, like a baby's, and not skinny at all, Sakina Bano mused in surprise, and how quick she is to show them.

She must do the same, she realized. Otherwise Hameeda would think she was afraid. She pulled up one leg of her *shalwar* tentatively, tucked it at the waist with one swift movement of her right hand, then looked about her sheepishly. Hameeda was laughing.

"The other one too, *Khala!*"

Who would want to look at her aged and scrawny legs? And her husband was not around to glare at her in remonstration. Gingerly the other leg of the *shalwar* was also lifted and tucked in. How funny her legs looked, the hair on them all gray now and curly, the calves limp. Now both women giggled like schoolgirls. And Raza would be amused, he would think she was having a good time, Sakina Bano told herself.

Raza and Jamil burst into laughter when they saw the women approach. They waved. Sakina Bano waved back.

Holding the front folds of her *shalwar* protectively, Sakina Bano strode toward the water. As she went past the other woman in the *sari* she smiled at her. The woman gave her a startled look, and then, dropping the hand with which she had been shielding her eyes from the sun, she let her arm fall away from her knees, and following Sakina Bano with her gaze, she returned her smile.

"Wait for me," Sakina Bano called to Hameeda in a loud, happy voice, "wait, girl."

Questions for Discussion and Writing

1. What observations does Sakina Bano make initially about her new surroundings in *Amreeka?* Sakina makes comparisons, most of them metaphors, about her experiences in the story to the life she knows in Pakistan. How do these metaphors help give us a sense of her home?

2. In what ways does Sakina's question of "profound thought preceded by profound scrutiny" (p. 253) help us to understand her? Why does she not ask Hameeda about it?

3. What significance does the movie (the "silly Urdu film") that Sakina saw in Pakistan continue to have in this experience at the beach?

4. What does Sakina fear is happening to her relationship with her son, and why or why not are her fears justified?

5. How do you interpret the end of the story? Through what patterns of values and attitudes is Sakina experiencing the beach? What patterns of values and attitudes underlie the actions of the Americans?

ANNE TYLER

Your Place Is Empty

When Anne Tyler writes about her life, she makes it seem as if her widely acclaimed novels and award-winning writing happen in the small bits of time—"the partitions" of her life she calls them—left between her trips to the pediatrician, the veterinarian, the schools of her children, and keeping the family home in repair. Accidental Tourist *(1985) is her best-known novel because of the film made from it.*

Born in 1941 in Minneapolis, she grew up in a number of Quaker communities in the Midwest and the South. It was this "setting-apart situation" and trying later on "to fit into the outside world" that helped mold Tyler into a writer. At age sixteen, she entered Duke University and there was guided by novelist Reynolds Price who, with Eudora Welty, became her greatest literary influence. "I don't talk well," she writes. "For me, writing something down was the only road out."

Tyler's father has been an important example to her. Even when he has had to give up critical goals and dreams, he's "whistled Mozart." Of his life Tyler writes, "It seems to me that the way my father lives (infinitely adapting and looking around him with a smile to say 'Oh! So this *is where I am!') is also the way to slip gracefully through a choppy life of writing novels, plastering the dining room ceiling, and presiding at slumber parties."*

Tyler lives with her husband, Taghi Modarressi, an Iranian-born psychiatrist and novelist, and their two daughters in Baltimore, Maryland. In "Your Place Is Empty," which first appeared in The New Yorker *(1976), the reader can gain insight into the ways in which fiction can grow out of a writer's life.*

"I think I was born with the impression that what happened in books was much more reasonable, and interesting, and real, *in some ways than what happened in life," Tyler writes. "I hated childhood,*

*and spent it sitting behind a book waiting for adulthood to arrive."
She has not been disappointed by adulthood. In fact she likes "every-
thing about it but the paperwork—the income tax and protesting the
Sears bill and renewing the Triple-A membership."*

*Writing is for Tyler "the most private of professions." She shuns
performing in public or telling her secrets to interviewers from
magazines: "I will write my books and raise the children. Anything
else just fritters me away."*

**Before you read "Your Place Is Empty," write about a time in your life when
a parent or someone close to you came to stay with you. Describe your and
the other person's expectations of the visit and how each of you felt about
it (frustrated, disappointed, surprised), and the reasons for feeling the ways
you did. Looking back on it now, why did you encounter the problems you
had? What were the reactions of the person who came to visit, and how did
you find them out, if you did?**

E arly in October, Hassan Ardavi invited his mother to come from Iran for
a visit. His mother accepted immediately. It wasn't clear how long the visit
was to last. Hassan's wife thought three months would be a good length of time.
Hassan himself had planned on six months, and said so in his letter of invitation.
But his mother felt that after such a long trip six months would be too short,
and she was counting on staying a year. Hassan's little girl, who wasn't yet two,
had no idea of time at all. She was told that her grandmother was coming but
she soon forgot about it.

Hassan's wife was named Elizabeth, not an easy word for Iranians to pronounce. She would have been recognized as American the world over—a blond,
pretty girl with long bones and an ungraceful way of walking. One of her strong
points was an ability to pick up foreign languages, and before her mother-in-law's
arrival she bought a textbook and taught herself Persian. *"Salaam aleikum,"* she
told the mirror every morning. Her daughter watched, startled, from her place
on the potty-chair. Elizabeth ran through possible situations in her mind and
looked up the words for them. "Would you like more tea? Do you take sugar?"
At suppertime she spoke Persian to her husband, who looked amused at the new
tone she gave his language, with her flat, factual American voice. He wrote his
mother and told her Elizabeth had a surprise for her.

Their house was a three-story brick Colonial, but only the first two stories were
in use. Now they cleared the third of its trunks and china barrels and *National
Geographics,* and they moved in a few pieces of furniture. Elizabeth sewed flowered curtains for the window. She was unusually careful with them; to a foreign
mother-in-law, fine seams might matter. Also, Hassan bought a pocket compass,
which he placed in the top dresser drawer. "For her prayers," he said. "She'll want
to face Mecca. She prays three times a day."

"But which direction is Mecca from here?" Elizabeth asked.

Hassan only shrugged. He had never said the prayers himself, not even as a child. His earliest memory was of tickling the soles of his mother's feet while she prayed steadfastly on; everyone knew it was forbidden to pause once you'd started.

Mrs. Ardavi felt nervous about the descent from the plane. She inched down the staircase sideways, one hand tight on the railing, the other clutching her shawl. It was night, and cold. The air seemed curiously opaque. She arrived on solid ground and stood collecting herself—a small, stocky woman in black, with a kerchief over her smooth gray hair. She held her back very straight, as if she had just had her feelings hurt. In picturing this moment she had always thought Hassan would be waiting beside the plane, but there was no sign of him. Blue lights dotted the darkness behind her, an angular terminal loomed ahead, and an official was herding the passengers toward a plate-glass door. She followed, entangled in a web of meaningless sounds such as those you might hear in a fever dream.

Immigration. Baggage Claims. Customs. To all she spread her hands and beamed and shrugged, showing she spoke no English. Meanwhile her fellow-passengers waved to a blur of faces beyond a glass wall. It seemed they all knew people here; she was the only one who didn't. She had issued from the plane like a newborn baby, speechless and friendless. And the customs official didn't seem pleased with her. She had brought too many gifts. She had stuffed her bags with them, discarding all but the most necessary pieces of her clothing so that she would have more room. There were silver tea sets and gold jewelry for her daughter-in-law, and for her granddaughter a doll dressed in the complicated costume of a nomad tribe, an embroidered sheepskin vest, and two religious medals on chains—one a disc inscribed with the name of Allah, the other a tiny gold Koran, with a very effective prayer for long life folded up within it. The customs official sifted gold through his fingers like sand and frowned at the Koran. "Have I done something wrong?" she asked. But of course he didn't understand her. Though you'd think, really, that if he would just *listen* hard enough, just meet her eyes once . . . it was a very simple language, there was no reason why it shouldn't come through to him.

For Hassan, she'd brought food. She had gathered all his favorite foods and put them in a drawstring bag embroidered with peacocks. When the official opened the bag he said something under his breath and called another man over. Together they unwrapped tiny newspaper packets and sniffed at various herbs. "Sumac," she told them. "Powder of lemons. Shambahleh." They gazed at her blankly. They untied a small cloth sack and rummaged through the kashk she had brought for soup. It rolled beneath their fingers and across the counter—hard white balls of yogurt curd, stuck with bits of sheep hair and manure. Some peasant had labored for hours to make that kashk. Mrs. Ardavi picked up one piece and replaced it firmly in the sack. Maybe the official understood her meaning: she was running out of patience. He threw up his hands. He slid her belongings down the counter. She was free to go.

Free to go where?

Dazed and stumbling, a pyramid of knobby parcels and bags, scraps of velvet and brocade and tapestry, she made her way to the glass wall. A door opened out of nowhere and a stranger blocked her path. "Khanom Jun," he said. It was a name that only her children would use, but she passed him blindly and he had to touch her arm before she would look up.

He had put on weight. She didn't know him. The last time she'd seen him he was a thin, stoop-shouldered medical student disappearing into an Air France jet without a backward glance. "Khanom Jun, it's me," this stranger said, but she went on searching his face with cloudy eyes. No doubt he was a bearer of bad news. Was that it? A recurrent dream had warned her that she would never see her son again—that he would die on his way to the airport, or had already been dead for months but no one wanted to break the news; some second or third cousin in America had continued signing Hassan's name to his cheerful, anonymous letters. Now here was this man with graying hair and a thick mustache, his clothes American but his face Iranian, his eyes sadly familiar, as if they belonged to someone else. "Don't you believe me?" he said. He kissed her on both cheeks. It was his smell she recognized first—a pleasantly bitter, herblike smell that brought her the image of Hassan as a child, reaching thin arms around her neck. "It's you, Hassan," she said, and then she started crying against his gray tweed shoulder.

They were quiet during the long drive home. Once she reached over to touch his face, having wanted to do so for miles. None of the out-of-focus snapshots he'd sent had prepared her for the way he had aged. "How long has it been?" she asked. "Twelve years?" But both of them knew to the day how long it had been. All those letters of hers: "My dear Hassan, ten years now and still your place is empty." "Eleven years and still . . ."

Hassan squinted through the windshield at the oncoming headlights. His mother started fretting over her kerchief, which she knew she ought not to have worn. She'd been told so by her youngest sister, who had been to America twice. "It marks you," her sister had said. But that square of silk was the last, shrunken reminder of the veil she used to hide beneath, before the previous Shah had banished such things. At her age, how could she expose herself? And then her teeth; her teeth were a problem too. Her youngest sister had said, "You ought to get dentures made, I'm sure there aren't three whole teeth in your head." But Mrs. Ardavi was scared of dentists. Now she covered her mouth with one hand and looked sideways at Hassan, though so far he hadn't seemed to notice. He was busy maneuvering his car into the right-hand lane.

This silence was the last thing she had expected. For weeks she'd been saving up stray bits of gossip, weaving together the family stories she would tell him. There were three hundred people in her family—most of them related to each other in three or four different ways, all leading intricate and scandalous lives she had planned to discuss in detail, but instead she stared sadly out the window. You'd think Hassan would ask. You'd think they could have a better conversation than this, after such a long time. Disappointment made her cross, and now she stubbornly refused to speak even when she saw something she wanted to comment on, some imposing building or unfamiliar brand of car sliding past her into the darkness.

By the time they arrived it was nearly midnight. None of the houses were lit but Hassan's—worn brick, older than she would have expected. "Here we are," said Hassan. The competence with which he parked the car, fitting it neatly into a small space by the curb, put him firmly on the other side of the fence, the American side. She would have to face her daughter-in-law alone. As they climbed the front steps she whispered, "How do you say it again?"

"Say what?" Hassan asked.

"Her name. Lizabet?"

"Elizabeth. Like Elizabeth Taylor. *You* know."

"Yes, yes, of course," said his mother. Then she lifted her chin, holding tight to the straps of her purse.

Elizabeth was wearing bluejeans and a pair of fluffy slippers. Her hair was blond as corn silk, cut short and straight, and her face had the grave, sleepy look of a child's. As soon as she had opened the door she said, *"Salaam aleikum."* Mrs. Ardavi, overcome with relief at the Persian greeting, threw her arms around her and kissed both cheeks. Then they led her into the living room, which looked comfortable but a little too plain. The furniture was straight-edged, the rugs uninteresting, though the curtains had a nice figured pattern that caught her eye. In one corner sat a shiny red kiddie car complete with license plates. "Is that the child's?" she asked. "Hilary's?" She hesitated over the name. "Could I see her?"

"Now?" said Hassan.

But Elizabeth told him, "That's all right." (Women understood these things.) She beckoned to her mother-in-law. They climbed the stairs together, up to the second floor, into a little room that smelled of milk and rubber and talcum powder, smells she would know anywhere. Even in the half-light from the hallway, she could tell that Hilary was beautiful. She had black, tumbling hair, long black lashes, and skin of a tone they called wheat-colored, lighter than Hassan's. "There," said Elizabeth. "Thank you," said Mrs. Ardavi. Her voice was formal, but this was her first grandchild and it took her a moment to recover herself. Then they stepped back into the hallway. "I brought her some medals," she whispered. "I hope you don't mind."

"Medals?" said Elizabeth. She repeated the word anxiously, mispronouncing it.

"Only an Allah and a Koran, both very tiny. You'll hardly know they're there. I'm not used to seeing a child without a medal. It worries me."

Automatically her fingers traced a chain around her neck, ending in the hollow of her collarbone. Elizabeth nodded, looking relieved. *"Oh* yes. Medals," she said.

"Is that all right?"

"Yes, of course."

Mrs. Ardavi took heart. "Hassan laughs," she said. "He doesn't believe in these things. But when he left I put a prayer in his suitcase pocket, and you see he's been protected. Now if Hilary wore a medal, I could sleep nights."

"Of course," Elizabeth said again.

When they re-entered the living room, Mrs. Ardavi was smiling, and she kissed Hassan on the top of his head before she sat down.

American days were tightly scheduled, divided not into morning and after-noon but into 9:00, 9:30, and so forth, each half hour possessing its own set activity. It was marvellous. Mrs. Ardavi wrote her sisters: "They're more orga-nized here. My daughter-in-law never wastes a minute." How terrible, her sisters wrote back. They were all in Teheran, drinking cup after cup of tea and idly guessing who might come and visit. "No, you misunderstand," Mrs. Ardavi protested. "I like it this way. I'm fitting in wonderfully." And to her youngest sister she wrote, "You'd think I was American. No one guesses otherwise." This wasn't true, of course, but she hoped it would be true in the future.

Hassan was a doctor. He worked long hours, from six in the morning until six at night. While she was still washing for her morning prayers she could hear him tiptoe down the stairs and out the front door. His car would start up, a distant rumble far below her, and from her bathroom window she could watch it swing out from beneath a tatter of red leaves and round the corner and disappear. Then she would sigh and return to her sink. Before prayers she had to wash her face, her hands, and the soles of her feet. She had to draw her wet fingers down the part in her hair. After that she returned to her room, where she swathed herself tightly in her long black veil and knelt on a beaded velvet prayer mat. East was where the window was, curtained by chintz and misted over. On the east wall she hung a lithograph of the Caliph Ali and a color snapshot of her third son, Babak, whose marriage she had arranged just a few months before this visit. If Babak hadn't married, she never could have come. He was the youngest, spoiled by being the only son at home. It had taken her three years to find a wife for him. (One was too modern, one too lazy, one so perfect she had been suspicious.) But finally the proper girl had turned up, modest and well-mannered and sufficiently wide of hip, and Mrs. Ardavi and the bridal couple had settled in a fine new house on the outskirts of Teheran. Now every time she prayed, she added a word of thanks that at last she had a home for her old age. After that, she unwound her veil and laid it carefully in a drawer. From another drawer she took thick cotton stockings and elastic garters; she stuffed her swollen feet into open-toed vinyl sandals. Unless she was going out, she wore a housecoat. It amazed her how wasteful Americans were with their clothing.

Downstairs, Elizabeth would have started her tea and buttered a piece of toast for her. Elizabeth and Hilary ate bacon and eggs, but bacon of course was unclean and Mrs. Ardavi never accepted any. Nor had it even been offered to her, except once, jokingly, by Hassan. The distinctive, smoky smell rose to meet her as she descended the stairs. "What does it taste like?" she always asked. She was dying to know. But Elizabeth's vocabulary didn't cover the taste of bacon; she only said it was salty and then laughed and gave up. They had learned very early to travel a well-worn conversational path, avoiding the dead ends caused by unfamiliar words. "Did you sleep well?" Elizabeth always asked in her funny, childish accent, and Mrs. Ardavi answered, "So-so." Then they would turn and watch Hilary, who sat on a booster seat eating scrambled eggs, a thin chain of Persian gold crossing the back of her neck. Conversation was easier, or even unnecessary, as long as Hilary was there.

In the mornings Elizabeth cleaned house. Mrs. Ardavi used that time for letter writing. She had dozens of letters to write, to all her aunts and uncles and her thirteen sisters. (Her father had had three wives, and a surprising number of children even for that day and age.) Then there was Babak. His wife was in her second month of pregnancy, so Mrs. Ardavi wrote long accounts of the American child-rearing methods. "There are some things I don't agree with," she wrote. "They let Hilary play outdoors by herself, with not even a servant to keep an eye on her." Then she would trail off and gaze thoughtfully at Hilary, who sat on the floor watching a television program called "Captain Kangaroo."

Mrs. Ardavi's own childhood had been murky and grim. From the age of nine she was wrapped in a veil, one corner of it clenched in her teeth to hide her face whenever she appeared on the streets. Her father, a respected man high up in public life, used to chase servant girls through the halls and trap them, giggling, in vacant bedrooms. At the age of ten she was forced to watch her mother bleed to death in childbirth, and when she screamed the midwife had struck her across the face and held her down till she had properly kissed her mother goodbye. There seemed no connection at all between her and this little overalled American. At times, when Hilary had one of her temper tantrums, Mrs. Ardavi waited in horror for Elizabeth to slap her and then, when no slap came, felt a mixture of relief and anger. "In Iran—" she would begin, and if Hassan was there he always said, "But this is not Iran, remember?"

After lunch Hilary took a nap, and Mrs. Ardavi went upstairs to say her noontime prayers and take a nap as well. Then she might do a little laundry in her bathtub. Laundry was a problem here. Although she liked Elizabeth, the fact was that the girl was a Christian, and therefore unclean; it would never do to have a Christian wash a Moslem's clothes. The automatic dryer was also unclean, having contained, at some point, a Christian's underwear. So she had to ask Hassan to buy her a drying rack. It came unassembled. Elizabeth put it together for her, stick by stick, and then Mrs. Ardavi held it under her shower and rinsed it off, hoping that would be enough to remove any taint. The Koran didn't cover this sort of situation.

When Hilary was up from her nap they walked her to the park—Elizabeth in her eternal bluejeans and Mrs. Ardavi in her kerchief and shawl, taking short painful steps in small shoes that bulged over her bunions. They still hadn't seen to her teeth, although by now Hassan had noticed them. She was hoping he might forget about the dentist, but then she saw him remembering every time she laughed and revealed her five brown teeth set wide apart.

At the park she laughed a great deal. It was her only way of communicating with the other women. They sat on the benches ringing the playground, and while Elizabeth translated their questions Mrs. Ardavi laughed and nodded at them over and over. "They want to know if you like it here," Elizabeth said. Mrs. Ardavi answered at length, but Elizabeth's translation was very short. Then gradually the other women forgot her, and conversation rattled on while she sat silent and watched each speaker's lips. The few recognizable words—"telephone," "television," "radio"—gave her the impression that American conversations were largely technical, even among women. Their gestures were wide and slow, disproving her youngest sister's statement that in America everyone was in a hurry. On the contrary, these women were dreamlike, moving singly or in twos across wide flat spaces beneath white November skies when they departed.

Later, at home, Mrs. Ardavi would say, "The red-haired girl, is she pregnant? She looked it, I thought. Is the fat girl happy in her marriage?" She asked with some urgency, plucking Elizabeth's sleeve when she was slow to answer. People's private lives fascinated her. On Saturday trips to the supermarket she liked to single out some interesting stranger. "What's the matter with that *jerky*-moving man? That girl, is she one of your dark-skinned people?" Elizabeth answered too softly, and never seemed to follow Mrs. Ardavi's pointing finger.

Supper was difficult; Mrs. Ardavi didn't like American food. Even when Elizabeth made something Iranian, it had an American taste to it—the vegetables still faintly crisp, the onions transparent rather than nicely blackened. "Vegetables not thoroughly cooked retain a certain acidity," Mrs. Ardavi said, laying down her fork. "This is a cause of constipation and stomach aches. At night I often have heartburn. It's been three full days since I moved my bowels." Elizabeth merely bent over her plate, offering no symptoms of her own in return. Hassan said, "At the table, Khanom? At the table?"

Eventually she decided to cook supper herself. Over Elizabeth's protests she began at three every afternoon, filling the house with the smell of dillweed and arranging pots on counters and cabinets and finally, when there was no more space, on the floor. She squatted on the floor with her skirt tucked between her knees and stirred great bowls of minced greens while behind her, on the gas range, four different pots of food bubbled and steamed. The kitchen was becoming more homelike, she thought. A bowl of yogurt brewed beside the stove, a kettle of rice soaked in the sink, and the top of the dishwasher was curlicued with the yellow dye from saffron. In one corner sat the pudding pan, black on the bottom from the times she had cooked down sugar to make a sweet for her intestines. "Now, this is your rest period," she always told Elizabeth. "Come to the table in three hours and be surprised." But Elizabeth only hovered around the kitchen, disturbing the serene, steam-filled air with clatter and slams as she put away pots, or pacing between stove and sink, her arms folded across her chest. At supper she ate little; Mrs. Ardavi wondered how Americans got so tall on such small suppers. Hassan, on the other hand, had second and third helpings. "I must be gaining five pounds a week," he said. "None of my clothes fit."

"That's good to hear," said his mother. And Elizabeth added something but in English, which Hassan answered in English also. Often now they broke into

English for paragraphs at a time—Elizabeth speaking softly, looking at her plate, and Hassan answering at length and sometimes reaching across the table to cover her hand.

At night, after her evening prayers, Mrs. Ardavi watched television on the living-room couch. She brought her veil downstairs and wrapped it around her to keep the drafts away. Her shoes lay on the rug beneath her, and scattered down the length of the couch were her knitting bag, her sack of burned sugar, her magnifying glass, and *My First Golden Dictionary*. Elizabeth read novels in an easy chair, and Hassan watched TV so that he could translate the difficult parts of the plot. Not that Mrs. Ardavi had much trouble. American plots were easy to guess at, particularly the Westerns. And when the program was boring—a documentary or a special news feature—she could pass the time by talking to Hassan. "Your cousin Farah wrote," she said. "Do you remember her? A homely girl, too dark. She's getting a divorce and in my opinion it's fortunate; he's from a lower class. Do you remember Farah?"

Hassan only grunted, his eyes on the screen. He was interested in American politics. So was she, for that matter. She had wept for President Kennedy, and carried Jackie's picture in her purse. But these news programs were long and dry, and if Hassan wouldn't talk she was forced to turn at last to her *Golden Dictionary*.

In her childhood, she had been taught by expensive foreign tutors. Her mind was her great gift, the compensation for a large, plain face and a stocky figure. But now what she had learned seemed lost, forgotten utterly or fogged by years, so that Hassan gave a snort whenever she told him some fact that she had dredged up from her memory. It seemed that everything she studied now had to penetrate through a great thick layer before it reached her mind. "Tonk you," she practiced. "Tonk you. Tonk you." "Thank you," Hassan corrected her. He pointed out useful words in her dictionary—grocery-store words, household words—but she grew impatient with their woodenness. What she wanted was the language to display her personality, her famous courtesy, and her magical intuition about the inside lives of other people. Nightly she learned "salt," "bread," "spoon," but with an inner sense of dullness, and every morning when she woke her English was once again confined to "thank you" and "NBC."

Elizabeth, meanwhile, read on, finishing one book and reaching for the next without even glancing up. Hassan chewed a thumbnail and watched a senator. He shouldn't be disturbed, of course, but time after time his mother felt the silence and the whispery turning of pages stretching her nerves until she had to speak. "Hassan?"

"Hmm."

"My chest seems tight. I'm sure a cold is coming on. Don't you have a tonic?"

"No," said Hassan.

He dispensed medicines all day; he listened to complaints. Common sense told her to stop, but she persisted, encouraged by some demon that wouldn't let her tongue lie still. "Don't you have some syrup? What about that liquid you gave me for constipation? Would that help?"

"No, it wouldn't," said Hassan.

He drove her on, somehow. The less he gave, the more she had to ask. "Well, aspirin? Vitamins?" Until Hassan said, "Will you just let me *watch?*" Then she could lapse into silence again, or even gather up the clutter of her belongings and bid the two of them good night.

She slept badly. Often she lay awake for hours, fingering the edge of the sheet and staring at the ceiling. Memories crowded in on her, old grievances and fears, injustices that had never been righted. For the first time in years she thought of her husband, a gentle, weak man given to surprising outbursts of temper. She hadn't loved him when she married him, and at his death from a liver ailment six years later her main feeling had been resentment. Was it fair to be widowed so young, while other women were supported and protected? She had moved from her husband's home back to the old family estate, where five of her sisters still lived. There she had stayed till Babak's wedding, drinking tea all day with her sisters and pulling the strings by which the rest of the family was attached. Marriages were arranged, funerals attended, childbirth discussed in fine detail; servants' disputes were settled, and feuds patched up and then restarted. Her husband's face had quickly faded, leaving only a vacant spot in her mind. But now she could see him so clearly—a wasted figure on his deathbed, beard untrimmed, turban coming loose, eyes imploring her for something more than an absentminded pat on the cheek as she passed through his room on her way to check the children.

She saw the thin faces of her three small boys as they sat on the rug eating rice. Hassan was the stubborn, mischievous one, with perpetual scabs on his knees. Babak was the cuddly one. Ali was the oldest, who had caused so much worry—weak, like his father, demanding, but capable of turning suddenly charming. Four years ago he had died of a brain hemorrhage, slumping over a dinner table in faraway Shīrāz, where he'd gone to be free of his wife, who was also his double first cousin. Ever since he was born he had disturbed his mother's sleep, first because she worried over what he would amount to and now, after his death, because she lay awake listing all she had done wrong with him. She had been too lenient. No, too harsh. There was no telling. Mistakes she had made floated on the ceiling like ghosts—allowances she'd made when she knew she shouldn't have, protections he had not deserved, blows which perhaps he had not deserved either.

She would have liked to talk to Hassan about it, but any time she tried he changed the subject. Maybe he was angry about the way he had heard of Ali's death. It was customary to break such news gradually. She had started a series of tactful letters, beginning by saying that Ali was seriously ill when in truth he was already buried. Something in the letter had given her away—perhaps her plans for a rest cure by the seaside, which she never would have considered if she'd had an ailing son at home. Hassan had telephoned overseas, taking three nights to reach her. "Tell me what's wrong," he said. "I know there's something. When her tears kept her from answering, he asked, "Is he dead?" His voice sounded angry, but that might have been due to a poor connection. And when he hung up, cutting her off before she could say all she wanted, she thought, I should have told him straight out. I had forgotten that about him. Now when she spoke of Ali he listened politely, with his face frozen. She would have told him anything, all about the death and burial and that witch of a wife throwing herself, too late, into the grave; but Hassan never asked.

Death was moving in on her. Oh, not on her personally (the women in her family lived a century or longer, burying the men one by one) but on everybody around her, all the cousins and uncles and brothers-in-law. No sooner had she laid away her mourning clothes than it was time to bring them out again. Recently she had begun to feel she would outlive her two other sons as well, and she fought off sleep because of the dreams it brought—Babak lying stiff and cold in his grave, Hassan crumpled over in some dark American alley. Terrifying images would zoom at her out of the night. In the end she had to wrap herself in her veil and sleep instead on the Persian rug, which had the dusty smell of home and was, anyway, more comfortable than her unsteady foreign mattress.

At Christmas time, Hassan and Elizabeth gave Mrs. Ardavi a brightly colored American dress with short sleeves. She wore it to an Iranian party, even leaving off her kerchief in a sudden fit of daring. Everyone commented on how nice she looked. "Really you fit right in," a girl told her. "May I write to my mother about you? She was over here for a year and a half and never once stepped out of the house without her kerchief." Mrs. Ardavi beamed. It was true she would never have associated with these people at home—children of civil servants and bank clerks, newly rich now they'd finished medical school. The wives called their husbands "Doctor" even in direct address. But still it felt good to be speaking so much Persian; her tongue nearly ran away with her. "I see you're expecting a baby," she said to one of the wives. "Is it your first? I could tell by your eyes. Now don't be nervous. I had three myself; my mother had seven and never felt a pain in her life. She would squat down to serve my father's breakfast and 'Eh?' she would say. 'Aga Jun, it's the baby!' and there it would be on the floor between her feet, waiting for her to cut the cord and finish pouring the tea." She neglected to mention how her mother had died. All her natural tact came back to her, her gift with words and her knowledge of how to hold an audience. She bubbled and sparkled like a girl, and her face fell when it was time to go home.

After the party, she spent two or three days noticing more keenly than ever the loss of her language, and talking more feverishly when Hassan came home in the evening. This business of being a foreigner was something changeable. Boundaries kept shifting, and sometimes it was she who was the foreigner but other times Elizabeth, or even Hassan. (Wasn't it true, she often wondered, that there was a greater distance between men and women than between Americans and Iranians, or even *Eskimos* and Iranians?) Hassan was the foreigner when she and Elizabeth conspired to hide a miniature Koran in his glove compartment; he would have laughed at them. "You see," she told Elizabeth, "I know there's nothing to it, but it makes me feel better. When my sons were born I took them all to the bath attendant to have their blood let. People say it brings long life. I know that's superstition, but whenever afterward I saw those ridges down their backs I felt safe. Don't you understand?" And Elizabeth said, "Of course." She smuggled the Koran into the car herself, and hid it beneath the Texaco maps. Hassan saw nothing.

Hilary was a foreigner forever. She dodged her grandmother's yearning hands, and when the grownups spoke Persian she fretted and misbehaved and pulled on Elizabeth's sleeve. Mrs. Ardavi had to remind herself constantly not to kiss the child too much, not to reach out for a hug, not to offer her lap. In this country people kept more separate. They kept so separate that at times she felt hurt. They tried to be so subtle, so undemonstrative. She would never understand this place.

In January they took her to a dentist, who made clucking noises when he looked in her mouth. "What does he say?" she asked. "Tell me the worst." But Hassan was talking in a low voice to Elizabeth, and he waved her aside. They seemed to be having a misunderstanding of some sort. "What does he *say*, Hassan?"

"Just a minute."

She craned around in the high-backed chair, fighting off the dentist's little mirror. "I have to know," she told Hassan.

"He says your teeth are terrible. They have to be extracted and the gums surgically smoothed. He wants to know if you'll be here for another few months; he can't schedule you till later."

A cold lump of fear swelled in her stomach. Unfortunately she *would* be here; it had only been three months so far and she was planning to stay a year. So she had to watch numbly while her life was signed away, whole strings of appointments made, and little white cards filled out. And Hassan didn't even look sympathetic. He was still involved in whatever this argument was with Elizabeth. The two of them failed to notice how her hands were shaking.

It snowed all of January, the worst snow they had had in years. When she came downstairs in the mornings she found the kitchen icy cold, crisscrossed by drafts. "The sort of cold enters your bones," she told Elizabeth. "I'm sure to fall sick." Elizabeth only nodded. Some mornings now her face was pale and puffy, as if she had a secret worry, but Mrs. Ardavi had learned that it was better not to ask about it.

Early in February there was a sudden warm spell. Snow melted and all the trees dripped in the sunshine. "We're going for a walk," Elizabeth said, and Mrs. Ardavi said, "I'll come too." In spite of the warmth, she toiled upstairs for her woolen shawl. She didn't like to take chances. And she worried over Hilary's bare ears. "Won't she catch cold?" she asked. "I think we should cover her head."

"She'll be all right," said Elizabeth, and then shut her face in a certain stubborn way she had.

In the park, Elizabeth and Hilary made snowballs from the last of the snow and threw them at each other, narrowly missing Mrs. Ardavi, who stood watching with her arms folded and her hands tucked in her sleeves.

The next morning, something was wrong with Hilary. She sat at the breakfast table and cried steadily, refusing all food. "Now, now," her grandmother said, "won't you tell old Ka Jun what's wrong?" But when she came close Hilary screamed louder. By noon she was worse. Elizabeth called Hassan, and he came home immediately and laid a hand on Hilary's forehead and said she should go to the pediatrician. He drove them there himself. "It's her ears, I'm sure of it," Mrs. Ardavi said in the waiting room. For some reason Hassan grew angry. "Do you always know better than the experts?" he asked her. "What are we coming to the doctor for? We could have talked to you and saved the trip." His mother lowered her eyes and examined her purse straps. She understood that he was anxious, but all the same her feelings were hurt and when they rose to go into the office she stayed behind.

Later Hassan came back and sat down again. "There's an infection in her middle ear," he told her. "The doctor's going to give her a shot of penicillin." His mother nodded, careful not to annoy him by reminding him she had thought as much. Then Hilary started crying. She must be getting her shot now. Mrs. Ardavi herself was terrified of needles, and she sat gripping her purse until her fingers turned white, staring around the waiting room, which seemed pathetically cheerful, with its worn wooden toys and nursery-school paintings. Her own ear ached in sympathy. She thought of a time when she had boxed Ali's ears too hard and he had wept all that day and gone to sleep sucking his thumb.

While Hassan was there she was careful not to say anything, but the following morning at breakfast she said, "Elizabeth dear, do you remember that walk we took day before yesterday?"

"Yes," said Elizabeth. She was squeezing oranges for Hilary, who'd grown cheerful again and was eating a huge breakfast.

"Remember I said Hilary should wear a hat? Now you see you should have been more careful. Because of you she fell sick; she could have died. Do you see that now?"

"No," said Elizabeth.

Was her Persian that scanty? Lately it seemed to have shrunk and hardened, like a stale piece of bread. Mrs. Ardavi sighed and tried again. "Without a hat, you see—" she began. But Elizabeth had set down her orange, picked up Hilary, and walked out of the room. Mrs. Ardavi stared after her, wondering if she'd said something wrong.

For the rest of the day, Elizabeth was busy in her room. She was cleaning out bureaus and closets. A couple of times Mrs. Ardavi advanced as far as the doorway, where she stood awkwardly watching. Hilary sat on the floor playing with a discarded perfume bottle. Everything, it seemed, was about to be thrown away—buttonless blouses and stretched-out sweaters, stockings and combs and empty lipstick tubes. "Could I be of any help?" Mrs. Ardavi asked, but Elizabeth said, "Oh, no. Thank you very much." Her voice was cheerful. Yet when Hassan came home he went upstairs and stayed a long time, and the door remained shut behind him.

Supper that night was an especially fine stew, Hassan's favorite ever since childhood, but he didn't say a word about it. He hardly spoke at all, in fact. Then later, when Elizabeth was upstairs putting Hilary to bed, he said, "Khanoum Jun, I want to talk to you."

"Yes, Hassan," she said, laying aside her knitting. She was frightened by his seriousness, the black weight of his mustache, and her own father's deep black eyes. But what had she done? She knotted her hands and looked up at him, swallowing.

"I understand you've been interfering," he said.

"I, Hassan?"

"Elizabeth isn't the kind you can do that with. And she's raising the child just fine on her own."

"Well, of course she is," said his mother. "Did I ever say otherwise?"

"Show it, then. Don't offer criticisms."

"Very well," she said. She picked up her knitting and began counting stitches, as if she'd forgotten the conversation entirely. But that evening she was unusually quiet, and at nine o'clock she excused herself to go to bed. "So early?" Hassan asked.

"I'm tired," she told him, and left with her back very straight.

Her room surrounded her like a nest. She had built up layers of herself on every surface—tapestries and bits of lace and lengths of Paisley. The bureau was covered with gilt-framed pictures of the saints, and snapshots of her sisters at family gatherings. On the windowsill were little plants in orange and aqua plastic pots—her favorite American colors. Her bedside table held bottles of medicine, ivory prayer beads, and a tiny brick of holy earth. The rest of the house was bare and shiny, impersonal; this room was as comforting as her shawl.

Still, she didn't sleep well. Ghosts rose up again, tugging at her thoughts. Why did things turn out so badly for her? Her father had preferred her brothers, a fact that crushed her even after all these years. Her husband had had three children by her and then complained that she was cold. And what comfort were children? If she had stayed in Iran any longer Babak would have asked her to move; she'd seen it coming. There'd been some disrespect creeping into his bride's behavior, some unwillingness to take advice, which Babak had overlooked even when his mother pointed it out to him. And Hassan was worse—always so stubborn, much too independent. She had offered him anything if he would just stay in Iran but he had said no; he was set on leaving her. And he had flatly refused to take along his cousin Shora as his wife, though everyone pointed out how lonely he would be. He was so anxious to break away, to get *going,* to come to this hardhearted country and take up with a Christian girl. Oh, she should have laughed when he left, and saved her tears for someone more deserving. She never should have come here, she never should have asked anything of him again. When finally she went to sleep it seemed that her eyes remained open, burning large and dry beneath her lids.

In the morning she had a toothache. She could hardly walk for the pain. It was only Friday (the first of her dental appointments was for Monday), but the dentist made time for her during the afternoon and pulled the tooth. Elizabeth said it wouldn't hurt, but it did. Elizabeth treated it as something insignificant, merely a small break in her schedule, which required the hiring of a babysitter. She wouldn't even call Hassan home from work. "What could he do?" she asked.

So when Hassan returned that evening it was all a surprise to him—the sight of his mother with a bloody cotton cylinder hanging out over her lower lip like a long tooth. "What *happened* to you?" he asked. To make it worse, Hilary was screaming and had been all afternoon. Mrs. Ardavi put her hands over her ears, wincing. "Will you make that child hush?" Hassan told Elizabeth. "I think we should get my mother to bed." He guided her toward the stairs, and she allowed herself to lean on him. "It's mainly my heart," she said. "You know how scared I am of dentists." When he had folded back her bedspread and helped her to lie down she closed her eyes gratefully, resting one arm across her forehead. Even the comfort of hot tea was denied her; she had to stay on cold foods for twelve hours. Hassan fixed her a glass of ice water. He was very considerate, she thought. He seemed as shaken at the sight of her as Hilary had been. All during the evening he kept coming to check on her, and twice in the night she heard him climbing the stairs to listen at her door. When she moaned he called, "Are you awake?"

"Of course," she said.

"Can I get you anything?"

"No, no."

In the morning she descended the stairs with slow, groping feet, keeping a tight hold on the railing. "It was a very hard night," she said. "At four my gum started throbbing. Is that normal? I think these American pain pills are constipating. Maybe a little prune juice would restore my regularity."

"I'll get it," Hassan said. "You sit down. Did you take the milk of magnesia?"

"Oh, yes, but I'm afraid it wasn't enough," she said.

Elizabeth handed Hassan a platter of bacon, not looking at him.

After breakfast, while Hassan and his mother were still sitting over their tea, Elizabeth started cleaning the kitchen. She made quite a bit of noise. She sorted the silverware and then went through a tangle of utensils, discarding bent spatulas and rusty tongs. "May I help?" asked Mrs. Ardavi. Elizabeth shook her head. She seemed to have these fits of throwing things away. Now she was standing on the counter to take everything from the upper cabinets—crackers, cereals, half-empty bottles of spices. On the very top shelf was a flowered tin confectioner's box with Persian lettering on it, forgotten since the day Mrs. Ardavi had brought it. "My!" said Mrs. Ardavi. "Won't Hilary be surprised!" Elizabeth pried the lid off. Out flew a cloud of insects, grayish-brown with V-shaped wings. They brushed past Elizabeth's face and fluttered through her hair and swarmed toward the ceiling, where they dimmed the light fixture. Elizabeth flung the box as far from her as possible and climbed down from the counter. "Goodness!" said Mrs.

Ardavi. "Why, *we* have those at home!" Hassan lowered his teacup. Mixed nuts and dried currants rolled every which way on the floor; more insects swung toward the ceiling. Elizabeth sat on the nearest chair and buried her head in her hands. "Elizabeth?" said Hassan.

But she wouldn't look at him. In the end she simply rose and went upstairs, shutting the bedroom door with a gentle, definite click, which they heard all the way down in the kitchen because they were listening so hard.

"Excuse me," Hassan said to his mother.

She nodded and stared into her tea.

After he was gone she went to find Hilary, and she set her on her knee, babbling various folk rhymes to her while straining her ears toward the silence overhead. But Hilary squirmed off her lap and went to play with a truck. Then Hassan came downstairs again. He didn't say a word about Elizabeth.

On the following day, when Mrs. Ardavi's tooth was better, she and Hassan had a little talk upstairs in her room. They were very polite with each other. Hassan asked his mother how long they could hope for her to stay. His mother said she hadn't really thought about it. Hassan said that in America it was the custom to have house guests for three months only. After that they moved to a separate apartment nearby, which he'd be glad to provide for her as soon as he could find one, maybe next week. "Ah, an apartment," said his mother, looking impressed. But she had never lived alone a day in her life, and so after a suitable pause she said that she would hate to put him to so much expense. "Especially," she said, "when I'm going in such a short time anyway, since I'm homesick for my sisters."

"Well, then," said Hassan.

At supper that night, Hassan announced that his mother was missing her sisters and would like to leave. Elizabeth lowered her glass. "Leave?" she said.

Mrs. Ardavi said, "And Babak's wife, of course, will be asking for me when the baby arrives."

"Well . . . but what about the dentist? You were supposed to start your appointments on Monday."

"It's not important," Mrs. Ardavi said.

"But we set up all those—"

"There are plenty of dentists she can see at home," Hassan told Elizabeth. "We have dentists in Iran, for God's sake. Do you imagine we're barbarians?"

"No," Elizabeth said.

On the evening of the third of March, Hassan drove his mother to the airport. He was worrying about the road, which was slippery after a snowfall. He couldn't find much to say to his mother. And once they had arrived, he deliberately kept the conversation to trivia—the verifying of tickets, checking of departure times, weighing of baggage. Her baggage was fourteen pounds overweight. It didn't make sense; all she had were her clothes and a few small gifts for her sisters. "Why is it so heavy?" Hassan asked. "What have you got in there?" But his mother only said, "I don't know," and straightened her shawl, looking elsewhere. Hassan bent to open a tooled-leather suitcase. Inside he found three empty urn-shaped wine bottles, the permanent-press sheets from her bed, and a sample box of detergent that had come in yesterday's mail. "Listen," said Hassan, "do you know how much I'd have to pay to fly these things over? What's the matter with you?"

"I wanted to show my sisters," his mother said.

"Well, forget it. Now, what else have you got?"

But something about her—the vague, childlike eyes set upon some faraway object—made him give in. He opened no more bags. He even regretted his sharpness, and when her flight was announced he hugged her closely and kissed the top of her head. "Go with God," he said.

"Goodbye, Hassan."

She set off down the corridor by herself, straggling behind a line of business-men. They all wore hats. His mother wore her scarf, and of all the travelers she alone, securely kerchiefed and shawled, setting her small shoes resolutely on the gleaming tiles, seemed undeniably a foreigner.

Questions for Discussion and Writing

1. The first four paragraphs of the story hint at or foreshadow a number of intercultural problems to come. What are they, and in what ways do they become problems?

2. To what cultural patterns in the United States does Mrs. Ardavi have difficulty adjusting, and why? What symptoms of culture shock is she experiencing? In what ways are her son, his wife, and his daughter involved in that shock?

3. What problems does Elizabeth have with the cultural assumptions of her mother-in-law? Why, or why not, would you expect the two women to be able to communicate eventually, given language proficiency?

4. What problems has Mrs. Ardavi not left behind in Iran, and what do they have to do with her relationship with her son Hassan now?

5. Language plays an important part in Mrs. Ardavi's adjustment, or lack of adjustment, in the United States. In what situations in the story does language become the focus of her attention, pleasure, or pain? What observations can you make about language as a result of your reading here, and why?

6. Whose place is empty, and why?

CARLOS BULOSAN

Be American

Carlos Bulosan was born in 1913, in Binalonan, Pangasinan province, in Luzon, in the central Philippines. After a childhood of working in the fields with his father and helping his mother sell salted
fish in the public market, he cut short his education to leave for
America in 1930. Landing in Seattle, he worked up and down the
West Coast, mostly as a migrant worker, becoming a union activist
to fight the persecution that he and other Filipinos were experiencing. During this time he also wrote—about peasant life in the Philippines and Filipino life in America.

Hospitalized for tuberculosis in 1936 for two years in Los Angeles
County Hospital, he read voraciously about America: ". . . books
opened all my world of intellectual possibilities—and a grand
dream of bettering society for the working man." His reading also
launched him on a decade of intensive writing. His major work,
America Is in the Heart, was published in 1946, though he continued
to write until his death in Seattle on September 13, 1956.

Bulosan represents vast numbers of Filipino immigrants who in
the 1930s arrived in this country expecting to be treated as equals,
discovering instead they were wanted only for their labor power.
Once in America, Filipinos were essentially exiles who had left their
home in the Philippines, an American colony; as subjects of a U.S.
colony, they were denied citizenship here.

The story/essay that follows, "Be American," comes from a collection of Bulosan's writing entitled If You Want to Know What We Are
(1983), in which he reconstructs the dream of an immigrant peasant
on his arrival and subsequent years in America. One of Bulosan's
aims as a writer was to help others like his cousin Consorcio to find
meaning in their suffering and struggle, and thus to transform the
history of the Filipinos.

274

Before you read "Be American," describe what you think it is like to be American. Describe the benefits you enjoy in your citizenship, the responsibilities it requires, the problems it creates, and the promises you think it holds—even if you feel they have not yet come your way. If you know someone well who has come here from another country, you could instead write about how that person feels about being an American.

It was not Consorcio's fault. My cousin was an illiterate peasant from the vast plains of Luzon. When he came off the boat in San Francisco, he could neither read nor write English or Ilocano, our dialect. I met him when he arrived, and right away he had bright ideas in his head.

"Cousin, I want be American," he told me.

"Good," I said. "That is the right thing to do. But you have plenty of time. You are planning to live permanently in the United States, are you not?"

"Sure, cousin," he said. "But I want be American right away. On the boat I say, 'Consorcio stoody Engleesh right away.' Good ideeyas, eh, cousin?"

"It is," I said. "But the first thing for you to do is look for a job."

"Sure, cousin. You have joob for me?"

I did. I took him to a countryman of ours who owned a small restaurant on Kearny Street. He had not done any dishwashing in the Philippines, so he broke a few dishes before he realized that the dishes were not coconut shells that he could flagrantly throw around the place, the way he used to do in his village where coconut shells were plates and carved trunks of trees were platters and his fingers were spoons. He had never seen bread and butter before, so he lost some weight before he realized that he had to eat these basic things like the rest of us, and be an American, which was his own idea in the first place. He had never slept in a bed with a mattress before, so he had to suffer from severe cold before he realized that he had to sleep inside the bed, under the blankets, but not on top of the spread, which was what he had done during his first two weeks in America. And of course he had never worn shoes before, so he had to suffer a few blisters on both feet before he realized that he had to walk light-footed, easy, and even graceful, but not the way he used to do it in his village, which was like wrestling with a carabao or goat.

All these natural things he had to learn during his first two weeks. But he talked about his Americanization with great confidence.

"You see, cousin," he told me, "I have earned mony quick. I poot the hoot dashes in the sink, wash-wash, day come, day out, week gone—mony! Simple?"

"Fine," I said.

"You know what I done with mony?"

"No."

"I spent it all."

"On what?"

"Books. Come see my room."

I went with him to his small room at the back of the restaurant where he was working, near the washrooms. And sure enough, he had lined the four walls of his room with big books. I looked at the titles. He had a cheap edition of the classics, books on science, law and mathematics. He even had some brochures on political and governmental matters. All were books that a student or even a professor would take time to read.

I turned to my cousin. He was smiling with pride.

"Well, I hope these big books will make you an American faster," I told him.

"Sure, cousin. How long I wait?"

"Five years."

"Five years?" There was genuine surprise in his dark peasant face. "Too long. I do not wait. I make faster—one year."

"It is the law," I assured him.

"No good law. One year enough for Consorcio. He make good American citizen."

"There is nothing you can do about it."

"I change law."

"Go ahead."

"You see, cousin."

But he was puzzled. So I left him. I left San Francisco. When I saw him a year later, he was no longer washing dishes. But he still had the pardonable naivete of a peasant from the plains of Luzon.

"Where are you working now?" I asked him.

"Bakery," he said. "I make da bread. I make da donot. I make da pys."

"Where?"

"Come, cousin. I show you."

It was a small shop, a three-man affair. Consorcio was the handyboy in the place, scrubbing the floor, washing the pots and pans; and he was also the messenger. The owner was the baker, while his wife was the saleswoman. My cousin lived at the back of the building, near the washrooms. He had a cot in a corner of the dark room. But the books were gone.

"What happened to your books?" I asked him.

He looked sad. Then he said, "I sold, cousin."

"Why?"

"I cannot read. I cannot understand. Words too big and too long."

"You should begin with simple grammar books."

"Those cannot read also. What to do now, cousin?"

"You still want to be an American citizen?"

"Sure."

"Go to night school."

"Is a place like that?"

"Yes."

"No use, cousin. No money."

"The school is free," I told him. "It is for foreign-born people. For adults, so they could study American history."

"Free? I go now."

"The school opens only at night."

"I work night."

"Well, work in the daytime. Look for another job. You still want to be an American, don't you?"

"Sure. But I like boss-man. What to do?"

"Tell him the truth."

"You help me?"

I did. We went to the boss-man. I explained the matter as truthfully as I could and he understood Consorcio's problems. But he asked me to find someone to take my cousin's place, which I did too, so we shook hands around and departed in the best of humor. I helped Consorcio register at the night school, [and] looked for another job for him as janitor in an apartment building. Then I left him, wishing him the best of luck.

I worked in Alaska the next two years. When I returned to the mainland, I made it my duty to pass through San Francisco. But my cousin had left his janitor job and the night school. I could not find his new address, and it seemed that no one knew him well enough in the Filipino community.

I did not think much of his disappearance because we are a wandering people due to the nature of our lowly occupations, which take us from place to place, following the seasons. When I received a box of grapes from a friend, I knew he was working in the grape fields in either Fresno or Delano, depending on the freight mark. When I received a box of asparagus, I knew he was working in Stockton. But when it was a crate of lettuce, he was working in Santa Maria or Salinas, depending on the freight mark again. And in the summertime when I received a large barrel of salmon, I knew he was working in the salmon canneries in Alaska. There were no letters, no post cards—nothing. But these surprising boxes, crates and barrels that arrived periodically were the best letters in the world. What they contained were lovingly distributed among my city friends. Similarly, when I was [on] one of my own wanderings, which were done in cities and large towns, I sent my friend or friends unsealed envelopes bursting with the colored pictures of actresses and other beautiful women. I addressed these gifts to poolrooms and restaurants in towns where my friends had lived or worked for a season, because they were bound to go to any of these havens of the homeless wanderer. However, when another curious wanderer opened the envelopes and pilfered the pictures, it was not a crime. The enjoyment which was originally intended for my friends was his and his friends.' That is the law of the nomad: finders keepers.

But Consorcio had not yet learned the unwritten law of the nomad. I did not expect him to send me boxes, crates, and barrels from faraway Alaska. So I did not know where I could locate him.

I wandered in and out of Los Angeles the next two years. At the beginning of the third year, when I was talking to the sleeping birds in Pershing Square, I felt a light hand on my shoulders. I was not usually curious about hands, but it was well after midnight and the cops were wandering in and out of the place. So I turned around—and found Consorcio.

I found a new Consorcio. He had aged and the peasant naivete was gone from his face. In his eyes was now a hidden fear. His hands danced and flew when he was talking, and even when he was not talking, as though he were slapping the wind with both hands or clapping with one hand. Have you ever heard the noise of one hand clapping?

That was Consorcio, after five years in America. He was either slapping the wind with both hands or clapping with one hand. So I guided him out of the dark place to the lighted place, where we had coffee until the city awoke to give us another day of hope. Of course, I sat in silence for a long time because it was the year of deep silence. And Consorcio sat for a long time too, because by now he had learned to hide in the deep silence that was flung like a mourning cloak across the face of the land. When we talked, our sentences were short and punctuated by long silences. So we conversed somewhat like this:

"Been wandering everywhere."

"No job."

"Nothing anywhere."

"Where have you been all these years?"

Silence.

"No finished school?"

Silence.

"Not American citizen yet?"

"You should have told me."

"Told you what?"

"Filipinos can't become American citizens."

"Well, I could have told you. But I wanted you to learn."

"At least I speak better English now."

"This is a country of great opportunity."

Silence.

"No work?"

"No work."

"How long?"

"I have forgotten."

"Better times will come."

"You have a wonderful dream, cousin," he told me and left. He left Los Angeles for a long time. Then, two years later, I received a crate of oranges from him. The freight mark was San Jose. Now I knew he was working and had learned the unwritten law of the wanderers on this troubled earth. So as I ate his oranges, I recalled his last statement: *You have a wonderful dream, cousin* . . .

I had a wonderful dream. But I dreamed it for both of us, for many of us who wandered in silence.

Then the boxes and crates became more frequent. Then a barrel of salmon came from Alaska. And, finally, the letters came. My cousin Consorcio, the one-time illiterate peasant from the vast plains of Luzon, had indeed become an American without knowing it. His letters were full of wondering and pondering about many things in America. Now he realized his naivete when he had landed in San Francisco. But he realized also that he could not ask too much in a strange land. And it was this realization that liberated him from his peasant prison, his heritage, and eventually led him to a kind of work to which he dedicated his time and life until the end.

I was in Oregon when I received a newspaper from Consorcio, postmarked Pismo Beach. It was the first issue of his publication for agricultural workers in California. It was in English. From then on, I received all issues of his publication. For five years it existed, defending the workers and upholding the rights and liberties of all Americans, native or foreign born, so that, as he began to understand the nature of American society, he became more belligerent in his editorials and had to go to jail a few times for his ideas about freedom and peace.

Yes, indeed, Consorcio: You have become an American, a real American. And this land that we have known too well is not yet denuded by the rapacity of men. Rolling like a beautiful woman with an overflowing abundance of fecundity and murmurous with her eternal mystery, there she lies before us like a great mother. To her we always return from our prodigal wanderings and searchings for an anchorage in the sea of life; from her we always draw our sustenance and noble thoughts, to add to her glorious history.

But the war came. And war ended Consorcio's newspaper work and his crusade for a better America. And it ended his life also. When he was brought back from overseas, he knew he would not last long. But he talked the way he had written his editorials, measured sentences that rang like music, great poetry, and soft, soft. He would not shed a tear; but his heart must have been crying, seeing eternal darkness coming toward him, deep, deep in the night of perpetual sleep. Yes, he would not shed a tear; but he must have been crying, seeing that there was so much to do with so little time left. There was in his voice a kindness for me—unhappy, perhaps, that he could not impart what he had learned from his wanderings on this earth; unhappy, also, because he knew that it would take all the people to unmake the unhappiness which had caught up with us. And now, fifteen years after his arrival in San Francisco, he was dying.

And he died. But at least he received his most cherished dream: American citizenship. He did realize later that he had become an American before he received his papers, when he began to think and write lovingly about *our* America. He gave up many things, and finally his own life, to realize his dream.

But Consorcio is not truly dead. He lives again in my undying love for the

American earth. And soon, when I see the last winter coming to the last leaf, I will be warm with the thought that another wanderer shall inherit the wonderful dream which my cousin and I had dreamed and tried to realize in America.

Questions for Discussion and Writing

1. Reflect on the importance of the first line of Bulosan's story: "It was not Consorcio's fault." What "fault" do you think the author has in mind here? What does this line imply? In what ways does it set the mood of the story?
2. What kinds of adjustments, small and large, did Consorcio have to make in living in the United States, and in what ways is each one of them significant?
3. What do you think Bulosan means when he writes, five years after Consorcio's arrival in America "he had learned to hide in the deep silence that was flung like a mourning cloak across the face of the land" (p. 278)? In what ways do the metaphors and images Bulosan uses throughout this story add to its meaning?
4. What are the "unwritten laws of the wanderers" or nomads, to which Bulosan refers (pp. 277, 278)? What cultural patterns and values from the Philippines have the men brought with them to America?
5. Why does his realization "that he could not ask too much in a strange land" (p. 279) liberate Consorcio? What does Bulosan imply it means to become "a real American" (p. 279)?

BHARATI MUKHERJEE

A Father

When Bharati Mukherjee moved to the United States from Canada and to there from India, she says she moved from "the aloofness of expatriation to the exuberance of immigration." The move meant that she stopped seeing her Indianness as a fragile identity to be preserved against obliteration and uses it now as a metaphor, "a particular way of partially comprehending the world" similar to American writers whose parents or grandparents have passed through Ellis Island.

The story that follows, "A Father," comes from a collection of Mukherjee's stories entitled Darkness *(1985), most of which were written in a three-month burst of energy when the author was writer-in-residence at Emory University in Atlanta, Georgia. "Until Atlanta," she writes, "I had thought of myself, in spite of a white husband and two assimilated sons, as an expatriate," wondering if she would ever belong. "If you have to wonder, if you keep looking for signs," she adds, "if you wait—surrendering little bits of a reluctant self every year, clutching the souvenirs of an ever-retreating past—you'll never belong, anywhere."*

Commenting on the energy with which she wrote the stories of Darkness, *she says, "For a writer, energy is aggression; urgency colliding with confidence. Suddenly, everything is possible. Excluded worlds are opened, secretive characters reveal themselves. The writing-self is somehow united with the universe."*

Before you read "A Father," write about a time in your life when you made a choice that shocked your parents, or when your parents made a choice that shocked you. (If you are a parent, you might write about a time when a child made a choice that shocked you—or you made a choice that shocked a child.) Describe the choice, why it was shocking, what cultural values were involved, and how it affected your relationship.

O   ne Wednesday morning in mid-May Mr. Bhowmick woke up as he usually
      did at 5:43 A.M., checked his Rolex against the alarm clock's digital
readout, punched down the alarm (set for 5:45), then nudged his wife awake.
She worked as a claims investigator for an insurance company that had an office
in a nearby shopping mall. She didn't really have to leave the house until 8:30,
but she liked to get up early and cook him a big breakfast. Mr. Bhowmick had
to drive a long way to work. He was a naturally dutiful, cautious man, and he
set the alarm clock early enough to accommodate a margin for accidents.

While his wife, in a pink nylon negligee she had paid for with her own
MasterCard card, made him a new version of French toast from a clipping
("Eggs-cellent Recipes!") Scotchtaped to the inside of a kitchen cupboard, Mr.
Bhowmick brushed his teeth. He brushed, he gurgled with the loud, hawking
noises that he and his brother had been taught as children to make in order to
flush clean not merely teeth but also tongue and palate.

After that he showered, then, back in the bedroom again, he recited prayers
in Sanskrit to Kali,* the patron goddess of his family, the goddess of wrath and
vengeance. In the pokey flat of his childhood in Ranchi, Bihar,† his mother had
given over a whole bedroom to her collection of gods and goddesses. Mr.
Bhowmick couldn't be that extravagant in Detroit. His daughter, twenty-six and
an electrical engineer, slept in the other of the two bedrooms in his apartment.
But he had done his best. He had taken Woodworking I and II at a nearby
recreation center and built a grotto for the goddess. Kali-Mata was eight inches
tall, made of metal and painted a glistening black so that the metal glowed like
the oiled, black skin of a peasant woman. And though Kali-Mata was totally nude
except for a tiny gilt crown and a garland strung together from sinners' chopped
off heads, she looked warm, cozy, *pleased,* in her makeshift wooden shrine in
Detroit. Mr. Bhowmick had gathered quite a crowd of admiring, fellow wood-
workers in those final weeks of decoration.

"Hurry it up with the prayers," his wife shouted from the kitchen. She was an
agnostic, a believer in ambition, not grace. She frequently complained that his
prayers had gotten so long that soon he wouldn't have time to go to work, play
duplicate bridge with the Ghosals, or play the tabla in the Bengali Association's
one Sunday per month musical soirees. Lately she'd begun to drain him in a
wholly new way. He wasn't praying, she nagged; he was shutting her out of his
life. There'd be no peace in the house until she hid Kali-Mata in a suitcase.

She nagged, and he threatened to beat her with his shoe as his father had
threatened his mother: it was the thrust and volley of marriage. There was no
question of actually taking off a shoe and applying it to his wife's body. She was
bigger than he was. And, secretly, he admired her for having the nerve, the
agnosticism, which as a college boy in backward Bihar he too had claimed.

"I have time," he shot at her. He was still wrapped in a damp terry towel.

*Kali: Hindu goddess.
†Ranchi, Bihar: city in the state of Bihar, one of the poorest of India's twenty-five states.

"You have time for everything but domestic life."

It was the fault of the shopping mall that his wife had started to buy pop psychology paperbacks. These paperbacks preached that for couples who could sit down and talk about their "relationship," life would be sweet again. His engineer daughter was on his wife's side. She accused him of holding things in.

"Face it, Dad," she said. "You have an affect deficit."

But surely everyone had feelings they didn't want to talk about or talk over. He definitely did not want to blurt out anything about the sick-in-the-guts sensations that came over him most mornings and that he couldn't bubble down with Alka-Seltzer or smother with Gas-X. The women in his family were smarter than him. They were cheerful, outgoing, more American somehow.

How could he tell these bright, mocking women that in the 5:43 A.M. darkness, he sensed invisible presences: gods and snakes frolicked in the master bedroom, little white sparks of cosmic static crackled up the legs of his pajamas. Something was out there in the dark, something that could invent accidents and coincidences to remind mortals that even in Detroit they were no more than mortal. His wife would label this paranoia and dismiss it. Paranoia, premonition: whatever it was, it had begun to undermine his composure.

Take this morning. Mr. Bhowmick had woken up from a pleasant dream about a man taking a Club Med vacation, and the postdream satisfaction had lasted through the shower, but when he'd come back to the shrine in the bedroom, he'd noticed all at once how scarlet and saucy was the tongue that Kali-Mata stuck out at the world. Surely he had not lavished such alarming detail, such admonitory colors on that flap of flesh.

Watch out, ambulatory sinners. Be careful out there, the goddess warned him, and not with the affection of Sergeant Esterhaus, either.

"French toast must be eaten hot-hot," his wife nagged.

"Otherwise they'll taste like rubber."

Mr. Bhowmick laid the trousers of a two-trouser suit he had bought on sale that winter against his favorite tweed jacket. The navy stripes in the trousers and the small, navy tweed flecks in the jacket looked quite good together. So what if the Chief Engineer had already started wearing summer cottons?

"I am coming, I am coming," he shouted back. "You want me to eat hot-hot, you start the frying only when I am sitting down. You didn't learn anything from Mother in Ranchi?"

"Mother cooked French toast from fancy recipes? I mean French Sandwich Toast with complicated filling?"

He came into the room to give her his testiest look. "You don't know the meaning of complicated cookery. And mother had to get the coal fire of the *chula* going first."

His daughter was already at the table. "Why don't you break down and buy her a microwave oven? That's what I mean about sitting down and talking things out." She had finished her orange juice. She took a plastic measure of

Slim-Fast out of its can and poured the powder into a glass of skim milk. "It's ridiculous."

Babli was not the child he would have chosen as his only heir. She was brighter certainly than the sons and daughters of the other Bengalis* he knew in Detroit, and she had been the only female student in most of her classes at Georgia Tech, but as she sat there in her beige linen business suit, her thick chin dropping into a polka-dotted cravat, he regretted again that she was not the child of his dreams. Babli would be able to help him out moneywise if something happened to him, something so bad that even his pension plans and his insurance policies and his money market schemes wouldn't be enough. But Babli could never comfort him. She wasn't womanly or tender the way that unmarried girls had been in the wistful days of his adolescence. She could sing Hindi film songs, mimicking exactly the high, artificial voice of Lata Mungeshkar, and she had taken two years of dance lessons at Sona Devi's Dance Academy in Southfield, but these accomplishments didn't add up to real femininity. Not the kind that had given him palpitations in Ranchi.

Mr. Bhowmick did his best with his wife's French toast. In spite of its filling of marshmallows, apricot jam and maple syrup, it tasted rubbery. He drank two cups of Darjeeling tea, said, "Well, I'm off," and took off.

All might have gone well if Mr. Bhowmick hadn't fussed longer than usual about putting his briefcase and his trenchcoat in the backseat. He got in behind the wheel of his Oldsmobile, fixed his seatbelt and was just about to turn the key in the ignition when his neighbor, Al Stazniak, who was starting up his Buick Skylark, sneezed. A sneeze at the start of a journey brings bad luck. Al Stazniak's sneeze was fierce, made up of five short bursts, too loud to be ignored.

Be careful out there! Mr. Bhowmick could see the goddess's scarlet little tongue tip wagging at him.

He was a modern man, an intelligent man. Otherwise he couldn't have had the options in life that he did have. He couldn't have given up a good job with perks in Bombay and found a better job with General Motors in Detroit. But Mr. Bhowmick was also a prudent enough man to know that some abiding truth lies bunkered within each wanton Hindu superstition. A sneeze was more than a sneeze. The heedless are carried off in ambulances. He had choices to make. He could ignore the sneeze, and so challenge the world unseen by men. Perhaps Al Stazniak had hayfever. For a sneeze to be a potent omen, surely it had to be unprovoked and terrifying, a thunderclap cleaving the summer skies. Or he could admit the smallness of mortals, undo the fate of the universe by starting over, and go back inside the apartment, sit for a second on the sofa, then re-start his trip.

Al Stazniak rolled down his window. "Everything okay?"

Mr. Bhowmick nodded shyly. They weren't really friends in the way neighbors

*Bengalis: people from the state of Bengal, in eastern India.

can sometimes be. They talked as they parked or pulled out of their adjacent parking stalls. For all Mr. Bhowmick knew, Al Stazniak had no legs. He had never seen the man out of his Skylark.

He let the Buick back out first. Everything was okay, yes, please. All the same he undid his seatbelt. Compromise, adaptability, call it what you will. A dozen times a day he made these small trade-offs between new-world reasonableness and old-world beliefs.

While he was sitting in his parked car, his wife's ride came by. For fifty dollars a month, she was picked up and dropped off by a hard up, newly divorced woman who worked at a florist's shop in the same mall. His wife came out the front door in brown K-Mart pants and a burgundy windbreaker. She waved to him, then slipped into the passenger seat of the florist's rusty Japanese car.

He was a metallurgist. He knew about rust and ways of preventing it, secret ways, thus far unknown to the Japanese.

Babli's fiery red Mitsubishi was still in the lot. She wouldn't leave for work for another eight minutes. He didn't want her to know he'd been undone by a sneeze. Babli wasn't tolerant of superstitions. She played New Wave music in her tapedeck. If asked about Hinduism, all she'd ever said to her American friends was that "it's neat." Mr. Bhowmick had heard her on the phone years before. The cosmos balanced on the head of a snake was like a beachball balanced on the snout of a circus seal. "This Hindu myth stuff," he'd heard her say, "is like a series of super graphics."

He'd forgiven her. He could probably forgive her anything. It was her way of surviving high school in a city that was both native to her, and alien.

There was no question of going back where he'd come from. He hated Ranchi. Ranchi was no place for dreamers. All through his teenage years, Mr. Bhowmick had dreamed of success abroad. What form that success would take he had left vague. Success had meant to him escape from the constant plotting and bitterness that wore out India's middle class.

Babli should have come out of the apartment and driven off to work by now. Mr. Bhowmick decided to take a risk, to dash inside and pretend he'd left his briefcase on the coffee table.

When he entered the living room, he noticed Babli's spring coat and large vinyl pocketbook on the sofa. She was probably sorting through the junk jewelry on her dresser to give her business suit a lift. She read hints about dressing in women's magazines and applied them to her person with seriousness. If his luck held, he could sit on the sofa, say a quick prayer and get back to the car without her catching on.

It surprised him that she didn't shout out from her bedroom, "Who's there?" What if he had been a rapist?

Then he heard Babli in the bathroom. He heard unladylike squawking noises. She was throwing up. A squawk, a spitting, then the horrible gurgle of a waterfall.

A revelation came to Mr. Bhowmick. A woman vomiting in the privacy of the bathroom could mean many things. She was coming down with the flu. She was nervous about a meeting. But Mr. Bhowmick knew at once that his daughter, his untender, unloving daughter whom he couldn't love and hadn't tried to love, was not, in the larger world of Detroit, unloved. Sinners are everywhere, even in the bosom of an upright, unambitious family like the Bhowmicks. It was the goddess sticking out her tongue at him.

The father sat heavily on the sofa, shrinking from contact with her coat and pocketbook. His brisk, bright engineer daughter was pregnant. Someone had taken time to make love to her. Someone had thought her tender, feminine. Someone even now was perhaps mooning over her. The idea excited him. It was so grotesque and wondrous. At twenty-six Babli had found the man of her dreams; whereas at twenty-six Mr. Bhowmick had given up on truth, beauty and poetry and exchanged them for two years at Carnegie Tech.

Mr. Bhowmick's tweed-jacketed body sagged against the sofa cushions. Babli would abort, of course. He knew his Babli. It was the only possible option if she didn't want to bring shame to the Bhowmick family. All the same, he could see a chubby baby boy on the rug, crawling to his granddaddy. Shame like that was easier to hide in Ranchi. There was always a barren womb sanctified by marriage that could claim sudden fructifying by the goddess Parvati. Babli would do what she wanted. She was headstrong and independent and he was afraid of her.

Babli staggered out of the bathroom. Damp stains ruined her linen suit. It was the first time he had seen his daughter look ridiculous, quite unprofessional. She didn't come into the living room to investigate the noises he'd made. He glimpsed her shoeless stockinged feet flip-flop on collapsed arches down the hall to her bedroom.

"Are you all right?" Mr. Bhowmick asked, standing in the hall. "Do you need Sinutab?"

She wheeled around. "What're you doing here?"

He was the one who should be angry. "I'm feeling poorly too," he said. "I'm taking the day off."

"I feel fine," Babli said.

Within fifteen minutes Babli had changed her clothes and left. Mr. Bhowmick had the apartment to himself all day. All day for praising or cursing the life that had brought him along with its other surprises an illegitimate grandchild.

It was his wife that he blamed. Coming to America to live had been his wife's idea. After the wedding, the young Bhowmicks had spent two years in Pittsburgh on his student visa, then gone back home to Ranchi for nine years. Nine crushing years. Then the job in Bombay had come through. All during those nine years his wife had screamed and wept. She was a woman of wild, progressive ideas—she'd called them her "American" ideas—and she'd been martyred by her neighbors for them. American *memsahib. Markin mem, Markin mem.* In bazaars the beggar boys had trailed her and hooted. She'd done provocative things. She'd hired a *chamar* woman who by caste rules was forbidden to cook for higher caste families, especially for widowed mothers of decent men. This had caused a blowup in the neighborhood. She'd made other, lesser errors. While other wives shopped and cooked every day, his wife had cooked the whole week's menu on weekends.

"What's the point of having a refrigerator, then?" She'd been scornful of the Ranchi women.

His mother, an old-fashioned widow, had accused her of trying to kill her by poisoning. "You are in such a hurry? You want to get rid of me quick-quick so you can go back to the States?"

Family life had been turbulent.

He had kept aloof, inwardly siding with his mother. He did not love his wife now, and he had not loved her then. In any case, he had not defended her. He felt some affection, and he felt guilty for having shunned her during those unhappy years. But he had thought of it then as revenge. He had wanted to marry a beautiful woman. Not being a young man of means, only a young man with prospects, he had had no right to yearn for pure beauty. He cursed his fate and after a while, settled for a barrister's daughter, a plain girl with a wide, flat plank of a body and myopic eyes. The barrister had sweetened the deal by throwing in an all-expenses-paid two years' study at Carnegie Tech to which Mr. Bhowmick had been admitted. Those two years had changed his wife from pliant girl to ambitious woman. She wanted America, nothing less.

It was his wife who had forced him to apply for permanent resident status in the U.S. even though he had a good job in Ranchi as a government engineer. The putting together of documents for the immigrant visa had been a long and humbling process. He had had to explain to a chilly clerk in the Embassy that, like most Indians of his generation, he had no birth certificate. He had to swear out affidavits, suffer through police checks, bribe orderlies whose job it was to move his dossier from desk to desk. The decision, the clerk had advised him, would take months, maybe years. He hadn't dared hope that merit might be rewarded. Merit could collapse under bad luck. It was for grace that he prayed.

While the immigration papers were being processed, he had found the job in Bombay. So he'd moved his mother in with his younger brother's family, and left his hometown for good. Life in Bombay had been lighthearted, almost fulfilling. His wife had thrown herself into charity work with the same energy that had offended the Ranchi women. He was happy to be in a big city at last. Bombay was the Rio de Janeiro of the East; he'd read that in a travel brochure. He drove out to Nariman Point at least once a week to admire the necklace of municipal lights, toss coconut shells into the dark ocean, drink beer at the Oberoi-Sheraton where overseas Indian girls in designer jeans beckoned him in sly ways. His nights were full. He played duplicate bridge, went to the movies, took his wife to Bingo nights at his club. In Detroit he was a lonelier man.

Then the green card had come through. For him, for his wife, and for the daughter who had been born to them in Bombay. He sold what he could sell, and put in his brother's informal trust what he couldn't to save on taxes. Then he had left for America, and one more start.

All through the week, Mr. Bhowmick watched his daughter. He kept furtive notes on how many times she rushed to the bathroom and made hawking, wrenching noises, how many times she stayed late at the office, calling her mother to say she'd be taking in a movie and pizza afterwards with friends.

He had to tell her that he knew. And he probably didn't have much time. She shouldn't be on Slim-Fast in her condition. He had to talk things over with her. But what would he say to her? What position could he take? He had to choose between public shame for the family, and murder.

For three more weeks he watched her and kept his silence. Babli wore shifts to the office instead of business suits, and he liked her better in those garments. Perhaps she was dressing for her young man, not from necessity. Her skin was pale and blotchy by turn. At breakfast her fingers looked stiff, and she had trouble with silverware.

Two Saturdays running, he lost badly at duplicate bridge. His wife scolded him. He had made silly mistakes. When was Babli meeting this man? Where? He must be American; Mr. Bhowmick prayed only that he was white. He pictured his grandson crawling to him, and the grandson was always fat and brown and buttery-skinned, like the infant Krishna. An American son-in-law was a terrifying notion. Why was she not mentioning men, at least, preparing the way for the major announcement? He listened sharply for men's names, rehearsed little lines like, "Hello, Bob, I'm Babli's old man," with a cracked little laugh. Bob, Jack, Jimmy, Tom. But no names surfaced. When she went out for pizza and a movie it was with the familiar set of Indian girls and their strange, unpopular, American friends, all without men. Mr. Bhowmick tried to be reasonable. Maybe she had already gotten married and was keeping it secret. "Well, Bob, you and Babli sure had Mrs. Bhowmick and me going there, heh-heh," he mumbled one night with the Sahas and Ghosals, over cards. "Pardon?" asked Pronob Saha. Mr. Bhowmick dropped two tricks, and his wife glared. "Such stupid blunders," she fumed on the drive back. A new truth was dawning; there would be no marriage for Babli. Her young man probably was not so young and not so available. He must be already married. She must have yielded to passion or been raped in the office. His wife seemed to have noticed nothing. Was he a murderer, or a conspirator? He kept his secret from his wife; his daughter kept her decision to herself.

Nights, Mr. Bhowmick pretended to sleep, but as soon as his wife began her snoring—not real snores so much as loud, gaspy gulpings for breath—he turned on his side and prayed to Kali-Mata.

In July, when Babli's belly had begun to push up against the waistless dresses she'd bought herself, Mr. Bhowmick came out of the shower one weekday morning and found the two women screaming at each other. His wife had a rolling pin in one hand. His daughter held up a *National Geographic* as a shield for her head. The crazy look that had been in his wife's eyes when she'd shooed away beggar kids was in her eyes again.

"Stop it!" His own boldness overwhelmed him. "Shut up! Babli's pregnant, so what? It's your fault, you made us come to the States."

Girls like Babli were caught between rules, that's the point he wished to make. They were too smart, too impulsive for a backward place like Ranchi, but not tough nor smart enough for sex-crazy places like Detroit.

"My fault?" his wife cried. "I told her to do hanky-panky with boys? I told her to shame us like this?"

She got in one blow with the rolling pin. The second glanced off Babli's shoulder and fell on his arm which he had stuck out for his grandson's sake.

"I'm calling the police," Babli shouted. She was out of the rolling pin's range. "This is brutality. You can't do this to me."

"Shut up! Shut your mouth, foolish woman." He wrenched the weapon from his wife's fist. He made a show of taking off his shoe to beat his wife on the face.

"What do you know? You don't know anything." She let herself down slowly on a dining chair. Her hair, curled overnight, stood in wild whorls around her head. "Nothing."

"And you do!" He laughed. He remembered her tormentors, and laughed again. He had begun to enjoy himself. Now *he* was the one with the crazy, progressive ideas.

"Your daughter is pregnant, yes," she said, "any fool knows that. But ask her the name of the father. Go, ask."

He stared at his daughter who gazed straight ahead, eyes burning with hate, jaw clenched with fury.

"Babli?"

"Who needs a man?" she hissed. "The father of my baby is a bottle and a syringe. Men louse up your lives. I just want a baby. Oh, don't worry—he's a certified fit donor. No diseases, college graduate, above average, and he made the easiest twenty-five dollars of his life—"

"Like animals," his wife said. For the first time he heard horror in her voice. His daughter grinned at him. He saw her tongue, thick and red, squirming behind her row of perfect teeth.

"Yes, yes, yes," she screamed, "like livestock. Just like animals. You should be happy—that's what marriage is all about, isn't it? Matching bloodlines, matching horoscopes, matching castes, matching, matching, matching . . ." and it was difficult to know if she was laughing or singing, or mocking and like a mad-woman.

Mr. Bhowmick lifted the rolling pin high above his head and brought it down hard on the dome of Babli's stomach. In the end, it was his wife who called the police.

Questions for Discussion and Writing

1. What signs or symbols in the story indicate Mr. and Mrs. Bhowmick's acceptance of American influence? What are the symbols of Mr. and Mrs. Bhowmick's holding onto their Indian patterns and values? In what ways do these different patterns collide in their lives?

2. Why does Mr. Bhowmick, in his daughter's words and eyes, have an "affect deficit" (p. 283)? In what ways could you argue that Babli's critical choice is the result of her father's attitude toward her?

3. What role does Hindu superstition play in this story? Why does Mr. Bhowmick make those "small trade-offs between new-world reasonableness and old-world beliefs" (p. 285)?

4. What are the elements of humor and irony in this story? In what ways do they intensify our response to each member of the Bhowmick family?

5. For Mr. Bhowmick, what is success? Why or why not has he found it in America? Do you think he would have been able to find success had he and his family remained in India? Explain. In what ways does his definition of success parallel or differ from yours?

6. What does Mr. Bhowmick mean when he thinks, "Girls like Babli were caught between rules" (p. 289)? In what ways is the Bhowmick family caught between rules?

SPENCER SHERMAN

The Hmong in America

"I don't think a day has gone by in the past decade where I did not come across a story worth telling. They are everywhere," Spencer Sherman claims. "All it takes is an inquisitive mind, a desire to tell an interesting story, and the effort to dig out the most compelling and fascinating facts."

Sherman has been writing stories for National Public Radio in Washington, D.C., from his new post in Tokyo, where he moved after two years in Seoul, Korea, as chief correspondent for United Press International. Since graduating from the University of California at Santa Cruz in 1978 with a bachelor's in American studies and political science, Sherman has been a journalist. He also looks to other forums, particularly magazines, where he can expand on the information he learns as a journalist.

The essay that follows had its beginnings when Sherman's neighborhood began to fill with Southeastern Asian refugees, and it became apparent to him that this influx involved the foot soldiers from the Vietnam War, "less educated, less rich, and less able to acclimate to life in America." In early 1981, Sherman went to Thailand to explore the problems of refugees, spending two weeks in refugee camps on the Thai-Cambodia and Thai-Laos borders. He began writing about the Hmong because he believed they needed the most help, and he found them a fascinating people. "By using the worst case," he explains, "I could most clearly show what problems were facing all refugees from Southeast Asia, to one degree or another." "The Hmong in America" was first published in National Geographic *in 1988.*

Before you read "The Hmong in America," write about what you imagine your city or town would look like to someone who suddenly arrived there without money, the skills needed to find work, or an understanding of the

language or cultural patterns that you take for granted. Of course, you'll have to explore the patterns that work beyond your awareness—the ones you take for granted.

"In the refugee camp in Thailand they say America has giants that eat Hmong people. Do I believe it? Well, I don't know . . . maybe yes. We have heard it many times," says Vas Seng Xiong, as he sinks back into the living room couch at his brother-in-law's home in Fresno, California. He laughs nervously, his thin body rattling as his voice cracks and fades into a dry cough. He is uncomfortable, and a little bewildered. He has been in the United States less than a week.

Vas Seng Xiong and the five other men sitting in a semicircle around him in this simple ranch-style house are Hmong from the northeastern highlands of Laos. They and about 97,000 other Hmong now live in the United States. Some 55,000 wait in refugee camps along the Mekong River border of Laos and Thailand to come to the United States or find some way to return home.

Anthropologists have described the Hmong as tribal mountain dwellers with strong clan loyalties, a people steeped in animistic ritual, bound by good and evil spirits to a way of life filled with the magical and mystical. Development specialists have called their agricultural life in Laos primitive and environmentally unsound. Narcotics officers have called them opium growers and dealers. The Communist leaders of Laos have called them barriers to national reconciliation. In the United States, refugee workers call their resettlement a worst-case situation.

The Hmong have one other attribute that makes them worthy of special note: They are Vietnam War veterans and, in the opinion of former Central Intelligence Agency Director William E. Colby, "damned good fighters."

Vas Seng Xiong and his brothers-in-law Nai and Chue Her were, for many years, foot soldiers in an army organized and trained by the CIA. It was a secret army; international treaties prohibited any foreign military presence in Laos. But at the height of the Vietnam War, 30,000 highland tribesmen, most of them Hmong, were supported by the CIA with arms, money, and personnel. Nearly as many died during the entire period from the early 1960s until 1973—10 percent of those who fought. If the same percentage of U.S. troops who fought in the war had been killed, the Vietnam Veterans Memorial in Washington, D.C., would commemorate some 270,000 dead and missing rather than the 58,156 fallen soldiers whose names are inscribed in the black wall today.

Not unlike many U.S. Vietnam veterans who felt abandoned by their country, many Hmong fighters feel they have been little rewarded for decades of service, cast adrift in a country so unfamiliar to them that they feel they have been "sent to the moon."

Since 1984 I have watched the Hmong adjust to life in the United States, seen the smallest of their tribal customs clash with American ways and often with U. S. laws. I have seen newly arrived Hmong ponder the use of stoves and refrigerators, and young Hmong spike their hair and wear chains in styles that they see on television. I have seen elderly Hmong depressed over their loss of authority, and illiterate working-age men puzzle over the tools of the industrial revolution as the rest of America marches into the computer age.

But I have also seen successes: In Merced, California, I met Blia Xiong, a dynamo looking for ways to succeed even if they conflict with her tribal origin. "I love to work. I wanted to try to get ahead. The places we can afford to live are surrounded by people on welfare, they are on some kinds of drugs, their kids don't have very good manners, and they use awful language," she said firmly.

Blia, sitting in her Hmong crafts shop in the downtown shopping district, recognizes that the unemployment rife in the Hmong community—though understandable—is dangerous: "When you are staying home on welfare, you begin to want to stay home. It is really hard to become who you want, but it is really easy to become lazy."

Or Vang Yee, who did not know how to use a stove when I first met him in 1985, but a year later had a job as an interpreter at a hospital, as well as a car, a two-bedroom house for his family, and a big new television set for his three kids.

The experiences of the men gathered in the Fresno house cover much of the range of Hmong success and failure in America. Sitting across from Vas Seng Xiong is Nai Her, owner of the house, who has been in the United States for five years. The contrast between the two is striking. Although Nai Her is a wiry, thin man, he has a well-fed look, clear-eyed and animated. Vas Seng Xiong is sallow, tired, and bone-protrudingly thin—as if he has just come through perilous surgery. In a sense he has: excising from himself the miseries of two years and eight months in a refugee camp.

"It is like a dream to him," said Nai Her, describing Vas Seng Xiong's first few days in America. "The sky and earth are so different here. He says he cannot walk because there are so many cars. When Americans speak, he doesn't hear."

And now Vas Seng Xiong must face the most serious barrier confronting the Hmong immigrants—language.

As a people without a written language until American and French missionaries invented one in the mid-1950s, the uneducated Hmong are forced to learn about the printed word in a tongue foreign to them. Like Nai Her, many other Hmong over 30 seem unable to master the task.

"Without the words I can't work," Nai Her laments. He is a trained mechanic, but his limited vocabulary has kept him out of most garages. He has survived mainly on refugee assistance and welfare, a situation mirrored by seven of every ten Hmong in Fresno and by 60 percent of his Hmong brethren elsewhere in the nation.

The newcomer Vas Seng Xiong has brought with him a view of the world incompatible with his new life. He knows little about America, and much of what he does know will have to be unlearned.

"I heard when I was a little boy that the Communists came to our village and said: 'We have to fight the Americans and the government and chase them away because they have let a giant come to our country.'"

If there were Hmong-eating giants in America, they would certainly stand out in Fresno. From this city of more than 500,000 people, set in the middle of California's San Joaquin Valley, not a hummock disturbs the horizon for more than a hundred miles in three directions. The foothills of the Sierra Nevada can be seen on clear days, an hour's drive to the east. The flat valley is perfect for growing food. More than half the Hmong in the U. S. live in California. Fresno, with 23,000 Hmong, is the second largest enclave in the world. Only Ban Vinai refugee camp in Thailand, with 34,000, is larger.

There are half a dozen reasons why so many Hmong came to the San Joaquin, like the Dust Bowl wanderers of John Steinbeck's *Grapes of Wrath* before them— reasons of economics and emotion, power and survival.

The initial settlement of the Hmong in America's cities was a failure. Cities isolated them from their countrymen and subjected them to the greatest possible contrast with the tribal, agriculture-centered lives of their past. Many Hmong were attacked by robbers or more subtly victimized for not knowing how to use money or call the police. They were unfamiliar with locked doors, light switches, modern plumbing. Some would use the toilet to clean rice, losing the precious kernels if the device was accidentally flushed. Refugee workers would find living rooms made into gardens, with soil brought in from the outside. Landlords would find Hmong using open cooking fires in the house, not knowing what the stove was for.

Mouachou Mouanoutoua, a Hmong community leader and evangelical minister in Santa Ana, California, told me the story of a Hmong who went looking for a job and wrote down the name of his street in case he got lost. When he did lose his way, he sought directions from a policeman, showing the officer the paper with the words: ONE WAY.

Sgt. Marvin Reyes of the Fresno city police told me of a Hmong man in a car jerking his way through an intersection one night. Pulled over by a policeman who figured him for a drunken driver, the Hmong man said he had been told to stop at every red light. It was late; the stoplight was blinking.

Compounding the adjustment problems of the Hmong was an adjustment problem of the United States government. Because of the tremendous number of refugees coming into the country in the late 1970s and early '80s (207,000 in 1980 alone, including 125,000 Cubans from the Mariel boatlift), the government was overwhelmed. Resettlement officials did not have time to consider the individual needs of each ethnic group among the 850,000 postwar Southeast Asian refugees, particularly the little-known Hmong. Few knew of the deep clan and tribal bonds that kept the Hmong together as a people, bonds that were torn when small groups were settled wherever sponsors could be found. Certain government policies exacerbated the problem. In one instance in 1982 federal officials issued a welfare regulation that would cut refugees from relief rolls if they had been in the U. S. for more than 18 months. Before the rule took effect in Oregon and Washington, some 4,000 Hmong moved to California, where state welfare programs offset the loss of federal funds.

Hmong politics also spurred the move to the San Joaquin. With their people spread out in a large country, leaders of the Hmong clans began to lose their hold. Younger people were beginning to take on responsibilities because of their greater command of English. Women, traditionally relegated to cooking, cleaning, and bearing children, were beginning to assert newfound rights in America. The traditional clan leaders began exerting pressure for the flock to come together again. The valley was also close to Santa Ana, California, where the famous Gen. Vang Pao, military leader of the Hmong during the war, had opened an office called Lao Family Community, Inc., that now has 12 branches nationwide.

For many Hmong such self-help groups serve as safety nets, teaching them living skills. For others they are a means of planning a return to Laos, to oust the Vietnamese-backed Communist government. That is Vang Pao's passion.

In a rare interview granted during Hmong New Year's festivities in Fresno, Gen. Vang Pao told me, his voice rising to a roar, "Laotians have nothing today. Between Laotian and Laotian we have no problems. We have the same blood, the same culture. But the North Vietnamese cannot dominate Laos, cannot control Laos, and must withdraw from Laos immediately!"

But the prospects of a return are not good. Though the general hints of support from several nations, including former foe China, he does not claim that any are offering funds, including his old ally, the United States. And support for the resistance is not even universal among the refugees. The words of one of them remain vivid: "I will not be involved with the dreams of angry men."

A return to agriculture was also an impetus for the migration to California. According to Cheu Thao, a top aide to Gen. Vang Pao, one question Hmong traditionally asked when considering a move to another site in Laos was "were your crops good this year?" From the few who had moved to the San Joaquin Valley as early as 1979, the answer was yes.

But finally the Hmong moved because it is a tenet of their tradition, like the Gypsies, that the response to adversity is to walk away.

"You want to know why the Hmong move from one mountain to another, why they always change their place?" asked Kou Yang, a Hmong social worker in Fresno who has given me much guidance on the Hmong and their ways. "Then go ask the deer who has been hurt why he defends himself. Ask the deer who changes forests why he changes his place. That is similar to the Hmong."

Migration had taken the Hmong to Laos. Many Hmong, hounded out of China early in the 19th century, fled to the high mountains between Vietnam and Laos, away from the cultivated lowlands. The strategic location of their mountain homeland, overlooking North Vietnam, forced them into the conflict between Communism and the West, first as scouts and fighters for the French, then as guerrillas for the United States. With the withdrawal of U.S. troops, they were forced to flee—first to camps in Thailand, then to low-income neighborhoods in the United States, France, and Australia.

"Sin City" is a four-square-block apartment complex formerly used to house Fresno State University students and nicknamed for their collegiate life-style. The Hmong migration has transformed Sin City into a refugee ghetto. The smell of hamburgers and hot dogs has been replaced by cilantro and ginger, and football games in the streets have been supplanted by kickball games among Hmong children. Agriculture drew the Hmong to the Fresno area, but their lack of money to buy the prime valley farmland and their dearth of skills to handle the modern mechanized farming for which the area is suited quickly forced most into reliance on welfare and the cheap housing of areas like Sin City.

"We used to farm crops for our family to consume. In this country you farm to make business. You farm to market, you have to produce good quality to compete with other farmers, and I think a lot of people didn't realize that," says Tony Vang, director of the Fresno office of Lao Family Community, Inc.

In Sin City today Hmong gardens fill the spaces between houses, and grandmothers watch hordes of young children whose mothers are away at work. As the 105-degree August heat beat down on a walkway between two Sin City apartment buildings, I was reminded of an alley in the Ban Vinai refugee camp in northern Thailand—the same stifling heat, the smell of boiled pig, the sight of half-bare babies and old wrinkled grandmothers in print sarongs.

Here, however, I soon passed a parade of carefully scrubbed Hmong children dressed in bright polo shirts and blue jeans, heading home from a summer day-care center at the nearby Wesley Methodist Church. It was there that Mike Morizono told me of the program that this church has set up to deal with the Hmong.

Part of the motivation for the day-care center was "just self-preservation." The children, he says, were climbing on the roof of the building and cutting up the lawns with their playing. Now, caring for the children has become a calling for the church, and every day the classes are packed with Hmong children cutting paper into designs and learning English-language ABCs.

For the adults in Sin City, life in many ways still resembles their existence in Ban Vinai. They are undoubtedly safer, healthier, and better fed here, but work is scarce. Unemployment is high among all residents of Fresno—13.3 percent as of last March, one of the worst rates in the nation. Among the Hmong, though, it is more than a third higher.

Trapped within the ghetto by economic forces, many of the formerly warm and welcoming Hmong have become insular and suspicious, leading to serious tensions with government officials. In the spring of 1986, for example, state welfare inspectors began unannounced home visits to investigate compliance with eligibility regulations. Officials soon reported death threats. The situation became so serious that Gen. Vang Pao traveled to a mass meeting of the Fresno Hmong to order the threats stopped.

The segregated Hmong communities do provide a safety net for the elderly and others who cannot adopt new ways. Those who have begun to change their lives, however, must learn to bridge a turbulent gap between the ghetto and outside society.

In April 1985 Kong Moua of Fresno decided to get married. He found the girl he wanted and proceeded as he thought he should: Kong Moua and a group of friends went to Fresno City College and took the girl from the campus to his house. That night he had sex with her.

In the Hmong culture Kong Moua had performed *zij poj niam:* marriage by capture. In the eyes of the police—called by the woman, Xeng Xiong—he had kidnapped and raped. Zij poj niam is not an everyday occurrence but is not unusual either. The roles of the traditional culture demand that the man appear strong, the woman resistant and virtuous.

Gene M. Gomes, the judge who heard Kong Moua's case, says he was "uncomfortable" acting as half judge, half anthropologist, but conceded that the unusual circumstances required unusual measures. He agreed to allow Kong Moua to plead to a lesser charge of false imprisonment, giving the court the "leeway to get into all these cultural issues and to try to tailor a sentence that would fulfill both our needs and the Hmong needs." Gomes ordered Kong Moua to pay a thousand dollars to the girl's family and to serve 90 days in jail.

Tou Lia Xiong, 21, handled his marriage differently. In 1985 he fell for Mai Vang Yang, and they secretly decided to wed. One day Mai and Tou Lia went to his home and a few hours later sent emissaries to her father's house to arrange the details of the marriage, as is customary. Her father was at first outraged at his daughter's attempt to marry without his permission, but he finally agreed, and Tou Lia made a ritual payment of $1,400.

In some ways Mai and Tou Lia are typical newlyweds. She goes to school during the day, and he works in the Fresno school district, explaining Hmong life to students to ease racial tensions. After school he works as a stock boy in a liquor store. They have a one-bedroom apartment, sparsely furnished except for a brand-new 21-inch color television set. "Next is a VCR," Tou Lia said, smiling.

But they are also bound to Hmong ways. They will not use birth control, for example, because Hmong, traditionally, must have many children. They know it is better for their future in America to limit their families, Mai Vang Yang said, but that would make her an outcast in her community. Mai says she might have only four children, but there is little conviction in her voice: It is hard to be sure of the future when you have just turned 14.

Tou Lu Thao of Fresno, a farmer, told me, "One of the big problems that we face in adjusting to this society is that in Laos it is really free. If you want to build a house in that corner, you just go and build a house. Or if you want to farm that land, if no one has farmed it, you just go do it. Here one of the hardest problems is that you have to go by rules and regulations."

Game warden Roger Reese agrees. He told me that the Hmong, along with other Southeast Asians, have caused a lot of trouble by poaching fish and wildlife. "To them, it's just harvesting. They don't care what species it is. If they can see it, they take it. They employ any means—nets, setlines, traps, snares, slingshots, even two-by-fours. And they're good at avoiding detection."

Lao Chu Cha, a Hmong community leader in the small Sierra Nevada foothill town of Porterville, offers a different explanation for the difficulties the Hmong have faced in Fresno. He says there are too many Hmong people grouped together.

In July 1983 Lao Chu drove to Porterville from San Diego with the idea of setting up a farming cooperative and experimenting with building a typical Hmong community. Other families of his clan, the Cha, and of related clans followed. There are now 80 Hmong families in the town—500 people.

Life in Porterville, Lao Chu Cha said, is better than in crowded Fresno. His community, however, shares some of the difficulties faced by the Hmong of the valley. The slash-and-burn agricultural techniques that the Hmong are accustomed to are environmentally disastrous and illegal in the United States, so they cannot farm without learning new techniques. They can go to school to learn U. S. farming, but working-age men and women—never schooled in Laos—cannot read or write in Hmong, let alone English. While they attend English classes, they live off welfare and plant little gardens for food. Only 20 Hmong in Porterville have jobs.

Buried under the seemingly overwhelming problems of resettling the Hmong, their successes are easy to ignore—until you meet a man like Kue Chaw and visit his community in the rural foothills of the Blue Ridge Mountains. With his family, Kue Chaw (a former captain in the Hmong secret army) weathered urban living in Philadelphia from 1976 to 1980. Then he went on a nationwide tour looking for a place to rebuild a life more like the one they had lost in Laos. He found it in a small North Carolina town called Marion.

"It had the trees, though not quite like Laos. It had lakes and cheap land for vegetables," he said. He sent word to his clan. Today nearly 600 Hmong live spread out over rural Burke and neighboring McDowell Counties.

As the leader, Kue Chaw exerts a powerful force on the people who come and stay. "If you come to Marion, you must work. This is what life in America is about," he told me in the office of the Hmong Natural Association. There is little choice, as the state provides virtually no welfare support, but there are enough nonskilled jobs available to keep the Hmong employed. Land and housing are also cheaper, making it possible to buy homes.

There was some resistance from local people when the Hmong began to arrive, and a short-lived letter-writing campaign to local newspapers stirred rumors of a Hmong invasion. But the number of letters soon dwindled, and the Hmong went on living quietly.

"I think you have to divide the Hmong transition in this country into two parts," said Yang Dao in St. Paul, Minnesota. The twin cities are home to 14,000 Hmong, second in concentration only to Fresno. As the first Hmong ever to receive a Ph.D., Yang Dao is the most respected Hmong intellectual in the nation. "When our people first came here in 1976, they were surprised by the modernization. Everything was totally different from the way of life they had known in Laos. They were happily surprised because life was better.

"Many Hmong in this country wrote back [to the refugee camps] saying: 'We are very happy in this country, this country is like heaven for us.' But after a while they realized it was not easy to adapt themselves to this country because they could not speak English and they could not find a job, and the stress started."

To cope with the transition, area Hmong come frequently to the Tong Vang farm north of the twin cities. There they hold traditional animal-sacrifice ceremonies to help ailing relatives or to assure that good spirits are watching over newborn children. Here too, in the cavernous barn, are held Hmong funeral ceremonies, elaborate affairs that often continue for four days amid organized wailing.

Yang Dao is not blind to the disintegration of much of Hmong culture in the United States, but thinks, in the final analysis, that the resettlement has been good for his people. "It is only here, in the United States, that the Hmong are able to learn, that the young can go to school and become important members of a society. Even if we someday go back to Laos, we will have the tools to play an important part in the nation, and not have to stick to the mountains.

"It is still the case, even in the United States, that you can go into a strange town and look in the telephone book for a Hmong name and call them. Even if you do not know them, you can stay at their house and they will feed you. This is something the other refugee groups do not have. It is something that keeps the Hmong together, as a group, as a people, as a clan."

I remember saying good-bye to social worker Kou Yang before his departure to China for six months as a visiting scholar from Fresno State University. His usual calm demeanor was cracking under the excitement as he pulled out books on China and Laos, pointing out their shared border and where he would go to find some of the estimated two million Hmong who never fled China to Laos: "The Hmong who have never been refugees," he said.

I asked how he could go freely back and forth between China and Fresno without a passport. He disappeared briefly, returning to display, proudly, his new naturalization papers. He is now an American citizen but still grapples with the question of whether a Hmong must cast off his past, like an adolescent casting off youth to become an adult, to be a true American. I told him I didn't think so and quoted to him the words of the Hmong refugee Mouachou Mouanoutoua in Santa Ana:

"Being an American is really espousing the founding principles of freedom, no matter whether you speak the language or not. And if I say I believe in the founding principles that make America, I think that is what makes an American. It is your love for it, your belief in it, and your labor to protect it. And I think the Hmong . . . know in their hearts that these principles are what they have fought for, even in Laos—the basic principles of freedom."

Kou Yang insists, however, that the Hmong must go a step further and cast off their refugee status. "We must start thinking like Hmong Americans. Take the best of Laos and the best of America and live like that, but stop thinking like refugees."

Whatever the future of the Hmong Americans, it most certainly belongs to people like Kou Yang.

Questions for Discussion and Writing

1. In what ways might the Hmong have been more effectively helped to prepare for the kind of cultural adjustments in patterns and values that they have had to make in the United States? In what ways might the United States have prepared more effectively to resettle the Hmong?

2. In what ways does the cultural, political, educational, and military history of the Hmong in Southeast Asia confuse and hamper their adjustment here? In what ways is their background valuable in their adjustment?

3. How does the case of King Moua of Fresno reflect the colliding patterns of intercultural values and attitudes?

4. What does it mean to "stop thinking like refugees" (p. 300)?

ISHMAEL REED

America: The Multinational Society

Born in 1938, Ishmael Reed grew up in Chattanooga, Tennessee, attended the University of Buffalo from 1957 to 1960, and has been a writer ever since. A novelist, poet, essayist, editor, and critic, Reed concerns himself especially with the ways in which politics, religion, and technology repress people. In 1973, his work Conjure *(1972) was nominated for the Pulitzer Prize in poetry and his novel* Mumbo Jumbo *(1972) for the National Book Award.*

Writing has always been a "coping mechanism" for Reed. People have paid attention to his words since he was a young boy: "It gave me power that other forms of expression didn't," he says. As a child he also became interested in reading what he calls "outlaw" intellectuals, black writers like J. A. Rogers who wrote about black culture in books never taught in schools.

Reed is regarded as one of the leading satirists in contemporary black literature. Today he is the editorial director of Reed and Cannon Communications Company, and a contributing writer to the New York Times, Los Angeles Times, Japan Times Weekly, LeMonde, San Francisco Examiner, *and* Newsday. *He has taught at Harvard, Yale, and Dartmouth, and for over twenty years has been a lecturer at the University of California at Berkeley.*

The essay that follows, "America: The Multinational Society," is taken from Reed's most recent book, Writin' Is Fightin', *published in 1988. In the book's introduction, Reed says that "a black boxer's career is the perfect metaphor for the career of a black male. Every day is like being in the gym, sparring with impersonal opponents as one faces the rudeness and hostility that a black male must confront in the United States, where he is the object of both fear and fascination. My difficulty in communicating this point of view used to really bewilder me," he explains, "but over the years I've learned that it takes an extraordinary amount of effort to understand someone from*

a background different from your own, especially when your life
really doesn't depend on it."

Before you read "America: The Multinational Society," write about how
you would classify or categorize yourself in terms of your citizenship, your
family's national and cultural heritage, and the cultural origins of major
influences in your life. Explain any confusion you encounter with your
categories.

> *At the annual Lower East Side Jewish Festival yesterday,*
> *a Chinese woman ate a pizza slice in front of Ty Thuan*
> *Duc's Vietnamese grocery store. Beside her a Spanish-*
> *speaking family patronized a cart with two signs: "Italian*
> *Ices" and "Kosher by Rabbi Alper." And after the pastrami*
> *ran out, everybody ate knishes.*
> NEW YORK TIMES, 23 JUNE 1983

O n the day before Memorial Day, 1983, a poet called me to describe a city
he had just visited. He said that one section included mosques, built by
the Islamic people who dwelled there. Attending his reading, he said, were large
numbers of Hispanic people, forty thousand of whom lived in the same city. He
was not talking about a fabled city located in some mysterious region of the
world. The city he'd visited was Detroit.

A few months before, as I was leaving Houston, Texas, I heard it announced
on the radio that Texas's largest minority was Mexican-American, and though a
foundation recently issued a report critical of bilingual education, the taped voice
used to guide the passengers on the air trams connecting terminals in Dallas
Airport is in both Spanish and English. If the trend continues, a day will come
when it will be difficult to travel through some sections of the country without
hearing commands in both English and Spanish; after all, for some western
states, Spanish was the first written language and the Spanish style lives on in the
western way of life.

Shortly after my Texas trip, I sat in an auditorium located on the campus of
the University of Wisconsin at Milwaukee as a Yale professor—whose original
work on the influence of African cultures upon those of the Americas has led to
his ostracism from some monocultural intellectual circles—walked up and down
the aisle, like an old-time southern evangelist, dancing and drumming the top
of the lectern, illustrating his points before some serious Afro-American intellectuals and artists who cheered and applauded his performance and his mastery of
information. The professor was "white." After his lecture, he joined a group of
Milwaukeeans in a conversation. All of the participants spoke Yoruban, though
only the professor had ever traveled to Africa.

One of the artists told me that his paintings, which included African and
Afro-American mythological symbols and imagery, were hanging in the local

McDonald's restaurant. The next day I went to McDonald's and snapped pictures of smiling youngsters eating hamburgers below paintings that could grace the walls of any of the country's leading museums. The manager of the local McDonald's said, "I don't know what you boys are doing, but I like it," as he commissioned the local painters to exhibit in his restaurant.

Such blurring of cultural styles occurs in everyday life in the United States to a greater extent than anyone can imagine and is probably more prevalent than the sensational conflict between people of different backgrounds that is played up and often encouraged by the media. The result is what the Yale professor, Robert Thompson, referred to as a cultural bouillabaisse, yet members of the nation's present educational and cultural Elect still cling to the notion that the United States belongs to some vaguely defined entity they refer to as "Western civilization," by which they mean, presumably, a civilization created by the people of Europe, as if Europe can be viewed in monolithic terms. Is Beethoven's Ninth Symphony, which includes Turkish marches, a part of Western civilization, or the late nineteenth- and twentieth-century French paintings, whose creators were influenced by Japanese art? And what of the cubists, through whom the influence of African art changed modern painting, or the surrealists, who were so impressed with the art of the Pacific Northwest Indians that, in their map of North America, Alaska dwarfs the lower forty-eight in size?

Are the Russians, who are often criticized for their adoption of "Western" ways by Tsarist dissidents in exile, members of Western civilization? And what of the millions of Europeans who have black African and Asian ancestry, black Africans having occupied several countries for hundreds of years? Are these "Europeans" members of Western civilization, or the Hungarians, who originated across the Urals in a place called Greater Hungary, or the Irish, who came from the Iberian Peninsula?

Even the notion that North America is part of Western civilization because our "system of government" is derived from Europe is being challenged by Native American historians who say that the founding fathers, Benjamin Franklin especially, were actually influenced by the system of government that had been adopted by the Iroquois hundreds of years prior to the arrival of large numbers of Europeans.

Western civilization, then, becomes another confusing category like Third World, or Judeo-Christian culture, as man attempts to impose his small-screen view of political and cultural reality upon a complex world. Our most publicized novelist recently said that Western civilization was the greatest achievement of mankind, an attitude that flourishes on the street level as scribbles in public restrooms: "White Power," "Niggers and Spics Suck," or "Hitler was a prophet," the latter being the most telling, for wasn't Adolf Hitler the archetypal monoculturalist who, in his pigheaded arrogance, believed that one way and one blood was so pure that it had to be protected from alien strains at all costs? Where did such an attitude, which has caused so much misery and depression in our national life, which has tainted even our noblest achievements, begin? An attitude that caused the incarceration of Japanese-American citizens during World War II, the persecution of Chicanos and Chinese-Americans, the near-extermination of the Indians, and the murder and lynchings of thousands of Afro-Americans.

Virtuous, hardworking, pious, even though they occasionally would wander off after some fancy clothes, or rendezvous in the woods with the town prostitute, the Puritans are idealized in our schoolbooks as "a hardy band" of no-nonsense patriarchs whose discipline razed the forest and brought order to the New World (a term that annoys Native American historians). Industrious, responsible, it was their "Yankee ingenuity" and practicality that created the work ethic. They were simple folk who produced a number of good poets, and they set the tone for the American writing style, of lean and spare lines, long before Hemingway. They worshiped in churches whose colors blended in with the New England snow, churches with simple structures and ornate lecterns.

The Puritans were a daring lot, but they had a mean streak. They hated the theater and banned Christmas. They punished people in a cruel and inhuman manner. They killed children who disobeyed their parents. When they came in contact with those whom they considered heathens or aliens, they behaved in such a bizarre and irrational manner that this chapter in the American history comes down to us as a late-movie horror film. They exterminated the Indians, who taught them how to survive in a world unknown to them, and their encounter with the calypso culture of Barbados resulted in what the tourist guide in Salem's Witches' House refers to as the Witchcraft Hysteria.

The Puritan legacy of hard work and meticulous accounting led to the establishment of a great industrial society; it is no wonder that the American industrial revolution began in Lowell, Massachusetts, but there was the other side, the strange and paranoid attitudes toward those different from the Elect.

The cultural attitudes of that early Elect continue to be voiced in everyday life in the United States: the president of a distinguished university, writing a letter to the *Times,* belittling the study of African civilizations; the television network that promoted its show on the Vatican art with the boast that this art represented "the finest achievements of the human spirit." A modern up-tempo state of complex rhythms that depends upon contacts with an international community can no longer behave as if it dwelled in a "Zion Wilderness" surrounded by beasts and pagans.

When I heard a schoolteacher warn the other night about the invasion of the American educational system by foreign curriculums, I wanted to yell at the television set, "Lady, they're already here." It has already begun because the world is here. The world has been arriving at these shores for at least ten thousand years from Europe, Africa, and Asia. In the late nineteenth and early twentieth centuries, large numbers of Europeans arrived, adding their cultures to those of the European, African, and Asian settlers who were already here, and recently millions have been entering the country from South America and the Caribbean, making Yale Professor Bob Thompson's bouillabaisse richer and thicker.

One of our most visionary politicians said that he envisioned a time when the

United States could become the brain of the world, by which he meant the repository of all of the latest advanced information systems. I thought of that remark when an enterprising poet friend of mine called to say that he had just sold a poem to a computer magazine and that the editors were delighted to get it because they didn't carry fiction or poetry. Is that the kind of world we desire? A humdrum homogeneous world of all brains and no heart, no fiction, no poetry; a world of robots with human attendants bereft of imagination, of culture? Or does North America deserve a more exciting destiny? To become a place where the cultures of the world crisscross. This is possible because the United States is unique in the world: The world is here.

Questions for Discussion and Writing

1. Explain what Reed means by the cultural "blurring" in the United States, or what Robert Thompson, a professor at Yale, calls the "cultural bouil-labaisse" (p. 303). In what ways does Reed support this assertion about cultural blurring? How might you use examples from your own experience to support his assertion? In what ways does your own experience not support his assertion?

2. What people and groups of people does Reed use to illustrate the dangers of thinking and behaving in monocultural patterns?

3. What cultural attitudes from the Puritans does Reed suggest still dominate our thinking in the United States?

4. What major question about our future does Reed raise at the end of the essay? For what reasons does he envision a "more exciting destiny" for North America? How do you think he uses the word *exciting* here? How would you define *exciting* in this context?

Chapter 5

CULTURAL EXCHANGES IN STUDY AND WORK

Ours is a century of mass migration set in motion by political upheavals and this, on such a scale is new; a formula of adaptation had to be invented, the past being unable to provide cues sufficiently valid for living today. No matter how strong the attachment to one's native land, one cannot live away from it very long and still resist what is seen every day—cannot go on complaining of the strangeness of the new language, mores, and institutions, straining sight and sound toward one's lost country. . . . Total uprootedness is contrary to our nature, and the human plant once plucked from the ground tries to send its roots into the ground onto which it is thrown. . . . Just as our hand reaches out and takes a pencil lying on a table, thus establishing a relationship between our body and what is outside it, our imagination extends us, establishing a sensory-visual relationship between us and a street, a town, a district, and a country.

**CZESLAW MILOSZ, winner of the Nobel Prize
for Literature in 1980, in
*"BIBLICAL HEIRS AND MODERN EVILS"***

BECAUSE THEY EXTEND OUR EXPERIENCE IN ANOTHER PLACE, IN-
tercultural study and work can offer the most thorough possibilities, short of immigration, of learning new cultures. The stages of cultural adaptation and shock move more slowly in extended stays in new places: the dazzle of the different and the exotic wears off, and we move inevitably from being a spectator to being a participant.

We do not have to go abroad to have the experience of intercultural study.

Look around the classroom and you will probably discover it there waiting for you. Students who come to the United States have the cultures here to learn, and those of us from the United States have the opportunities, if we take them, to begin learning theirs without leaving school. In the first selection in this chapter, "Nothing in Our Hands but Age," Raquel Puig Zaldívar shows us what can happen when we don't take the opportunity to learn about another culture. Her essay/story reflects a classroom in Florida in which American students are put off by the peculiar ways of an older wife and husband from Cuba who suddenly appear in the class and as a result nearly miss knowing them.

Once students from other places begin adapting to their new culture—wherever it is—that culture begins to seep into the patterns and values of their lives whether they choose it or not, as it does for Yearn Hong Choi, a student from Korea, in "Bloomington, Fall 1971." The toll of graduate students' returning to their own countries after years in the United States can be enormous too, as James R. Corey explains in "Cultural Shock in Reverse."

With work as well as with study, we do not have to go abroad for the intercultural experience. Our colleagues may provide all the insights we need into seeing the complexities of work from different cultural perspectives. In "Señor Payroll," William E. Barrett reflects the need of managers to learn about the cultural assumptions and expectations of their employees—the same idea that Lawrence Stessin emphasizes in "Culture Shock and the American Businessman Overseas." Work also makes its own intercultural demands on Dahn, the character in Similih M. Corder's "A Farewell to the Old Order," who moves from his rural past into a high administrative post in the city of Monrovia, without even leaving his country.

In "How Datsun Discovered America," David Halberstam explores the intricacies of intercultural gaps in the case of a man from Japan who became his company's leading representative in the United States. The essay explores the pressures such people face in making their company's product acceptable to and appropriate for a new set of needs and values in another culture, and the difficulties they can encounter in explaining such differences to the home office a world away, for whom such adjustments can seem a triviality, a luxury, or a waste.

RAQUEL PUIG ZALDÍVAR

Nothing in Our Hands but Age

Born in Cuba in 1950, Raquel Puig Zaldívar moved with her family to Florida in 1961. As an undergraduate she studied journalism and education; she received her masters degree in Spanish literature. In 1974, Zaldívar began teaching at Miami Dade Community College. Although she had wanted to be a writer since her college days, she became disenchanted with writing because she found it so hard "to reach the people," and in 1979, decided she would quit. Wanting to make a clean break with it, she eventually attended law school, graduating in 1987, when her son Robert was three years old.

Today Zaldívar continues to teach at Miami Dade, has a part-time legal practice, and writes during the summer months. Her son has inspired her to write children's stories in Spanish and English, and her legal practice has given her material for a novel she is currently writing, called Custody.

"Nothing in Our Hands but Age," published in 1980, is a fictionalized account of two students whose presence and influence in class Zaldívar could not forget.

Before you read "Nothing in Our Hands but Age," write about a time when a student in your class seemed strange to you. (You might instead write about yourself, if you felt you were that "strange" student.) Describe the factors that made the student seem strange to you and how you and your classmates reacted. What did you find out about that person, if anything, to make you reassess your initial reaction? How did the situation resolve itself?

"And since I have realized that many people go through life without thinking, my most important goal in this course will be to teach you to think, and, hopefully, help you make a habit of it." I paused to catch my breath and the door behind me clacked to announce the arrival of a new student. The first day of classes it is very difficult to gather all of them at the same time. They cruise in and out of several wrong rooms before they finally reach the proper destination. I was quiet without looking back. As usually, I expected the student to sit down before continuing my lecture. The door did not clack back right away and I had to turn around.

A heavy set, dark-haired woman was holding the door open, waiting for someone else to come in. She had an over-sized flowery plastic bag hanging from her arm and a fairly large brown paper bundle firmly grasped with her hand. At this point the whole class was interested in who or what was finally going to enter. The door, with a personality of its own, struggled with the woman's arm, but she was victorious. A frail-looking man, dragging his feet, entered and glanced at us triumphantly a little out of breath. The woman let go of the door and approached me energetically. The man I suspected to be her husband trailed along with much effort, unable to keep up. "Alicia Pérez de Roca"; she pronounced every syllable carefully and pointed to herself as she opened her enormous eyes even wider. "Antonio Roca," she said pointing to her husband who had not quite reached us.

The group was starting to get restless. Some were speaking to their friends and others were just staring at the newcomers and laughing. I glared at them and for once it worked. They straightened up and looked respectful once more. Then I turned my attention to the couple:

"Mrs. Roca," I began.

"Pérez de Roca," she interrupted; "Alicia Pérez de Roca, Antonio Roca," she added pointing to her husband.

"All right, Mrs. Pérez de Roca, please sit down and I will speak to you again after class." I tried my best to be calm.

It took them five more minutes to settle down. I was able to add a few comments about the grading system and the books that were required for the course, but it was time to leave before I realized it.

"If you have any questions please come to my office. If not, I'll see you Thursday. Have a nice day."

One by one the students gathered their belongings and emptied the room, all of them except the Roca couple, who were standing up and slowly making it to the front. I was waiting for them and felt an unexpected gush of tenderness. Alicia was not very tall, somewhat wide around the hips and the bustline. She was probably past sixty but had a very white, clear complexion on which the years had not cared to leave too many traces. Antonio could have been approximately ten years her senior. He was obviously weak but did not lack enthusiasm. His small eyes glowed with excitement; they were younger than the rest of him and very ill-matched with the multiple folds surrounding his eyes and lips and the wart that sat ungraciously on his nose.

Their attire was spotless, old but well-preserved. It had been ironed and starched with careful, experienced hands. She wore a long black skirt with a pleat in the back. Her white blouse was completely embroidered in the front with what had been colorful threads, the type of work that was imported years ago from the Canary Islands. He wore a firmly starched *guayabera* with long sleeves, four pockets and tiny pleats, the kind Cubans used to wear on grand occasions. There was no doubt in my mind that they were my countrymen.

"You see, professor," she automatically emphasized her *r*'s, "wee come from Cuba and my hoosband was a pharmacist and I was a doctor of pheelosophee and we come to the Junited States of America to find freedom and the social worker tell us we can come to the school for the, the, revalidation of our title . . . ," she looked uncertain.

"Degree," I corrected; "you want to study to revalidate your degrees to continue in your professions." Smiling she nodded profusely; Antonio followed doubtful. "Do you wish to speak Spanish? I'm Cuban, too. I can understand."

"Oh no," she shook her head back and held the heavy plastic bag with both her hands in front of her stomach. "Wee want to comprehend English better, wee have to revalidate in English. This is pheelosophee, correct?"

"Yes."

"My hoosband and me have mooch experience of many years with pheelosophee, we love it very mooch and we want to do good in yourr class."

"Do you know the titles of the books?" I asked.

"Mmmmmm, wee were not able to grasp those names. The vision I don't have it very well and you speek too fast. Wee may come to yourr offiz, yes?"

"Of course, come right up and I'll give you all the details."

I smiled and left the room ahead of them. Where did these people get their energy? They apparently were honest about the whole thing and were seriously considering a new beginning at a point when most individuals are realizing they have to face the end. I wondered how they would pass my course, but decided not to worry about it so soon.

My office was locked. I opened the door, turned on the lights and barely had time to sit down when they appeared at the threshold and asked permission to come in.

"Of course, come right in and sit down," I said as cheerfully as I knew how. They accepted my invitation and looked at me with all their attention.

"Mrs. Roca."

"Pérez de Roca. You know, professor, in Cuba the married ladies keep the father's name. That for me is Pérez."

"Mrs. Pérez de Roca and Mr. Roca, this is a course divided in two parts: philosophy and drama."

"Excellent, excellent," said Antonio and smiled.

"It is not an easy course," I stressed; "you will have to read a lot."

"No problem, we have a good bilingual dictionary," she said.

"There will be weekly quizzes." Mrs. Pérez de Roca wrote everything I said in her new notebook. They could not be dissuaded.

"Alicia, ¿no se te parece a la niña?" The old man's expression became very soft and he looked at me insistently. I understood him perfectly, but:

"My hoosband says you are alike that our daughter." I smiled at him; he was obviously pleased.

"Is your daughter here?" I asked not knowing what else to say.

"In Cuba, in Cuba." Antonio understood for the first time.

"Wee come to the school for her. She come here very soon and then she is goin to need our help."

"When did you see her last?"

"Oh, fifteen years ago, but now she is goin to come very, very soon."

Weeks later Alicia barely passed the first test and Antonio failed miserably but neither of them became discouraged. It was close to impossible for them to understand the lectures. The terminology was difficult and I know I went too fast for them. I realized, however, that they enjoyed the small group sessions the most. Once a week the students were supposed to meet with me in groups of no more than twelve to discuss the assignments. It was here where Alicia gave all her comments and Antonio listened attentively. Most of the students didn't mind them, but others expressed their disgust very openly, and disagreed with them constantly.

"I don't think men need goals," said Matt discussing a passage from *Siddhartha*. "Why can't we just live and take things as they come, and not worry? We spend too much time planning for the future and forget our present."

"I disagree," answered Alicia. Her husband nodded faithfully in the back. "When I was a young woman I wanted to care for my family the best way and wanted to teech history. I had a goal and that made me continue in life and do thins and brin out a family and be happy."

"But what for? We all can do something but without living only for that," insisted the younger man. "In our society we waste our lives in futile things."

"Futile?" asked Alicia. A student who sat next to her translated the word into Spanish.

"Well, maybe goals should be there, we must have one, but we shouldn't devote all our lives to them. Don't you think, Mrs. Morales?" asked another student.

"I don't want to influence your opinions. I know what I believe in, but I want you to do your own thinking."

"Futile not!" refuted Mrs. Pérez de Roca with conviction. "No goals and when you arrive to be as old as me, you see yourr life behind you and you don't have . . . Mmmmm . . . How is it that you say? Anythin to show."

"Is that so?" said Matt sarcastically; "then what do you have to show? If your goals had worked you wouldn't be here. Your circumstances have put you here, goals or no goals. Goals, what they do is chain you, don't let you be free."

"Goals do not chain, they direct," Alicia turned very solemn.

"Well," I interrupted; "we're beginning to talk in circles and besides our time is up. Read the next ten pages for Monday and have a nice day."

The students left immediately. Alicia and Antonio stayed behind as usual. They took a little longer standing up and picking up their belongings. I felt a bit attached to these two souls. They came from the country to which I belong, but of which I have no memory. Sometimes they came to my office and talked to me about the street vendors, the *guajiros* or peasants and the tall palm trees, always in "carrreful" English. More than one time their tales made me smile.

"Do not worry about the commentaries this children make. Wee are not offended. Wee know wee are too old but wee talk because wee have somethin to . . . Mmmmmm!! . . . How do you say? Compart?"

"Share," I corrected.

"Correct, 'share'. Wee share, they share too. This new method of teachin is very new and it function well. When I was a teacher I only taught from the outside. You teech from the inside also."

While the woman talked, Antonio looked at me with affection. Often, as I left, I heard him discuss with his wife how much I resembled their daughter.

"Where do you live, Alicia?" I asked one morning.

"In the block of apartments in Seventh and Thirteen. Nice place but no good to stay there all the day. Very sad, many old people with no family. Wee are not sad," she explained. "Wee have our daughter. She is far away but she is close here." She indicated her heart and nodded resolutely opening her eyes and smiling.

"Did she arrive yet?"

"No, not yet, but she is comin soon. Wee don't see her since fifteen years ago. She cannot write often. It's a little problem. But when she come, we're goin to help an awful mooch."

"An awful lot, Alicia."

"Da's correct," she stopped as if looking for the right words. "You know, wee already bought for her all for the house. All new thins. Wee save and wee buy little by little. Pillows and mantels . . ."

"Tablecloths."

"Correct! and dishes and towels. Everysin, her father and me buy it for her. When she comes."

"Is she married?" I asked.

"No, she had all prepared. You know," she smacked her lips in a sorrowful gesture; "but she was prisioned, you know, to the . . . Mmmmm . . . How do you say it?"

"Jail?"

"Dat is it, to the jail. She is forty years old now. It happened fifteen years ago on March. But she is gettin out on dis year. Then she is comin to us. She is our family, you know? Nobody else," she shook her head.

They weren't as disturbed by their jailed daughter as I was. The idea was already part of them and nothing mattered but the fact that she would be free again next March. Fifteen years! My body went cold with the thought.

Humanities 202 continued as usual. The Rocas were never absent. They knew they were slow settling down and they made it a point to arrive early. When I got to class they were usually excited, with new questions and comments to make. The course was more than halfway through when we began discussing *Macbeth*.

"Well, class, how could you describe the character of Macbeth?"

"Imaginative," said Justo.

"Courageous," answered another student.

"Ambitious," exclaimed Alicia.

"What was it that he most desired?"

"Power," explained Justo.

"Why do you suppose he wanted power?" Sometimes it was very hard to make the students talk.

"He wanted to control others and make them do what he wanted," said the young man.

"He was willing to go to any extreme to achieve this," added another one.

"He assessinated the king and his friend B . . . B . . . Bbb . . ."

"Banquo," I said, helping Alicia. She nodded. "Does he represent men of his time or mankind as a whole?"

"Menkind," Alicia was quick to reply. "Dere are," she rolled her *r*'s mercilessly, "men in our world today dat are equal to Macbeth. For example, you know in Cuba know, wee have a man in the power dat kills many people to be powerfool and dominate the whole nation." I knew the subject matter was getting touchy but it was my policy to accept any comments students made and I had to listen and pray the situation wouldn't get out of hand.

"It's not at all the same," answered Jenny; "Macbeth did it to satisfy his own desire. In Cuba it's being done for a purpose, to help the poor." I wished I could have stopped them but I couldn't. That would have been going against my own rules. I remained quiet.

"No, Jenny, you are mistaken," said another one. "Killing and destruction are wrong. We mustn't consider the purpose for which those things are committed."

"You know, people, what I consider is valuable?" Justo was wondering out loud. "My freedom to express any disagreement, man." Several classmates assented.

"Well, that's necessary," Jenny was quick to reply; "but that's allowed in Cuba today, any fool knows that."

"I am not in accordance." This time Alicia stood up as she always did when she was going to say something she considered important. "Nobody can express his opinions in my country today."

"Oh, there she goes again!" I heard someone whisper in boredom. Alicia paid no heed. She wasn't excited; her voice was soft, her words paused. Only a competent observer could have noticed she trembled a little. Antonio usually sat motionless behind her. He knew enough English to realize that things were getting rough for his wife.

"You know, Miss, I know a young woman who was only a little bit older dat you and very pretty also," she smiled and nodded; "and she has espent many years in a prision for the only mistake dat she did not want to teech the wrong way to little childrens."

"Ah!" Jenny exclaimed with exaggerated disgust. "We have learned enough in this class to know that words like 'wrong' are relative." Alicia simply ignored her.

"She went to the country, you know, with the farmers, to teech dem the grammar and the aritmetic and the oder sings importants. She did not desire to teech Communist doctrine." The class became very quiet. "She said dis to her chief and asked to leave the country and she was incarcelated, in prision, you know? For fifteen years."

"Well, that's all a nice tale, a story," answered Jenny stubbornly; "but they are always things that people make up. Rumors. How do you know they are true?" The whole class, including me, was paying close attention to the discussion. We followed with our heads the words that, like arrows, went from one end of the room to the other.

"Dat is not correct. Dis is not a rumor. It is a true story." Alicia's words were paused.

"That's what they always say," rebutted Jenny.

"I know dis is true," the old woman's tone was forgiving, not defiant. "You see, I am espeakin about my daughter."

Everyone was still. Any movement would have wounded the woman's solemn declaration. Moments later other students began trying to enter the room for their next class and we had to leave. Nobody, however, even bothered to speak.

Cuba was never again discussed in that class. We finished with Shakespeare, with Ibsen, with Bernard Shaw, but Cuba was never again touched. Justo, Jenny and the others were sensitive enough to imagine the burden the old couple bore. They stopped raising their eyebrows and sighing hard enough to be noticed every time Alicia spoke. A certain respect grew out of that experience and even though the discussions continued and the disagreements were frequent, the atmosphere of the class was less tight, more pleasant.

Mrs. Pérez de Roca passed the course with few problems. Her test grades were very humble, but throughout the discussions she showed me that she read the material. Her husband Antonio didn't make it. I wondered what tests, group discussions and classes like mine were supposed to mean when a man like Antonio Roca, a college graduate, a man who had supported his family with dignity so many years, did not manage to pass it. I blamed his age but quickly dismissed from my mind the "F" I entered in the gradebook.

When the last class was over, they came to my office one morning.

"Mrs. Morales, wee want to show our appreciacion for yourr pacience and help." She sounded as if she had memorized the lines the night before. "Yesterday I ovened some pastries."

"Baked," I said.

"Correct; baked some *guayaba* pastries for you and yourr family. Wee learned very mooch in yourr class. Our grades are not so good but wee learned English, and wee learned what young people sink today and many, many sings, Mrs. Morales. Wee are grateful." Antonio assented and handed me the homemade pastries wrapped in wax paper.

"Wee want to ask one last question."

"By all means, Alicia, and please don't say the last, I hope you come back and visit me very often." Both of them smiled.

"Our friend told us dat somesin very useful for a teacher is a en-cy-clo-pe-dia. It is somesin good to have in the home and check a correct date or find out somesin important. Is that correct?"

"Of course! An encyclopedia is something very useful to own, even if you are not a teacher. The information is right there all the time."

"Exactly like ourr friend says. You know, wee want to buy one for ourr daughter which is comin very soon. You know, it is already April so she must be gettin everysin ready now. Wee sent her all the money and everysin wiz an agency and she is goin to need a en-cy-clo-pe-dia. Correct? When she wants to be a teacher again."

"It is a very good idea." I looked at both of them and thought there was something beautiful in their hopeful, wrinkled stares.

We shook hands and they left. Alicia, as usual, walking ahead with her determined attitude, her very clean embroidered old blouse, and Antonio trailing not too close behind with his spotless *guayabera* and shiny laced shoes.

◄►

At the beginning of the fall term it was Jenny who telephoned me one morning and said Antonio had died.

"I heard it over the radio, the Spanish radio station announces such things," she said.

"I know. When did you hear it?"

"Oh, it was last week but I couldn't call you then. You weren't in school and I didn't know your home number. Know what?"

"What is it, Jenny?"

"I'd sure like to go and visit Alicia. Do you know where she lives?"

"She said once that she lived in those government projects on Seventh and Thirteenth. Yes, it must be there."

"Wanna come and look for her?"

"Sure!" I was happy to see the young girl taking an interest.

"Pick you up at lunch time tomorrow?"

"At twelve thirty," I answered.

Alicia opened the door the following afternoon looking the same as always. Her big eyes, less energetic perhaps, were grateful yet silent. She stepped aside; wiping her hands in her apron, she asked us in. It was a very small efficiency apartment with the kitchen and the bedroom separated from the main living area by tall wooden superimposed walls. The tiny coffee table was monopolized by a picture of a young woman—"their daughter," I thought—with lively dark eyes looking far away. In one of the corners of the picture, Alicia secured to the frame an instant shot of Antonio sitting in a rocking chair, wearing a *guayabera*.

There was a map of Cuba hanging from a wall and on top of the sewing machine a statue of Our Lady of Charity, Cuba's patron saint, with lit candles in front of it. By far the most spectacular piece in the room was a very simple bookcase with the complete set of the *Encyclopaedia Britannica*.

"Sit down, pliz. Sank you very mooch for comin, Jenny," she looked at her. "Mrs. Morales," she said facing me, "it is very sad for me, therefore do not say you are sorry. It is all right, Antonio was an old man."

"You are not alone, Alicia. You are an energetic woman. You have a lot to give and you can still help other people," Jenny said.

"You are not alone. Your daughter will be coming soon and she will need you to help her begin. Life is very important you know." Everything I said was unfit and I was concerned.

"Correct. Wee know all about estarting all over. You know when Antonio married me I was a telephone operator and he was a estudent. Wee lived in a esmall room. Oh yes, esmaller dan dis. I helped him become a pharmacist and when he was finished I began estudyin at the University to become a professor. Of history," she didn't look at us, she stared at her lap. "It was a very hard task. He worked and saved penny after penny. I finished when ourr daughter was born. Wee had an apartment at that time. It was in La Víbora. Do you know La Víbora? Nice place. Wee were happy. When my daughter went to eschool, I too worked teachin history of Cuba. Many years pass and den wee had enough money to buy a pharmacy. Antonio was a good man. He was happy with the new pharmacy."

I was wondering why she didn't cry. She stared at her black skirt but not a drop fell.

"Wee were honest people, dat is why wee could not underestand dat the government came and dey took the pharmacy, and two houses wee had bought for, you know, how is it dat you say? gainin money I sink. It was so eslow, when wee woke up one day it was the law dat wee couldn't have nosing. Only ourr careers, ourr titles, degree like you say, Mrs. Morales. Wee were there because ourr daughter, you know, she like the system and she was happy dat the rich was sharin with the poor and . . . Well she was ourr daughter and wee love her very mooch and wee want to be wiz her. Den she left for the country and she saw what she did not like and complained and when the chiefs did not hear her complaints she was a counter-revolutionary. She was put in prision, for fifteen years, in a prision with oders bad womans and little food and all dirty. . . . One friend tol us to come to the Junited States and save all the money we can get to send ourr daughter the passage—she meant the ticket—when she was out of the prision. Ourr daughter said yes, one day when wee saw her. Wee were old, the government did not want us, we lef. Here wee estart, like when wee were young, nosing in our hand, but wee had the age, very important and very bad. You know, Mrs. Morales. I tol you when I was yourr estudent."

"You are really praiseworthy, Alicia, both you and your husband. You still have such energy, desire to become a better person." I wanted to sound convincing because I meant what I said. "Forget the past, forget . . ." I knew I was telling her to forget her whole life and I felt ridiculous. ". . . what you lost. Think ahead, think of how you will help your daughter, you are the only thing she has here. Don't lose your spirit, your vitality."

"You see, it is difficult to be the same. One month ago, a woman prisioner dat was inside with my daughter. She has liberty now, she wrote and she tells us that ourr daughter is no longer alive." Alicia looked at us, put her hand on the encyclopedia and tightened her lips.

Questions for Discussion and Writing

1. What techniques does Zaldívar use to create Mrs. Pérez de Roca and Mr. Roca? What are their dominant characteristics? How do you think and feel about this couple as a result? What clues does the title give you in these considerations?
2. What personal attitudes and values do the characters bring with them? What cultural attitudes might they reflect? On what bases do you yourself interpret what is personal and what is cultural?
3. What personal attitudes does Jenny bring with her to class? What cultural attitudes might she reflect, and why?
4. What has Jenny learned at the end of the story? Why or why not does the story's ending work for you? For what reasons might you assume the writer chose to end it as she did?

YEARN HONG CHOI

Bloomington, Fall 1971

Yearn Hong Choi was a young Korean poet when he came to the United States for advanced study. His poems have been translated into Portuguese and published in Brazil. He continues to write short stories and poetry in both Korean and English. His literary works have been published in many journals and newspapers. "Bloomington, Fall 1971" was published in Short Story International *in 1988.*

In his time off from writing, Dr. Choi is a professor of public administration.

Before you read "Bloomington, Fall 1971," write about a time in your life, if there was one, when you fell in love with the wrong person, at least according to your family's assessment. Describe the situation, the cultural differences involved, and how the relationship was resolved. What have you learned about love, family constraints, and decision-making as a result?

S ummer vacation was almost over. Mr. and Mrs. Shin invited me to dinner at their apartment as they had done from time to time. It was an established custom for the married Korean students to invite single, particularly male, students to dinner at Indiana University. Korean men often didn't know how to cook.

Mr. Shin was a graduate student in music. He had taught at Seoul National University. He was about ten years older than most Korean students.

After dinner he asked me, "Mr. Kim, are you going to marry a Korean girl?"

It was a totally unexpected question. He hadn't asked that kind of question before. It might be reflecting the fact that I liked to date American girls. The question was really two questions in sequence: are you going to marry? If so, are you going to marry a Korean girl, or an American girl?

"Mr. Kim, if you decide to marry, I truly advise you to marry a Korean girl.

I like you; you are a most able young man. You want to enter the field of Korean politics. You can do many good things for our country, many more than for the United States."

I replied with a grin, "If I can find a beautiful girl, yes . . ."

"That is good."

It was a strange response to my words.

"Well, there is good news for you. A very beautiful girl is coming from Korea to attend Indiana University. She is a graduate of Seoul National University. She was one of my best students. She is from a very good family, and I know her parents well. They called me this morning and asked me to find them a future son-in-law. They told me that she will be too old for marriage after she earns her Ph.D. degree. She will be here this Saturday. I will pick you up on the way to the airport."

He was not kidding. Teachers, parents and students form a close triad in Korean society.

I listened to him with some interest and told him, "I don't have a gold ring for her yet, nor money to buy it."

He smiled.

I was poor. I relied on a fifteen-hour-a-week campus job and $150 monthly from my parents. A gold ring for a wedding ceremony was beyond my reach.

"Don't worry! You don't need to worry about money or a gold ring. Her father is a tycoon."

The days were getting shorter, and the twilight after the sunset was as pretty as an oil painting. In the darkness of my apartment, I was reflecting on my long single life, and felt that my single voyage was ending. I was 27, working on my dissertation. Marriage had been far from my thoughts before dinner that evening. In Korea, a decent job was a pre-condition for marriage. A decent job meant a decent income. A gold wedding band was a necessary indicator of a man's condition. He should be able to buy a gold ring or a diamond ring for his bride. Student status was not a proper status for marriage.

Indiana was thousands of miles away from Korea. But I was still a Korean influenced by Korean custom, tradition, and inertia even though I liked American culture and dynamics.

I liked to see young American couples being married in churches or courthouses, without decent jobs or gold wedding rings. Their marriages start as healthy as their bodies. But many of their marriages often break up and end in divorce. Whether they have decent jobs or not, whether they have bought gold rings or not, they often break up and end in divorce. Marriage is not a serious thing to Americans, but is to Koreans.

I had planned to come to the United States since I was in high school. The more I had been attracted to the American lifestyle, the more I had disliked the Korean way of life. I had rejected Korean authoritarianism, formalism and "seriousness." I had protested against college teachers who tried to dominate students with age and gray hair, not knowledge and wisdom. I had rebelled against my father who had tried to teach me the words of Confucius. I had even come to dislike the smallness of Korea's territory, and missed the Manchuan territory of the Koguryo dynasty.

Upon arrival in the United States, however, I discovered the virtue of Korean things. Actually, I was a prisoner of Korea. I missed my college, the narrow streets of Seoul, the tearoom, friends and, of course, my family.

I liked the American lifestyle, but had not acquired it. The distance between me and the United States was still thousands of miles.

Typing my dissertation was the major work in my little nest. But I could not concentrate on typing. One mistake, and two. Three on one page. I gave up typing and went out into the darkness of the summer night, the still, hot and humid Midwestern summer night.

I don't mind the single's life. I couldn't commit myself to one woman among so many beautiful and smart women. I thought I could continue a bachelor's life with dignity. Gold ring, money and status were merely excuses.

Gary Capp's girls had also changed my views of girls, American girls. Gary, my friend, changed girls every night, nearly every night. I called his girls "common market" girls. I had looked long upon girls as "angels." Gary was a carefree man who was concerned about me, the foreign student next door to him. He was kind. He sometimes worked at a construction site as a laborer. When he had enough money for three months' rent and groceries, he stayed in his apartment and played the saxophone all day. Many college girls came to him and slept with him. He sent girls over to me. I did not like such an arrangement, and some girls complained.

"You don't like American girls?"

"I like American girls more than any American boy!"

Jane, an English literature graduate student from Boston, tried to interpret the "common market" girl as unladylike.

"Kim, oh, I know what that means. That means I am not a lady you want to sleep with." She was smart.

Freedom, freedom from sexual restraint, prevailed.

She told me, "Kim, sex is like a meal here in the United States. We should eat."

Saturday afternoon, Mr. Shin picked me up on the way to the airport. It was a fine day. He was somewhat embarrassed by my casual dress. For this occasion, I was supposed to be dressed up. I was deliberately showing my unpreparedness to the girl who was to be landing soon at Bloomington.

"Why don't you dress up?" he said. "We still have enough time."

I insisted, "What I am wearing is O.K."

He was a bit disappointed.

In his car, there were two women. One was Mrs. Shin, and the other was a Korean girl whom I hadn't met before. She was a stranger, an attractive stranger. Sexy, glamorous. Mr. Shin introduced her to me.

"Mr. Kim, this is Miss Kyoung Sook Kim. She arrived here a week ago to attend music school. She is a classmate of Young Sil's."

Young Sil was the girl I was going to greet at the airport.

Kyoung Sook smiled.

In response to her smile, I joked, "The music school will be crowded with Korean girls."

Indiana University is known for its music school. And Korea is known as a nation of musical talent. Koreans are a very virile, passionate and temperamental people, which makes for ideal musicians. Many Korean students come to Indiana.

Young Sil arrived at the small airport on time. It was awkward . . . I didn't know what to say or how to greet her. Silence on that occasion was not very comfortable. I was uneasy all the way to Mr. Shin's apartment.

From our dinner conversation, I learned that Young Sil was the niece of Dr. Chon, a lawyer specializing in international commerce at the Asian Development Bank in Manila. I had met him during my one-year stint in Manila before I came to the United States.

The world is small for Koreans. Korea is a small country. Many times when first meeting, Koreans find they have mutual friends after five minutes' talk. The same town, the same high school, the same college, the same military duty might be found between any two Korean people. If they didn't share the same town, they might have lived in the same province. Province is smaller than country. If they didn't share the same high school, their high schools might have been in neighboring towns.

Young Sil and I became more comfortable when we sipped coffee.

Kyoung Sook politely left right after dinner. I stayed until late at Mr. Shin's apartment.

Registration began the following Monday. Thirty thousand students suddenly flooded the town, a campus town. The field house looked like the Stock Exchange in New York City. It was hell to many foreign students. Long waiting, slow processing. Slow proceeding.

I met Kyoung Sook there. We had the same last name, Kim.

I rescued her and helped her complete the registration process. I remember how I had felt in the same field house three years before. I had been lonely and terribly confused. I couldn't understand the registration instructions; I couldn't speak English very well. I was scared. Helpless.

When we left the field house, Kyoung Sook spoke to me as if she were one of my younger sisters.

"Mr. Kim, you should know what day today is."

"Wednesday."

"No," she said. "It is my birthday."

I smiled at her.

I could not go off and leave her there. It was only noon.

We went to the student union. I had an unexpected luncheon in the Commons at the Memorial Union with a Korean girl. It was my first date with a Korean girl. She expressed her thanks with her eyes.

I was glad to treat her on her birthday, her first birthday in the United States, away from her home and home country.

The university quickly forgot the summer vacation. School was full of young bodies and minds. Vitality and rhythm. I was just one of these 30,000 souls. Other than dissertation writing, I was idle.

The first Friday evening after school opened, I had to meet the new international student senator who would succeed me. Gabriel, from a Latin American country, had asked my advice and suggestions for his leadership of the 1500 foreign students from 80 different nations. I had helped him get elected.

I was about to leave for the meeting with Gabriel when the telephone rang. It was from Kyoung Sook. She asked me to come to her place for dinner.

"Yes, I will be there soon."

It was strange. I was supposed to meet with Gabriel. And, moreover, I had to see Young Sil, not Kyoung Sook. I was not supposed to see Kyoung Sook.

She looked fresh and happy when she opened the door for me. She wore an apron. I discovered the beauty of an apron for the first time. She was shy. She justified this sudden invitation as a return for my treat on her birthday. The justification made me uncomfortable.

I smiled at her. "You don't need to justify any act. You are an opera student, not a political science student, my fair lady!"

We quickly became friends; we were already very close. I held her hand. We shared Bach, Rainer Maria Rilke's poetry, and our lives in Korea and at Indiana University. We discussed the Beatles, hippies, and an underground newspaper. I was a contributor to the underground campus newspaper which had been born during a turbulent time in the late 1960s; it was against the Vietnam War and the Establishment, and was popular and well-circulated to town students, not to the Greek house students.

The underground newspaper printed my poems . . . I didn't know whether a poet could be a good friend to a singer.

She invited me to come see her the following Saturday. We called each other every night. We got together everyday. We shared many events on the university calendar: opera, art, the tavern, strolls in the woods.

I told her, "You are Madame Butterfly."

She told me, "You are Hamlet and Don Quixote."

We laughed. We shared many, many laughs.

She liked my poems and I liked her songs. Her favorite poem was:

To a Violinist

The pain of fingers is not enough.
Agonies from soul.
He assembled himself
by a piano, under a Miro
abstract painting.
He is supported by
the strings and bow.
Space and vacuum
are filled with image.
An hour is translated into
time infinite.
Is he a magician
offering the meaning
to the object(s)?

I spent every evening with her. She was a good cook. I didn't know how to cook. For the previous three years I had only opened cans, or gone to the cafeteria for a cheeseburger. I was tired of canned food and fast food. She seemed happy to cook for me. She told me that she did not like cooking for only herself.

After dinner, we often took a long walk across the meadow. There was a small railroad station at the end of the meadow. We saw an old man working there. The train did not stay very long. We did not see any passengers in or out the station. We did not know where the train went to, where the railroad ended.

We seemed to be perfect lovers in a most romantic and classical background. When we returned from the long walk, we listened to Bach. One night I confessed to her, "I like Bach. I still like Beethoven and Mozart. I also like the Beatles. Maybe I need a religion."

She responded, "You are a fragile man. I want you to go to church with me. Anyway, man is fragile, whereas woman is resilient."

She smiled. I laughed.

Kyoung Sook was dreaming of becoming a prima donna at the New York Metropolitan Opera. I became Rudolfo and she became Mimi. We were going into an opera. Music was a splendid thing.

I wrote a long letter to my mother about Kyoung Sook and my vague plans to marry her. I needed her blessing. Long before, I had determined not to marry any woman without her blessing, if I married. She had sacrificed her life for me, for my schooling here especially. She hadn't bought any nice clothes since I left Korea. My sister wrote me that my family did not buy meat regularly anymore, and mother prayed every night for my health, my studies, and my success in a country far from her. All mothers are great. I claimed that my mother was greater than any other.

Our secret love was no longer a secret in the campus town. We were spotted by many Korean students. Indiana University is a town. We were all there together, whether we liked it or not. We could be easily seen by other Korean students in the cafeteria, library, opera house, and woods. We were sensational news to them, whether we liked it or not. But we didn't mind. They needed a love story for good entertainment in their simple and monotonous foreign student lives. They confined themselves to the university dormitory, library, classroom, and the struggle for good grades for four years or longer. Most Korean students had only one objective—their Ph.D. degree. Most single students, both men and women, did not find each other attractive romantically. They were all stoic scholars.

My mother's letter came. It was a shock! A bomb! She did her best to convince me that Kyoung Sook should not be my bride. Her explanation created darkness and fears for our future. And the future included the present. She wrote me that Kyoung Sook was talented and beautiful, but her family background was not acceptable.

My mother had gone to the Seoul National University of Music and met Kyoung Sook's former professors. She had met her mother who was a hairdresser and her father who was a policeman. She emphasized and reemphasized that her family background would be detrimental to our marriage. She ended her letter by urging that I should set an example to my younger brother and sisters.

Family and the family name were the most important considerations to my parents' generation. Birth and education were the two most important factors in judging a man and a woman in Korean society. The landlord-gentry class produced royal bureaucrats for centuries in the Korean dynasty. Their grandchildren, my father and mother, no longer owned vast tracks of land, but maintained the old pride and honor of the dynastic class system, or more accurately, the caste system. The landlord-gentry class had been replaced by the merchant-entrepreneur class. My parents had lost their land, but culturally and socially remained in the gentry class.

I loved and respected my mother more than anyone in this world. I attributed my luck, my health, and my life in this foreign country to her prayers. She sent me $150 monthly, which was every cent she could afford. She was always gentle and kind. My father was like a stormy sea whereas my mother was the sunshine after a stormy night.

I went to Kyoung Sook's apartment that evening, not for supper. She noticed something was wrong, and asked me to tell her what it was. I could not at first. I asked her out to eat. We drank beer at a tavern with our cheeseburgers. A crowd was there, but the crowd and the tavern's dim light could not change my feelings. Maybe I could not hide myself in the crowd. On the way to her apartment, I said to her, "I received a letter from my mother."

"I know what the letter said about me."

She was very upset.

"What does my family background matter? I am myself," she burst out in anger. "Our relationship is a mistake. I never thought you were that kind of outdated man. I thought you were a modern man."

She cried.

Near her apartment, she stopped crying and said calmly, "I don't want to see you again. I don't love you anymore. I don't know anything anymore. Please leave me alone."

It was near midnight. On the way to my apartment, I knocked on the door of Mr. Shin's apartment. For the first time I felt the need to talk to him about our romance. He and his wife were not surprised by my late night visit. They understood very well my state of mind. They were as kind as they had always been.

"Mr. Kim, marriage is not as simple as you think. Family background is an important factor that you should consider. When you are passionate, you cannot distinguish fire from water. Calm down, and think it all over again."

Mrs. Shin added, "One or two months are very short compared with the rest of your life. You and Kyoung Sook went too fast. We knew it. This town knew it. Marriage is a lifelong commitment. It is not like affairs, affairs are sweet. But marriage is not an affair."

Pain, sorrow, sadness and loneliness invaded me. I tried to defend myself from the invasion. I tried to forget her and to blank out the last two months' relationship. Nothing worked for me. I tried harder to forget her, but my attempts were futile. Every night I dreamed of her. I was running to her. She came to me with her smile. She was already a part of my life. I dialed her number and hung up before the phone rang. I dialed again, again, and hung up again, again, So many times a day.

I wrote a poem:

Untitled

I cannot listen to your songs,
and you cannot read my poems
even though others listen and read
our songs and poems.
A long walk to the railroad station
on a fine evening is beautiful
as is counting the railroad ties beautiful.
Do you still remember how many?
Remembering is not so good
after we leave Bloomington.
I just wonder whether
you know nostalgia is an arrow
not just passing by.
The shadows on the wall,
they are like lovers in
an opera.

My pain soothed at the opera house. We saw each other at a Leontyne Price recital. Of course, we did not arrange that meeting. We happened to see each other.

Outside the opera house, we hesitated. Then we walked by a small stream, across a wooden bridge and down a narrow brick road in the woods where we used to walk. No words were spoken. We couldn't talk. Instead, I squeezed her hand. At last, I spoke to her, trying to control my emotions.

"How are you?"

I did not show any pain. I tried to control my emotions.

She stared at me, her eyes showing tears.

As we left the woods, she spoke.

"Next week, I am going to audition for *Don Giovanni*. Will you come to the audition?"

"Then, next, next week, you will go to the New York Metropolitan Opera?"

"Don't be ridiculous!"

"I mean it. You don't know how to speak English yet, but you are now ready for the university audition."

We continued our walk through the woods, stopping at the Observatory. We used to stop at the Observatory and sit on the benches of the Well House. We were surrounded by Japanese maples, tulip trees, Norway maples, and American beeches.

In the woods, we tried to hide our happiness at our reunion, but we could not completely hide the sadness inside us. We stared at each other as if we were staring at a broken vase we once owned. After the walk we could not say good-bye to each other. I realized that I loved her more than anyone or anything.

I asked myself whether I should consider my mother's advice against her. There was no easy answer. Conflict, pain, the broken vase. No conflict resolution, no pain resolution. Insomnia.

Kyoung Sook was chosen to be Donna Anna in *Don Giovanni*. *The Daily Student* printed the cast of the opera on its front page. I was happy when I saw Kyoung Sook's name in the newspaper. But I could not call her or approach her. Insomnia continued. I would be awake for forty-eight hours, then asleep for two or three hours.

I had a seat in the opera house. I was extremely tired. I could not watch Kyoung Sook's performance. I just stared. I could hear her voice, but as if it were coming from a distant land. I was almost unconscious. I had no bouquet for her.

After the final curtain, I went backstage to congratulate her. I kissed her on her lips. I didn't know whether the kiss was hot or cold. We went out into the darkness of the night again where the crisp air surrounded us. We were crying. Darkness helps a man cry. I said good-bye at her apartment door, and walked the two miles to my own. A long walk. When I entered my apartment, the telephone was ringing. It was Kyoung Sook.

"Please come!"

Her voice was faint and trembling. She could not manage her loneliness, the vast loneliness after her prima donna debut. I went to her.

At the door, we embraced.
"Don't leave me!"
"I will not, Kyoung Sook!"
The next morning, we went to the courthouse to get our marriage license. Kyoung Sook told me, "Diamonds are not useful in our lives now."
It was a fine autumn day.

Questions for Discussion and Writing

1. What Korean cultural assumptions, values, and attitudes does Yearn Hong Choi establish in his essay/story?
2. What American influences play a part in his eventual problems over Kyoung Sook? What become the central conflicts that he must face and make choices about?
3. What has Choi lost and what has he gained in his decision at the end of the story? What decision would you have made in the same situation, and why?
4. At the end of the essay, when Choi and Kyoung Sook are walking in the woods, Choi writes, "We stared at each other as if we were staring at a broken vase we once owned" (p. 327). What do you make of this comparison between the couple and the image of the vase? Does the author use other images in similar ways elsewhere in the story, and if so, how do they work? What does Choi's writing style tell you about him? Use brief passages to support your response.

JAMES R. COREY

Cultural Shock in Reverse

Born in 1937, James R. Corey grew up in a small farming and ranching community in Montana. He received his undergraduate and master's degrees from Montana State University and the University of Montana, both in English, and went on to earn his doctoral degree at Washington State University in American studies.

When Corey left the United States to teach in Saudi Arabia in 1969, he boarded an airplane for the first time. He taught at the University of Petroleum and Minerals in Saudi Arabia until 1977. The late King Faisal had decided in the 1960s against sending young Saudi men to the United States for their education, fearing Western influences on them. Instead, the king organized a university in which professors—Corey among them as part of a two-man humanities team—were imported to teach on the Saudis' turf. In spite of the King's plan, many Saudi students still came to the United States to earn their graduate degrees. When these students returned to Saudi Arabia, sometimes ten years later, Corey witnessed their great difficulty in readjusting to conservative Muslim customs. This experience prompted him to write "Cultural Shock in Reverse" in 1979.

When Corey returned to the United States in 1977, he joined the faculty of the New Mexico Institute of Mining and Technology, where he is a professor of humanities and American literature today. He also directs a program in technical communications for people who want to be trained in writing and editing for computer, engineering, scientific, and environmental companies.

In 1986, Corey returned to the Middle East, this time to Jordan for a year on a Fulbright scholarship at Yarmouk University.

Before you read "Cultural Shock in Reverse," write about a time in your life when returning home (especially after time away at school) was more of an adjustment for you than entering the world you had left home to visit. Explain why this reentry was difficult.

W hen an American university confers a doctoral degree upon a student from an underdeveloped country, it often does so with the expectation that the student will return home and become an instrument of change, of progress in his native land. We educators see the foreign student as a bearer of technological and cultural light from America. We see his future as effecting technological development and putting an end to ignorance, superstition, and other kinds of cultural backwardness.

The student, too, believes in this idea. Anyone who has met and talked with many third-world students knows the zeal with which that dream is held. However, not many American educators have the opportunity to see exactly what becomes of the new Ph.D., to observe what happens to his dream when he tries to realize it at home.

From 1969 to 1977, I taught in a university program in one of the world's most conservative developing countries—Saudi Arabia. I witnessed the return from America of the first significantly large group of Saudi Ph.D.'s. Virtually all of them held the ideal that I described above: to move Saudi Arabia into industrial utopia and out of cultural backwardness.

So far each of these young men has been confronted with the same cruel dilemma: If he wishes to assume a role in the prosperous and challenging area of technological development, he must give up any plans to tamper directly with the cultural life of the country. In other words, he must buy his future wealth and position at the price of wearing blinders to the cultural problems around him. It is a purchase that produces more and more personal tension, frustration, and bitterness as years go by.

The young Saudi Ph.D. returning home after a lengthy stay in the U.S. experiences something akin to reverse cultural shock. At 28 to 30 years of age, he has often spent up to 10 years—a third of his life—in America. When he steps off the plane in Jeddah or Riyadh or Dhahran, he re-enters an environment that is now foreign to him. Though Saudi Arabia has made progress toward modernity during the 10 years of his absence, it is only as an external mark on the landscape. At her cultural heart, she is as restrictive, as narrow, as apparently ignorant as she ever was when he was a youth.

Cultural traditions that he never questioned as a boy growing up in a squatty, brown village now dismay him by their barbarity and irrationality. He is shocked by the backwardness: His mother and sisters still cannot go out in the streets without covering themselves from head to foot in an ugly, black veil, or *abayah*. His sisters have no choice of whom or when they marry. He himself will marry a girl he has probably never spoken to nor seen. Women he knows will die because their men will not allow male doctors to examine and treat them.

Or consider what the young man faces in the business and legal sectors of the culture. The economic machinery of the country is almost without regulations; it is controlled by men's signatures. The question of what is possible in business is not answered by an examination of commercial codes and regulations, as would be the case in a developed country. Rather, the question of what is possible is directly proportional to a man's standing with those who control the economic machinery. Such a situation is ready-made for exploitation by the unscrupulous. In fact, that is precisely what the young returning Saudi sees: a business environment where paying off the men of influence is the accepted mode of operation, and a legal system that is inadequate to cope with the corruption.

In other areas the situation is just as bad. Deaths attributable to engineering incompetence occur daily. A girls' school collapsed recently, killing a score of youngsters. The highway-accident death rate in Saudi Arabia is appalling.

The problems of corruption and incompetence are the most devastating ills of a developing country, but the returning Ph.D. is almost powerless to do anything about them. He is paralyzed by time-honored cultural patterns. For example, direct criticism is culturally taboo, unless the criticizing is done by the "right" sort of person—but even then the critic may be as likely to suffer cultural ostracism as is the one criticized. A young Saudi who has been tainted by exposure to a foreign culture does not dare to criticize.

To be bothered by payoffs and influence-peddling is to be an exception in the culture. I recall, for example, trying to explain to a group of Saudi students why Vice-President Spiro Agnew was forced out of office. When I explained that Agnew, while governor of Maryland, was alleged to have accepted influence money from various contractors doing business with the state, my audience was unable to comprehend the offense. As one student put it, Why should a man want to be a governor except to use his position for personal financial gain?

As for criticism of incompetence, the critic will constantly confront the argument that the school collapsed or the car accident occurred because it was God's will that it should happen. Death, so the argument goes, is not something attributable to the engineer's or the builder's incompetence; death is the carrying out of God's plan.

Faced with those and similar cultural circumstances, the young idealist has few options. He can throw himself enthusiastically into a money-making area of the country's development, but to do so he must don a mask of cultural conservatism for the sake of the society around him. The mask will include wearing the correct national dress and disdaining foreign clothing styles, trimming his hair and moustache to the proper length and shape, marrying a local girl, speaking Arabic in public, and paying full lip service to the national religion.

But behind the mask he will live a quite different life. Within his own home, he will surround himself with the people and objects of his American life. His friends will be young and either foreigners or foreign-educated Arabs. He will speak English, his second language, almost as frequently as he will his native tongue. He will indulge his tastes for American food, drink, music, and reading material. Most importantly, he will escape from his own culture as often as possible. In fact, he will take as many business and vacation trips to the U.S. as he can possibly arrange.

This dual existence will not be without its adverse effects. I have often observed its results. It produces a tension which for some individuals is intolerable. Many cease to be able to perform productive work because their creative energies become paralyzed. Others discard whatever ideals they once had and become hedonists or alcoholics. A few live in self-imposed exile in the U.S. or elsewhere, waiting for a time when cultural changes will bring the country's technological and cultural advances abreast of each other.

But for most, the mask quickly becomes the true face of the man. Unable to cope for long with the tension of a dual existence, incapable of sustaining a "foreign" identity in his native land, the young Ph.D. simply reaccepts the culture. He allows himself to become an influence peddler and an incompetent. And when the next wave of young idealists arrives, they will find the first group standing in the way of their plan for social reform.

Saudi Arabia is, I am sure, not unique among the developing wealthy nations of the world. The same conditions apply throughout the Arabian peninsula—in Kuwait, Abu Dhabi, Dubai, Qatar, and the emirates of southern Arabia. They also exist in other emerging oil-rich countries—Libya, Algeria, Nigeria, and Iran, for example. It is those countries that are sending increasing numbers of graduate students to the U.S. Thus it may be possible for something to be done in the American universities to prepare these students to cope more effectively with reverse cultural shock.

I can suggest at least three steps.

First, foreign graduate students should not be encouraged to stay on in the U.S. for extended periods. They should return to their home countries for summer vacations at four-year intervals, at a minimum. Two-year intervals would be even better, given the rapid pace of industrial change in their home countries. Currently, it is common for foreign students to spend eight or ten or even more years in the U.S., taking courses the year round. Many universities even urge this pattern on the students, in an effort to help them overcome language problems and course deficiencies from their previous educational backgrounds.

Such students are the ones who experience the profoundest shock upon returning home. Certainly, the present level of airline service around the world should make it easy for nearly all of them to go home for the summer every few years and see their country's culture first-hand.

Second, professors themselves could do more to help such students cope with their frustrating futures. Too often graduate courses are offered in such a way as to imply that their content has no relevance to particular cultural, geographical, political, or economic contexts. Subjects are presented as though they are to be practiced in an ideal world, uninfluenced by outside factors. Fields like money and banking or highway design or public health—or a hundred others—do not respond to absolute laws, although they are often taught as if they do.

In fact, the usefulness of such courses to the student is directly proportional to the student's understanding of how *relative* their content is. The foreign student needs to be encouraged to go beyond the American applications of his subjects. He needs to think about money and banking under conditions where all banking interest is considered usury, about highway engineering where drifting sand and wandering camels are the main menaces to moving traffic, about public health where camel's urine is still believed to be the only disinfectant that really works. The student needs to be encouraged to see his courses in the context of his native environment, not just in terms of American applications.

Finally, the foreign student needs to realize that American solutions to political problems like corruption and incompetence will not necessarily work when he gets home. I know several students who have spent a few years in jail because they apparently forgot that they left American-style freedom behind when they flew east from Kennedy Airport.

Reverse cultural shock is a real problem for many foreign students. It is time for American universities to undertake measures to counteract its effects. Any diminishing of the effects of reverse cultural shock will, in the end, benefit all the parties involved.

Questions for Discussion and Writing

1. Explain the line of argument Corey develops in this essay: What are the problems he addresses, the causes of those problems, and the conclusions he reaches about their possible solutions?
2. What cultural differences between the United States and Saudi Arabia do Saudi students encounter when they return to their country, and what do they have to do with the students' goals and even dreams?
3. What problems do the students encounter as a result of what Corey calls a "dual existence" upon returning home? Explain in your own words what the author means when he writes, "But for most, the mask quickly becomes the true face of the man" (p. 332).
4. If there are students in your class who have had experiences similar to those Corey describes, ask them for their own analyses of reverse culture shock.

WILLIAM E. BARRETT

Señor Payroll

William E. Barrett's career began in 1923 at Westinghouse, where he served as advertising manager for six years. He turned to free-lance writing after that, becoming a prolific writer whose books often address the issues of social justice. His best-known novels, The Left Hand of God *(1951, reprinted 1976) and* The Lilies of the Field *(1962), were both made into popular films.*

Barrett's stories typically have happy endings. Of this pattern The New York Times *quotes him as saying: "I believe that life produces more happy endings than unhappy endings. . . . Happiness is always cheated in the census because people count their miseries carefully . . . , accepting their blessings without thought."*

Barrett died in September 1986, in Denver, Colorado, where he had spent the greater part of his eighty-six years. Following his duty with the American Air Force in 1942, he became an amateur pilot and a consultant in aerospace for the Denver Public Library. His life reflects the diverse corners and commitments into which a writer can also reach, given enough time.

In "Señor Payroll," published in 1943 in Southwestern Review, *Barrett makes a good case for the need of managers to learn about the cultural expectations, habits, and attitudes of the people who work for them.*

Before you read "Señor Payroll," write about a time when your manager or boss failed to gain the input of employees when attempting to solve some problem at the workplace. Describe how you and your co-workers tried to outwit or at least ignore the company's rules and with what results. How might the problem have been solved in another, more direct way and to everyone's satisfaction?

L arry and I were Junior Engineers in the gas plant, which means that we were clerks. Anything that could be classified as paper work came to the flat double desk across which we faced each other. The Main Office downtown sent us a bewildering array of orders and rules that were to be put into effect.

Junior Engineers were beneath the notice of everyone except the Mexican laborers at the plant. To them we were the visible form of a distant, unknowable paymaster. We were Señor Payroll.

Those Mexicans were great workmen; the aristocrats among them were the stokers, big men who worked Herculean eight-hour shifts in the fierce heat of the retorts. They scooped coal with huge shovels and hurled it with uncanny aim at tiny doors. The coal streamed out from the shovels like black water from a high-pressure nozzle, and never missed the narrow opening. The stokers worked stripped to the waist, and there was pride and dignity in them. Few men could do such work, and they were the few.

The Company paid its men only twice a month, on the fifth and on the twentieth. To a Mexican, this was absurd. What man with money will make it last fifteen days? If he hoarded money beyond the spending of three days, he was a miser—and when, Señor, did the blood of Spain flow in the veins of misers? Hence, it was the custom for our stokers to appear every third or fourth day to draw the money due to them.

There was a certain elasticity in the Company rules, and Larry and I sent the necessary forms to the Main Office and received an "advance" against a man's pay check. Then, one day, Downtown favored us with a memorandum:

"There have been too many abuses of the advance-against-wages privilege. Hereafter, no advance against wages will be made to any employee except in a case of genuine emergency."

We had no sooner posted the notice when in came stoker Juan Garcia. He asked for an advance. I pointed to the notice. He spelled is through slowly, then said, "What does this mean, this 'genuine emergency'?"

I explained to him patiently that the Company was kind and sympathetic, but that it was a great nuisance to have to pay wages every few days. If someone was ill or if money was urgently needed for some other good reason, then the Company would make an exception to the rule.

Juan Garcia turned his hat over and over slowly in his big hands. "I do not get my money?"

"Next payday, Juan. On the twentieth."

He went out silently and I felt a little ashamed of myself. I looked across the desk at Larry. He avoided my eyes.

In the next hour two other stokers came in, looked at the notice, had it explained and walked solemnly out; then no more came. What we did not know was that Juan Garcia, Pete Mendoza, and Francisco Gonzalez had spread the word, and that every Mexican in the plant was explaining the order to every other

Mexican. "To get money now, the wife must be sick. There must be medicine for the baby."

The next morning Juan Garcia's wife was practically dying, Pete Mendoza's mother would hardly last the day, there was a veritable epidemic among children, and, just for variety, there was one sick father. We always suspected that the old man was really sick; no Mexican would otherwise have thought of him. At any rate, nobody paid Larry and me to examine private lives; we made out our forms with an added line describing the "genuine emergency." Our people got paid.

That went on for a week. Then came a new order, curt and to the point: "Hereafter, employees will be paid ONLY on the fifth and the twentieth of the month. No exceptions will be made except in the cases of employees leaving the service of the Company."

The notice went up on the board, and we explained its significance gravely. "No, Juan Garcia, we cannot advance your wages. It is too bad about your wife and your cousins and your aunts, but there is a new rule."

Juan Garcia went out and thought it over. He thought out loud with Mendoza and Gonzales and Ayala, then, in the morning, he was back. "I am quitting this company for different job. You pay me now?"

We argued that it was a good company and that it loved its employees like children, but in the end we paid off, because Juan Garcia quit. And so did Gonzalez, Mendoza, Obregon, Ayala and Ortez, the best stokers, men who could not be replaced.

Larry and I looked at each other; we knew what was coming in about three days. One of our duties was to sit on the hiring line early each morning, engaging transient workers for the handy gangs. Any man was accepted who could walk up and ask for a job without falling down. Never before had we been called upon to hire such skilled virtuosos as stokers for handy-gang work, but we were called upon to hire them now.

The day foreman was wringing his hands and asking the Almighty if he was personally supposed to shovel this condemned coal, while there in a stolid, patient line were skilled men—Garcia, Mendoza, and others—waiting to be hired. We hired them, of course. There was nothing else to do.

Every day we had a line of resigning stokers, and another line of stokers seeking work. Our paper work became very complicated. At the Main Office they were jumping up and down. The procession of forms showing Juan Garcia's resigning and being hired over and over again was too much for them. Sometimes Downtown had Garcia on the payroll twice at the same time when someone down there was slow in entering a resignation. Our phone rang early and often.

Tolerantly and patiently we explained: "There's nothing we can do if a man wants to quit, and if there are stokers available when the plant needs stokers, we hire them."

Out of chaos, Downtown issued another order. I read it and whistled. Larry looked at it and said, "It is going to be very quiet around here."

The order read: "Hereafter, no employee who resigns may be rehired within a period of 30 days."

Juan Garcia was due for another resignation, and when he came in we showed him the order and explained that standing in line the next day would do him no good if he resigned today. "Thirty days is a long time, Juan."

It was a grave matter and he took time to reflect on it. So did Gonzalez, Mendoza, Ayala and Ortez. Ultimately, however, they were all back—and all resigned.

We did our best to dissuade them and we were sad about the parting. This time it was for keeps and they shook hands with us solemnly. It was very nice knowing us. Larry and I looked at each other when they were gone and we both knew that neither of us had been pulling for Downtown to win this duel. It was a blue day.

In the morning, however, they were all back in line. With the utmost gravity, Juan Garcia informed me that he was a stoker looking for a job.

"No dice, Juan," I said. "Come back in thirty days. I warned you."

His eyes looked straight into mine without a flicker. "There is some mistake, Señor," he said. "I am Manuel Hernandez. I work as the stoker in Pueblo, in Santa Fe, in many places."

I stared back at him, remembering the sick wife and the babies without medicine, the mother-in-law in the hospital, the many resignations and the rehirings. I knew that there was a gas plant in Pueblo, and that there wasn't any in Santa Fe; but who was I to argue with a man about his own name? A stoker is a stoker.

So I hired him. I hired Gonzalez, too, who swore that his name was Carrera, and Ayala, who had shamelessly become Smith.

Three days later the resigning started.

Within a week our payroll read like a history of Latin America. Everyone was on it: Lopez and Obregon, Villa, Diaz, Batista, Gomez, and even San Martín and Bolívar. Finally Larry and I, growing weary of staring at familiar faces and writing unfamiliar names, went to the Superintendent and told him the whole story. He tried not to grin, and said, "Damned nonsense!"

The next day the orders were taken down. We called our most prominent stokers into the office and pointed to the board. No rules any more.

"The next time we hire you hombres," Larry said grimly, "come in under the names you like best, because that's the way you are going to stay on the books."

They looked at us and they looked at the board; then for the first time in the long duel, their teeth flashed white. "Si, Señores," they said.

And so it was.

Questions for Discussion and Writing

1. Larry and the narrator, whose name we never know, work for a gas plant. What do we learn about the attitudes and policies of the company, both directly and indirectly, from the things the narrator tells us?

2. What were the company's policies of paying its laborers? What cultural assumptions are involved in these policies, and why?
3. What cultural assumptions did the laborers have regarding their pay, and why?
4. What changes in understanding would it have taken on the company's part to have avoided the intercultural problems it encountered with its laborers? What changes would it have taken on the laborers' part?
5. Why were the employees able to outwit the company? Why or why not do you find Barrett's story funny? Which group—the employees or the company managers—carries the greater responsibility to change, and why?

LAWRENCE STESSIN

Culture Shock and the American Businessman Overseas

The authority and experience on which Lawrence Stessin draws in the following essay spans a long, professional life in a variety of disciplines. For seven years (1934–1941) he was a writer for The New York Times; *he was also an editor for ten years at Row Features in New York, a company he then owned for six years (1951–1957). In 1958, Stessin became a professor of management at Hofstra University in Hempstead, New York, where he is now professor emeritus. He has also worked for the U.S. State Department's International Cooperation executive development program as mission chief in the Middle East (1956–1959).*

Stessin's published works include numerous magazine articles and books, including The Practice of Personnel and Industrial Relations: A Casebook *(1964) and* The Disloyal Employee *(1967).*

"Culture Shock and the American Businessman Overseas" reflects the experience and expertise of the author's multifaceted career. It first appeared in Exchange Magazine *(1973), a publication from International Educational and Cultural Exchange, and later in a collection of essays entitled* Toward Internationalism *(1979).*

A note to readers: Stessin wrote about the American "businessman" at the time he wrote this article in 1973. Today he would most likely include the American businesswoman as well—an example through language of the ways in which cultural assumptions evolve and change.

Before you read "Culture Shock and the American Businessman Overseas," write about the patterns of values and attitudes that you think shape American business practices. Imagine yourself as a businessperson—what primary policies would you have for your company, and from what influences in your life have you gained them?

T he American businessman overseas often operates under demanding conditions. He suffers the hardship of giving up cold martinis for warm beer as one way to integrate into the English business community. He must keep his mind on business during the rounds of Geisha houses as a prelude to concluding a deal in Japan. And if he operates in Spain, he must brace himself for the rigors of 11 P.M. dinners and negotiations that continue into the small hours.

In an age of hangups, the American entrepreneur venturing into overseas lands soon discovers his. It is what the anthropologists call the "culture shock,"[1] a series of jolts that await even the wariest American when he encounters the wide variety of customs, value systems, attitudes, and work habits which make it difficult for him to move comfortably in a foreign commercial environment.

Some adjust and survive; others retreat to the familiar atmosphere of a service club in Hometown, U.S.A.

The Culture Gap

American companies spend millions to immunize their about-to-go-overseas personnel against culture shock. In some companies,[2] executives pegged for foreign assignments are put through cross-cultural operations courses. Almost every graduate business school with a curriculum in international trade includes "Comparative Business Cultures" in its teaching and research disciplines. Donald Stone, former dean of the University of Pittsburgh's Graduate School of Public and International Affairs, remembers an experience he had which illustrates how subtle and intimately subversive the culture gap can be:

> In the Middle East, I was once with an American oil refinery which had installed an American-type canteen. The employees were shown how to queue up, extend their trays to the help behind the counters and have them fill their cups and plates with nourishing food. The management were perplexed when only a few workers responded. A visiting sociologist discovered the reason. The holding of a cup and a plate in outstretched manner was viewed by the natives as a symptom of begging. The management rearranged the serving line so that the food could be dispensed while the tray rested on a railing. Only then did the employees take advantage of the free lunches offered by the employer.

The executive assigned to ply his trade overseas must face an abrasive adjustment to what seems to him to be an exaggerated sensitivity of foreigners to certain forms of American etiquette. The practice of shaking hands to establish a cordial relationship with a stranger is part of the Western cultural repertory. It is a sign of warmth and friendship. Yet in India he meets a businessman who either won't shake hands or gives him a limp welcome that Americans associate with femininity.[3]

The stereotype of the American—hail fellow, well-met, cordial, friendly, outgoing, and gregarious—does not mesh with the discomfort he feels and often shows in his contacts with Latin Americans and Middle Easterners. There, people crowd close to him to talk, and in Latin America his host is likely to greet him with a warm abrazo, suggesting unfamiliar intimacy. Anyone who has ever attended a party or a reception in Latin America must surely have observed the self-consciousness of the uninitiated stateside visitor, who keeps backing away from his native host to whom it is natural to carry on a conversation separated by inches. Last year at a businessmen's club in Brazil, where many receptions are held for newly arrived U.S. executives, the railings on the terrace had to be reinforced because so many American businessmen fell into the garden as they backed away.

Differing Religious Customs

Culturally, the criterion for success in overseas assignments is the ability of the executive to dilute his American outlook and view alien ways as not being bad, but just different. In particular, religious beliefs and rituals and how they totally embrace the workaday lives of many peoples of the world create unforeseen problems for American management abroad. A U.S. company setting up a facility in the Arab countries must plan its productivity objectives in the face of over 20 religious holidays a year. [3] In Western countries religion and work are segregated, and to ask an employee to come in on a Sunday does not carry with it the same sacrilege it does when a Mohammedan or a Hindu is requested to put in work-time on one of his holy days.

In Germany one motor company faced a sticky religious situation when, a few years ago, it decided to import some 2000 Turkish workers to ease the firm's serious manpower shortages. It's been the experience of American companies that Turkish men make good factory employees. They train easily, take instructions well, and love to punch a time clock—this being a symbol of having outgrown the condition of peasantry from which most of them have been recruited. As everyone knows, the efficient production of an automobile depends on the continuity of the assembly line. A minute's stoppage is counted in many dollars lost. When the Turkish workers were put to the task of manning several hundred positions along a moving belt, the line began to go awry with stop-watch regularity—three times a day. Cars came off in disassemblement that would cross the eyes of a Ralph Nader. What happened? Came prayer time, the more devout Turkish employees forsook whatever it was they were doing, faced east, and gave a five-minute homage to Allah. And no amount of pleading from management could stay them from their appointed periods of devotion.

Here was a problem to be solved and the company solved it. It rescheduled the work of its religiously dedicated Turkish employees so that each man could take a "prayer break." He was allowed to leave his post and go to specially built prayer rooms with interiors simulating Turkish mosques. During the prayer breaks, relief squads of Italians and Germans filled in. The added manpower cost was minimal. Turkish employees willingly sacrificed the Western-oriented coffee break and lunch hour—it being proper for them to squeeze in a snack while giving thanks to their God.

An Oft-repeated Story

Every calling has its "hot stove league" where buffs meet and exchange experiences. One does not delve long into the life and times of the American businessman overseas without running into the story of the dislocated latrines.

It happened in a village which, until three years ago, was a journey into the unchangeable. Here a man lived and died in a hovel of mud, rocks, bone-dry timber, and rice straw under a cluster of poplar trees stripped bare by ravenous locusts. The village square was laid in uneven cobblestones and pockmarked by treacherous cesspools. Women wrapped their newborn infants in newspapers, and running water meant a canal flowing through the public streets—the gully reserved for drinking, washing, ablutions, and even worse. The industrial community—to use a gratuitous phrase—was a prison-like compound of crumbling shanties where a few rugs and some crude pottery were produced for the sidewalk market in the hope that some adventurous tourist would stumble by—and buy.

But apparently the village was not destined for an eternity of the mud and the crud of a feudal economy. American geologists, scratching the sun-dried earth, discovered a rich vein of copper deposits. Within a year the village was on its way to becoming a bubbling oasis. A consortium of American companies set up operations. Peasants from 50 nearby villages were recruited, hired, and trained, but the principal drawback to urbanization was a slow-moving government which tied up the installation of a transportation system to take workers to and from work. Many of the employees trod 8 to 10 miles to get to their jobs. The American companies took the initiative and planned a series of modest homes where the employees and their families could live near the mining sites without the hardship of crude commuting by foot and mule.

Back in America, bids were solicited from construction companies. In a short time plans were drawn and approved, and construction was started for 300 homes with architects and builders flown in for the project from the United States. The dwellings were built of concrete, and inside each one there was a kitchen, a bathroom, running water, and lights that turned on at the flick of a switch. When the compound was finished, the project was dedicated with elaborate ceremonies. American executives and local officials who came from a town a hundred miles away hailed the new homes as another forward step in the industrialization of the country. The country's leader, who had vowed to his people and to Allah that he would devote his life to modernizing his lands, sent his blessing. The workers were given a tour of the housing units and then asked to select the apartments they preferred. None applied. It was obvious that something about the houses bruised local sensibilities. It turned out that the latrines faced the wrong way. People had their backs facing east—Mecca—a sinful position for a good Moslem. The toilets were torn out and turned around.

Among the managerial imperatives of the big American companies establishing business bases overseas is to train and develop the nationals of the country to manage the enterprises. There are over 250,000 such foreign managers working for American firms,[4] and it's standard policy for many companies to bring some of these people to the United States for periods of orientation in modern management. Those selected for such training obviously relish the opportunity to observe and learn American skills from the "horse's mouth." Sometimes the foreign manager returns overly converted to the American way—like the English marketing man who came back to London after six months with his U.S. counterparts in the headquarters offices. He spouted the American jargon. He invited customers to his home and committed the social "gaff" of talking business at dinner. His "Americanization" annoyed his colleagues. One day when he came into his office, there on his desk was a sign: "YANKEE GO HOME!"

Manager Learns New Skills

There are cases where the cultural differences between Americans and foreigners are so marked that no amount of indoctrination will rub off on the native manager. Recently when I was in Tangiers, I was invited to tour one American company's plant by its local manager. He was most intelligent, urbane, and proud of his association with one of the elite in multicountry manufacturing. He had lived all his life in Morocco and was educated in its schools. He began his business career as a supervisor in a nearby factory and had been recruited to head up the company's Middle Eastern subsidiary. He talked most enthusiastically about his recent visit to the United States, where he was put through an intensive training course in the "5 M's" of management—how to handle Men, Money, Methods, Machinery, and Motivation. When the course was finished, he was asked if there was anything else in the way of training and development he felt he needed.

"I told them yes—all my life I had the desire to go to the Harvard School of Business. When I told this to the vice president, he granted my wish."

He left for Cambridge and was enrolled in the six-week "Advanced Management Development" course, which is the worldwide model of business training. As he was recounting his experience at Harvard, name-dropping the jargon of the managerial trade—"human relations," "the decision tree," "management by objectives," "the art of delegation"—I noticed a worker off in the distance reading a newspaper and leaving his machine unattended. This is a serious violation of company rules in any country, and I wondered what managerial skills this man would use to handle this situation. He was indeed up to the task. He stopped, caught the eye of a foreman nearby, and beckoned him to act. The supervisor tiptoed over and gave the employee a swift kick in the pants. The man jumped, dropped his paper, and unprotestingly took his position at the machine. My host nodded, pleased.

Don't Bring Chrysanthemums!

The traumas that emerge from even the small deviations from conventional norms are quite likely to sound as if the American had wandered through the looking glass. Here's what some Americans had to say:

A banker: "The head of a company here does business in a strange way. Draw up a contract and he signs it right away. He reads the small print later at his convenience. He expects you to do the same."

A construction foreman: "How can you train these people? Tell a carpenter to cut a piece of wood and he *pulls* the saw. Now everybody knows that the only *right* way to cut a board is to *push* the saw."

A plant manager: "Now I've heard everything! I offered my assistant a raise and he turned it down. He said he would rather be allowed to come in a half-hour later every morning. It would give him more status."

A company president: "When you do business here, the chances are you will be invited for dinner to the businessman's house, which means that the deal has gone through. Be sure to bring flowers to the hostess. But for goodness sake, be careful what you bring. Not roses, because these are the flowers that a lover brings to his sweetheart. And not chrysanthemums—they're for funerals."

So I asked, "Is this what they taught you at the Harvard Business School?" "Oh, yes," he replied, surprised at my question. "I used to kick the men myself, but since I went to Harvard, I now *delegate* the task to my foreman."

The Impatient American

The trait that blurs the American image overseas is the impatience of the U.S. businessman. From Mark Twain's *Innocents Abroad* to *The Ugly American,* this equation has caused cultural trouble for the Yankee trader. His compulsion for action was caricatured by a commercial attaché who said: "Tell the American businessman in a hurry that Rome wasn't built in a day and he'll reply, 'That's because they didn't have an American foreman on the job.' " A European hunter who has led many Americans on safaris embellished this portrait with the remark, "The American is a fast, bang-bang-bang person. He expects to see and shoot the rarest gazelle in Africa within the first half-hour."

If in Europe the pace of business dealing seems maddeningly slow to the stateside businessman, in Japan it is excruciatingly stagnant. "It's the transition from the rat race to the turtle race," remarked one American businessman who finally made it by slowing down. It's an "in" joke among the Japanese that if Americans are kept waiting long enough, they will agree to do anything.

What's more, in Japan it is not unusual in the middle of a deal to have sudden periods of silence, sometimes lasting more than half an hour. To an American, brought up on a business culture of "the pitch and the sell," the lack of verbal communication can be unsettling indeed.

Differing Concepts of Time

Much of the rhythm of international trade is generated by the social circuit, and the American businessman is known the world over as a gracious, outgoing host. His wife, as hostess, is more the anxious type, for she must plan dinners without knowing who is going to show up when—if at all. If an American executive sets dinner for eight o'clock, his U.S. colleagues will arrive between five and fifteen minutes after the hour. They will find that the Norwegian guest is already there—most likely having ingratiated himself with his hostess by bringing her a small gift. The Latin American visitor will knock at about nine—apologizing for having arrived too early. An Ethiopian businessman might enter at about eleven, too polite to ask why everyone is already sipping after-dinner cordials. A Japanese, though he has accepted the invitation to avoid losing face by refusing, may not come at all.

Business appointments can be equally uncertain. Edward Hall, the anthropologist, calls "time" part of the "silent language."[5]

> Everywhere in the world, people use time to communicate with each other. In the United States, giving a person a deadline is a way of indicating the degree of urgency or relative importance of the work. But in the Middle East and in Latin America and Japan, the American runs into a cultural trap the minute he opens his mouth. "Mr. Azuz will have to make up his mind in a hurry because my board of directors meets next week and I have to have an answer by then" is overly demanding and is exerting undue pressure. "I'm going to Damascus tomorrow morning and I'll have to have my car tonight" is a sure way to get a mechanic to stop working, because to give another person a deadline in many parts of the world is to be rude, pushy and demanding.

An American suggesting a noon appointment with an Argentine businessman will often hear in response, "La hora latina? O la hora norteamericana?"—our time or your time?

Status Symbols

In America, a man's office is a symbol of where he is and where he is going on the corporate ladder. His rug on the floor, his name on the door, whether it is private or shared—the office is a cultural index of his position in the pecking order. When assigned overseas, his status syndromes on this point begin to show. He frets at the fact that in France a high officer occupies a space half the size of a U.S. executive. But more disquieting is that the French manager is sharing his office with half-a-dozen assistants—the only sign of his authority being that his desk is in the middle of the room. Negotiations are conducted to a cacophony of noise, interruptions, and traffic. It's simply that the place where a man conducts his daily business affairs is not considered an important image-builder in the commercial mores of many countries.

But not in Germany. The compulsion for orderliness and formality is an ingredient of the German culture, and their offices reflect these national characteristics. For one thing, the Germans take their office doors very seriously. They are heavy, solid, soundproof. A German executive assigned to an office will, even before he inspects the interior, test the click of the latch just as Americans kick a tire or slam the door of a car to listen for a tinny rebound. American companies which have opened branch offices or subsidiaries in Germany have had to act as arbiters of clashes between U.S. executives and German managers over the issue of the "closed door vs. the open door." Americans keep their doors open; German[s], solidly shut. A whole generation of American businessmen has grown up in a tradition that the "open door" is a democratic virtue. To Germans, open doors are sloppy and disorderly and reflect an unbusinesslike air, where, to the Americans, the closed door conveys a conspiratorial atmosphere.

Chairs also create a culture chasm between Americans and German businessmen. Here the phrase "pull up a chair" is an invitation to informality. Among Germans, it is a violation of mores to change the distance between a chair and a desk. It is said that the great architect, Ludwig Mies van der Rohe, so rebelled against the American habit of moving chairs closer for conversation that he had his visitor's chair bolted to the floor and enjoyed watching the rupturous gymnastics of his American friends when they encountered the immovable seat. [5]

Employee Relations

The American executive runs into sweeping unorthodoxy (by U.S. standards) in employee and labor relations. It would not appear so at first. Men on an assembly line turn a bolt, weld a fender, inflate a tire in the same stance the world over. There is not a European or Asian way to run an American-made bulldozer or tractor. Textile production is so automated that workers are little more than standbys, and the ennui of policing the warps and woofs by sitting in a chair or pacing up and down an aisle equally afflicts those in developed and underdeveloped countries.

But surface standardization is deceiving. The newly assigned manager of a plant in Barcelona will soon discover that workers air their grievances in eerie fashion. When employees are unhappy over a managerial policy or decision, they gather in the courtyard of the plant and stare in silence into the window of the managing director.

"This silent treatment is right out of the Spanish Inquisition," an executive complained. "They just stand there and stare and stare for hours—or days. When you enter and leave the plant, you have a thousand eyes following you—and not a single word. It's damn effective, too. When a dispute comes up, I settle it right away even though I know that if I waited, I could negotiate a better deal."

In France and Italy, where many unions are Communist-dominated, the American manager is likely to find a red flag implanted in the center of the bargaining table, and he negotiates with a hammer and sickle fluttering in his face. The union's demands must sound strange indeed to a Detroit-trained manager brought up in the pragmatism of a Walter Reuther where the issues can be equated easily in terms of money.[6]

"Money is the least of our problems when we deal with French unions," an American vice president in Paris reflected. "On these demands we settle quickly. But tell me—what is a company supposed to do about ending the Viet-Nam war, breaking up the military industrial complex in the United States, or firing Mayor Daly?"

The Tea Break

If the American in Paris thinks he has labor problems, he hasn't heard about the U.S.-owned company in England which was forced out of business because it tampered with the tea break. Back in 1965 a North Carolina company got the entrepreneurial bug to go international and bought up—at a bargain—a 150-year-old textile machinery company near Birmingham. Its hopes were to modernize the decrepit piece of property and to use its output as a springboard into the foreign market. The plant was made operational in 18 months, but efficiency lagged. What bothered and bewildered the management was the mountain of work rules that plague all of English industry.

"All that endless talk over whether a machinist can lift an oil can to lubricate a part or wait for a maintenance man to come around in his own sweet time to do it," lamented one of the production superintendents sent over by the States to "do something."

All the nitty-gritty stuff was gradually solved until one day the production head decided to "do something" about the big problem that was hampering output—the tea break. Among English workers this custom is a precious institution, and the American boss, a veteran of culture shocks on other assignments, approached the issue with due caution. In England tea breaks can take a half-hour per man, as each worker brews his own leaves to his particular taste and sips out of a large, pint-sized vessel with the indulgence of a wine-taster.

The rate of sipping is not constant, so that coordinated production does not return to its full rhythm until the slowest sipper has shuffled back to his job. The first meeting called by the management suggested to the union that perhaps it could use its good offices to speed up the "sipping time" to ten minutes a break. This is pretty much in line with the coffee-break time in America. The union agreed to try, but failed. Several employees were disciplined for overextending their tea breaks. They received one- or two-day suspensions, but after each decision, a wildcat strike ensued until the men were given back pay for their enforced layoffs. Then one Monday morning, the workers rioted. Windows were broken, epithets greeted the executives as they entered the plant and police had to be called to restore order. It seems the company went ahead and installed a tea-vending machine—just put a paper cup under a spigot and out pours a standard brew. The pint-sized container was replaced by a five-ounce cup imprinted—as they are in America—with morale-building messages imploring greater dedication to the job and loyalty to the company.

"Looking back, I could shoot myself for approving such an installation," the company president said.

The plant never did get back into production. Even after the tea-brewing machine was hauled out, workers boycotted the company and it finally closed down.

Recruiting Problems

The problem of staffing—recruiting and selecting local personnel for the middle and the top of the hierarchy—is a walking-on-eggs experience for American businessmen. In almost every country he must be overly careful to skirt what foreigners consider to be the abrasive approaches of American hiring practices. Advertising for help—though coming into its own in some countries—draws only the dregs in the manpower market in other parts of the world. Job-changing is a culturally accepted road to promotion in America, and every management hopeful has a roving eye and a cocked ear for new opportunities. In Europe, this manner of career development is viewed as disloyal and unethical.[7] A special contempt is reserved for the American practice of submitting applicants to the intimacies of the personality test or the "depth interview"—a form of psychic undress which is criticized as an American vulgarism. One Englishman walked out on an interview when an American recruiter asked the seemingly harmless question, "What clubs do you belong to?" "None of your bloody business," was the indignant reply. The American practice of interviewing wives of prospective employees to determine whether they fit into the organization arouses the harshest reactions among foreigners. One marketing vice president, in considering an Italian for a sales manager's job, said: "I think you will do well in our organization, but before I make a final decision, I would like to see your wife." The man flushed angrily, stood up and rendered the American a salivary shower he didn't quickly forget.

When an American company ventures into Japan, the recruitment problem is doubly complex. A job is a commitment for life—to both the employee and the employer. Layoffs are unknown, discharges are rare, and job-hopping an occupational aberration.

All of these culture patterns faced one company when it decided to staff a subsidiary to produce and sell beds in Japan. The market was surely enticing—74 percent of the islanders sleep on floor pallets called futons. Here indeed was a potential bed of roses for a company which had successfully pierced difficult selling areas before. Finding a plant site and recruiting factory help was no problem. But putting together a sales force of bright, educated young men was something else again. Most Japanese firms recruit their marketing people from the colleges. University graduates are often reluctant to accept jobs with American firms because if they do not pan out, the employee cannot move into a Japanese company where progress is strictly by seniority. So, in this instance management felt that it would do better in smaller colleges and high schools outside the sophisticated Tokyo area, and its hunch was right. In six months it hired a small cadre of salesmen, filled their attaché cases with price lists and brochures, and sent them off to wholesalers and department stores to interest them in marketing American-type beds. When day after day the young men returned with blank order books, the company suspected a flaw in its sales program. And a flaw it found. When asked by prospective buyers about the product, the salesmen's answers had to be vague. None had ever slept in a bed before!

Notes

1. Cleveland, Mangone, and Adams, *The Overseas Americans,* p. 26, McGraw-Hill, 1960.
2. R. Farmer, *International Management,* p. 37, Dickenson, 1968.
3. Arensberg and Niehoff, *Introducing Social Change,* pp. 59, 32, Aldine, 1964.
4. "American Technical Assistants Abroad," *Annals of the American Academy of Political and Social Science,* November 1966, pp. 40–49.
5. E. Hall, *The Silent Language,* pp. 247, 287, Doubleday, 1959.
6. S. Barkin, *International Labor,* p. 213, Harper & Row, 1970.
7. R. Lewis and R. Stewart, *The Managers,* p. 214, Mentor, 1969.

Questions for Discussion and Writing

1. In what ways does Stessin show us how difficult it is for an American to do business in another country, even for one with the best of motives?
2. Why are some of the examples Stessin uses of intercultural gaffes and misunderstandings funny to us? Why or why not would they be funny to the people in the culture from which they are taken?
3. What trait does Stessin claim most "blurs the American image overseas" (p. 344)? In what ways does he persuade us about the problems and effects of this trait in conducting business overseas?
4. In what ways can Americans prepare for problems involving concepts of time, space, and employee relations in doing business overseas?
5. In what ways does this essay directly and indirectly emphasize the need for intercultural understanding in business dealings? What does the business-person without it stand to lose?

SIMILIH M. CORDOR

A Farewell to the Old Order

*Born in 1946 in northern Liberia, Similih M. Cordor writes fiction
and studies African mass communications, literature, and politics.
He is also a journalist, political activist, and university professor.
Cordor's writings have been published in anthologies and periodi-
cals in Liberia, South Africa, England, Denmark, and the United
States.*

In "A Farewell to the Old Order," published in Short Story International *in 1988, Cordor tells us the story of a man who encounters
intercultural problems at work even though he never leaves his country.*

Before you read "A Farewell to the Old Order," write about a time when
a situation in your life demanded that you give up someone or something
important from your past or lose someone or something important in your
present situation. Describe the choice you faced, why you faced it, and what
you thought the rewards would be if you gave up the someone or something
from your past. What choice did you finally make, and why? What have you
learned from having made the choice?

T he choice was hard to make. It was between my new job in a powerful
government ministry and my two unlettered wives, the mothers of my five
children: three by Kau and two by Yei. The two ropes were tightly tied on my
waist and it was rather difficult to decide on which one to pull down.

I had gone to the university, studied various disciplines including economics,
public administration, and personnel management, and got a couple of college
degrees. And right after my graduate studies, I got this government job, but my
two non-literate women became a problem almost immediately. The whole affair
emerged rather casually and then developed into an open crisis between me and
our chief minister.

The frequent visits to my office by my wives were the first thing that unveiled

the distaste my colleagues had for my marital status. Each time my wives came
to the office, people would ask:

"Whom these country women always coming to here?"

To me of course.

When it became known that I was married to two unlettered women, my
co-workers, including some of my senior staff members, began to ask again:

"With all his university education, James Dahn is living with country women?"

What is wrong with a country man living with country women in a country way?

I began to feel a little uneasy about the situation but I tried to tolerate it. Then
one Tuesday morning, one of my senior planning officers walked into my office
as soon as my two wives had entered. It seems that he had been running behind
them from the hallway.

"Chief, these girls are quite charming," he said and stared at the women.

They bent their heads down to avoid his eyes.

"Is that what brought you here this morning?"

"Well, you're our Chief, and we come in here anytime."

"But you don't usually run into my office like that."

"Anyway, who are these beautiful girls to you, Chief?" the young man asked
and looked at the women again.

They tried to avoid his eyes but he kept them firmly on the two girls, who were
dressed in modern African style. Both wore *lappas* and *bubas* made of Fante cloth.

Who are these women to you?

I hesitated to answer the question.

"But, Chief, tell me who are these fine girls to you; don't blame me if I tried
to push my hand around one of them."

The girls laughed.

"They are my women," I said finally, almost blurting.

I waited for another statement because I knew my planning officer would say
something else.

"Women . . . or *wives,* Minister Dahn?" he asked.

I tried to avoid frowning.

"Yes, my man, they're my wives . . . Don't you know?"

When did I ever introduce any of my wives to my staff members?

The gentleman let out a queer laugh that greatly irritated me.

"The two of them, Chief? You mean you *alone* have these two fine girls? And
you want to keep both?"

I ignored the series of questions from my planning officer. He looked at the
girls for the last time and walked out of my office quietly, perhaps slightly
embarrassed about the brief encounter.

I looked at my wives who sat innocently. They didn't appear to be upset, at
least not as much as I had been.

After this incident, my uneasiness about the frequent visits to my office by my
wives increased. Then several other junior and senior officials began to joke and

tease me. Their jokes made me feel rather uncomfortable and indignant about the whole affair. But I couldn't think of dropping my wives at the moment, neither was I contemplating quitting my ministerial job. My appointment as Assistant Minister for Personnel and Planning in the Ministry of Presidential Affairs was too great a milestone in my career to let it go like that. In our country, top administrative positions in national government hardly went to people like me. And this had come to me not particularly for my academic brilliance and professional training, but because of a social connection I had established with an elitist family in Monrovia. Now the same elite was on me about some aspects of my social life.

After some time, I called Kau, my senior wife, and talked to her about their visits to my office. I felt that this was necessary because the problem kept rising steadily.

"Kau, I think you people will have to keep at home now," I said to her.

"But we don't walk about in the city," she said, quite surprised by my statement. "Aye, my people who saw us in the street? Who want to put us in trouble with you, Dahn?"

"No, Kau," I said quickly, "I mean coming to my office."

"What about coming to your office?"

"I told you the last time that our work was rather delicate and receiving visitors was inconvenient on many occasions . . . You have seen me working with all kinds of papers and people in my office before . . ."

Kau sighed and looked at me with some sort of amazement. She probably did not expect this from me. When this ministerial job was given to me, my wives were quite enthusiastic about it. In fact all my people were crazy about the idea that someone from our area suddenly had been pushed into the political limelight.

"But people go to other offices quite frequently," Kau said to me.

"Yes, that's true, Kau, but you people will have to stay home now, and not be running to my office as before."

"Is your office different from other people's?"

"Yes, it is quite different, Kau; you know it is the Presidential Ministry, right in the building with the President of the country . . ."

When last did I discuss the various types of government ministries and their functions with Kau?

"Dahn, you must be up to something now; I don't understand. Maybe you want to be taking your *kwii* women or school girls to your office now. Anyway, it is your office. We will stay home and be eating our *pusawa* and you and your *kwii* women can have your office . . ."

"Don't talk like that, Kau," I said; "you people should be able to understand."

"Dahn, do what you want to do."

"Tell Yei about it."

"Don't worry about Yei. If I don't go to your office or didn't send her there, she won't be seen there at all."

Kau sent her big son to call Yei. When she came, Kau wasted no time in telling her the news about visiting my office. Yei frowned immediately and joined Kau in suspecting me of being up to something. We talked about it briefly and then they resorted to quiet resignation.

I could see the discontent in their faces about stopping them from visiting my office, where they usually went together. Kau and Yei apparently enjoyed their visits to the Ministry of Presidential Affairs in the Presidential Palace. The colossal building was the most modern and beautiful in the whole country. Our government was still paying on the 108 million dollar loan that went into the construction of the statuesque edifice.

My wives enjoyed stepping into the beautiful hallways of the Palace; they loved to ride the elevators to my sixteenth floor office. Walking into the air-conditioned office became so great a pleasure that they were there every week. Sometimes they brought me food, sometimes they brought their friends and relatives to see the beauty and magnificence of their husband's office. But other times they came simply to greet me and see me punching the adding machine and hitting the electric typewriter behind my desk. Now they missed all of these things.

The curtailing of visits to my office by Kau and Yei and their relatives and friends did not solve my problem at all. Some of my office mates, especially those higher than me including our chief minister, Edward J. Barclay, continued to joke and tease me occasionally, sometimes quite strongly. I tried to tolerate the jokes and make them rather amusing, but I couldn't continue this for long. I began to think about what to do under the circumstances.

I took a report to Minister Barclay's office one afternoon. He had not sent for it but I knew he needed it for the forthcoming staff meeting on recruitment of planning officers for our ministry.

"Thank you for the report, Minister Dahn," Mr. Barclay said when I gave him the booklet. "You brought it just in time. You're a brilliant young man and you usually do smart and neat job."

A contented smile crossed my face.

"Dahn, how is the Personnel and Planning Office?"

"It's all right, Mr. Barclay," I said. "We're trying."

"That's fine, Dahn; you are quite brilliant as I just said, and that is why when my uncle and his wife recommended you to me, I didn't hesitate to forward your name to the President of the Republic for the ministerial appointment you now hold. You know I bypassed all formalities to push your appointment through."

I grinned appreciatively. Minister Barclay was not a man who easily expressed commendation to workers, and whenever he did, one felt flattered and highly delighted.

Then a brief silence fell on us. I stared into Mr. Barclay's face. It seemed that he was thinking about something and I suspected that he was about to plunge into my domestic life. Minister Barclay had joined the teasing group and gone deeper into it. He usually confronted me with the issue on certain occasions, often informally, but sometimes embarrassingly.

"I saw you people at the party the other day," he said, smiling.

My guess proved correct. I knew the subject would come up. And, as usual, it emerged casually and as a byproduct of our conversation.

I said nothing to the minister about my going to a party with anyone.

"How are your people, Minister Dahn?" he asked.

"Which people?" I asked, of course knowing exactly to whom he was referring.

"You don't know whom I'm talking about? I mean your native women, especially your headwife I saw with you at the party over the weekend . . . I know you didn't expect me at that party, not so?"

I didn't answer but it was true that I did not think Minister Barclay would attend such a party. It was rather a small social affair, the type that he hardly attended.

"Well, they are all right, Minister Barclay," I said finally.

"Dahn, aren't you tired of those poor country women yet?"

I looked into his face again. I had wanted to ask him: "Minister Barclay, aren't you tired of your wife now?"

"When will you get a civilized wife, I mean an educated woman to take to parties and other kinds of social and political functions?"

I hesitated to respond to his question, and he didn't press me for an immediate answer.

"Minister Barclay, what about attending important occasions without a lady?" I asked.

"Just so you can keep your country women?"

"No, Mr. Barclay."

"Well, that's even worse, Dahn. Just imagine a government official like you—a whole Assistant Minister, not just a clerk or a head of a bureau—without a wife, I mean a decent *kwii* wife, attending important functions like one of those irresponsible single boys around town. That would not look good at all."

There was an air of joviality in our talks but Mr. Barclay firmly held his officialdom behind his words. Each time I appeared a little resentful he threw his official weight behind his words, forcing me to retreat to give way to him.

I continued in my job amidst the pressure on me to marry a literate woman. After a year, a vacancy occurred: the Deputy Minister for Personnel and Planning was dismissed for what was termed as "administrative reasons." I became immediately excited. My rise to power and eminence in government service on the national level was about to take another thrust. I was sure of succeeding my immediate boss for the mere fact that I was next in line of succession and I thought I had all the necessary qualifications and experience. I began to calculate the increase in salary and fringe benefits, the traveling allowance, and the little tips received during recruitment of workers in our ministry, which my former boss used to enjoy.

What happened next?

My excitement died down as suddenly as it had arisen when Minister Barclay hinted that he would not consider any person for such a position whose social life did not reflect modern living. The minister did not define the term "modern living," neither did he mention me by name. But everybody knew what the term signified as far as Minister Barclay was concerned. And it was also apparent that the first person his mind had run to was me—James K. Dahn.

Minister Barclay instructed me to take over the duties of the former deputy minister until further ordered. I did all the work of my ex-chief without extra compensation and without much difficulty until I received a pamphlet on budgetary appropriations for the new fiscal year. I took it to Minister Barclay.

"What's that, Minister Dahn?" he asked.

"The budgetary appropriations and the new superannuation scheme for our ministry," I said.

"What am I supposed to do with it, Dahn?"

"Well, Chief, I need some clarification on it."

"My goodness!" the minister sighed. "I think we need a Deputy Minister for Personnel and Planning," he said, and sat up in his chair.

He looked at me after his statement, perhaps to see if I was offended by it.

"Let's see what it is all about, Dahn."

I put the document before the minister on his desk.

He skimmed through it.

"Sit down, Mr. Dahn," he said after skimming. "We have to examine the statistical calculations carefully . . . This seems to be a complicated document."

You don't have to tell me that; I know it.

I drew a chair to the desk and sat. For a good thirty minutes we went over the huge amounts and the various notations in the document. Minister Barclay seemed exhausted. He took his head away from the pamphlet, got a cigarette from his coat pocket and lit it.

Then he stared at me for a few seconds.

"My man, how are things at your home?" he asked, and leaned back in his chair.

What the hell had he to do with my home?

Well, Minister Barclay often asked about the homes of his employees including his subministers. It was a habit of his, and most of us were no longer reluctant to tell him all about our homes. Usually there was no malice in his intrusion into the affairs of other people.

"My home is all right, Minister," I said.

"All your people all right, Dahn?"

"Yes sir, thanks to the Lord."

He lit another cigarette and began smoking.

"My man, when will you get into real modern living?" he asked, smiling rather generously.

"I'm a modern man and I am sure I live a modern life," I said and began preparations because the battle over my social life was about to be resumed.

"Even when it comes to marriage?"

I didn't want to answer him on this topic but I later decided to.

"Well, I have been married for some time now."

"You mean to those native women? Don't tell me that."

"But what can I say again?"

"Say something better than that, Dahn."

"What else do you want me to say, Minister Barclay?"

"A whole Assistant Minister like you?"

"Mr. Barclay . . ."

"I say, tell me something better than that, Dahn."

I adjusted my body in the chair and gathered momentum. The battle was now in full swing. I had fought it several times and I was prepared to continue it.

"Is that all you can say, Dahn?"

"What do you want me to say again, Minister Barclay? After all, that is the way I want things to be with me. I don't have anything more to say on this topic, Minister . . ."

I sounded defiant. I suddenly seemed to have courage to speak out on my domestic affairs.

"Don't you think all these things count when it comes to higher government positions?"

Even that of the Deputy Minister for Personnel and Planning in our ministry?

"Well, I am speaking only in your own interest . . . You have to do something about your domestic life. With all these educated girls around town looking for husbands with tears in their eyes, you telling me that you are married to a pile of country women? You better do something or you won't have me to blame . . ."

"Minister Barclay, some people are married according to the traditional African way and are working in government offices."

"But they know what offices to work in," the minister said, "and what positions to hold, too."

"Well, look, Minister Barclay . . ."

"Dahn, not in this ministry, right in the Presidential Palace."

"But Minister . . ."

"Dahn, this is not the office for such people."

"So there is none in our ministry?"

"You mean besides you?"

"Well, yes."

"At least not in any ministerial position. Maybe some of our drivers, mechanics, janitors, and people like that, but not you and me."

I seemed to be losing the battle but I struggled on.

"We are all Africans, Minister Barclay," I said.

"And so what?" he replied rather quickly.

"Well . . ."

"Look, Dahn, we surely are all Africans, but this is a modern age. We have to bid a farewell to old Africa. In fact, we expect people like you with higher

Western education to lead the way, but you seem to be looking towards traditional African life with glorification. You see, Dahn, you have been to the university and have college degrees, an opportunity which we did not get in our day."

Who's to be blamed for that?

The minister looked into my face again. He said a few more things and lit another cigarette. Then he picked up the document from his desk. We went over the rest of the pages after the battle over my social life.

"Minister Dahn, go and look over the figures again," Mr. Barclay noted. "You need to study this document carefully. You see, when it comes to professional training and academic qualifications, you've got them, but try to do something about yourself, Dahn. You see, you boys from the interior ought to get some political appointments now, because we want to bring some country people into the government. But you all have to do away with some of those primitive things from the hinterland. We're in the modern world now . . . I hope you will see about yourself as soon as possible."

Who are the country people?

Three months later the vacancy for the deputy minister in our ministry was filled by another person outside the ministry. I was disappointed but not surprised that the position was not given to me. But another promotion came up and that passed by me the way June passes by July every year.

However, I continued in my same portfolio and kept on hoping to rise to higher positions in the government bureaucracy. Then something came up again. Minister Barclay received a few fellowships for senior staff training in the United States of America. He sent for me.

"Minister Dahn, we have something again," Mr. Barclay said, when I came to his office that morning.

"Again?" I said.

"Well, yes, something again," he said, laughing.

"What is it this time?"

"We have some fellowships from the American Cultural and Educational Foundation in Monrovia for senior staff members to improve themselves. Of course, you've got your B.A., M.A., and M.Sc., but you might want to take one of these to America to go and enjoy those colored girls in the States . . ."

"That will be fine, sir," I said, after thinking about the fellowships for a while. "I won't mind taking one if you people agree to offer me one."

The Minister laughed.

"If we agree? Well, Dahn, you know your trouble. You don't want to leave those poor *country things* and live a modern life."

"Well, Minister, I thought I promised to do something about the matter very soon."

"Well, you have to . . . I hope you will put an end to the problem soon. You see, everything that comes your way is always missing you."

"I know, Mr. Barclay."

"If another promotion comes again, where will you be?"

Where have I been all this time?

"You see, we have to know the kind of persons we are giving higher government positions to," he said to me.

Minister Barclay sounded as if government positions were a legacy of a particular group of people—perhaps the elitist sector of our population.

"Well, if our advice continues to fall on deaf ears, don't be surprised if something unfavorable happens to your job here."

"You mean my present job?" I asked rather quickly.

Minister Barclay laughed and said, "Of course, yes."

Was he thinking about replacing me now because of my social life?

"Since you're interested in the fellowships, I will see if we can give you one. Anyway, they are not for this year. They won't be available until about three to five months from now. I hope things will be all right with you by then."

"I think so, Minister Barclay."

"That's fine, Dahn; I hope everything comes through."

"Thank you, sir," I said to Minister Barclay, and left his office.

When I walked out of Mr. Barclay's office, I wondered why he and his senior staff members could not understand my position. It was not too strange a life to live but they kept bugging me about my unlettered wives, whom I had acquired some years ago. I got Kau during my high school days and Yei when I was doing my undergraduate studies at the state university in Monrovia. For Kau, I went upcountry to collect her; my mother had completed all negotiations for her and all I had to do was to pay the bride price and bring her with me to the city. As for Yei, I didn't even have to travel; I only sent the bride price and she was sent to me like one of those big parcels that come to us in the city from our people in the rural areas. Nothing was unusual about such an act.

Each time the pressure on me to marry according to Western custom mounted, I took refuge at my brother's home in Sinkor. So when Minister Barclay told me about the fellowships and what would happen to my present position if I didn't do something about my social life, I went to Brother Dolo.

"Hello, Brother Dolo," I greeted him when I entered his house that evening.

He responded and offered me a seat in the sitting room.

I sat down and looked around.

"How are things this way, Brother?" I asked.

"Well, things are so-so," Dolo said, smiling. "We look up to you big, big people in the country."

We laughed.

"What's the news in the big office—the Presidential Palace, Brother Dahn?"

"Brother Dolo, we are there-O."

"Ah, you people stay there-O," he said laughing.

Brother Dolo sent for a few bottles of club beer and we began drinking. His wives came and greeted me. The children came and did the same thing.

"So everything is all right with you at work?" Dolo asked, as we sat drinking the beer.

"Well, yes, except this one marriage business."

My brother laughed and stared at me. He refilled my glass and then picked up his. I sent for more beer for us.

"The same thing still around," Dolo said.

"Yes, Brother Dolo, the same *kwii* marriage business. All the talk is about my marriage business as if I am the only person in such shoes."

"Dahn, the way I see it, it looks like your ministers will never get tired about this one marriage business."

"Well, my marriage business and my job are like two ropes hanging on my waist, and I have to try to pull one down."

"I think so myself, Brother Dahn. You have to make up your mind and pull down one of the ropes and let the other one go. In any case, we have talked about this before."

"That's true, Brother Dolo," I said. "Everyday, we're just talking about the same thing . . . In fact something new has come on top of it."

"What is that, Dahn?"

"Foreign travel and training for senior staff members."

"That's fine, and I hope you won't miss this time. We are proud of you, Dahn; it is a great thing to see you in that Presidential Palace. All our people look up to you as our part, the *big shot* in the government. All the chiefs from our home come to Monrovia to see you. We all pray that you will remain in such a big position all the time. So you must do something about this one marriage business. You have to do what your ministers want you to do, Dahn."

I lay back in my chair as my mind wandered. Dolo wasn't compromising any longer as he used to do before. He had joined my senior ministers in calling for a farewell to the old order. The pressure on me had taken on a new front. Now everybody wanted me to marry according to Western custom: one man, one wife in public and several women in secret; church ceremonies, wearing of rings; cutting of cakes, and having an elaborate wedding reception that usually takes the newly married couple a year round to pay for.

"You're right, Brother Dolo," I finally concurred, rather painfully. "My senior ministers keep bugging me all the time. In fact, I am fed up with the whole mess now."

I wanted to tell my brother that I was now thinking of resigning my ministerial post and that would automatically put an end to the pressure. I would be out of their way for good. But where in the world could I find such employment with comparable rank and remuneration? Many persons from the rural areas with a similar amount of Western education and even more usually ended up becoming only teachers, clerks, and general office workers. But here I was in an administrative position with the hope of rising to higher posts in the near future. I knew many people were envious of me and would take my portfolio at any moment.

"Well, Brother Dolo, we have talked about Kau and Yei and the children, over and over," I said. "But I don't seem to have any clear cut solution to the problem . . ."

"Except to send them back to their people, as we have discussed sometime ago."

"But Brother Dolo, my wives have born five children for me."

"And so what?" Dolo said quickly. "Other men have had more than ten children and as many as a dozen wives, but they left them all and got married to civilized women."

What a wickedness!

"Your friend Bill Paasewe and Kato separated. Whoever thought they would? Brother Dolo asked.

Nobody, not even myself. I could not believe that Paasewe could abandon Kato, after fifteen years together and with nine children, for a little schoolgirl. But he did.

"Explain to your wives, Brother Dahn; they should understand the situation."

"Well, up to now, they have not understood it."

"Everything is up to you, Dahn. You see, you people have put your hand in this civilized business, so you must try to live up to it in every way."

"But all these so-called civilized people in higher positions or offices are doing all kinds of things. You and I know that these cabinet ministers, legislators, jurists, and people like that have several women—both civilized and natives—in various parts of the town or country. They are running to them regularly and paying huge bills for them."

"So you prefer to have them under one roof?" Brother Dolo said.

We laughed.

"I know that, Brother Dahn, but despite that, they have their *kwii* women at home, of course as a show-off business."

"So you want me to marry according to Western custom and have a big party?"

"Yes, so we can get boozed up that day."

We laughed again.

"Anyway, Brother Dolo, I have to do something about these girls," I told my brother.

"Well, it is all up to you, Brother Dahn. Me, I got my five women and have no trouble with any one. I can keep as many as my pocket can afford."

But your case is different; you are not a government minister or official like me.

Brother Dolo and I discussed the issue at length, but I still felt undecided. I told him that I would need some time to make a choice between my job and my wives—the two ropes that were tied tightly on my waist.

Kau and I sat face to face again. The same marriage business was our topic for discussion. It was about a few months before the fellowships at my ministry would be granted.

"Kau, the marriage business is catching hell again," I said to her at the beginning of our discussion that night.

She looked into my face and sighed deeply. There was much sadness in her face. I was terribly upset about the whole thing. And it seemed that Kau noticed that I was very desperate that night. This was the first time Kau and I had talked so seriously and so lengthily on the matter.

"Well, I have told you what I had to say on this marriage business," Kau said.

"Kau, I have been thinking of what to do with you and Yei, especially you, who have served me so long and so well."

"Dahn, do as your Brother Dolo has always told you: send us back to our people . . . we will go."

"How can I do that?"

"It's all right; our people will never refuse us."

"I know that, but we have been together for so long now and we have children . . ."

"And so what, Dahn?"

"Kau, you people helped me to become what I am today . . . This very house we live in now, my small taxi transport business and other things, the two of you helped to get them all."

"Yes, and this is our pay now we are getting . . . Well, so God say."

I saw tears rolling down her cheeks. From this point on, she sobbed intermittently throughout our discussion that night and that deepened my grief.

"You and Yei did all kinds of things for us to live in this hard city when I was going to college right here in Monrovia. I was not working for money except the little jobs I used to cut here and there. You people made market and got money, and when I went to America for school, for two years you people took care of the house and the children."

"Well, you either drop us or leave your government job."

Leave my government portfolio?

"That's hard to decide, Kau," I said. "You people can't go like that, and I can't leave my job like that, either."

Kau almost laughed.

"You have to choose between us and the government office so you can live your *kwii* life . . . It is now that you are so civilized to see us around you."

She burst into tears again.

"I'm not the one causing all this trouble, Kau," I said to her. "You should understand my situation."

"I think we will never understand this one. We can't go to school tonight and finish book tomorrow."

I wish they could, especially Kau.

I waited for a moment as she wiped her face and hauled down her *buba* and tied her *lappa* around her waist. Then I began thinking about the series of proposals I had made up a week ago to present to Kau. I took my time to present them to her one by one.

"Kau, suppose I get a place in town for you to stay? Won't that be all right for you?" I said, and listened carefully to her reply to my first proposal.

"Suppose *you do what?*" she asked quickly and stared at me.

I hesitated to answer her. She appeared a little skeptical of the first plan. I explained the deal to her and then added:

"You have seen this many times in Monrovia, right?"

She did not answer; she only sighed deeply.

"What about Yei?" Kau asked.

Yes, poor, young but innocent Yei.

"I can take care of her problem easily. Yei's uncle is in town and he knows the trouble I am going through at my office. He will understand the situation."

"Well, do anything that will get us out of your way."

"You can have the house we were building near my uncle's place in Sinkor," I announced my next plan.

"Who is coming to take that unfinished house?"

Kau seemed to be doubtful of my deals.

"Finishing the house is no problem," I said. "I can arrange that quite easily with my position in government. And I will be supporting you, doing everything for you . . ."

"And you will be doing what?" Kau cut me off.

Her eyes were up into mine again. She showed more skepticism about my next deal.

"You will be supporting me until when?" she asked.

"Should there be any time limit to supporting you?"

"Yes, because it will depend on the *kwii* wife you're going to get. You know these civilized women are troublesome. They don't like to share men with other women but they like to take people good, good men from them. I know that some of them finished putting all these ideas into your head."

"No, no, Kau, no woman is cooking my head. Anyway, the woman I will marry will have to share me with you and Yei; after all, my children's mothers have to live, too."

"Oh, my children!" Kau cried out loudly.

"Don't cry about the children business," I comforted her.

As Kau cried, I tried to figure out which of the two ropes on my waist I should pull down in the final analysis. On the right were Kau, Yei, and their children; at the end of the left were my ministerial rank and my possible rise to eminence on the national political scene.

"You know these *kwii* women don't like to take good care of other people's children . . . they make servants out of them . . . I want my children to be with me wherever I will go."

"Don't worry about the children, Kau," I repeated my assurance. "I will take good care of them. You can come to the house sometimes to see them."

"Who wants to come to your *kwii* house for your civilized woman to be abusing for nothing?"

"Well, you may see me at my office, then . . ."

"What? The same office you finished driving us away? No, my man, you don't mean that."

"What about my brother Dolo's house?"

"That your brother who has been behind you ever since to throw us away?"

Well, where should we meet then?

"Anyway, those kids will be properly cared for, Kau. Don't have any fear about them."

"We shall see what will happen in the future."

"So I will finish the house and you can go in immediately. I will send Yei to her uncle whom I have already explained everything to, and I am glad he is in sympathy with me in this marriage trouble."

"Anything you do will be all right with me . . . I will stay at the house; if you don't come to see me, it is okay with me. If you don't let my children come to see me, it is fine with me . . . God will help me."

"Who says I will forget about you? I will forever be grateful to you people for all what you and Yei did for me. I promise you sincerely on all these things. In fact I will give you some money, about three to four hundred dollars, to start a big market or you can have a shop at the house . . . I will put a shop room on it. Won't that be fine, Kau?"

Kau only nodded her answer. I had expected her to smile after I had talked about giving her some money, but she didn't. Instead, she continued sobbing.

"Well, everything is all right, now, Kau," I said.

"What makes everything all right? Because we are going and leaving behind everything we have suffered for?"

"Don't talk like that, Kau. Don't you want to consider all what I have been telling you the whole night?" I said and looked at my watch; it was after midnight, indicating that we had now talked for more than five hours.

I looked at Kau and reflected on the number of years we had been together; I thought of the pressure on me from my minister to marry a literate woman. Then I sighed deeply. We had reached the end of the affair; of course, I was determined to finalize everything about this marriage business. I had presented all my deals in a grand style, amidst Kau's skepticism and hesitation in accepting them. But I had comforted and assured her sincerely that I would not forget her and Yei.

After a moment of brief but awesome silence, Kau raised her eyes up into mine.

"Oh, Dahn, so this is the end of us now, after all the years with you?" she said and burst into tears.

Well, what to do?

Kau wept bitterly as one of the two ropes on my waist came down solemnly.

Questions for Discussion and Writing

1. On what cultural assumptions and values do Kau and Yei operate? From what background has each woman come, and how do her assumptions grow out of that background?

2. Although Dahn, the narrator, never leaves Liberia, in what ways does he cross cultures nevertheless? What are the cultural assumptions and values under which Mr. Barclay and his department operate? In what ways are Barclay's demands of Dahn justified? In what ways are they not justified?

3. What is really at stake in this story, both for Dahn and for Barclay, and why? What does the "old order" have to recommend it; what does the new way offer?

4. What elements do you respond to, effective or detracting, in Cordor's writing style? Explain your response.

DAVID HALBERSTAM

How Datsun Discovered America

Born in 1934, David Halberstam graduated from Harvard University in 1955 and has been involved with writing ever since. He has worked as a reporter for the New York Times *(1956–1960) and as a staff writer and foreign correspondent for the newspaper in the Congo (now Zaire) from 1961 to 1962. He also spent a year each in Vietnam (1962–1963), Warsaw, Poland (1965), and Paris, France (1966). In 1964, Halberstam won a Pulitzer Prize for his reporting on the Vietnam War. His two best-selling books,* The Best and the Brightest *(1972) and* The Powers That Be *(1979), have been widely praised and criticized as examples of new journalism.*

"How Datsun Discovered America," published in Esquire *in October 1986, also exemplifies this new journalism approach to reporting. Fellow new journalist Tom Wolfe describes this kind of nonfiction writing as one in which techniques ordinarily confined to the novel or short story are used "to create in one form both the kind of objective reality of journalism and the subjective reality that people have always gone to the novel for." New journalism often has a colorful style, extensive description, personal commentary from the writer, juxtaposed facts creating a desired dramatic effect, and a narrative that brings us inside the minds of the characters.*

Halberstam is a thorough writer. In preparing his subject, he says, "I talk to everybody. I don't just see the generals—what I call four-star interviews where everything is all set up for you. I start with the privates so that when I get to the top, I know what I'm talking about."

Before you read "How Datsun Discovered America," write about a situation at work involving a well-liked and even competent co-worker who was nevertheless eventually let go. Describe the situation of the person at work, why the person was removed, and what factors you think caused his or her removal. If you haven't encountered a situation like this, write instead about a time when you or someone you know encountered a difficult situation at work. Describe what happened and why.

Yutaka Katayama was sent to America in 1960 to handle Nissan's first exports to that distant and pervasively rich land, not because he was a rising star but because he was in disgrace in Tokyo, and this assignment was a form of exile. What better place for a Japanese auto executive in disgrace than the world's greatest center of automobile manufacturing, where success was dubious and failure highly likely?

Katayama was a conservative man of upper-class origins, and his privileged childhood had made him somewhat different from other Japanese. For one thing, it had given him a desire for a higher level of independence. For another, it had made him an absolute car nut. His father had owned two very sporty cars, and it was Katayama's love of cars that brought him to work at Nissan: it was about cars, and he was about cars, and he not only wanted to drive them, he wanted to build them. At one point, frustrated with the politics of Nissan, he had even designed his own car, an ultralight auto for a country where gas was extremely expensive. The Flying Feather, it was called, and he and a friend put it together in the second story of a Tokyo building but couldn't get it out for a trial run. In a nation filled with laws and restrictions and inhibitions, racing around in a sports car was to Katayama the highest form of freedom.

By the late Fifties, he had fallen into disgrace with his superiors because of his opposition to the company's new, powerful, management-propelled union. Katayama, a man of the old order, was essentially antiunion. In his perfect world, managers would deal with workers in an honorable Japanese manner that reflected well on both labor and management and that accorded both sides dignity. In a slightly less perfect world where there had to be unions, management would make the decisions, and labor would go through the motions of pretending that it had fought valiantly to improve things. That kind of relationship he could understand. Labor as an extension of management was something he could not. In the early Fifties, when Nissan had been under assault from a leftist union, Katayama had opposed the leftists. That had not bothered his superiors. But his crucial mistake was to oppose the new management-sponsored union, which had crushed the leftist one. That had sealed his fate.

His friends warned him to keep his mouth shut, but he never listened. When almost everyone else in middle management was joining the union, Katayama stood on the sidelines.

In 1958, desperate to get away from the company's politics, Katayama led a triumphant team of Nissan drivers through an arduous auto rally in Australia. He returned a national hero—only to find that his job had been given away to a union member. Two years later, when management asked him to check out Nissan's prospects in California, he jumped at the chance. The decision to try exporting had been partially inspired by his success in Australia, and though he knew he was being banished, he was delighted nonetheless.

As a student Katayama had been sent to America by his father to expand his horizons, and he had loved it. Now, as a grown man living in Los Angeles, he was struck again by the sense of freedom. Americans believed they could do whatever they wanted, the way they wanted, when they wanted. The lack of formality, symbolized by the absence of blue suits, cheered him. In Japan, if you were to transact serious commerce, you wore a blue suit. If you were not entitled to wear a blue suit, you wore a laborer's work clothes. But in America there was no telling what a man did by looking at his clothes.

In addition, and most miraculously, it did not seem to matter that he was Japanese; what mattered to the Americans was what he was selling and what the terms were: Was it a good deal? An American trying to do business in Japan, he was sure, would never have found as many doors open as Katayama was finding open to him. Yutaka Katayama, to his amazement, found himself more at home in California than he had been in Tokyo. Soon the American job became a permanent one. No one else seemed eager to go to America, that alien, often terrifying place, so he was placed in charge of Nissan's operations in the western United States. He sent for his family. What was supposed to have been a brief tour lasted seventeen years.

He was poor in America at first, barely able to survive on his salary, yet he knew that every dollar he spent represented real sacrifice for the company. To save money he had his regional salesman call in every day at certain prescribed hours; if the phone rang three times and then stopped, it meant that the salesman had nothing to report. It was typical of his operation.

Katayama's big problem in the early days was that the car he was selling was simply terrible, crude and underpowered. There were those who believed that Nissan, realizing how bad its car was, had declined to put the company's name on it, calling it the Datsun in America, so that if the car failed there would be less loss of face.

But Tokyo was beginning to send over engineers to modify the Datsun for American requirements, and Katayama pounced on them, relentlessly indoctrinating them in his view of the Datsun's shortcomings and the need for improvements, creating allies for the debates he was already carrying on with the home office. He worked the engineers over so hard that they called his sessions Katayama University. He thought the task ahead was much more difficult than Tokyo realized, and he had already found Tokyo very slow to accept the gravity of its problems in America.

Katayama decided the first thing to do was to study the American market and find out what it would take. He learned a number of things very quickly. The first was that he was probably lucky to be on the West Coast rather than on the East, for people in California were less fixed in their habits. The second and more important thing Katayama learned was that in America the dealer network was critical. In Japan Nissan dealers played almost no part in the selling of cars. In America they would have to be the true customers of the company. If they were strong and vital, the company might succeed.

For those he chose, he made the deal quite profitable, giving them about 19 percent of the gross profit. The American companies were paying dealers only 12 or 13 percent, which was one reason why they preferred selling large cars and why America both manufactured and sold more big cars than little. It was a habit based on the difference between 13 percent of $2,000 and 13 percent of $5,000. Katayama paid considerably more, partly because he had no alternative, but also because he realized that the only way the company could prosper was if the dealers got rich.

From the start, Nissan in Tokyo judged Katayama negatively. The home-office managers remembered his old affronts to the union, and, worse, decided he had gone American. That did not bother Katayama. He was having too much fun. Even when business was awful, when the cars were bad and his prospects bleak, he had no regrets. He thought himself lucky. In Japan, where he had always been perceived as incautious and somewhat aggressive, he made enemies; in America people responded to his openness and exuberance, and he made friends. Almost immediately, and for the first time in years, he was enjoying his work. Sometimes he went house to house in the Japanese sections of Los Angeles trying to sell pickup trucks to Japanese gardeners. Many of them were among the city's poorer citizens, but they were usually sympathetic and also alert to the possibility that the pickup was a good buy.

His English was not very good; as one friend noted, he spoke a language of his own, a kind of "Janglish." But he was so winning that many Americans reached out to help him. He loved the openings of Datsun dealerships, loved the hoopla of these American ceremonies—a barbecue in Texas (he would inevitably show up in a ten-gallon hat), a fish fry in Louisiana, or a Mexican dinner in San Diego. The Americans did not call him Katayama—that was too long and too foreign—but Mr. K, and he loved that too.

Amid all the fun, he was taking careful sights on the national market. Importers, he reasoned, would have to leave the center of the country alone for a while; it was a vast, underpopulated region of great distances where people needed big cars, and that was what the American companies did best. If the Japanese poured their energy and resources into every section of the country, they would surely fail. The Japanese were wise to begin on the coasts, creating their beachheads there, slowly earning the money to spend on advertising, and only then expanding into selected areas of the Heartland. "What we should do," he told his American associates, "is get better and creep up slowly, so that we'll be good—and the customers will think we're good—before Detroit even knows about us."

In the beginning almost no one knew about them. By American standards there was virtually no advertising, just simple black-and-white brochures printed in Tokyo with florid English-language descriptions of the cars. Katayama hired a Los Angeles adman named John Parker because he was young, did not cost much, and seemed bright. When Nissan needed to shoot still photos, Parker and his family served as models. The first television commercial was shot in 1963, for a four-wheel-drive wagon called the Nissan Patrol. Hiring a friend who was an

L.A. Police Department photographer and who had a 16-mm camera, Parker drove a Patrol into the canyons and shot a sixty-second ad; Parker himself was again the model. The next year they heard that Roy Rogers, the cowboy actor, liked the Nissan Patrol, and Parker asked him to do the company's first full-fledged commercial. "I can't offer you any money, Roy," Parker said, "but we'll give you a Patrol, two pickups, and all the glory a man could want." As the cars began to sell, there began to be a budget for TV ads.

Katayama was absolutely convinced that, even more than advertising, the key to success was providing service. The American market, he decided, was in some ways a prisoner of the country's wealth. The system seemed designed to produce a car that would last three or four years and that, when it began to deteriorate, would be shuttled off to a poorer segment of the population. Katayama knew, though, that these Americans were potentially good customers. They included young people, elderly people, and some poorer people, all of whom badly needed durable, fuel-efficient cars.

Already Volkswagen was doing well with these customers, the ones ignored by Detroit, providing a reasonably priced alternative source of good transportation, good mileage, and good service. Katayama realized that VW customers believed they were treated better, *respected* more, than they would be if they were trying to buy at the lower end of the American lines. (Generally the first thing that happened was that some salesmen wanted to talk them into buying something grander.) VW became the model for Katayama. At that time, 1961, it seemed invincible. It was at the height of its success (in another decade it would begin to slip), and it was doing everything right, selling 177,000 cars a year, a remarkable 46.8 percent of the import market.

Of course, the first Datsun in America was a disaster. It sold for $1,616, and Katayama often wondered why anyone bothered to buy it. He had direct knowledge of the car's problems, for in the beginning his was truly a shoestring operation; if a Datsun broke down—and one often did—he sometimes ended up doing the repair work himself. If worse came to worst and the car could not be fixed, he might even lend the enraged owner his own car.

The salesmen called the Datsuns mobile coffins because of the unbearable heat inside the car. There was no real heater; the car was heated—unintentionally—by the engine all the time. The worst thing about the Datsun was that its engine was simply too small—only 1,189 cc. Even the VW's was 1,300, and the typical American cars in those heady pre-oil-crunch days were coming in with engines of 5,000 and 6,000 cc. With the Datsun's little engine, its acceleration was poor, a real problem on the entrance ramps of the California freeways. Also, the brakes were weak. That was not all. The Datsun was designed for Japanese winters, which, by and large, are milder than American ones, and the car was very difficult to start because the battery was too small and did not throw much of a charge. For the Datsuns in the more northern sections on each coast, this morning sluggishness was a major problem. In the East, the Datsuns were selling mainly to blue-collar people who could not afford better cars. These were people who got up early, when the engines were coldest and the batteries weakest. Masataka Usami, a Nissan executive who lived in Greenwood Lake, New Jersey, and whose own car would not start in cold weather, reported back to Tokyo that Nissan could not have a car that started only two out of ten times. Tokyo was not very helpful. The alleged starting problems were impossible, the home office insisted, since it had checked and Hokkaido—Japan's northernmost island, where Datsuns started without difficulty—was just as cold as New Jersey. Usami replied that in Hokkaido those few Japanese who were privileged to own cars lovingly put blankets over the hoods every night. Tokyo asked why Americans didn't do the same thing. Usami explained that to the Japanese a car was a privilege, but to Americans it was an appliance, and they expected it to work without pampering.

Katayama's attempt to get Tokyo to upgrade and Americanize the car was a constant struggle. Even on the small matter of the floor carpets there was a problem. The Japanese tended to clean their cars incessantly and thus preferred to take the floor mat out, the better to pursue every last speck; the Americans were more casual, at best giving the floors a quick vacuuming, and they wanted the mats permanently attached, an attitude the home office found inexplicable. Whatever Katayama asked for, whether it was a more powerful motor, better acceleration, or better brakes, Tokyo resisted. What the Americans wanted above all, power and particularly styling, the Japanese were not yet ready for. In 1961, the year after he arrived in America, Katayama estimated that it would take until 1970 to get the right car for the American market, one with at least a 1,600 cc engine, real performance, and some style. He was off by a few years. The first really viable Datsun was the 1968.

What saved the company in the meantime, though Tokyo was loath to admit it, was Nissan's little pickup truck. It was small, it was inexpensive, and it exploited the single Japanese automotive strength—durability. Even more significant was the fact that, as Katayama soon learned, in western America and especially in California the pickup had a function different from the one it had elsewhere. Here it was both truck *and* passenger vehicle. Many Americans worked their small patches of farmland for an hour or two in the morning before driving off to a factory job. Some who no longer worked on the farm kept a pickup nonetheless, as if to sustain their sense of self. Other, older Americans preferred pickups because they held up well; younger ones liked them because of the image of ruggedness they projected. People who owned small companies, maybe just one or two employees or maybe just themselves, needed a pickup for work and liked the Datsuns because they were cheap and tough.

The pickups sold right from the start. They sold without advertising. They sold because the men and women who came in to look at them could sense that they were well made. They sold because the word of mouth was phenomenal. These funny little trucks, owners told their friends, lasted forever, and nothing ever went wrong—they were a real buy. The sales were so good that Nissan's West Coast office soon had twice the total volume of the East Coast's. In 1963, for example, a critical year when Datsun was just beginning to get a foothold in the

American market (late that year it moved into the top ten importers in terms of monthly sales), the western division outsold the eastern 2,781 vehicles to 1,151. Of the western division's sales, 1,597 came from small trucks.

Tokyo was ambivalent about this desperately needed success. Nissan had wanted to arrive in America and be classy and sell cars and make a reputation; it had not wanted to come and sell trucks. So when Katayama kept talking about the need to improve the trucks, management refused to listen. Katayama was trying to tell the home office that more than half of these Datsun trucks were used for commuting, that they were, in effect, being used as cars, and that the market would explode if Nissan simply upgraded them a little. But Tokyo would not budge. A truck was a truck, and Americans had no right to use one to drive to work, particularly to offices. That was wrong of them. The trucks should be used for carting heavy goods. Katayama suggested certain changes that would permit owners to convert them rather readily for family use, and again Tokyo vetoed him. Families had no business riding around in pickup trucks. Katayama sometimes wondered how many more pickups might have sold if Tokyo had listened.

What also helped carry the company in those days was Takashi Ishihara. Like Katayama, he was in a form of genteel exile, although he was a far more senior and powerful figure in the company, the heir apparent at one time to the president, Katsuji Kawamata, himself. Ishihara was export manager of Nissan in the fall of 1960, when he was made president of the American branch. Though for a time their purposes coincided, there was no love lost between him and Katayama. There was, after all, an ocean between them, because Ishihara chose not to live in America. To Katayama he seemed just one more of that legion of insular Japanese businessmen who looked upon America simply as a place from which to take something, either knowledge or technology or perhaps some hard currency.

Nonetheless, he was an extremely powerful ally for Katayama. For though they might differ on specific tactics and ambitions, and though Katayama might be more willing to adopt a truly American business style, they were as one on the central goal, which was the success of the American enterprise. That gave Katayama a lever he otherwise sorely lacked. For Ishihara's troubles with Kawamata notwithstanding, he was *of* the company as Katayama was not. Though his background was in finance, he was still considered more of a car man than Katayama, and his recommendations had a great deal more impact. Once, early in the course of the American venture, during a visit to California, Ishihara took Katayama to dinner. The question of Tokyo's reluctance to accept suggestions from America hung heavily in the air. It was very hard to make Tokyo respond to America's needs, Ishihara agreed. "I am the only one who can do it, who can push it through," he said, "and I can do it only from Tokyo. Always remember that."

There was soon ample evidence of it. Nissan had capitalized the American company at $1 million. To the Japanese that seemed an enormous amount of money. There were strict governmental limits on how much a company could spend overseas, and they were sure $1 million would last five years. But America turned out to be a terribly expensive place. Breakfast at a hotel could cost the unwary traveler several dollars. Advertising on radio and television was like burning money. Even arranging dealerships turned out to cost money, for lawyers were expensive. There was no way to save. Within two years there was only $100,000 left of the original $1 million. In late 1962 Ishihara went back to the board, hat in hand, and asked for another $500,000. There was no real challenge to him. The board voted the money rather readily, and he felt very little heat. But the American operation continued to be costly, and results remained hard to come by. A year later he had to go back and ask for another $500,000. This time he knew he was going against the wishes of the board. Some board members suggested he had been careless and that for so much money there ought to be more to show. Ishihara replied politely that he was still confident they could attain their objective, that Nissan could make a car that would do well in the American market. Indeed, he was willing to bet his career on it. If we don't make it with this request, he added, I will resign from the company.

The eyes on him at the meeting, he thought, were as cold as stone, and he could even see some pleasure in the faces of some potential adversaries. The board again gave him $500,000, but it left no doubt that he was not to come back again.

It was, he often reflected later, a very close call. In 1964 the company began to show a profit, about $200,000. Years later, when Ishihara was president of Nissan and was frequently congratulated on the brilliance of its performance in America, he was always mildly amused, for he knew how near they had come to failure.

To Katayama, Ishihara was simply someone in Tokyo who had responsibility for America. He was an asset, an ally, but not a colleague. To most of the people in America who had any encounter with Nissan's American operation, it was still Katayama's company. He was there every day, impassioned, pushing for dealers, trying to sell cars. He often delivered them to the dealers himself, because it was cheaper and because it gave him a chance to hear what they were saying.

Katayama had nothing but contempt for most of the other Japanese businessmen he met in America. When some of the younger ones came to him for guidance, he scorned their insularity. Too many of them, he said, when they came to America, knew only the map of Japan, and thought only of the people in the home office, and trusted only other Japanese. Sometimes, out for a meal with a few American friends, he would spot a group of Japanese businessmen seated nearby, five or six of them, no Americans. "Look at them," he would say, "afraid to be in America." Worse, when Japanese like these talked about Americans among themselves, they still used the hateful Japanese word for "foreigners," *gaijin*. They did not go out and get to know the market; they sat in their offices being very Japanese, trying not to make mistakes, trying not to be different. Timid rabbits, he thought.

"I am Katayama of Nissan," he would say when checking into a hotel or arriving at a meeting, and that was enough. He was the head of a company just as Lee Iacocca and Pete Estes were heads of companies, though of course he made about $25,000 a year, or about one thirtieth of what they made, and soon about one thirtieth of what some of his own dealers made. This did not bother him. The other auto executives traveled with great retinues, and there was always someone to meet them at the airport, someone to get them a drink, someone to light a cigar, someone to make sure that when they went to their favorite restaurant they got their favorite table. He preferred to travel alone; he could learn more that way. He could meet people on planes and in restaurants and bars, and not be separated from them and the truth by underlings eager to protect him from the truth. He ventured forth constantly, savoring and studying the country. There was not a sports event in Los Angeles that he did not find interesting, and he became a devoted football and baseball fan. He was a great hiker, and there was no mountain worthy of the name in the West that he did not climb. He became a devoted fisherman and he worked the rivers and the lakes in the Pacific Northwest, fishing there with his dealers and their friends. He was a good amateur painter, and wherever he went he took his paint kit and sketched the American landscape. Each year he would take the sketch he liked best and make it into his Christmas card. By the end of his tour, his Christmas list had ten thousand names. Nothing, his friends thought, told more about him than this; here was a man who had come from a country where there was no strong tradition of Christmas cards, and he had compiled what surely must be one of the nation's longest lists. Few Americans understood the modern American Christmas-card ritual as well, or practiced it as personally.

He was a man, said his longtime friend and speechwriter, Mayfield Marshall, who wanted nothing less than to shrink the Pacific Ocean. Like many Japanese he loved flying kites, and those Americans who worked for him had to be prepared to leave the office at almost any hour and fly kites (just as the Japanese who came to work for him had to be prepared to go to a barbecue for dinner or to watch a professional football game—to most of them a semibarbaric sport only dimly understood). When, after a few years in Los Angeles, he had the company buy a large plot of land off the San Diego Freeway, someone asked him what it was for. "One day it will be our headquarters building," he replied, "but for now it is our field for flying kites." He corresponded with innumerable American kite freaks, and one of his proudest days was when the editors of *Road & Track* invited him to their offices near Newport Beach, held a kite-flying contest, and then awarded him an inscribed winner's trophy. The trophy was of a bird dog and was supposed to go to a dog breeder, but the editors had gotten a small brass kite and stuffed it in the dog's mouth, which pleased Katayama immensely. That day, he told his friends, the East had met the West. He was fascinated by the difference in the way Americans and Japanese flew their kites:

even here, he thought, the Americans were frontiersmen, finding the wind current and charging into it as fast as they could, challenging it. The Japanese were more delicate about it; they would find the wind, turn their backs to it, and gently let their kites out.

He was a rare man. He brought a face to the Japanese mercantile presence; meeting him, Americans felt that they knew, understood, and liked the Japan that was behind his products. If he took pride in the growing success of Nissan America, it was a quiet pride in showing what modern Japan could do, and in the success he had helped bring to his dealers. He seemed to gain special pleasure from his work with them. After all, he had taken these ordinary and indeed often unsuccessful men, who had had nothing but their ambition and their willingness to take a chance, and helped turn them into millionaires. Years later, in his tiny office in Tokyo, he liked to point at a map of the western part of the United States. It was covered with little dots. "Each dot is a millionaire I made," he would say. The dealers loved him because he listened to them and fought for them. He wanted to find out not so much what the sales were but what was behind them and how ordinary people in America really felt. The only thing about America he did not understand and truly hated and feared was lawsuits. When even a minor suit was filed, he began to shiver. Suitcases, he called them, because his lawyer was always talking about the suit and the case. "You have to save me from these suitcases," he would say. "They want to kill me with them."

Suitcases aside, the mid-Sixties were joyous years for Katayama. Slowly, the Datsun was getting better. At first he thought it was not jaunty enough, and he argued with Tokyo to make it sportier, but Tokyo was stuffy, regarding him as too much of a sports-car buff. He also argued with the home office over naming the cars. Tokyo kept coming up with terrible names like Bluebonnet, Cedric, and Fairlady. Katayama, who increasingly fancied himself an expert on American taste, wanted more virile names, like Lion or Tiger. The problem, of course, was that Tokyo's names were the personal choices of Kawamata, who seemed to have some odd, hidden streak of anglophilia. Fairlady had been so decreed because Kawamata had once seen and apparently liked the musical *My Fair Lady.* Generally Katayama accepted his defeats on nomenclature reasonably well, but in 1969, when the first Japanese sports car arrived in America and he saw with horror that it had actually been called the Fairlady, he and his men simply pried the name tag off the car and replaced it with one using the company's internal designation for the car, 240Z. It was far more appropriate, they decided, and it was the only way to change the name without being insubordinate.

It was also during the Sixties that Katayama began to sense a change in customer attitudes, an increasingly powerful undercurrent of resentment. The objections to Detroit, he decided, were no longer just about the size and the price of the cars but about the quality and, even more important, about Detroit's response to legitimate complaints. Detroit's attitude seemed to be that if the customer was truly a good American, he would stop complaining and do the right thing, which was to buy a new car.

In the fall of 1964 Datsun made it into the annual list of the top ten importers for the first time, a list absolutely dominated by Volkswagen. VW had 63 percent of the import market with 307,000 cars sold, an average of more than 25,000 a month. In July 1965, Datsun's sales reached 1,000 a month. Back in Japan sales were rising quickly, which allowed Nissan to keep cutting the price; success was begetting success. The American market now looked more and more promising, though Volkswagen still appeared awesome. Steadily, Nissan, and then Toyota, gained on the other imports. In 1966 Nissan was fourth, with total sales of 22,000, while the VW bug sold 420,000. By 1967 Nissan had sales of 33,000; in 1969 it was still fourth, but with 58,000.

The cars were getting better, but Katayama still needed one critical addition—a jump to a 1,600 cc engine. At 1,400 cc, the current cars simply were not powerful enough. Eventually, he kept telling Tokyo, if they did not upgrade the engine, they would level off in the market. Worse, if they leveled off, they would not stay level; they would inevitably decline. On this Tokyo remained surprisingly resistant; if 1,400 cc was good enough for Japan, it was good enough for America. Katayama pleaded. He tried shock tactics, pointing out that Toyota, with a 1,600 cc model, was making sizable inroads where Datsun had once been strong. Even this failed. He had never felt so frustrated. "Why does no one listen?" he asked those around him.

Then he got an extraordinary break. In the fall of 1965 a man named Keiichi Matsumura joined Nissan. He came over from the Ministry of International Trade and Industry, where he had been MITI's man on automobiles. There was a tradition of this in Japan. A high MITI official, his career completed, would go over into the industry that he had served—the Japanese called it *amakudari,* "descending from heaven." In the spring of 1966 Matsumura visited America, and he and Katayama began a series of conversations about problems the company was having.

Katayama knew immediately that this was his great chance to upgrade the engine, so he pushed as hard as he could with Matsumura about the need for the 1,600 cc. At the end of their first long session Matsumura said, "Write a letter for me, and I will sign it." Then he changed his mind. "Make it a telex," he said. "There's a board meeting coming up soon." The next day a long, impassioned telex message, which everyone at Nissan knew was from Katayama, went out over Matsumura's name. Almost immediately Katayama got an angry message from Yuji Shimamoto, who was a key man in the export department. Shimamoto had been his chief tormentor in the past and had strenuously fought him on his repeated requests to upgrade the engine. This time Shimamoto was complaining bitterly and publicly of Katayama's failure to ask him for the 1,600 cc engine any earlier. That night, April 8, 1966, Katayama wrote in his diary:

> I do not know how many times I have asked the head office for more [engine] power. In fact I have been begging for it, but we always had to shut up because their answer was that it was impossible. Now Shimamoto tells me that everyone including Kawamata was shocked by Matsumura's telex. It is we who should be shocked, not him.

A few days later Kawamata arrived in Los Angeles with his wife. Katayama was nervous that the president might be angry with him, but Kawamata seemed not to mind the telex at all; indeed he affected to take it as a normal request. It was, of course, immediately approved, and the 1,600 cc engine went into production, which made it ready for the new 1968 model called the 510. It was a remarkable car, in any real sense Yutaka Katayama's car, a personal victory of exceptional magnitude in any auto company and particularly in a Japanese one. The 510 marked the beginning of the end of the Japanese small car as a clumsy, flimsy econobox. It was the fulfillment in that sense of Katayama's vision, of taking the best of modern European engineering and marrying it to Japanese manufacturing expertise.

In the months when the car was in its final engineering design, Katayama was on the phone to Japan constantly; one of his American associates thought he was more like an expectant mother than an auto executive. He went sleepless the night before it arrived, and when the ship was finally docking in San Pedro he was more nervous than anyone had ever seen him. As soon as the first one came off the ship, he himself drove it out of the parking facility. "Finally!" he exclaimed to the friend riding next to him. "Finally they did it! I thought it would take ten years, but they did it in seven!"

For the first few months he was like a kid with a new toy. He made everyone drive it, first his colleagues at the office, then journalists, then anyone who walked near the showroom. He loved the car, and it was inconceivable to him that anyone who touched it would not be equally excited.

In essence, as one high Nissan executive admitted at the time, the 510 was a brilliant knockoff of the BMW 1600, the main difference being that the BMW cost roughly $4,000 and the Nissan 510 about $1,800. The 510 had four-wheel independent suspension, an overhead camshaft, and a 1,600 cc engine with 96 horsepower. It was very strong, well put together, fuel efficient. It was almost immediately a hot car. The professional auto magazines were unusually enthusiastic. Car nuts loved the new Datsuns. Dealers could not keep them on the floor, and for a time there were the inevitable charges that some dealers were taking bribes in order to save cars for customers. In Detroit few of the people at the top of the auto companies took the 510 very seriously, though among the engineering people there was a sudden realization that the Japanese could be more than functional, they could be *good*.

In 1970, Datsun jumped into third place among the importers, with 150,000 pieces sold. The 510 alone sold more than 300,000 pieces in five years, and to anyone paying attention it was a sure sign that the Japanese had arrived.

It had always been a part of the basic theology of Detroit that it could roll back the foreigners anytime it wanted. The idea had always been that the imports could have 5 percent of the market, nothing more; if the foreigners went above that magic figure, Detroit would strike back. But in 1968 the figure neared 10 percent, with VW getting 54 percent of the total import market. Detroit executives were not really worried, they were making too much money for that. All they had to do whenever they wanted, they assured each other, was tool up some small cars. Soon the Detroit companies were bringing out their new compacts and subcompacts; Ford had the Maverick in 1969 and the ill-fated Pinto in 1970, and GM had the equally ill-fated Vega in 1970. But the import sales did not, as in the past, collapse. What Katayama and others had suspected was becoming true. Bonds of loyalty were being severed. It was no longer, as in the past, just an issue of size and price. The issues now were also quality and integrity.

If the first oil shock, after the Yom Kippur War in 1973, enraged and discomfited the Americans, who suddenly had to pay more for gasoline, then it truly frightened the Japanese. For it was not some temporary inconvenience; it was a crisis imperiling their society. The Japanese economy was entirely built upon oil, of which Japan, unlike the United States, had minuscule domestic supplies. What followed was pure panic. There was immediate hoarding of nearly everything, stores were mobbed, and the government had to promise that there would be enough toilet paper for everyone. A quickie book entitled *The Oil Is Cut* instantly became a best seller. Companies decreed emergency measures to conserve energy; the paint ovens at most of the auto factories, for example, were redesigned so that they needed less heat. Throughout the world of business, faucets in the lavatories produced only cold water.

The recovery came slowly. But it soon became clear that Japan was going to be the beneficiary of this crisis. Some Nissan executives claimed it was actually a blessing, because it had badly shaken the younger workers who had taken the company's success for granted and had become arrogant and spoiled, and it had made them properly grateful for their jobs. Above all, there was now a greater need for smaller, gas-efficient cars.

Soon after the Arab embargo began, the people at Nissan found out that the U.S. Environmental Protection Agency had completed its first mileage test and that the Datsun 1200, the company's smallest car, one that had been around for several years and that the executives were anxious to phase out, had scored the best mileage. John Parker and Mayfield Marshall, sensing that a very good commercial might be made from this, took a crew and started filming the 1200 going from California to Maine, where it finally drove up to a lobsterman standing amid a pile of lobster pots. A team of independent authorities went along to check how much gas the 1200 used. The EPA study had rated it at thirty-three miles to the gallon; the independent officials certified that on this trip the 1200 had gotten forty. The last line of the commercial was simply: "Datsun Saves."

Even if there were few 1200s left to sell, Datsun was able to push its low-cost replacement, the 210. Fifteen years of hard work and constant upgrading of both performance and quality were now paying off. The Germans, because they had stayed with the Beetle, appealed to only a fraction of the new market and were unable to exploit the new opportunities. For the American auto companies, production in 1974 was down 23 percent. In the beginning, the Japanese had

378 Cultural Exchanges in Study and Work

trouble, too, in finding the oil to keep their factories going, coping with depleted steel production, and shipping the cars they were making. But in due course the first oil shock allowed the Japanese to solidify their position in America. The real benefits came in 1975. That was the year Toyota passed Volkswagen as the leading import car. VW fell behind Toyota (268,000 to 284,000) and was only 15,000 units ahead of Nissan. (In fact, Nissan was some 67,000 vehicles ahead of VW if truck sales were included.) Even more significant, imported passenger cars went to 18.3 percent of the market in 1975, and more than half of those cars were Japanese.

Yutaka Katayama watched this startling success and knew that it marked the end of his freedom. As long as Nissan America was small, profitable, and making progress (but not too much progress), he was relatively safe in his job. But, if anything, his growing accomplishment and the considerable publicity he was receiving were reminders back home that he was getting out of control and accepting credit that was not, it was felt, rightly his. He had no sponsor in Tokyo, no one to speak up for him. Over the years, as he had begun to do well in America, friends had begged him to go see Ichiro Shioji, the powerful Nissan labor boss, during his visits to Tokyo and pay homage. The phrase they used, for in the old days the labor office was right across the river from the old Nissan headquarters, was "go across the bridge." Shioji was susceptible to courtship, they said; the relationship could still be patched up. But Katayama stubbornly refused to try. His East Coast counterpart, Soichi Kawazoe, was not doing as well in sales, but he had maintained his strong connection with Shioji and thus was still well thought of. (Kawazoe, Katayama once said, had always had a gift for playing poker with the right people.) Finally, somewhat reluctantly, on one trip home, Katayama went across the bridge to see Shioji. Shioji was an hour late for the meeting. In a country where people are extremely prompt, there was no doubt of the lesson Shioji was teaching Katayama.

As the American operation became increasingly successful, more and more bright young men began to arrive from Tokyo to help Katayama. He was extremely wary of some of them. "This one," he might say, "is here to spy on me. Watch out for him. Tell him nothing." At first some of Katayama's American associates thought he was being a little paranoid; later, as they learned more of the complexity of the company's politics, they were not so sure. When Kawamata or Ishihara showed up in America, they seemed cold and disapproving, and Katayama, in turn, usually so exuberant, became reserved. The Americans in the office thought Katayama was doing a brilliant job, and they found it odd that when they took these visiting officials out to some appointment and, making small talk, mentioned something about how well Mr. K was doing, the visitors never responded, never said a kind word about him. For Katayama had been much too visible in America, had taken too much pleasure in what he had done, had not played the role of the modest Japanese businessman who owes all to his superiors. They would not lightly forgive him for that.

Katayama himself knew that from their point of view there had been too many

American articles about this wonderful entrepreneurial Japanese businessman in Los Angeles who had made Nissan such a success, who had become so Americanized, and who was, it seemed, an honorary sheriff in half the counties in Texas. Too many people had said that it was Katayama's company and that the 510 was Katayama's car. All that, he knew, would hurt in Tokyo, but he did not care. He knew that they thought he had gone too American, that his clothes were considered too sporty and his manner too informal, and that every request he made to modify the car, no matter how valid, and no matter that Tokyo followed up on it, would eventually help to undo him back home. There he was seen as a spokesman for America against Japan, a man who had been implicitly critical of the existing Datsuns. He had had no illusion about his position from the start. "Everything I do right here," he told his closest American associates, "will be considered something I did wrong by Tokyo."

When he bought a house in Palos Verdes, he knew it would be held against him, that he would be charged with high living. He knew he would never be able to make Tokyo understand that whereas in Japan—because housing was so bad and perhaps because women were not a part of the business world—businessmen entertained by taking one another out for extravagantly expensive nights on the Ginza; in the United States, with its wonderful housing, Americans entertained in their homes. He paid a mere $25,000 for the house, and he loved entertaining there, barbecuing steak like an American but serving sushi beforehand. By American standards the house was very nice, but by Japanese standards it was extraordinarily grand, far grander than those in which his superiors lived at home. The house was always a sticking point. Tokyo never really accepted the idea of the house. A steady stream of high Nissan executives passed through California, looked at it, and held it against him, concluding that if Katayama had a house this splendid, he was in some way ripping off the company. When Katayama retired, his successor sold the house at a profit of about $50,000, and if he had held on a few years more, it would have been nearly $2 million.

The end for him began when Hiroshi Majima showed up in 1975. Majima became president, and Katayama became chairman. Japanese executives had arrived in the past, and Katayama had always been able to deal with them. Majima was different. He was Ishihara's man, an executive with clout and connections. It was clear from the start that he was there to replace Katayama and that his coming signaled the close of the era. It was an uncomfortable time for everyone. Katayama, of course, knew a lot more about America and doing business there, and Majima, just as clearly, outranked Katayama by light-years and was under orders to take the company back from him. Majima did not speak English, and to the Americans at headquarters his manner seemed chilly and evasive. It was hard to get a quick and clear answer from him. He was not comfortable with Americans, only with other Japanese, and he brought more and more of them into the Los Angeles office. For some of the Americans it was their first real recognition that they were working for a Japanese company.

Katayama knew his time was running out. He had stayed on in America past retirement anyway, and now Tokyo was catching up. In early 1977 he received a cable imperiously summoning him home, without explanation. It was as if he had suddenly disappeared. On arrival in Tokyo he was informed that he had retired a few days earlier. His friends back in Los Angeles did not know what was happening but feared the worst. Mayfield Marshall, probably Katayama's closest friend in the company, cabled him in Tokyo. "Hope they give you more than a gold watch," he said. A few weeks later Katayama returned. He looked at Marshall and held up his wrist. On it was a gold watch. It was about the only thing they gave him.

He did not particularly want to return to Japan and for a time considered staying on in America in a different business. But he did go back, and in Tokyo, Nissan wanted to hide him. It was almost as if he had come home in disgrace. There was no reward for the job he had done. He was not put on the board. He did not make vice-president. He was given a minor job in an advertising subsidiary. "I was farmed out," he wrote his friends in America. "At least I am beyond the reach of the union." Nissan tried to minimize any publicity in Japan about the role he had played. When American writers wanting to talk about the American operation showed up, the Nissan public relations people would come up with a short list of names, and though Kawazoe's was on the list, Katayama's was notable by its absence.

Not everyone ignored him; in April of 1977 Katayama was awarded a blue ribbon by MITI for his work in behalf of Japanese trade in America. That was a particularly high honor, and it pleased some of his friends back in America, for to them it was as if he had won it in spite of Nissan. But he took little pleasure in the award; to him it had a slightly bitter taste. He sensed that the Nissan people, embarrassed by his success in America and their own failure to recognize it by putting him on the board, had gotten MITI to do their work for them. It was partly a scam, he thought, and he felt oddly detached on the day of the presentation. Later he could not even remember whether or not he had celebrated with a few friends that night. A few months later there was a party in his honor given by about 150 of his friends and colleagues; they had had to pay for the party themselves, he noted acidly.

In America, Nissan moved quickly against those who had been his nearest associates. Within a few months it got rid of John Parker, whose agency had handled the Nissan account since the first commercial. But in a way Katayama got his revenge. For in America he had become not just popular, not just admired, but mythic. In 1983, *Car and Driver,* lamenting that Nissan products, though still durable, had become boring ("Nissan remains innovative only in financial matters," the magazine noted), published a special tribute to Katayama as a human being and as a car man. By dint of a rare human vision, he had helped make a small, incompetent Japanese company an exciting one, pushing it relentlessly to produce its best. What Nissan needed most now, *Car and Driver* asserted, was another such man. The title of the article said it all: WHERE HAVE YOU GONE, YUTAKA KATAYAMA?

Questions for Discussion and Writing

1. For what reasons, obvious and subtle, did Nissan send Yutaka Katayama to work in the United States?
2. Under what major cultural assumptions, values, and attitudes did Nissan make its decisions about its operations in the United States and its handling of Katayama?
3. In what ways did Katayama reflect his company's patterns of assumptions, values, and attitudes? What kinds of cultural assumptions, values, and attitudes did he encounter in the United States? What were his own dominant assumptions and values? In what other ways might he have handled the problems he encountered?
4. For what reasons and what audience do you imagine Halberstam wrote this essay? Support your answer with brief passages.
5. In what ways does the essay qualify as new journalism? What writing techniques might you be able to learn and adapt from it? Use details and brief passages to support your response.
6. If you were assigned to work in another country or culture, what lessons from this essay would you find most helpful?

Chapter 6

MATTERS OF LOVE
AND FAMILY

It was a love that asks nothing and gives everything—intelligence, will power, strength. A love without merchandising, without trade, without pounds of flesh or vials of fragrance, without barter of secret effusions. Without collections, calculations, or receipts. A clean, pure, new love without hands, nor words, nor lips. Mute and secret, it neither comes nor goes. It is fixed nowhere; it only is. It never reaches realization. It is like the quiet air that never becomes an impure wind. There is no vanity. There is no narcissism. It is all sweet, throbbing pain. It is a love that is death without desires or hopes of being reborn. Love must kill, to a greater or lesser degree. If it does not kill, it is not love; it is something else. Only a child is capable of complete love.

SABINE ULIBARRÍ, *from*
"FORGE WITHOUT FIRE"

THE FAMILY IS A MICROCOSM OF CULTURE—THE SMALL ARENA IN which we first learn the attitudes and values that we take with us into the adult world. The family unit gives its members their patterns of assumptions about the world, patterns that each person will mold to fit particular needs. Our lives are a combination of imitating and rejecting the early patterns we grew up with in the family.

As a microcosm of culture, the family is not only the source of our earliest learning but also a mirror of the larger culture of which it is a part. Thus, one way to get a small-scale picture of a different culture is to study the patterns and values of its families. Within the family we express our worst and best, our most intimate selves.

Cultures differ enormously in their patterns and customs of family. The stories in this chapter bring us into the lives of particular, rather than typical, families; a "typical" family in any culture remains a concept, not a reality.

Family patterns and customs are not always the warm affairs that American television is fond of portraying. In Juanita Platero and Siyowin Miller's story, "Chee's Daughter," a Navajo father loses his baby girl to tribal custom and his late wife's parents. In Julio Cortázar's "The Health of the Sick," family members go to great and humorous lengths to spare their ailing family matriarch the knowledge of her son's death. The three generations in Aharon Megged's "The Name" struggle with each other over the losses and history of their family's past, to decide how a child in Israel will be named.

Our American convictions that marriage should involve romantic love remain peculiar and unconvincing to many cultures of the world where marriages of children arranged by parents are still the rule. Zhang Jie infuriated people in the People's Republic of China with her story "Love Must Not Be Forgotten," which suggests that marriage needs to involve love—a lesson a daughter thinks she learns from her late mother's life. In Ann Petry's "Solo on the Drums," Kid Jones deals with the pain of his failing marriage through jazz—on his drums. And in V. Goryushkin's "Before Sunrise," a Russian soldier, mutilated by war, reflects the potential of marital love even in a nearly destroyed body.

The intimacy of family, or the lack thereof, is perhaps most obvious, ironically, at the time of a person's death. Gabriel García Márquez's "Big Mama's Funeral" is a party, Colombian style—reflecting more than Big Mama might have chosen to witness—of her extended family's feeling for her. In Linda Hogan's "Making Do," three generations of a Chickasaw Indian family struggle with loss, attempt to comfort each other, and make do in the ways they have learned from their culture and the truths of their own lives.

JUANITA PLATERO AND
SIYOWIN MILLER

Chee's Daughter

Long before collaborative writing was recognized for its value, Juanita Platero and Siyowin Miller were writing together, having met in California in 1929 through Chief Standing Bear. In 1930, Juanita Platero moved to New Mexico to live with her husband's people on the reservation, and Siyowin Miller traveled between California and New Mexico to write with her.

The story "Chee's Daughter" comes from a publication of the 1940s entitled Common Ground, *a periodical that published the work of writers from many cultures. Platero and Miller had earlier published a story in that journal called "Warrior Returning." The biographical information given with this story announced that in 1940 the coauthors were at work on a book entitled* The Winds Erase Your Footprints, *reflecting the struggle that Juanita and Luciano Platero faced in finding a middle path between the Anglo and Navajo cultures. No trace of the book can be found today.*

Before you read "Chee's Daughter," write about a time in your life when you had to make a difficult sacrifice because of a custom or pattern important to your family. Describe the situation, the ways you tried to defy the requirement if you did, and what happened as a result. If you have not encountered such a situation, you might write about someone you know who has. Another possibility is to write about those customs in your family that no one is supposed to defy—what they are and what you think would happen if a family member were to reject them.

T he hat told the story, the big, black, drooping Stetson. It was not at the proper angle, the proper rakish angle for so young a Navaho. There was no song, and that was not in keeping either. There should have been at least a humming, a faint, all-to-himself "he he he heya," for it was a good horse he was riding, a slender-legged, high-stepping buckskin that would race the wind with light knee-urging. This was a day for singing, a warm winter day, when the touch of the sun upon the back belied the snow high on distant mountains.

Wind warmed by the sun touched his high-boned cheeks like flicker feathers, and still he rode on silently, deeper into Little Canyon, until the red rock walls rose straight upward from the stream bed and only a narrow piece of blue sky hung above. Abruptly the sky widened where the canyon walls were pushed back to make a wide place, as though in ancient times an angry stream had tried to go all ways at once.

This was home—this wide place in the canyon—levels of jagged rock and levels of rich red earth. This was home to Chee, the rider of the buckskin, as it had been to many generations before him.

He stopped his horse at the stream and sat looking across the narrow ribbon of water to the bare-branched peach trees. He was seeing them each springtime with their age-gnarled limbs transfigured beneath veils of blossom pink; he was seeing them in autumn laden with their yellow fruit, small and sweet. Then his eyes searched out the indistinct furrows of the fields beside the stream, where each year the corn and beans and squash drank thirstily of the overflow from summer rains. Chee was trying to outweigh today's bitter betrayal of hope by gathering to himself these reminders of the integrity of the land. Land did not cheat! His mind lingered deliberately on all the days spent here in the sun caring for the young plants, his songs to the earth and to the life springing from it— ". . . In the middle of the wide field . . . Yellow Corn Boy . . . He has started both ways . . . ," then the harvest and repayment in full measure. Here was the old feeling of wholeness and of oneness with the sun and earth and growing things.

Chee urged the buckskin toward the family compound where, secure in a recess of overhanging rock, was his mother's dome-shaped hogan, red rock and red adobe like the ground on which it nestled. Not far from the hogan was the half-circle of brush like a dark shadow against the canyon wall—corral for sheep and goats. Farther from the hogan, in full circle, stood the horse corral made of heavy cedar branches sternly interlocked. Chee's long thin lips curved into a smile as he passed his daughter's tiny hogan squatted like a round Pueblo oven beside the corral. He remembered the summer day when together they sat back on their heels and plastered wet adobe all about the circling wall of rock and the woven dome of piñon twigs. How his family laughed when the Little One herded the bewildered chickens into her tiny hogan as the first snow fell.

Then the smile faded from Chee's lips and his eyes darkened as he tied his horse to a corral post and turned to the strangely empty compound. "Someone has told them," he thought, "and they are inside weeping." He passed his mother's deserted loom on the south side of the hogan and pulled the rude wooden door toward him, bowing his head, hunching his shoulders to get inside.

His mother sat sideways by the center fire, her feet drawn up under her full skirts. Her hands were busy kneading dough in the chipped white basin. With her head down, her voice was muffled when she said, "The meal will soon be ready, son."

Chee passed his father sitting against the wall, hat over his eyes as though asleep. He passed his older sister who sat turning mutton ribs on a crude wire grill over the coals, noticed tears dropping on her hands. "She cared more for my wife than I realized," he thought.

Then because something must be said sometime, he tossed the black Stetson upon a bulging sack of wool and said, "You have heard, then." He could not shut from his mind how confidently he had set the handsome new hat on his head that very morning, slanting the wide brim over one eye: he was going to see his wife and today he would ask the doctors about bringing her home; last week she had looked so much better.

His sister nodded but did not speak. His mother sniffled and passed her velveteen sleeve beneath her nose. Chee sat down, leaning against the wall. "I suppose I was a fool for hoping all the time. I should have expected this. Few of our people get well from the coughing sickness. But *she* seemed to be getting better."

His mother was crying aloud now and blowing her nose noisily on her skirt. His father sat up, speaking gently to her.

Chee shifted his position and started a cigarette. His mind turned back to the Little One. At least she was too small to understand what had happened, the Little One who had been born three years before in the sanitarium where his wife was being treated for the coughing sickness, the Little One he had brought home to his mother's hogan to be nursed by his sister whose baby was a few months older. As she grew fat-cheeked and sturdy-legged, she followed him about like a shadow; somehow her baby mind had grasped that of all those at the hogan who cared for her and played with her, he—Chee—belonged most to her. She sat cross-legged at his elbow when he worked silver at the forge; she rode before him in the saddle when he drove the horses to water; often she lay wakeful on her sheep-pelts until he stretched out for the night in the darkened hogan and she could snuggle warm against him.

Chee blew smoke slowly and some of the sadness left his dark eyes as he said, "It is not as bad as it might be. It is not as though we are left with nothing."

Chee's sister arose, sobs catching in her throat, and rushed past him out the doorway. Chee sat upright, a terrible fear possessing him. For a moment his mouth could make no sound. Then: "The Little One! Mother, where is she?"

His mother turned her stricken face to him. "Your wife's people came after her this morning. They heard yesterday of their daughter's death through the trader at Red Sands."

Chee started to protest but his mother shook her head slowly. "I didn't expect they would want the Little One either. But there is nothing you can do. She is a girl child and belongs to her mother's people; it is custom."

Frowning, Chee got to his feet, grinding his cigarette into the dirt floor. "Custom! When did my wife's parents begin thinking about custom? Why, the hogan where they live doesn't even face the East!" He started toward the door. "Perhaps I can overtake them. Perhaps they don't realize how much we want her here with us. I'll ask them to give my daughter back to me. Surely, they won't refuse."

His mother stopped him gently with her outstretched hand. "You couldn't overtake them now. They were in the trader's car. Eat and rest, and think more about this."

"Have you forgotten how things have always been between you and your wife's people?" his father said.

That night, Chee's thoughts were troubled—half-forgotten incidents became disturbingly vivid—but early the next morning he saddled the buckskin and set out for the settlement of Red Sands. Even though his father-in-law, Old Man Fat, might laugh, Chee knew that he must talk to him. There were some things to which Old Man Fat might listen.

Chee rode the first part of the fifteen miles to Red Sands expectantly. The sight of sandstone buttes near Cottonwood Spring reddening in the morning sun brought a song almost to his lips. He twirled his reins in salute to the small boy herding sheep toward many-colored Butterfly Mountain, watched with pleasure the feathers of smoke rising against tree-darkened western mesas from the hogans sheltered there. But as he approached the familiar settlement sprawled in mushroom growth along the highway, he began to feel as though a scene from a bad dream was becoming real.

Several cars were parked around the trading store which was built like two log hogans side by side, with red gas pumps in front and a sign across the tarpaper roofs: *Red Sands Trading Post—Groceries Gasoline Cold Drinks Sandwiches Indian Curios.* Back of the trading post an unpainted frame house and outbuildings squatted on the drab, treeless land. Chee and the Little One's mother had lived there when they stayed with his wife's people. That was according to custom—living with one's wife's people—but Chee had never been convinced that it was custom alone which prompted Old Man Fat and his wife to insist that their daughter bring her husband to live at the trading post.

Beside the Post was a large hogan of logs, with brightly painted pseudo-Navaho designs on the roof—a hogan with smoke-smudged windows and a garish blue door which faced north to the highway. Old Man Fat had offered Chee a hogan like this one. The trader would build it if he and his wife would live there and Chee would work at his forge making silver jewelry where tourists could watch him. But Chee had asked instead for a piece of land for a cornfield and help in building a hogan far back from the highway and a corral for the sheep he had brought to this marriage.

A cold wind blowing down from the mountains began to whistle about Chee's ears. It flapped the gaudy Navaho rugs which were hung in one long bright line to attract tourists. It swayed the sign *Navaho Weaver at Work* beside the loom where Old Man Fat's wife sat hunched in her striped blanket, patting the colored thread of a design into place with a wooden comb. Tourists stood watching the weaver. More tourists stood in a knot before the hogan where the sign said: *See Inside a Real Navaho Home 25c.*

Then the knot seemed to unravel as a few people returned to their cars; some had cameras; and there against the blue door Chee saw the Little One standing uncertainly. The wind was plucking at her new purple blouse and wide green skirt; it freed truant strands of soft dark hair from the meager queue into which it had been tied with white yarn.

"Isn't she cunning!" one of the women tourists was saying as she turned away.

Chee's lips tightened as he began to look around for Old Man Fat. Finally he saw him passing among the tourists collecting coins.

Then the Little One saw Chee. The uncertainty left her face and she darted through the crowd as her father swung down from his horse. Chee lifted her in his arms, hugging her tight. While he listened to her breathless chatter, he watched Old Man Fat bearing down on them, scowling.

As his father-in-law walked heavily across the gravelled lot, Chee was reminded of a statement his mother sometimes made: "When you see a fat Navaho, you see one who hasn't worked for what he has."

Old Man Fat was fattest in the middle. There was indolence in his walk even though he seemed to hurry, indolence in his cheeks so plump they made his eyes squint, eyes now smoldering with anger.

Some of the tourists were getting into their cars and driving away. The old man said belligerently to Chee, "Why do you come here? To spoil our business? To drive people away?"

"I came to talk with you," Chee answered, trying to keep his voice steady as he faced the old man.

"We have nothing to talk about," Old Man Fat blustered and did not offer to touch Chee's extended hand.

"It's about the Little One." Chee settled his daughter more comfortably against his hip as he weighed carefully all the words he had planned to say. "We are going to miss her very much. It wouldn't be so bad if we knew that *part* of each year she could be with us. That might help you too. You and your wife are no longer young people and you have no young ones here to depend upon." Chee chose his next words remembering the thriftlessness of his wife's parents, and their greed. "Perhaps we could share the care of this little one. Things are good with us. So much snow this year will make lots of grass for the sheep. We have good land for corn and melons."

Chee's words did not have the expected effect. Old Man Fat was enraged. "Farmers, all of you! Long-haired farmers! Do you think everyone must bend his back over the short-handled hoe in order to have food to eat?" His tone changed as he began to brag a little. "We not only have all the things from cans at the trader's, but when the Pueblos come past here on their way to town we buy their salty jerked mutton, young corn for roasting, dried sweet peaches."

Chee's dark eyes surveyed the land along the highway as the old man continued to brag about being "progressive." *He* no longer was tied to the land. He and his wife made money easily and could *buy* all the things they wanted. Chee realized too late that he had stumbled into the old argument between himself and his wife's parents. They had never understood his feeling about the land— that a man took care of his land and it in turn took care of him. Old Man Fat and his wife scoffed at him, called him a Pueblo farmer, all during that summer when he planted and weeded and harvested. Yet they ate the green corn in their mutton stews, and the chili paste from the fresh ripe chilis, and the tortillas from the cornmeal his wife ground. None of this working and sweating in the sun for Old Man Fat, who talked proudly of his easy way of living—collecting money from the trader who rented this strip of land beside the highway, collecting money from the tourists.

Yet Chee had once won that argument. His wife had shared his belief in the integrity of the earth, that jobs and people might fail one but the earth never would. After that first year she had turned from her own people and gone with Chee to Little Canyon.

Old Man Fat was reaching for the Little One. "Don't be coming here with plans for my daughter's daughter," he warned. "If you try to make trouble, I'll take the case to the government man in town."

The impulse was strong in Chee to turn and ride off while he still had the Little One in his arms. But he knew his time of victory would be short. His own family would uphold the old custom of children, especially girl children, belonging to the mother's people. He would have to give his daughter up if the case were brought before the Headman of Little Canyon, and certainly he would have no better chance before a strange white man in town.

He handed the bewildered Little One to her grandfather who stood watching every movement suspiciously. Chee asked, "If I brought you a few things for the Little One, would that be making trouble? Some velvet for a blouse, or some of the jerky she likes so well . . . this summer's melon?"

Old Man Fat backed away from him. "Well," he hesitated, as some of the anger disappeared from his face and beads of greed shone in his eyes. "Well," he repeated. Then as the Little One began to squirm in his arms and cry, he said, "No! No! Stay away from here, you and all your family."

The sense of his failure deepened as Chee rode back to Little Canyon. But it was not until he sat with his family that evening in the hogan, while the familiar bustle of meal preparing went on about him, that he began to doubt the wisdom of the things he'd always believed. He smelled the coffee boiling and the oily fragrance of chili powder dusted into the bubbling pot of stew; he watched his mother turning round crusty fried bread in the small black skillet. All around him was plenty—a half of mutton hanging near the door, bright strings of chili drying, corn hanging by the braided husks, cloth bags of dried peaches. Yet in his heart was nothing.

He heard the familiar sounds of the sheep outside the hogan, the splash of water as his father filled the long drinking trough from the water barrel. When his father came in, Chee could not bring himself to tell a second time of the day's happenings. He watched his wiry, soft-spoken father while his mother told the story, saw his father's queue of graying hair quiver as he nodded his head with sympathetic exclamations.

Chee's doubting, acrid thoughts kept forming: Was it wisdom his father had passed on to him or was his inheritance only the stubbornness of a long-haired Navaho resisting change? Take care of the land and it will take care of you. True, the land had always given him food, but now food was not enough. Perhaps if he had gone to school he would have learned a different kind of wisdom, something to help him now. A schoolboy might even be able to speak convincingly to this government man whom Old Man Fat threatened to call, instead of sitting here like a clod of earth itself—Pueblo farmer indeed. What had the land to give that would restore his daughter?

In the days that followed, Chee herded sheep. He got up in the half-light, drank the hot coffee his mother had ready, then started the flock moving. It was necessary to drive the sheep a long way from the hogan to find good winter forage. Sometimes Chee met friends or relatives who were on their way to town or to the road camp where they hoped to get work; then there was friendly banter and an exchange of news. But most of the days seemed endless; he could not walk far enough or fast enough from his memories of the Little One or from his bitter thoughts. Sometimes it seemed his daughter trudged beside him, so real he could almost hear her footsteps—the muffled pad-pad of little feet clad in deerhide. In the glare of a snow bank he would see her vivid face, brown eyes sparkling. Mingling with the tinkle of sheep bells he heard her laughter.

When, weary of following the small sharp hoof marks that crossed and recrossed in the snow, he sat down in the shelter of a rock, it was only to be reminded that in his thoughts he had forsaken his brotherhood with the earth and sun and growing things. If he remembered times when he had flung himself against the earth to rest, to lie there in the sun until he could no longer feel where he left off and the earth began, it was to remember also that now he sat like an alien against the same earth; the belonging together was gone. The earth was one thing and he was another.

It was during the days when he herded sheep that Chee decided he must leave Little Canyon. Perhaps he would take a job silversmithing for one of the traders in town. Perhaps, even though he spoke little English, he could get a job at the road camp with his cousins; he would ask them about it.

◄►

Springtime transformed the mesas. The peach trees in the canyon were shedding fragrance and pink blossoms on the gentled wind. The sheep no longer foraged for the yellow seeds of chamiso but ranged near the hogan with the long-legged new lambs, eating tender young grass.

Chee was near the hogan on the day his cousins rode up with the message for which he waited. He had been watching with mixed emotions while his father and his sister's husband cleared the fields beside the stream.

"The boss at the camp says he needs an extra hand, but he wants to know if you'll be willing to go with the camp when they move it to the other side of the town?" The tall cousin shifted his weight in the saddle.

The other cousin took up the explanation. "The work near here will last only until the new cut-off beyond Red Sands is finished. After that, the work will be too far away for you to get back here often."

That was what Chee had wanted—to get away from Little Canyon—yet he found himself not so interested in the job beyond town as in this new cut-off which was almost finished. He pulled a blade of grass, split it thoughtfully down the center as he asked questions of his cousins. Finally he said: "I need to think more about this. If I decide on this job I'll ride over."

Before his cousins were out of sight down the canyon Chee was walking toward the fields, a bold plan shaping in his mind. As the plan began to flourish, wild and hardy as young tumbleweed, Chee added his own voice softly to the song his father was singing: ". . . In the middle of the wide field . . . Yellow Corn Boy . . . I wish to put in."

Chee walked slowly around the field, the rich red earth yielding to his footsteps. His plan depended upon this land and upon the things he remembered most about his wife's people.

Through planting time Chee worked zealously and tirelessly. He spoke little of the large new field he was planting because he felt so strongly that just now this was something between himself and the land. The first days he was ever stooping, piercing the ground with the pointed stick, placing the corn kernels there, walking around the field and through it, singing, ". . . His track leads into the ground . . . Yellow Corn Boy . . . his track leads into the ground." After that, each day Chee walked through his field watching for the tips of green to break through; first a few spikes in the center and then more and more until the corn in all parts of the field was above ground. Surely, Chee thought, if he sang the proper songs, if he cared for this land faithfully, it would not forsake him now, even though through the lonely days of winter he had betrayed the goodness of the earth in his thoughts.

Through the summer Chee worked long days, the sun hot upon his back, pulling weeds from around young corn plants; he planted squash and pumpkin; he terraced a small piece of land near his mother's hogan and planted carrots and onions and the moisture-loving chili. He was increasingly restless. Finally he told his family what he hoped the harvest from this land would bring him. Then the whole family waited with him, watching the corn: the slender graceful plants that waved green arms and bent to embrace each other as young winds wandered through the field, the maturing plants flaunting their pollen-laden tassels in the sun, the tall and sturdy parent corn with new-formed ears and a froth of purple, red and yellow corn-beards against the dusty emerald of broad leaves.

Summer was almost over when Chee slung the bulging packs across two pack ponies. His mother helped him tie the heavy rolled pack behind the saddle of the buckskin. Chee knotted the new yellow kerchief about his neck a little tighter, gave the broad black hat brim an extra tug, but these were only gestures of assurance and he knew it. The land had not failed him. That part was done. But this he was riding into? Who could tell?

When Chee arrived at Red Sands, it was as he had expected to find it—no cars on the highway. His cousins had told him that even the Pueblo farmers were using the new cut-off to town. The barren gravel around the Red Sands Trading Post was deserted. A sign banged against the dismantled gas pumps *Closed until further notice.*

Old Man Fat came from the crude summer shelter built beside the log hogan from a few branches of scrub cedar and the sides of wooden crates. He seemed almost friendly when he saw Chee.

"Get down, my son," he said, eyeing the bulging packs. There was no bluster in his voice today and his face sagged, looking somewhat saddened; perhaps because his cheeks were no longer quite full enough to push his eyes upward at the corners. "You are going on a journey?"

Chee shook his head. "Our fields gave us so much this year, I thought to sell or trade this to the trader. I didn't know he was no longer here."

Old Man Fat sighed, his voice dropping to an injured tone. "He says he and his wife are going to rest this winter; then after that he'll build a place up on the new highway."

Chee moved as though to be traveling on, then jerked his head toward the pack ponies. "Anything you need?"

"I'll ask my wife," Old Man Fat said as he led the way to the shelter. "Maybe she has a little money. Things have not been too good with us since the trader closed. Only a few tourists come this way." He shrugged his shoulders. "And with the trader gone—no credit."

Chee was not deceived by his father-in-law's unexpected confidences. He recognized them as a hopeful bid for sympathy and, if possible, something for nothing. Chee made no answer. He was thinking that so far he had been right about his wife's parents: their thriftlessness had left them with no resources to last until Old Man Fat found another easy way of making a living.

Old Man Fat's Wife was in the shelter working at her loom. She turned rather wearily when her husband asked with noticeable deference if she would give him money to buy supplies. Chee surmised that the only income here was from his mother-in-law's weaving.

She peered around the corner of the shelter at the laden ponies, and then she looked at Chee. "What do you have there, my son?"

Chee smiled to himself as he turned to pull the pack from one of the ponies, dragged it to the shelter where he untied the ropes. Pumpkins and hardshelled squash tumbled out, and the ears of corn—pale yellow husks fitting firmly over plump ripe kernels, blue corn, red corn, yellow corn, many-colored corn, ears and ears of it—tumbled into every corner of the shelter.

"Yooooh," Old Man Fat's Wife exclaimed as she took some of the ears in her hands. Then she glanced up at her son-in-law. "But we have no money for all this. We have sold almost everything we own—even the brass bed that stood in the hogan."

Old Man Fat's brass bed. Chee concealed his amusement as he started back for another pack. That must have been a hard parting. Then he stopped, for, coming from the cool darkness of the hogan was the Little One, rubbing her eyes as though she had been asleep. She stood for a moment in the doorway and Chee saw that she was dirty, barefoot, her hair uncombed, her little blouse shorn of all its silver buttons. Then she ran toward Chee, her arms outstretched. Heedless of Old Man Fat and his wife, her father caught her in his arms, her hair falling in a dark cloud across his face, the sweetness of her laughter warm against his shoulder.

It was the haste within him to get this slow waiting game played through to the finish that made Chee speak unwisely. It was the desire to swing her before him in the saddle and ride fast to Little Canyon that prompted his words. "The money doesn't matter. You still have something. . . ."

Chee knew immediately that he had overspoken. The old woman looked from him to the corn spread before her. Unfriendliness began to harden in his father-in-law's face. All the old arguments between himself and his wife's people came pushing and crowding in between them now.

Old Man Fat began kicking the ears of corn back onto the canvas as he eyed Chee angrily. "And you rode all the way over here thinking that for a little food we would give up our daughter's daughter?"

Chee did not wait for the old man to reach for the Little One. He walked dazedly to the shelter, rubbing his cheek against her soft dark hair and put her gently into her grandmother's lap. Then he turned back to the horses. He had failed. By his own haste he had failed. He swung into the saddle, his hand touching the roll behind it. Should he ride on into town?

Then he dismounted, scarcely glancing at Old Man Fat, who stood uncertainly at the corner of the shelter, listening to his wife. "Give me a hand with this other pack of corn, Grandfather," Chee said, carefully keeping the small bit of hope from his voice.

Puzzled, but willing, Old Man Fat helped carry the other pack to the shelter, opening it to find more corn as well as carrots and round pale yellow onions. Chee went back for the roll behind the buckskin's saddle and carried it to the entrance of the shelter where he cut the ropes and gave the canvas a nudge with his toe. Tins of coffee rolled out, small plump cloth bags; jerked meat from several butcherings spilled from a flour sack, and bright red chilis splashed like flames against the dust.

"I will leave all this anyhow," Chee told them. "I would not want my daughter nor even you old people to go hungry."

Old Man Fat picked up a shiny tin of coffee, then put it down. With trembling hands he began to untie one of the cloth bags—dried sweet peaches.

The Little One had wriggled from her grandmother's lap, unheeded, and was on her knees, digging her hands into the jerked meat.

"There is almost enough food here to last all winter," Old Man Fat's Wife sought the eyes of her husband.

Chee said, "I meant it to be enough. But that was when I thought you might send the Little One back with me." He looked down at his daughter noisily sucking jerky. Her mouth, both fists were full of it. "I am sorry that you feel you cannot bear to part with her."

Old Man Fat's Wife brushed a straggly wisp of gray hair from her forehead as she turned to look at the Little One. Old Man Fat was looking too. And it was not a thing to see. For in that moment the Little One ceased to be their daughter's daughter and became just another mouth to feed.

"And why not?" the old woman asked wearily.

Chee was settled in the saddle, the barefooted Little One before him. He urged the buckskin faster, and his daughter clutched his shirtfront. The purpling mesas flung back the echo: ". . . My corn embrace each other. In the middle of the wide field . . . Yellow Corn Boy embrace each other."

Questions for Discussion and Writing

1. What are the customs and laws under which the crises of this story have taken place and are taking place? How does Chee feel about following those laws, and why?
2. How does the reader know that the grandparents do not really believe the old teachings and are invoking the laws of the Navajos for other reasons? Why do they want Chee's daughter?
3. In what ways do the tourists have a role in the conflicts of this story?
4. Why are the grandparents finally willing to give up the child? Why, or why not, do you think that their doing so is consistent with their characters as described earlier in the story?
5. In what ways do Platero and Miller create and show Chee's belief in "the integrity of the earth" (p. 390)? Are the writers successful? Explain your response.

JULIO CORTÁZAR

The Health of the Sick

Julio Cortázar was born in Brussels, Belgium, in 1914, while his parents were abroad on business there. The family returned to Buenos Aires when he was four years old. As a young man, Cortázar taught French literature, protested the Argentinian dictator Juan Perón, was jailed for a short time because of those protests, later became a director of a publishing company, and, in 1952, moved to Paris where he became a free-lance interpreter for UNESCO. He still lives and writes in Paris today.

A master of the fantastic short story, Cortázar has published his stories in six collections. Many of his short stories depict the everyday lives of common people whose peaceful existence is subtly and mysteriously subverted. Often his stories are based on his dreams, nightmares, and hallucinations brought on by illness or obsession. The author has said that his short stories serve him as exorcisms of "repressed, irrational instincts and phobias."

Much of Cortázar's fame rests on his second novel, Rayuela *(1963) in Spanish, or* Hopscotch *(1966) in English, a book that became famous to American readers after it was made into a popular and disturbing film. Its title comes from the author's innovative use of language and narration in the novel, in which the reader, led by the narrator's directions, can jump forward and backward through the book as if playing hopscotch. Cortázar, one critic claims, "wants to open up the closed literary order, to establish an open order that offers multiple perspectives. Even more, he chiefly wants disorder, the breaking of logical and discursive expression into a disconnected and fragmented story, which he feels can best be compared to a kaleidoscope."*

"The Health of the Sick" was published in Spanish in 1966 as part of a collection of Cortázar's stories entitled Todos los fuegos el fuego, *and in English in 1973 as* All Fires the Fire and Other Stories.

Before you read "The Health of the Sick," write about a time in your life when people in your family kept a secret from one of the family members, substituting a cover-up instead. You could also write about a time when you were the person keeping the secret. Describe the secret, why it needed to be concealed, and what it took to make the cover-up plausible.

W hen Aunt Clelia unexpectedly felt ill, there was a moment of panic in the family, and for several hours no one seemed able to face the situation and discuss a plan of action, not even Uncle Roque, who was always finding the most sensible way out. They called Carlos on the phone at the office, Rosa and Pepa dismissed their piano pupils, and even Aunt Clelia was more worried about Mama than about herself. She was sure that what she felt wasn't serious, but you couldn't give Mama upsetting news with her blood pressure and sugar content. They all very well knew that Doctor Bonifaz had been the first to understand and to approve their hiding from Mama what had happened to Alejandro. If Aunt Clelia had to be confined to bed, they would have to figure out something so that Mama wouldn't suspect she was sick, but already what had happened to Alejandro had become so difficult, and now this to boot; the slightest mistake, and she would find out the truth. The house was big, but you still had to keep in mind Mama's keen ear and her disturbing capacity for guessing where everyone was. Pepa, who had called Doctor Bonifaz from the upstairs telephone, warned her brother and sister that the doctor would come right away and that they should leave the front door ajar so he could enter without ringing. While Rosa and Uncle Roque attended to Aunt Clelia, who had fainted twice and was complaining of an unbearable headache, Carlos stayed with Mama to tell her about the new developments in the diplomatic conflict with Brazil and to read her the latest news. Mama was in a good mood that afternoon, and her back didn't hurt as it almost always did at siesta time. She asked each one of them what was the matter, they seemed so nervous, and everyone seemed to be talking about low air pressure and the horrid effects of additives in bread. At teatime, Uncle Roque came to chat with Mama so that Carlos could take a bath and wait downstairs for the doctor. Aunt Clelia was feeling better now, but it was an effort for her to move around in bed and she had almost no interest in what had worried her so much when she came out of the first dizzy spell. Pepa and Rosa took turns by her side, offering her tea and water without getting an answer; the house calmed down at dusk, and the brother and sisters thought that perhaps Aunt Clelia's [illness] wasn't serious and that the next afternoon she would again go into Mama's room as if nothing had happened.

With Alejandro, things had been worse, because Alejandro had been killed in a car accident shortly after reaching Montevideo, where he was expected at the house of an engineer friend. Already almost a year had passed since then, but it was always the first day for the family, for all except Mama. For Mama, Alejandro was in Brazil, where a Recife business firm had commissioned him to set up a cement factory. The idea of preparing Mama, of hinting to her that Alejandro had had an accident and was slightly wounded, had not occurred to them, even after Doctor Bonifaz's warnings. Even María Laura, beyond all understanding in those first hours, had admitted that it was impossible to break the news to Mama. Carlos and María Laura's father went to Uruguay to bring back Alejandro's body, while the family, as usual, took care of Mama, who was distressed and difficult that day. The engineering club agreed to have the wake at its headquarters, and Pepa, the one most occupied with Mama, didn't even get to see Alejandro's coffin, while the others took turns every hour and accompanied the poor María Laura, lost in a tearless horror. As almost always, it was up to Uncle Roque to do the thinking. Early in the morning, he spoke to Carlos, who was crying silently for his brother with his head on the green cover of the dining room table, where they had so often played cards. Then Aunt Clelia joined them, because Mama slept the whole night, and they didn't have to worry about her. With Rosa's and Pepa's tacit agreement, they decided the first measures, beginning with the abduction of *La Nación*—at times, Mama got up the strength to read the newspaper for a few minutes—and all agreed with what Uncle Roque had thought up. It was that a Brazilian company had given Alejandro a contract to spend a year in Recife, and in a matter of hours Alejandro had to give up his brief vacation at the house of an engineer friend, pack his suitcase, and jump on the first plane. Mama had to understand that these were new times, that industrialists didn't know from sentiments, but that Alejandro would soon find a way to take a week's vacation in the middle of the year and come down to Buenos Aires. All this seemed very well to Mama, although she cried a little, and they had to bring her smelling salts. Carlos, who knew how to make her laugh, told her it was shameful to cry about their kid brother's first success and that Alejandro wouldn't like it if he knew they acted that way when they received the news of his contract. Then Mama calmed down and said that she would drink a bit of sherry to Alejandro's health. Carlos abruptly went out to get the wine, but it was Rosa who brought it and who toasted with Mama.

Mama's life was difficult, and although she seldom complained, they had to keep her company and distract her as much as possible. When, the day after Alejandro's funeral, she wondered why María Laura had not come to visit her as on every Thursday, Pepa went to the Novallis' house in the afternoon to speak to María Laura. At that hour, Uncle Roque was in a lawyer friend's study, explaining the situation to him; the lawyer promised to write immediately to his brother, who was working in Recife (cities were not chosen by chance in Mama's house), and organize the letter end. Doctor Bonifaz had already visited Mama as if by chance, and, after examining her sight, he found her considerably improved, but asked her to abstain from reading newspapers for a few days. Aunt Clelia was in charge of summarizing the most interesting news for her; luckily, Mama didn't like the radio newscasts, because they were common and every few minutes there were commercials on dubious medicines that people took come what may, and that's how they went.

María Laura came Friday afternoon and talked about all that she had to study for the architecture exams.

"Yes, my dear", Mama said, looking at her affectionately. "Your eyes are red from reading, and that's bad. Put some boric acid compresses on them—that's the best there is."

Rosa and Pepa were constantly there to assist during the conversation, and María Laura managed to endure it and even smiled when Mama started to go on about that naughty fiancé who went so far away and almost without warning. That was today's youth for you, the world had gone crazy, and everybody was in a hurry and had no time for anything. Then Mama lost the thread in the already well-known anecdotes about parents and grandparents, and the coffee came, and then Carlos came in with jokes and stories, and at one point Uncle Roque stood in the door of the bedroom and looked at them in his good-natured way, and everything went as it always did until it was time for Mama's rest.

The family got used to it; it was harder for María Laura, but then again she had to see Mama only on Thursdays. One day, Alejandro's first letter arrived (Mama had already wondered twice about his silence), and Carlos read it at the foot of the bed. Alejandro was delighted with Recife, he talked about the port and the parrot-sellers and the delicious cold drinks. Everybody's mouth watered in the family when they found out that pineapples didn't cost a thing and that the coffee there was the real McCoy and had a fragrance . . . Mama asked them to show her the envelope and told them to give the stamp to the Marolda boy, who was a stamp collector, although she didn't approve of boys playing around with stamps, because afterwards they didn't wash their hands, and the stamps had been all over the place.

"They lick them to glue them on," Mama would always say, "and the germs stay on their tongue and incubate—it's a well-known fact. But give it to him anyway, he has so many already that one more . . ."

The next day Mama called Rosa in and dictated a letter for Alejandro, asking him when he'd be able to take a vacation and if the trip wouldn't cost too much. She explained how she felt and spoke of the promotion they had just given Carlos and of the prize that one of Pepa's pupils had won. She also told him that María Laura visited her every Thursday without fail, but that she studied too much, and that was bad for the eyes. When the letter was written, Mama signed it at the bottom in pencil and gently kissed the paper. Pepa got up with the pretext of going for an envelope, and Aunt Clelia came in with the five o'clock pills and some flowers for the vase on the bureau.

It was not easy, because during that time Mama's blood pressure went up even more, and the family got to wondering if there wasn't some unconscious influence, something that showed from their behavior, an anxiety and depression that did Mama harm, despite the precautions and false gaiety. But it couldn't be, because just by pretending to laugh they all had ended up by really laughing with Mama, and at times they made jokes and cuffed each other even when they weren't with her and then looked at each other as if suddenly waking up, and Pepa got very red, and Carlos lit a cigarette with his head slouched. The only thing that mattered though was that time pass and that Mama not realize anything. Uncle Roque had spoken with Doctor Bonifaz, and everybody agreed that they had to continue the merciful comedy, as Aunt Clelia called it, indefinitely. The only problem was María Laura's visits, because Mama naturally insisted upon talking about Alejandro. She wanted to know if they would get married as soon as he came back from Recife or if that crazy son of hers was going to accept another contract somewhere faraway and for such a long time again. The only thing to do was to constantly go into the bedroom and distract Mama and remove María Laura, who would keep very still in her chair, squeezing her hands so tight that she'd hurt herself, but one day, Mama asked Aunt Clelia why everybody rushed in like that when María Laura came to see her, as if it were the only opportunity they had to be with her. Aunt Clelia laughed and said that they all saw a little of Alejandro in María Laura, and that's why they liked to be with her when she came.

"You're right. María Laura is so good," Mama said. "That rascally son of mine doesn't deserve her, believe you me."

"Look who's talking," Aunt Clelia said. "Why, you drool every time you mention your son."

Mama also laughed and remembered that they would be getting a letter from Alejandro any day then. The letter came, and Uncle Roque brought it with the five o'clock tea. This time, Mama wanted to read the letter and asked for her reading glasses. She read industriously, as if each sentence were a tasty morsel that she had to savor slowly.

"The boys today don't have respect," she said, without giving it too much importance. "All right, so in my time they didn't use those machines, but still I would never have dared write to my father that way, and you neither."

"Of course not," Uncle Roque said. "With the temper the old man had."

"When will you stop saying 'the old man,' Roque. You know I don't like to hear you say that, but you don't care. Remember how Mama would get."

"O.K., take it easy. 'The old man' is just a manner of speaking, it has nothing to do with respect."

"It's very strange," Mama said, taking off her glasses and looking at the moldings on the ceiling. "We've already gotten five or six letters from Alejandro, and in none of them has he called me . . . Oh, it's a secret between the two of us. It's strange, you know. Why hasn't he called me that, not even once?"

"Maybe the boy thinks it's silly to put it on paper. Saying is one thing . . . what is it he says? . . ."

"It's a secret," Mama said. "A secret between my little son and myself."

Neither Pepa nor Rosa knew what it was, and Carlos shrugged his shoulders when they asked him.

"What more do you want, Uncle? The most I can do is forge his signature. Mama will forget about it in time, don't take it so much to heart."

Four or five months later, after a letter from Alejandro in which he explained how much he had to do (although he was happy because it was a great opportunity for a young engineer), Mama insisted it was time he took a vacation and came down to Buenos Aires. It seemed to Rosa, who was writing Mama's answer, that she was dictating more slowly, as if she had been thinking each sentence out.

"Who knows if the poor thing will be able to come?" Rosa commented, trying to sound offhand. "It would be a shame for him to make a wrong move precisely when it's going so well for him and he's so happy."

Mama continued the dictation as if she hadn't heard. Her health left much to be desired, and she would like to see Alejandro, even if it were only for a few days. Alejandro also had María Laura to think about—not that she thought he was neglecting his fiancée, but affection doesn't live on pretty words and promises alone. So, she hoped Alejandro would write soon with good news. Rosa noticed that Mama didn't kiss the paper after signing, but that she stared at the letter as if she wanted to record it in her memory. "Poor Alejandro," thought Rosa and then crossed herself quickly so that Mama wouldn't see.

"Look," Uncle Roque said to Carlos when they were alone that night for their domino game, "this is going to get serious. We've got to invent something plausible, or in the end she's going to realize."

"What can I say, Uncle? The best thing is for Alejandro to answer in a way that will keep her happy a while longer. The poor thing is in such delicate condition, you can't even think of . . ."

"Nobody said anything about that, boy. But I'm telling you, your mother is the kind that doesn't give up. I know, it runs in the family."

Mama read Alejandro's evasive letter without comment; he would try to get a vacation as soon as he handed in the plans for the first sector of the factory. When María Laura arrived that afternoon, Mama asked her to entreat Alejandro to come to Buenos Aires, even if for no more than a week. María Laura told Rosa afterwards that Mama had asked that of her at the only moment when no one else could hear her. Uncle Roque was the first to suggest what all of them had already thought so many times without daring to come out and say it, and when Mama dictated to Rosa another letter to Alejandro, insisting that he come, it was decided that the only thing left to do was to try and see if Mama was in good shape to receive the first disagreeable news. Carlos consulted Doctor Bonifaz, who prescribed prudence and a few drops. They let the necessary time pass, and one afternoon Uncle Roque came to sit at the foot of Mama's bed, while Rosa prepared maté and looked out the window of the balcony, beside the medicine chest.

"How do you like that? Now I'm starting to understand a little why this devil of a nephew can't make up his mind to come and see us," Uncle Roque said. "The thing is, he just didn't want to upset you, knowing that you're still not well."

Mama looked at him as if she didn't understand.

"The Novallis phoned today. It seems that María Laura received news from Alejandro. He's fine, but he won't be able to travel for a few months."

"Why won't he be able to travel?" Mama asked.

"Because there's something wrong with his foot, it seems. The ankle, I think. We'll have to ask María Laura to find out what it is. Old man Novalli mentioned a fracture or something like that."

"Ankle fracture?" Mama said.

Before Uncle Roque could answer, Rosa was there with the bottle of salts. Doctor Bonifaz came immediately, and it was all over in a few hours, but they were long hours, and Doctor Bonifaz didn't leave the family until well into the night. Only two days later did Mama feel well enough to ask Pepa to write to Alejandro. When Pepa, who hadn't understood, came as always with the block and the pencil holder, Mama closed her eyes and refused with a nod.

"You write to him. Tell him to take good care of himself."

Pepa obeyed, not knowing why she was writing one sentence after another, since Mama wasn't going to read the letter. That night, she told Carlos that all the time she was writing at Mama's bedside, she was absolutely sure that Mama wasn't going to read or sign that letter. Her eyes remained closed, and she didn't open them until it was time for her medicinal tea; she seemed to have forgotten, to be thinking of other things.

Alejandro answered with the most natural tone in the world, explaining that he hadn't wanted to tell her about the fracture so as not to upset her. At first, they had made a mistake and put on a cast that had to be changed, but now he was better, and in a few weeks he'd be able to start walking again. Altogether he had some two months to go, although the worst part was that his work had been greatly delayed at the busiest moment, and . . .

Carlos, who read the letter out loud, had the impression that Mama wasn't listening to him like other times. From time to time, she looked at the clock, which in her was a sign of impatience. At seven, Rosa had to bring her the broth with Doctor Bonifaz's drops, and it was five after seven.

"Well", Carlos said, folding the letter. "Now you see that everything's O.K. Nothing's seriously wrong with the kid."

"Of course," Mama said. "Look, tell Rosa to hurry, will you?"

Mama listened attentively while María Laura told her all about Alejandro's fracture and even advised her to recommend some ankle rubs, which had done his father so much good the time he fell off a horse in Matanzas. Almost immediately, as if it were part of the same sentence, she asked if they couldn't give her some orange blossom water, which always cleared her head.

The first to speak was María Laura, that very afternoon. She said it to Rosa in the drawing room, before going, and Rosa stood there looking at her as if she couldn't believe her ears.

"Please," Rosa said, "how can you imagine such a thing?"

"I'm not imagining it, it's the truth," María Laura said. "And I'm not going there any more, Rosa. Ask me all you want, but I'm not going back to that room again."

When you get right down to it, María Laura's notion didn't seem that ridiculous, but Aunt Clelia summed up everyone's sentiment when she said that in a home like theirs a duty was a duty. It was Rosa's turn to go to the Novallis', but María Laura had such a fit of hysterics that they would just have to respect her decision; that same afternoon, Pepa and Rosa began to comment on how much the poor girl had to study and how tired she was. Mama didn't say anything, and when Thursday came along she didn't ask for María Laura. That Thursday marked ten months since Alejandro left for Brazil. The company was so satisfied with his services, that some weeks later they proposed a renewal of his contract for another year, providing he go to Belén immediately to install another factory. Uncle Roque thought this was just wonderful, a great triumph for a boy so young.

"Alejandro was always the smartest one," Mama said. "Just as Carlos is the most tenacious."

"You're right," Uncle Roque said, wondering what could have gotten into María Laura that day. "The truth is you've turned out some wonderful children, sister."

"Oh yes, I can't complain. Their father would have liked to have seen them grown up. The girls, so good, and poor Carlos, such a homebody."

"And Alejandro, with so much future ahead of him."

"Ah, yes," Mama said.

"Why, that new contract alone that they're offering him . . . Oh well, you'll answer your son when you're in the mood, I suppose; he must be going around with his tail between his legs thinking the news of the renewal isn't going to please you."

"Ah, yes," Mama said again, looking at the ceiling. "Tell Pepa to write to him, she knows."

Pepa wrote, without being very sure of what she should say to Alejandro, but convinced that it was always better to have a complete text to avoid contradictions in the answers. As for Alejandro, he was very happy that Mama appreciated what an opportunity they were offering him. The ankle was doing fine, and he would ask for a vacation as soon as he could, to come and spend two weeks with them. Mama assented with a slight nod and asked if *La Razón* had arrived yet, so that Carlos could read her the cable news. Everything began to run smoothly in the house, now that there seemed to be no more surprises in store, and Mama's health remained stationary. Her children took turns at keeping her company; Uncle Roque and Aunt Clelia were constantly going in and out. Carlos read Mama the newspaper at night, and Pepa in the morning. Rosa and Aunt Clelia took care of the medications and baths; Uncle Roque had maté in her room two or three times a day. Mama was never alone and never asked for María Laura; every three weeks she received news of Alejandro without comment; she'd tell Pepa to answer and talk about something else, always intelligent and attentive and distant.

It was around then that Uncle Roque began to read her the news about tensions with Brazil. He had written the first reports on the edges of the newspapers, but Mama didn't care about the perfection of the reading, so after a few days Uncle Roque got used to improvising. At first, he accompanied the disturbing cablegrams with some comment on the problems this situation could cause Alejandro and the other Argentines in Brazil, but as Mama didn't seem to worry, he stopped insisting, although every few days the situation grew a little worse. In Alejandro's letter, the possibility of a break in diplomatic relations was mentioned, although the boy was as optimistic as ever and convinced that the chancellors would mend the dispute.

Mama would make no comments, perhaps because it was still a long time before Alejandro could request leave, but one night she suddenly asked Doctor Bonifaz if the situation with Brazil was as bad as the newspapers said.

"Brazil? Well, yes, things aren't going too well," the doctor said. "Let's hope that the statesmen have the good sense . . ."

Mama looked at him as if surprised that he had answered without hesitating. She sighed softly and changed the subject. That night, she was in better spirits than usual, and Doctor Bonifaz left satisfied. The next day, Aunt Clelia fell ill; the fainting spells seemed like a passing thing, but Doctor Bonifaz spoke to Uncle Roque and advised them to put Aunt Clelia in a hospital. They told Mama, who was at that moment listening to the news about Brazil which Carlos brought with the evening paper, that Aunt Clelia was in bed with a migraine. They had the whole night to think about what they would do, but Uncle Roque was rather crushed after speaking to Doctor Bonifaz, and it was up to Carlos and the girls to decide. Rosa thought of Manolita Valle's villa and the good country air; the second day of Aunt Clelia's migraine, Carlos led the conversation so well that it was as if Mama herself had advised a spell in Manolita's villa, which would do Clelia so much good. An office companion of Carlos' offered to take her in his car, since the train would be tiring with that migraine. Aunt Clelia was the first to want to say goodbye to Mama, and between them, Carlos and Uncle Roque led her step by step, so that Mama could tell her not to catch cold in those automobiles they have today and to remember to take her fruit laxative at night.

"Clelia looked red in the face," Mama said to Pepa that afternoon. "She looked bad to me, you know."

"Oh, after a few days in the country she'll be fine again. She's been a bit tired these last few months; I remember Manolita telling her she should come keep her company at the villa."

"Really? That's strange, she never told me."

"So as not to upset you, I suppose."

"And how long is she going to stay, dear?"

Pepa didn't know, but she would ask Doctor Bonifaz, who was the one who had advised the change of air. Mama didn't speak of the matter again until some days later. (Aunt Clelia had just had a stroke in the hospital, and Rosa took turns at keeping her company with Uncle Roque.)

"I wonder when Clelia's coming back," Mama said.

"Come on, the one time the poor thing makes up her mind to leave you and get a change of air . . ."

"Yes, but what she had was nothing, you all said."

"Of course it's nothing. She must be staying on because she likes it, or to keep Manolita company; you know what good friends they are."

"Phone the villa and find out when she's coming back," Mama said.

Rosa phoned the villa, and they told her that Aunt Clelia was better, but that she still felt a bit weak, so that she would take the opportunity to stay. The weather was splendid in Olavarría.

"I don't like that at all," Mama said. "Clelia should have come home by now."

"Please, Mama, don't worry so much. Why don't you get better as soon as you can and go sunbathe with Clelia and Manolita at the villa?"

"Me?" Mama said, looking at Carlos as if astonished, outraged, insulted. Carlos laughed to hide what he felt (Aunt Clelia was in critical condition, Pepa had just phoned) and kissed her on the cheek as if she were a naughty child.

"Silly little Mama," he said, trying not to think of anything.

That night, Mama slept badly and at daybreak asked for Clelia, as if they could have heard from the villa at that hour. (Aunt Clelia had just died, and they had decided to have her wake at the funeral home.) At eight o'clock, they called the villa from the living room telephone, so that Mama could listen to the conversation, and luckily Aunt Clelia had had a good night, although Manolita's doctor advised her to stay while the good weather continued. Carlos was very happy, since the office was closed for the annual financial statement, and he came in, in pajamas, to have his maté at the foot of Mama's bed and chat with her.

"Look," Mama said, "I think we should write to Alejandro and tell him to come see his aunt. He was always Clelia's favorite, and it's only right that he should come."

"But Aunt Clelia doesn't have anything, Mama. If Alejandro hasn't been able to come and see you, imagine . . ."

"That's up to him," Mama said. "You write and tell him that Clelia is sick and that he should come see her."

"But how many times do we have to tell you that what Aunt Clelia has isn't serious?"

"All the better. But it won't do any harm to write him."

They wrote that same afternoon and read the letter to Mama. During the days when Alejandro's letter would be arriving (Aunt Clelia was still doing fine, but Manolita's doctor insisted that she take advantage of the good country air), the diplomatic situation with Brazil got even worse, and Carlos told Mama that it wouldn't be surprising if Alejandro's letters were delayed.

"It would almost seem on purpose," Mama said. "Now you'll see that he won't be able to come either."

None of them could make up his mind to read her Alejandro's letter.

All together at the dining room table, they looked at Aunt Clelia's empty place, then looked at each other, hesitating.

"This is ridiculous. We're so used to this comedy already, that one scene more or less . . ."

"Then you take it to her," Pepa said, while her eyes filled with tears and she dried them with her napkin.

"Whatever you do, there's something wrong somehow. Each time I go into her room now it feels like I'm expecting a surprise, a trap, almost."

"It's María Laura's fault," Rosa said. "She put the idea into our heads, and we can't act naturally anymore. And to top it off, Aunt Clelia . . ."

"Well, now that you mention it, I think it would be a good idea to talk to María Laura," Uncle Roque said. "It would be the most logical thing for her to come visit after her exams and bring your mother the news that Alejandro won't be able to come."

"But doesn't it make your blood run cold that Mama doesn't ask for María Laura anymore, even though Alejandro mentions her in all his letters?"

"The temperature of my blood has nothing to do with it," Uncle Roque said. "You either do it or don't do it, and that's that."

It took Rosa two hours to convince María Laura, but she was her best friend, and María Laura loved them all dearly, even Mama, although she had frightened her. They had to prepare a new letter, which María Laura brought along with a bouquet of flowers and the mandarine orange drops that Mama liked. Yes, luckily the worst exams were over, and she could go to San Vicente for a few weeks to rest.

"The country air will do you good," Mama said. "Now with Clelia . . . Did you call the villa today, Pepa? Oh yes, I remember that you told me . . . Well, it's been three weeks since Clelia left, and just look . . ."

María Laura and Rosa made the obvious comments, the tea tray came, and María Laura read Mama some paragraphs from Alejandro's letter with the news of the temporary imprisonment of all foreign technicians, and how funny he thought it was to be living in a splendid hotel at the government's expense, while waiting for the chancellors to mend the dispute. Mama made no comment, drank her cup of linden flower tea and became sleepy. The girls continued their conversation in the living room, relieved. María Laura was about to go, when she suddenly thought of the telephone and told Rosa. It seemed to Rosa that Carlos, too, had thought of that, and later she spoke to Uncle Roque, who shrugged his shoulders. Faced with something like that, the only thing you could do was to keep reading the newspaper. But Rosa and Pepa also told Carlos about it, who refused to look for a solution except that of accepting what nobody wanted to accept.

"We'll see," Carlos said. "She still may think of that and ask for it. In which case . . ."

But Mama never asked them to bring her the telephone so that she could speak personally with Aunt Clelia. Every morning she asked if there was news from the villa and then returned to her silence, where time seemed to be measured in doses of medicine and medicinal tea. She wasn't displeased when Uncle Roque came with *La Razón* to read the latest news about the conflict with Brazil, but neither did she seem to care if the newsboy was late or if Uncle Roque was more occupied than usual with a chess problem. Rosa and Pepa became convinced that Mama didn't care if they read her the news, or phoned the villa, or brought a letter from Alejandro. But you couldn't be sure, because sometimes Mama raised her head and looked at them with that same profound look, in which there was no change, no acceptance. Routine took over, and for Rosa, phoning a black hole at the end of the line was as simple and everyday as reading false cable news on a background of sales advertisements or soccer news was for Uncle Roque, or as coming in with stories of his visit to the Olavarría villa and of the baskets of fruit Manolita and Aunt Clelia sent them was for Carlos. Not even during Mama's last months did they change their habits, although they had little importance by then. Doctor Bonifaz told them that, fortunately, Mama would not suffer at all and that she would pass away without feeling it. But Mama remained clear-headed until the end, when her children came around her, unable to hide what they felt.

"How good you were to me," Mama said. "All that trouble you went through so I wouldn't suffer."

Uncle Roque was sitting beside her and he caressed her hand cheerfully, saying how silly she was. Pepa and Rosa, pretending to look for something in the bureau, now knew that María Laura had been right; they knew what in some way they had always known.

"Such good care of me . . .," Mama said, and Pepa squeezed Rosa's hand, because, after all, those five words put everything back into order, reestablished the long and necessary comedy. But Carlos, at the foot of the bed, looked at Mama as if he knew she was going to say something further.

"Now you'll all be able to relax," Mama said. "We won't give you any more trouble."

Uncle Roque was going to protest, to say something, but Carlos went to him and violently squeezed his shoulder. Mama was slipping gradually into a doze, and it was better not to bother her.

Three days after the funeral, Alejandro's last letter arrived, in which, as always, he asked about Mama's and Aunt Clelia's health. Rosa opened it and began reading without a second thought, and when she raised her eyes because they were suddenly blinded with tears, she realized that while she was reading, she had been thinking about how she was going to break the news to Alejandro that Mama was dead.

Translated by Suzanne Jill Levine

Questions for Discussion and Writing

1. As this story unfolds, it is difficult to follow all that is happening and to identify who each character is, especially in relationship to each other. Keep track of all the questions you have as you read; fill in the answers as you come upon them. Then write about why you think Cortázar wrote the story in this way. Discuss what this confusion has to do with the meaning of the story.

2. What are the motivations behind the patterns of secrecy in this family? When you've come up with the obvious answers, probe further for more subtle possibilities.

3. Does Mama know the real situation? Support your response with details and brief passages from the story.

4. Near the end of the story Cortázar writes, " 'Such good care of me . . .,' Mama said, and Pepa squeezed Rosa's hand, because, after all, those five words put everything back into order, reestablished the long and necessary comedy" (p. 407). Considering this ending to the story, explain *(1)* how the story could be seen as a "long and necessary comedy," and *(2)* in what ways we might read this line ironically.

AHARON MEGGED

The Name

Born in Wloclawek, Poland, in 1920, Aharon Megged moved to
Palestine (now Israel) as a young boy, graduating from high school
there in 1937. Hebrew was his family's language even in Poland,
where his father had been a Hebrew teacher. Only when his grandmother came to Israel did Megged learn Yiddish, falling in love with
the language through her.

Writing began for Megged in notebooks he filled with poetry when
he was eight or nine years old. He published his first short story, "A
Load of Oxen," at the age of twenty, exploring in it his experiences
as a stevedore at the Haifa harbor and the relationships there among
Arab and Jewish workers. Although writing has always been his
focus, Megged was a founding member of S'dot Yam, a fishing kib-
butz where he spent twelve years (1938–1950). Since 1950, he has
lived in Tel Aviv, working as editor of the weekly literary supplement of the newspaper Lamerhav, with time away from 1968 to 1971
as cultural attaché to London and, in 1984, as an international
writer in the writing program at the University of Iowa. In Israel,
Megged has won several prizes for his work as a writer.

"The Name," one of Megged's earlier stories from the 1950s, was
written in reaction against those Israelis who believed they were
starting a nation with connections only to an ancient past, rejecting
in the process the cultures and histories that the Diaspora—or scattering of Jews around the world—had created in the intervening
centuries. The story explores Grandfather Zisskind's pain in what
Megged calls "the failure of continuity" in place and culture and in
the history of the family itself. "If you live in the same place over
time," he explains, "you walk through centuries even as you live your
daily life." Many Israelis have had to confront this failure of continuity—a two-thousand-year gap between their present and their
past.

Before you read "The Name," write about an older person in your life who wants you and others to act and think in a different way—that is, the way in which that older person acts or thinks. Describe the person's demands on you and your reaction to those demands. Then discuss how you might understand those demands by looking at the world through that older person's eyes.

Grandfather Zisskind lived in a little house in a southern suburb of the town. About once a month, on a Saturday afternoon, his granddaughter Raya and her young husband Yehuda would go and pay him a visit.

Raya would give three cautious knocks on the door (an agreed signal between herself and her grandfather ever since her childhood, when he had lived in their house together with the whole family) and they would wait for the door to be opened. "Now he's getting up," Raya would whisper to Yehuda, her face glowing, when the sound of her grandfather's slippers was heard from within, shuffling across the room. Another moment, and the key would be turned and the door opened.

"Come in," he would say somewhat absently, still buttoning up his trousers, with the rheum of sleep in his eyes. Although it was very hot he wore a yellow winter vest with long sleeves, from which his wrists stuck out—white, thin, delicate as a girl's, as was his bare neck with its taut skin.

After Raya and Yehuda had sat down at the table, which was covered with a white cloth showing signs of the meal he had eaten alone—crumbs from the Sabbath loaf, a plate with meat leavings, a glass containing some grape pips, a number of jars and so on—he would smooth the crumpled pillows, spread a cover over the narrow bed and tidy up. It was a small room, and its obvious disorder aroused pity for the old man's helplessness in running his home. In the corner was a shelf with two sooty kerosene burners, a kettle and two or three saucepans, and next to it a basin containing plates, knives and forks. In another corner was a stand holding books with thick leather bindings, leaning and lying on each other. Some of his clothes hung over the backs of the chairs. An ancient walnut cupboard with an empty buffet stood exactly opposite the door. On the wall hung a clock which had long since stopped.

"We ought to make Grandfather a present of a clock," Raya would say to Yehuda as she surveyed the room and her glance lighted on the clock; but every time the matter slipped her memory. She loved her grandfather, with his pointed white silky beard, his tranquil face from which a kind of holy radiance emanated, his quiet, soft voice which seemed to have been made only for uttering words of sublime wisdom. She also respected him for his pride, which had led him to move out of her mother's house and live by himself, accepting the hardship and trouble and the affliction of loneliness in his old age. There had been a bitter quarrel between him and his daughter. After Raya's father had died, the house had lost its grandeur and shed the trappings of wealth. Some of the antique furniture which they had retained—along with some crystalware and jewels, the dim lustre of memories from the days of plenty in their native city—had been sold, and Rachel, Raya's mother, had been compelled to support the home by working as a dentist's nurse. Grandfather Zisskind, who had been supported by the family ever since he came to the country, wished to hand over to his daughter his small capital, which was deposited in a bank. She was not willing to accept it. She was stubborn and proud like him. Then, after a prolonged quarrel and several weeks of not speaking to each other, he took some of the things in his room and the broken clock and went to live alone. That had been about four years ago. Now Rachel would come to him once or twice a week, bringing with her a bag full of provisions, to clean the room and cook some meals for him. He was no longer interested in expenses and did not even ask about them, as though they were of no more concern to him.

"And now . . . what can I offer you?" Grandfather Zisskind would ask when he considered the room ready to receive guests. "There's no need to offer us anything, Grandfather; we didn't come for that," Raya would answer crossly.

But protests were of no avail. Her grandfather would take out a jar of fermenting preserves and put it on the table, then grapes and plums, biscuits and two glasses of strong tea, forcing them to eat. Raya would taste a little of this and that just to please the old man, while Yehuda, for whom all these visits were unavoidable torment, the very sight of the dishes arousing his disgust, would secretly indicate to her by pulling a sour face that he just couldn't touch the preserves. She would smile at him placatingly, stroking his knee. But Grandfather insisted, so he would have to taste at least a teaspoonful of the sweet and nauseating stuff.

Afterwards Grandfather would ask about all kinds of things. Raya did her best to make the conversation pleasant, in order to relieve Yehuda's boredom. Finally would come what Yehuda dreaded most of all and on account of which he had resolved more than once to refrain from these visits. Grandfather Zisskind would rise, take his chair and place it next to the wall, get up on it carefully, holding on to the back so as not to fall, open the clock and take out a cloth bag with a black cord tied round it. Then he would shut the clock, get off the chair, put it back in its place, sit down on it, undo the cord, take out of the cloth wrapping a bundle of sheets of paper, lay them in front of Yehuda and say:

"I would like you to read this."

"Grandfather," Raya would rush to Yehuda's rescue, "but he's already read it at least ten times. . . ."

But Grandfather Zisskind would pretend not to hear and would not reply, so Yehuda was compelled each time to read there and then that same essay, spread over eight, long sheets in a large, somewhat shaky handwriting, which he almost knew by heart. It was a lament for Grandfather's native town in the Ukraine which had been destroyed by the Germans, and all its Jews slaughtered. When he had finished, Grandfather would take the sheets out of his hand, fold them, sigh and say:

"And nothing of all this is left. Dust and ashes. Not even a tombstone to bear witness. Imagine, of a community of twenty thousand Jews not even one survived to tell how it happened . . . Not a trace."

Then out of the same cloth bag, which contained various letters and envelopes, he would draw a photograph of his grandson Mendele, who had been twelve years old when he was killed; the only son of his son Ossip, chief engineer in a large chemical factory. He would show it to Yehuda and say:

"He was a genius. Just imagine, when he was only eleven he had already finished his studies at the Conservatory, won a scholarship from the Government and was considered an outstanding violinist. A genius! Look at that forehead. . . ." And after he had put the photograph back he would sigh and repeat "Not a trace."

A strained silence of commiseration would descend on Raya and Yehuda, who had already heard these same things many times over and no longer felt anything when they were repeated. And as he wound the cord round the bag the old man would muse: "And Ossip was also a prodigy. As a boy he knew Hebrew well, and could recite Bialik's poems by heart. He studied by himself. He read endlessly, Gnessin, Frug, Bershadsky . . . You didn't know Bershadsky; he was a good writer . . . He had a warm heart, Ossip had. He didn't mix in politics, he wasn't even a Zionist, but even when they promoted him there he didn't forget that he was a Jew . . . He called his son Mendele, of all names, after his dead brother, even though it was surely not easy to have a name like that among the Russians . . . Yes, he had a warm Jewish heart . . ."

He would turn to Yehuda as he spoke, since in Raya he always saw the child who used to sit on his knee listening to his stories, and for him she had never grown up, while he regarded Yehuda as an educated man who could understand someone else, especially inasmuch as Yehuda held a government job.

Raya remembered how the change had come about in her grandfather. When the war was over he was still sustained by uncertainty and hoped for some news of his son, for it was known that very many had succeeded in escaping eastwards. Wearily he would visit all those who had once lived in his town, but none of them had received any sign of life from relatives. Nevertheless he continued to hope, for Ossip's important position might have helped to save him. Then Raya came home one evening and saw him sitting on the floor with a rent in his jacket. In the house they spoke in whispers, and her mother's eyes were red with weeping. She, too, had wept at Grandfather's sorrow, at the sight of his stricken face, at the oppressive quiet in the rooms. For many weeks afterwards it was as if he had imposed silence on himself. He would sit at his table from morning to night, reading and re-reading old letters, studying family photographs by the hour as he brought them close to his shortsighted eyes, or leaning backwards on his chair, motionless, his hand touching the edge of the table and his eyes staring through the window in front of him, into the distance, as if he had turned to stone. He was no longer the same talkative, wise and humorous grandfather who interested himself in the house, asked what his granddaughter was doing, instructed her, tested her knowledge, proving boastfully like a child that he knew

more than her teachers. Now he seemed to cut himself off from the world and
entrench himself in his thoughts and his memories, which none of the household
could penetrate. Later, a strange perversity had taken hold of him which it was
hard to tolerate. He would insist that his meals be served at his table, apart, that
no one should enter his room without knocking at the door, or close the shutters
of his window against the sun. When any one disobeyed these prohibitions he
would flare up and quarrel violently with his daughter. At times it seemed that
he hated her.

When Raya's father died, Grandfather Zisskind did not show any signs of grief,
and did not even console his daughter. But when the days of mourning were past
it was as if he had been restored to new life, and he emerged from his silence.
Yet he did not speak of his son-in-law, nor of his son Ossip, but only of his
grandson Mendele. Often during the day he would mention the boy by name
as if he were alive, and speak of him familiarly, although he had seen him only
on photographs—as though deliberating aloud and turning the matter over, he
would talk of how Mendele ought to be brought up. It was hardest of all when
he started criticizing his son and his son's wife for not having foreseen the
impending disaster, for not having rushed the boy away to a safe place, not having
hidden him with non-Jews, not having tried to get him to the Land of Israel in
good time. There was no logic in what he said; this would so infuriate Rachel
that she would burst out with, "Oh, do stop! Stop it! I'll go out of my mind with
your foolish nonsense!" She would rise from her seat in anger, withdraw to her
room, and afterwards, when she had calmed down, would say to Raya, "Sclerosis,
apparently. Loss of memory. He no longer knows what he's talking about."

One day—Raya would never forget this—she and her mother saw that Grandfather was wearing his best suit, the black one, and under it a gleaming white
shirt; his shoes were polished, and he had a hat on. He had not worn these
clothes for many months, and the family was dismayed to see him. They thought
that he had lost his mind. "What holiday is it today?" her mother asked. "Really,
don't you know?" asked her grandfather. "Today is Mendele's birthday!" Her
mother burst out crying. She too began to cry and ran out of the house.

After that, Grandfather Zisskind went to live alone. His mind, apparently, had
become settled, except that he would frequently forget things which had occurred a day or two before, though he clearly remembered, down to the smallest
detail, things which had happened in his town and to his family more than thirty
years ago. Raya would go and visit him, at first with her mother and, after her
marriage, with Yehuda. What bothered them was that they were compelled to
listen to his talk about Mendele his grandson, and to read that same lament for
his native town which had been destroyed.

Whenever Rachel happened to come there during their visit, she would scold
Grandfather rudely. "Stop bothering them with your masterpiece," she would
say, and herself remove the papers from the table and put them back in their bag.
"If you want them to keep on visiting you, don't talk to them about the dead.
Talk about the living. They're young people and they have no mind for such

things." And as they left his room together she would say, turning to Yehuda in order to placate him, "Don't be surprised at him. Grandfather's already old. Over seventy. Loss of memory."

When Raya was seven months pregnant, Grandfather Zisskind had in his absent-mindedness not yet noticed it. But Rachel could no longer refrain from letting him share her joy and hope, and told him that a great-grandchild would soon be born to him. One evening the door of Raya and Yehuda's flat opened, and Grandfather himself stood on the threshold in his holiday clothes, just as on the day of Mendele's birthday. This was the first time he had visited them at home, and Raya was so surprised that she hugged and kissed him as she had not done since she was a child. His face shone, his eyes sparkled with the same intelligent and mischievous light they had in those far-off days before the calamity. When he entered he walked briskly through the rooms, giving his opinion on the furniture and its arrangement, and joking about everything around him. He was so pleasant that Raya and Yehuda could not stop laughing all the time he was speaking. He gave no indication that he knew what was about to take place, and for the first time in many months he did not mention Mendele.

"Ah, you naughty children," he said, "is this how you treat Grandfather? Why didn't you tell me you had such a nice place?"

"How many times have I invited you here, Grandfather?" asked Raya.

"Invited me? You ought to have *brought* me here, dragged me by force!"

"I wanted to do that too, but you refused."

"Well, I thought that you lived in some dark den, and I have a den of my own. Never mind, I forgive you."

And when he took leave of them he said:

"Don't bother to come to me. Now that I know where you're to be found and what a palace you have, I'll come to you . . . if you don't throw me out, that is."

Some days later, when Rachel came to their home and they told her about Grandfather's amazing visit, she was not surprised:

"Ah, you don't know what he's been contemplating during all these days, ever since I told him that you're about to have a child . . . He has one wish—that if it's a son, it should be named . . . after his grandson."

"Mendele?" exclaimed Raya, and involuntarily burst into laughter. Yehuda smiled as one smiles at the fond fancies of the old.

"Of course, I told him to put that out of his head," said Rachel, "but you know how obstinate he is. It's some obsession and he won't think of giving it up. Not only that, but he's sure that you'll willingly agree to it, and especially you, Yehuda."

Yehuda shrugged his shoulders. "Crazy. The child would be unhappy all his life."

"But he's not capable of understanding that," said Rachel, and a note of apprehension crept into her voice.

Raya's face grew solemn. "We have already decided on the name," she said. "If it's a girl she'll be called Osnath, and if it's a boy—Ehud."

Rachel did not like either.

The matter of the name became almost the sole topic of conversation between Rachel and the young couple when she visited them, and it infused gloom into the air of expectancy which filled the house.

Rachel, midway between the generations, was of two minds about the matter. When she spoke to her father she would scold and contradict him, flinging at him all the arguments she had heard from Raya and Yehuda as though they were her own, but when she spoke to the children she sought to induce them to meet his wishes, and would bring down their anger on herself. As time went on, the question of a name, to which in the beginning she had attached little importance, became a kind of mystery, concealing something preordained, fearful, and pregnant with life and death. The fate of the child itself seemed in doubt. In her inner-most heart she prayed that Raya would give birth to a daughter.

"Actually, what's so bad about the name Mendele?" she asked her daughter. "It's a Jewish name like any other."

"What are you talking about, Mother"—Raya rebelled against the thought—"a Ghetto name, ugly, horrible! I wouldn't even be capable of letting it cross my lips. Do you want me to hate my child?"

"Oh, you won't hate your child. At any rate, not because of the name . . ."

"I should hate him. It's as if you'd told me that my child would be born with a hump! And anyway—why should I? What for?"

"You have to do it for Grandfather's sake," Rachel said quietly, although she knew that she was not speaking the whole truth.

"You know, Mother, that I am ready to do anything for Grandfather," said Raya. "I love him, but I am not ready to sacrifice my child's happiness on account of some superstition of his. What sense is there in it?"

Rachel could not explain the "sense in it" rationally, but in her heart she rebelled against her daughter's logic which had always been hers too and now seemed very superficial, a symptom of the frivolity afflicting the younger generation. Her old father now appeared to her like an ancient tree whose deep roots suck up the mysterious essence of existence, of which neither her daughter nor she herself knew anything. Had it not been for this argument about the name, she would certainly never have got to meditating on the transmigration of souls and the eternity of life. At night she would wake up covered in cold sweat. Hazily, she recalled frightful scenes of bodies of naked children, beaten and trampled under the jackboots of soldiers, and an awful sense of guilt oppressed her spirit.

Then Rachel came with a proposal for a compromise: that the child should be named Menachem. A Hebrew name, she said; an Israeli one, by all standards. Many children bore it, and it occurred to nobody to make fun of them. Even Grandfather had agreed to it after much urging.

Raya refused to listen.

"We have chosen a name, Mother," she said, "which we both like, and we won't change it for another. Menachem is a name which reeks of old age, a name which for me is connected with sad memories and people I don't like. Menachem you could call only a boy who is short, weak and not good-looking. Let's not talk about it any more, Mother."

Rachel was silent. She almost despaired of convincing them. At last she said:

"And are you ready to take the responsibility of going against Grandfather's wishes?"

Raya's eyes opened wide, and fear was reflected in them:

"Why do you make such a fateful thing of it? You frighten me!" she said, and burst into tears. She began to fear for her offspring as one fears the evil eye.

"And perhaps there *is* something fateful in it . . ." whispered Rachel without raising her eyes. She flinched at her own words.

"What is it?" insisted Raya, with a frightened look at her mother.

"I don't know . . ." she said. "Perhaps all the same we are bound to retain the names of the dead . . . in order to leave a remembrance of them . . ." She was not sure herself whether there was any truth in what she said or whether it was merely a stupid belief, but her father's faith was before her, stronger than her own doubts and her daughter's simple and understandable opposition.

"But I don't always want to remember all those dreadful things, Mother. It's impossible that this memory should always hang about this house and that the poor child should bear it!"

Rachel understood. She, too, heard such a cry within her as she listened to her father talking, sunk in memories of the past. As if to herself, she said in a whisper:

"I don't know . . . at times it seems to me that it's not Grandfather who's suffering from loss of memory, but ourselves. All of us."

About two weeks before the birth was due, Grandfather Zisskind appeared in Raya and Yehuda's home for the second time. His face was yellow, angry, and the light had faded from his eyes. He greeted them, but did not favor Raya with so much as a glance, as if he had pronounced a ban upon the sinner. Turning to Yehuda he said, "I wish to speak to you."

They went into the inner room. Grandfather sat down on the chair and placed the palm of his hand on the edge of the table, as was his wont, and Yehuda sat, lower than he, on the bed.

"Rachel has told me that you don't want to call the child by my grandchild's name," he said.

"Yes . . ." said Yehuda diffidently.

"Perhaps you'll explain to me why?" he asked.

"We . . ." stammered Yehuda, who found it difficult to face the piercing gaze of the old man. "The name simply doesn't appeal to us."

Grandfather was silent. Then he said, "I understand that Mendele doesn't appeal to you. Not a Hebrew name. Granted! But Menachem—what's wrong

with Menachem?" It was obvious that he was controlling his feelings with difficulty.

"It's not . . ." Yehuda knew that there was no use explaining; they were two
generations apart in their ideas. "It's not an Israeli name . . . it's from the *Golah*"*

"*Golah*," repeated Grandfather. He shook with rage, but somehow he maintained his self-control. Quietly he added, "We all come from the *Golah*. I, and
Raya's father and mother. Your father and mother. All of us."

"Yes . . ." said Yehuda. He resented the fact that he was being dragged into
an argument which was distasteful to him, particularly with this old man whose
mind was already not quite clear. Only out of respect did he restrain himself from
shouting: That's that, and it's done with! . . . "Yes, but we were born in this
country," he said aloud; "that's different."

Grandfather Zisskind looked at him contemptuously. Before him he saw a
wretched boor, an empty vessel.

"You, that is to say, think that there's something new here," he said, "that
everything that was there is past and gone. Dead, without sequel. That you are
starting everything anew."

"I didn't say that. I only said that we were born in this country. . . ."

"You were born here. Very nice . . ." said Grandfather Zisskind with rising
emotion. "So what of it? What's so remarkable about that? In what way are you
superior to those who were born *there*? Are you cleverer than they? More cultured? Are you greater than they in Torah or good deeds? Is your blood redder
than theirs?" Grandfather Zisskind looked as if he could wring Yehuda's neck.

"I didn't say that either. I said that *here* it's different. . . ."

Grandfather Zisskind's patience with idle words was exhausted.

"You good-for-nothing!" he burst out in his rage. "What do you know about
what was there? What do you know of the *people* that were there? The communities? The cities? What do you know of the *life* they had there?"

"Yes," said Yehuda, his spirit crushed, "but we no longer have any ties with
it."

"You have no ties with it?" Grandfather Zisskind bent towards him. His lips
quivered in fury. "With what . . . with what *do* you have ties?"

"We have . . . with this country," said Yehuda and gave an involuntary smile.

"Fool!" Grandfather Zisskind shot at him. "Do you think that people come
to a desert and make themselves a nation, eh? That you are the first of some new
race? That you're not the son of your father? Not the grandson of your grandfather? Do you want to forget them? Are you ashamed of them for having had a
hundred times more culture and education than you have? Why . . . why,
everything here"—he included everything around him in the sweep of his arm—
"is no more than a puddle of tapwater against the big sea that was there! What
have you here? A mixed multitude! Seventy languages! Seventy distinct groups!

*Golah: Diaspora—the whole body of Jews living dispersed among the Gentiles.

Customs? A way of life? Why, every home here is a nation in itself, with its own customs and its own names! And with this you have ties, you say . . ."

Yehuda lowered his eyes and was silent.

"I'll tell you what ties are," said Grandfather Zisskind calmly. "Ties are remembrance! Do you understand? The Russian is linked to his people because he remembers his ancestors. He is called Ivan, his father was called Ivan and his grandfather was called Ivan, back to the first generation. And no Russian has said: From today onwards I shall not be called Ivan because my fathers and my fathers' fathers were called that; I am the first of a new Russian nation which has nothing at all to do with the Ivans. Do you understand?"

"But what has that got to do with it?" Yehuda protested impatiently. Grandfather Zisskind shook his head at him.

"And you—you're ashamed to give your son the name Mendele lest it remind you that there were Jews who were called by that name. You believe that his name should be wiped off the face of the earth. That not a trace of it should remain . . ."

He paused, heaved a deep sigh and said:

"O children, children, you don't know what you're doing . . . You're finishing off the work which the enemies of Israel began. They took the bodies away from the world, and you—the name and the memory . . . No continuation, no evidence, no memorial and no name. Not a trace . . ."

And with that he rose, took his stick and with long strides went towards the door and left.

The new-born child was a boy and he was named Ehud, and when he was about a month old, Raya and Yehuda took him in the carriage to Grandfather's house.

Raya gave three cautious knocks on the door, and when she heard a rustle inside she could also hear the beating of her anxious heart. Since the birth of the child Grandfather had not visited them even once. "I'm terribly excited," she whispered to Yehuda with tears in her eyes. Yehuda rocked the carriage and did not reply. He was now indifferent to what the old man might say or do.

The door opened, and on the threshold stood Grandfather Zisskind, his face weary and wrinkled. He seemed to have aged. His eyes were sticky with sleep, and for a moment it seemed as if he did not see the callers.

"Good Sabbath, Grandfather," said Raya with great feeling. It seemed to her now that she loved him more than ever.

Grandfather looked at them as if surprised, and then said absently, "Come in, come in."

"We've brought the baby with us!" said Raya, her face shining, and her glance traveled from Grandfather to the infant sleeping in the carriage.

"Come in, come in," repeated Grandfather Zisskind in a tired voice. "Sit down," he said as he removed his clothes from the chairs and turned to tidy the disordered bedclothes.

Yehuda stood the carriage by the wall and whispered to Raya, "It's stifling for him here." Raya opened the window wide.

"You haven't seen our baby yet, Grandfather!" she said with a sad smile.

"Sit down, sit down," said Grandfather, shuffling over to the shelf, from which he took the jar of preserves and the biscuit tin, putting them on the table.

"There's no need, Grandfather, really there's no need for it. We didn't come for that," said Raya.

"Only a little something. I have nothing to offer you today. . . ." said Grandfather in a dull, broken voice. He took the kettle off the kerosene burner and poured out two glasses of tea which he placed before them. Then he too sat down, said "Drink, drink," and softly tapped his fingers on the table.

"I haven't seen Mother for several days now," he said at last.

"She's busy . . ." said Raya in a low voice, without raising her eyes to him. "She helps me a lot with the baby. . . ."

Grandfather Zisskind looked at his pale, knotted and veined hands lying helplessly on the table; then he stretched out one of them and said to Raya, "Why don't you drink? The tea will get cold."

Raya drew up to the table and sipped the tea.

"And you—what are you doing now?" he asked Yehuda.

"Working as usual," said Yehuda, and added with a laugh, "I play with the baby when there's time."

Grandfather again looked down at his hands, the long thin fingers of which shook with the palsy of old age.

"Take some of the preserves," he said to Yehuda, indicating the jar with a shaking finger. "It's very good." Yehuda dipped the spoon in the jar and put it to his mouth.

There was a deep silence. It seemed to last a very long time. Grandfather Zisskind's fingers gave little quivers on the white tablecloth. It was hot in the room, and the buzzing of a fly could be heard.

Suddenly the baby burst out crying, and Raya started from her seat and hastened to quiet him. She rocked the carriage and crooned, "Quiet, child, quiet, quiet . . ." Even after he had quieted down she went on rocking the carriage back and forth.

Grandfather Zisskind raised his head and said to Yehuda in a whisper:

"You think it was impossible to save him . . . it was possible. They had many friends. Ossip himself wrote to me about it. The manager of the factory had a high opinion of him. The whole town knew them and loved them. . . . How is it they didn't think of it . . . ?" he said, touching his forehead with the palm of his hand. "After all, they knew that the Germans were approaching . . . It was still possible to do something . . ." He stopped a moment and then added, "Imagine that a boy of eleven had already finished his studies at the Conservatory—wild beasts!" He suddenly opened eyes filled with terror. "Wild beasts! To take little children and put them into wagons and deport them . . ."

When Raya returned and sat down at the table, he stopped and became silent, and only a heavy sigh escaped from deep within him.

Again there was a prolonged silence, and as it grew heavier Raya felt the oppressive weight on her bosom increasing till it could no longer be contained. Grandfather sat at the table tapping his thin fingers, and alongside the wall the infant lay in his carriage; it was as if a chasm gaped between a world which was passing and a world that was born. It was no longer a single line to the fourth generation. The aged father did not recognize the great-grandchild whose life would be no memorial.

Grandfather Zisskind got up, took his chair and pulled it up to the clock. He climbed on to it to take out his documents.

Raya could no longer stand the oppressive atmosphere.

"Let's go," she said to Yehuda in a choked voice.

"Yes, we must go," said Yehuda, and rose from his seat. "We have to go," he said loudly as he turned to the old man.

Grandfather Zisskind held the key of the clock for a moment more, then he let his hand fall, grasped the back of the chair and got down.

"You have to go. . . ." he said with a tortured grimace. He spread his arms out helplessly and accompanied them to the doorway.

When the door had closed behind them the tears flowed from Raya's eyes. She bent over the carriage and pressed her lips to the baby's chest. At that moment it seemed to her that he was in need of pity and of great love, as though he were alone, an orphan in the world.

Translated by Minna Givton

Questions for Discussion and Writing

1. What are Grandfather Zisskind's motivations for wanting Raya and Yehuda's baby named after his grandson, Mendele? Explore in your answer both the obvious and subtle possibilities suggested in the story.
2. In what ways is his daughter Rachel caught between the generation of her father and that of her children? What are her own convictions in these matters, and how do we as readers come to discover them?
3. What does the name chosen for the baby—Ehud—symbolize in the story? For what reasons do you support Raya and Yehuda's choice to use their own preferred name for the child? For what reasons do you feel that they might have submitted to Grandfather Zisskind's desires and convictions? What do you think the baby will gain in the name? What will he lose?

ZHANG JIE

Love Must Not Be Forgotten

Born in 1937, Zhang Jie grew up with a passion for music and literature, but was persuaded to study economics instead because it was considered of more use to the New China. After graduating from the People's University, she worked for some years in an industrial bureau and then in a film studio, where she got a chance to write two film scripts. "I once thought I was like a darting dragonfly, with no goals in life and no substantial pursuits," Jie has said of her first forty years in an essay entitled "My Boat." "Only through literature did I discover myself."

Jie began her real life as a writer after the fall of the "Gang of Four" and the end of the Cultural Revolution. She was then forty years old. Her earlier stories address the problems of Chinese youth and love. She had divorced her husband because he maltreated her, and in a society still influenced by traditional ideas, her decision stigmatized her.

With her strong sense of social responsibility and her "complete faith in socialism," Jie tackles sensitive issues in her writing without regard for her own welfare. "Love Must Not Be Forgotten" caused a furor in her country when it was published in 1979, because it justifies love outside marriage, albeit of the spirit and not the physical. It also suggests that a woman should remain single unless she finds a man she loves and respects. Ironically, at least to most Western readers, critics accused Jie of undermining social morality.

Zhang Jie believes that most of the world's troubles arise from misunderstanding—from lack of communication—and that modern Chinese writers are the people best suited to introduce their country abroad.

Before you read "Love Must Not Be Forgotten," write about a time in your life when something you learned unexpectedly about the life of someone in

your family caused you to rethink your choices about an important decision.
If you haven't learned something unexpectedly, write about a time when you
used a lesson from someone else's life to make an important decision.

I am thirty, the same age as our People's Republic. For a republic thirty is still
young. But a girl of thirty is virtually on the shelf.

Actually, I have a bonafide suitor. Have you seen the Greek sculptor Myron's
Discobolus? Qiao Lin is the image of that discus thrower. Even the padded
clothes he wears in winter fail to hide his fine physique. Bronzed, with clear-cut
features, a broad forehead and large eyes, his appearance alone attracts most girls
to him.

But I can't make up my mind to marry him. I'm not clear what attracts me
to him, or him to me. I know people are gossiping behind my back, "Who does
she think she is, to be so choosy?" To them, I'm a nobody playing hard to get.
They take offense at such preposterous behavior.

Of course, I shouldn't be captious. In a society where commercial production
still exists, marriage like most other transactions is still a form of barter.

I have known Qiao Lin for nearly two years, yet still cannot fathom whether
he keeps so quiet from aversion to talking or from having nothing to say. When,
by way of a small intelligence test, I demand his opinion of this or that, he says
"good" or "bad" like a child in kindergarten.

Once I asked, "Qiao Lin, why do you love me?" He thought the question over
seriously for what seemed an age. I could see from his normally smooth but now
wrinkled forehead that the little grey cells in his handsome head were hard at
work cogitating. I felt ashamed to have put him on the spot.

Finally he raised his clear childlike eyes to tell me, "Because you're good!"

Loneliness flooded my heart. "Thank you, Qiao Lin!" I couldn't help wondering, if we were to marry, whether we could discharge our duties to each other
as husband and wife. Maybe, because law and morality would have bound us
together. But how tragic simply to comply with law and morality! Was there no
stronger bond to link us?

When such thoughts cross my mind I have the strange sensation that instead
of being a girl contemplating marriage I am an elderly social scientist.

Perhaps I worry too much. We can live like most married couples, bringing
up children together, strictly true to each other according to the law. . . .
Although living in the seventies of the twentieth century, people still consider
marriage the way they did millennia ago, as a means of continuing the race, a
form of barter or a business transaction in which love and marriage can be
separated. Since this is the common practice, why shouldn't we follow suit?

But I still can't make up my mind. As a child, I remember, I often cried all
night for no rhyme or reason, unable to sleep and disturbing the whole household. My old nurse, a shrewd though uneducated woman, said an ill wind had
blown through my ear. I think this judgment showed prescience, because I still
have that old weakness. I upset myself over things which really present no

problem, upsetting other people at the same time. One's nature is hard to change.

I think of my mother too. If she were alive, what would she say about my attitude to Qiao Lin and my uncertainty about marrying him? My thoughts constantly turn to her, not because she was such a strict mother that her ghost is still watching over me since her death. No, she was not just my mother but my closest friend. I loved her so much that the thought of her leaving me makes my heart ache.

She never lectured me, just told me quietly in her deep, unwomanly voice about her successes and failures, so that I could learn from her experience. She had evidently not had many successes—her life was full of failures.

During her last days she followed me with her fine, expressive eyes, as if wondering how I would manage on my own and as if she had some important advice for me but hesitated to give it. She must have been worried by my naiveté and sloppy ways. She suddenly blurted out, "Shanshan, if you aren't sure what you want, don't rush into marriage—better live on your own!"

Other people might think this strange advice from a mother to her daughter, but to me it embodied her bitter experience. I don't think she underestimated me or my knowledge of life. She loved me and didn't want me to be unhappy.

"I don't want to marry, mother!" I said, not out of bashfulness or a show of coyness. I can't think why a girl should pretend to be coy. She had long since taught me about things not generally mentioned to girls.

"If you meet the right man, then marry him. Only if he's right for you!"

"I'm afraid no such man exists!"

"That's not true. But it's hard. The world is so vast, I'm afraid you may never meet him." Whether married or not was not what concerned her, but the quality of the marriage.

"Haven't you managed fine without a husband?"

"Who says so?"

"I think you've done fine."

"I had no choice. . . ." She broke off, lost in thought, her face wistful. Her wistful lined face reminded me of a withered flower I had pressed in a book.

"Why did you have no choice?"

"You ask too many questions," she parried, not ashamed to confide in me but afraid that I might reach the wrong conclusion. Besides, everyone treasures a secret to carry to the grave. Feeling a bit put out, I demanded bluntly, "Didn't you love my dad?"

"No, I never loved him."

"Did he love you?"

"No, he didn't."

"Then why get married?"

She paused, searching for the right words to explain this mystery, then answered bitterly, "When you're young you don't always know what you're looking for, what you need, and people may talk you into getting married. As you grow older and more experienced you find out your true needs. By then, though, you've done many foolish things for which you could kick yourself. You'd give anything to be able to make a fresh start and live more wisely. Those content with their lot will always be happy, they say, but I shall never enjoy that happiness." She added self-mockingly, "A wretched idealist, that's all I am."

Did I take after her? Did we both have genes which attracted ill winds?

"Why don't you marry again?"

"I'm afraid I'm still not sure what I really want." She was obviously unwilling to tell me the truth.

I cannot remember my father. He and Mother split up when I was very small. I just recall her telling me sheepishly that he was a fine handsome fellow. I could see she was ashamed of having judged by appearances and made a futile choice. She told me, "When I can't sleep at night, I force myself to sober up by recalling all those stupid blunders I made. Of course it's so distasteful that I often hide my face in the sheet for shame, as if there were eyes watching me in the dark. But distasteful as it is, I take some pleasure in this form of atonement."

I was really sorry that she hadn't remarried. She was such a fascinating character, if she'd married a man she loved, what a happy household ours would surely have been. Though not beautiful, she had the simple charm of an ink landscape. She was a fine writer too. Another author who knew her well used to say teasingly, "Just reading your works is enough to make anyone love you!"

She would retort, "If he knew that the object of his affection was a white-haired old crone, that would frighten him away." At her age, she must have known what she really wanted, so this was obviously an evasion. I say this because she had quirks which puzzled me.

For instance, whenever she left Beijing on a trip, she always took with her one of the twenty-seven volumes of Chekov's stories published between 1950 and 1955. She also warned me, "Don't touch these books. If you want to read Chekov, read that set I bought you." There was no need to caution me. Having a set of my own why should I touch hers? Besides, she'd told me this over and over again. Still she was on her guard. She seemed bewitched by those books.

So we had two sets of Chekov's stories at home. Not just because we loved Chekov, but to parry other people like me who loved Chekov. Whenever anyone asked to borrow a volume, she would lend one of mine. Once, in her absence, a close friend took a volume from her set. When she found out she was frantic, and at once took a volume of mine to exchange for it.

Ever since I can remember, those books were on her bookcase. Although I admire Chekov as a great writer, I was puzzled by the way she never tired of reading him. Why, for over twenty years, had she had to read him every single day? Sometimes, when tired of writing, she poured herself a cup of strong tea and sat down in front of the bookcase, staring raptly at that set of books. If I went into her room then it flustered her, and she either spilt her tea or blushed like a girl discovered with her lover.

I wondered: Has she fallen in love with Chekov? She might have if he'd still been alive.

When her mind was wandering just before her death, her last words to me were: "That set . . ." She hadn't the strength to give it its complete title. But I knew what she meant. "And my diary . . . 'Love Must Not Be Forgotten.' . . . Cremate them with me."

I carried out her last instruction regarding the works of Chekov, but couldn't bring myself to destroy her diary. I thought, if it could be published, it would surely prove the most moving thing she had written. But naturally publication was out of the question.

At first I imagined the entries were raw material she had jotted down. They read neither like stories, essays, a diary or letters. But after reading the whole I formed a hazy impression, helped out by my imperfect memory. Thinking it over, I finally realized that this was no lifeless manuscript I was holding, but an anguished, loving heart. For over twenty years one man had occupied her heart, but he was not for her. She used these diaries as a substitute for him, a means of pouring out her feelings to him, day after day, year after year.

No wonder she had never considered any eligible proposals, had turned a deaf ear to idle talk whether well-meant or malicious. Her heart was already full, to the exclusion of anybody else. "No lake can compare with the ocean, no cloud with those on Mount Wu." Remembering those lines I often reflected sadly that few people in real life could love like this. No one would love me like this.

I learned that toward the end of the thirties, when this man was doing underground work for the Party in Shanghai, an old worker had given his life to cover him, leaving behind a helpless wife and daughter. Out of a sense of duty, of gratitude to the dead and deep class feeling, he had unhesitatingly married the daughter. When he saw the endless troubles of couples who had married for "love," he may have thought, "Thank Heaven, though I didn't marry for love, we get on well, able to help each other." For years, as man and wife they lived through hard times.

He must have been my mother's colleague. Had I ever met him? He couldn't have visited our home. Who was he?

In the spring of 1962, Mother took me to a concert. We went on foot, the theater being quite near. On the way a black limousine pulled up silently by the pavement. Out stepped an elderly man with white hair in a black serge tunic-suit. What a striking shock of white hair! Strict, scrupulous, distinguished, transparently honest—that was my impression of him. The cold glint of his flashing eyes reminded me of lightning or swordplay. Only ardent love for a woman really deserving his love could fill cold eyes like those with tenderness.

He walked up to Mother and said, "How are you, Comrade Zhong Yu? It's been a long time."

"How are you!" Mother's hand holding mine suddenly turned icy cold and trembled a little.

They stood face to face without looking at each other, each appearing upset, even stern. Mother fixed her eyes on the trees by the roadside, not yet in leaf. He looked at me. "Such a big girl already. Good, fine—you take after your mother."

Instead of shaking hands with Mother he shook hands with me. His hand was as icy as hers and trembling a little. As if transmitting an electric current, I felt a sudden shock. Snatching my hand away I cried, "There's nothing good about that!"

"Why not?" he asked with the surprised expression grown-ups always have when children speak out frankly.

I glanced at Mother's face. I did take after her, to my disappointment. "Because she's not beautiful!"

He laughed, then said teasingly, "Too bad that there should be a child who doesn't find her own mother beautiful. Do you remember in '53, when your mother was transferred to Beijing, she came to our ministry to report for duty? She left you outside on the veranda, but like a monkey you climbed all the stairs, peeped through the cracks in doors, and caught your finger in the door of my office. You sobbed so bitterly that I carried you off to find her."

"I don't remember that." I was annoyed at his harking back to a time when I was still in open-seat pants.

"Ah, we old people have better memories." He turned abruptly and remarked to Mother, "I've read that last story of yours. Frankly speaking, there's something not quite right about it. You shouldn't have condemned the heroine. . . . There's nothing wrong with falling in love, as long as you don't spoil someone else's life. . . . In fact, the hero might have loved her too. Only for the sake of a third person's happiness, they had to renounce their love. . . ."

A policeman came over to where the car was parked and ordered the driver to move on. When the driver made some excuse, the old man looked around. After a hasty "Goodbye" he strode back to the car and told the policeman, "Sorry. It's not his fault, it's mine. . . ."

I found it amusing watching this old cadre listening respectfully to the policeman's strictures. When I turned to Mother with a mischievous smile, she looked as upset as a first-form primary schoolchild standing forlornly in front of the stern headmistress. Anyone would have thought she was the one being lectured by the policeman. The car drove off, leaving a puff of smoke. Very soon even this smoke vanished with the wind, as if nothing at all had happened. But the incident stuck in my mind.

Analyzing it now, I realize he must have been the man whose strength of character won Mother's heart. That strength came from his firm political convictions, his narrow escapes from death in the revolution, his active brain, his drive at work, his well-cultivated mind. Besides, strange to say, he and Mother both liked the oboe. Yes, she must have worshipped him. She once told me that unless she worshipped a man, she couldn't love him even for one day.

But I could not tell whether he loved her or not. If not, why was there this entry in her diary?

> "This is far too fine a present. But how did you know that Chekov's my favorite writer?"
> "You said so."
> "I don't remember that."
> "I remember. I heard you mention it when you were chatting with someone."

So he was the one who had given her the *Selected Stories of Chekov*. For her that was tantamount to a love letter. Maybe this man, who didn't believe in love, realized by the time his hair was white that in his heart was something which could be called love. By the time he no longer had the right to love, he made the tragic discovery of this love for which he would have given his life. Or did it go deeper even than that?

This is all I remember about him.

How wretched Mother must have been, deprived of the man to whom she was devoted! To catch a glimpse of his car or the back of his head through its rear window, she carefully figured out which roads he would take to work and back. Whenever he made a speech, she sat at the back of the hall watching his face rendered hazy by cigarette smoke and poor lighting. Her eyes would brim with tears, but she swallowed them back. If a fit of coughing made him break off, she wondered anxiously why no one persuaded him to give up smoking. She was afraid he would get bronchitis again. Why was he so near yet so far?

He, to catch a glimpse of her, looked out of the car window every day straining his eyes to watch the streams of cyclists, afraid that she might have an accident. On the rare evenings on which he had no meetings, he would walk by a roundabout way to our neighborhood, to pass our compound gate. However busy, he would always make time to look in papers and journals for her work. His duty had always been clear to him, even in the most difficult times. But now confronted by this love he became a weakling, quite helpless. At his age it was laughable. Why should life play this trick on him?

Yet when they happened to meet at work, each tried to avoid the other, hurrying off with a nod. Even so, this would make Mother blind and deaf to everything around her. If she met a colleague named Wang she would call him Guo and mutter something unintelligible.

It was a cruel ordeal for her. She wrote:

> We agreed to forget each other. But I deceived you, I have never forgotten. I don't think you've forgotten either. We're just deceiving each other, hiding our misery. I haven't deceived you deliberately, though; I did my best to carry out our agreement. I often stay far away from Beijing, hoping time and distance will help me to forget you. But when I return, as the train pulls into the station, my head reels. I stand on the platform looking round intently, as if someone were waiting for me. Of course there is no one. I realize then

that I have forgotten nothing. Everything is unchanged. My love is like a tree the roots of which strike deeper year after year—I have no way to uproot it.

At the end of every day, I feel as if I've forgotten something important. I may wake with a start from my dreams wondering what has happened. But nothing has happened. Nothing. Then it comes home to me that you are missing! So everything seems lacking, incomplete, and there is nothing to fill up the blank. We are nearing the ends of our lives, why should we be carried away by emotion like children? Why should life submit people to such ordeals, then unfold before you your lifelong dream? Because I started off blindly I took the wrong turning, and now there are insuperable obstacles between me and my dream.

Yes, Mother never let me go to the station to meet her when she came back from a trip, preferring to stand alone on the platform and imagine that he had met her. Poor mother with her greying hair was as infatuated as a girl.

Not much space in the diary was devoted to their romance. Most entries dealt with trivia: why one of her articles had not come off; her fear that she had no real talent; the excellent play she missed by mistaking the time on the ticket; the drenching she got by going out for a stroll without her umbrella. In spirit they were together day and night, like a devoted married couple. In fact, they spent no more than twenty-four hours together in all. Yet in that time they experienced deeper happiness than some people in a whole lifetime. Shakespeare makes Juliet say, "I cannot sum up half my sum of wealth." And probably that is how Mother felt.

He must have been killed in the Cultural Revolution. Perhaps because of the conditions then, that section of the diary is ambiguous and obscure. Mother had been so fiercely attacked for her writing, it amazed me that she went on keeping a diary. From some veiled allusions I gathered that he had questioned the theories advanced by that "theoretician" then at the height of favor, and had told someone, "This is sheer Rightist talk." It was clear from the tear-stained pages of Mother's diary that he had been harshly denounced; but the steadfast old man never knuckled under to the authorities. His last words were, "When I go to meet Marx, I shall go on fighting my case!"

That must have been in the winter of 1969, because that was when Mother's hair turned white overnight, though she was not yet fifty. And she put on a black arm-band. Her position then was extremely difficult. She was criticized for wearing this old-style mourning, and ordered to say for whom she was in mourning.

"For whom are you wearing that, Mother?" I asked anxiously.

"For my lover." Not to frighten me she explained, "Someone you never knew."

"Shall I put one on too?" She patted my cheeks, as she had when I was a child. It was years since she had shown me such affection. I often felt that as she aged, especially during these last years of persecution, all tenderness had left her, or was concealed in her heart, so that she seemed like a man.

She smiled sadly and said, "No, you needn't wear one." Her eyes were as dry as if she had no more tears to shed. I longed to comfort her or do something to please her. But she said, "Off you go."

I felt an inexplicable dread, as if dear Mother had already half left me. I blurted out, "Mother!"

Quick to sense my desolation, she said gently, "Don't be afraid. Off you go. Leave me alone for a little."

I was right. She wrote:

> You have gone. Half my soul seems to have taken flight with you.
>
> I had no means of knowing what had become of you, much less of seeing you for the last time. I had no right to ask either, not being your wife or friend. . . . So we are torn apart. If only I could have borne that inhuman treatment for you, so that you could have lived on! You should have lived to see your name cleared and take up your work again, for the sake of those who loved you. I knew you could not be a counter-revolutionary. You were one of the finest men killed. That's why I love you—I am not afraid now to avow it.
>
> Snow is whirling down. Heavens, even God is such a hypocrite, he is using this whiteness to cover up your blood and the scandal of your murder.
>
> I have never set store by my life. But now I keep wondering whether anything I say or do would make you contract your shaggy eyebrows in a frown. I must live a worthwhile life like you, and do some honest work for our country. Things can't go on like this—those criminals will get what's coming to them.
>
> I used to walk alone along that small asphalt road, the only place where we once walked together, hearing my footsteps in the silent night. . . . I always paced to and fro and lingered there, but never as wretchedly as now. Then, though you were not beside me, I knew you were still in this world and felt that you were keeping me company. Now I can hardly believe that you have gone.
>
> At the end of the road I would retrace my steps, then walk along it again. Rounding the fence I always looked back, as if you were still standing there waving goodbye. We smiled faintly, like casual acquaintances, to conceal our undying love. That ordinary evening in early spring a chilly wind was blowing as we walked silently away from each other. You were wheezing a little because of your chronic bronchitis. That upset me. I wanted to beg you to slow down, but somehow I couldn't. We both walked very fast, as if some important business were waiting for us. How we prized that single stroll we had together, but we were afraid we might lose control of ourselves and burst out with "I love you"—those three words which had tormented us for years. Probably no one else could believe that we never once even clasped hands!

No, Mother, I believe it. I am the only one able to see into your locked heart. Ah, that little asphalt road, so haunted by bitter memories. We shouldn't overlook the most insignificant spots on earth. For who knows how much secret grief and joy they may hide. No wonder that when tired of writing, she would pace slowly along that little road behind our window. Sometimes at dawn after a sleepless night, sometimes on a moonless, windy evening. Even in winter during howling gales which hurled sand and pebbles against the window pane. . . . I thought this was one of her eccentricities, not knowing that she had gone to meet him in spirit.

She liked to stand by the window, too, staring at the small asphalt road. Once

I thought from her expression that one of our closest friends must be coming to call. I hurried to the window. It was a late autumn evening. The cold wind was stripping dead leaves from the trees and blowing them down the small empty road.

She went on pouring out her heart to him in her diary as she had when he was alive. Right up to the day when the pen slipped from her fingers. Her last message was:

> I am a materialist, yet I wish there were a Heaven. For then, I know, I would find you there waiting for me. I am going there to join you, to be together for eternity. We need never be parted again or keep at a distance for fear of spoiling someone else's life. Wait for me, dearest, I am coming—

I do not know how, on her death bed, Mother could still love so ardently with all her heart. To me it seemed not love but a form of madness, a passion stronger than death. If undying love really exists, she reached its extreme. She obviously died happy, because she had known true love. She had no regrets.

Now these old people's ashes have mingled with the elements. But I know that no matter what form they may take, they still love each other. Though not bound together by earthly laws or morality, though they never once clasped hands, each possessed the other completely. Nothing could part them. Centuries to come, if one white cloud trails another, two grasses grow side by side, one wave splashes another, a breeze follows another . . . believe me, that will be them.

Each time I read that diary "Love Must Not Be Forgotten" I cannot hold back my tears. I often weep bitterly, as if I myself experienced their ill-fated love. If not a tragedy it was too laughable. No matter how beautiful or moving I find it, I have no wish to follow suit!

Thomas Hardy wrote that "the call seldom produces the comer, the man to love rarely coincides with the hour for loving." I cannot judge them by conventional moral standards. What I deplore is that they did not wait for a "missing counterpart" to call them. If everyone could wait, instead of rushing into marriage, how many tragedies could be averted!

When we reach communism, will there still be cases of marriage without love? Perhaps . . . since the world is so vast, two kindred spirits may never be able to answer each other's call. But how tragic! Could it be that by then we will have devised ways to escape such tragedies? But this is all conjecture.

Maybe after all we are accountable for these tragedies. Who knows? Should we take the responsibility for the old ideas handed down from the past? Because, if you choose not to marry, your behavior is considered a direct challenge to these ideas. You will be called neurotic, accused of having guilty secrets or having made political mistakes. You may be regarded as an eccentric who looks down on ordinary people, not respecting age-old customs—a heretic. In short they will trump up endless vulgar and futile charges to ruin your reputation. Then you have to succumb to those ideas and marry regardless. But once you put the chains of an indifferent marriage around your neck, you will suffer for it for the rest of your life.

I long to shout: "Mind your own business! Let us wait patiently for our counterparts. Even waiting in vain is better than loveless marriage. To live single is not such a fearful disaster. I believe it may be a sign of a step forward in culture, education and the quality of life."

Translated by Gladys Yang

Questions for Discussion and Writing

1. The young woman who narrates the story says near the beginning that "marriage like most other transactions is still a form of barter" (p. 422). In what ways does she consider her relationship with Qiao Lin to be a form of barter? What would she gain from marriage with him, and what would she lose?

2. In many ways the narrator's story is more one of her mother's life than her own. What issues of love do the narrator's discoveries about her mother raise about both their lives? How do these issues reflect cultural influences? In what ways do the issues transcend cultural boundaries?

3. For what reasons do you think Jie wrote this story? What overtones in the story suggest that the writer is carrying out her strong sense of social responsibility? In what ways are her messages about love compatible with, or incompatible with, her faith in socialism?

ANN PETRY

Solo on the Drums

Born in 1912 in Old Saybrook, Connecticut, Ann Petry studied phar-macy at the University of Connecticut and later worked in her fam-ily's drugstore before moving to Harlem, New York, where she worked for several social agencies. Petry began writing as a reporter for The People's Voice, *and published her first novel,* The Street, *in 1946, written on a Houghton Mifflin Literary Fellowship.*

With the publication of that novel, Petry became the first black female author to address the problems faced by black women strug-gling to cope with urban life. She has been praised for her ability to understand and depict people—especially people weakened and disillusioned by poverty and by racial and sexual stereotypes.

Petry's later novels take place in small, middle-class New England towns, a change that critic Carl Hughes describes as Petry's "asser-tion of freedom as a creative artist with the whole of humanity in the American scene as her province."

In "Solo on the Drums," published in 1966, Petry explores the pain of failing love as it is expressed through music.

Before you read "Solo on the Drums," remember a time when your emo-tions ran high—in one direction or the other. Now imagine you are beating a drum to express those emotions but the sound that results is in words and sentences rather than in drumbeats. Try to write of this time as if you are a drummer, beating out the words of your feelings.

T he orchestra had a week's engagement at the Randlert Theater at Broad-way and Forty-second Street. His name was picked out in lights on the marquee. The name of the orchestra and then his name underneath by itself. There had been a time when he would have been excited by it. And stopped

432

to let his mind and his eyes linger over it lovingly. Kid Jones. The name—his name—up there in lights that danced and winked in the brassy sunlight. And at night his name glittered up there on the marquee as though it had been sprinkled with diamonds. The people who pushed their way through the crowded street looked up at it and recognized it and smiled.

He used to eat it up. But not today. Not after what happened this morning. He just looked at the sign with his name on it. There it was. Then he noticed that the sun had come out, and he shrugged, and went on inside the theater to put on one of the cream-colored suits and get his music together.

After he finished changing his clothes, he glanced in the long mirror in his dressing room. He hadn't changed any. Same face. No fatter and no thinner. No gray hair. Nothing. He frowned. Because he felt that the things that were eating him up inside ought to show. But they didn't.

When it was time to go out on the stage, he took his place behind the drums, not talking, just sitting there. The orchestra started playing softly. He made a mental note of the fact that the boys were working together as smoothly as though each one had been oiled.

The long gray curtains parted. One moment they were closed. And then they were open. Silently. Almost like magic. The high-powered spots flooded the stage with light. He could see specks of dust gliding down the wide beams of light. Under the bands of light the great space out front was all shadow. faces slowly emerged out of it—disembodied heads and shoulders that slanted up and back, almost to the roof.

He hit the drums lightly. Regularly. A soft, barely discernible rhythm. A background. A repeated emphasis for the horns and the piano and the violin. The man with the trumpet stood up, and the first notes came out sweet and clear and high.

Kid Jones kept up the drum accompaniment. Slow. Careful. Soft. And he felt his left eyebrow lift itself and start to twitch as the man played the trumpet. It happened whenever he heard the trumpet. The notes crept up, higher, higher, higher. So high that his stomach sucked in against itself. Then a little lower and stronger. A sound sustained. The rhythm of it beating against his ears until he was filled with it and sighing with it.

He wanted to cover his ears with his hands because he kept hearing a voice that whispered the same thing over and over again. The voice was trapped somewhere under the roof—caught and held there by the trumpet. "I'm leaving I'm leaving I'm leaving."

The sound took him straight back to the rain, the rain that had come with the morning. He could see the beginning of the day—raw and cold. He was at home. But he was warm because he was close to her, holding her in his arms. The rain and the wind cried softly outside the window.

And now—well, he felt as though he were floating up and up and up on that long blue note of the trumpet. He half closed his eyes and rode up on it. It had stopped being music. It was that whispering voice, making him shiver. Hating it and not being able to do anything about it. "I'm leaving it's the guy who plays the piano I'm in love with him and I'm leaving now today." Rain in the streets. Heat gone. Food gone. Everything gone because a woman's gone. It's everything you ever wanted, he thought. It's everything you never got. Everything you ever had, everything you ever lost. It's all there in the trumpet—pain and hate and trouble and peace and quiet and love.

The last note stayed up in the ceiling. Hanging on and on. The man with the trumpet had stopped playing but Kid Jones could still hear that last note. In his ears. In his mind.

The spotlight shifted and landed on Kid Jones—the man behind the drums. The long beam of white light struck the top of his head and turned him into a pattern of light and shadow. Because of the cream-colored suit and shirt, his body seemed to be encased in light. But there was a shadow over his face, so that his features blended and disappeared. His hairline receding so far back that he looked like a man with a face that never ended. A man with a high, long face and dark, dark skin.

He caressed the drums with the brushes in his hands. They responded with a whisper of sound. The rhythm came over but it had to be listened for. It stayed that way for a long time. Low, insidious, repeated. Then he made the big bass drum growl and pick up the same rhythm.

The Marquis of Brund, pianist with the band, turned to the piano. The drums and the piano talked the same rhythm. The piano high. A little more insistent than the drums. The Marquis was turned sideway on the piano bench. His left foot tapped out the rhythm. His cream-colored suit sharply outlined the bulki-ness of his body against the dark gleam of the piano. The drummer and the pianist were silhouetted in two separate brilliant shafts of light. The drums slowly dominated the piano.

The rhythm changed. It was faster. Kid Jones looked out over the crowded theater as he hit the drums. He began to feel as though he were the drums and the drums were he.

The theater throbbed with the excitement of the drums. A man sitting near the front shivered, and his head jerked to the rhythm. A sailor put his arm around the girl sitting beside him, took his hand and held her face still and pressed his mouth close over hers. Close. Close. Close. Until their faces seemed to melt together. Her hat fell off and neither of them moved. His hand dug deep into her shoulder and still they didn't move.

A kid sneaked in through a side door and slid into an aisle seat. His mouth was wide open, and he clutched his cap with both hands, tight and hard against his chest as he listened.

The drummer forgot he was in the theater. There was only he and the drums and they were far away. Long gone. He was holding Lulu, Helen, Susie, Mamie close in his arms. And all of them—all those girls blended into that one girl who was his wife. The one who said, "I'm leaving." She had said it over and over again, this morning, while rain dripped down the window panes.

When he hit the drums again it was with the thought that he was fighting with the piano player. He was choking the Marquis of Brund. He was putting a knife in clean between his ribs. He was slitting his throat with a long straight blade. Take my woman. Take your life.

The drums leaped with the fury that was in him. The men in the band turned their heads toward him—a faint astonishment showed in their faces.

He ignored them. The drums took him away from them, took him back, and back, and back, in time and space. He built up an illusion. He was sending out the news. Grandma died. The foreigner in the litter has an old disease and will not recover. The man from across the big water is sleeping with the chief's daughter. Kill. Kill. Kill. The war goes well with the men with the bad smell and the loud laugh. It goes badly with the chiefs with the round heads and the peacock's walk.

It is cool in the deep track in the forest. Cool and quiet. The trees talk softly. They speak of the dance tonight. The young girl from across the lake will be there. Her waist is slender and her thighs are rounded. Then the words he wanted to forget were all around Kid Jones again. "I'm leaving I'm leaving I'm leaving."

He couldn't help himself. He stopped hitting the drums and stared at the Marquis of Brund—a long, malevolent look, filled with hate.

There was a restless, uneasy movement in the theater. He remembered where he was. He started playing again. The horn played a phrase. Soft and short. The drums answered. The horn said the same thing all over again. The drums repeated it. The next time it was more intricate. The phrase was turned around, it went back and forth and up and down. And the drums said it over, exactly the same.

He knew a moment of panic. This was where he had to solo again and he wasn't sure he could do it. He touched the drums lightly. They quivered and answered him.

And then it was almost as though the drums were talking about his own life. The woman in Chicago who hated him. The girl with the round, soft body who had been his wife and who had walked out on him, this morning, in the rain. The old woman who was his mother, the same woman who lived in Chicago, and who hated him because he looked like his father, his father who had seduced her and left her, years ago.

He forgot the theater, forgot everything but the drums. He was welded to the drums, sucked inside them. All of him. His pulse beat. His heart beat. He had become part of the drums. They had become part of him.

He made the big bass rumble and reverberate. He went a little mad on the big bass. Again and again he filled the theater with a sound like thunder. The sound seemed to come not from the drums but from deep inside himself; it was a sound that was being wrenched out of him—a violent, raging, roaring sound. As it issued from him he thought, this is the story of my love, this is the story of my hate, this is all there is left of me. And the sound echoed and re-echoed far up under the roof of the theater.

When he finally stopped playing, he was trembling; his body was wet with sweat. He was surprised to see that the drums were sitting there in front of him. He hadn't become part of them. He was still himself. Kid Jones. Master of the drums. Greatest drummer in the world. Selling himself a little piece at a time. Every afternoon. Twice every evening. Only this time he had topped all his other performances. This time, playing like this after what had happened in the morning, he had sold all of himself—not just a little piece.

Someone kicked his foot. "Bow, you ape. Whassamatter with you?"

He bowed from the waist, and the spotlight slid away from him, down his pants legs. The light landed on the Marquis of Brund, the piano player. The Marquis' skin glistened like a piece of black seaweed. Then the light was back on Kid Jones.

He felt hot and he thought, I stink of sweat. The talcum he had dabbed on his face after he shaved felt like a constricting layer of cement. A thin layer but definitely cement. No air could get through to his skin. He reached for his handkerchief and felt the powder and the sweat mix as he mopped his face.

Then he bowed again. And again. Like a—like one of those things you pull the string and it jerks, goes through the motion of dancing. Pull it again and it kicks. Yeah, he thought, you were hot all right. The jitterbugs ate you up and you haven't any place to go. Since this morning you haven't had any place to go. "I'm leaving it's the guy who plays the piano I'm in love with the Marquis of Brund he plays such sweet piano I'm leaving leaving leaving—"

He stared at the Marquis of Brund for a long moment.

Then he stood up and bowed again. And again.

Questions for Discussion and Writing

1. What do we learn about Kid Jones directly? What do we learn about him indirectly, and in what ways? How does Petry evoke our empathy for him?
2. Analyze the ways in which words work in the story to beat out the rhythms of Kid Jones's life, thoughts, and feelings. Use brief passages in support of your analysis.
3. What, if anything, has Kid Jones decided at the end of the story, and on what factors do you base your interpretation?

V. GORYUSHKIN

Before Sunrise

V. Goryushkin is a writer living in Moscow; little else is known of him. The story that follows comes from a collection entitled Russia's Other Writers, Selections from Samizdat Literature *(1970). "Samizdat" is a Russian abbreviation for "self-publishing" and, at the same time, an ironic allusion to "Gosizdat," the standard abbreviation of the State Publishing House. The stories in the book were gathered from a Russian-language review called* Grani, *a literary magazine published by a Soviet expatriate organization in Frankfurt-am-Main, Germany.*

Before its publication in Grani *in 1967, "Before Sunrise" appeared, in Icelandic translation, in the Reykjavik newspaper* Morgunbladid *in December 1966.*

Soviet literature typically reflects a mixture of literary and political concerns. In a country where politics impinge on everything, a tradition of political pressure on literature cannot be ignored. Censors of literature do not necessarily work in comprehensible ways, so some of the Soviet Union's finest literature must be published abroad in Samizdat sources. Even a story like "Before Sunrise," with its emphasis on compassion and optimism rather than on overt political concerns, has nevertheless not seen publication in the Soviet Union.

Before you read "Before Sunrise," write about a time in your life when a problem, physical or mental, made you at least temporarily unable to speak. If you have not experienced such a problem, write instead about a time when some other disability prevented you from expressing yourself or from achieving your goals. What has the experience taught you?

A kim awoke, and a few pale watery stars shone in the sky. Beside him was the warm body of his wife, but he couldn't put his arms round her, for they were missing from the elbow. . . . So he lay without stirring. He would have told her how much he loved her, remembering how easily he once made the

437

words come; but he could not. Akim had lost his tongue long since, it had been carried away by a shell in the war.

The windows of his hut were open. Outside it was July and the lime tree was in blossom. From an iron hook by the stove hung a cradle. In it was his son, the son of Akim the Cripple. Akim had no hands and no legs, his tongue was useless, but he possessed a son. His son had hands; and legs; and a voice to be marvelled at.

Akim smiled with quiet joy, remembering his dream. The dream had been of an enormous field, so huge and boundless that it took your breath away to look at it. . . . He was on a tractor, hands over the steering wheel, his foot down on the accelerator, a song bursting from his throat. Then Akim realised he was shouting with the voice of his son, that he had long since forgotten the sound of his own.

Akim closed his eyes again. He would have given anything to see himself in that field with those hands, those legs, that song. He would not ask for anything more, to save his life.

Soon his wife would wake up, slip quietly from under the covers and go to milk the cow in her nightgown. She would leave the outer door open, and he would hear her say a reassuring word to the cow. Then the streams of milk would start banging into the pail, and the chickens would wake up and start clucking. . . .

Akim loved the summer, because in the summer his wife carried him out on to the verandah, where he sat until dinner. And there was a lot to see before dinner. . . .

Their neighbour usually sent his cow out to join the herd, but the herd was already grazing in the ravine for he had overslept. Hastily he greeted Akim in a voice still hoarse from sleep and went frowning on his way, wondering why Akim the cripple should have a wife, while he, the healthy one, had none. Akim felt sorry for his neighbour, he wanted to say a comforting word, but all he could do was wrinkle his left eyebrow; and besides, perhaps it was better that way, because Akim didn't know why his wife loved him.

The peasant women greeted him as they went by with their hayrakes and the cheekiest winked and whispered a few ardent words in his ear, asking when she could come and see him; she knew that Akim wouldn't tell his wife, of course, because he couldn't. The women burst out laughing and Akim blushed and grinned like a little boy. Because the women were a cheerful crowd, and they made him feel good.

In the yard the cock came to life, ruffling his feathers, and inviting the hens on to the dungheap he had discovered. A succession of roosters' war-cries rolled through the village, now dying away and now flaring up again. Fluffy clouds, like stray ducklings, dawdled over the village; the sky was a deep and peaceful blue. A swallow flew in under the verandah roof and placed a worm in the yellow gape of its young.

Vasya the blacksmith, who had grown up and fought together with Akim, came by on his way to the forge and said:

"Your whiskers are growing, Akim, my old son. When I knock off work, I'll come and shave you. My razor's a beauty—I've still got the one I had in the war."

He ran his hand upwards over Akim's face. "What a lovely day it is. . . ." And the blacksmith rubbed the unshaven cheeks, sighed, and went off to the forge where his mate and the blazing hearth awaited him, to earn his and his children's daily bread.

The grass along the road was sickly, just single blades, but there was an abundance of dense green plantains and they were all in flower, covered with little beads of white. The dust on the road was soft and hot and the sparrows fluttered and bathed in it. And Akim knew that if he were to crawl down the path through the garden and down the slope beyond, he would see the spring, with an oak water trough which he and his dad had chiselled out themselves. As a youth he had fought with Vasya the blacksmith by that spring and both had drawn blood. Akim no longer remembered what that fight had been over, but he had won it, and not with tricks or sticks, but honestly.

"But what had honesty to do with it?" thought Akim. "One was weaker, the other stronger, that was all the honesty about it. And why did this happen to me, especially to me? How is one to take such things? . . ."

The thatched huts flowed on somewhere across the ravine and beyond Akim's horizon. He wanted to see where the village ended, how he longed to see where it ended. But perhaps the village didn't end. Perhaps it stretched over the whole world, round the round earth and back again the other side, like a line round the rubber ball that the kids played with.

Over the village floated the ringing of the forge, dissolving in the greater bell of the deep blue sky, overflowing, echoed by the song of the lark. How he longed to take off and fly over the world, see the whole earth as it really was, but the only trouble was—he had no wings. Once when the dew was still white on the fields, Akim had suddenly felt that the time had come. He breathed in the air of the wide open spaces, shut his eyes and then—and then he was flying and flying; or perhaps he wasn't, who knows? But he wasn't going to open his eyes until he suddenly heard the schoolmaster's voice:

"You're a lucky fellow, Akim," he said, and Akim knew that the schoolmaster wasn't making mock of him, but really meant it. His face was wreathed in a respectful grimace. Looking at the schoolmaster, Akim was reminded of a mare, emaciated by a long winter and a neglectful master. "You've time to contemplate. You live on a higher plane, unattainable to us ordinary mortals. It's not as if we lead frantically busy lives, but all the same. . . ." The schoolmaster shook his head. "Did you say 'sanctity of labour'? What does 'labour' mean when, because of it, we scurry about all over the place like insects, and before we've time to look around, it's winter, time to die. And why did we rush all over the place—nobody knows. Just the same, I studied, dreamed, thought I would see a better world. But when I sit down to mark my tests, my hands are covered in dung. . . ."

"He's jealous," thought Akim, "and who is he jealous of? Me, a limbless torso. What's going on in the world, what's going on?"

"I thought the purpose of life was work, serving other people. . . . But that's just dogma! Terrifying, life-killing dogma. And you're allowed no doubts, and no confirmations either. You're like a horse bitted and bridled, shafts on either side, and as for turning left or right—not a hope, that's what the whip is for."

"If only I had hands," Akim was thinking, "I'd plough up the earth with my fingers."

"Contemplation," the schoolmaster went on, "is the greatest blessing given to man, his highest spiritual state. But here am I talking to you, while my sick wife is expecting me home—the sow is due to farrow, and somebody must see she doesn't eat the litter. Isn't that a joke—my children's future, my wonderful ideals, my relations with my wife, all depend on a sow in-pig. . . ."

The schoolmaster wasn't directing his questions at Akim, but talking to himself, to that winged cripple that lives inside every one of us. But Akim wasn't bored, he was looking along the village, trying to see to the far end.

Then the schoolmaster's wife appeared, bony and perpetually pregnant. Seeing her husband, she called out tenderly, pleadingly: "Kolya! Kolya, my love!" Even in Akim's presence she contained herself, but at home she gave free rein to her feelings, shouting about her ruined life, weeping, hissing: "Tramp, good-for-nothing, intellectual!" But now she stood by the mountain ash hedge, with a sickly smile on her face: "Kolya, my love!" The schoolmaster painfully suppressed a cough, saying as he left: "I try to feel that my pupils need me—I immerse myself in the life of my children—I try to get by somehow. The most terrible thing of all is—impotence."

"There goes a man who can read and write, who's got arms and legs, and still tortures himself. Why?" Akim asked himself for the umpteenth time, without finding an answer. Along the road marched a platoon of soldiers, raising swirls of dust behind them as they sang about Sergeant Kolya, who had lost the gift of speech at the sight of dark-browed Masha. Grubby urchins marched alongside, joining in the choruses.

Akim stopped dreaming about the verandah, and turned over like a caterpillar, painfully but very carefully, so as not to wake his wife before time. She must be worn out . . . alone the whole time . . . twenty years as if alone. She slept deeply, breathing heavily, as if weeping. Weeping. He could not weep, could not say to her, "Stop it, why mess up your life?" He could only grunt and roll his eyes; but if he could have spoken, he would have said: "They've got special homes where they keep people like us, who've suffered for the motherland. Those that haven't arms can dance, those that haven't legs can play dominoes, those that haven't arms or legs can sing songs, those that can't sing gaze at the sky, those that can't see . . . I'd like it there, it would be nice and peaceful. So what if you loved me when I was a whole man? So what if I was once the breadwinner and built this house for us—I was well then. But all I'm good for is begging in the church porch. Don't ruin your beautiful life, no one obliged you to saddle yourself with a hopeless cripple. . . ."

Marya had brought Akim home across the fields on a little sledge one cold

January night, the stars like wolves' eyes blotted out by his wife's back. The squeaky snowy path suddenly gave way under the runners, Akim bellowed, his face in a snowdrift. Marya had lifted him out, murmuring, "My own Aki-mushka," wiped the froth from his lips, replaced him on the sledge, and the brilliant crackle of the snow rose triumphantly again to the stars. But Akim's bellow and his wife's tears remained there, on earth.

Winter was like the torments of hell, unending as the snowy wastes outside, in the half-dark hut with the weeping candle end and the mournful cricket. Marya was busy with her housework, with all her cares, while he was on his back, looking for weeks on end at a little lump of tow which had come loose from under a board. Whichever way you looked at it, it had to be pushed in, the hut would be chilled, firewood would be wasted. It wasn't very high, if you stood up on your leg-stumps and pointed with your arm stumps . . . but then it was right up under the ceiling, perhaps you wouldn't be able to reach.

Akim grunted, pointing with his arm, but Marya didn't understand, she looked at the ceiling and fussed about straightening the pillow and bringing water, and finally she sat down and burst into tears. How was she to spot that tiny piece of caulking? But the cripple could think of only one thing, raging uncontrollably and beating his stump against the log wall. Marya wiped away her tears: "Aki-mushka, what is it? The ceiling? The roof? Are you hungry?" Akim shook his head. "Wrong, wrong. . . ."

Marya planted her beetroot and potatoes, thinking to herself: "What can he want?" And when the following winter came, the cripple would begin again, and Marya would ask once more: "Is it the roof? The sky?" Akim felt his head would split. His face was purple, the sweat stood out on his forehead, his lips were drawn. He twitched, then grew still, his breathing became inaudible—was he alive or dead? Marya looked into her husband's open eyes, but saw nothing, only a stale, unfulfilled longing; she asked with a sigh, "Is it God?" The short sharp word was like a slap in the face. But the cripple remained calm and quietly shook his head.

In the sixth year the caulking that had so long occupied Akim's thoughts worked its way out and fell somewhere behind the bed, and Akim began to think that Marya would understand him at last. He was inexpressibly glad, contented and good tempered; but not for long. . . .

Akim's nostrils widened and turned white, the smell of his sick body tormented him, he felt that he stank worse than pig's dung. Marya bathed him with scented soap, while Akim inspected his sores, comparing himself to some loathsome may-fly grub, twisting and wriggling.

Now and then he would remember his medals. He would start to grunt, thumping his bloated chest with his stump, and Marya would know immediately and reach for the box where the medals were kept, along with her buttons and thread. Akim had a lot of medals and decorations—enough to go right across his chest. On public holidays, Marya would pin them on his old jacket and sit Akim outside on the verandah. Sometimes at night he was unable to restrain himself, and would wake Marya, pointing to his chest as if to say: "Where are those medals of mine?"

The hut was warm and quiet, and by the light of the guttering candle Akim had been looking at his medals all night, a month, a year, ten years. . . . Marya became fearful when she looked at Akim. Then one day, Akim crawled over to the window, butted his head through the glass and put his neck on the jagged edge. All winter he lay ill and barely conscious. Marya's expression hardened and when the spring thaw came, and the roads turned to mud, the cripple's ears caught a conversation in undertones, carried by chance on the wind.

"Fate's played you a cruel trick, Marya, but we've all been in the war, we could all have been like that. You're a woman, you need someone to lean on, a man's help." A man's hoarse voice was persuading, pleading. "What does it matter to him? There are homes for people like that. . . . Don't ruin my life, Marya. . . ."

Akim strained his ears, afraid to miss a word.

"Look at me—hands, feet, a fine smallholding, but what use is that in God's name without you? Special homes. . . . All luck, a trick of fate. . . ."

"What do you know about fate? . . ."

Then Akim heard a scuffling by the hedge, as of geese flapping their wings, and the sound of heavy breathing, and his wife whispering: "Let me go, do you hear? I love him, do you hear?"

The July nights were short and the breath of the lime trees was sweet.

Akim pressed closer to his wife's flowing hair, let down for the night, and recalled how she had carried him on to the verandah and blushingly told him about the baby. He had thrown himself off the verandah into the puddle in front of the house, tipped his face into the mud, kissed the earth.

From the depths of the ravine the mist rose, drifting and spreading, as if seeking shelter, catching at the bushes and tops of the trees: "Help me, take me in. . . ." wept the mist, leaving tears on the broad leaves of the indifferent burdocks. But everything was quiet. In a little while the sun would come up. The dew in the meadows would vanish and day would forget that the mist had wept—until it was time for the next sunrise.

Translated by Michael Scammell

Questions for Discussion and Writing

1. In what ways does Goryushkin help us to feel Akim's struggles, doubts, and despair? Use examples from the story to show and support your ideas. What dynamics of writing can we learn from this story?

2. In what ways do you suspect that this story could offend Soviet censors? How can the character of Akim be read politically and thus symbolically?

3. "Contemplation," the schoolmaster says, "is the greatest blessing given to man, his highest spiritual state" (p. 440). In what ways does the story support this idea? In what ways does it refute it? What do you see as the main function of the schoolmaster's role in talking to Akim?

4. What effects does Akim's physical state have on the relationship between him and his wife? In what ways does his condition help us to see the world in new patterns?
5. What meanings does the word *disabled* have for you? In what ways have you observed people suffering disabilities, and what weapons might each person use against them? How does the culture in which you live influence your ideas about what being disabled means?

GABRIEL GARCÍA MÁRQUEZ

Big Mama's Funeral

"For a long time, of course, things did not work out for me—almost the first forty years of my life," says 1982 Colombian Nobel Laureate Gabriel García Márquez. "I had financial problems; I had work problems. I had not made it as a writer or anything else. . . . I had the idea that I was like an extra, that I did not count anywhere. And then, with [the novel] One Hundred Years of Solitude, *things turned." As a result of that novel and his now well-known short stories, García Márquez has been credited with putting Latin America on the literary map. Macondo, the name of the city in "Big Mama's Funeral" and the setting for* One Hundred Years of Solitude, *is often understood by critics to be Latin America in microcosm.*

Asked about what he loves now in his life and what he dreams about, García Márquez says "the world of the farandula, *of show business, nightlife. . . . I'd like to run around with many beautiful women, different every day. And never work. To be a bum. To get up at any hour, without thinking." A pause. "But then I couldn't write. And the only thing I ever wanted to do in life was write."*

Born in 1928 in Aracataca, Colombia, García Márquez has long been interested in writing—first as a journalist in Latin America, Europe, and the United States (1947–1965), and then as a full-time writer of short stories, novels, and plays. Critics place his literature in a category they call magic or marvelous realism. "It always amuses me," the author says, "that the biggest praise for my work comes for the imagination while the truth is that there's not a single line in all my work that does not have a basis in reality. The problem is that Caribbean reality resembles the wildest imagination."

Before you read "Big Mama's Funeral," write about a time when an important person died—it can be but doesn't need to be someone you knew well. Describe the details you remember before the death, at the time of death, and following the death. What struck you as odd, funny, ironic, or sad, and why?

This is, for all the world's unbelievers, the true account of Big Mama, absolute sovereign of the Kingdom of Macondo, who lived for ninety-two years, and died in the odor of sanctity one Tuesday last September, and whose funeral was attended by the Pope.

Now that the nation, which was shaken to its vitals, has recovered its balance; now that the bagpipers of San Jacinto, the smugglers of Guajira, the rice planters of Sinú, the prostitutes of Caucamayal, the wizards of Sierpe, and the banana workers of Aracataca have folded up their tents to recover from the exhausting vigil and have regained their serenity, and the President of the Republic and his Ministers and all those who represented the public and supernatural powers on the most magnificent funeral occasion recorded in the annals of history have regained control of their estates; now that the Holy Pontiff has risen up to Heaven in body and soul; and now that it is impossible to walk around in Macondo because of the empty bottles, the cigarette butts, the gnawed bones, the cans and rags and excrement that the crowd which came to the burial left behind; now is the time to lean a stool against the front door and relate from the beginning the details of this national commotion, before the historians have a chance to get at it.

Fourteen weeks ago, after endless nights of poultices, mustard plasters, and leeches, and weak with the delirium of her death agony, Big Mama ordered them to seat her in her old rattan rocker so she could express her last wishes. It was the only thing she needed to do before she died. That morning, with the intervention of Father Anthony Isabel, she had put the affairs of her soul in order, and now she needed only to put her worldly affairs in order with her nine nieces and nephews, her sole heirs, who were standing around her bed. The priest, talking to himself and on the verge of his hundredth birthday, stayed in the room. Ten men had been needed to take him up to Big Mama's bedroom, and it was decided that he should stay there so they should not have to take him down and then take him up again at the last minute.

Nicanor, the eldest nephew, gigantic and savage, dressed in khaki and spurred boots, with a .38-caliber long-barreled revolver holstered under his shirt, went to look for the notary. The enormous two-story mansion, fragrant from molasses and oregano, with its dark apartments crammed with chests and the odds and ends of four generations turned to dust, had become paralyzed since the week before, in expectation of that moment. In the long central hall, with hooks on the walls where in another time butchered pigs had been hung and deer were slaughtered on sleepy August Sundays, the peons were sleeping on farm equipment and bags of salt, awaiting the order to saddle the mules to spread the bad news to the four corners of the huge hacienda. The rest of the family was in the living room. The women were limp, exhausted by the inheritance proceedings and lack of sleep; they kept a strict mourning which was the culmination of countless accumulated mournings. Big Mama's matriarchal rigidity had surrounded her fortune and her name with a sacramental fence, within which uncles married the daughters of their nieces, and the cousins married their aunts, and brothers their sisters-in-law, until an intricate mesh of consanguinity was formed, which turned procreation into a vicious circle. Only Magdalena, the youngest of the nieces, managed to escape it. Terrified by hallucinations, she made Father Anthony Isabel exorcise her, shaved her head, and renounced the glories and vanities of the world in the novitiate of the Mission District.

On the margin of the official family, and in exercise of the *jus primae noctis,* the males had fertilized ranches, byways, and settlements with an entire bastard line, which circulated among the servants without surnames, as godchildren, employees, favorites, and protégés of Big Mama.

The imminence of her death stirred the exhausting expectation. The dying woman's voice, accustomed to homage and obedience, was no louder than a bass organ pipe in the closed room, but it echoed in the most far-flung corners of the hacienda. No one was indifferent to this death. During this century, Big Mama had been Macondo's center of gravity, as had her brothers, her parents, and the parents of her parents in the past, in a dominance which covered two centuries. The town was founded on her surname. No one knew the origin, or the limits or the real value of her estate, but everyone was used to believing that Big Mama was the owner of the waters, running and still, of rain and drought, and of the district's roads, telegraph poles, leap years, and heat waves, and that she had furthermore a hereditary right over life and property. When she sat on her balcony in the cool afternoon air, with all the weight of her belly and authority squeezed into her old rattan rocker, she seemed, in truth, infinitely rich and powerful, the richest and most powerful matron in the world.

It had not occurred to anyone to think that Big Mama was mortal, except the members of her tribe, and Big Mama herself, prodded by the senile premonitions of Father Anthony Isabel. But she believed that she would live more than a hundred years, as did her maternal grandmother, who in the War of 1885 confronted a patrol of Colonel Aureliano Buendía's, barricaded in the kitchen of the hacienda. Only in April of this year did Big Mama realize that God would not grant her the privilege of personally liquidating, in an open skirmish, a horde of Federalist Masons.

During the first week of pain, the family doctor maintained her with mustard plasters and woolen stockings. He was a hereditary doctor, a graduate of Montpellier, hostile by philosophical conviction to the progress of his science, whom Big Mama had accorded the lifetime privilege of preventing the establishment in Macondo of any other doctors. At one time he covered the town on horseback, visiting the doleful, sick people at dusk, and Nature had accorded him the privilege of being the father of many another's children. But arthritis kept him stiff-jointed in bed, and he ended up attending to his patients without calling on them, by means of suppositions, messengers, and errands. Summoned by Big Mama, he crossed the plaza in his pajamas, leaning on two canes, and he installed himself in the sick woman's bedroom. Only when he realized that Big Mama was dying did he order a chest with porcelain jars labeled in Latin brought, and for three weeks he besmeared the dying woman inside and out with all sorts of academic salves, magnificent stimulants, and masterful suppositories. Then he applied bloated toads to the site of her pain, and leeches to her kidneys, until the early morning of that day when he had to face the dilemma of either having her bled by the barber or exorcised by Father Anthony Isabel.

Nicanor sent for the priest. His ten best men carried him from the parish house to Big Mama's bedroom, seated on a creaking willow rocker, under the mildewed canopy reserved for great occasions. The little bell of the Viaticum in the warm September dawn was the first notification to the inhabitants of Macondo. When the sun rose, the little plaza in front of Big Mama's house looked like a country fair.

It was like a memory of another era. Until she was seventy, Big Mama used to celebrate her birthday with the most prolonged and tumultuous carnivals within memory. Demijohns of rum were placed at the townspeople's disposal, cattle were sacrificed in the public plaza, and a band installed on top of a table played for three days without stopping. Under the dusty almond trees, where, in the first week of the century, Colonel Aureliano Buendía's troops had camped, stalls were set up which sold banana liquor, rolls, blood puddings, chopped fried meat, meat pies, sausage, yucca breads, crullers, buns, corn breads, puff paste, *longanizas,* tripes, coconut nougats, rum toddies, along with all sorts of trifles, gewgaws, trinkets, and knicknacks, and cockfights and lottery tickets. In the midst of the confusion of the agitated mob, prints and scapularies with Big Mama's likeness were sold.

The festivities used to begin two days before and end on the day of her birthday, with the thunder of fireworks and a family dance at Big Mama's house. The carefully chosen guests and the legitimate members of the family, generously attended by the bastard line, danced to the beat of the old pianola which was equipped with the rolls most in style. Big Mama presided over the party from the rear of the hall in an easy chair with linen pillows, imparting discreet instructions with her right hand, adorned with rings on all her fingers. On that night the coming year's marriages were arranged, at times in complicity with the lovers, but almost always counseled by her own inspiration. To finish off the jubilation, Big Mama went out to the balcony, which was decorated with diadems and Japanese lanterns, and threw coins to the crowd.

That tradition had been interrupted, in part because of the successive mournings of the family and in part because of the political instability of the last few years. The new generations only heard stories of those splendid celebrations. They never managed to see Big Mama at High Mass, fanned by some functionary of the Civil Authority, enjoying the privilege of not kneeling, even at the moment of the elevation, so as not to ruin her Dutch-flounced skirt and her starched cambric petticoats. The old people remembered, like a hallucination out of their youth, the two hundred yards of matting which were laid down from the manorial house to the main altar the afternoon on which Maria del Rosario Castañeda y Montero attended her father's funeral and returned along the matted street endowed with a new and radiant dignity, turned into Big Mama at the age of twenty-two. That medieval vision belonged then not only to the family's past but also to the nation's past. Ever more indistinct and remote, hardly visible on her balcony, stifled by the geraniums on hot afternoons, Big Mama was melting into her own legend. Her authority was exercised through Nicanor. The tacit promise existed, formulated by tradition, that the day Big Mama sealed her will the heirs would declare three nights of public merrymaking. But at the same time it was known that she had decided not to express her last wishes until a few hours before dying, and no one thought seriously about the possibility that Big Mama was mortal. Only this morning, awakened by the tinkling of the Viaticum, did the inhabitants of Macondo become convinced not only that Big Mama was mortal but also that she was dying.

Her hour had come. Seeing her in her linen bed, bedaubed with aloes up to her ears, under the dust-laden canopy of Oriental crêpe, one could hardly make out any life in the thin respiration of her matriarchal breasts. Big Mama, who until she was fifty rejected the most passionate suitors, and who was well enough endowed by Nature to suckle her whole issue all by herself, was dying a virgin and childless. At the moment of extreme unction, Father Anthony Isabel had to ask for help in order to apply the oils to the palms of her hands, for since the beginning of her death throes Big Mama had had her fists closed. The attendance of the nieces was useless. In the struggle, for the first time in a week, the dying woman pressed against her chest the hand bejeweled with precious stones and fixed her colorless look on the nieces, saying, "Highway robbers." Then she saw Father Anthony Isabel in his liturgical habit and the acolyte with the sacramental implements, and with calm conviction she murmured, "I am dying." Then she took off the ring with the great diamond and gave it to Magdalena, the novice, to whom it belonged since she was the youngest heir. That was the end of a tradition: Magdalena had renounced her inheritance in favor of the Church.

At dawn Big Mama asked to be left alone with Nicanor to impart her last instructions. For half an hour, in perfect command of her faculties, she asked about the conduct of her affairs. She gave special instructions about the disposition of her body, and finally concerned herself with the wake. "You have to keep your eyes open," she said. "Keep everything of value under lock and key, because many people come to wakes only to steal." A moment later, alone with the priest, she made an extravagant confession, sincere and detailed, and later on took Communion in the presence of her nieces and nephews. It was then that she asked them to seat her in her rattan rocker so that she could express her last wishes.

Nicanor had prepared, on twenty-four folios written in a very clear hand, a scrupulous account of her possessions. Breathing calmly, with the doctor and Father Anthony Isabel as witnesses, Big Mama dictated to the notary the list of her property, the supreme and unique source of her grandeur and authority. Reduced to its true proportions, the real estate was limited to three districts, awarded by Royal Decree at the founding of the Colony; with the passage of time, by dint of intricate marriages of convenience, they had accumulated under the control of Big Mama. In that unworked territory, without definite borders, which comprised five townships and in which not one single grain had ever been sown at the expense of the proprietors, three hundred and fifty-two families lived as tenant farmers. Every year, on the eve of her name day, Big Mama exercised the only act of control which prevented the lands from reverting to the state: the collection of rent. Seated on the back porch of her house, she personally received the payment for the right to live on her lands, as for more than a century her ancestors had received it from the ancestors of the tenants. When the three-day collection was over, the patio was crammed with pigs, turkeys, and chickens, and with the tithes and first fruits of the land which were deposited there as gifts. In reality, that was the only harvest the family ever collected from a territory which had been dead since its beginnings, and which was calculated on first examination at a hundred thousand hectares. But historical circumstances had brought it about that within those boundaries the six towns of Macondo district should grow and prosper, even the county seat, so that no person who lived in a house had any property rights other than those which pertained to the house itself, since the land belonged to Big Mama, and the rent was paid to her, just as the government had to pay her for the use the citizens made of the streets.

On the outskirts of the settlements, a number of animals, never counted and even less looked after, roamed, branded on the hindquarters with the shape of a padlock. This hereditary brand, which more out of disorder than out of quantity had become familiar in distant districts where the scattered cattle, dying of thirst, strayed in summer, was one of the most solid supports of the legend. For reasons which no one had bothered to explain, the extensive stables of the house had progressively emptied since the last civil war, and lately sugarcane presses, milking parlors, and a rice mill had been installed in them.

Aside from the items enumerated, she mentioned in her will the existence of three containers of gold coins buried somewhere in the house during the War of Independence, which had not been found after periodic and laborious excavations. Along with the right to continue the exploitation of the rented land, and to receive the tithes and first fruits and all sorts of extraordinary donations, the heirs received a chart kept up from generation to generation, and perfected by each generation, which facilitated the finding of the buried treasure.

Big Mama needed three hours to enumerate her earthly possessions. In the stifling bedroom, the voice of the dying woman seemed to dignify in its place each thing named. When she affixed her trembling signature, and the witnesses affixed theirs below, a secret tremor shook the hearts of the crowds which were beginning to gather in front of the house, in the shade of the dusty almond trees of the plaza.

The only thing lacking then was the detailed listing of her immaterial possessions. Making a supreme effort—the same kind that her forebears made before they died to assure the dominance of their line—Big Mama raised herself up on her monumental buttocks, and in a domineering and sincere voice, lost in her memories, dictated to the notary this list of her invisible estate:

The wealth of the subsoil, the territorial waters, the colors of the flag, national sovereignty, the traditional parties, the rights of man, civil rights, the nation's leadership, the right of appeal, Congressional hearings, letters of recommendation, historical records, free elections, beauty queens, transcendental speeches, huge demonstrations, distinguished young ladies, proper gentlemen, punctilious military men, His Illustrious Eminence, the Supreme Court, goods whose importation was forbidden, liberal ladies, the meat problem, the purity of the language, setting a good example, the free but responsible press, the Athens of South America, public opinion, the lessons of democracy, Christian morality, the shortage of foreign exchange, the right of asylum, the Communist menace, the ship of state, the high cost of living, republican traditions, the underprivileged classes, statements of political support.

She didn't manage to finish. The laborious enumeration cut off her last breath. Drowning in the pandemonium of abstract formulas which for two centuries had constituted the moral justification of the family's power, Big Mama emitted a loud belch and expired.

That afternoon the inhabitants of the distant and somber capital saw the picture of a twenty-year-old woman on the first page of the extra editions, and thought that it was a new beauty queen. Big Mama lived again the momentary youth of her photograph, enlarged to four columns and with needed retouching, her abundant hair caught up atop her skull with an ivory comb and a diadem on her lace collar. That image, captured by a street photographer who passed through Macondo at the beginning of the century, and kept in the newspaper's morgue for many years in the section of unidentified persons, was destined to endure in the memory of future generations. In the dilapidated buses, in the elevators at the Ministries, and in the dismal tearooms hung with pale decorations, people whispered with veneration and respect about the dead personage in her sultry, malarial region, whose name was unknown in the rest of the country a few hours before—before it had been sanctified by the printed word. A fine drizzle covered the passers-by with misgiving and mist. All the church bells tolled for the dead. The President of the Republic, taken by surprise by the news when on his way to the commencement exercises for the new cadets, suggested to the War Minister, in a note in his own hand on the back of the telegram, that he conclude his speech with a minute of silent homage to Big Mama.

The social order had been brushed by death. The President of the Republic himself, who was affected by urban feelings as if they reached him through a purifying filter, managed to perceive from his car in a momentary but to a certain extent brutal vision the silent consternation of the city. Only a few low cafés remained open; the Metropolitan Cathedral was readied for nine days of funeral rites. At the National Capitol, where the beggars wrapped in newspapers slept in the shelter of the Doric columns and the silent statues of dead Presidents, the lights of Congress were lit. When the President entered his office, moved by the vision of the capital in mourning, his Ministers were waiting for him dressed in funereal garb, standing, paler and more solemn than usual.

The events of that night and the following ones would later be identified as a historic lesson. Not only because of the Christian spirit which inspired the most lofty personages of public power, but also because of the abnegation with which dissimilar interests and conflicting judgments were conciliated in the common goal of burying the illustrious body. For many years Big Mama had guaranteed the social peace and political harmony of her empire, by virtue of the three trunks full of forged electoral certificates which formed part of her secret estate. The men in her service, her protégés and tenants, elder and younger, exercised not only their own rights of suffrage but also those of electors dead for a century. She exercised the priority of traditional power over transitory authority, the predominance of class over the common people, the transcendence of divine wisdom over human improvisation. In times of peace, her dominant will approved and disapproved canonries, benefices, and sinecures, and watched over the welfare of her associates, even if she had to resort to clandestine maneuvers or election fraud in order to obtain it. In troubled times, Big Mama contributed secretly for weapons for her partisans, but came to the aid of her victims in public. That patriotic zeal guaranteed the highest honors for her.

The President of the Republic had not needed to consult with his advisers in order to weigh the gravity of his responsibility. Between the Palace reception hall and the little paved patio which had served the viceroys as a *cochère,* there was an interior garden of dark cypresses where a Portuguese monk had hanged himself out of love in the last days of the Colony. Despite his noisy coterie of bemedaled officials, the President could not suppress a slight tremor of uncertainty when he passed that spot after dusk. But that night his trembling had the strength of a premonition. Then the full awareness of his historical destiny dawned on him, and he decreed nine days of national mourning, and posthumous honors for Big Mama at the rank befitting a heroine who had died for the fatherland on the field of battle. As he expressed it in the dramatic address which he delivered that morning to his compatriots over the national radio and television network, the Nation's Leader trusted that the funeral rites for Big Mama would set a new example for the world.

Such a noble aim was to collide nevertheless with certain grave inconveniences. The judicial structure of the country, built by remote ancestors of Big Mama, was not prepared for events such as those which began to occur. Wise Doctors of Law, certified alchemists of the statutes, plunged into hermeneutics and syllogisms in search of the formula which would permit the President of the Republic to attend the funeral. The upper strata of politics, the clergy, the financiers lived through entire days of alarm. In the vast semicircle of Congress, rarefied by a century of abstract legislation, amid oil paintings of National Heroes and busts of Greek thinkers, the vocation of Big Mama reached unheard-of proportions, while her body filled with bubbles in the harsh Macondo September. For the first time, people spoke of her and conceived of her without her rattan rocker, her afternoon stupors, and her mustard plasters, and they saw her ageless and pure, distilled by legend.

Interminable hours were filled with words, words, words, which resounded throughout the Republic, made prestigious by the spokesmen of the printed word. Until, endowed with a sense of reality in that assembly of aseptic lawgivers, the historic blahblahblah was interrupted by the reminder that Big Mama's corpse awaited their decision at 104° in the shade. No one batted an eye in the face of that eruption of common sense in the pure atmosphere of the written law. Orders were issued to embalm the cadaver, while formulas were adduced, viewpoints were reconciled, or constitutional amendments were made to permit the President to attend the burial.

So much had been said that the discussions crossed the borders, traversed the ocean, and blew like an omen through the pontifical apartments at Castel Gandolfo. Recovered from the drowsiness of the torpid days of August, the Supreme Pontiff was at the window watching the lake where the divers were searching for the head of a decapitated young girl. For the last few weeks, the evening newspapers had been concerned with nothing else, and the Supreme Pontiff could not be indifferent to an enigma located such a short distance from his summer residence. But that evening, in an unforeseen substitution, the newspapers changed the photographs of the possible victims for that of one single twenty-year-old woman, marked off with black margins. "Big Mama," exclaimed the Supreme Pontiff, recognizing instantly the hazy daguerreotype which many years before had been offered to him on the occasion of his ascent to the Throne of Saint Peter. "Big Mama," exclaimed in chorus the members of the College of Cardinals in their private apartments, and for the third time in twenty centuries there was an hour of confusion, chagrin, and bustle in the limitless empire of Christendom, until the Supreme Pontiff was installed in his long black limousine en route to Big Mama's fantastic and far-off funeral.

The shining peach orchards were left behind, the Via Appia Antica with warm movie stars tanning on terraces without as yet having heard any news of the commotion, and then the somber promontory of Castel Sant' Angelo on the edge of the Tiber. At dusk the resonant pealing of St. Peter's Basilica mingled with the cracked tinklings of Macondo. Inside his stifling tent across the tangled reeds and the silent bogs which marked the boundary between the Roman Empire and the ranches of Big Mama, the Supreme Pontiff heard the uproar of the monkeys agitated all night long by the passing of the crowds. On his nocturnal itinerary, the canoe had been filled with bags of yucca, stalks of green bananas, and crates of chickens, and with men and women who abandoned their customary pursuits to try their luck at selling things at Big Mama's funeral. His Holiness suffered that night, for the first time in the history of the Church, from the fever of insomnia and the torment of the mosquitoes. But the marvelous dawn over the Great Old Woman's domains, the primeval vision of the balsam apple and the iguana, erased from his memory the suffering of his trip and compensated him for his sacrifice.

Nicanor had been awakened by three knocks at the door which announced the imminent arrival of His Holiness. Death had taken possession of the house. Inspired by successive and urgent Presidential addresses, by the feverish controversies which had been silenced but continued to be heard by means of conventional symbols, men and congregations the world over dropped everything and with their presence filled the dark hallways, the jammed passageways, the stifling attics; and those who arrived later climbed up on the low walls around the church, the palisades, vantage points, timberwork, and parapets, where they accommodated themselves as best they could. In the central hall, Big Mama's cadaver lay mummifying while it waited for the momentous decisions contained in a quivering mound of telegrams. Weakened by their weeping, the nine nephews sat the wake beside the body in an ecstasy of reciprocal surveillance.

And still the universe was to prolong the waiting for many more days. In the city-council hall, fitted out with four leather stools, a jug of purified water, and a burdock hammock, the Supreme Pontiff suffered from a perspiring insomnia, diverting himself by reading memorials and administrative orders in the lengthy, stifling nights. During the day, he distributed Italian candy to the children who approached to see him through the window, and lunched beneath the hibiscus arbor with Father Anthony Isabel, and occasionally with Nicanor. Thus he lived for interminable weeks and months which were protracted by the waiting and the heat, until the day Father Pastrana appeared with his drummer in the middle of the plaza and read the proclamation of the decision. It was declared that Public Order was disturbed, ratatatat, and that the President of the Republic, ratatatat, had in his power the extraordinary prerogatives, ratatatat, which permitted him to attend Big Mama's funeral, ratatatat, tatatat, tatat, tatat.

The great day had arrived. In the streets crowded with carts, hawkers of fried foods, and lottery stalls, and men with snakes wrapped around their necks who peddled a balm which would definitively cure erysipelas and guarantee eternal life; in the mottled little plaza where the crowds had set up their tents and unrolled their sleeping mats, dapper archers cleared the Authorities' way. There they were, awaiting the supreme moment: the washerwomen of San Jorge, the pearl fishers from Cabo de la Vela, the fishermen from Ciénaga, the shrimp fishermen from Tasajera, the sorcerers from Mojajana, the salt miners from Manaure, the accordionists from Valledupar, the fine horsemen of Ayapel, the ragtag musicians from San Pelayo, the cock breeders from La Cueva, the improvisers from Sábanas de Bolívar, the dandies from Rebolo, the oarsmen of the Magdalena, the shysters from Monpox, in addition to those enumerated at the beginning of this chronicle, and many others. Even the veterans of Colonel Aureliano Buendía's camp— the Duke of Marlborough at their head, with the pomp of his furs and tiger's claws and teeth—overcame their centenarian hatred of Big Mama and those of her line and came to the funeral to ask the President of the Republic for the payment of their veterans' pensions which they had been waiting for for sixty years.

A little before eleven the delirious crowd which was sweltering in the sun, held back by an imperturbable élite force of warriors decked out in embellished jackets and filigreed morions, emitted a powerful roar of jubilation. Dignified, solemn in their cutaways and top hats, the President of the Republic and his Ministers, the delegations from Parliament, the Supreme Court, the Council of State, the traditional parties and the clergy, and representatives of Banking, Commerce, and Industry made their appearance around the corner of the telegraph office. Bald and chubby, the old and ailing President of the Republic paraded before the astonished eyes of the crowds who had seen him inaugurated without knowing who he was and who only now could give a true account of his existence. Among the archbishops enfeebled by the gravity of their ministry, and the military men with robust chests armored with medals, the Leader of the Nation exuded the unmistakable air of power.

In the second rank, in a serene array of mourning crêpe, paraded the national queens of all things that have been or ever will be. Stripped of their earthly splendor for the first time, they marched by, preceded by the universal queen: the soybean queen, the green-squash queen, the banana queen, the meal yucca queen, the guava queen, the coconut queen, the kidney-bean queen, the 255-mile-long-string-of-iguana-eggs queen, and all the others who are omitted so as not to make this account interminable.

In her coffin draped in purple, separated from reality by eight copper turnbuckles, Big Mama was at that moment too absorbed in her formaldehyde eternity to realize the magnitude of her grandeur. All the splendor which she had dreamed of on the balcony of her house during her heat-induced insomnia was fulfilled by those forty-eight glorious hours during which all the symbols of the age paid homage to her memory. The Supreme Pontiff himself, whom she in her delirium imagined floating above the gardens of the Vatican in a resplendent carriage, conquered the heat with a plaited palm fan, and honored with his Supreme Dignity the greatest funeral in the world.

Dazzled by the show of power, the common people did not discern the covetous bustling which occurred on the rooftree of the house when agreement was imposed on the town grandees' wrangling and the catafalque was taken into the street on the shoulders of the grandest of them all. No one saw the vigilant shadow of the buzzards which followed the cortege through the sweltering little streets of Macondo, nor did they notice that as the grandees passed they left a pestilential train of garbage in the street. No one noticed that the nephews, godchildren, servants, and protégés of Big Mama closed the doors as soon as the body was taken out, and dismantled the doors, pulled the nails out of the planks, and dug up the foundations to divide up the house. The only thing which was not missed by anyone amid the noise of that funeral was the thunderous sigh of relief which the crowd let loose when fourteen days of supplications, exaltations, and dithyrambs were over, and the tomb was sealed with a lead plinth. Some of those present were sufficiently aware as to understand that they were witnessing the birth of a new era. Now the Supreme Pontiff could ascend to Heaven in body and soul, his mission on earth fulfilled, and the President of the Republic could sit down and govern according to his good judgment, and the queens of all things that have been or ever will be could marry and be happy and conceive and give birth to many sons, and the common people could set up their tents where they damn well pleased in the limitless domains of Big Mama, because the only one who could oppose them and had sufficient power to do so had begun to rot beneath a lead plinth. The only thing left then was for someone to lean a stool against the doorway to tell this story, lesson and example for future generations, so that not one of the world's disbelievers would be left who did not know the story of Big Mama, because tomorrow, Wednesday, the garbage men will come and will sweep up the garbage from her funeral, forever and ever.

Translated by J. S. Bernstein

Questions for Discussion and Writing

1. Death allows those living to focus on the life and meaning of the person who has died. How would you describe Big Mama's dominant characteristics, and on the basis of what details in the story? What are the feelings of the people of Macondo toward Big Mama, and for what reasons has her life engendered those feelings?
2. How would you describe the tone of this story—the narrator's attitude toward his subject? What aspects of García Márquez's style especially draw your attention? Use brief passages to illustrate your responses. Where your interest lags in reading it, if it does, examine the causes of your disengagement. In what ways might they have something to do with Big Mama herself?
3. "The problem is that Caribbean reality resembles the wildest imagination," García Márquez has said. What details in the story resemble the "wildest imagination" for you? Given that the author has never written "a single line in all [his] work that does not have a basis in reality," in what ways does this story help you to gain insight into Colombian culture?
4. How do you interpret the end of the story? What is its "lesson and example for future generations" (p. 455)?

LINDA HOGAN

Making Do

Although she grew up with the stories that her Chickasaw Indian father and his brother Uncle Wesley told, Linda Hogan, born in 1947 in Denver, Colorado, thought of writing as "high art," belonging to another time, to an older language. "None of the literature came from us. None of it was written by Indians or working-class people. Nothing in it was about our ordinary life," she says.

Eventually Hogan came to believe that "writing came from people and went back to people—that life could be made beautiful in words." Working as a teacher's aide, she discovered a poem by Kenneth Rexroth about a cow; for her it was magical stuff. "I can do that," she said, "I know some cows." She took her first writing class after that discovery in 1975, became hooked on writing, began publishing her work, and received her masters degree in creative writing from the University of Colorado at Boulder in 1978. Hogan has been writing and teaching writing ever since.

Although Hogan was born and now lives in Colorado, she says Oklahoma is the home of her heart. She and her family still return there often in what she calls a "great migration." Her experiences in Oklahoma—a state once called Indian Territory—gave her a sense of difference from the dominant culture that she has, in her adult years, come to value. As she has met indigenous people from other tribes and countries in the world, Hogan recognizes the same binding values: the sense of oneness with the land; the effects of being colonized and broken; and the struggle to hold on to a culture after it's been broken.

Today Hogan writes as many hours as the day allows. In addition to her writing, she teaches at the University of Colorado, cares for her daughter, does workshops in writing fiction and poetry, and gives readings. She also teaches nature writing and works as a volunteer at a facility for injured birds of prey because of her concerns about the environment. "The birds are so big they could be dangerous," she says, "but they are so gentle. They keep me grounded in physical labor. I need time when I'm not working around ideas."

"Making Do" appeared as part of a collection of traditional tales and contemporary writing entitled Spider Woman's Granddaughters (1989). In her introduction to the writers and writing of the book, editor Paula Gunn Allen said of the selection: "I have been moved by few works as completely as I was by 'Making Do'."

Before you read "Making Do," write about the ways in which you or your family "make do"—choose from the most difficult of life's circumstances to the most trivial. How, in other words, do you use the resources you do have to compensate for what you don't have? If you've never thought of yourself as "making do," write about what this discovery might mean to you.

R oberta James became one of the silent people in Seeker County when her daughter, Harriet, died at six years of age.

Harriet died of what they used to call consumption.

After the funeral, Grandmother Addie went to stay with Roberta in her grief, as she had done over the years with her children and grandchildren. Addie, in fact, had stayed with Roberta during the time of her pregnancy with Harriet, back when the fifteen-year-old girl wore her boyfriend's black satin jacket that had a map of Korea on the back. And she'd visited further back than that, back to the days when Roberta wore white full skirts and white blouses and the sun came in the door, and she lay there in that hot sun like it was ironed flat against the floor, and she felt good with clean hair and skin and singing a little song to herself. There were oak trees outside. She was waiting. Roberta was waiting there for something that would take her away. But the farthest she got was just outside her skin, that black jacket against her with its map of Korea.

Addie never told Roberta a word of what she knew about divided countries and people who wear them on their backs, but later Roberta knew that her grandmother had seen way down the road what was coming, and warned her in little ways. When she brushed Roberta's dark hair, she told her, "You were born to a different life, Bobbie."

After the funeral, Roberta's mother offered comfort in her own way. "Life goes on," Neva said, but she herself had long belonged to that society of quiet Indian women in Seeker, although no one would have guessed this of the woman who wore Peach Promise lipstick, smiled generously, and kissed the bathroom mirror, leaving a message for Roberta that said, "See you in the a.m. Love."

Grandma Addie tended Angela, Roberta's younger daughter. She fed the baby Angela spoonsful of meal, honey, and milk and held her day and night while Roberta went about the routines of her life. The chores healed her a little; perking coffee and cleaning her mother's lipstick off the mirror. She swept away traces of Harriet with the splintered broom, picking up threads from the girl's dress, black hair from her head, wiping away her footprints.

Occasionally Neva stopped in, clasped her daughter's thin cold hands between her warm ones, and offered advice. "That's why you ought to get married," she said. She wrapped Roberta's shoulders in a large gray sweater. "Then you'd have some man to help when things are down and out. Like Ted here. Well, anyway, Honey," she said at eye level to Roberta, "you sure drew a good card when Harriet was born. Didn't she, Ted?"

"Sure sugar, an ace."

But when Roberta wasn't looking, Neva shook her head slowly and looked down at the floor, and thought their lives were all hopeless.

Roberta didn't get married like her mother suggested. She did take some comfort on those long nights by loving Tom Wilkins. Each night she put pieces of cedar inside his Red Wing boots, to keep him close, and neatly placed them beneath her bed. She knew how to care for herself with this man, keeping him close in almost the same space Harriet had abandoned. She wept slightly at night after he held her and he said, "There now. There now," and patted her on the back.

He brought her favorite Windmill cookies with him from town and he sang late at night so that the ghost of Harriet could move on more easily, like he eventually moved on when Roberta stopped placing cedar in his boots.

"Why didn't that Wilkins boy come back?" Grandma asked. "Choctaw, wasn't he?"

Roberta shrugged as if she hadn't left his boots empty of cedar. "He was prettier than me." She pushed her straggly hair back from her face to show Grandma what she meant.

A month later, Roberta was relieved when the company summoned Tom Wilkins to Louisiana to work on a new oil field and she didn't have to run into him at the store any longer.

Roberta's next child, a son she named Wilkins after the father, died at birth, strangled on his own cord. Roberta had already worn a dark shawl throughout this pregnancy. She looked at his small roughbox and said, "He died of life and I know how that can happen."

She held on to her grandmother's hand.

Grandma Addie and Neva talked about Roberta. "A woman can only hold so much hurt," Grandma said.

"And don't think I don't know it," said Neva.

Roberta surfaced from her withdrawal a half year later, in the spring of 1974, when Angela looked at her like a little grandmother and said, "Mother, I know it is hard, but it's time for me to leave you" and immediately became feverish. Roberta bathed her with alcohol and made blessing-root tea, which she dropped into little Angela's rose-petal mouth with an eye dropper. She prayed fervently to God or Jesus, she had never really understood which was which, and to all the stones and trees and gods of the sky and inner earth that she knew well, and to the animal spirits, and she carried her little Angel to the hospital in the middle of praying, to that house made of brick and window and cinders where dying bodies were kept alive, carried the girl with soft child skin in a small quilt decorated with girls in poke bonnets, and thought how funny it was to wrap a dying child in such sweetness as those red-cheeked girls in the calico bonnets. She blamed herself for ignoring Angela in her own time of grief. Four days later Angela died, wearing a little corn necklace Roberta made, a wristlet of glass beads, and covered with that quilt.

"She even told Roberta she was about to die," Neva told Ted. "Just like an old woman, huh, Bert?"

Roberta went on with her silence through this third death, telling herself over and over what had happened, for the truth was so bad she could not believe it. The inner voice of the throat spoke and repeated the words of loss and Roberta listened hard. "My Angel. My Harriet. All my life gone and broken while I am so young. I'm too young for all this loss."

She dreamed of her backbone and even that was broken in pieces. She dreamed of her house in four pieces. She was broken like the country of Korea or the land of the tribe.

They were all broken, Roberta's thin-skinned father broken by the war. He and Neva raised two boys whose parents had "gone off" as they say of those who come under the control of genie spirits from whiskey bottles, and those boys were certainly broken. And Neva herself who had once been a keeper of the gates; she was broken.

In earlier days she read people by their faces and bodies. She was a keeper of gates, opening and closing ways for people to pass through life. "This one has been eating too much grain," she'd say, or "That one was born too rich for her own good and is spoiled. That one is broken in the will to live by this and that." She was a keeper of the family gates as well. She closed doors on those she disliked, if they were dishonest, say, or mean, or small. There was no room for smallness in her life, but she opened the doors wide for those who moved her slightly, in any way, with stirrings of love or pity. She had lusty respect for belligerence, political rebellion, and for vandalism against automobiles or businesses or bosses, and those vandals were among those permitted inside her walls.

And now she was broken, by her own losses and her loneliness.

Roberta cried against Addie's old warm shoulder and Grandma Addie stayed on, moving in all her things, cartons of canning jars, a blue-painted porcelain horse, her dark dresses and aprons, pictures of her grandchildren and great-grandchildren, rose-scented candles of the virgin of Guadalupe, even though she was never a Catholic, and the antlers of the deer.

Roberta ignored her cousins from the churches of the brethren of this and that when they came to comfort her in their ways, telling her that all things were meant to be and that the Lord gives and takes.

Uncle James was older and so he said nothing, and she sat with him, those silent ones together.

Roberta's mother left messages on the bathroom mirror. "There is a time for everything in heaven."

With Grandma there to watch over Neva and the house, Roberta decided one day to pack her dishes, blankets, and clothes into the old Chevy she had bought from Ted, and she drove away from the little square tombstones named Angela, Wilkins, and Harriet, though it nearly broke her heart to leave them. She drove away from all those trying to comfort her with what comforted them. The sorrow in her was like a well too deep for young ground; the sides caved in with anger, but Roberta planned still to return for Grandma Addie. She stopped once, in the flat, neutral land of Goodland, Kansas, and telephoned back.

"You sure you don't want to come with me? It's kind of pretty out this way, Grandma," she lied. She smelled truck exhaust from the phone booth and she watched the long, red-faced boys walking past, those young men who had eaten so much cattle they began to look like them.

"Just go and get settled. I'll be out to visit as soon as you get the first load of laundry hung on the line."

Roberta felt her grandma smile. She hung up the phone and headed back to the overloaded, dusty white car.

She headed for Denver, but wound up just west of there, in a mountain town called The Tropics. Its name was like a politician's vocabulary, a lie. In truth, The Tropics was arid. It was a mine town, uranium most recently. Dust devils whirled sand off the mountains. Even after the heaviest of rains, the water seeped back into the ground, between stones, and the earth was parched again. Still, *Tropics* conjured up visions of tall grasses in outlying savannas, dark rivers, mists, and deep green forests of ferns and trees and water-filled vines. Sometimes it seemed like they were there.

Roberta told herself it was God's acres, that it was fate she had missed the Denver turn-offs from the freeway, that here she could forgive and forget her losses and get on with living. She rented a cabin, got a part-time job working down at the Tropics Grocery where she sold single items to customers who didn't want to travel to town. She sold a bag of flour to one, a can of dog food to another, candy to schoolchildren in the afternoon. She sold boxed doughnuts and cigarettes to work crews in the mornings and 3.2 beer to the same crews after five. She dusted and stacked the buckling shelves, and she had time to whittle little birds, as her Uncle James had done. She whittled them and thought of them as toys for the spirits of her children and put them in the windows so the kids would be sure and see them. "This one's for Harriet," she'd tell no one in particular.

When she didn't work she spent her time in bed, completely still and staring straight at the ceiling. They used to say if a person is motionless, their soul will run away from the body, and Roberta counted on that. They say that once a soul decides to leave, it can't be recalled. Roberta lay in that room with its blue walls and blue-flowered blanket. She lay there with her hair pulled back from her round forehead. She held the sunbonnet quilt in her hands and didn't move.

To her disappointment, she remained alive. Every night she prayed to die and join her kids, but every morning she was still living, breathing. Some mornings she pulled at her flesh just to be certain, she was so amazed and despairing to be still alive.

Her soul refused to leave. It had a mind of its own. So Roberta got up and began a restless walking. There were nights in The Tropics that she haunted the dirt roads like a large-shouldered, thin-hipped ghost, like a tough girl with her shoulders held high to protect her broken heart. Roberta Diane James with her dark hair that had been worn thin from the hours she spent lying down trying to send her soul away. Roberta, with her eyes the color of dark river water after a storm when the gold stirs up in it. The left eye still held the trace of a wink in it, despite the thinness of skin stretched over her forehead, the smell of ivory soap on her as she tried over and over to wash the grief from her flesh.

2

When I first heard how bad things were going for Roberta, I thought about going home, but I heard my other voices tell me it wasn't time. "There is a season for all things," Mom used to say, and I knew Mom would be telling Roberta just that, in her own words, and that Roberta would be fuming inside as I had done with Mom's fifty-cent sayings.

I knew this much: Roberta would need to hold on to her grief and her pain.

Us Chickasaws have lost so much we hold on to everything. Even our muscles hold on to their aches. We love our lovers long after they are gone, better than when they were present.

When we were girls, Roberta and I saved the tops of Coke bottlecaps and covered them with purple cloth like grapes. We made clusters of grapes sitting out there on the porch, or on tire swings in the heat, and we sewed the grapes together. We made do. We drank tea from pickle jars. We used potato water to starch our clothes. We even used our skinny dark legs as paper for tic-tac-toe. Now the girls turn bleach containers into hats, cutting them in fours and crocheting them together.

Our Aunt Bell is famous for holding on and making do. There's a nail in her kitchen for plastic six-pack rings, a box for old jars, a shelf or box for everything, including all the black and white shoes she's worn out as a grown woman. Don't think those boxes or nails mean she's neat, either. She's not. She has hundreds of dusty salt and pepper shakers people gave her, and stacks of old magazines and papers, years of yellowed history all contained in her crowded rooms, and I love her for it, for holding on that way. I have spent hours of my younger life looking at those shakers and reading those papers. Her own children tell her it is a miracle the viruses of science aren't growing to maturity in there.

We save ourselves from loss in whatever ways we can, collecting things, going out to Danceland, getting drunk, reading westerns or finding new loves, but the other side of all this salvation is that we deny the truth. When some man from town steals our land, we say, "Oh, he wouldn't do that. Jimmy Slade is a good old boy. I knew his folks. I used to work for the Slades during the Depression." Never mind that the Slades were not the hungry ones back then.

Some of us southern Indians used to have ranches and cattle. They were all lost piece by piece, or sold to pay for taxes on some land that was also lost. Now and then someone comes around and tells us we should develop our land like we once did. Or they tell us just to go out in the world. We nod and smile at them.

Now and then some of us young people make a tidal wave in the ocean of our history, an anxiety attack in the heart monitor of our race. We get angry and scream out. We get in the news. We strip ourselves bare in the colleges that recruited us as their minority quota and we run out into the snowstorm naked and we get talked about for years as the crazy Indian that did this or that, the one that drove to the gas station and went on straight to Canada, the girl who took out the garbage and never turned and went back. We made do.

I knew some people from up north. You could always tell they were from up north because my friend's daughter had a wall-eye with a hook tattooed on her forearm. Once we went to a pow-wow together and some of the women of the People wore jingle dresses, with what looked like bells. "What are those?" I asked my friend.

They were snuff can lids. Those women of the forests and woodlands, so much making do just like us, like when we use silver salt cans in our dances instead of turtle-shell rattles. We make music of those saltshakers, though now and then some outsider decides we have no culture because we use store-bought shakers and they are not traditional at all.

I defy them: Salt is the substance of our blood, sweat, our secretions, our semen. It is the ocean of ourselves.

Once I saw a railroad engineer's hat in a museum. It was fully beaded. I thought it was a new style like the beaded tennis shoes or the new beaded truckers' hats. But it was made in the late 1800s when the Lakota were forbidden to make traditional items. The mothers took to beading whatever was available, hats of the engineers of death. They covered colony cotton with their art.

We make art out of our loss.

That's why when I heard Roberta was in Colorado and was carving wooden birds, I figured it made sense. Besides, we come from a long line of whittlers and table carvers, people who work with wood, including the Mexican great-grandfather who made santos and a wooden mask that was banned by the priests. Its presence got him excommunicated.

Uncle James carves chains out of trees. We laugh and say it sounds like something *they* would do.

Roberta was carving wooden birds, crows, mourning doves, and even a scissor-tail or two. She sent some of the birds back home to have Aunt Bell put them on the graves of her little ones.

I think she was trying to carve the souls of her children into the birds. She was making do.

Questions for Discussion and Writing

1. In what ways does Hogan re-create Roberta's grief and pain? What images, metaphors, and descriptions in the story reflect the intensity of her feelings most strikingly for you, and why? Use brief passages from the story to support your answer.
2. What observations can you make about the values and roles of the family in each other's lives? In what ways do the values here remind you of your own family's, and in what ways do they diverge? If you were to choose three or four lines from this story for their insights, which ones would they be, and why? With whom would you want to share them, and why?
3. What influences of other cultures do you find in the story, and in what ways are they significant?
4. Who is the speaker in part two, and what purposes does this part serve in the story?
5. In what ways does the story probe and show the meaning of its title?
6. What is the significance of Roberta's carved birds?

Chapter 7

DEPARTURES, JOURNEYS, AND (SOMETIMES) RETURNS

You think a person you know has got through death and illness and being broke and living on commodity rice will get through anything. Then they fold and you see how fragile were the stones that underpinned them. You see how instantly the ground can shift you thought was solid. You see the stop signs and the yellow dividing markers of roads you traveled and all the instructions you had played according to vanish. You see how all the everyday things you counted on was just a dream you had been having by which you run your whole life.

LOUISE ERDRICH, from
LOVE MEDICINE, words spoken by the character Lipsha Morrissey

WE TRAVEL FOR MANY REASONS AND IN MANY WAYS. THE TITLE OF this book suggests the journeys we make through reading and writing to new places and new insights. Journeys, both real and metaphorical, outward and inward, begin in one place and end in another. Yet we never can quite return to the place we left. Often we choose not to try.

Journeys are always tied to place—to leaving some place, to arriving at some place. The history of a people reflects the journeys they have made over land, ideas, and the shared and changing patterns of their lives. The story of a single person is a journey, too, from birth to death and all points in between.

In the essays and stories of this chapter, we experience a variety of departures: the end of a place and a childhood in My Van Vu's "The Village We Left Behind"; a young boy's early morning confrontation with death in southern Africa, in which he loses his innocence, in Doris Lessing's "Sunrise on the Veld."

Some of us are forced to make the journey from our homes and childhood, whereas others choose the departure with pleasure. The young woman in Jamaica Kincaid's "Poor Visitor" has left home in Antigua to embark on a new life in the United States, where she discovers homesickness and, for the first time, a sunny day that has no warmth. Piluk, the young woman in Richard K. Nelson's "Tingiivik Tatqiq: The Moon When Birds Fly South (September)," is returning to the place of her childhood—an Eskimo village—and, ironically, discovering her disconnectedness with her past. The young man in Graham Sheil's "The Picking Season" has chosen to leave home too, but in his journey he discovers the meaning of the family he's renounced through knowing Alf, a German who has no home at all.

The trips we take are never predictable. When we leave familiar ground, both physical and mental, we are vulnerable to strange forces. In Milan Kundera's "The Hitchhiking Game," a Czechoslovakian couple on a tightly scheduled holiday engage in an unscheduled game, through which they embark on an experimental journey that they can neither control nor stop. The man in Massud Farzan's "The Plane Reservation," who returns to Iran to visit his parents, discovers another twist in the journeys of our lives: the familiar past, revisited, can be too foreign to handle.

In the last selection in this chapter, "Grandmother's Country," N. Scott Momaday returns to the places of his father's people, the Kiowa Indians, and in particular, to the knoll called Rainy Mountain and the old home of the woman who was for him the last of the Kiowas, his grandmother. In his journeys, he is able briefly to return, but he must move on.

Journeys tie together where we are and who we are.

MY VAN VU

The Village We Left Behind

In November 1952, My Van Vu was born in the village of Thanh Phu, Kien Tuong province, Vietnam. For him the war in Vietnam began when he was eight; three years later his family had to leave their village to move to Saigon, where his father worked as a carpenter in a small furniture shop until his death from overwork and exhaustion. Vu's older brother, still in Vietnam, works as a mechanic.

After finishing high school, like many other Vietnamese youth, Vu joined the South Vietnamese army in the fight to protect his country. When South Vietnam fell to the Communists in April 1975, he lived as an outlaw, drifting from one Communist prison to another. In 1980, after escaping from the Vung Tau prison, he married and tried to settle down. He and his wife had one daughter and she was pregnant with their second child when Vu fled his pursuers once again. He spent two years in Indonesia before resettling in the United States in 1985. "Now I have my precious thing—freedom," he says, "but I also lost another one: my family. In a dark night in March, 1986, my wife and my two children tried to escape from Vietnam by boat, but they never reached their destination."

"The Village We Left Behind" was written in response to an assignment in Vu's English Composition class in 1987 to write about an important place in his life. The essay has been published for the first time in this anthology.

Vu is now a student of electrical engineering at the University of Washington. His mother, younger brother, and younger sister have joined him in Seattle. He hopes someday to write a small book about his country, "to write about the feelings of a vagabond, a family lost, a country-lost person, to explain why our fellow people would rather die in the open sea than live under the Communist regime."

Before you read "The Village We Left Behind," write about the place and time of your childhood using whatever details and perspective come to mind.

My village was located in the Mekong Delta, the most fertile land of South Vietnam, providing more than eighty percent of the rice for the nation. Sixty miles south of Saigon, the area was called the "barn of South Vietnam." Like most Vietnamese villages, my village was fringed with green bamboo hedges. Its back leaned on the left bank of the Mekong River, and its face looked out on the vast rice fields running side by side to the horizon.

On the road leading to the main gate of the village, two old tamarind tree rows spread their large branches, providing the shaded resting places for the farmers when the sun was giving off its hottest shine. Behind the main gate stood the ancient temple with the curved tiled roof, the most important place in the village. The temple served as the celebrating location for the festivals during the year, and also as the elementary school for the children. Here, through early lessons, I learned about and loved my country.

Inside the village, the red-tiled roofs emerged from the grey-thatched ones, the flower fences, the fruit trees, and the vegetable yards separating the houses. The villagers were simple and assiduous farmers, their lives tied to the yellow rice fields, the green bamboo hedges, the cows and cattle. They worried about the irregular weather; they rejoiced with the successful crops. Festivals took place all year long. The villagers prayed before and thanked God after each crop. Life in my village was as peaceful as the tranquil flowing of the Mekong River.

Everyday, when the birds started singing to the sun, the whole village awakened. Group after group of farmers and buffalos left for the fields. In the orange sunshine, the silhouettes of my father and Can, our buffalo, disappeared behind the bamboo hedges at the end of the village. My mother also left for the rural market in the nearby village. My brother and I went to school.

At noon, I used to stand at the main gate and look out at the road, waiting for my mother. I could recognize the small, thin, familiar shape from a far distance. My mother never forgot to bring me something, either a small rice cake or a pack of candies each day. She wiped her wet face and fanned herself by the *non la,* the well-known Vietnamese hat, while I ate the cake. The sweetness of the cake seemed packed with all motherlove to me.

In the evening, when the sun set westward, the grey smoke floating from the thatched roofs mixed with the snow-white clouds in the sky. The flutes, attached to the kites high in the air, sounded a beautiful melody accompanied by the singing of the flocks of birds returning to their warm nests. On the road, the farmers and the buffalos came back from the fields. The laughing of people, the noise of the animals—all those sounds in the air brought relaxation to the village.

At dusk, my brother and I joined the children in the village playing at the dam near the river. We were competing in raising kites. Our kite used to be the most beautiful, the highest kite with the sweetest sound. For making the kites, I had to spend all of my savings to buy colored papers and two spools of thread in the small town nearby. My brother had to spend many days to build the kite frame from the selected bamboo tree, and stick the colored papers on it. Finally, we attached the small bamboo flute my father made to the kite to create the sound.

Now the kite with its parallelogram shape and motley tails was ready to fly in the blue sky. When my brother raised the kite at its highest, I took the string on my brother's hand to control the kite. Inspired by the admiring eyes of the village children, my pride and happiness flew as high as the kite in the blue sky.

Our villagers used to cultivate two crops in a year: the first crop from the end of October to April, and the second from May to the end of September. In October, after the second crop was finished, it was time for fishing. Here and there on the river, the brown sails emerged from the coconut tree rows on both sides of the river banks. "Ho," a kind of popular song, sung by groups of fishermen and rural girls in challenging each other, echoed everywhere on the river. On our boat, I sat near the stove in the middle, trying to build a fire. My brother rowed the oars in the rear, while my father, standing on the front of the boat, threw down the net. When the moon spread its ivory light over the river, our baskets were full of fish. We let the boat drift with the current and began our meal. My father chose the most delicious fish to bake on the stove, and we enjoyed the tasteful fish while my father drank a small cup of *de,* a kind of alcohol made from rice, and softly sung his favorite poems.

Then, one day, the cane of war stirred up the peaceful life in my village. More and more people left the village to find another, safer place. I, myself, had just known the word "war" in spelling until an event happened: the death of Can, our beloved buffalo.

I still remember Can coming to my family. Like most Vietnamese farmers, my father had a dream of owning a buffalo. When Can's mother, the buffalo of our neighbor, got pregnant, each day after he finished working, my father had to work for our neighbor to trade his labor for the infant buffalo. At that time, my mother raised a group of chickens, and I used to have an egg for breakfast before going to school. One morning, my mother put all the chickens in cages, loaded them in our neighbor's buffalo cart, and headed to the market. That noon, I received more candies than ever, but I also had no more eggs after that.

After Can was born, my father brought him home and I was jealous of him. Everybody in my family took good care of Can and forgot me. My milk had to be shared with Can. My father hung mosquito nets to protect Can every night; my mother warmed him with my patched clothes. Even my brother, my closest friend, was interested in Can instead. I tried in vain to regain the attention of my loved ones, and failing, hated the buffalo.

Gradually, my childish hatred faded away and I was happy to play with the buffalo. Can carried my brother and me, traveling from field to field to seek the green grass fields. Can enjoyed the finest green grass while my brother and I enjoyed the baked sweet potatoes remaining after the harvest; then my brother and I let Can lazily bathe in the muddy pools while we swam in the river.

When Can grew up, two and a half years later, he became a co-worker with my father in our small field. During the leisure time between the crops, Can towed the cart loaded with fruit baskets and us to the fairs at the nearby city. He was a member of my family; he shared the hard labor with my father in cultivating the crops, and the pleasure with my brother and me in the sunshine fields. In my mind, I had thought that nothing could separate me from the buffalo, the green bamboo hedges, the yellow rice fields, and the light blue Mekong River.

One night, I was awakened by the thunder of all kinds of guns. My whole family sought shelter under the wooden bed. Shuddering in my mother's arms, I was so panicked that I could not utter a word. The thunder was closer and closer, and an explosion shined brightly in our house. Above the thunder, the cry of our poor Can made my father forget the danger. My father ran toward the stable and tried by all the means to save Can, but he made no difference. The sound of the buffalo in agony made my mother burst into tears.

To end Can's suffering, my father many times raised high the hammer, but many times he lowered it down. The red eyes of Can, tears running down unceasingly, made my father hesitate. Finally, with all his effort, my father hit the hammer at Can's neck. The buffalo fell down and my father fell down too. At the corners of my father's eyes glittered the teardrops. This was the first time in my life that I had seen my father cry. He cried for our poor Can, and also for the collapse of his dream—the very ordinary dream of a Vietnamese farmer. Instantly, I realized that my golden childhood was over.

Questions for Discussion and Writing

1. In what ways does Vu re-create his village for us?
2. What ideas does this essay reflect about the life of Can, not only to its writer but to you?
3. For what reasons do you think Vu wrote this essay? If you were to share the essay with three people, who would they be, and why?
4. In what ways does Vu handle the pain of his memories, and how does he communicate that pain to his readers?
5. Reread the quotation of Mohm Phat that opens Chapter 3 (p. 143). In what ways do you think Vu might relate to what Phat says there about expressing herself in English? Use brief passages from Vu's essay to support your ideas.

DORIS LESSING

Sunrise on the Veld

Born in 1919 in Kermanshah, Persia (now Iran), Doris (Taylor) Lessing moved with her parents in 1925 to southern Rhodesia (now Zimbabwe), where her father purchased land that had recently been taken from Africans who had been put onto reservations. She attended school in Salisbury, England, until she was fourteen, when she began working as a nursemaid and then as a secretary. She was married and divorced twice, four years each time; although she came to decide that marriage is not among her talents, she retained the name of Lessing from her second marriage. Today Lessing lives and continues to write in London, enjoying England because she says it is "quiet and unstimulating and leaves you in peace."

"Sunrise on the Veld" comes from her book African Stories, *originally published in 1951. "Africa gives you the knowledge that man is a small creature among other creatures, in a large landscape," Lessing says of the continent. Her life there taught her not only about the ways in which white exiles oppressed black natives, but also about the conflict—the "necessary cruelty"—that results among all living things in the struggle to achieve what is right for each life. Because of what Lessing has written about the conflicts between whites and blacks in southern Africa, she has been banned from returning to either Zimbabwe or South Africa by their governments.*

Lessing became serious about writing in her late twenties. She struggles in all her stories and novels to capture the truths of her life. Believing that the greatest writers have a "climate of ethical judgment" and humanistic values in common, Lessing has said that getting a story or a novel published is "an attempt to impose one's personality and beliefs on other people. If a writer accepts this responsibility," she says, "he must see himself . . . as an architect of the soul."

471

Before you read "Sunrise on the Veld," write about your earliest, conscious realization of death and the meaning of that encounter for you.

E very night that winter he said aloud into the dark of the pillow: Half-past four! Half-past four! till he felt his brain had gripped the words and held them fast. Then he fell asleep at once, as if a shutter had fallen; and lay with his face turned to the clock so that he could see it first thing when he woke.

It was half-past four to the minute, every morning. Triumphantly pressing down the alarm-knob of the clock, which the dark half of his mind had outwitted, remaining vigilant all night and counting the hours as he lay relaxed in sleep, he huddled down for a last warm moment under the clothes, playing with the idea of lying abed for this once only. But he played with it for the fun of knowing that it was a weakness he could defeat without effort; just as he set the alarm each night for the delight of the moment when he woke and stretched his limbs, feeling the muscles tighten, and thought: Even my brain—even that! I can control every part of myself.

Luxury of warm rested body, with the arms and legs and fingers waiting like soldiers for a word of command! Joy of knowing that the precious hours were given to sleep voluntarily!—for he had once stayed awake three nights running, to prove that he could, and then worked all day, refusing even to admit that he was tired; and now sleep seemed to him a servant to be commanded and refused.

The boy stretched his frame full-length, touching the wall at his head with his hands, and the bedfoot with his toes; then he sprang out, like a fish leaping from water. And it was cold, cold.

He always dressed rapidly, so as to try and conserve his night-warmth till the sun rose two hours later; but by the time he had on his clothes his hands were numbed and he could scarcely hold his shoes. These he could not put on for fear of waking his parents, who never came to know how early he rose.

As soon as he stepped over the lintel, the flesh of his soles contracted on the chilled earth, and his legs began to ache with cold. It was night: the stars were glittering, the trees standing black and still. He looked for signs of day, for the greying of the edge of a stone, or a lightening in the sky where the sun would rise, but there was nothing yet. Alert as an animal he crept past the dangerous window, standing poised with his hand on the sill for one proudly fastidious moment, looking in at the stuffy blackness of the room where his parents lay.

Feeling for the grass-edge of the path with his toes, he reached inside another window further along the wall, where his gun had been set in readiness the night before. The steel was icy, and numbed fingers slipped along it, so that he had to hold it in the crook of his arm for safety. Then he tiptoed to the room where the dogs slept, and was fearful that they might have been tempted to go before him; but they were waiting, their haunches crouched in reluctance at the cold, but ears and swinging tails greeting the gun ecstatically. His warning undertone kept them secret and silent till the house was a hundred yards back: then they bolted off into the bush, yelping excitedly. The boy imagined his parents turning in their beds and muttering: Those dogs again! before they were dragged back in sleep; and he smiled scornfully. He always looked back over his shoulder at the house before he passed a wall of trees that shut it from sight. It looked so low and small, crouching there under a tall and brilliant sky. Then he turned his back on it, and on the frosting sleepers, and forgot them.

He would have to hurry. Before the light grew strong he must be four miles away; and already a tint of green stood in the hollow of a leaf, and the air smelled of morning and the stars were dimming.

He slung the shoes over his shoulder, veld *skoen* that were crinkled and hard with the dews of a hundred mornings. They would be necessary when the ground became too hot to bear. Now he felt the chilled dust push up between his toes, and he let the muscles of his feet spread and settle into the shapes of the earth; and he thought: I could walk a hundred miles on feet like these! I could walk all day, and never tire!

He was walking swiftly through the dark tunnel of foliage that in day-time was a road. The dogs were invisibly ranging the lower travelways of the bush, and he heard them panting. Sometimes he felt a cold muzzle on his leg before they were off again, scouting for a trail to follow. They were not trained, but free-running companions of the hunt, who often tired of the long stalk before the final shots, and went off on their own pleasure. Soon he could see them, small and wild-looking in a wild strange light, now that the bush stood trembling on the verge of colour, waiting for the sun to paint earth and grass afresh.

The grass stood to his shoulders; and the trees were showering a faint silvery rain. He was soaked; his whole body was clenched in a steady shiver.

Once he bent to the road that was newly scored with animal trails, and regretfully straightened, reminding himself that the pleasure of tracking must wait till another day.

He began to run along the edge of a field, noting jerkily how it was filmed over with fresh spiderweb, so that the long reaches of great black clods seemed netted in glistening grey. He was using the steady lope he had learned by watching the natives, the run that is a dropping of the weight of the body from one foot to the next in a slow balancing movement that never tires, nor shortens the breath; and he felt the blood pulsing down his legs and along his arms, and the exultation and pride of body mounted in him till he was shutting his teeth hard against a violent desire to shout his triumph.

Soon he had left the cultivated part of the farm. Behind him the bush was low and black. In front was a long vlei, acres of long pale grass that sent back a hollowing gleam of light to a satiny sky. Near him thick swathes of grass were bent with the weight of water, and diamond drops sparkled on each frond.

The first bird woke at his feet and at once a flock of them sprang into the air calling shrilly that day had come; and suddenly, behind him, the bush woke into song, and he could hear the guinea fowl calling far ahead of him. That meant they would now be sailing down from their trees into thick grass, and it was for them he had come: he was too late. But he did not mind. He forgot he had come to shoot. He set his legs wide, and balanced from foot to foot, and swung his gun up and down in both hands horizontally, in a kind of improvised exercise, and let his head sink back till it was pillowed in his neck muscles, and watched how above him small rosy clouds floated in a lake of gold.

Suddenly it all rose in him: it was unbearable. He leapt up into the air, shouting and yelling wild, unrecognisable noises. Then he began to run, not carefully, as he had before, but madly, like a wild thing. He was clean crazy, yelling mad with the joy of living and a superfluity of youth. He rushed down the vlei under a tumult of crimson and gold, while all the birds of the world sang about him. He ran in great leaping strides, and shouted as he ran, feeling his body rise into the crisp rushing air and fall back surely on to sure feet; and thought briefly, not believing that such a thing could happen to him, that he could break his ankle any moment, in this thick tangled grass. He cleared bushes like a duiker, leapt over rocks; and finally came to a dead stop at a place where the ground fell abruptly away below him to the river. It had been a two-mile-long dash through waist-high growth, and he was breathing hoarsely and could no longer sing. But he poised on a rock and looked down at stretches of water that gleamed through stooping trees, and thought suddenly, I am fifteen! Fifteen! The words came new to him; so that he kept repeating them wonderingly, with swelling excitement; and he felt the years of his life with his hands, as if he were counting marbles, each one hard and separate and compact, each one a wonderful shining thing. That was what he was: fifteen years of this rich soil, and this slow-moving water, and air that smelt like a challenge whether it was warm and sultry at noon, or as brisk as cold water, like it was now.

There was nothing he couldn't do, nothing! A vision came to him, as he stood there, like when a child hears the word "eternity" and tries to understand it, and time takes possession of the mind. He felt his life ahead of him as a great and wonderful thing, something that was his; and he said aloud, with the blood rising to his head: all the great men of the world have been as I am now, and there is nothing I can't become, nothing I can't do; there is no country in the world I cannot make part of myself, if I choose. I contain the world. I can make of it what I want. If I choose, I can change everything that is going to happen: it depends on me, and what I decide now.

The urgency, and the truth and the courage of what his voice was saying exulted him so that he began to sing again, at the top of his voice, and the sound went echoing down the river gorge. He stopped for the echo, and sang again: stopped and shouted. That was what he was!—he sang, if he chose; and the world had to answer him.

And for minutes he stood there, shouting and singing and waiting for the lovely eddying sound of the echo; so that his own new strong thoughts came back and washed round his head, as if someone were answering him and encouraging him; till the gorge was full of soft voices clashing back and forth from rock to rock over the river. And then it seemed as if there was a new voice. He listened, puzzled, for it was not his own. Soon he was leaning forward, all his nerves alert, quite still: somewhere close to him there was a noise that was no joyful bird, nor tinkle of falling water, nor ponderous movement of cattle.

There it was again. In the deep morning hush that held his future and his past, was a sound of pain, and repeated over and over: it was a kind of shortened scream, as if someone, something, had no breath to scream. He came to himself, looked about him, and called for the dogs. They did not appear: they had gone off on their own business, and he was alone. Now he was clean sober, all the madness gone. His heart beating fast, because of that frightened screaming, he stepped carefully off the rock and went towards a belt of trees. He was moving cautiously, for not so long ago he had seen a leopard in just this spot.

At the edge of the trees he stopped and peered, holding his gun ready; he advanced, looking steadily about him, his eyes narrowed. Then, all at once, in the middle of a step, he faltered, and his face was puzzled. He shook his head impatiently, as if he doubted his own sight.

There, between two trees, against a background of gaunt black rocks, was a figure from a dream, a strange beast that was horned and drunken-legged, but like something he had never even imagined. It seemed to be ragged. It looked like a small buck that had black ragged tufts of fur standing up irregularly all over it, with patches of raw flesh beneath . . . but the patches of rawness were disappearing under moving black and came again elsewhere; and all the time the creature screamed, in small gasping screams, and leaped drunkenly from side to side, as if it were blind.

Then the boy understood: it *was* a buck. He ran closer, and again stood still, stopped by a new fear. Around him the grass was whispering and alive. He looked wildly about, and then down. The ground was black with ants, great energetic ants that took no notice of him, but hurried and scurried towards the fighting shape, like glistening black water flowing through the grass.

And, as he drew in his breath and pity and terror seized him, the beast fell and the screaming stopped. Now he could hear nothing but one bird singing, and the sound of the rustling, whispering ants.

He peered over at the writhing blackness that jerked convulsively with the jerking nerves. It grew quieter. There were small twitches from the mass that still looked vaguely like the shape of a small animal.

It came into his mind that he should shoot it and end its pain; and he raised the gun. Then he lowered it again. The buck could no longer feel; its fighting was a mechanical protest of the nerves. But it was not that which made him put down the gun. It was a swelling feeling of rage and misery and protest that expressed itself in the thought: if I had not come it would have died like this: so why should I interfere? All over the bush things like this happen; they happen all the time; this is how life goes on, by living things dying in anguish. He gripped the gun between his knees and felt in his own limbs the myriad swarming pain of the twitching animal that could no longer feel, and set his teeth, and said over and over again under his breath: I can't stop it. I can't stop it. There is nothing I can do.

He was glad that the buck was unconscious and had gone past suffering so that he did not have to make a decision to kill it even when he was feeling with his whole body: this is what happens, this is how things work.

It was right—that was what he was feeling. *It was right and nothing could alter it.*

The knowledge of fatality, of what has to be, had gripped him and for the first time in his life; and he was left unable to make any movement of brain or body, except to say: "Yes, yes. That is what living is." It had entered his flesh and his bones and grown in to the furthest corners of his brain and would never leave him. And at that moment he could not have performed the smallest action of mercy, knowing as he did, having lived on it all his life, the vast unalterable, cruel veld, where at any moment one might stumble over a skull or crush the skeleton of some small creature.

Suffering, sick, and angry, but also grimly satisfied with his new stoicism, he stood there leaning on his rifle, and watched the seething black mound grow smaller. At his feet, now, were ants trickling back with pink fragments in their mouths, and there was a fresh acid smell in his nostrils. He sternly controlled the uselessly convulsing muscles of his empty stomach, and reminded himself: the ants must eat too! At the same time he found that the tears were streaming down his face, and his clothes were soaked with the sweat of that other creature's pain.

The shape had grown small. Now it looked like nothing recognisable. He did not know how long it was before he saw the blackness thin, and bits of white showed through, shining in the sun—yes, there was the sun, just up, glowing over the rocks. Why, the whole thing could not have taken longer than a few minutes.

He began to swear, as if the shortness of the time was in itself unbearable, using the words he had heard his father say. He strode forward, crushing ants with each step, and brushing them off his clothes, till he stood above the skeleton, which lay sprawled under a small bush. It was clean-picked. It might have been lying there years, save that on the white bone were pink fragments of gristle. About the bones ants were ebbing away, their pincers full of meat.

The boy looked at them, big black ugly insects. A few were standing and gazing up at him with small glittering eyes.

"Go away!" he said to the ants, very coldly. "I am not for you—not just yet, at any rate. Go away." And he fancied that the ants turned and went away.

He bent over the bones and touched the sockets in the skull; that was where the eyes were, he thought incredulously, remembering the liquid dark eyes of a buck. And then he bent the slim foreleg bone, swinging it horizontally in his palm.

That morning, perhaps an hour ago, this small creature had been stepping proud and free through the bush, feeling the chill on its hide even as he himself had done, exhilarated by it. Proudly stepping the earth, tossing its horns, frisking a pretty white tail, it had sniffed the cold morning air. Walking like kings and conquerors it had moved through this free-held bush, where each blade of grass grew for it alone, and where the river ran pure sparkling water for its slaking.

And then—what had happened? Such a swift surefooted thing could surely not be trapped by a swarm of ants?

The boy bent curiously to the skeleton. Then he saw that the back leg that lay uppermost and strained out in the tension of death, was snapped midway in the thigh, so that broken bones jutted over each other uselessly. So that was it! Limping into the ant-masses it could not escape, once it had sensed the danger. Yes, but how had the leg been broken? Had it fallen, perhaps? Impossible, a buck was too light and graceful. Had some jealous rival horned it?

What could possibly have happened? Perhaps some Africans had thrown stones at it, as they do, trying to kill it for meat, and had broken its leg. Yes, that must be it.

Even as he imagined the crowd of running, shouting natives, and the flying stones, and the leaping buck, another picture came into his mind. He saw himself, on any one of these bright ringing mornings, drunk with excitement, taking a snap shot at some half-seen buck. He saw himself with the gun lowered, wondering whether he had missed or not; and thinking at last that it was late, and he wanted his breakfast, and it was not worth while to track miles after an animal that would very likely get away from him in any case.

For a moment he would not face it. He was a small boy again, kicking sulkily at the skeleton, hanging his head, refusing to accept the responsibility.

Then he straightened up, and looked down at the bones with an odd expression of dismay, all the anger gone out of him. His mind went quite empty: all around him he could see trickles of ants disappearing into the grass. The whispering noise was faint and dry, like the rustling of a cast snakeskin.

At last he picked up his gun and walked homewards. He was telling himself half defiantly that he wanted his breakfast. He was telling himself that it was getting very hot, much too hot to be out roaming the bush.

Really, he was tired. He walked heavily, not looking where he put his feet. When he came within sight of his home he stopped, knitting his brows. There was something he had to think out. The death of that small animal was a thing that concerned him, and he was by no means finished with it. It lay at the back of his mind uncomfortably.

Soon, the very next morning, he would get clear of everybody and go to the bush and think about it.

Questions for Discussion and Writing

1. What is the young boy proving to himself in his early morning exploits? Support your analysis with phrases and images from the story.
2. What truths does the boy begin to discover through his encounter with the buck, and why?

3. Explain what the knowledge of fatality has to do with the boy's understanding of living in this passage: "The knowledge of fatality, of what has to be, had gripped him and for the first time in his life; and he was left unable to make any movement of brain or body, except to say: 'Yes, yes. That is what living is' " (page 476).
4. What has the boy lost by the story's end? What has he gained? Why do you suppose he remains nameless?

JAMAICA KINCAID

Poor Visitor

Born in 1949, Jamaica Kincaid grew up in Antigua, West Indies, the home she writes about in her book A Small Place *(1988). At the age of seventeen she left the lush, tropical island to work and study abroad. Her book* Annie John *(1983) re-creates much of her childhood.*

"My mother kept everything I ever wore," Kincaid explains, "and basically until I was quite grown up my past was sort of a museum to me. Clearly, the way I became a writer was that my mother wrote my life for me and told it to me. I can't help but think that it made me interested in the idea of myself as an object. I can't account for the reason I became a writer in any other way. . . . I thought writing was something that people just didn't do anymore, that went out of fashion, like the bustle." Although Kincaid left Antigua to continue her education, she says she did "sort of go to college but it was such a dismal failure. I just educated myself, if that's possible." In "Poor Visitor," published in 1989 in The New Yorker, *the author recounts her feelings of homesickness as she began her new life in the United States. "Poor Visitor" will appear in Kincaid's latest book,* Lucy *(Farrar, Straus & Giroux: 1990).*

Since 1976, Kincaid has been a staff writer for The New Yorker. *She now writes and lives in Vermont with her husband and two children. Yet the West Indies, she says, continues to provide the material for her writing, not the United States. "It's just not in my imagination. What I really feel about America is that it's given me a place to be myself—but myself as I was formed somewhere else."*

Before you read "Poor Visitor," write about your first experience with homesickness. Describe where you were at the time, your original plans and dreams about being there, what you found strange about the new place, and why your home suddenly seemed like the best place to be.

I t was my first day. I had come the night before, a gray-black and cold night before—as it was expected to be in the middle of January, though I didn't know that at the time—and I could not see anything clearly on the way in from the airport, even though there were lights everywhere. As we drove along, someone would single out to me a famous building, an important street, a park, a bridge that when built was thought to be a spectacle. In a daydream I used to have, all these places were points of happiness to me; all these places were lifeboats to my small drowning soul, for I would imagine myself entering and leaving them, and just that—entering and leaving over and over again—would see me through a bad feeling I did not have a name for. I only knew it felt a little like sadness. Now that I saw these places, they looked ordinary, dirty, worn down by so many people entering and leaving them in real life, and it occurred to me that I could not be the only person in the world for whom they were a fixture of fantasy. It was not my first bout with the disappointment of reality and it would not be my last. The undergarments that I wore were all new, bought for my journey, and as I sat in the car, twisting this way and that to get a good view of the sights before me, I was reminded of how uncomfortable the new can make you feel.

I got into an elevator, something I had never done before, and then I was in an apartment and seated at a table, eating food just taken from a refrigerator. In Antigua, where I came from, I had always lived in a house, and my house did not have a refrigerator in it. Everything I was experiencing—the ride in the elevator, being in an apartment, eating day-old food that had been stored in a refrigerator—was such a good idea that I could imagine I would grow used to it and like it very much, but at first it was all so new that I had to smile with my mouth turned down at the corners. I slept soundly that night, but it wasn't because I was happy and comfortable—quite the opposite; it was because I didn't want to take in anything else.

That morning, the morning of my first day, the morning that followed my first night, was a sunny morning. It was not the sort of bright sun-yellow making everything curl at the edges, almost in fright, that I was used to, but a pale-yellow sun, as if the sun had grown weak from trying too hard to shine; but still it was sunny, and that was nice and made me miss my home less. And so, seeing the sun, I got up and put on a dress, a gay dress made out of madras cloth—the same sort of dress that I would wear if I were at home and setting out for a day in the country. It was all wrong. The sun was shining but the air was cold. It was the middle of January, after all. But I did not know that the sun could shine and the air remain cold; no one had ever told me. What a feeling that was! How can I explain? Something I had always known—the way I knew my skin was the color brown of a nut rubbed repeatedly with a soft cloth, or the way I knew my own name—something I took completely for granted, "the sun is shining, the air is warm," was not so. I was no longer in a tropical zone, and this realization now entered my life like a flow of water dividing formerly dry and solid ground, creating two banks, one of which was my past—so familiar and predictable that even my unhappiness then made me happy now just to think of it—the other my future, a gray blank, an overcast seascape on which rain was falling and no boats were in sight. I was no longer in a tropical zone and I felt cold inside and out, the first time such a sensation had come over me.

In books I had read—from time to time, when the plot called for it—someone would suffer from homesickness. A person would leave a not very nice situation and go somewhere else, somewhere a lot better, and then long to go back where it was not very nice. How impatient I would become with such a person, for I would feel that I was in a not very nice situation myself, and how I wanted to go somewhere else. But now I, too, felt that I wanted to be back where I came from. I understood it, I knew where I stood there. If I had had to draw a picture of my future then, it would have been a large gray patch surrounded by black, blacker, blackest.

What a surprise this was to me, that I longed to be back in the place that I came from, that I longed to sleep in a bed I had outgrown, that I longed to be with people whose smallest, most natural gesture would call up in me such a rage that I longed to see them all dead at my feet. Oh, I had imagined that with my one swift act—leaving home and coming to this new place—I could leave behind me, as if it were an old garment never to be worn again, my sad thoughts, my sad feelings, and my discontent with life in general as it presented itself to me. In the past, the thought of being in my present situation had been a comfort, but now I did not even have this to look forward to, and so I lay down on my bed and dreamt that I was eating a bowl of pink mullet and green figs cooked in coconut milk, and it had been cooked by my grandmother, which was why the taste of it pleased me so, for she was the person I liked best in all the world and those were the things I liked best to eat also.

The room in which I lay was a small room just off the kitchen—the maid's room. I was used to a small room, but this was a different sort of small room. The ceiling was very high and the walls went all the way up to the ceiling, enclosing the room like a box—a box in which cargo travelling a long way should be shipped. But I was not cargo. I was only an unhappy young woman living in a maid's room, and I was not even the maid. I was the young girl who watches over the children and goes to school at night. How nice everyone was to me, though, saying that I should regard them as my family and make myself at home. I believed them to be sincere, for I knew that such a thing would not be said to a member of their real family. After all, aren't family the people who become the millstone around your life's neck? On the last day I spent at home, my cousin—a girl I had known all my life, an unpleasant person even before her parents forced her to become a Seventh-Day Adventist—made a farewell present to me of her own Bible, and with it she made a little speech about God and goodness and blessings. Now it sat before me on a dresser, and I remembered how when we were children we would sit under my house and terrify and torment each other by reading out loud passages from the Book of Revelations, and I wondered if ever in my whole life a day would go by when these people I had left behind, my own family, would not appear before me in one way or another.

There was also a small radio on this dresser, and I had turned it on. At that moment, almost as if to sum up how I was feeling, a song came on some of the words of which were "Put yourself in my place, if only for a day; see if you can stand the awful emptiness inside." I sang these words to myself over and over, as if they were a lullaby, and I fell asleep again. This time I dreamt that I was holding in my hands one of my old cotton-flannel nightgowns, and it was printed with beautiful scenes of children playing with Christmas-tree decorations. The scenes printed on my nightgown were so real that I could actually hear the children laughing. I felt compelled to know where this nightgown came from, and I started to examine it furiously, looking for the label. I found it just where a label usually is, in the back, and it read "Made in Australia." I was awakened from this dream by the actual maid, a woman who had let me know right away, on meeting me, that she did not like me, and gave as her reason the way I talked. I thought it was because of something else, but I did not know what. As I opened my eyes, the word "Australia" stood between our faces, and I remembered then that Australia was settled as a prison for bad people, people so bad that they couldn't be put in a prison in their own country.

My waking hours soon took on a routine. I walked four small girls to their school, and when they returned at midday I gave them a lunch of soup from a tin, and sandwiches. In the afternoon, I read to them and played with them. When they were away, I studied my books, and at night I went to school. I was unhappy. I looked at a map. The Atlantic Ocean stood between me and the place I came from, but would it have made a difference if it had been a teacup of water? I could not go back.

Outside, always it was cold, and everyone said that it was the coldest winter they had ever experienced; but the way they said it made me think they said this every time winter came around. And I couldn't blame them for not really remembering each year how unpleasant, how unfriendly winter weather could be. The trees with their bare, still limbs looked dead, and as if someone had just placed them there and planned to come back and get them later; all the windows of the houses were shut tight, the way windows are shut up when a house will be empty for a long time; when people walked on the streets they did it quickly, as if they were doing something behind someone's back, as if they didn't want to draw attention to themselves, as if being out in the cold too long would cause them to dissolve. How I longed to see someone lingering on a corner, trying to draw my attention to him, trying to engage me in conversation, someone complaining to himself in a voice I could overhear about a god whose love and mercy fell on the just and the unjust.

I wrote home to say how lovely everything was, and I used flourishing words and phrases, as if I were living life in a greeting card—the kind that has a satin ribbon on it, and quilted hearts and roses, and is expected to be so precious to the person receiving it that the manufacturer has placed a leaf of plastic on the front to protect it. Everyone I wrote to said how nice it was to hear from me, how nice it was to know that I was doing well, that I was very much missed, and that they couldn't wait until the day came when I returned.

One day the maid who said she did not like me because of the way I talked told me that she was sure I could not dance. She said that I spoke like a nun, I walked like one also, and that everything about me was so pious it made her feel at once sick to her stomach and sick with pity just to look at me. And so, perhaps giving way to the latter feeling, she said that we should dance, even though she was quite sure I didn't know how. There was a little portable record-player in my room, the kind that when closed up looked like a ladies' vanity case, and she put on a record she had bought earlier that day. It was a song that was very popular at the time—three girls, not older than I was, singing in harmony and in a very insincere and artificial way about love and so on. It was very beautiful all the same, and it was beautiful because it was so insincere and artificial. She enjoyed this song, singing at the top of her voice, and she was a wonderful dancer—it amazed me to see the way in which she moved. I could not join her and I told her why: the melodies of her song were so shallow, and the words, to me, were meaningless. From her face, I could see she had only one feeling about me: how sick to her stomach I made her. And so I said that I knew songs, too, and I burst into a calypso about a girl who ran away to Port-au-Spain, Trinidad, and had a good time, with no regrets.

The household in which I lived was made up of a husband, a wife, and the four girl children. The husband and wife looked alike and their four children looked just like them. In photographs of themselves, which they placed all over the house, their six yellow-haired heads of various sizes were bunched as if they were a bouquet of flowers tied together by an unseen string. In the pictures, they smiled out at the world, giving the impression that they found everything in it unbearably wonderful. And it was not a farce, their smiles. From wherever they had gone, and they seemed to have been all over the world, they brought back some tiny memento, and they could each recite its history from its very beginning. Even when a little rain fell, they would admire the way it streaked through the blank air.

At dinner, when we sat down at the table—and did not have to say grace (such a relief; as if they believed in a God that did not have to be thanked every time you turned around)—they said such nice things to each other, and the children were so happy. They would spill their food, or not eat any of it at all, or make up rhymes about it that would end with the words "smelt bad." How they made me laugh, and I wondered what sort of parents I must have had, for even to think of such words in their presence I would have been scolded severely, and I vowed that if I ever had children I would make sure that the first words out of their mouths were bad ones.

It was at dinner one night not long after I began to live with them that they began to call me the Visitor. They said I seemed not to be a part of things, as if I didn't live in their house with them, as if they weren't like a family to me, as if I were just passing through, just saying one long Hallo!, and soon would be saying a quick Goodbye! So long! It was very nice! For look at the way I looked at them eating, Lewis said. Had I never seen anyone put a forkful of French-cut green beans in his mouth before? This made Mariah laugh, but almost everything Lewis said made Mariah happy, and so she would laugh. When I didn't laugh also, Lewis said, Poor Visitor, poor Visitor, over and over, a sympathetic tone to his voice, and then he told me a story about an uncle he had who had gone to Canada and raised monkeys, and of how after a while the uncle loved monkeys so much and was so used to being around them that he found actual human beings hard to take. He had told me this story about his uncle before, and while he was telling it to me this time I was remembering a dream I had had about them: Lewis was chasing me around the house. I wasn't wearing any clothes. The ground on which I was running was yellow, as if it had been paved with cornmeal. Lewis was chasing me around and around the house, and though he came close he could never catch up with me. Mariah stood at the open windows saying, Catch her, Lewis, catch her. Eventually I fell down a hole, at the bottom of which were some silver and blue snakes.

When Lewis finished telling his story, I told them my dream. When I finished, they both fell silent. Then they looked at me and Mariah cleared her throat, but it was obvious from the way she did it that her throat did not need clearing at all. Their two yellow heads swam toward each other and, in unison, bobbed up and down. Lewis made a clucking noise, then said, Poor, poor Visitor. And Mariah said, Dr. Freud for Visitor. Then they laughed in a soft, kind way. I had meant by telling them my dream that I had taken them in, because only people who were very important to me had ever shown up in my dreams, and I could see that they already understood that.

Questions for Discussion and Writing

1. In what ways does Kincaid not only show what she was experiencing in being foreign but also help us as readers to feel it?
2. What are the surprises and contrasts of this new world with Kincaid's past? In what ways does her home of Antigua now assume new meaning?
3. What meanings does the title convey, both obvious and subtle? What surprises do you find in Kincaid's writing? Use brief passages from her essay to support your response.
4. What cultural gaps exist between the Poor Visitor and the family she is working for? Between the author and the Australian maid? How does the dream that Kincaid shares with the family at the end of the essay help us to experience the cultural differences between her and the family?

RICHARD K. NELSON

Tingiivik Tatqiq: The Moon When Birds Fly South (September)

Born in Wisconsin in 1941, Richard K. Nelson earned his bachelors and masters degrees from the University of Wisconsin. He was a research fellow in anthropology at the University of California at Santa Barbara from 1968 to 1971, and in 1971 he received his doctorate. Since then Nelson has taught anthropology at a number of universities from Newfoundland to California to Alaska.

Nelson's primary interests center on four extended ethnographic field studies among Alaskan Eskimos and Athapaskan Indians; he has written several books about these cultures. The story that follows comes from his book Shadow of the Hunter: Stories of Eskimo Life, *published in 1980. The book's stories are arranged according to month. Although the author uses names and occasional words from Eskimo life unfamiliar to us, he always makes the meanings of these words clear as they occur.*

Before you read "Tingiivik Tatqiq: The Moon When Birds Fly South (September)," write about a time when you or someone you know was torn between returning home and remaining in a place of extended stay. What purpose took you or the other person away, what skills and ideas were gained in those years away, what aspects of childhood life did you no longer appreciate as an adult, and what decision was made as a result of these struggles? You might, for example, attempt to see your parents and their ideas in a new light, based on what you've learned as an adult.

Main Characters

KILUK (*Kee*-look)	a young woman
MASU (*Mah*-soo)	Kiluk's adoptive grandmother
NAURUK (*Now*-rook)	Masu's adult son

ITIRUK (It-*tir*-ook)	Nauruk's wife
SAKIAK (Sah-*kee*-uk)	an old man
PATIK (*Pah*-tik)	Sakiak's grandson

K iluk was wet, cold, and miserable. Icy raindrops beat relentlessly against her cheeks and forehead. The canvas tarpaulin that covered her lap had soaked through and water saturated her legs, so she huddled against the gunwale of the *umiaq* trying to shelter them from the blowing rain. A drop of water slid down the soggy fur of her parka ruff and hung from a cluster of matted hairs. She watched it shiver a moment in the wind before it flew away. Behind her the outboard engine droned monotonously, as it had done for several hours.

There was no chance of going back now, she thought, her gloom almost as dark as the ragged scud that raced overhead. At least the water had calmed somewhat since they passed the mouth of the Ivisauraq River, so brackish spray no longer blew in over the bow. The great estuary of the Kuk River had begun to narrow, and Nauruk kept the boat near its protecting south bank. She thought of him sitting in the stern, far more exposed to the weather and unable even to turn his face from it. He would never complain, she knew. He was like all the others—tough, proud, and stoic.

She could say the same for old Masu, Nauruk's mother and her own adoptive grandmother, who sat quietly beside the opposite gunwale. Surely Masu was as wet and chilled as she, but her aged face reflected no discomfort. In fact, it seemed she was either asleep or thinking placidly with her eyes closed.

And in the bow, seated so she faced them, was Nauruk's wife Itiruk. Never one to be idle, she was repairing tears in a fishnet, deftly weaving the shuttle and tying the special knots that would not slip. Kiluk watched her glistening wet hands and wondered how they could remain supple when hers were stiff and numb even inside sealskin mittens.

Both Masu and Itiruk looked quite at peace, while Kiluk suffered. She should have resisted their urgings to join them at fish camp far up the Kuk River. After all, she had refused all their other suggestions—that she learn to scrape hides, to sew boots and parkas, to prepare food in the old ways. "Come now, you try it," they always said. "You will learn to be a real Eskimo woman at last." Itiruk, who was younger and more direct, would add pointed remarks: "School taught you many things, but never how to *live*. What good is all that reading if you cannot sew and catch fish?"

The words hurt Kiluk, sometimes even angered her; but she was enough of an Eskimo to shadow her emotions behind silence and an expressionless face. What did she care for the endless labors of an Eskimo woman, working hours each day with needle and braided sinew, or bent over dried skins with a scraper . . . or shivering in the fall rain in an open boat? Eight grades in the village school had kept her away from all that; and four years at a high school for Indians and Eskimos nearly a thousand miles from Ulurunik; and even a start at college. After so much education, it was hard to be told that little you knew was of any value.

When criticism failed to change Kiluk, Masu would try other approaches. Learning the skills and ways of her people would be fun, exciting—it was a better way to live than having a job or just doing nothing. "You will see if you come with us to fish camp," she had said a few days earlier. "The river at Nunavik will be full of fish, thousands of them. We will eat fresh whitefish and grayling, and perhaps there will be caribou herds as well. When you start catching fish you will know why we love to go there."

Masu had spoken it all in her labored English, even though she knew Kiluk understood Eskimo perfectly. Kiluk had been raised with the language of her people, but after the years away at school she spoke it with a strange accent and sometimes she stumbled over the long word-phrases. People had laughed at her, so she retreated into English, which she could speak far better than they.

It was one of her few points of clear superiority. They knew little of the *Tanik's* world, and she knew it well. She had proved that by living so long away. But her heart had yearned for the familiarity of home, for people who would not insult her with foolish questions about living in igloos and rubbing noses. She had been lonely there. And now she had to admit that she was lonely here, too, that although she was no *Tanik* she was not fully Eskimo either. There were other young ones like her in Ulurunik, others who lived the same dilemma. Some stayed and some did not, but nearly all felt lost wherever they were.

Only Patik seemed to know exactly what he wanted. The years in school never took away his consuming desire to be a hunter, and to be all that went along with it. No amount of teasing by the elders for his inexperience, or jealousy from his less settled friends, could turn him from that course. Patik wanted to hunt, to drive dogs alone across the tundra, to dance in front of the drummers, to speak *Inupiat*—to be clearly and preeminently an Eskimo.

And there was something else Patik wanted. It showed in his eyes and in the way he teased her. Patik wanted Kiluk.

That thought pulled her suddenly back to the present, to the wetness that saturated her thick cloth parka and the gusts of wind that leaned intermittently against her. She looked far ahead through the haze and drizzle and saw a black speck on the river. That was Sakiak's boat, and Patik was its steersman. The old man had requested that his grandson come with him to help out in the fish camp and to further his learning. Sakiak must have had another motive too, Kiluk thought. Somehow he knew of Patik's interest in her—nothing could be hidden from him.

Of course they were all wasting their time. Patik would need quite a different kind of woman for the life he wanted—"a real Eskimo woman." She let herself think those words, but with sarcasm and a brief flush of bitterness. A woman who had never sewn even a pair of fur socks would hardly do for Patik. And a man who wished only to go to fish camp and to hunt for caribou was not what Kiluk had in mind.

Tired of such thoughts, now colder and even less happy than before, Kiluk leaned against the heap of gear that filled the *umiaq* behind her. She pulled her hood farther up so it deflected some of the rain and stared with tear-filled eyes over the gray water. The riverbank was muddy and black in the muted light, and the tundra sloped away above it, fading into the chill mist. Before she closed her eyes, she saw a patch of willows at the water's edge, their bare, twisted branches shaking in the wind.

Kiluk ascended slowly to the edge of wakefulness. She heard a flapping noise, first softly, then growing louder as she became conscious. It was wind on loose canvas. And there was a hissing sound of windblown drizzle against the tent walls and roof. She opened her eyes and gazed into the dim light. Someone breathed heavily nearby. It was early morning, and the others were still asleep.

Cold air crept into the opening of her sleeping bag, as it had done all night. She remembered shivering for hours in the darkness, breathing inside the bag to warm it, while the others slept soundly. Finally she had drifted into a fitful sleep, awakening often and wondering if daylight would ever come. Now it had come at last, and she lifted the tent wall just enough to peek outside. A chill breeze puffed in underneath, and a few big snowflakes came with it. She could see patches of wet snow clinging to the windward sides of tussocks, but the drizzle was eating them away and they would probably vanish soon. She also saw another tent—Sakiak's—just a few yards away.

Kiluk snuggled back down into her sleeping bag, grateful for even the modest warmth it provided. She remembered last night, arriving here in the half-darkness, everyone rushing to unload the boats during a merciful break in the rain. "This is Kangich," Nauruk had shouted to her over the wind, "the old village where your grandparents lived." All her life she had been told about this place, that her ancestors had had a sod house here, that Masu and Ulimaun often camped here to fish, that its name meant "meeting-of-rivers"—the Qaolaq and Avalik, with the Qitiq just upstream. The others had seemed excited just to be here, as if Kangich was a very special place. But to Kiluk it had seemed like any other empty spot on the flat and dismal land, meaningful only because they were finally going to stop here and shelter themselves.

A short while later she heard movement beside her, then Masu's voice. She was talking softly to herself about sleeping too late, about the chill as she crawled from her sleeping bag, and then about how fine it was to be at Kangich again after a whole year's passage. This awakened Nauruk and Itiruk, who also shared the cramped little tent. "Granddaughter, are you sleeping?" the old woman asked. "We are at Kangich! And the sun is shining." She laughed at the last remark, as Eskimos often did to be sure no one ever mistook a tease for a deliberate deception.

Kiluk stretched and wearily peeked out. "Come, hurry," Nauruk admonished gruffly. "We have a long trip today while the weather is so fine." He cocked his head and looked down at her, smiling broadly. Everyone knew how wretched she had been yesterday, and now they were teasing her for it. She rolled toward the tent wall and said nothing.

"Sakiak! Patik! Wake up before the morning is gone." Masu's shrill voice filled the tent; and in a moment they heard Sakiak's reply: "I am well awake and drinking hot coffee. Only this young man sleeps, when he should be out looking for caribou. Perhaps you will come to my tent; there is plenty of coffee here."

Masu and the others had already gone by the time Kiluk got up, slipped on her parka, and ran the few yards to Sakiak's tent. She felt a rush of warmth as she stepped inside, and rich smells of fresh coffee and boiling meat mixed heavily in the air. Everyone sat around the walls, leaning against the clutter of gear, clothes, and caribou hides. Kiluk shook the water from her parka before sitting down and accepting coffee from Itiruk. The cup felt wonderfully warm between her palms, and she relished her first sips.

After several minutes of silence, Sakiak began thinking aloud: "This is poor weather for traveling farther upriver. The wind has shifted to the north and the rain is heavy. If we wait here, the water may rise and it will be easier to cross the shallows below Nunavik." Kiluk could have shouted her joy at hearing these words, but she was young and a woman, so she remained silent. It was for Masu to agree, and she did. She was anxious to see her camp, she said, but she could wait another day or two. Plenty of work could be done here, especially on the nets.

Old people were the final authorities on such matters, and so even Nauruk was quiet. He was the biggest and most powerful man in Ulurunik, one of the most successful hunters, and leader of his own whaling crew—but he always showed deference to his elders. Among Eskimos, wisdom was the most treasured virtue; and wisdom came only with age.

This was true for men and women alike, but there was also a difference. Old men eventually weakened and could not hunt or travel, so their only asset was their knowledge. But old women could still cut patterns and fit and sew, usually far better than their younger counterparts. Perhaps this was why their personalities and assertiveness often strengthened with age. None showed this better than Masu, who administered the household of Ulimaun as tightly as she stitched her seams.

Steaming caribou meat was drawn from the pot, and everyone ate enthusiastically. Even Kiluk felt almost contented afterward, and she listened closely as Sakiak recounted the history of Kangich: "When I was a boy, this was a gathering place for the *Kugmiut*—the Kuk River people—who used to make a big camp here each fall when the fish ran thick. One day they would look across the land and see people walking toward them from the south. These were the Utoqaq River people, who traveled the long overland trail so they could trade at Kangich, and dance and play games. It was especially fine for the young ones, who made new friends here, or arranged trading partnerships, or even met someone they would later marry." Kiluk was sure that she saw a mischievous twinkle in the old man's eyes when he said those last words.

Masu then interjected: "It was that way for your real grandparents, Kiluk. Atuk, your grandmother, was a *Kugmiut*, and her husband Ivrulik was from the Utoqaq. They came here with their parents, and their mothers arranged that they should marry. So when your grandfather's people left after the snows, he stayed with the *Kugmiut*. He was scarcely a man then, but already a fine hunter; and your grandmother loved to fish. Perhaps that is why they spent much of their lives here, in the country around Kangich. Both of them died long before you were born, from a sickness that came with the whaling ships. Your real mother nearly died with them, and she never was strong after that."

Masu looked to Sakiak for confirmation, then continued: "Your mother had two children already when you began growing inside her, and no one knew how she would feed you. So she and your real father, who was an unlucky hunter, asked if Ulimaun and I would raise another baby, our own children being older by that time. We agreed, and you were given to us; and although we are uncle and aunt to your parents you have always called us grandfather and grandmother."

"By your birth you are a Kangich person," Sakiak added, "because your family has always camped here. Until your mother died she came here each year, and just after your birth she brought you with her. She stayed with your father in a sod house that stood above the bank where the rivers join. It is gone now, and only a shallow pit remains. I can show it to you."

Thoughts of the cold and misery left Kiluk as she lost herself in these stories of her life and her special connection with Kangich. The bleak emptiness of the place gave way, in her mind, to something more meaningful. The land here was a part of her, and she a part of it. The earth seemed warmer in a sense, less forbidding and foreign.

Kiluk had been told the story of her adoption before, but never in such detail. She felt no antipathy toward her mother, no sense of rejection, because children were often given to others for adoption. If her mother and father were still alive, they would remain special for her and she for them. A child was given away lovingly, to a couple who could provide well but who had no children or whose children were grown up.

But sometimes, as Sakiak now pointed out, parents could not support a new child and had no one to give it to. "Long ago, in the spring of a year with little food, a woman was about to give birth. But she already had a child at her breast, and three others who were still small. Perhaps she did not ask if someone could take her new baby when it was born because it was a hard season and the burden would be too much. So when it came from her she took it outside the house, dug a hole in the snow, and left it to die quickly.

"A man and his wife were camped nearby, and the woman heard a baby crying outside. She listened for a long time, knowing what it was and thinking. She had wished for a child, but none was ever born to her. If she adopted an infant now, before summer came and the animals arrived, it would mean difficulty or even danger of starvation for her and her husband. But she kept hearing the baby and it was hard for her to wait until its crying stopped. Finally her power to resist was gone, and so she rushed out and took the infant from the snow.

"Her name was Aliksik, and she has always been very special indeed for me. You see, I was the baby and she became my mother."

There was a brief, thoughtful silence, and then Masu continued: "In the old days, before we had rifles and such things as the *Taniks* brought, there were starvation times. When food ran out in one place, people had to move, and they kept moving until they found something to eat. A woman with a baby needed more food, and she moved less easily than the others. So, although it was a terribly sad thing, she sometimes had to let her newborn infant die. She did this as soon as it was born, because if she waited she would be unable to let it go."

Infant girls were more often left this way than boys, because hunters were essential to the family's survival. But many more boys died before they became adults, because they faced the great dangers of traveling on the sea ice and hunting far over the tundra. So, although more boys were raised in an Eskimo society, more girls lived beyond adolescence; and by the time of adulthood the numbers of men and women were almost equal. Thus, as in most realms of Eskimo life, the practical dictates of survival held sway above all else. Nowadays things were less difficult, and so children never had to be left this way any longer.

Masu and Sakiak continued exchanging stories for some time, until finally the old woman said she must go to her work. "I want to be ready for fishing when we reach Nunavik," she declared. "We will set our nets quickly so we can eat fresh, fat fish. And in a few days the river will freeze and we will start hooking. Then you young ones will know what it means to fish!" Kiluk could see how real Masu's enthusiasm was, but it made little sense to her. Fishing on the ice all day sounded cold and utterly boring.

By late afternoon she felt the same way about sitting inside the tent with rain beating ceaselessly against it. She huddled in a corner, half-covered by her sleeping bag, watching the others work. Itiruk spent hours with her shuttle, gradually closing a multitude of holes in an old gill net she had borrowed from her brother's wife. In return for its use she would give a portion of the fish she caught in it. As her fingers darted in and out of the webbing she sang Eskimo songs to herself.

From time to time Masu would join in, swaying with the music and smiling in pure delight. She was sewing a pair of waterproof sealskin boots for Nauruk, fancy ones with the silvery fur outside and geometric designs stitched from hide pieces around the tops. Few younger women knew how to make such boots, and Kiluk noticed that Itiruk was watching closely as they took shape. Masu loved to talk, and so she gave a running account of her work as she proceeded, sometimes complaining when she felt her stitch was uneven or too loose.

Twice she spoke softly to Kiluk without looking up from her work: "My granddaughter, come and let Itiruk show you how to mend the net. It will be easy to learn the knots, and time will pass quickly if you are busy." But Kiluk made no reply, just wrinkled her nose as children did to say no. She was not entirely uninterested, but she would be inept at first and the women would tease her. Masu was silent when Kiluk refused; but she hurt inside, thinking that this girl who meant so much to her wanted nothing of the life she loved.

That evening they all ate in Sakiak's tent, and afterward the men began carving new sinkers for the net Itiruk had repaired. The sinkers were made from pieces of caribou antler, cut to the length of a man's palm and drilled at each end. These were tied at intervals along the net's bottom edge; and along the top they placed floats carved from driftwood chunks. Patik watched his grandfather and Nauruk for a while, then began carving too. The older men corrected his errors, and Nauruk had a great laugh when he split a float in half just before it was finished. Patik only smiled and started over, determined to do it right the next time.

Kiluk sat beside Masu, who had insisted she help braid sinew for tomorrow's sewing. They peeled long filaments from a strip of dried caribou sinew and braided them into thick, strong thread. Twice when Kiluk glanced toward the men she saw Patik looking at her. She flushed and quickly resumed her work, feeling both perplexed and flattered by his apparent liking for her. He was very pleasant and singularly handsome, and she had to admit that she admired his willingness to become absorbed in the Eskimo ways. It was not for her, but perhaps he was fortunate because he knew who he wanted to be. She found herself looking at him again, bent to his carving, pulling the sharp blade of his knife through the weathered wood.

That night, while she lay awake listening to the wind buffet and winnow over the tundra, Kiluk thought she heard a lone wolf howling in the distance. The sound came to her briefly and faded, carried off by the swirling gusts. She wondered if perhaps it was not a wolf at all; perhaps, as Masu often said, those who lived at Kangich long ago had never left. Kiluk stared into the darkness. The storm pressed heavily around the tent, and the wind moaned and whispered and breathed, alive with something she felt but did not know. She was afraid and wished to be in the safe familiarity of the village.

The next day was much like the one before, except that the north wind strengthened and the rain turned to showers of snow. Everyone worked inside the tents, and Kiluk helped with the cooking to relieve her boredom. Confinement made her feel nervous and sullen, so near midday she went outside to look around. She walked along the steeply cut riverbank, which stood slightly higher than the surroundings. Snow had whitened the landscape, and the converging rivers stood out like streaks of black ash. Sakiak came out and showed her where her parents' house had been. The river had cut into it, and fragments of bone sled runner protruded from the mud. She wondered if they might have been from her father's sled, and she felt a growing sadness as she lingered in that silent place. Finally she returned, shivering, to the tents.

That afternoon the wind diminished, but mixed snow and rain fell heavily from a somber sky. Sakiak went to get something from his tent, and on his way back he stopped and shouted toward the sky: "Sun! Sun! Your smell is getting bad."

"*Aana* [grandmother], what does he mean?" Kiluk asked. The old woman put her sewing aside and spoke slowly: "To understand this, you must know about the beginnings of the world. A long time ago, the things we see around us were not as they are today. For example, the animals were like people and could talk. Also, the moon was a man and the sun was his wife. One day they had a terrible argument, and the moon man cut her with his knife. She ran away, up a rainbow into the sky, and there she became the sun. Her husband chased after her, and he became the moon. Today he still follows her around the sky, and sometimes he comes close enough so that we can see both of them at the same time.

"The sun is still a woman today, and she can hear us if we talk to her. When she insists on hiding behind the clouds, as she often does in the summer and fall, men sometimes insult her by saying that she will smell bad inside if she does not come out. Many times I have seen the sky clear after someone shouted at the sun this way."

When Masu had finished, Itiruk added, "These are not just stories; they are as true as the Bible." Kiluk had heard the old people tell *ulipqaat*—ancestral stories—many times before, and she knew how strongly they held them as essential truths about the world. They had accepted the missionaries' Christian teachings, but without abandoning all their traditional beliefs. They kept their Eskimo ways to themselves, however, and let the *Taniks* believe that such things were lost long ago. Only the young people, like Kiluk, seemed to care little for the old religion. She listened respectfully to the stories but was not at all sure there was truth in them.

The day passed slowly. Evening finally came, and darkness fell early beneath the heavy curtain of clouds. Kiluk withdrew to her sleeping bag while the others played cards with a ragged old deck, drinking tea and laughing far into the night. She wondered why she did not join them, but somehow she resented their easy, simple pleasure. Alone and full of self-pity, she stared at the pattern of stains and watermarks on the tent roof, dimly lit by the gasoline lantern. One was a caribou; another was a bird flying away alone.

"Wake up in there! The wind is gone and the sky is clearing. Time to load the boats and head for Nunavik." It was Sakiak, poking his head into the tent. "Come, Nauruk. . . . You sleep too much. There is ice on the water's edge and I want to see *fish* today." Kiluk awakened slowly and saw shadows on the tent wall—the sun. She thought of yesterday's stories as she yawned and rubbed her eyes.

An hour later they slid the two *umiaqs* into the river, loaded mountains of gear inside, and pushed away from the hard-frozen bank. Cold outboards slowly came to life as the boats turned up the Avalik River. On both sides the tundra mosaic of snow white and patches of vibrant brown lifted away in protracted sweeps. High above a golden eagle circled in ascending spirals, a tiny fleck weaving its way upward in the cold blue ocean of sky.

When they had traveled only a few miles, the current increased and the river became shallow. Crystal water ran swiftly over gravel shoals, and before long the boats scraped bottom. "*Azaah,* too shallow," Sakiak complained. "We will have to drag the boats upstream until we reach deep water again. Masu and Kiluk should wade to shore and walk ahead on the bank."

The river bottom was tricky and uneven, and within a few steps Kiluk slipped and icy water soaked one of her feet. It was a bad way to start a long trek upriver. She found herself feeling miserable again, wishing this would all end quickly so she could go back home. How many miles were they going to walk? And would the others be able to pull the boats over the riffles she saw ahead? It seemed that Eskimos had to do everything the hard way, and she wished they could just live on food from grocery stores like *Taniks* in the cities.

The ground was covered with frozen tussocks that made walking very difficult indeed. But old Masu trudged along happily, sometimes singing Eskimo songs to herself and sometimes telling stories about the places they passed. She paused occasionally to look over the land for caribou and was disappointed that there were none. Near one place called Tasiq, she stopped abruptly, listened, then gazed at the sky overhead. "Do you remember," she asked, "that Sakiak told you we have nearly reached the end of *Tingiivik tatqiq,* the moon when birds fly south?" Now she pointed, and Kiluk finally saw what it was—very high above them she could make out a long skein of Canada geese, so high that they barely seemed to be moving. The old woman watched them for a time, and then mused with a soft smile. "They must be the last ones to fly away from us this year; but if I am still alive I will see them again in the spring."

When they had gone about a mile, she led Kiluk away from the bank, promising a surprise. Shortly she stopped and gestured toward the ground. "Look, *akpik!"* she exclaimed with obvious delight. Poking up through the snow was a profusion of beautiful orange cloudberries—one of the few edible plant species found on the tundra—a favorite Eskimo treat. Both of them set to work immediately, picking berries and putting them in the large front pouches of their cloth parka covers. They rewarded themselves liberally as they went along, savoring the cold, sweet, succulent berries.

Kiluk's wet foot was aching with cold by the time they finished and walked back to the river. The boats were close by now, but they were stuck in very shallow water and the others had partly unloaded them. "Come, granddaughter," Masu urged. "We are strong enough to help." And without hesitating she went down the bank and waded in. Kiluk followed reluctantly, wondering how she could be so unlucky, wishing they had just stayed at Kangich.

"Ah, good, now we have plenty of power," Nauruk declared laughingly. "This young woman has been resting for two days and must be very strong. *Ki . . .* go up near the bow, where Patik can help you if you fall." Nauruk had gone too far with his joking, but the others were ready, so Kiluk had to stumble quickly alongside and start pulling.

The *umiaqs* very slowly began moving upstream, their resilient sealskin covers flexing as they slid over the rocks. When they were about halfway through the riffle, Kiluk slipped and filled her boots with numbing water again. She could have cried, but no one stopped, and she could only keep splashing ahead. The water became shallower, the load heavier, and she was almost gasping for breath.

"Whoa!" Nauruk shouted as if he were driving a dog team. "Look there, ahead of us in the river—fish!" Kiluk saw nothing for a moment, just the gentle rush of water over the shallows. Then suddenly she realized that it was deeper ahead, and what looked like scattered rapids were fish, thousands and thousands of them, huge, dense schools frothing the surface as they dashed away from the boats. The entire river, from bank to bank, for a hundred yards upstream, swarmed with fish.

Kiluk suddenly forgot her agony, and when Nauruk gave the word she pulled as hard as the rest. The boat moved more easily now, and she glanced up to watch the spectacle of the fleeing fish. For a moment the water would be calm; then it would suddenly explode as the frenzied mass scattered first one way, then another. She had never seen such an abundance of anything, never imagined it possible.

Finally the boats floated free, and they all went to shore. "Now you have seen the fish!" Nauruk triumphed, looking at both Kiluk and Patik. "And before long you will have the fun of catching them." He punctuated that by crunching his boot through the thin layer of ice along the shore, indicating that the river would soon freeze. "Come, let's go for the gear. We have an easy ride to fish camp from here."

Kiluk was thoroughly exhausted by the time they had carried all the gear to the *umiaqs.* Her back hurt, her arms were rubbery, and every time she took a step her boots sloshed loudly. Sakiak noticed her forlorn expression as she pulled her boots off and poured water from them. "Ah, you work like a young man," he congratulated, "but you don't watch for the deep holes." Then he sat beside her, took off his own boots, and dumped an equal amount of water from them. "And look at that old woman . . . and my foolish grandson." Now Kiluk saw them all begin emptying their boots and realized that everyone was suffering like her. Sakiak began laughing; and he laughed harder and harder, until tears began streaming down his cheeks. The others could not help joining, and finally even Kiluk laughed.

Like a real Eskimo, she laughed with the others—at the absurdity of their misfortune, at their icy feet and their aching backs, at the shallow water that had tricked them all into hard work and suffering. And they laughed, too, at the pleasure of seeing the multitude of fish, which promised good fortune and good times ahead. They laughed as those who came before them had learned to laugh, toasting a hard life in a hard land, that took from them payment in labor and pain and rewarded them with the inestimable riches of freedom.

It was not long before they approached Nunavik, traveling swiftly on placid waters that mirrored the riverbanks and tundra in detailed perfection. A few upright poles marked the campsite, beside a small creek that flowed into the river. The water was very deep, Masu said, and the fish congregated here before going farther upstream to spawn. Her face glowed with excitement as they eased in to the shore, and she almost ran up the bank to look over the land. "We are here!" she sang out. "Come, old man—you, Sakiak—come and look at Nunavik again."

Everyone worked hard to set up camp quickly, but the sun touched the horizon before they finished. It was a beautiful evening, the sky aflame with orange and magenta, the air still and cold, and the indigo water dimpled with occasional swirls of fish. Patik walked far off across the tundra before darkness came, searching for signs of caribou. When he returned he found Kiluk alone by the river. He said he had seen nothing, and they sat together talking until there was no more light.

When they entered Masu's tent, where everyone had gathered to eat, they felt clumsy and embarrassed. Kiluk expected Nauruk to make a joke about them, but instead he asked Patik what he had seen and said perhaps they would walk farther to look around tomorrow. Masu added that young men were supposed to tire quickly, but somehow this one still had the energy to hunt after a long day. "*Azahaa,* you're a man," Nauruk whispered, smiling and feigning exaggerated admiration. In the end, he could not resist a tease.

After they had eaten their supper of caribou meat with seal oil, they all talked for a while and then retired to their sleeping bags. Kiluk laid awake in the stillness, thinking of the day's events and feeling almost too tired to sleep. She wondered when the first deep snow would fall so that dog teams would come from Ulurunik and she could go back to the comforts of home. But there was a vague feeling of excitement in her too; she could not deny it, thinking of all those fish. . . . When she was on the verge of sleep she thought of Patik, walking alone across the tundra in the last glow of twilight.

The sharp noise of rifle shots somewhere nearby startled Kiluk awake the next morning. She sat up and blinked at the brightness of high sun on the tent wall. *Crack!* Another shot, then silence. A few minutes later she heard Masu's voice down by the river: "Look, daughter-in-law," she called to Itiruk, "that old man can still shoot." Curious now, and knowing she had slept very late, Kiluk got up and peeked out the tent door.

Sakiak was walking along the bank, carrying two plump little animals. "*Sikrik,*" he called to her. "Ground squirrels. Fat ones ready to hibernate. They were half-asleep in the sunshine outside their burrows." Kiluk pulled on her parka and stepped outside, stiff from yesterday's hard work. Itiruk was already preparing to skin the squirrels, and Sakiak had gone down the bank to help Masu with a fishnet. "For several years I have been saving *sikrik* hides," Itiruk said as she carefully removed one of the small skins. "Someday I will use them to make a fancy parka, decorated with tails and stitched designs."

"And today we can eat fresh boiled *sikrik,*" Masu called out, "perhaps some fish too." She and Sakiak had a gill net stretched along the beach and were discussing where to set it. "Your *aana* wants it right here, but Sakiak says it should be farther upstream," Itiruk explained. "Of course she will win, because she is always the boss at Nunavik, and she perhaps knows the fish better than anyone else."

Itiruk was soon proved right. Sakiak fetched a tiny skin-covered boat that he had brought upriver from the village. Then he took one end of the net and pulled it out into the deep eddy, while Masu tended the beach end. When the net was stretched completely out, Sakiak dropped a rock anchor that would hold it in place. At the same time Masu tied the other end to a stake on the beach. A line of floats marked the top of the net, and the carved antler weights along its bottom edge made it hang vertically underwater.

Kiluk sat with Itiruk, eating a breakfast of cold meat with her coffee, watching the two elders work. They quickly prepared two more nets, then set them in the spots Masu insisted upon. When they finished, Masu puffed up the bank looking completely pleased with herself. "My *qatangan* wants to put the nets in all the wrong places," she laughed. "But then, who knows where the fish may choose to swim?"

Itiruk saw Kiluk's quizzical expression and knew immediately what to ask. "Do you know why she calls the old man *qatangan?*" Without waiting for an answer, she explained: "Your *aana* and Sakiak have always been fishing partners, but they have another special relationship as well. Long ago, before the *Taniks* changed things, men sometimes exchanged wives for a short while. Often these men were trading partners from different villages, and they might agree to the exchange without asking their wives first. After this was carried out, the children of both couples always called each other *qatangan;* and they were obligated to help each other like brothers and sisters.

"The missionaries said such things were a sin," she mused, "and because I am a woman I think it is better that husbands no longer have this right. But I have heard that *Taniks* are not free of such sins themselves, and I often wonder if their children become *qatangan* like Masu and Sakiak. I am always too shy to ask."

This started Masu on stories of her childhood, and then stories about Nunavik and the events that had taken place here. For several hours she talked, and Kiluk surprised herself by listening carefully the entire time. It was only because there was nothing else to do, she told herself. Things were especially quiet without Patik and Nauruk, who had left at dawn to search farther inland for caribou.

Late in the afternoon, Masu saw the net floats jiggling. "Many fish have entangled themselves already," she surmised. "We should check the nets—I am too anxious to wait any longer." It took almost an hour to pull all the slippery, wiggling fish from the meshes, and when they finished they had almost filled a large tub with silvery whitefish and a few grayling trout. Masu and Sakiak's enthusiasm was contagious, and when they began cleaning fish to hang on the drying rack Kiluk let them teach her how it was done.

They were so busy that Patik and Nauruk walked into camp unnoticed. Suddenly Nauruk's voice boomed behind Kiluk, "*Azahaa,* look at this young woman cutting fish." His broad hand took one of hers from the slimy fish it held, and he scrutinized it. "Well, no fingers cut off yet. I see you are learning how to do something important, just like this funny little man here." He looked mockingly at Patik, who would have blushed except that his cheeks were already red from the cold. Nauruk's voice was hard and gruff, but in fact teasing was his way of showing affection. No matter how tough he sounded, there was always a gentle look in his eyes.

"Well, what did you see?" Masu interrupted. "Nothing except a few ptarmigan," he replied, "and a brown bear's tracks near Avalitqoq Creek." He recounted the details of their day and then announced that he and Patik had eaten nothing except a few berries since morning. So they all filed into Masu's tent to boil a huge pot of freshly caught fish.

In the hushed chill of evening, Kiluk walked to the riverbank. On the pretext of getting water from the river, Patik followed shortly afterward, and they sat together as night flooded the sky. For a while they spoke of unimportant things, then about their lives away from Ulurunik and their reasons for coming back. Patik was not one to speak of sadness, but his voice showed that he had struggled with the same confusion that Kiluk knew in herself. Finally he said, "I am an Eskimo, and I belong here. I have seen the cities, where there is no open land to travel, no game to hunt, and no freedom to choose your own trail in the morning. Others may leave, but I will stay where I have all those things, and where I can laugh with people who know me well."

Stars lit the sky, and a new moon skirted the horizon. While the others played cards and drank tea in Masu's tent, Kiluk and Patik sat alone on the bank. Later, when the moon vanished, they slipped quietly into the other tent.

Hidden by the deepening darkness, an owl hovered on silent wings above the camp, then swept away in an exultant rush of flight over the undulating land.

Days seemed to pass quickly in the Nunavik camp, although the routine varied little. Fish came in greater and greater numbers, and gunnysacks beside the tents bulged with the catch. For a few days it was warm enough to allow some fermentation, which would give the fish the tangy flavor Eskimos liked. But then they began to freeze, and flurries of snow made little drifts around the gunnies.

Kiluk learned how to set and check the gill nets, and one day Masu convinced her to help with a pair of mittens she was sewing. But she still missed the comfort of the village—regular baths (even though they were in a small washtub), warm houses, well-washed clothes, and the excitement of having many people around. Sakiak said that a good snow could come any day now, and dog teams would surely follow immediately afterward to haul fish. Then, she knew, she could ride back to the village . . . if she wanted to. Kiluk startled herself by thinking of it that way.

Perhaps it was Patik—she knew that something was happening to her, but she would forget about it when she left. Fish camp had become a fairly pleasant interlude, but not a life. She and Patik spent their evenings by the river, and the others let them be alone. Nauruk, of course, could not help teasing whenever he had a chance, but it was easy to see that he was pleased.

Then one dawn Sakiak woke the camp, shouting happily from outside the tents that the river had frozen. The ice was only a fragile skin of crystal, but it would thicken quickly in the growing cold. That afternoon they broke lanes with the little boat to remove their nets. Masu was almost beside herself with anticipation, and she spent the evening at work on her fishhooks and jigging lines. "Now, at last, the *fun* is here. I have a line ready for you, granddaughter, and a warm caribou skin for you to kneel on."

The next morning Kiluk awoke early, because it was very cold inside the tent. She decided to light the gasoline stove for warmth, and when she did she noticed that Masu and Itiruk were gone. Only Nauruk was there, snoring blissfully. Once the stove was lighted and coffee water was on, she poked her head out the tent flap to look for the women. A dusting of snow had fallen, and the world was a sheet of white. Footprints led toward the riverbank and onto the ice. There they were, two dark figures bent over newly chopped holes, rhythmically jigging their fishing lines.

A short while later she walked down to join them. The sun broke intermittently through running clouds, mottling the snow-covered land with patterns of bright and shadow. "At last you have come," Itiruk declared. "We checked the ice at dawn, and when we found it safe we didn't hesitate even long enough for hot coffee. Look, your grandmother has many fish already, and even I have a few." Itiruk was being overly modest, although the old woman had indeed caught considerably more.

Masu immediately called for Kiluk. "Come, granddaughter, I will show you how to fish. You can sit here and I will chop a new hole nearby." Kiluk was reluctant to try, feeling that she would be inept and the others would laugh at her. And to make things worse, Sakiak and Patik were now coming down onto the ice, the old man carrying a tangle of fishing gear. "These women must have fished all night in the darkness," he laughed. "Grandson, run quickly; get me a caribou skin to sit on, and bring one for yourself."

Kiluk escaped to the tent, with the excuse of getting her heavy caribou parka and boots. But, instead of hiding there, she encountered a wide-awake Nauruk, who immediately asked how many fish she had caught and why she was in the tent when she should be out jigging. Reluctantly she resigned herself to the inevitable. She would try for a while, so they would have to leave her alone.

Masu taught her in typical Eskimo fashion—by handing her the jigging rod and telling her to fish. The hook looked like a small piece of ivory, slender and curved, with a sharp metal barb set out from its lower end. It was carved from a dog's tooth, Masu explained, while Kiluk lowered her line into the black water and began jigging. Much to her surprise, the old woman only laughed a little at her first clumsy attempts, and by pantomime she demonstrated how to move the line properly.

Kiluk held the jigging rod in one hand and a short stick in the other. If she caught a fish, which she thought unlikely, she was to lift the line, then loop it over the stick to pull it from the water. That way she would never have to touch the wet line. Not far away, she saw Patik making his own beginning; and when he looked at her she could not help smiling. He would surely catch many fish, she thought, and she would catch nothing. She moved her arm up and down, imitating the motion her grandmother had used. But nothing happened.

Then suddenly she felt a hard jerk on the rod, and more jerks, as the line zipped in circles around the fishing hole. She was so startled that she nearly lost the rod, but Itiruk shouted, "Pull it up . . . quickly!" In a moment a fat, shiny grayling flopped on the ice beside her. She shook it from the hook as she had seen Itiruk do earlier, then just sat there looking at her catch with a huge smile on her face.

"Azahaa," Sakiak called from the river's far side, "a fish already. Go ahead, drop your line again." Kiluk almost quivered in her excitement, realizing she had actually caught a fish. And before she had calmed down, the line tugged again. This time she laughed with pure delight as her fish dropped onto the ice. The next fish took longer, and she lost it by pulling it up too slowly. But she had another out of the water a short while later.

"This young woman seems to be lucky with fish," Itiruk called to Masu. "Look, Patik has yet to catch his first, and I have caught only one, while she has got three." Masu replied in a matter-of-fact voice, "Kiluk is almost certain to catch many fish. She was born just after the death of old man Kiluk, who was from the Utoqaq people and was known as a great fisherman. His name was given to her, and so we must expect that she will show something of him."

In the Eskimo world, each person's name was imbued with its own soul. When someone died, the soul wandered aimlessly, sometimes maliciously, until it was given an abode in a newborn child. Eventually the child would behave in some way like his or her namesake, when the soul manifested itself. This bequeathed a kind of immortality or promise of reincarnation to the Eskimo people. That was why Amiksuk, who was old Kiluk's grandson, sometimes greeted Kiluk as *ataataga,* "my grandfather," even though she was young and a woman.

The fishing went on for hours and hours, with occasional breaks for hot food, tea, and the tent's welcome warmth. Everyone had caught a little pile of fish, and even Patik was quite successful. Only Masu had more fish than Kiluk, who never retreated to the tent until her hands and feet were freezing and her teeth chattered. *"Aana,"* she once called to Masu, "I am having great fun, and someday perhaps I will catch as many fish as you." The old woman only laughed, but tears of happiness stood in her eyes. In all the time since Kiluk had returned, she had never before shown pleasure in learning the ways of her own people.

When dusk came, Patik and Kiluk were the last to pull out their lines and walk up the bank. Everyone else was in Masu's tent, celebrating the day with laughter and stories. The two stood for a moment listening, then went to Sakiak's tent. Eskimos had lived for many generations in small family camps, and the elders understood the need to be alone. Sakiak would not return to his tent tonight, and Nauruk would even resist teasing through the thin canvas walls . . . at least until tomorrow.

Days melted together where the calendar had little relevance. Each was a bit shorter than the one before, as they descended toward the time when no sun would appear at all. And each was a bit colder. Life at Nunavik was filled with fishing—and more fishing. Kiluk awoke with the women each morning, sometimes even before them, and fished until dusk. With Masu's help, she cut caribou leg skins for a pair of warm fishing mittens, which she would try to sew herself.

Nauruk and Patik, and sometimes Sakiak, searched far for caribou but found none. Then a blizzard came and deep snow packed hard around the tents. The next day they found caribou tracks nearby, and that night they heard the clicking of hooves almost within the camp. When they awoke the following morning caribou were everywhere, scattered herds of a few hundred each, moving north-ward over the tundra plain. The fall migration had reached them at last, and the men began hunting immediately. They concealed themselves below the riverbank and shot only the best animals, the fat cows and young bulls, as they walked near the tents. When they had enough they stopped shooting and everybody helped to butcher the catch. Kiluk joined in the work, though she had never touched an animal's warm insides before.

The evening of the caribou, they heard distant shots from the east, and they knew that hunters were coming. After dusk, under a high full moon that made shadows on the drifts, Patik and Kiluk saw a dog team coming slowly over the nearest rise. Two more followed, and soon they heaved into camp. It was Sakiak's oldest son Kuvlu, together with Migalik and Talimat, who were sons of Masu. Amid the joy and excitement of greeting. Migalik's dogs pulled over to the sacks of fish and managed to tear one open. Migalik shooed them off and laughingly warned that they would pull the fish home on the sled, not in their bellies.

"Tomorrow I head back to Ulurunik, younger sister," he called to Kiluk. "Perhaps you will ride on my sled and keep me company. Your friends have missed you in the village." Her heart jumped, and she saw Patik turn and walk to his tent.

Everyone stayed awake very late that night, eating fresh meat and fish, exchang-ing news, and telling stories. Finally, as the moon descended along the sky's eastern edge, they turned off the lanterns and slept. Only Kiluk remained awake, thinking of the weeks past and agonizing toward a decision. She had longed for the village; she was tired of hard work and cold; and she was almost afraid, as a matter of principle, to stay in the camp. Deep inside, she felt she was losing her former self—but what was that to lose, she wondered? Perhaps a storm would come and she would have more time to think.

Dawn light smoldered dimly along the far horizon, beneath the prodigious blackness of the sky. The dense quiet was broken by a hollow boom, as the river ice cracked in the pinch of deepening cold. Beyond the eastern bank, a resting caribou twitched its ears at the sound, lifted its warm muzzle to the breeze, and stared into the chasm of darkness.

Migalik's voice abruptly ended Kiluk's sleep, which seemed to have just begun. "Come, sister, wake up and eat. I will load my sled soon and start for Ulurunik. The sun is bright and there is little wind; a fine day to travel." Migalik had a curious gleam in his smile, as if he was teasing her, or perhaps taunting her. "Go away," she whispered hoarsely, still only half-awake. But a few minutes later she slowly crept out of her sleeping bag.

Kiluk dressed in her warmest clothes and walked to the riverbank, where she could look across the river and the lift of tundra beyond. She saw a small herd of caribou in the distance, and another far upriver. The snow-covered ice was dotted with fishing holes and laced with a network of footprints. Brilliant sun reflected from the white land. It was so quiet, she thought, so peaceful, here in this Eskimo place far removed from all other worlds.

She turned abruptly and hurried toward the camp, then pulled open the flap of Sakiak's tent. Patik looked up at her and their eyes met for a long moment. "Hurry," Migalik said, "Talimat is already loading the sled and I . . . ."

"I will stay!" she blurted, a huge smile brightening the beauty of her face. *"Aulagnaitchunga!"* She said it again, in Eskimo this time, because it also explained her reasons. "I will stay until I have caught enough fish to feel satisfied, and until I have finished a pair of mittens, and until everyone else is leaving."

Migalik looked down at his soup, trying to hide his satisfied grin. Patik pretended to be busy with his boot ties. And old Sakiak just looked at her with a pleased light in his eyes.

Kiluk walked slowly away from the tent. An icy breeze hushed over the drifts and stung her cheeks. She turned away for a moment, but then she faced the wind and smiled. Suddenly she thought of herself in the boat a few weeks earlier, crying tears of anger at the cold and loneliness. Now the chill felt like a friend to her, and the breeze like a reassuring hand. The land that once seemed so empty had become rich with life and meaning. She was no longer a stranger here. She was an Eskimo.

Kiluk looked over at the tents and saw a young hunter coming toward her.

Questions for Discussion and Writing

1. Setting is an important factor in our reading of this story. In what ways does Nelson help us to feel, see, smell, hear, and taste the setting, and why is it critical to make it so real?

2. What are the cultural values and assumptions of the people in the story? What cultural values and assumptions did Kiluk acquire during her years of education in the town of Ulurunik?

3. What relationships exist between the setting or place of the Eskimo culture and the underlying values that you observe and interpret in the story? Use brief passages to support your analysis.

4. Why or why not would you have made the same decision that Kiluk makes at the end of the story? In what ways might your cultural background influence your decision?

GRAHAM SHEIL

The Picking Season

Born in 1938 in Melbourne, Australia, Graham Sheil describes himself as a compulsive writer whose short stories are published "by just about everyone in Australia who publishes short stories." When he left school at fifteen, his universities became "the optical workshops of Melbourne, and the bikeracing sports carnivals of rural Australia." In spite of his working his way from laborer and miner to owner of an optical wholesale company, Sheil has never been able to subdue the need in his life to write. A number of his stories celebrate work, which he believes is "one of the great expressions of human endeavor."

"The Picking Season" reflects a time in the 1950s when migrants were coming to Australia to work; the time that Sheil spent as a picker was one of his few departures from the optical business as well as his first acquaintance with Germans. The constant traveling that Sheil still does in his optical business throws him into contact with an immense range of people and situations—"from crowded one-room sweatshops in Hong Kong to a factory of 40,000 workers in East Germany, from bush eye hospitals in New Guinea to fashion spectacle manufacturers in Cologne."

Sheil's stories often reflect his experiences of work and travel in diverse cultures. His fascination with the stories of other peoples, cultures, and places comes from a recognition that his aspiration in making stories is "to grasp and hold to what is constant in a world where what is most constant is change."

Before you read "The Picking Season," write about a time in your life when, away from your home, the experience of observing or living with another person from a different background or culture made you reassess your own attitudes toward your life and family.

B eyond the window of the single-carriage train, twin concrete cylinders of a wheat silo loomed above the low Mallee scrub; another of the pickers said, "This's it."

When I wheeled my bike along the platform, pickers with their suitcases clustered around the spike-topped gate. Beyond the gate, dried leathery faces regarded us from beneath turned-down hat brims.

"I'll take the kid with a bike."

The gate swung open; and I awkwardly wheeled the bike forward. A hand closed around mine holding the suitcase and took it from me.

"Name's Ron," he said. "Ron Quin."

I followed to a dented utility truck caked in red mud, and hefted the bike in on top of the case.

We drove from the railway station and the silos, the car splashing through puddles in potholes. Late afternoon sun drew steam from rain-darkened bitumen. We continued past shops hooded by verandas and a pub; then the low Mallee scrub began.

"Rain," Ron Quin said. "F' eight months y'd go down on yer knees f' rain—'n' don't sight a cloud. Once the fruit's on the vines, y'd rather sight a debt collector than rain, but down she comes! With rain in this heat, the fruit rots while yer watchin' it."

Ahead were sprawling branches and foliage of river gums, then a bridge over the wide greenish river. There the bitumen ended. A red sandy track went on, through spindly stunted scrub.

"Specially with the pickers I won," he said, continuing his previous statement, after a distance of some miles. "One, Australian, had the shakes—walked off. T'other two 're German. They're awright. As fellas. But they don't like the dust, they don't like the heat, they won't get down on their knees. Let me tell y' somethin'. You stand-'n'-bend—like them Germans—you won't make wages. An' I won't get enough o' this crop off t' *pay* wages!"

He was in his thirties, short and sinewy; his limbs, emerging from stain-streaked shirt and shorts, were the color of the red sandy track darkened by rain.

As for myself, I was then seventeen. I was putting distance between me and my father's resentment at me fuzzing my apprenticeship; putting behind me, too, the hostility between my mother's religion and my grandfather's determination to face his impending death with none of religion's consolations; getting away from my seven-year-old sister's embarrassing, if gratifying, hero-worship: I was, that is, cutting loose from home and family.

The track emerged from the stunted scrub. Rows of vines along waist-high wires filled an uncannily flat landscape. Among the green were pickers and tractors pulling trailers loaded with rectangular iron buckets.

We turned in at a gateway, around behind a fibro-cement house. Ron indicated a corrugated iron hut beyond drying racks.

"Two spare bunks in there; take either one."

I wheeled the bike to the side wall, then back for the suitcase. My new employer had stepped from the *ute*'s cabin, straight to a tractor. From the house—the sound of a door slamming. A woman came down steps below a flywire door, crossed the bare-ground yard to where Ron cranked the tractor into life. She was tall, and wide across at shoulders and hips; and leaned back as she walked to ballast her pregnancy.

Inside the hut, bunks had been made by threading saplings through hessian bags. Above me, I hung clothes from nails driven into the unlined framework; I stacked tinned food in an empty fruit box.

From outside, the sound of voices.

The lowering sun had tinged the vines in mauve light. There was a stillness in which distant sounds of tractors seemed to hang in the mauve air.

Two figures walked slowly between the rows of vines. One was short and heavy, wearing a hat, shorts, boots; his body was burned brown by the sun.

"Huh!" he called to me. "You're new for picking d' grapes—huh?"

Nearer, he thrust out his hand: "Helmut."

Now I looked at the other man. He was taller, lighter built. He wore a long-sleeved shirt buttoned at the wrists; and all down the front of the shirt and trousers were dark, stiff stains. Around his neck was a bandage.

Helmut was saying he had been in Australia before.

"But him," he indicated the other, "I tell on d' boat: I will learn you English. But he all-a-time at night in d' cabin with lady. Daytime he so weak he on hands and foots like a dog."

Helmut dropped to all fours, his head hanging down, tongue out, and panting. Abruptly he lifted his head high to emit yelps and howls.

I'd begun to laugh at Helmut's clowning—when the taller German shouted something at him. There was no need to comprehend the language to get the meaning: if Helmut thought of the shipboard romance as a dog-in-heat affair, the other did not.

Not till Helmut had gone to the side of the hut where a shower had been rigged beneath a tank stand, did the other turn to me.

"Alf."

He took off his boots outside the hut. Inside he took off his trousers. With bitter humor he demonstrated the trousers would stand—almost—unsupported. He took off his shirt.

Alf must have commenced picking in just shorts, for his back was covered in watery blisters of sunburn. Down the backs of his legs, skin was peeling away. When he turned to me, I saw his thighs were covered in blisters that had burst, then an irritation—from the grape juice or the red dust—had set up an inflammation. He unwound the bandage around his neck, and at the back and sides of his neck were blisters margined by inflammation.

In the open fireplace of the hut, he got a fire going. He heated water, then bathed his blisters. Later, Helmut returned from the house where their meat was kept in the 'fridge; he cooked the meat and mashed potatoes with fat in which the steak had been fried. Throughout the meal, Alf barely spoke. When Helmut took out a pack of cards, Alf pointedly took out a book.

Only once did Alf make any definite remark; and then it was to me. I had joined Helmut in playing cards for matches, and in spite of the fire had to go to my case for a jumper. Then Alf, sitting on his bunk with blankets pulled about his shoulders, rummaged his stock of English to say:

"Daytime—Sahara; nighttime—Siberia."

He threw off his blankets, stoked the fire, and went out of the hut.

Helmut was telling me that in Germany after the war he had been a trotting driver. He spoke of races he'd been rigged out of winning or robbed of in photo-finishes, of the crookedness of drivers, trainers, bookmakers, judges. To escape, I stood and indicated I had to go outside.

As I closed the door, cold engulfed me with such intensity that it was minutes before I could breathe freely. Hugging arms to chest, I walked through the gateway to the road. I began to run. In the moonless sky, myriad stars flared with icy brilliance. But running caused the cold to burn in my throat with the taste of nausea, and I walked back the way I had run.

I was almost at the gateway when I saw someone among the vines. The figure stood motionless, just beyond the tongue of light that licked out from the one illuminated window of the house.

Standing side-on to the watcher and the house, I could not see what it was he saw. When cold sent me to the hut and the fire there, Helmut was already asleep. I lay newspapers between blankets on my bunk and got into bed. Sleep came immediately. Yet some sound must have woken me, for I momentarily saw Alf huddled over the fire before sleep again overwhelmed me.

In the cold of early morning, Ron took me out among the vines. By the time the sun was belting down from halfway up the sky, dried juice from rotting grapes had stiffened my shirt front and thighs of pants. But, kneeling, I was making faster progress on my row than the two Germans were together, as they stood and stooped and moved buckets by hand.

At midday we washed faces and hands, scraped boots, went to the house and in at the flywire door. Our meal of cold meat, salad and bread was on the kitchen table.

Ron introduced me to his wife. There was nothing pretty about Wendy, yet she did possess a big-boned handsomeness. During the meal she spoke to Ron, to all of us, in bossy ridiculing phrases, but in a half-joking tone, as though she did not expect what she said to be taken at full value.

As she clattered dishes into the sink, she said: "You three better get yer bum down an' feet up before yer out again in that bugger of a sun."

It was then—as she poured water from a kettle into the sink in front of the kitchen's solitary window—that it came to me: the illuminated window of last night had not been, as I'd supposed, the bedroom window.

Just what breed of queer was it, I wondered, who gets kicks worth freezing for out of looking in at a *kitchen* window?

Twice that afternoon it rained. We all ran to roll covers down the sides of drying racks and cover fruit drying on tarred paper on the ground. When the rain passed, the steamy heat was made even more oppressive by the stench of grapes fermenting as they rotted.

That night, the three of us had cleaned and eaten when Ron pushed open the door. He had continued dipping and spreading grapes after we knocked off, then worked on his erratically-running tractor. So he stood in juice-stained shirt and shorts and with grease-smeared hands, as he asked if we'd work the weekend.

I affected disinterest to see if he would offer a higher rate. Helmut translated to Alf, who emphatically shook his head. Helmut said he wouldn't either.

Ron turned to the door. I quickly said I'd pick through the weekend. I calculated I could make more money than ever I'd made, and it wasn't going to last. Not with the rain.

At that, Ron was apparently encouraged to try an appeal.

"The blockie who had this before me loaded his wife 'n' kids an' his kitchen table onto a truck—an' he lit out. A bank later repossessed the truck, but they never got him in their sights. I got this block with a loan the size o' his debts. I'd one fair season . . . two bad . . . now this . . . Looked like a bumper—till the rain. Now it's a race against rot t' get enough off t' keep the bank from selling me up . . . So-o-o, what about it?"

I don't know how much of that Alf followed, but he knew he was being put on to work the weekend. He indicated neck and thighs. Through Helmut he said he wanted Saturday and Sunday out of sun and dirt. Helmut lamely said the rain must stop.

Then Ron said it was he who had to sign their return rail voucher.

The return rail voucher, that employment officers issued to pickers, had to be endorsed by the employer before a free rail pass was issued. But as long as a picker stuck out the season, the blockie couldn't refuse to sign.

Perhaps the bluff did work for Helmut began urging Alf. Alf shook his head. Helmut urged more emphatically, and Alf nodded. Then Helmut put to Ron that they would work Saturday morning, provided he drove them eight miles to a pub in the afternoon. They would not work Sunday.

As it happened, neither on Saturday nor Sunday did it rain. It was past lunch time Monday when dark slate clouds began to muster; Ron punched on the *ute*'s horn to bring us running.

Throughout that week it rained sporadically. And twice that week, Alf went to stand motionless among the vines, staring in at the kitchen window.

When Ron asked us to work the weekend, Helmut put the same proposition as the week before.

On the Sunday, Helmut and Alf slept through the morning; in the afternoon, they sat in the shade of almond trees, dozing and drinking beer.

From the west, clouds blew in with such suddenness that though Ron roared the tractor between the rows—and I jumped onto the trailer—rain was falling before we reached the racks. Neither Helmut nor Alf moved to help. Then the flywire door slammed, and Wendy was running in bare feet toward fruit drying on tarred paper on the ground.

That brought Alf to his feet and running. In now driving rain, he shouted at Wendy, pointing toward the house. She jerked a thumb at him, and dragged a tarpaulin to cover drying fruit, then ran for spare sheets of tarred paper. Alf abandoned his remonstrations to run and drag and cover drying fruit beside her. By the time Ron and I unrolled covers on the drying racks, Wendy and Alf had fruit on tarred paper covered.

Splashing through puddles, we all ran to the east side of the hut. Wendy made no attempt to stand against the wall. With bare feet in puddles, red mud splashed up her legs, her dress clinging to her, outlining her pregnancy, she seemed to take a perverse pleasure from standing in the driving rain.

"That," she said, "has buggered it. There's as much chance of us keeping this place now—as there is me being made Queen of England."

Helmut had been first against the hut wall. He laughed hugely at Wendy's assertion.

Alf wanted to know what the joke was. He seemed not to comprehend either in English nor in translation. Then Helmut elaborated, going into a clowning act of Wendy as Queen, of subjects curtsying before her. When Alf understood Wendy's meaning, it appalled him.

"Home," he said, directly to Ron. He swept his arm around to include Wendy, her pregnancy, the house and fruit block.

"Home . . . finished?"

In his tight-lipped way, Ron said there was a chance yet.

"Huh!" It was Wendy's derisive exclamation. "Some chance!"

She stomped off, through rain and red mud and puddles, up steps and in at the flywire door.

Helmut must have decided he had some squaring-off to do, because after the rain passed and Ron and I finished work, he offered to share with us what was left of the beer.

When Ron had cleaned and eaten, he brought to the hut a cold bottle of his own, which was better than Helmut's two warm ones.

I asked Ron about the war in New Guinea, but when we got that—or any other subject—running, it was lapped at bolting pace by Helmut's trotting horses. Helmut slapped a photograph onto the fruit box used as a table, and was jabbing a finger at horses distorted by the angle of the photograph, claiming the photograph proved he had won but the judges had . . .

"Uhh!" Alf swept Helmut's photograph from the fruit box. "All times horses trotting! Trotting horses!"

Where Helmut's photograph had been, Alf slapped down one of his own.

In the creased and curled print was a family scene. Before a narrow-fronted, two-story house, stood a family in what surely was fancy dress. The father and a youth of, perhaps, twelve wore hats with narrow brims and feathers in the bands, white shirts beneath a bib-and-brace top of leather joining to leather shorts. The mother and daughter wore scooped-neck blouses with puffed sleeves, tight-laced garments from waist to chest, and wide skirts: an outfit Helmut consented to tell us was called a *dirndle*.

Ron wanted to know if those were really the clothes they wore. With sullen help from Helmut, Alf said those clothes were worn in country districts and in Bavaria. Not in northern cities. Not in Hanover where he lived. But in Hitler's time the government encouraged everyone to dress like that on Sundays and when there were political rallies. The photograph was taken during the first year of war, on the day when for the first time they all dressed like that.

It was the girl in the photograph who took my interest. She was eight or nine—a year or so older than my own sister—and I fancied a similarity: both were fair, both had smallboned facial features.

Alf told he had started to learn English at school. He remembered one lesson:

I . . . go . . . to . . . the . . . window.
I . . . go . . . to . . . the . . . door.
I . . . come . . . from . . . the . . . window.
I . . . come . . . from . . . the . . . door.

But the lessons were stopped, he couldn't recall why.

What he remembered clearly were Sunday mornings. He and his sister slept in one room, where they would lie listening for their father to go from the other bedroom to the kitchen. The two then ran to jump into the big bed with their mother. Their father would turn on the wireless—there was a program of brass band music on Sunday mornings—and bring coffee to their mother. He always affected surprise at finding them in the bed. When Alf asked for coffee for himself and his sister because it was Sunday, their father sternly lectured them hot coffee was not for growing children, then went to the kitchen for the two cups already poured for them.

Helmut, in filling in where Alf's English failed him, added to the telling to say Hanover was a big city: more people than Perth, more than Adelaide, though it did not spread so far.

There was little damage to the city when Alf, at sixteen, was trucked south to man anti-aircraft guns surrounding the Mercedes factory at Stuttgart.

There he met Helmut. They were in the same gun crew. Few bombing raids penetrated so far south; there was little damage either to the Mercedes works or the city.

Two months after the war ended, Alf was able to make his way north. He found the city which had been bigger than Perth or Adelaide, a waste of fire-blackened rubble. Of the more than six hundred thousand living within the city less than a year before, there now existed like rats among rubble, no more than two hundred. Thirty huddled at night in the unroofed shell of a church. From these he learnt of nights when the whole city roared and blazed in flames, and above the flames and the smoke, the sky filled with bombers.

For days he went to wherever he was told someone was living; but none could answer what he asked. Nor was it even possible to discover where individual streets had been. So he left his boyhood city without even the certainty he had found where his home had been.

During the dozen years since then, he moved from place to place throughout Germany, forming no lasting relationships until a chance meeting with Helmut, back from two years in Australia.

The following week Helmut gained a second topic of conversation. Ron had returned from the one local store with two letters: one from my mother (asking why her previous letter was unanswered) with a postscript from my sister; the other, for Alf.

In his elation at receiving the letter, Alf told Helmut. Helmut, of course, told us. The lady of Alf's shipboard romance was working as a nursing aid in Melbourne. She wrote she had moved out from the migrant hostel to a flat near the hospital.

Helmut clowned his dog-in-heat act during smokos. When he once got a laugh from Wendy by saying after the picking season Alf would start working hard in the night, he said the same thing every lunch time.

Alf took this with more forbearance than he'd previously shown. But one lunch time Ron told Helmut he better give it a rest. When the next day he said the same thing again, Wendy bellowed at him to put a bloody sock in it. That gained us a rest from Helmut throughout a week of oppressive humidity and sudden, brief, showers.

Alf's back and legs healed. Yet he had only to work a day without the bandage for new blisters to rise on top of old infections. He never seemed to adjust to the heat, nor to the fall in temperature at night; nor could he accept as normal the red mud when it rained, the red dust when it didn't, the stain and stench of rotting grapes.

During that week, Alf stayed in the hut at night. Then on a night of full moon, a night not as cold as others had been, I stalked him among the vines. From a dozen rows of vines behind him, I watched Alf as he watched the window.

Framed in the kitchen window was Wendy at the sink. Beyond her Ron supported his head with one hand over what would have been the kitchen table. His other hand came to his head, holding a pencil. Wendy apparently finished washing the dishes, for she went from the sink, then reappeared. She threw a tea towel at Ron. He made no move to catch it, and it landed across his head. After some time Ron took the towel and moved to the sink to dry dishes. Possibly they had a wireless playing, for Wendy did some dance steps around Ron, tapping him on the head as though to music. At all events, that tight-lipped man looked at her and grinned.

That was about all. Ron returned to the table, Wendy went from the window, though she must have remained in the room for at times Ron looked up and spoke.

Alf made his way to the hut. I stooped among the vines to the road, then I walked miles through a flat, moonwashed landscape.

After Alf's second letter came, he crossed from the hut to where Ron and I were unrolling covers on the racks. In words he had apparently rehearsed, he said:

"Saturday. I go to back to Melbourne."

Ron went on unrolling the covers as though nothing had been said.

Next morning Alf was waiting beside the tractor when Ron came from the house. Word for word he made the same statement, adding that on Tuesday he would "come to back to here."

Ron stepped to the tractor and cranked the motor without the least indication he had heard. But when he brought black tea in a thermos for afternoon smoko, Ron thrust a slip of paper at Alf.

"That's the buckets you an' Helmut 've picked. S'pose y'want a check f' your half b'fore you go?"

Alf nodded.

Ron stepped up onto the tractor which he'd left idling during smoko. He revved the motor and rammed the gear lever forward so that the tractor lurched forward to career off between the vines.

That night Ron brought the check and Alf's rail voucher, signed, to the hut. As Alf had not worked the season, Ron wasn't required to sign the voucher. Now Alf would travel to Melbourne free; but if he was coming back, he was up for the fare both ways.

Some chance! I thought.

Alf began talking about coming back on Tuesday.

"So y' keep tellun me," Ron said.

Ron told Alf about the trains; and it was actually Friday afternoon when he drove Alf to the station.

Ron and I worked the Saturday and Sunday with Helmut wandering over to talk. When a shower blew up, Helmut helped us cover drying fruit. While we waited for the rain to pass, Helmut went through his dog-in-heat antics. And when, lunch time Tuesday, Helmut started on his piece about Alf working hard in the night, even Helmut could interpret the look he got from Ron.

That afternoon I heard the tractor motor die away, the *ute* start up, and drive out along the road.

I was on my bunk, trying to summon energy to get clean and cook dinner, when I heard the *ute* return.

Only one door slammed. And that, hard.

Next afternoon, Ron again drove to meet the train. Again returned alone.

When he drove off on the Thursday, it wasn't the train he was heading for; it was the employment office. There he was told there wouldn't be any more pickers, not this late in the season.

The Friday was very still, the oppressive humidity threatening a storm all day. Both Helmut and I worked late, then I went into the hut ahead of Helmut.

And there was Alf. He was sitting on the edge of his bunk.

Helmut, following me, blurted questions, repeating the answers to me. Yes, Alf had come on today's train. He hadn't got a lift. He'd walked. Walked? Carrying his coat and case? In this heat? . . . *"Ja,"* Alf said, *"ja, ja, ja."*

He lay back on his bunk staring up at the unlined roof.

I went among the vines to tell Ron. He hesitated in loading buckets of grapes onto the trailer, but that was the only indication that he'd heard.

That night the hut door was pushed open and Ron stood there holding two bottles of beer. Wendy was behind him. She had two more bottles, glasses, the battery wireless from the house. Neither said anything about Alf coming back. Ron held out his hand to Helmut for an opener, and got the tops off the bottles.

Alf sat up on the bed. Helmut, as always responding to an audience, got maximum effect by clowning as he asked questions in German, then leeringly translated for us.

Yes, Alf stayed in the lady's flat. Yes, it had been like on the boat. Yes, she'd planned on him staying, she'd arranged a job for him at the hospital.

Then Alf spoke directly to Ron and Wendy. "She did not want home, children and like that," he said. She wanted him to live with her.

Helmut didn't see any problem about that. He went down on hands and knees, lifting his head high to howl.

Alf stood, and he kicked Helmut. The kick thudded into Helmut's lower stomach and would have put most men in hospital. It didn't do that to Helmut. He got to his feet, one hand holding his stomach, the other clenched into a fist and he came at Alf. Ron stepped in front, thrust a glass at Helmut's hand. Wendy flung an arm around Helmut's neck and laughed. Helmut stopped his rush. He stood, puzzled. Then he must have decided the laugh was on Alf, for he skoaled the beer and roared laughing. Wendy kept the momentum of that going by switching on the wireless, turning through static and stations until she had music. She held out her arms for Helmut to dance with her.

To a strident beat they danced something between a jive and a jitterbug. Wendy tossed off a glass of beer as she danced, without missing a beat. Helmut, laughing, stuck out his belly in clowning imitation of Wendy's pregnancy.

The music ended with Wendy laughing, breathless, and perspiring. Ron filled glasses while Wendy fiddled with the wireless. The music she now found was more sedate. Alf came to Ron to quite formally ask if he could dance with Wendy. Ron jerked his head in a go-to-it gesture.

The dance of Wendy and Alf didn't work very well. Alf tried to dance something like a waltz, then more like a foxtrot. They couldn't get the steps right. Alf became embarrassed because of Wendy's protruding belly against him. Then Wendy became embarrassed because he was.

When the music ended, Alf led Wendy to Ron. He went to his case for a parcel which he handed to Wendy saying it was for the baby. Opening the gift, Wendy took out a tiny blouse, jacket, skirt: miniatures of what Alf's mother and sister wore in the photograph, and which Helmut had said was called a *dirndle*.

The gift struck me as ridiculous. The baby might not be a girl! Even if it was, a *dirndle*, here, would be as misplaced as a *didgeridoo* in a military brass band.

Wendy seemed mystified by the present, too. Oh, she thanked him—kissed him full on the lips—and Ron clapped his shoulder in thanks. But plainly she did not know what she would ever do with it. What, later that night, she did do, was to dance with it. Holding the dirndle in front of her, she jived to a pulsating beat from the wireless.

We'd all had a couple of glasses by then, and the three of us stood around her, clapping and shouting to the beat as she—incredibly for her size and state—went to it. She stomped, rocked hips, shoulders, shook arms and breasts, her hair flying out, her head tossed back in laughter. Ron did not stand and clap. He sat grinning at Wendy's dance and at our applause: in his own way taking more from it than any of us.

Past Wendy, I saw the grin go from Ron. He reached for the wireless, switched it off. In abrupt silence, we all heard it. Rain. Rain not yet on the iron roof, but advancing, tramping across the rows of vines. Then it was upon us, larruping on the iron roof and walls, holding us silent within its kettledrum rat-ta-tat of sound.

That ended the party. We drank what was left of the beer, Wendy and Ron went to the door. Ron asked Alf if he'd be going back to his lady friend when the picking ended. Alf said he might. Then he said he might not. Then—he didn't know.

That rain really ended the picking season, too. It dragged on for another ten days; but it was that rain which finished it.

To me it capped the futility of Alf's return; an army of Alf's in a month without rain couldn't save that fruit block now. Not from being sold up over Ron's head. And Wendy and Ron had even less idea of what they were going to do than Alf.

As for Alf, within days he was back to bathing and bandaging blisters and with morose humor demonstrating his pants would stand—almost—unsupported. But now he worked on his knees, through that last week and two weekends.

On the Sunday before Easter, Ron abandoned the picking. He signed my rail voucher, and I sold it for half value to Alf, then arranged for Ron to rail home my case.

At midday I rode out between the gateposts, along the red sandy track. Flat monotonous miles of stunted scrub fell away beneath my pedals, then country sparse with trees and with salt lakes in shallow depressions. That night I slept in a football pavilion. The next day I reached Bendigo.

I intended staying in Bendigo until after Easter, to watch the bike-racing carnival. But after a day, something from those past weeks goaded me to continue on.

Leaving Bendigo, I was heading toward my own home. Climbing and free-wheeling through hills, Alf's return no longer came to me as pointless nor his gift as ridiculous. These now seemed the expression of sympathy toward two who would lose what they had tried to make a home—by one who had lost all trace of home and hearth and family, except an ideal of it.

Questions for Discussion and Writing

1. What does the seventeen-year-old narrator learn about each person in the story, and in what ways does this learning influence him? In what ways does the menace of the weather become part of his lessons?
2. What cultural values and history have shaped Alf? In what ways does the writer re-create his past, and how do the bits and pieces of this past change the narrator's understanding of the man?
3. For what reasons do you suppose Alf is stealing glimpses into Ron and Wendy's kitchen?
4. What is the significance of the gift Alf brings back for the baby? What does the narrator learn as a result?

MILAN KUNDERA

The Hitchhiking Game

*Born in 1929, the Czechoslovakian writer Milan Kundera has writ-
ten, "All my life long I have been protesting the mutilation of works
of art in the name of an ideological doctrine as practiced in the
socialist countries of Europe." With the Soviet invasion of his country in August 1968, Kundera lost his hope that censorship might be
abolished. He also lost his job at the Prague Film Faculty, his plays
were no longer produced, and his books were banned. When the
University of Rennes in France offered him a job in 1975, he obtained permission to move to that country, where he continues to live
today. Kundera still writes in his native tongue, from which his
books are translated and published around the world.*

*Living away from his home of Czechoslovakia, Kundera has
learned that great writing must have a universal application: "To
depict human situations in a way which makes it impossible for
them to be understood beyond the frontiers of any single country is
a disservice to the readers of that country too. By so doing we prevent
them from looking further than their own backyard, we force them
into a straitjacket of parochialism."*

*"The Hitchhiking Game" is taken from a collection of Kundera's
stories entitled* Laughable Loves *(1974), one of only a few books he
is allowed to publish in Czechoslovakia. Only in subtle ways does the
story suggest political concerns.*

Before you read "The Hitchhiking Game," write about a time in your life
when you decided to take on a persona—a different personality. What made
you decide, consciously or unconsciously, to change yourself, who was directly involved with your decision, and what happened as a result of the
change?

1

The needle on the gas gauge suddenly dipped toward empty and the young driver of the sports car declared that it was maddening how much gas the car ate up. "See that we don't run out of gas again," protested the girl (about twenty-two), and reminded the driver of several places where this had already happened to them. The young man replied that he wasn't worried, because whatever he went through with her had the charm of adventure for him. The girl objected; whenever they had run out of gas on the highway it had, she said, always been an adventure only for her. The young man had hidden and she had had to make ill use of her charms by thumbing a ride and letting herself be driven to the nearest gas station, then thumbing a ride back with a can of gas. The young man asked the girl whether the drivers who had given her a ride had been unpleasant, since she spoke as if her task had been a hardship. She replied (with awkward flirtatiousness) that sometimes they had been *very* pleasant but that it hadn't done her any good as she had been burdened with the can and had had to leave them before she could get anything going. "Pig," said the young man. The girl protested that she wasn't a pig, but that he really was. God knows how many girls stopped him on the highway, when he was driving the car alone! Still driving, the young man put his arm around the girl's shoulders and kissed her gently on the forehead. He knew that she loved him and that she was jealous. Jealousy isn't a pleasant quality, but if it isn't overdone (and if it's combined with modesty), apart from its inconvenience there's even something touching about it. At least that's what the young man thought. Because he was only twenty-eight, it seemed to him that he was old and knew everything that a man could know about women. In the girl sitting beside him he valued precisely what, until now, he had met with least in women: purity.

The needle was already on empty, when to the right the young man caught sight of a sign, announcing that the station was a quarter of a mile ahead. The girl hardly had time to say how relieved she was before the young man was signaling left and driving into a space in front of the pumps. However, he had to stop a little way off, because beside the pumps was a huge gasoline truck with a large metal tank and a bulky hose, which was refilling the pumps. "We'll have to wait," said the young man to the girl and got out of the car. "How long will it take?" he shouted to the man in overalls. "Only a moment," replied the attendant, and the young man said: "I've heard that one before." He wanted to go back and sit in the car, but he saw that the girl had gotten out the other side. "I'll take a little walk in the meantime," she said. "Where to?" the young man asked on purpose, wanting to see the girl's embarrassment. He had known her for a year now but she would still get shy in front of him. He enjoyed her moments of shyness, partly because they distinguished her from the women he'd met before, partly because he was aware of the law of universal transience, which made even his girl's shyness a precious thing to him.

2

The girl really didn't like it when during the trip (the young man would drive for several hours without stopping) she had to ask him to stop for a moment somewhere near a clump of trees. She always got angry when, with feigned surprise, he asked her why he should stop. She knew that her shyness was ridiculous and old-fashioned. Many times at work she had noticed that they laughed at her on account of it and deliberately provoked her. She always got shy in advance at the thought of how she was going to get shy. She often longed to feel free and easy about her body, the way most of the women around her did. She had even invented a special course in self-persuasion: she would repeat to herself that at birth every human being received one out of the millions of available bodies, as one would receive an allotted room out of the millions of rooms in an enormous hotel; that, consequently, the body was fortuitous and impersonal, only a ready-made, borrowed thing. She would repeat this to herself in different ways, but she could never manage to feel it. This mind-body dualism was alien to her. She was too much one with her body; that is why she always felt such anxiety about it.

She experienced this same anxiety even in her relations with the young man, whom she had known for a year and with whom she was happy, perhaps because he never separated her body from her soul and she could live with him *wholly.* In this unity there was happiness, but right behind the happiness lurked suspicion, and the girl was full of that. For instance, it often occurred to her that the other women (those who weren't anxious) were more attractive and more seductive and that the young man, who did not conceal the fact that he knew this kind of woman well, would someday leave her for a woman like that. (True, the young man declared that he'd had enough of them to last his whole life, but she knew that he was still much younger than he thought.) She wanted him to be completely hers and she to be completely his, but it often seemed to her that the more she tried to give him everything, the more she denied him something: the very thing that a light and superficial love or a flirtation gives to a person. It worried her that she was not able to combine seriousness with lightheartedness.

But now she wasn't worrying and any such thoughts were far from her mind. She felt good. It was the first day of their vacation (of their two-week vacation, about which she had been dreaming for a whole year), the sky was blue (the whole year she had been worrying about whether the sky would really be blue), and he was beside her. At his, "Where to?" she blushed, and left the car without a word. She walked around the gas station, which was situated beside the highway in total isolation, surrounded by fields. About a hundred yards away (in the direction in which they were traveling), a wood began. She set off for it, vanished behind a little bush, and gave herself up to her good mood. (In solitude it was possible for her to get the greatest enjoyment from the presence of the man she loved. If his presence had been continuous, it would have kept on disappearing. Only when alone was she able to *hold on* to it.)

When she came out of the wood onto the highway, the gas station was visible. The large gasoline truck was already pulling out and the sports car moved forward toward the red turret of the pump. The girl walked on along the highway and only at times looked back to see if the sports car was coming. At last she caught sight of it. She stopped and began to wave at it like a hitchhiker waving at a stranger's car. The sports car slowed down and stopped close to the girl. The young man leaned toward the window, rolled it down, smiled, and asked, "Where are you headed, miss?" "Are you going to Bystritsa?" asked the girl, smiling flirtatiously at him. "Yes, please get in," said the young man, opening the door. The girl got in and the car took off.

3

The young man was always glad when his girl friend was gay. This didn't happen too often; she had a quite tiresome job in an unpleasant environment, many hours of overtime without compensatory leisure and, at home, a sick mother. So she often felt tired. She didn't have either particularly good nerves or self-confidence and easily fell into a state of anxiety and fear. For this reason he welcomed every manifestation of her gaiety with the tender solicitude of a foster parent. He smiled at her and said: "I'm lucky today. I've been driving for five years, but I've never given a ride to such a pretty hitchhiker."

The girl was grateful to the young man for every bit of flattery; she wanted to linger for a moment in its warmth and so she said, "You're very good at lying."

"Do I look like a liar?"

"You look like you enjoy lying to women," said the girl, and into her words there crept unawares a touch of the old anxiety, because she really did believe that her young man enjoyed lying to women.

The girl's jealousy often irritated the young man, but this time he could easily overlook it for, after all, her words didn't apply to him but to the unknown driver. And so he just casually inquired, "Does it bother you?"

"If I were going with you, then it would bother me," said the girl and her words contained a subtle, instructive message for the young man; but the end of her sentence applied only to the unknown driver, "but I don't know you, so it doesn't bother me."

"Things about her own man always bother a woman more than things about a stranger" (this was now the young man's subtle, instructive message to the girl), "so seeing that we are strangers, we could get on well together."

The girl purposely didn't want to understand the implied meaning of his message, and so she now addressed the unknown driver exclusively:

"What does it matter, since we'll part company in a little while?"

"Why?" asked the young man.

"Well, I'm getting out at Bystritsa."

"And what if I get out with you?"

At these words the girl looked up at him and found that he looked exactly as she imagined him in her most agonizing hours of jealousy. She was alarmed at how he was flattering her and flirting with her (an unknown hitchhiker), and *how becoming it was to him*. Therefore she responded with defiant provocativeness, "What would *you* do with me, I wonder?"

"I wouldn't have to think too hard about what to do with such a beautiful woman," said the young man gallantly and at this moment he was once again speaking far more to his own girl than to the figure of the hitchhiker.

But this flattering sentence made the girl feel as if she had caught him at something, as if she had wheedled a confession out of him with a fraudulent trick. She felt toward him a brief flash of intense hatred and said, "Aren't you rather too sure of yourself?"

The young man looked at the girl. Her defiant face appeared to him to be completely convulsed. He felt sorry for her and longed for her usual, familiar expression (which he used to call childish and simple). He leaned toward her, put his arm around her shoulders, and softly spoke the name with which he usually addressed her and with which he now wanted to stop the game.

But the girl released herself and said: "You're going a bit too fast!"

At this rebuff the young man said: "Excuse me, miss," and looked silently in front of him at the highway.

4

The girl's pitiful jealousy, however, left her as quickly as it had come over her. After all, she was sensible and knew perfectly well that all this was merely a game; now it even struck her as a little ridiculous that she had repulsed her man out of jealous rage; it wouldn't be pleasant for her if he found out why she had done it. Fortunately she had the miraculous ability to change the meaning of her actions after the event. Using this ability, she decided that she had repulsed him not out of anger but so that she could go on with the game, which, with its whimsicality, so well suited the first day of their vacation.

So again she was the hitchhiker, who had just repulsed the overenterprising driver, but only so as to slow down his conquest and make it more exciting. She half turned toward the young man and said caressingly:

"I didn't mean to offend you, mister!"

"Excuse me, I won't touch you again," said the young man.

He was furious with the girl for not listening to him and refusing to be herself when that was what he wanted. And since the girl insisted on continuing in her role, he transferred his anger to the unknown hitchhiker whom she was portraying. And all at once he discovered the character of his own part: he stopped making the gallant remarks with which he had wanted to flatter his girl in a roundabout way, and began to play the tough guy who treats women to the coarser aspects of his masculinity: willfulness, sarcasm, self-assurance.

This role was a complete contradiction of the young man's habitually solicitous approach to the girl. True, before he had met her, he had in fact behaved roughly rather than gently toward women. But he had never resembled a heartless tough guy, because he had never demonstrated either a particularly strong will or ruthlessness. However, if he did not resemble such a man, nonetheless he had *longed* to at one time. Of course it was a quite naive desire, but there it was. Childish desires withstand all the snares of the adult mind and often survive into ripe old age. And this childish desire quickly took advantage of the opportunity to embody itself in the proffered role.

The young man's sarcastic reserve suited the girl very well—it freed her from herself. For she herself was, above all, the epitome of jealousy. The moment she stopped seeing the gallantly seductive young man beside her and saw only his inaccessible face, her jealousy subsided. The girl could forget herself and give herself up to her role.

Her role? What was her role? It was a role out of trashy literature. The hitchhiker stopped the car not to get a ride, but to seduce the man who was driving the car. She was an artful seductress, cleverly knowing how to use her charms. The girl slipped into this silly, romantic part with an ease that astonished her and held her spellbound.

5

There was nothing the young man missed in his life more than lightheartedness. The main road of his life was drawn with implacable precision: his job didn't use up merely eight hours a day, it also infiltrated the remaining time with the compulsory boredom of meetings and home study, and, by means of the attentiveness of his countless male and female colleagues, it infiltrated the wretchedly little time he had left for his private life as well; this private life never remained secret and sometimes even became the subject of gossip and public discussion. Even two weeks' vacation didn't give him a feeling of liberation and adventure; the gray shadow of precise planning lay even here. The scarcity of summer accommodations in our country compelled him to book a room in the Tatras six months in advance, and since for that he needed a recommendation from his office, its omnipresent brain thus did not cease knowing about him even for an instant.

He had become reconciled to all this, yet all the same from time to time the terrible thought of the straight road would overcome him—a road along which he was being pursued, where he was visible to everyone, and from which he could not turn aside. At this moment that thought returned to him. Through an odd and brief conjunction of ideas the figurative road became identified with the real highway along which he was driving—and this led him suddenly to do a crazy thing.

"Where did you say you wanted to go?" he asked the girl.

"To Banska Bystritsa," she replied.

"And what are you going to do there?"

"I have a date there."

"Who with?"

"With a certain gentleman."

The car was just coming to a large crossroads. The driver slowed down so he could read the road signs, then turned off to the right.

"What will happen if you don't arrive for that date?"

"It would be your fault and you would have to take care of me."

"You obviously didn't notice that I turned off in the direction of Nove Zamky."

"Is that true? You've gone crazy!"

"Don't be afraid, I'll take care of you," said the young man.

So they drove and chatted thus—the driver and the hitchhiker who did not know each other.

The game all at once went into a higher gear. The sports car was moving away not only from the imaginary goal of Banska Bystritsa, but also from the real goal, toward which it had been heading in the morning: the Tatras and the room that had been booked. Fiction was suddenly making an assault upon real life. The young man was moving away from himself and from the implacable straight road, from which he had never strayed until now.

"But you said you were going to the Low Tatras!" The girl was surprised.

"I am going, miss, wherever I feel like going. I'm a free man and I do what I want and what it pleases me to do."

6

When they drove into Nove Zamky it was already getting dark.

The young man had never been here before and it took him a while to orient himself. Several times he stopped the car and asked the passersby directions to the hotel. Several streets had been dug up, so that the drive to the hotel, even though it was quite close by (as all those who had been asked asserted), necessitated so many detours and roundabout routes that it was almost a quarter of an hour before they finally stopped in front of it. The hotel looked unprepossessing, but it was the only one in town and the young man didn't feel like driving on. So he said to the girl, "Wait here," and got out of the car.

Out of the car he was, of course, himself again. And it was upsetting for him to find himself in the evening somewhere completely different from his intended destination—the more so because no one had forced him to do it and as a matter of fact he hadn't even really wanted to. He blamed himself for this piece of folly, but then became reconciled to it. The room in the Tatras could wait until tomorrow and it wouldn't do any harm if they celebrated the first day of their vacation with something unexpected.

He walked through the restaurant—smoky, noisy, and crowded—and asked for the reception desk. They sent him to the back of the lobby near the staircase, where behind a glass panel a superannuated blonde was sitting beneath a board full of keys. With difficulty, he obtained the key to the only room left.

The girl, when she found herself alone, also threw off her role. She didn't feel ill-humored, though, at finding herself in an unexpected town. She was so devoted to the young man that she never had doubts about anything he did, and confidently entrusted every moment of her life to him. On the other hand the idea once again popped into her mind that perhaps—just as she was now doing— other women had waited for her man in his car, those women whom he met on business trips. But surprisingly enough this idea didn't upset her at all now; in fact, she smiled at the thought of how nice it was that today she was this other woman, this irresponsible, indecent other woman, one of those women of whom she was so jealous; it seemed to her that she was cutting them all out, that she had learned how to use their weapons; how to give the young man what until now she had not known how to give him: lightheartedness, shamelessness, and dissoluteness; a curious feeling of satisfaction filled her, because she alone had the ability to be all women and in this way (she alone) could completely captivate her lover and hold his interest.

The young man opened the car door and led the girl into the restaurant. Amid the din, the dirt, and the smoke he found a single, unoccupied table in a corner.

7

"So how are you going to take care of me now?" asked the girl provocatively.

"What would you like for an aperitif?"

The girl wasn't too fond of alcohol, still she drank a little wine and liked vermouth fairly well. Now, however, she purposely said: "Vodka."

"Fine," said the young man. "I hope you won't get drunk on me."

"And if I do?" said the girl.

The young man did not reply but called over a waiter and ordered two vodkas and two steak dinners. In a moment the waiter brought a tray with two small glasses and placed it in front of them.

The man raised his glass, "To you!"

"Can't you think of a wittier toast?"

Something was beginning to irritate him about the girl's game; now sitting face to face with her, he realized that it wasn't just the *words* which were turning her into a stranger, but that her *whole persona* had changed, the movements of her body and her facial expression, and that she unpalatably and faithfully resembled that type of woman whom he knew so well and for whom he felt some aversion.

And so (holding his glass in his raised hand), he corrected his toast: "O.K., then I won't drink to you, but to your kind, in which are combined so successfully the better qualities of the animal and the worse aspects of the human being."

"By 'kind' do you mean all women?" asked the girl.

"No, I mean only those who are like you."

"Anyway it doesn't seem very witty to me to compare a woman with an animal."

"O.K.," the young man was still holding his glass aloft, "then I won't drink to your kind, but to your soul. Agreed? To your soul, which lights up when it descends from your head into your belly, and which goes out when it rises back up to your head."

The girl raised her glass. "O.K., to my soul, which descends into my belly."

"I'll correct myself once more," said the young man. "To your belly, into which your soul descends."

"To my belly," said the girl, and her belly (now that they had named it specifically), as it were, responded to the call; she felt every inch of it.

Then the waiter brought their steaks and the young man ordered them another vodka and some soda water (this time they drank to the girl's breasts), and the conversation continued in this peculiar, frivolous tone. It irritated the young man more and more how *well able* the girl was to become the lascivious miss; if she was able to do it so well, he thought, it meant that she really *was* like that; after all, no alien soul had entered into her from somewhere in space; what she was acting now was she herself; perhaps it was that part of her being which had formerly been locked up and which the pretext of the game had let out of its cage. Perhaps the girl supposed that by means of the game she was *disowning* herself, but wasn't it the other way around? wasn't she becoming herself only through the game? wasn't she freeing herself through the game? no, opposite him was not sitting a strange woman in his girl's body; it was his girl, herself, no one else. He looked at her and felt growing aversion toward her.

However, it was not only aversion. The more the girl withdrew from him *psychically,* the more he longed for her *physically;* the alienation of her soul drew attention to her body; yes it turned her body into a body; as if until now it had been hidden from the young man within clouds of compassion, tenderness, concern, love, and emotion, as if it had been lost in these clouds (yes, as if this body had been *lost!*). It seemed to the young man that today he was *seeing* his girl's body for the first time.

After her third vodka and soda the girl got up and said flirtatiously, "Excuse me."

The young man said, "May I ask you where you are going, miss?"

"To piss, if you'll permit me," said the girl and walked off between the tables back toward the plush screen.

8

She was pleased with the way she had astounded the young man with this word, which—in spite of all its innocence—he had never heard from her; nothing seemed to her truer to the character of the woman she was playing than this flirtatious emphasis placed on the word in question; yes, she was pleased, she was in the best of moods; the game captivated her. It allowed her to feel what she had not felt till now: *a feeling of happy-go-lucky irresponsibility.*

She, who was always uneasy in advance about her every next step, suddenly felt completely relaxed. The alien life in which she had become involved was a life without shame, without biographical specifications, without past or future, without obligations; it was a life that was extraordinarily free. The girl, as a hitchhiker, could do anything: *everything was permitted her;* she could say, do, and feel whatever she liked.

She walked through the room and was aware that people were watching her from all the tables; it was also a new sensation, one she didn't recognize: *indecent joy caused by her body.* Until now she had never been able to get rid of the fourteen-year-old girl within herself who was ashamed of her breasts and had the disagreeable feeling that she was indecent, because they stuck out from her body and were visible. Even though she was proud of being pretty and having a good figure, this feeling of pride was always immediately curtailed by shame; she rightly suspected that feminine beauty functioned above all as sexual provocation and she found this distasteful; she longed for her body to relate only to the man she loved; when men stared at her breasts in the street it seemed to her that they were invading a piece of her most secret privacy which should belong only to herself and her lover. But now she was the hitchhiker, the woman without a destiny. In this role she was relieved of the tender bonds of her love and began to be intensely aware of her body; and her body became more aroused the more alien the eyes watching it.

She was walking past the last table when an intoxicated man, wanting to show off his worldliness, addressed her in French: *"Combien, mademoiselle?"*

The girl understood. She thrust out her breasts and fully experienced every movement of her hips, then disappeared behind the screen.

9

It was a curious game. This curiousness was evidenced, for example, in the fact that the young man, even though he himself was playing the unknown driver remarkably well, did not for a moment stop seeing his girl in the hitchhiker. And it was precisely this that was tormenting; he saw his girl seducing a strange man, and had the bitter privilege of being present, of seeing at close quarters how she looked and of hearing what she said when she was cheating on him (when she had cheated on him, when she would cheat on him); he had the paradoxical honor of being himself the pretext for her unfaithfulness.

This was all the worse because he worshipped rather than loved her; it had always seemed to him that her inward nature was *real* only within the bounds of fidelity and purity, and that beyond these bounds it simply didn't exist; beyond these bounds she would cease to be herself, as water ceases to be water beyond the boiling point. When he now saw her crossing this horrifying boundary with nonchalant elegance, he was filled with anger.

The girl came back from the rest room and complained: "A guy over there asked me: *Combien, mademoiselle?*"

"You shouldn't be surprised," said the young man, "after all, you look like a whore."

"Do you know that it doesn't bother me in the least?"

"Then you should go with the gentleman!"

"But I have you."

"You can go with him after me. Go and work out something with him."

"I don't find him attractive."

"But in principle you have nothing against it, having several men in one night."

"Why not, if they're good-looking."

"Do you prefer them one after the other or at the same time?"

"Either way," said the girl.

The conversation was proceeding to still greater extremes of rudeness; it shocked the girl slightly but she couldn't protest. Even in a game there lurks a lack of freedom; even a game is a trap for the players. If this had not been a game and they had really been two strangers, the hitchhiker could long ago have taken offense and left. But there's no escape from a game. A team cannot flee from the playing field before the end of the match, chess pieces cannot desert the chessboard: the boundaries of the playing field are fixed. The girl knew that she had to accept whatever form the game might take, just because it was a game. She knew that the more extreme the game became, the more it would be a game and the more obediently she would have to play it. And it was futile to evoke good sense and warn her dazed soul that she must keep her distance from the game and not take it seriously. Just because it was only a game her soul was not afraid, did not oppose the game, and narcotically sank deeper into it.

The young man called the waiter and paid. Then he got up and said to the girl, "We're going."

"Where to?" The girl feigned surprise.

"Don't ask, just come on," said the young man.

"What sort of way is that to talk to me?"

"The way I talk to whores," said the young man.

10

They went up the badly lit staircase. On the landing below the second floor a group of intoxicated men was standing near the rest room. The young man caught hold of the girl from behind so that he was holding her breast with his hand. The men by the rest room saw this and began to call out. The girl wanted to break away, but the young man yelled at her: "Keep still!" The men greeted this with general ribaldry and addressed several dirty remarks to the girl. The young man and the girl reached the second floor. He opened the door of their room and switched on the light.

It was a narrow room with two beds, a small table, a chair, and a washbasin. The young man locked the door and turned to the girl. She was standing facing him in a defiant pose with insolent sensuality in her eyes. He looked at her and tried to discover behind her lascivious expression the familiar features which he loved tenderly. It was as if he were looking at two images through the same lens, at two images superimposed one upon the other with the one showing through the other. These two images showing through each other were telling him that *everything* was in the girl, that her soul was terrifyingly amorphous, that it held faithfulness and unfaithfulness, treachery and innocence, flirtatiousness and chastity. This disorderly jumble seemed disgusting to him, like the variety to be found in a pile of garbage. Both images continued to show through each other and the young man understood that the girl differed only on the surface from other women, but deep down was the same as they: full of all possible thoughts, feelings, and vices, which justified all his secret misgivings and fits of jealousy. The impression that certain outlines delineated her as an individual was only a delusion to which the other person, the one who was looking, was subject— namely himself. It seemed to him that the girl he loved was a creation of his desire, his thoughts, and his faith and that the *real* girl now standing in front of him was hopelessly *alien,* hopelessly *ambiguous.* He hated her.

"What are you waiting for? Strip," he said.

The girl flirtatiously bent her head and said, "Is it necessary?"

The tone in which she said this seemed to him very familiar; it seemed to him that once long ago some other woman had said this to him, only he no longer knew which one. He longed to humiliate her. Not the hitchhiker, but his own girl. The game merged with life. The game of humiliating the hitchhiker became only a pretext for humiliating his girl. The young man had forgotten that he was playing a game. He simply hated the woman standing in front of him. He stared at her and took a fifty-crown bill from his wallet. He offered it to the girl. "Is that enough?"

The girl took the fifty crowns and said: "You don't think I'm worth much."

The young man said: "You aren't worth more."

The girl nestled up against the young man. "You can't get around me like that! You must try a different approach, you must work a little!"

She put her arms around him and moved her mouth toward his. He put his fingers on her mouth and gently pushed her away. He said: "I only kiss women I love."

"And you don't love me?"

"No."

"Whom do you love?"

"What's that got to do with you? Strip!"

11

She had never undressed like this before. The shyness, the feeling of inner panic, the dizziness, all that she had always felt when undressing in front of the young man (and she couldn't hide in the darkness), all this was gone. She was standing in front of him self-confident, insolent, bathed in light, and astonished at where she had all of a sudden discovered the gestures, heretofore unknown to her, of a slow, provocative striptease. She took in his glances, slipping off each piece of clothing with a caressing movement and enjoying each individual stage of this exposure.

But then suddenly she was standing in front of him completely naked and at this moment it flashed through her head that now the whole game would end, that since she had stripped off her clothes, she had also stripped away her dissimulation, and that being naked meant that she was now herself and the young man ought to come up to her now and make a gesture with which he would wipe out everything and after which would follow only their most intimate love-making. So she stood naked in front of the young man and at this moment stopped playing the game. She felt embarrassed and on her face appeared the smile which really belonged to her: a shy and confused smile.

But the young man didn't come to her and didn't end the game. He didn't notice the familiar smile; he saw before him only the beautiful, alien body of his own girl, whom he hated. Hatred cleansed his sensuality of any sentimental coating. She wanted to come to him, but he said: "Stay where you are, I want to have a good look at you." Now he longed only to treat her as a whore. But the young man had never had a whore and the ideas he had about them came from literature and hearsay. So he turned to these ideas and the first thing he recalled was the image of a woman in black underwear (and black stockings) dancing on the shiny top of a piano. In the little hotel room there was no piano, there was only a small table covered with a linen cloth leaning against the wall. He ordered the girl to climb up on it. The girl made a pleading gesture, but the young man said, "You've been paid."

When she saw the look of unshakable obsession in the young man's eyes, she tried to go on with the game, even though she no longer could and no longer knew how. With tears in her eyes she climbed onto the table. The top was scarcely three feet square and one leg was a little bit shorter than the others so that standing on it the girl felt unsteady.

But the young man was pleased with the naked figure, now towering above him, and the girl's shy insecurity merely inflamed his imperiousness. He wanted to see her body in all positions and from all sides, as he imagined other men had seen it and would see it. He was vulgar and lascivious. He used words that she had never heard from him in her life. She wanted to refuse, she wanted to be released from the game. She called him by his first name, but he immediately yelled at her that she had no right to address him so intimately. And so eventually in confusion and on the verge of tears, she obeyed, she bent forward and squatted according to the young man's wishes, saluted, and then wiggled her hips as she did the Twist for him; during a slightly more violent movement, when the cloth slipped beneath her feet and she nearly fell, the young man caught her and dragged her to the bed.

He had intercourse with her. She was glad that at least now finally the unfortunate game would end and they would again be the two people they had been before and would love each other. She wanted to press her mouth against his. But the young man pushed her head away and repeated that he only kissed women he loved. She burst into loud sobs. But she wasn't even allowed to cry, because the young man's furious passion gradually won over her body, which then silenced the complaint of her soul. On the bed there were soon two bodies in perfect harmony, two sensual bodies, alien to each other. This was exactly what the girl had most dreaded all her life and had scrupulously avoided till now: love-making without emotion or love. She knew that she had crossed the forbidden boundary, but she proceeded across it without objections and as a full participant; only somewhere, far off in a corner of her consciousness, did she feel horror at the thought that she had never known such pleasure, never so much pleasure as at this moment—beyond that boundary.

12

Then it was all over. The young man got up off the girl and, reaching out for the long cord hanging over the bed, switched off the light. He didn't want to see the girl's face. He knew that the game was over, but didn't feel like returning to their customary relationship; he feared this return. He lay beside the girl in the dark in such a way that their bodies would not touch.

After a moment he heard her sobbing quietly; the girl's hand diffidently, childishly touched his; it touched, withdrew, then touched again, and then a pleading, sobbing voice broke the silence, calling him by his name and saying, "I am me, I am me . . ."

The young man was silent, he didn't move, and he was aware of the sad emptiness of the girl's assertion, in which the unknown was defined by the same unknown.

And the girl soon passed from sobbing to loud crying and went on endlessly repeating this pitiful tautology: "I am me, I am me, I am me . . ."

The young man began to call compassion to his aid (he had to call it from afar, because it was nowhere near at hand), so as to be able to calm the girl. There were still thirteen days' vacation before them.

Translated by Suzanne Rappaport and revised by Kundera

Questions for Discussion and Writing

1. In what ways would you describe the couple's relationship as the story begins? What were their feelings toward each other? What were their fears about each other? What were their feelings about themselves? Use brief passages from the story to support your responses.

2. What role does each character assume in the hitchhiking game? For what reasons did they become these new personae? What did they discover about their game once it began?

3. In what ways does the setting of Czechoslovakia and the conditions of the couple's lives influence their two-week holiday and the game they are playing? What influence does the idea of responsibility have on them in that game?
4. What discoveries does the man make about the body and the psyche (or spirit)? What discoveries does the woman make in this connection?
5. How would you predict the last thirteen days of their vacation, based on all that has happened in the story? Support your prediction with brief passages from the story.
6. What has the couple gained and lost through the hitchhiking game? Why does the girl keep repeating the "pitiful tautology: 'I am me, I am me, I am me . . .'" (p. 528) near the end of the story? What truths have you gained from the story?

MASSUD FARZAN

The Plane Reservation

*Born in 1936 in Tabriz, Iran, Massud Farzan was educated at Tabriz
University, receiving his undergraduate degree there in 1958. At the
University of Michigan he earned his masters in 1961 and his doctorate in 1964. In the United States, Farzan has been on the faculties
of English departments at several universities; since 1982, he has
been visiting professor of English at Boston University and a teacher
of writing at Harvard University. Between 1973 and the beginning
of the Iranian revolution in 1980, he also taught English and comparative literature at Pahlavi University (now Shiraz University) in
Shiraz, Iran.*

*Farzan has written, edited, and translated a number of books. One
of his books, a collection of his poems and poems in translation,
published by Pahlavi University Press in 1974 (second edition,
1977), is entitled* Kashan to Kalamazoo. *The title reflects with good
humor the two worlds that Farzan has made home, both in his life
and his writing.*

*Most of Farzan's work concerns itself with intercultural dilemmas,
although not by conscious design. "It was one of those stories that
had to be written," Farzan says of "The Plane Reservation," "because
in no other way could I bring the ambivalence to resolution.
Strangely," he explains further, "the process continued beyond the
writing. Soon after the story was published, a number of Iranian
journals printed it in Persian translation. One of those versions got
into the hands of my father who, much to my surprise, was affected
by it in a very positive manner. Whether by coincidence or not,
thereafter the relationship between my father and mother improved
noticeably."*

**Before you read "A Plane Reservation," write about a time in your life
when, upon returning home, you realized that although things were still the**

same there, you were not quite the same. What happened to make you see things differently, and what did you decide to do?

W e lived on 23 Sadness Street. But it was a narrow street—cars couldn't enter—so I asked the cabdriver to drop me on the corner of Sadness and Pomegranate Blossoms. I paid the fare we had settled at the airport, plus a generous tip. The driver asked for more, speaking slowly and with funny gestures. I said no, and why do you speak like that, I am not a foreigner; I am just a Persian like yourself. He became embarrassed and I paid him a little more. He then helped me carry the heavy suitcase as far as 23 Sadness Street.

I knocked the horseshoe knocker that dangled in the afternoon breeze. An old woman opened the door a crack, peeped and immediately ran back into the house. "Khanom, my baksheesh! Mr. Morad come!" I recognized the voice of the old laundress and remembered how I used to eavesdrop her conversations with herself. I passed the dark vestibule, knocked my head on the transom overhead and figured out how much taller I must have gotten since I had last passed under it. The little brick-covered yard, surrounded by four big walls, had been watered for coolness. In front of the yard stood the two little flowerbeds with flowers of many colors and with assorted vegetables. In the middle there was the little pond. A goldfish hung from the water surface, eating bubbles.

My mother rushed through the sitting room window to the yard, her prayer chador safety-pinned under her chin. "My son! Thanks Allah!" She opened her arms. My head down, I saw her shoulders shake. I stood wordless, without tears of happiness. I did not feel happy.

"Have you lost some weight, Morad? You look so different. Come through the window. That's all right, you needn't take off your shoes."

The living room was covered with thick native rugs, from wall to wall. There was no furniture except for a chair in a corner. Against the wall facing the yard and the flowerbeds there were two cushions. In the middle of the room my mother's prayer-spread lay open on the floor.

"You aren't through with your prayer, Mom. Go ahead and finish it first."

"I am going to. But first let me fix you a glass of quince sharbat, it is good for the heart. Why did you sit on the floor? We have put the chair for you."

"I don't need to sit on the chair, Mom. It feels so good to spread my legs on these thick rugs."

"Drink your sharbat, it is good for the heart."

"All right. You go ahead and finish your prayer now."

She stood before her prayer-spread, facing Mecca, and began to move her lips. I noticed that she was saying her prayer slowly and deliberately and that her chador reached the floor, covering her entire feet. I remembered that she didn't used to wear her chador so long. Nor was her rosary so big. Mother must be getting old.

Outside, a man was selling ice. And in a distance a voice called out: THIS EVENING! IT WILL HAPPEN THIS EVENING AT EIGHT!

I sipped the quince sharbat and watched the yard. The flowerbeds were certainly my father's work; carefully cultivated and yet going wild and wayward. So many things in that ten by fifteen feet. Vivid green spotted with flowers red and yellow, pink and blue. Red roses surrounded by lettuce. Little violets at the foot of delpheniums. Petunias everywhere.

Four walls, thick and tall, surrounded the yard, keeping out whatever rays there were left of the setting sun.

A little clay-roofed closet huddled back in the corner, on the other side of the flowerbeds. It was the toilet. It had no stool, no toilet seat. You merely squatted over a funnel-shaped pit, dark and deep. You could keep the door open, if you wished, watching the flowers, the rooftops, and the sky. Nobody to see you except maybe a couple of sparrows or a lone pigeon. I remembered how my father used to sit there, sometimes for half an hour or more. My mother would then go to wash her hands in the pond and call out, "Aren't you going to come out of that toilet?" Or, "Do you know you have been sitting in there for forty minutes?" My father wouldn't say anything. I knew that he didn't want to come out. He liked very much to think or meditate without being disturbed. My mother would make snide remarks whenever she caught him in deep reflection. "Inventing again, eh?" she would say and disturb his thoughts.

My father was an inventor. He had invented many things, although none of them had worked out. With each invention, he thought that he would make lots of money. He never told anybody what he would do once he got rich. But I knew what he would do. He would buy a house with a bigger yard, perhaps a garden, with a big pond; have a lot of goldfish; cultivate a great variety of flowers and vegetables. He would go on pilgrimage to Mecca and give to the poor. He would elicit respect from those he didn't like. He would cease to worry about his future in this world and beyond. But with each invention something would go wrong at the last moment, and he would abandon it only to start inventing something else. That would make my mother bolder and warier. She thought that whenever my father was silent and staring into the blank, he was conceiving a new invention. So she was always on the watch for those moments.

One day my father had come home with a big box under his arms. He had bought a radio. We all rejoiced. Every evening we sat on the rugs and listened. My father seemed to listen more attentively than everyone else. But it did not take long before my mother discovered what he was really doing. I think what gave him away was the faraway look in his eyes and the faint motionless smile on his face. My mother called him a sneak, a hopeless dreamer and other names. My father looked quite embarrassed. From then on he used to spend more time in the toilet at the corner of the yard.

That was many years ago. My mother was getting old; my father must be getting older. Maybe now they understood their common lot and forgave each other's foibles.

Once again the voice outside called out: IT WILL HAPPEN THIS EVE-NING AT EIGHT!

My mother finished her prayer. She carefully folded the prayer-spread and put it away on the shelf by the radio. "Tell me what you'd like to eat and I'll cook it for you. You really look so dark and thin."

I didn't know what to answer. "Am I? Maybe that's because I am now taller than I was when I left."

"As a boy you were so good looking," she went on. "We were all thinking you would come back from America fat and white."

Suddenly it occurred to me that she was blaming me.

"Look at that picture of your brother over your head. See the belly, *mashallah?* Isn't that something? He's married, that's right. Maybe that is the reason. Which reminds me, you haven't gotten married, have you?"

"No, Mom, not yet. As a matter of fact, I may get married here."

"Good, I tell everybody that you are my wisest son. Is that why you came back?"

"Well, not really. To be frank, Mom, I came back in order to see what I can do for, I mean to have a close look at you and Pop and make sure that you are happy together. Now tell me, how are you getting along? How is Pop?"

"Don't worry about him. The bad vessel is seldom broken, as the saying goes."

THIS EVENING. . . .

My mother turned to the door. "He's not inventing anymore, if that's what you mean, but he's taken something else."

I listened.

"He's now buying lottery tickets *every* week. He also writes poetry. He thinks that—"

Just then the door opened and my father came in, holding a full grocery bag under his chin and a melon in the curve of his arm. The melon rolled on the floor; we salaamed and embraced.

"You've kept yourself pretty well," I lied. "You look good, Pop."

"Do I really?" He smiled diffidently and watched my mother from the corner of his eye. "How do you find our little house? I mean next to American houses. Modest, eh?"

"I never saw flowerbeds like this anywhere," I said. My father smiled with mild contentment. "You should've seen it last month, Morad, we had roses as big as sunflowers." He walked to the window and gently threw the melon into the pond to get cool there.

THIS EVENING AT EIGHT! The voice was now very close, loud and clear.

"What does that mean?" I asked.

My father's face lit up. My mother looked at him reproachfully. "He's selling lottery tickets," he finally said. "The draw is this evening at eight." He stole a look at the clock on the radio.

My mother went out to the kitchen. I thought it was time to ask him if he was happy in his job and at home, whether he got along well with Mom. But just then he took his ashtray and cushion and sat beside me. "There is something I wanted to tell you," he began in a low, confidential tone, "I hope you won't mind it. What I wanted to say, Morad, you see, maybe you've forgotten all this time you were abroad, but in this country people look at your appearance and judge you accordingly; as the poet said: Feel the skin of a melon/Before thou purchaseth one. You see, if you were fat and white, if you had a nice double chin and a potbelly, then there wouldn't be any problem and I wouldn't take up your time telling you all this. I mean people would then think that you're rich; you would be respected wherever you went in the country. But unfortunately you and I are the wiry type and rather dark. It would be a blasphemy to complain about it. Allah must have wanted it to be that way and we just can't do anything about it. But there is something we *can* do."

He leaned over and whispered, "Buy yourself a nice new suit and change your necktie. What is that you're wearing? As the poet said: What is in my weary heart/That while I'm quiet, it's in turmoil? Maybe that is not the appropriate poem; there is a better one in Sa'di's *Rose Garden*. I can't remember it now, but it doesn't matter. What I am trying to tell you, Morad, I'm really ashamed to mention it, but the barber on the corner of Pomegranate Street wears a better tie than yours. I always watch him closely when he cuts my hair, he wears genuine Silka tie, I am not lying to you. And his shoes are always polished. I myself can't afford to be very well dressed, but at least I can have a crease in my trousers. I can afford to have a shoeshine once in a while. I'll be darned if I can tell when it was last you got a shoeshine."

His face was quite somber. Apparently he wasn't any more pleased with his returning son than my mother was. Why did they keep asking me to go back? What made them believe that I would return someone other than I was, fatter and whiter than I was, as young as I was ten years ago? One thing was clear—they were disillusioned at the one who had returned. But I didn't resent that at all. If only I could make sure that they got along together, that they were a bit happier than I remembered them to be.

My father put half a cigarette in a cigarette holder. "That's all I wanted to say, Morad. But I am not a narrow-minded old man; you'll of course do whatever you choose. As the poet has said: I advise whatever methinks fit/You either profit by it or resent it."

Just then my mother came, hugging the big copper tray of supper. "What were you whispering to each other?" she asked.

"I was just telling Morad how he would look like a real gentleman if he had his shoes shined."

She said she agreed with him on that. I fetched the melon from the pond.

After supper my mother went to the kitchen to do the dishes. My father took a pencil and a piece of paper. He then turned on the radio. "I have a little lottery ticket. Who knows, Morad, maybe you've brought good luck to our house tonight."

At eight o'clock the radio chimed eight times, followed by a minute of silence. Then the announcer said that the draw procedures were being broadcast live from the Horizon Hall. My father took out his ticket and put it upside down on the floor beside his cigarette case and abacus. He then began to jot down the winning numbers on the sheet of paper.

My mother finished the dishes while the draw was still going on. She came in with a small tray of green beans and sat down to string them. I noticed that she was watching my father from the corner of her eye.

Having written all the winning numbers, my father turned over the ticket and began to check its number against the winning numbers. He started with the top prize and went down. His hand hovered over each number for a second before going to the next. The pencil trembled a little. My mother held a bean and forgot to string it. My eyes raced from him to her and back to him.

Suddenly my father threw the pencil up in the air. "Ten tumans! won ten tumans!" Immediately I made a mental calculation: one dollar and twenty-five cents. My mother was now bending over the tray, stringing rapidly; she didn't want father to see the broad smile that had spread all over her face.

I found myself outside in the yard. The night had fallen. I had to think. I sat over the deep pit. I left the door open. There was a full moon and the crickets sang. I sat there for several minutes, my chin propped in my hand. I wanted to sit more, but I thought that they might wonder where I was and get worried. I went back to the living room. My father was now sitting beside my mother, helping her string the beans; I dropped a bulb into my Agfa and snapped a picture. They smiled. I hurried back to the yard. The goldfish was motionless at the bottom of the pond. The night smelled of petunias. I sat over the pit again. I thought, what a marvelous picture that will be. Stringing beans together in peace and harmony!

In the morning I would get my shoes shined. I would also buy a few fish for the pond and make a plane reservation.

Questions for Discussion and Writing

1. What are the conflicts of this story? In what ways are they generational— the inevitable differences between the lives of parents and their children? In what ways are they cultural—the result of the son living in another country for a long time?
2. Why does the son return to Iran? Why does he leave so soon?
3. What symbols does Farzan use to create the feelings and moods of the son's return, the setting, and the family relationships? How do these symbols create meaning in the story?

N. SCOTT MOMADAY

Grandmother's Country

N. Scott Momaday was born in 1934 in Lawton, Oklahoma, the son of parents who successfully bridged the gulf between Kiowa Indian and white ways, but remained Indian. Momaday has made the same choice himself. As a writer, he uses his mother's language, English, to tell his story in the manner of his father's people, moving freely among legend, myth, and history.

Momaday teaches on the faculty of the Department of English at the University of Arizona in Tucson. He received his bachelor's degree in 1958 from the University of New Mexico, and his masters and doctoral degrees from Stanford University in 1960 and 1963, respectively. In addition to his writing, Momaday is a painter like his mother, and exhibits his work in galleries. He has won numerous awards for his writing, including the Pulitzer Prize for fiction in 1969. He writes novels, nonfiction, books on the Kiowas, and poetry.

The essay that follows, originally published in The Reporter *in 1967, is now the introduction to one of Momaday's most acclaimed books,* The Way to Rainy Mountain *(1969). The book relates the story of the Kiowa Indians' journey three hundred years ago from the Yellowstone down onto the plains. This essay is about Momaday's grandmother, who was present at the last and abortive Kiowa Sun Dance in 1887. For Momaday, she is the last of the Kiowas.*

Before you read "Grandmother's Country," write about a grandparent or another older person who has had a significant influence in your life. What traditions does that person's life represent, and what are some of the moments you remember best about that person?

A single knoll rises out of the plain in Oklahoma, north and west of the Wichita Range. For my people, the Kiowas, it is an old landmark, and they gave it the name Rainy Mountain. The hardest weather in the world is there. Winter brings blizzards, hot tornadic winds arise in the spring, and in summer the prairie is an anvil's edge. The grass turns brittle and brown, and it cracks beneath your feet. There are green belts along the rivers and creeks, linear groves of hickory and pecan, willow and witch hazel. At a distance in July or August the steaming foliage seems almost to writhe in fire. Great green and yellow grasshoppers are everywhere in the tall grass, popping up like corn to sting the flesh, and tortoises crawl about on the red earth, going nowhere in the plenty of time. Loneliness is an aspect of the land. All things in the plain are isolate; there is no confusion of objects in the eye, but *one* hill or *one* tree or *one* man. To look upon that landscape in the early morning, with the sun at your back, is to lose the sense of proportion. Your imagination comes to life, and this, you think, is where Creation was begun.

I returned to Rainy Mountain in July. My grandmother had died in the spring, and I wanted to be at her grave. She had lived to be very old and at last infirm. Her only living daughter was with her when she died, and I was told that in death her face was that of a child.

I like to think of her as a child. When she was born, the Kiowas were living the last great moment of their history. For more than a hundred years they had controlled the open range from the Smoky Hill River to the Red, from the headwaters of the Canadian to the fork of the Arkansas and Cimarron. In alliance with the Comanches, they had ruled the whole of the southern Plains. War was their sacred business, and they were among the finest horsemen the world has ever known. But warfare for the Kiowas was preeminently a matter of disposition rather than of survival, and they never understood the grim, unrelenting advance of the U.S. Cavalry. When at last, divided and ill-provisioned, they were driven onto the Staked Plains in the cold rains of autumn, they fell into panic. In Palo Duro Canyon they abandoned their crucial stores to pillage and had nothing then but their lives. In order to save themselves, they surrendered to the soldiers at Fort Sill and were imprisoned in the old stone corral that now stands as a military museum. My grandmother was spared the humiliation of those high gray walls by eight or ten years, but she must have known from birth the affliction of defeat, the dark brooding of old warriors.

Her name was Aho, and she belonged to the last culture to evolve in North America. Her forebears came down from the high country in western Montana nearly three centuries ago. They were a mountain people, a mysterious tribe of hunters whose language has never been positively classified in any major group. In the late seventeenth century they began a long migration to the south and east. It was a journey toward the dawn, and it led to a golden age. Along the way the Kiowas were befriended by the Crows, who gave them the culture and religion of the Plains. They acquired horses, and their ancient nomadic spirit was suddenly free of the ground. They acquired Tai-me, the sacred Sun Dance doll, from that moment the object and symbol of their worship, and so shared in the divinity of the sun. Not least, they acquired the sense of destiny, therefore courage and pride. When they entered upon the southern Plains they had been transformed. No longer were they slaves to the simple necessity of survival; they were a lordly and dangerous society of fighters and thieves, hunters and priests of the sun. According to their origin myth, they entered the world through a hollow log. From one point of view, their migration was the fruit of an old prophecy, for indeed they emerged from a sunless world.

Although my grandmother lived out her long life in the shadow of Rainy Mountain, the immense landscape of the continental interior lay like memory in her blood. She could tell of the Crows, whom she had never seen, and of the Black Hills, where she had never been. I wanted to see in reality what she had seen more perfectly in the mind's eye, and traveled fifteen hundred miles to begin my pilgrimage.

Yellowstone, it seemed to me, was the top of the world, a region of deep lakes and dark timber, canyons and waterfalls. But, beautiful as it is, one might have the sense of confinement there. The skyline in all directions is close at hand, the high wall of the woods and deep cleavages of shade. There is a perfect freedom in the mountains, but it belongs to the eagle and the elk, the badger and the bear. The Kiowas reckoned their stature by the distance they could see, and they were bent and blind in the wilderness.

Descending eastward, the highland meadows are a stairway to the plain. In July the inland slope of the Rockies is luxuriant with flax and buckwheat, stonecrop and larkspur. The earth unfolds and the limit of the land recedes. Clusters of trees, and animals grazing far in the distance, cause the vision to reach away and wonder to build upon the mind. The sun follows a longer course in the day, and the sky is immense beyond all comparison. The great billowing clouds that sail upon it are shadows that move upon the grain like water, dividing light. Farther down, in the land of the Crows and Blackfeet, the plain is yellow. Sweet clover takes hold of the hills and bends upon itself to cover and seal the soil. There the Kiowas paused on their way; they had come to the place where they must change their lives. The sun is at home on the plains. Precisely there does it have the certain character of a god. When the Kiowas came to the land of the Crows, they could see the dark lees of the hills at dawn across the Bighorn River, the profusion of light on the grain shelves, the oldest deity ranging after the solstices. Not yet would they veer southward to the caldron of the land that lay below; they must wean their blood from the northern winter and hold the mountains a while longer in their view. They bore Tai-me in procession to the east.

A dark mist lay over the Black Hills, and the land was like iron. At the top of a ridge I caught sight of Devil's Tower upthrust against the gray sky as if in the birth of time the core of the earth had broken through its crust and the motion of the world was begun. There are things in nature that engender an awful quiet in the heart of man; Devil's Tower is one of them. Two centuries ago, because they could not do otherwise, the Kiowas made a legend at the base of the rock. My grandmother said:

> Eight children were there at play, seven sisters and their brother. Suddenly the boy was struck dumb; he trembled and began to run upon his hands and feet. His fingers became claws, and his body was covered with fur. Directly there was a bear where the boy had been. The sisters were terrified; they ran,

and the bear after them. They came to the stump of a great tree, and the tree spoke to them. It bade them climb upon it, and as they did so it began to rise into the air. The bear came to kill them, but they were just beyond its reach. It reared against the tree and scored the bark all around with its claws. The seven sisters were borne into the sky, and they became the stars of the Big Dipper.

From that moment, and so long as the legend lives, the Kiowas have kinsmen in the night sky. Whatever they were in the mountains, they could be no more. However tenuous their well-being, however much they had suffered and would suffer again, they had found a way out of the wilderness.

My grandmother had a reverence for the sun, a holy regard that now is all but gone out of mankind. There was a wariness in her, and an ancient awe. She was a Christian in her later years, but she had come a long way about, and she never forgot her birthright. As a child she had been to the Sun Dances; she had taken part in those annual rites, and by them she had learned the restoration of her people in the presence of Tai-me. She was about seven when the last Kiowa Sun Dance was held in 1887 on the Washita River above Rainy Mountain Creek. The buffalo were gone. In order to consummate the ancient sacrifice—to impale the head of a buffalo bull upon the medicine tree—a delegation of old men journeyed into Texas, there to beg and barter for an animal from the Goodnight herd. She was ten when the Kiowas came together for the last time as a living Sun Dance culture. They could find no buffalo; they had to hang an old hide from the sacred tree. Before the dance could begin, a company of soldiers rode out from Fort Sill under orders to disperse the tribe. Forbidden without cause the essential act of their faith, having seen the wild herds slaughtered and left to rot upon the ground, the Kiowas backed away forever from the medicine tree. That was July 20, 1890, at the great bend of the Washita. My grandmother was there. Without bitterness, and for as long as she lived, she bore a vision of deicide.

Now that I can have her only in memory, I see my grandmother in the several postures that were peculiar to her: standing at the wood stove on a winter morning and turning meat in a great iron skillet; sitting at the south window, bent above her beadwork, and afterwards, when her vision failed, looking down for a long time into the fold of her hands; going out upon a cane, very slowly as she did when the weight of age came upon her; praying. I remember her most often at prayer. She made long, rambling prayers out of suffering and hope, having seen many things. I was never sure that I had the right to hear, so exclusive were they of all mere custom and company. The last time I saw her she prayed standing by the side of her bed at night, naked to the waist, the light of a kerosene lamp moving upon her dark skin. Her long, black hair, always drawn and braided in the day, lay upon her shoulders and against her breasts like a shawl. I do not speak Kiowa, and I never understood her prayers, but there was something inherently sad in the sound, some merest hesitation upon the syllables of sorrow. She began in a high and descending pitch, exhausting her breath to silence; then again and again—and always the same intensity of effort, of something that is, and is not, like urgency in the human voice. Transported so in the dancing light among the shadows of her room, she seemed beyond the reach of time. But that was illusion; I think I knew then that I should not see her again.

Houses are like sentinels in the plain, old keepers of the weather watch. There, in a very little while, wood takes on the appearance of great age. All colors wear soon away in the wind and rain, and then the wood is burned gray and the grain appears and the nails turn red with rust. The windowpanes are black and opaque; you imagine there is nothing within, and indeed there are many ghosts, bones given up to the land. They stand here and there against the sky, and you approach them for a longer time than you expect. They belong in the distance; it is their domain.

Once there was a lot of sound in my grandmother's house, a lot of coming and going, feasting and talk. The summers there were full of excitement and reunion. The Kiowas are a summer people; they abide the cold and keep to themselves, but when the season turns and the land becomes warm and vital they cannot hold still; an old love of going returns upon them. The aged visitors who came to my grandmother's house when I was a child were made of lean and leather, and they bore themselves upright. They wore great black hats and bright ample shirts that shook in the wind. They rubbed fat upon their hair and wound their braids with strips of colored cloth. Some of them painted their faces and carried the scars of old and cherished enmities. They were an old council of warlords, come to remind and be reminded of who they were. Their wives and daughters served them well. The women might indulge themselves; gossip was at once the mark and compensation of their servitude. They made loud and elaborate talk among themselves, full of jest and gesture, fright and false alarm. They went abroad in fringed and flowered shawls, bright beadwork and German silver. They were at home in the kitchen, and they prepared meals that were banquets.

There were frequent prayer meetings, and great nocturnal feasts. When I was a child I played with my cousins outside, where the lamplight fell upon the ground and the singing of the old people rose up around us and carried away into the darkness. There were a lot of good things to eat, a lot of laughter and surprise. And afterwards, when the quiet returned, I lay down with my grandmother and could hear the frogs away by the river and feel the motion of the air.

Now there is a funeral silence in the rooms, the endless wake of some final word. The walls have closed in upon my grandmother's house. When I returned to it in mourning, I saw for the first time in my life how small it was. It was late at night, and there was a white moon, nearly full. I sat for a long time on the stone steps by the kitchen door. From there I could see out across the land; I could see the long row of trees by the creek, the low light upon the rolling plains, and the stars of the Big Dipper. Once I looked at the moon and caught sight of a strange thing. A cricket had perched upon the handrail, only a few inches away from me. My line of vision was such that the creature filled the moon like a fossil. It had gone there, I thought, to live and die, for there, of all places, was its small definition made whole and eternal. A warm wind rose up and purled like the longing within me.

The next morning I awoke at dawn and went out on the dirt road to Rainy Mountain. It was already hot, and the grasshoppers began to fill the air. Still, it was early in the morning, and the birds sang out of the shadows. The long yellow grass on the mountain shone in the bright light, and a scissortail hied above the land. There, where it ought to be, at the end of a long and legendary way, was my grandmother's grave. Here and there on the dark stones were ancestral names. Looking back once, I saw the mountain and came away.

Questions for Discussion and Writing

1. Throughout this portrait of his grandmother, Momaday uses images of nature and animals. Describe these images and the kinds of meaning they create in her portrait.
2. What relationships do you discover between the Kiowas' adaptation to new surroundings and their evolving culture?
3. In what ways did myth and story shape the cultural habits and values of the Kiowas? In what ways does Momaday show his grandmother as the last of the Kiowas?
4. What unspoken quest do you think Momaday is making in this return to his grandmother's home? For whom do you think Momaday wrote this essay, and why?

Chapter **8**

DEFINING OURSELVES AND OTHERS

I am an invisible man. No, I am not a spook like those who haunted Edgar Allan Poe; nor am I one of your Hollywood-movie ectoplasms. I am a man of substance, of flesh and bone, fiber and liquids—and I might even be said to possess a mind. I am invisible, understand, simply because people refuse to see me. Like the bodiless heads you see sometimes in circus sideshows, it is as though I have been surrounded by mirrors of hard, distorting glass. When they approach me they see only my surroundings, themselves, or figments of their imagination—indeed, everything and anything except me.

RALPH ELLISION,
INVISIBLE MAN

I have more to live for than what you think I ought to be about.

PROFESSOR DORIS GINN of Jackson State University,
in a lecture to a class on black culture and Ellison's
INVISIBLE MAN

HOW DO WE DEFINE FOR OURSELVES WHAT WE THINK WE OUGHT TO be about? How do we take the measure of another man or woman? How do we consider a people or a culture? How do we accept a world made richer by its variety when we struggle so hard to assert and hold onto what is ours? The essays and stories in this chapter examine these questions and raise new ones.

Physical characteristics provide the easiest way to categorize ourselves and others. Skin color, for example, is obvious and inescapable. In "I'm Black, You're

White, Who's Innocent?" Shelby Steele explores the ways in which blacks and whites struggle for power and definition through issues of race and what he calls "presumed innocence."

We also define people politically, often projecting our biases rather than theirs on them. In the selection by Feng Jicai, political definition by others in the People's Republic of China shatters the lives of "The Tall Woman and Her Short Husband." Political definition can also improve a life—as it does for the man in Richard Rive's "The Bench"—when it appears to strike at the truth.

In "An Image of Africa," Chinua Achebe examines the power of literature to define and measure people—in the case of Africa, a whole continent of people—using Joseph Conrad's *Heart of Darkness* as an example.

Definitions of others, patterned by years and centuries of history, can reduce our understanding to what Norman Mailer calls a scenario in his essay, "A Country, Not a Scenario." His trip to Russia forces him to see that country and its people, ironically, in ways not so different than he sees his own.

Those forces—racial, historical, political, and literary—that define others from the outside may not be as pervasive, however, as the social structures of definition we create within cultures. In Premchand's story "A Coward," we experience the effects of the Indian Hindu caste system on two families' lives—a system that orders the world from birth, conferring privilege and degradation before a human being even learns to say "I am."

In the Egyptian play "Not a Thing Out of Place," Tewfiq al-Hakim helps us to consider who is doing the defining about whom and what we think and believe is sane and insane. Depending on the definer, the answers shock, amuse, confuse, or, sometimes, threaten our destruction.

In the last selection, "Communication in a Global Village," Dean Barnlund emphasizes that the question of understanding and defining ourselves and our neighbors is more than an exercise in trying to figure out who we all are. Intercultural understanding and communication may be our hope of survival as technology reduces the space and distance between people and cultures to a metaphoric village.

SHELBY STEELE

I'm Black, You're White, Who's Innocent?

Born in Chicago in 1946, Shelby Steele grew up with parents deeply involved in the civil rights movement, walking picket lines from the time he can remember. As a young boy, he attended a segregated primary school in Phoenix, Illinois, a black suburb of Chicago, was denied a job at a golf course as caddy, and had to swim in segregated pools. Nevertheless, Steele explains, "I was not angry. This life was all I knew at that time." His legacy from both his parents' and his own experiences has been the pursuit of issues of social justice.

As an undergraduate at Coe College in Cedar Rapids, Iowa, Steele studied political science. He received his masters degree in sociology from Southern Illinois University, and his doctorate in English from the University of Utah. That Ph.D. was the result of Steele's finally realizing what he calls his "predilection—a love of literature. Before that, I had been accepted to law school, visited law school, saw what lawyers did, and saw that it was not interesting."

Since receiving his doctorate in 1974, Steele has taught English at San Jose State University. He sees his work there as an opportunity to "get students to discover and be involved in the vision of a particular writer." He teaches half-time, spending the other half as a writer of both fiction and essays, exploring his own perceptions and visions.

In "I'm Black, You're White, Who's Innocent?" published in 1988 in Harper's Magazine, *Steele explores the relationships among race, power, and innocence.*

Before you read "I'm Black, You're White, Who's Innocent?" write about a situation in your life when, in the middle of an otherwise happy social time, someone (maybe even you) unexpectedly made a controversial or offensive comment that changed the course of the occasion. Describe the comment, why it was offensive, how people responded or didn't respond to it, and the

result of their response or lack response. As you think back on it now, what
is your analysis (or as Steele might call it, the autopsy) of the whole experience?

I t is a warm, windless California evening, and the dying light that covers the
redbrick patio is tinted pale orange by the day's smog. Eight of us, not close
friends, sit in lawn chairs sipping chardonnay. A black engineer and I (we had
never met before) integrate the group. A psychologist is also among us, and her
presence encourages a surprising openness. But not until well after the lovely
twilight dinner has been served, when the sky has turned to deep black and the
drinks have long since changed to scotch, does the subject of race spring awkwardly upon us. Out of nowhere the engineer announces, with a coloring of
accusation in his voice, that it bothers him to send his daughter to a school where
she is one of only three black children. "I didn't realize my ambition to get ahead
would pull me into a world where my daughter would lose touch with her
blackness," he says.

Over the course of the evening we have talked about money, infidelity, past
and present addictions, child abuse, even politics. Intimacies have been revealed,
fears named. But this subject, race, sinks us into one of those shaming silences
where eye contact terrorizes. Our host looks for something in the bottom of his
glass. Two women stare into the black sky as if to locate the Big Dipper and point
it out to us. Finally, the psychologist seems to gather herself for a challenge, but
it is too late. "Oh, I'm sure she'll be just fine," says our hostess, rising from her
chair. When she excuses herself to get the coffee, the two sky gazers offer to help.

With three of us now gone, I am surprised to see the engineer still silently
holding his ground. There is a willfulness in his eyes, an inner pride. He knows
he has said something awkward, but he is determined not to give a damn. His
unwavering eyes intimidate me. At last the host's head snaps erect. He has an
idea. "The hell with coffee," he says. "How about some of the smoothest brandy
you ever tasted?" An idea made exciting by the escape it offers. Gratefully we
follow him back into the house, quickly drink his brandy, and say our good-byes.

An autopsy of this party might read: death induced by an abrupt and lethal
injection of the American race issue. An accurate if superficial assessment. Since
it has been my fate to live a rather integrated life, I have often witnessed sudden
deaths like this. The threat of them, if not the reality, is a part of the texture of
integration. In the late 1960s, when I was just out of college, I took a delin-
quent's delight in playing the engineer's role, and actually developed a small
reputation for playing it well. Those were the days of flagellatory white guilt; it
was such great fun to pinion some professor or housewife or, best of all, a large
group of remorseful whites, with the knowledge of both their racism and their
denial of it. The adolescent impulse to sneer at convention, to startle the middle-
aged with doubt, could be indulged under the guise of racial indignation. And
how could I lose? My victims—earnest liberals for the most part—could no more
crawl out from under my accusations than Joseph K. in Kafka's *Trial* could escape

the amorphous charges brought against him. At this odd moment in history the world was aligned to facilitate my immaturity.

About a year of this was enough: the guilt that follows most cheap thrills caught up to me, and I put myself in check. But the impulse to do it faded more slowly. It was one of those petty talents that is tied to vanity, and when there were ebbs in my self-esteem the impulse to use it would come alive again. In integrated situations I can still feel the faint itch. But then there are many youthful impulses that still itch, and now, just inside the door of mid-life, this one is least precious to me.

In the literature classes I teach, I often see how the presence of whites all but seduces some black students into provocation. When we come to a novel by a black writer, say Toni Morrison, the white students can easily discuss the human motivations of the black characters. But, inevitably, a black student, as if by reflex, will begin to set in relief the various racial problems that are the background of these characters' lives. This student's tone will carry a reprimand: the class is afraid to confront the reality of racism. Classes cannot be allowed to die like dinner parties, however. My latest strategy is to thank that student for his or her moral vigilance, and then appoint the young man or woman as the class's official racism monitor. But even if I get a laugh—I usually do, but sometimes the student is particularly indignant, and it gets uncomfortable—the strategy never quite works. Our racial division is suddenly drawn in neon. Overcaution spreads like spilled paint. And, in fact, the black student who started it all does become a kind of monitor. The very presence of this student imposes a new accountability on the class.

I think those who provoke this sort of awkwardness are operating out of a black identity that obliges them to badger white people about race almost on principle. Content hardly matters. (For example, it made no sense for the engineer to expect white people to sympathize with his anguish over sending his daughter to school with *white* children.) Race indeed remains a source of white shame; the goal of these provocations is to put whites, no matter how indirectly, in touch with this collective guilt. In other words, these provocations I speak of are *power* moves, little shows of power that try to freeze the "enemy" in self-consciousness. They gratify and inflate the provocateur. They are the underdog's bite. And whites, far more secure in their power, respond with a self-contained and tolerant silence that is, itself, a show of power. What greater power than that of non-response, the power to let a small enemy sizzle in his own juices, to even feel a little sad at his frustration just as one is also complimented by it. Black anger always, in a way, flatters white power. In America, to know that one is not black is to feel an extra grace, a little boost of impunity.

I think the real trouble between the races in America is that the races are not just races but competing power groups—a fact that is easily minimized perhaps because it is so obvious. What is not so obvious is that this is true quite apart from the issue of class. Even the well-situated middle-class (or wealthy) black is never completely immune to that peculiar contest of power that his skin color subjects him to. Race is a separate reality in American society, an entity that carries its own potential for power, a mark of fate that class can soften considerably but not eradicate.

The distinction of race has always been used in American life to sanction each race's pursuit of power in relation to the other. The allure of race as a human delineation is the very shallowness of the delineation it makes. Onto this shallowness—mere skin and hair—men can project a false depth, a system of dismal attributions, a series of malevolent or ignoble stereotypes that skin and hair lack the substance to contradict. These dark projections then rationalize the pursuit of power. Your difference from me makes you bad, and your badness justifies, even demands, my pursuit of power over you—the oldest formula for aggression known to man. Whenever much importance is given to race, power is the primary motive.

But the human animal almost never pursues power without first convincing himself that he is *entitled* to it. And this feeling of entitlement has its own precondition: to be entitled one must first believe in one's innocence, at least in the area where one wishes to be entitled. By innocence I mean a feeling of essential goodness in relation to others and, therefore, superiority to others. Our innocence always inflates us and deflates those we seek power over. Once inflated we are entitled; we are in fact licensed to go after the power our innocence tells us we deserve. In this sense, *innocence is power*. Of course, innocence need not be genuine or real in any objective sense, as the Nazis demonstrated not long ago. Its only test is whether or not we can convince ourselves of it.

I think the racial struggle in America has always been primarily a struggle for innocence. White racism from the beginning has been a claim of white innocence and, therefore, of white entitlement to subjugate blacks. And in the '60s, as went innocence so went power. Blacks used the innocence that grew out of their long subjugation to seize more power, while whites lost some of their innocence and so lost a degree of power over blacks. Both races instinctively understand that to lose innocence is to lose power (in relation to each other). Now to be innocent someone else must be guilty, a natural law that leads the races to forge their innocence on each other's backs. The inferiority of the black always makes the white man superior; the evil might of whites makes blacks good. This pattern means that both races have a hidden investment in racism and racial disharmony, despite their good intentions to the contrary. Power defines their relations, and power requires innocence, which, in turn, requires racism and racial division.

I believe it was this hidden investment that the engineer was protecting when he made his remark—the white "evil" he saw in a white school "depriving" his daughter of her black heritage confirmed his innocence. Only the logic of power explained this—he bent reality to show that he was once again a victim of the white world and, as a victim, innocent. His determined eyes insisted on this. And the whites, in their silence, no doubt protected their innocence by seeing him as an ungracious troublemaker—his bad behavior underscoring their goodness.

I can only guess how he was talked about after the party. But it isn't hard to imagine that his blunder gave everyone a lift. What none of us saw was the underlying game of power and innocence we were trapped in, or how much we needed a racial impasse to play that game.

When I was a boy of about twelve, a white friend of mine told me one day that his uncle, who would be arriving the next day for a visit, was a racist. Excited by the prospect of seeing such a man, I spent the following afternoon hanging around the alley behind my friend's house, watching from a distance as this uncle worked on the engine of his Buick. Yes, here was evil and I was compelled to look upon it. And I saw evil in the sharp angle of his elbow as he pumped his wrench to tighten nuts, I saw it in the blade-sharp crease of his chinos, in the pack of Lucky Strikes that threatened to slip from his shirt pocket as he bent, and in the way his concentration seemed to shut out the human world. He worked neatly and efficiently, wiping his hands constantly, and I decided that evil worked like this.

I felt a compulsion to have this man look upon me so that I could see evil—so that I could see the face of it. But when he noticed me standing beside his toolbox, he said only, "If you're looking for Bobby, I think he went up to the school to play baseball." He smiled nicely and went back to work. I was stunned for a moment, but then I realized that evil could be sly as well, could smile when it wanted to trick you.

Need, especially hidden need, puts a strong pressure on perception, and my need to have this man embody white evil was stronger than any contravening evidence. As a black person you always hear about racists but never meet any. And I needed to incarnate this odious category of humanity, those people who hated Martin Luther King Jr. and thought blacks should "go slow" or not at all. So, in my mental dictionary, behind the term "white racist," I inserted this man's likeness. I would think of him and say to myself, "There is no reason for him to hate black people. Only evil explains unmotivated hatred." And this thought soothed me; I felt innocent. If I hated white people, which I did not, at least I had a reason. His evil commanded me to assert in the world the goodness he made me confident of in myself.

In looking at this man I was *seeing for innocence*—a form of seeing that has more to do with one's hidden need for innocence (and power) than with the person or group one is looking at. It is quite possible, for example, that the man I saw that day was not a racist. He did absolutely nothing in my presence to indicate that he was. I invested an entire afternoon in seeing not the man but in seeing my innocence through the man. *Seeing for innocence* is, in this way, the essence of racism—the use of others as a means to our own goodness and superiority.

The loss of innocence has alwys to do with guilt, Kierkegaard tells us, and it has never been easy for whites to avoid guilt where blacks are concerned. For whites, *seeing for innocence* means seeing themselves and blacks in ways that minimize white guilt. Often this amounts to a kind of white revisionism, as when President Reagan declares himself "color-blind" in matters of race. The President, like many of us, may aspire to racial color blindness, but few would grant that he has yet reached this sublimely guiltless state. The statement clearly revises reality, moves it forward into some heretofore unknown America where all racial determinism will have vanished. I do not think that Ronald Reagan is a racist, as that term is commonly used, but neither do I think that he is capable of seeing color without making attributions, some of which may be negative—nor am I, or anyone else I've ever met.

So why make such a statement? I think Reagan's claim of color blindness with regard to race is really a claim of racial innocence and guiltlessness—the preconditions for entitlement and power. This was the claim that grounded Reagan's campaign against special entitlement programs—affirmative action, racial quotas, and so on—that black power had won in the '60s. Color blindness was a strategic assumption of innocence that licensed Reagan's use of government power against black power.

I do not object to Reagan's goals in this so much as the presumption of innocence by which he rationalized them. I, too, am strained to defend racial quotas and any affirmative action that supersedes merit. And I believe there is much that Reagan has to offer blacks. His emphasis on traditional American values—individual initiative, self-sufficiency, strong families—offers what I think is the most enduring solution to the demoralization and poverty that continue to widen the gap between blacks and whites in America. Even his de-emphasis of race is reasonable in a society where race only divides. But Reagan's posture of innocence undermines any beneficial interaction he might have with blacks. For blacks instinctively sense that a claim of racial innocence always precedes a power move against them. Reagan's pretense of innocence makes him an adversary, and makes his quite reasonable message seem vindictive. You cannot be innocent of a man's problem and expect him to listen.

I'm convinced that the secret of Reagan's "teflon" coating, his personal popularity apart from his policies and actions, has been his ability to offer mainstream America a vision of itself as innocent and entitled (unlike Jimmy Carter, who seemed to offer only guilt and obligation). Probably his most far-reaching accomplishment has been to reverse somewhat the pattern by which innocence came to be distributed in the '60s, when outsiders were innocent and insiders were guilty. Corporations, the middle class, entrepreneurs, the military—all villains in the '60s—either took on a new innocence in Reagan's vision or were designated as protectors of innocence. But again, for one man to be innocent another man must be bad or guilty. Innocence imposes, *demands,* division and conflict, a right/wrong view of the world. And this, I feel, has led to the underside of Reagan's achievement. His posture of innocence draws him into a partisanship that undermines the universality of his values. He can't sell these values to blacks and others because he has made blacks into the bad guys and outsiders who justify his power. It is humiliating for a black person to like Reagan because Reagan's power is so clearly derived from a distribution of innocence that leaves a black with less of it, and the white man with more.

Black Americans have always had to find a way to handle white society's presumption of racial innocence whenever they have sought to enter the American mainstream. Louis Armstrong's exaggerated smile honored the presumed innocence of white society—I will not bring you your racial guilt if you will let me play my music. Ralph Ellison calls this "masking"; I call it bargaining. But whatever it's called, it points to the power of white society to enforce its innocence. I believe this power is greatly diminished today. Society has reformed and transformed—Miles Davis never smiles. Nevertheless, this power has not faded altogether; blacks must still contend with it.

Historically, blacks have handled white society's presumption of innocence in two ways: they have bargained with it, granting white society its innocence in exchange for entry into the mainstream; or they have challenged it, holding that innocence hostage until their demand for entry (or other concessions) was met. A bargainer says, *I already believe you are innocent (good, fair-minded) and have faith that you will prove it.* A challenger says, *If you are innocent, then prove it.* Bargainers *give* in hope of receiving; challengers *withhold* until they receive. Of course, there is risk in both approaches, but in each case the black is negotiating his own self-interest against the presumed racial innocence of the larger society.

Clearly the most visible black bargainer on the American scene today is Bill Cosby. His television show is a perfect formula for black bargaining in the '80s. The remarkable Huxtable family—with its doctor/lawyer parent combination, its drug-free, college-bound children, and its wise yet youthful grandparents—is a blackface version of the American dream. Cosby is a subscriber to the American identity, and his subscription confirms his belief in its fair-mindedness. His vast audience knows this, knows that Cosby will never assault their innocence with racial guilt. Racial controversy is all but banished from the show. The Huxtable family never discusses affirmative action.

The bargain Cosby offers his white viewers—I will confirm your racial innocence if you accept me—is a good deal for all concerned. Not only does it allow whites to enjoy Cosby's humor with no loss of innocence, but it actually enhances their innocence by implying that race is not the serious problem for blacks that it once was. If anything, the success of this handsome, affluent black family points to the fair-mindedness of whites who, out of their essential goodness, changed society so that black families like the Huxtables could succeed. Whites can watch *The Cosby Show* and feel complimented on a job well done.

The power that black bargainers wield is the power of absolution. On Thursday nights, Cosby, like a priest, absolves his white viewers, forgives and forgets the sins of the past. (Interestingly, Cosby was one of the first blacks last winter to publicly absolve Jimmy the Greek for his well-publicized faux pas about black athletes.) And for this he is rewarded with an almost sacrosanct status. Cosby benefits from what might be called a gratitude factor. His continued number-one rating may have something to do with the (white) public's gratitude at being offered a commodity so rare in our time; he tells his white viewers each week that they are okay, and that this black man is not going to challenge them.

When a black bargains, he may invoke the gratitude factor and find himself cherished beyond the measure of his achievement; when he challenges, he may draw the dark projections of whites and become a source of irritation to them. If he moves back and forth between these two options, as I think many blacks do today, he will likely baffle whites. It is difficult for whites to either accept or reject such blacks. It seems to me that Jesse Jackson is such a figure—many whites see Jackson as a challenger by instinct and a bargainer by political ambition. They are uneasy with him, more than a little suspicious. His powerful speech at the 1984 Democratic convention was a masterpiece of bargaining. In it he offered a Kinglike vision of what America could be, a vision that presupposed Americans had the fair-mindedness to achieve full equality—an offer in hope of a return. A few days after this speech, looking for rest and privacy at a lodge in Big Sur, he and his wife were greeted with standing ovations three times a day when they entered the dining room for meals. So much about Jackson is deeply American— his underdog striving, his irrepressible faith in himself, the daring of his ambition, and even his stubbornness. These qualities point to his underlying faith that Americans can respond to him despite his race, and this faith is a compliment to Americans, an offer of innocence.

But Jackson does not always stick to the terms of his bargain—he is not like Cosby on TV. When he hugs Arafat, smokes cigars with Castro, refuses to repudiate Farrakhan, threatens a boycott of major league baseball, or, more recently, talks of "corporate barracudas," "pension-fund socialism," and "economic violence," he looks like a challenger in bargainer's clothing, and his positions on the issues look like familiar protests dressed in white-paper formality. At these times he appears to be revoking the innocence so much else about him seems to offer. The old activist seems to come out of hiding once again to take white innocence hostage until whites prove they deserve to have it. In his candidacy there is a suggestion of protest, a fierce insistence on his *right* to run, that sends whites a message that he may secretly see them as a good bit less than innocent. His dilemma is to appear the bargainer while his campaign itself seems to be a challenge.

There are, of course, other problems that hamper Jackson's bid for the Democratic presidential nomination. He has held no elective office, he is thought too flamboyant and opportunistic by many, there are rather loud whispers of "character" problems. As an individual he may not be the best test of a black man's chances for winning so high an office. Still, I believe it is the aura of challenge surrounding him that hurts him most. Whether it is right or wrong, fair or unfair, I think no black candidate will have a serious chance at his party's nomination, much less the presidency, until he can convince white Americans that he can be trusted to preserve *their* sense of racial innocence. Such a candidate will have to use his power of absolution; he will have to flatly forgive and forget. He will have to bargain with white innocence out of a genuine belief that it really exists. There can be no faking it. He will have to offer a vision that is passionately raceless, a vision that strongly condemns any form of racial politics. This will require the most courageous kind of leadership, leadership that asks all the people to meet a new standard.

Now the other side of America's racial impasse: How do blacks lay claim to their racial innocence?

The most obvious and unarguable source of black innocence is the victimization that blacks endured for centuries at the hands of a race that insisted on black inferiority as a means to its own innocence and power. Like all victims, what blacks lost in power they gained in innocence—innocence that, in turn, entitled them to pursue power. This was the innocence that fueled the civil rights movement of the '60s, and that gave blacks their first real power in American life—victimization metamorphosed into power via innocence. But this formula carries a drawback that I believe is virtually as devastating to blacks today as victimization once was. It is a formula that binds the victim to his victimization by linking his power to his status as a victim. And this, I'm convinced, is the tragedy of black power in America today. It is primarily a victim's power, grounded too deeply in the entitlement derived from past injustice and in the innocence that Western/ Christian tradition has always associated with poverty.

Whatever gains this power brings in the short run through political action, it undermines in the long run. Social victims may be collectively entitled, but they are all too often individually demoralized. Since the social victim has been oppressed by society, he comes to feel that his individual life will be improved more by changes *in* society than by his own initiative. Without realizing it, he makes society rather than himself the agent of change. The power he finds in his victimization may lead him to collective action against society, but it also encourages passivity within the sphere of his personal life.

This past summer I saw a television documentary that examined life in Detroit's inner city on the twentieth anniversary of the riots there in which forty-three people were killed. A comparison of the inner city then and now showed a decline in the quality of life. Residents feel less safe than they did twenty years ago, drug trafficking is far worse, crimes by blacks against blacks are more frequent, housing remains substandard, and the teenage pregnancy rate has skyrocketed. Twenty years of decline and demoralization, even as opportunities for blacks to better themselves have increased. This paradox is not peculiar to Detroit. By many measures, the majority of blacks—those not yet in the middle class—are further behind whites today than before the victories of the civil rights movement. But there is a reluctance among blacks to examine this paradox, I think, because it suggests that racial victimization is not our real problem. If conditions have worsened for most of us as racism has receded, then much of the problem must be of our own making. But to fully admit this would cause us to lose the innocence we derive from our victimization. And we would jeopardize the entitlement we've always had to challenge society. We are in the odd and self-defeating position where taking responsibility for bettering ourselves feels like a surrender to white power.

So we have a hidden investment in victimization and poverty. These distressing conditions have been the source of our only real power, and there is an unconscious sort of gravitation toward them, a complaining celebration of them. One sees evidence of this in the near happiness with which certain black leaders recount the horror of Howard Beach and other recent (and I think over-celebrated) instances of racial tension. As one is saddened by these tragic events, one is also repelled at the way some black leaders—agitated to near hysteria by the scent of victim-power inherent in them—leap forward to exploit them as evidence of black innocence and white guilt. It is as though they sense the decline of black victimization as a loss of standing and dive into the middle of these incidents as if they were reservoirs of pure black innocence swollen with potential power.

Seeing for innocence pressures blacks to focus on racism and to neglect the individual initiative that would deliver them from poverty—the only thing that finally delivers anyone from poverty. With our eyes on innocence we see racism everywhere and miss opportunity even as we stumble over it. About 70 percent of black students at my university drop out before graduating—a flight from opportunity that racism cannot explain. It is an injustice that whites can *see for innocence* with more impunity than blacks can. The price whites pay is a certain blindness to themselves. Moreover, for whites *seeing for innocence* continues to engender the bad faith of a long-disgruntled minority. But the price blacks pay is an ever-escalating poverty that threatens to make the worst off of them a permanent underclass. Not fair, but real.

Challenging works best for the collective, while bargaining is more the individual's suit. From this point on, the race's advancement will come from the efforts of its individuals. True, some challenging will be necessary for a long time to come. But bargaining is now—today—a way for the black individual to *join* the larger society, to make a place for himself or herself.

"Innocence is ignorance," Kierkegaard says, and if this is so, the claim of innocence amounts to an insistence on ignorance, a refusal to know. In their assertions of innocence both races carve out very functional areas of ignorance for themselves—territories of blindness that license a misguided pursuit of power. Whites gain superiority by *not* knowing blacks; blacks gain entitlement by *not* seeing their own responsibility for bettering themselves. The power each race seeks in relation to the other is grounded in a double-edged ignorance, ignorance of the self as well as the other.

The original sin that brought us to an impasse at the dinner party I mentioned at the outset occurred centuries ago, when it was first decided to exploit racial difference as a means to power. It was the determinism that flowed karmically from this sin that dropped over us like a net that night. What bothered me most was our helplessness. Even the engineer did not know how to go forward. His challenge hadn't worked, and he'd lost the option to bargain. The marriage of race and power depersonalized us, changed us from eight people to six whites and two blacks. The easiest thing was to let silence blanket our situation, our impasse.

I think the civil rights movement in its early and middle years offered the best way out of America's racial impasse: in this society, race must not be a source of advantage or disadvantage for anyone. This is fundamentally a *moral* position, one that seeks to breach the corrupt union of race and power with principles of fairness and human equality: if all men are created equal, then racial difference cannot sanction power. The civil rights movement was conceived for no other reason than to redress that corrupt union, and its guiding insight was that only a moral power based on enduring principles of justice, equality, and freedom could offset the lower impulse in man to exploit race as a means to power. Three hundred years of suffering had driven the point home, and in Montgomery, Little Rock, and Selma, racial power was the enemy and moral power the weapon.

An important difference between genuine and presumed innocence, I believe, is that the former must be earned through sacrifice, while the latter is unearned and only veils the quest for privilege. And there was much sacrifice in the early civil rights movement. The Gandhian principle of non-violent resistance that gave the movement a spiritual center as well as a method of protest demanded sacrifice, a passive offering of the self in the name of justice. A price was paid in terror and lost life, and from this sacrifice came a hard-earned innocence and a credible moral power.

Non-violent passive resistance is a bargainer's strategy. It assumes the power that is the object of the protest has the genuine innocence to morally respond, and puts the protesters at the mercy of that innocence. I think this movement won so many concessions precisely because of its belief in the capacity of whites to be moral. It did not so much demand that whites change as offer them relentlessly the opportunity to live by their own morality—to attain a true innocence based on the sacrifice of their racial privilege, rather than a false innocence based on presumed racial superiority. Blacks always bargain with or challenge the larger society; but I believe that in the early civil rights years, these forms of negotiation achieved a degree of integrity and genuineness never seen before or since.

In the mid-'60s all this changed. Suddenly a sharp *racial* consciousness emerged to compete with the moral consciousness that had defined the movement to that point. Whites were no longer welcome in the movement, and a vocal "black power" minority gained dramatic visibility. Increasingly, the movement began to seek racial as well as moral power, and thus it fell into a fundamental contradiction that plagues it to this day. Moral power precludes racial power by denouncing race as a means to power. Now suddenly the movement itself was using race as a means to power, and thereby affirming the very union of race and power it was born to redress. In the end, black power can claim no higher moral standing than white power.

It makes no sense to say this shouldn't have happened. The sacrifices that moral power demands are difficult to sustain, and it was inevitable that blacks would tire of these sacrifices and seek a more earthly power. Nevertheless, a loss of genuine innocence and moral power followed. The movement, splintered by a burst of racial militancy in the late '60s, lost its hold on the American conscience and descended more and more to the level of secular, interest-group politics. Bargaining and challenging once again became racial rather than moral negotiations.

You hear it asked, why are there no Martin Luther Kings around today? I think one reason is that there are no black leaders willing to resist the seductions of racial power, or to make the sacrifices moral power requires. King understood that racial power subverts moral power, and he pushed the principles of fairness and equality rather than black power because he believed those principles would bring blacks their most complete liberation. He sacrificed race for morality, and his innocence was made genuine by that sacrifice. What made King the most powerful and extraordinary black leader of this century was not his race but his morality.

Black power is a challenge. It grants whites no innocence; it denies their moral capacity and then demands that they be moral. No power can long insist on itself without evoking an opposing power. Doesn't an insistence on black power call up white power? (And could this have something to do with what many are now calling a resurgence of white racism?) I believe that what divided the races at the dinner party I attended, and what divides them in the nation, can only be bridged by an adherence to those moral principles that disallow race as a source of power, privilege, status, or entitlement of any kind. In our age, principles like fairness and equality are ill-defined and all but drowned in relativity. But this is the fault of people, not principles. We keep them muddied because they are the greatest threat to our presumed innocence and our selective ignorance. Moral principles, even when somewhat ambiguous, have the power to assign responsibility and therefore to provide us with knowledge. At the dinner party we were afraid of so severe an accountability.

What both black and white Americans fear are the sacrifices and risks that true racial harmony demands. This fear is the measure of our racial chasm. And though fear always seeks a thousand justifications, none is ever good enough, and the problems we run from only remain to haunt us. It would be right to suggest courage as an antidote to fear, but the glory of the word might only intimidate us into more fear. I prefer the word effort—relentless effort, moral effort. What I like most about this word are its connotations of everydayness, earnestness, and practical sacrifice. No matter how badly it might have gone for us that warm summer night, we should have talked. We should have made the effort.

Questions for Discussion and Writing

1. Steele establishes a relationship among issues of race, power, and innocence in his essay. What are the major ideas he suggests about that relationship? In whay ways does this relationship explain the results of the black engineer's comment at the party?

2. Define what Steele means by the word *innocence* and the phrase *seeing for innocence* in his essay. In what ways and for what reasons do blacks understand that they are innocent? In what ways do whites understand that they are innocent? What price does each racial group pay for its own presumed innocence?

3. In telling the story of his friend's racist uncle, Steele writes: "Need, especially hidden need, puts a strong pressure on perception" (p. 549). What does the author mean by this assertion? In what ways does he illustrate its implications and truth throughout the essay?

4. Steele explores the significance of blacks involved in both bargainer and challenger roles. What are the major characteristics of each role, and what are its major strengths and weaknesses? What examples does the author use to illustrate the differences between bargaining and challenging?

5. What distinctions does Steele make between genuine and presumed innocence near the end of the essay? What distinctions does he make between racial power and moral power? How might these distinctions help us to define the problems of race differently?

6. How would Steele answer this question: In what ways is race a dangerous basis for defining or seeing a person? How would you answer that question, based on your reading and your own ideas?

FENG JICAI

The Tall Woman and Her Short Husband

Born in 1942 in Tianjin, Feng Jicai is one of China's best-known writers. His career as a writer evolved after he was injured as an athlete. Following that injury, the Chinese government transferred Jicai to work in the Chinese Traditional Painting Press in Tianjin, where he began to paint and write. In 1974, he was appointed to teach Chinese traditional painting at the Tianjin Workers' College of Decorative Art, and continued to write in his spare time. Four years later, he became a professional, full-time writer.

Since 1976, Jicai has published several novels, novellas, and short stories. "The Tall Woman and Her Short Husband" gives us glimpses into one family's life following the Cultural Revolution in China (1966–1976), when the country was torn apart by the rampaging Red Guards in the name of rejecting all Western influence and Chinese "capitalists." The tailor's wife, described in the story as the "neighborhood activist," is a holdover from the cruel controls of those years, when such people were given legal status to make decisions concerning the lives of those in their immediate neighborhoods.

Before you read "The Tall Woman and Her Short Husband," write about a time in your life when you experienced or observed a group's rejection of the behavior of another person based on the group's perceptions or force of habit, which turned out to be invalid, perhaps even cruel. Describe who was involved, the circumstances, and what happened to the victims. What has the experience taught you?

S ay you have a small tree in your yard and are used to its smooth trunk. If one day it turns twisted and gnarled it strikes you as awkward. As time goes by, however, you grow to like it, as if that was how this tree should always have been. Were it suddenly to straighten out again you would feel indescribably put out. A trunk as dull and boring as a stick! In fact it would simply have reverted to its original form, so why should you worry?

Is this force of habit? Well, don't underestimate "habit." It runs through everything done under the sun. It is not a law to be strictly observed, yet flouting it is simply asking for trouble. Don't complain though if it proves so binding that sometimes, unconsciously, you conform to it. For instance, do you presume to throw your weight about before your superiors? Do you air your views recklessly in front of your seniors? When a group photograph is taken, can you shove celebrities aside to stand swaggering and chortling in the middle? You can't, of course you can't. Or again, would you choose a wife ten years older than you, heftier than you or a head taller than you? Don't be in a rush to answer. Here's an instance of such a couple.

2

She was seventeen centimetres taller than he.

One point seven five metres in height, she towered above most of her sex like a crane over chickens. Her husband, a bare 1.58 metres, had been nicknamed Shorty at college. He came up to her ear-lobes but actually looked two heads shorter.

And take their appearances. She seemed dried up and scrawny with a face like an unvarnished pingpong bat. Her features would pass, but they were small and insignificant as if carved in shallow relief. She was flat-chested, had a ramrod back and buttocks as scraggy as a scrubbing-board. Her husband on the other hand seemed a rubber rolypoly: well-fleshed, solid and radiant. Everything about him—his calves, insteps, lips, nose and fingers—were like pudgy little meatballs. He had a soft skin and a fine complexion shining with excess fat and ruddy because of all the red blood in his veins. His eyes were like two high-voltage little light bulbs, while his wife's were like glazed marbles. The two of them just did not match, formed a marked contrast. But they were inseparable.

One day some of their neighbours were having a family reunion. After drinking his fill the grandfather put a tall, thin empty wine bottle on the table next to a squat tin of pork.

"Who do these remind you of?" he asked. Before anyone could guess he gave the answer, "That tall woman downstairs and that short husband of hers."

Everyone burst out laughing. Went on laughing all through the meal.

What had brought such a pair together?

This was a mystery to the dozens of households living in Unity Mansions. Ever since this couple moved in, the old residents had eyed them curiously. Some registered a question-mark in their minds, others put their curiosity into words. Tongues started wagging. Especially in wet weather, when the two of them went out and it was always Mrs. Tall who held the umbrella. If anything dropped to the ground, though, it was simple for Mr. Short to pick it up. Some old ladies at a loose end would gesticulate, finding this comic, or splutter with laughter. This set a bad example for the children who would burst out laughing at sight of the pair and hoot, "Long carrying-pole; big, low stool!" Husband and wife pretended not to hear and kept their tempers, paying no attention. But maybe for this reason their relations with their neighbours remained rather cool. The few less officious ones simply nodded a greeting when they met. This made it hard for those really intrigued by them to find out more about them. For instance, how did they hit it off? Why had they married? Which gave way to the other? They could only speculate.

This was an old-fashioned block of flats with large sunny rooms and wide, dark corridors. It stood in a big courtyard with a small gatehouse. The man who lived there was a tailor, a decent fellow. His wife, who brimmed over with energy, liked to call on her neighbours and gossip. Most of all she liked to ferret out their secrets. She knew exactly how husbands and wives got on, why sisters-in-law quarrelled, who was lazy, who hard-working, and how much everyone earned. If she was unclear about anything she would leave no stone unturned to get at the truth. The thirst for knowledge makes even the ignorant wise. And in this respect she was outstanding. She analyzed conversations, watched expressions, and could even tell what people were secretly thinking. Simply by using her nose, she knew which household was eating meat or fish, and from that could deduce their income. For some reason or other, ever since the sixties each housing estate had chosen someone like this as a "neighbourhood activist," giving legal status to these nosey-parkers so that their officiousness could have full play. It seems the Creator will never waste any talent.

Though the tailor's wife was indefatigable she failed to discover how this incongruous couple who passed daily before her eyes had come to marry. She found this most frustrating; it posed a formidable challenge. On the base of her experience, however, by racking her brains she finally came up with a plausible explanation: either husband or wife must have some physiological deficiency. Otherwise no one would marry someone a whole head taller or shorter. Her grounds for this reasoning were that after three years of marriage they still had no children. The inmates of Unity Mansions were all convinced by this brilliant hypothesis.

But facts are merciless. The tailor's wife was debunked and lost face when Mrs. Tall appeared in the family way. Her womb could be seen swelling from day to day, for being relatively far from the ground it was all too evident. Regardless of their amazement, misgivings or embarrassment, she gave birth to a fine baby. When the sun was hot or it rained and the couple went out, Mrs. Tall would carry the baby while the holding of the umbrella devolved on Mr. Short. He plodded along comically on his plump legs, the umbrella held high, keeping just behind his wife. And the neighbours remained as intrigued as at the start by this ill-assorted, inseparable couple. They went on making plausible conjectures, but could find no confirmation for any of them.

The tailor's wife said, "They must have something to hide, those two. Why else should they keep to themselves? Well, it's bound to come to light some day, just wait and see."

One evening, sure enough, she heard the sound of smashing from their flat. On the pretext of collecting the money for sweeping the yard she rushed to knock on their door, sure that their long hidden feud had come to a head and avid to watch the confrontation between them. The door opened. Mrs. Tall asked her in with a smile. Mr. Short was smiling too at a smashed plate on the floor—that was all the tailor's wife saw. She hastily collected the money and left to puzzle over what had happened. A plate smashed, yet instead of quarrelling they had treated it as a joke. How very strange!

Later the tailor's wife became the residents' representative for Unity Mansions. When she helped the police check up on living permits, she at last found the answer to this puzzle. A reliable and irrefutable answer. The tall woman and her short husband both worked in the Research Institute of the Ministry of Chemical Industry. He as chief engineer, with a salary of over 180 yuan! She as an ordinary laboratory technician earning less than sixty yuan; and her father was a hard-working low-paid postman. So that explained why she had married a man so much shorter. For status, money and an easy life. Right! The tailor's wife lost no time in passing on this priceless information to all the bored old ladies in Unity Mansions. Judging others by themselves, they believed her. At last this riddle was solved. They saw the light. Rich Mr. Short was congenitally deficient; poor Mrs. Tall, a money-grabber on the make. When they discussed the good luck of this tall woman who looked so like a horse, they often voiced resentment—especially the tailor's wife.

3

Sometimes good luck turns into bad.

In 1966, disaster struck China. Great changes came into the lives of all the residents in Unity Mansions, which was like a microcosm of the whole country. Mr. Short as chief engineer was the first to suffer. His flat was raided, his furniture moved out, he was struggled against and confined in his institute. And worse was to come. He was accused of smuggling out the results of his researches to write up at home in the evenings, with a view to fleeing the country to join a wealthy relative abroad. This preposterous charge of passing on scientific secrets to foreign capitalists was widely believed. For in that period of lunacy people took leave of their senses and cruelly made up groundless accusations in order to find some Hitler in their midst. The institute kept a stranglehold on its chief engineer. He was threatened, beaten up, put under all kinds of pressure; and his wife was ordered to hand over that manuscript which no one had ever seen. But to no effect. Then someone proposed holding a struggle meeting against them both in the courtyard of Unity Mansions. As everyone dreads losing face in front of relatives and friends, this would put more pressure on them. Since all else had failed, it was at least worth trying.

Never before had Unity Mansions been the scene of such excitement.

In the afternoon the institute sent people to fix up ropes between two trees in the yard, on which to hang a poster with the name of Mr. Short on it—crossed out. Inside and outside the yard they pasted up threatening slogans, and on the wall put up eighteen more posters listing the engineer's "crimes." As the meeting was to be held after supper, an electrician was sent to fix up four big 500-watt bulbs. By now the tailor's wife, promoted to be the chairman of the Neighbour-hood's Public Security Committee, was a powerful personage, full of self-impor-tance, and much fatter than before. She had been busy all day bossing the other women about, helping to put up slogans and make tea for the revolutionaries from the institute. The wiring for the lights had been fixed up from her gate-house. Really as if she were celebrating a wedding!

After supper the tailor's wife assembled all the residents in the yard, lit up as brilliantly as a sportsground at night. Their shadows, magnified ten-fold, were thrown on the wall of the building. These shadows stayed stock-still, not even the children daring to play about. The tailor's wife led a group also wearing red armbands, in those days most awe-inspiring, to guard the gate and keep outsiders out. Presently a crowd from the institute, wearing armbands and shouting slo-gans, marched in the tall woman and her short husband. He had a placard hung round his neck, she had none. The two of them were marched in front of the platform, and stood there side by side with lowered heads.

The tailor's wife darted forward. "This wretch is too short for the revolutionary masses at the back to see," she cried. "I'll soon fix that." She dashed into the gatehouse, her fat shoulders heaving, to fetch a soapbox which she turned upside down. Mr. Short standing on this was the same height as his wife. But at this point little attention was paid to the relative heights of this couple facing disaster.

The meeting followed the customary procedure. After slogans had been shouted, passionate accusations were made, punctuated by more slogans. The pressure built up. First Mrs. Tall was ordered to come clean, to produce that "manuscript." Questions and denunciations were fired at her, hysterical screams, angry shouts and threatening growls. But she simply shook her head gravely and sincerely. What use was sincerity? To believe in her would have made the whole business a farce.

No matter what bullies sprang forward to shake their fists at her, or what tricky questions were asked to try to trap her, she simply shook her head. The members of the institute were at a loss, afraid that if this went on the struggle meeting would fizzle out and end up a fiasco.

The tailor's wife had listened with mounting exasperation. Being illiterate she took no interest in the "manuscript" they wanted, and felt these research workers were too soft-spoken. All of a sudden she ran to the platform. Raising her right arm with its red armband she pointed accusingly at Mrs. Tall.

"Say!" she screeched. "Why did you marry him?"

The members of the institute were staggered by this unexpected question. What connection had it with their investigation?

Mrs. Tall was staggered too. This wasn't the sort of question asked these days. She looked up with surprise on her thin face which showed the ravages of the last few months.

"So you don't dare answer, eh?" The tailor's wife raised her voice. "I'll answer for you! You married this scoundrel, didn't you, for his money? If he hadn't had money who'd want such a short fellow!" She sounded rather smug, as if she alone had seen through Mrs. Tall.

Mrs. Tall neither nodded nor shook her head. She had seen through the tailor's wife too. Her eyes glinted with derision and contempt.

"All right, you won't admit it. This wretch is done for now, he's a broken reed. Oh, I know what you're thinking." The tailor's wife slapped her chest and brandished one hand gloatingly. Some other women chimed in.

The members of the institute were flummoxed. A question like this was best ignored. But though these women had strayed so far from the subject, they had livened up the meeting. So the institute members let them take the field. The women yelled:

"How much has he paid you? What has he bought you? Own up!"

"Two hundred a month isn't enough for you, is it. You have to go abroad!"

"Is Deng Tuo* behind you?"

"That day you made a long-distance call to Beijing, were you ringing up the Three Family Village?"†

The success of a meeting depends on the enthusiasm worked up. The institute members who had convened this meeting saw that the time was ripe now to shout a few more slogans and conclude it. They then searched Mrs. Tall's flat, prising up floorboards and stripping off wallpaper. When they discovered nothing, they marched her husband away, leaving her behind.

Mrs. Tall stayed in all the next day but went out alone after dark, unaware that though the light in the gatehouse was out the tailor's wife was watching her from the window. She trailed her out of the gate and past two crossroads till Mrs. Tall stopped to knock softly on a gate. The tailor's wife ducked behind a telegraph pole and waited, holding her breath, as if to pounce on a rabbit when it popped out of its burrow.

The gate creaked open. An old woman led out a child.

"All over, is it?" she asked.

Mrs. Tall's answer was inaudible.

"He's had his supper and a sleep," the old woman said. "Take him home quickly now."

The tailor's wife realized that this was the woman who minded their little boy. Her excitement died down as Mrs. Tall turned back to lead her son home. All was silence apart from the sound of their footsteps. The tailor's wife stood motionless behind the telegraph pole till they had gone, then scurried home herself.

The next morning when Mrs. Tall led her son out, her eyes were red. No one would speak to her, but they all saw her red, swollen eyes. Those who had

---

*Deng Tuo (1912–1966), historian, poet and essayist, was the party secretary of Beijing in charge of cultural and educational work, who was considered a counterrevolutionary after the start of the Cultural Revolution in 1966.
†In 1961, Deng Tuo, Wu Han (a historian) and Liao Mosha (a writer) started a magazine column "Notes from the Three Family Village" and published many essays that were well received. During the Cultural Revolution, the three writers were falsely charged as "The Three Family Village."

denounced her the previous day had a strange feeling of guilt. They turned away so as not to meet her eyes.

4

After the struggle meeting Mr. Short was not allowed home again. The tailor's wife, who was in the know, said he had been imprisoned as an active counter-revolutionary. That made Mrs. Tall the lowest of the low, naturally unfit to live in a roomy flat. She was forced to change places with the tailor's wife and moved into the little gatehouse. This didn't worry her, as it meant she could avoid the other residents who snubbed her. But they could look through her window and see her all alone there. Where she had sent her son, they didn't know, he only came home for a few days at a time. Ostracized by all, she looked older than a woman in her thirties.

"Mark my words," the tailor's wife said, "she can only keep this up for at most a year. Then if Shorty doesn't get out she'll have to remarry. If I were her I'd get a divorce and remarry. Even if he's let out his name will be mud, and he won't have any money."

A year went by, still Mr. Short didn't come back and Mrs. Tall kept to herself. In silence she went to work, came back, lit her stove and went out with a big shabby shopping basket. Day after day she did this, the whole year round. . . . But one day in autumn Mr. Short reappeared—thinly clad, his head shaved, his whole appearance changed. He seemed to have shrunk and his skin no longer gleamed with health. He went straight to his old flat. Its new master, the honest tailor, directed him to the gatehouse. Mrs. Tall was squatting in the doorway chopping firewood. At the sound of his voice she sprang up to stare at him. After two years' separation both were appalled by the change in the other. One was wrinkled, the other haggard; one looked taller than before, the other shorter. After gazing at each other they hastily turned away, and Mrs. Tall ran inside. When finally she came out again he had picked up the axe and squatted down to chop firewood, until two big boxes of wood had been chopped into kindling, as if he feared some new disaster might befall them at any moment. After that they were inseparable again, going to work together and coming back together just as before. The neighbours, finding them unchanged, gradually lost interest in them and ignored them.

One morning Mrs. Tall had an accident. Her husband rushed frantically out and came back with an ambulance to fetch her. For days the gatehouse was empty and dark at night. After three weeks Mr. Short returned with a stranger. They were carrying her on a stretcher. She was confined to her room. He went to work as usual, hurrying back at dusk to light the stove and go out with the shopping basket. This was the same basket she had used every day. In his hand it looked even bigger and nearly reached the ground.

When the weather turned warmer Mrs. Tall came out. After so long in bed her face was deathly white, and she swayed from side to side. She held a cane in her right hand and kept her left elbow bent in front of her. Her half-paralysed left leg made walking difficult. She had obviously had a stroke. Every morning and every evening Mr. Short helped her twice round the yard, painfully and slowly. By hunching up his shoulders he was able to grip her crooked arm in both hands. It was hard for him, but he smiled to encourage her. As she couldn't raise her left foot, he tied a rope round it and pulled this up when she wanted to take a step forward. This was a pathetic yet impressive sight, and the neighbours were touched by it. Now when they met the couple they nodded cordially to them.

5

Mrs. Tall's luck had run out: she was not to linger long by the side of the short husband who loved her so dearly. Death and life were equally cruel to her. Life had struck her down and now death carried her off. Mr. Short was left all alone.

But after her death fortune smiled on him again. He was rehabilitated, his confiscated possessions were returned, and he received all his back pay. Only his flat, occupied by the tailor's wife, was not given back to him. The neighbours watched to see what he would do. It was said that some of his colleagues had proposed finding him another wife, but he had declined their offers.

"I know the kind of woman he wants," said the tailor's wife. "Just leave it to me!"

Having passed her zenith she had become more subdued. Stripped of her power she had to wear a smile. With a photograph of a pretty girl in her pocket she went to the gatehouse to find Mr. Short. The girl in the picture was her niece.

She sat in the gatehouse sizing up its furnishings as she proposed this match to rich Mr. Short. Smiling all over her face she held forth with gusto until suddenly she realized that he had said not a word, his face was black, and behind him hung a picture of him and Mrs. Tall on their wedding day. Then she beat a retreat without venturing to produce the photograph of her niece.

Since then several years have passed. Mr. Short is still a widower, but on Sundays he fetches his son home to keep him company. At sight of his squat lonely figure, his neighbours recall all that he has been through and have come to understand why he goes on living alone. When it rains and he takes an umbrella to go to work, out of force of habit perhaps he still holds it high. Then they have the strange sensation that there is a big empty space under that umbrella, a vacuum that nothing on earth can fill.

Translated by Gladys Yang

Questions for Discussion and Writing

1. In what ways does Jicai's story show us the complexities of attempting to define the truths about another person's life or relationship? In what ways does the brief first section relate to the story that follows or have to do with "force of habit" (p. 559)?

2. What connections does Jicai create between the personal husband–wife relationship and the larger social and political ways of thinking in the community?
3. What possibilities of defining or interpreting the couple does the community neglect to consider? What truths about the couple and the community does the author want to convey? Use brief passages from the story to support your answer.

RICHARD RIVE

The Bench

Born in 1931 in the ghettos of District Six, Cape Town, South Africa, Richard Rive began his storytelling early, at the age of twelve, when he used to read Shakespeare and Dickens and retell the stories to his friends. As a "coloured" in South Africa, the official designation for descendants of African natives and white settlers, Rive has lived the cruelties of apartheid there for most of his life.

Following his graduation from the University of Cape Town in 1962, Rive studied abroad in the United States and in England, eventually receiving his doctorate from Oxford University. He returned to South Africa and a teaching position at the University of Cape Town, where he was one of two nonwhite faculty members among a staff of six hundred at the time. Because Rive's writing explores the problems and injustices of life in South Africa, his novels and stories are not available there.

Before his writing attracted the attention of the South African government, "The Bench" appeared in a collection entitled African Voices *(1958), by Drum Publications, Johannesburg. In the story, Rive reflects the awakening to the small and large injustices that men like Karlie had too often lived and accepted as part of the pattern of their lives.*

Before you read "The Bench," write about a time when someone communicated an idea that significantly changed your life, that gripped you for its truth. Describe the situation, the person and his or her idea, and how the idea changed you at first and over time.

"We form an integral part of a complex society, a society complex in that a vast proportion of the population are denied the very basic privileges of existence, a society that condemns a man to an inferior position because he has the misfortune to be born black, a society that can only retain its precarious social and economic position at the expense of an enormous oppressed proletariat!"

Karlie's eyes shone as he watched the speaker. Those were great words, he thought, great words and true. The speaker paused for a moment and sipped some water from a glass. Karlie sweated. The hot October sun beat down mercilessly on the gathering. The trees on the Grand Parade afforded very little shelter and his handkerchief was already soaked where he had placed it between his neck and shirt collar. Karlie stared round him at the sea of faces. Every shade of colour was represented, from shiny ebony to the one or two whites in the crowd. He stared at the two detectives who were busily making shorthand notes of the speeches, and then turned to stare back at the speaker.

"It is up to us to challenge the rights of any groups who wilfully and deliberately condemn a fellow group to a servile position. We must challenge the rights of any people who see fit to segregate human beings solely on grounds of pigmentation. Your children are denied the rights which are theirs by birth. They are segregated socially, economically. . . ."

Ah, thought Karlie, that man knows what he is speaking about. He says I am as good as any other man, even a white man. That needs much thinking. I wonder if he thinks I have the right to go into any bioscope or eat in any restaurant, or that my children can go to any school? These are dangerous ideas and need much thinking; I wonder what Ou Klaas would say to this. Ou Klaas said God made the white man and the black man separately and the one must always be *"baas"* and the other *"jong."* But this man says different things and somehow they seem true.

Karlie's brow was knitted as he thought. On the platform were many speakers, both white and black, and they were behaving as if there were no difference of colour between them. There was a white woman in a blue dress offering a cigarette to Nxeli. That could never happen at Bietjiesvlei. Old Lategan at the store would have fainted if his Annatjie had offered Witbooi a cigarette. And Annatjie had no such pretty dress. These were new things, and he, Karlie, had to be careful before he accepted them. But why shouldn't he accept them? He was not coloured any more, he was a human being. The speaker had said so. He remembered seeing pictures in the newspaper of people who defied laws which relegated them to a particular class, and those people were smiling as they went to prison. This was a strange world.

The speaker continued and Karlie listened intently. His speech was obviously carefully prepared and he spoke slowly, choosing his words. This is a great man, Karlie thought.

The last speaker was the white lady in the blue dress, who asked them to challenge any discriminatory laws or measures in every possible manner. Why should she speak like that? thought Karlie. She could go to the best bioscopes, and swim at the best beaches. Why, she was even more beautiful than Annatjie Lategan. They had warned him in Bietjiesvlei about coming to the city. He had seen the *Skollies* in District Six and knew what to expect there. Hanover Street held no terrors for him. But no one had told him about this. This was new, this set one's mind thinking, yet he felt it was true. She said one should challenge. He would challenge. He, Karlie, would astound old Lategan and Balie at the dairy farm. They could do what they liked to him after that. He would smile like those people in the newspaper.

The meeting was almost over when Karlie threaded his way through the crowd. The words of the speakers were still milling through his head. It could never happen in Bietjiesvlei, he thought, or could it? The sudden screech of a car pulling to a hurried stop whirled him back to his senses. A white head was angrily thrust through the window. "Look where you're going, you black bastard!"

Karlie stared dazedly at him. Surely this white man had never heard what the speakers had said. He could never have seen the white woman offering Nxeli a cigarette. Karlie could never imagine the white lady shouting those words at him. It would be best to catch a train and think these things over.

He saw the station in a new light. Here was a mass of human beings, some black, some white, and some brown like himself. Here they mixed with one another, yet each mistrusted the other with an unnatural fear. Each treated the other with suspicion, each moved in a narrow, haunted pattern of its own manufacture. One must challenge these things the speaker had said . . . in one's own way. Yet how in one's own way? How was one to challenge? Slowly it dawned upon him. Here was his chance, *the bench*. The railway bench with the legend "Europeans Only" neatly painted on it in white. For one moment it symbolized all the misery of the plural South African society. Here was a challenge to his rights as a man. There it stood, a perfectly ordinary wooden railway bench, like hundreds of thousands of others in South Africa. His challenge. That bench, now, had concentrated in it all the evils of a system he could not understand. It was the obstacle between himself and humanity. If he sat on it he was a man. If he was afraid he denied himself membership as a human in a human society. He almost had visions of righting the pernicious system if only he sat on that bench. Here was his chance. He, Karlie, would challenge.

He seemed perfectly calm when he sat down on the bench, but inside his heart was thumping wildly. Two conflicting ideas now throbbed through him. The one said, "I have no right to sit on this bench"; the other said, "Why have I no right to sit on this bench?" The one voice spoke of the past, of the servile position he had occupied on the farms, of his father and his father's father who were born black, lived like blacks and died like oxen. The other voice spoke of the future and said, "Karlie, you are a man. You have dared what your father would not have dared. You will die like a man!"

Karlie took out a cigarette and smoked. Nobody seemed to notice his sitting there. This was an anti-climax. The world still pursued its monotonous way. No voice shouted "Karlie has conquered!" He was a normal human being sitting on a bench on a busy station, smoking a cigarette. Or was this his victory, the fact that he was a normal human being? A well-dressed white woman walked down the platform. Would she sit on the bench, Karlie wondered. And then that gnawing voice, "You should stand and let the white woman sit." Karlie narrowed his eyes and gripped tighter at his cigarette. She swept past him without the slightest twitch of an eyelid and walked on down the platform. Was she afraid to challenge, to challenge his right to be a human? Karlie now felt tired. A third conflicting emotion was now creeping in, a compensatory emotion which said, "You do not sit on this bench to challenge, you sit there because you are tired. You are tired; therefore you sit." He would not move because he was tired, or was it because he wanted to sit where he liked?

People were now pouring out of a train that had pulled into the station. There were so many people pushing and jostling one another that nobody noticed him. This was his train. It would be quite easy to step into the train and ride off home, but that would be giving in, suffering defeat, refusing the challenge, in fact admitting that he was not a human being. He sat on. Lazily he blew the cigarette smoke into the air, thinking . . . his mind was far from the meeting and the bench, he was thinking of Bietjiesvlei and Ou Klaas, how he had insisted that Karlie should come to Cape Town. Ou Klaas could look so quizzically at one and suck at his pipe. He was wise to know and knew much. He had said one must go to Cape Town and learn the ways of the world. He would spit and wink slyly when he spoke of District Six and the women he knew in Hanover Street. Ou Klaas knew everything. He said God made us white or black and we must therefore keep our places.

"Get off this seat!"

Karlie did not hear the gruff voice. Ou Klaas would be on the land now, waiting for his tot of cheap wine.

"I said get off the bench, you swine!"

Karlie suddenly whipped back to reality. For a moment he was going to jump up, then he remembered who he was and why he was sitting there. Suddenly he felt very tired. He looked up slowly into a very red face that stared down at him.

"Get up! I said, there are benches down there for you!"

Karlie stared up and said nothing. He stared up into very sharp, cold grey eyes.

"Can't you hear me speaking to you, you black swine!"

Slowly and deliberately Karlie puffed at his cigarette. So this was his test. They both stared at each other, challenged with the eyes, like two boxers, each knowing that they must eventually trade blows yet each afraid to strike first.

"Must I dirty my hands on scum like you?"

Karlie said nothing. To speak would be to break the spell, the supremacy he felt he was slowly gaining. An uneasy silence. Then,

"I will call a policeman rather than kick a Hotnot like you! You can't even open your black jaw when a white man speaks to you!"

Karlie saw the weakness. The white youth was afraid to take action himself. He, Karlie, had won the first round of the bench dispute!

A crowd now collected. "Afrika!" shouted one joker. Karlie ignored the remark. People were now milling around, staring at the unusual sight of a black man sitting on a white man's bench. Karlie merely puffed on.

"Look at the black ape! That's the worst of giving these Kaffirs too much rope!"

"I can't understand it, they have their own benches!"

"Don't get up, you have every right to sit there!"

"He'll get hell when a policeman comes!"

"Mind you, I can't see why they shouldn't sit where they please!"

"I've said before, I've had a native servant, and a more impertinent. . . ."

Karlie sat and heard nothing. Irresolution had now turned to determination. Under no condition was he going to rise. They could do what they liked.

"So this is the fellow, hey, get up there! Can't you read?" The policeman was towering over him. Karlie could see the crest on his buttons and the thin wrinkles on his neck.

"What is your name and address?"

Karlie still maintained his obstinate silence. It took the policeman rather unawares. The crowd was growing every minute.

"You have no right to speak to this man in such a manner!" It was the white lady in the blue dress.

"Mind your own business! I'll ask your help when I need it. It is people like you who make Kaffirs think they're as good as white people!"

Then addressing Karlie, "Get up, you!"

"I insist that you treat him with proper respect!"

The policeman turned red. "This . . . this. . . ." He was at a loss for words.

"Kick up the Hotnot if he won't get up!" shouted a spectator. Rudely a white man laid hands on Karlie. "Get up you bloody bastard!"

Karlie turned to resist, to cling to the bench, his bench. There were more than one man now pulling at him. He hit out wildly and then felt a dull pain as somebody rammed a fist into his face. He was now bleeding and wild-eyed. He would fight for it. The constable clapped a pair of handcuffs round Karlie's wrists and tried to clear a way through the crowds. Karlie was still struggling. A blow or two landed on him. Suddenly he relaxed and slowly struggled to his feet. It was useless fighting any longer. Now it was his turn to smile. He had challenged and won. Who cared at the result?

"Come on, you swine!" said the policeman, forcing Karlie through the crowd.

"Certainly," said Karlie for the first time, and stared at the policeman with the arrogance of one who dared to sit on a "European" bench.

Questions for Discussion and Writing

1. What do we learn, directly and indirectly, about Karlie's patterns of defining himself and others before he hears the speakers at the rally?
2. In what ways is the bench an appropriate symbol and place for carrying out his new convictions? Who is Karlie by the story's end?
3. What elements of humor make us smile in spite of the cruelty Karlie experiences? For what purposes do you think Rive evokes humor in his story?

CHINUA ACHEBE

An Image of Africa

Born in 1930 in Ogidi, Nigeria, Chinua Achebe today lives and works in Nsukka, Nigeria, as head of the Department of English at the University of Nigeria. Considered by many critics to be one of the best contemporary African novelists, Achebe has traveled and lectured all over the world. He is particularly concerned with three aspects of African life: the legacy of colonialism, using English as a language of national and international exchange, and the responsibilities of the writer both to the society in which he lives and to his art.

On the issue of using English as an African writer, Achebe explains that, although the language embodies the values of the foreign, colonial culture, it gives the African writer "the facility for mutual communication . . . [and thus he] should aim at fashioning out an English which is at once universal and able to carry his experience." Achebe has been praised by critics for maintaining this delicate balance of communicating in English in his own voice as an African. In most of his writing, the theme he has made his own involves the tragic consequences of Africa's encounter with Europe, and the subsequent confusion in the African consciousness.

The world that interests Achebe most is the African village, especially the kind of village that his people, the Ibo, have created: "We think what is safest and best is a system in which everybody knows everybody else," he explains, a world in which "when a man got up to talk to his fellows, they knew who he was, they knew exactly whether he was a thief, an honest man, or whatever."

"An Image of Africa" appeared in Achebe's book Hopes and Impediments, *published in 1988, and* Chant of Saints, *published in 1979.*

Before you read "An Image of Africa," write down the images that come to mind when you think of that continent. Be as descriptive and thorough

as you can in your free associations. After you've described your images of Africa and the feelings you associate with them, explain what sources of reading or experience shaped your understanding. In what ways do you suspect your images are stereotypical? If you've been to Africa or come from Africa, describe the dominant features of the place you know, especially as they contrast with stereotypes you've encountered in Europe or the United States.

I t was a fine autumn morning at the beginning of this academic year such as encouraged friendliness to passing strangers. Brisk youngsters were hurrying in all directions, many of them obviously freshmen in their first flush of enthusiasm. An older man, going the same way as I, turned and remarked to me how very young they came these days. I agreed. Then he asked me if I was a student too. I said no, I was a teacher. What did I teach? African literature. Now that was funny, he said, because he never had thought of Africa as having that kind of stuff, you know. By this time I was walking much faster. "Oh well," I heard him say finally, behind me, "I guess I have to take your course to find out."

A few weeks later I received two very touching letters from high school children in Yonkers, New York, who—bless their teacher—had just read *Things Fall Apart.* One of them was particularly happy to learn about the customs and superstitions of an African tribe.

I propose to draw from these rather trivial encounters rather heavy conclusions which at first sight might seem somewhat out of proportion to them: But only at first sight.

The young fellow from Yonkers, perhaps partly on account of his age but I believe also for much deeper and more serious reasons, is obviously unaware that the life of his own tribesmen in Yonkers, New York, is full of odd customs and superstitions and, like everybody else in his culture, imagines that he needs a trip to Africa to encounter those things.

The other person being fully my own age could not be excused on the grounds of his years. Ignorance might be a more likely reason; but here again I believe that something more willful than a mere lack of information was at work. For did not that erudite British historian and Regius Professor at Oxford, Hugh Trevor Roper, pronounce a few years ago that African history did not exist?

If there is something in these utterances more than youthful experience, more than a lack of factual knowledge, what is it? Quite simply it is the desire—one might indeed say the need—in Western psychology to set up Africa as a foil to Europe, a place of negations at once remote and vaguely familiar in comparison with which Europe's own state of spiritual grace will be manifest.

This need is not new: which should relieve us of considerable responsibility and perhaps make us even willing to look at this phenomenon dispassionately. I have neither the desire nor, indeed, the competence to do so with the tools of the social and biological sciences. But, I can respond, as a novelist, to one famous book of European fiction, Joseph Conrad's *Heart of Darkness,* which better than any other work I know displays that Western desire and need which I have just spoken about. Of course, there are whole libraries of books devoted to the same purpose, but most of them are so obvious and so crude that few people worry about them today. Conrad, on the other hand, is undoubtedly one of the great stylists of modern fiction and a good storyteller into the bargain. His contribution therefore falls automatically into a different class—permanent literature— read and taught and constantly evaluated by serious academics. *Heart of Darkness* is indeed so secure today that a leading Conrad scholar has numbered it "among the half-dozen greatest short novels in the English language."[1] I will return to this critical opinion in due course because it may seriously modify my earlier suppositions about who may or may not be guilty in the things of which I will now speak.

Heart of Darkness projects the image of Africa as "the other world," the antithesis of Europe and therefore of civilization, a place where a man's vaunted intelligence and refinement are finally mocked by triumphant bestiality. The book opens on the River Thames, tranquil, resting peacefully "at the decline of day after ages of good service done to the race that peopled its banks." But the actual story takes place on the River Congo, the very antithesis of the Thames. The River Congo is quite decidedly not a River Emeritus. It has rendered no service and enjoys no old-age pension. We are told that "going up that river was like travelling back to the earliest beginning of the world."

Is Conrad saying then that these two rivers are very different, one good, the other bad? Yes, but that is not the real point. What actually worries Conrad is the lurking hint of kinship, of common ancestry. For the Thames, too, "has been one of the dark places of the earth." It conquered its darkness, of course, and is now at peace. But if it were to visit its primordial relative, the Congo, it would run the terrible risk of hearing grotesque, suggestive echoes of its own forgotten darkness, and of falling victim to an avenging recrudescence of the mindless frenzy of the first beginnings.

I am not going to waste your time with examples of Conrad's famed evocation of the African atmosphere. In the final consideration it amounts to no more than a steady, ponderous, fake-ritualistic repetition of two sentences, one about silence and the other about frenzy. An example of the former is "It was the stillness of an implacable force brooding over an inscrutable intention" and of the latter, "The steamer toiled along slowly on the edge of a black and incomprehensible frenzy." Of course, there is a judicious change of adjective from time to time so that instead of "inscrutable," for example, you might have "unspeakable," etc., etc.

The eagle-eyed English critic, F. R. Leavis, drew attention nearly thirty years ago to Conrad's "adjectival insistence upon inexpressible and incomprehensible mystery." That insistence must not be dismissed lightly, as many Conrad critics have tended to do, as a mere stylistic flaw. For it raises serious questions of artistic good faith. When a writer, while pretending to record scenes, incidents and their impact, is in reality engaged in inducing hypnotic stupor in his readers through a bombardment of emotive words and other forms of trickery, much more has to be at stake than stylistic felicity. Generally, normal readers are well armed to detect and resist such underhand activity. But Conrad chose his subject well—one which was guaranteed not to put him in conflict with the psychological predisposition of his readers or raise the need for him to contend with their resistance. He chose the role of purveyor of comforting myths.

The most interesting and revealing passages in *Heart of Darkness* are, however, about people. I must quote a long passage from the middle of the story in which representatives of Europe in a steamer going down the Congo encounter the denizens of Africa:

> We were wanderers on a prehistoric earth, on an earth that wore the aspect of an unknown planet. We could have fancied ourselves the first of men taking possession of an accursed inheritance, to be subdued at the cost of profound anguish and of excessive toil. But suddenly, as we struggled round a bend, there would be a glimpse of rush walls, of peaked grass-roofs, a burst of yells, a whirl of black limbs, a mass of hands clapping, of feet stamping, of bodies swaying, of eyes rolling, under the droop of heavy and motionless foliage. The steamer toiled along slowly on the edge of a black and incomprehensible frenzy. The prehistoric man was cursing us, praying to us, welcoming us—who could tell? We were cut off from the comprehension of our surroundings; we glided past like phantoms, wondering and secretly appalled, as sane men would be before an enthusiastic outbreak in a madhouse. We could not remember because we were travelling in the night of first ages, of those ages that are gone, leaving hardly a sign—and no memories.
>
> The earth seemed unearthly. We are accustomed to look upon the shackled form of a conquered monster, but there—there you could look at a thing monstrous and free. It was unearthly, and the men were—No, they were not inhuman. Well, you know, that was the worst of it—this suspicion of their not being inhuman. It would come slowly to one. They howled and leaped, and spun, and made horrid faces; but what thrilled you was just the thought of your remote kinship with this wild and passionate uproar. Ugly. Yes, it was ugly enough; but if you were man enough you would admit to yourself that there was in you just the faintest trace of a response to the terrible frankness of that noise, a dim suspicion of there being a meaning in it which you—you so remote from the night of first ages—could comprehend.

Herein lies the meaning of *Heart of Darkness* and the fascination it holds over the Western mind: "What thrilled you was just the thought of their humanity—like yours. . . . Ugly."

Having shown us Africa in the mass, Conrad then zeros in on a specific example, giving us one of his rare descriptions of an African who is not just limbs or rolling eyes:

> And between whiles I had to look after the savage who was fireman. He was an improved specimen; he could fire up a vertical boiler. He was there below me, and, upon my word, to look at him was as edifying as seeing a dog in a parody of breeches and a feather hat, walking on his hind legs. A few months of training had done for that really fine chap. He squinted at the steam gauge and at the water gauge with an evident effort of intrepidity—and he had filed his teeth, too, the poor devil, and the wool of his pate shaved

into queer patterns, and three ornamental scars on each of his cheeks. He ought to have been clapping his hands and stamping his feet on the bank, instead of which he was hard at work, a thrall to strange witchcraft, full of improving knowledge.

As everybody knows, Conrad is a romantic on the side. He might not exactly admire savages clapping their hands and stamping their feet but they have at least the merit of being in their place, unlike this dog in a parody of breeches. For Conrad, things (and persons) being in their place is of the utmost importance.

Towards the end of the story, Conrad lavishes great attention quite unexpectedly on an African woman who has obviously been some kind of mistress to Mr. Kurtz and now presides (if I may be permitted a little imitation of Conrad) like a formidable mystery over the inexorable imminence of his departure:

> She was savage and superb, wild-eyed and magnificent . . . She stood looking at us without a stir and like the wilderness itself, with an air of brooding over an inscrutable purpose.

This Amazon is drawn in considerable detail, albeit of a predictable nature, for two reasons. First, she is in her place and so can win Conrad's special brand of approval; and second, she fulfills a structural requirement of the story; she is a savage counterpart to the refined, European woman with whom the story will end:

> She came forward, all in black with a pale head, floating towards me in the dusk. She was in mourning. . . . She took both my hands in hers and murmured, "I had heard you were coming" . . . She had a mature capacity for fidelity, for belief, for suffering.

The difference in the attitude of the novelist to these two women is conveyed in too many direct and subtle ways to need elaboration. But perhaps the most significant difference is the one implied in the author's bestowal of human expression to the one and the withholding of it from the other. It is clearly not part of Conrad's purpose to confer language on the "rudimentary souls" of Africa. They only "exchanged short grunting phrases" even among themselves but mostly they were too busy with their frenzy. There are two occasions in the book, however, when Conrad departs somewhat from his practice and confers speech, even English speech, on the savages. The first occurs when cannibalism gets the better of them:

> "Catch 'im," he snapped, with a bloodshot widening of his eyes and a flash of sharp white teeth—"catch 'im. Give 'im to us." "To you, eh?" I asked; "what would you do with them?" "Eat 'im!" he said curtly . . .

The other occasion is the famous announcement:

> Mistah Kurtz—he dead.

At first sight, these instances might be mistaken for unexpected acts of generosity from Conrad. In reality, they constitute some of his best assaults. In the case of the cannibals, the incomprehensible grunts that had thus far served them for speech suddenly proved inadequate for Conrad's purpose of letting the European glimpse the unspeakable craving in their hearts. Weighing the necessity for consistency in the portrayal of the dumb brutes against the sensational advantages of securing their conviction by clear, unambiguous evidence issuing out of their own mouth, Conrad chose the latter. As for the announcement of Mr. Kurtz's death by the "insolent black head in the doorway," what better or more appropriate *finis* could be written to the horror story of that wayward child of civilization who willfully had given his soul to the powers of darkness and "taken a high seat amongst the devils of the land" than the proclamation of his physical death by the forces he had joined?

It might be contended, of course, that the attitude to the African in *Heart of Darkness* is not Conrad's but that of his fictional narrator, Marlow, and that far from endorsing it Conrad might indeed be holding it up to irony and criticism. Certainly, Conrad appears to go to considerable pains to set up layers of insulation between himself and the moral universe of his story. He has, for example, a narrator behind a narrator. The primary narrator is Marlow but his account is given to us through the filter of a second, shadowy person. But if Conrad's intention is to draw a *cordon sanitaire* between himself and the moral and psychological malaise of his narrator, his care seems to me totally wasted because he neglects to hint however subtly or tentatively at an alternative frame of reference by which we may judge the actions and opinions of his characters. It would not have been beyond Conrad's power to make that provision if he had thought it necessary. Marlow seems to me to enjoy Conrad's complete confidence—a feeling reinforced by the close similarities between their careers.

Marlow comes through to us not only as a witness of truth, but one holding those advanced and humane views appropriate to the English liberal tradition which required all Englishmen of decency to be deeply shocked by atrocities in Bulgaria or the Congo of King Leopold of the Belgians or wherever. Thus Marlow is able to toss out such bleeding-heart sentiments as these:

> They were all dying slowly—it was very clear. They were not enemies, they were not criminals, they were nothing earthly now—nothing but black shadows of disease and starvation, lying confusedly in the greenish gloom. Brought from all the recesses of the coast in all the legality of time contracts, lost in uncongenial surroundings, fed on unfamiliar food, they sickened, became inefficient, and were then allowed to crawl away and rest.

The kind of liberalism espoused here by Marlow/Conrad touched all the best minds of the age in England, Europe, and America. It took different forms in the minds of different people but almost always managed to sidestep the ultimate question of equality between white people and black people. That extraordinary missionary, Albert Schweitzer, who sacrificed brilliant careers in music and theology in Europe for a life of service to Africans in much the same area as Conrad writes about, epitomizes the ambivalence. In a comment which I have often quoted but must quote one last time Schweitzer says: "The African is indeed my brother but my junior brother." And so he proceeded to build a hospital appropriate to the needs of junior brothers with standards of hygiene reminiscent of medical practice in the days before the germ theory of disease came into being. Naturally, he became a sensation in Europe and America. Pilgrims flocked, and I believe still flock even after he has passed on, to witness the prodigious miracle in Lamberene, on the edge of the primeval forest.

Conrad's liberalism would not take him quite as far as Schweitzer's, though. He would not use the word "brother" however qualified; the farthest he would go was "kinship." When Marlow's African helmsman falls down with a spear in his heart he gives his white master one final disquieting look.

> And the intimate profundity of that look he gave me when he received his hurt remains to this day in my memory—like a claim of distant kinship affirmed in a supreme moment.

It is important to note that Conrad, careful as ever with his words, is not talking so much about *distant kinship* as about someone *laying a claim* on it. The black man lays a claim on the white man which is well-nigh intolerable. It is the laying of this claim which frightens and at the same time fascinates Conrad, ". . . the thought of their humanity—like yours . . . Ugly."

The point of my observations should be quite clear by now, namely, that Conrad was a bloody racist. That this simple truth is glossed over in criticism of his work is due to the fact that white racism against Africa is such a normal way of thinking that its manifestations go completely undetected. Students of *Heart of Darkness* will often tell you that Conrad is concerned not so much with Africa as with the deterioration of one European mind caused by solitude and sickness. They will point out to you that Conrad is, if anything, less charitable to the Europeans in the story than he is to the natives. A Conrad student told me in Scotland last year that Africa is merely a setting for the disintegration of the mind of Mr. Kurtz.

Which is partly the point: Africa as setting and backdrop which eliminates the African as human factor. Africa as a metaphysical battlefield devoid of all recognizable humanity, into which the wandering European enters at his peril. Of course, there is a preposterous and perverse kind of arrogance in thus reducing Africa to the role of props for the breakup of one petty European mind. But that is not even the point. The real question is the dehumanization of Africa and Africans which this age-long attitude has fostered and continues to foster in the world. And the question is whether a novel which celebrates this dehumanization, which depersonalizes a portion of the human race, can be called a great work of art. My answer is: No, it cannot. I would not call that man an artist, for example, who composes an eloquent instigation to one people to fall upon another and destroy them. No matter how striking his imagery or how beautifully his cadences fall, such a man is no more a great artist than another may be called a priest who reads the mass backwards or a physician who poisons his patients.

All those men in Nazi Germany who lent their talent to the service of virulent racism whether in science, philosophy or the arts have generally and rightly been condemned for their perversions. The time is long overdue for taking a hard look at the work of creative artists who apply their talents, alas often considerable as in the case of Conrad, to set people against people. This, I take it, is what Yevtushenko is after when he tells us that a poet cannot be a slave trader at the same time, and gives the striking examples of Arthur Rimbaud, who was fortunately honest enough to give up any pretenses to poetry when he opted for slave trading. For poetry surely can only be on the side of man's deliverance and not his enslavement; for the brotherhood and unity of all mankind and against the doctrines of Hitler's master races or Conrad's "rudimentary souls."

Last year was the 50th anniversary of Conrad's death. He was born in 1857, the very year in which the first Anglican missionaries were arriving among my own people in Nigeria. It was certainly not his fault that he lived his life at a time when the reputation of the black man was at a particularly low level. But even after due allowances have been made for all the influences of contemporary prejudice on his sensibility, there remains still in Conrad's attitude a residue of antipathy to black people which his peculiar psychology alone can explain. His own account of his first encounter with a black man is very revealing:

> A certain enormous buck nigger encountered in Haiti fixed my conception of blind, furious, unreasoning rage, as manifested in the human animal to the end of my days. Of the nigger I used to dream for years afterwards.

Certainly, Conrad had a problem with niggers. His inordinate love of that word itself should be of interest to psychoanalysts. Sometimes his fixation on blackness is equally interesting as when he gives us this brief description:

> A black figure stood up, strode on long black legs, waving long black arms. [2]

as though we might expect a black figure striding along on black legs to wave *white* arms! But so unrelenting is Conrad's obsession.

As a matter of interest Conrad gives us in *A Personal Record* what amounts to a companion piece to the buck nigger of Haiti. At the age of sixteen Conrad encountered his first Englishman in Europe. He calls him "my unforgettable Englishman" and describes him in the following manner:

> [his] calves exposed to the public gaze . . . dazzled the beholder by the splendor of their marble-like condition and their rich tone of young ivory . . . The light of a headlong, exalted satisfaction with the world of men . . . illumined his face . . . and triumphant eyes. In passing he cast a glance of kindly curiosity and a friendly gleam of big, sound, shiny teeth . . . his white calves twinkled sturdily. [3]

Irrational love and irrational hate jostling together in the heart of that tormented man. But whereas irrational love may at worst engender foolish acts of indiscretion, irrational hate can endanger the life of the community. Naturally, Conrad is a dream for psychoanalytic critics. Perhaps the most detailed study of him in this direction is by Bernard C. Meyer, M.D. In this lengthy book, Dr. Meyer follows every conceivable lead (and sometimes inconceivable ones) to explain Conrad. As an example, he gives us long disquisitions on the significance of hair and hair-cutting in Conrad. And yet not even one word is spared for his attitude to black people. Not even the discussion of Conrad's anti-Semitism was enough to spark off in Dr. Meyer's mind those other dark and explosive thoughts. Which only leads one to surmise that Western psychoanalysts must regard the kind of racism displayed by Conrad as absolutely normal despite the profoundly important work done by Frantz Fanon in the psychiatric hospitals of French Algeria.

Whatever Conrad's problems were, you might say he is now safely dead. Quite true. Unfortunately, his heart of darkness plagues us still. Which is why an offensive and totally deplorable book can be described by a serious scholar as "among the half dozen greatest short novels in the English language," and why it is today perhaps the most commonly prescribed novel in the twentieth-century literature courses in our own English Department here. Indeed the time is long overdue for a hard look at things.

There are two probable grounds on which what I have said so far may be contested. The first is that it is no concern of fiction to please people about whom it is written. I will go along with that. But I am not talking about pleasing people. I am talking about a book which parades in the most vulgar fashion prejudices and insults from which a section of mankind has suffered untold agonies and atrocities in the past and continues to do so in many ways and many places today. I am talking about a story in which the very humanity of black people is called in question. It seems to me totally inconceivable that great art or even good art could possibly reside in such unwholesome surroundings.

Secondly, I may be challenged on the grounds of actuality. Conrad, after all, sailed down the Congo in 1890 when my own father was still a babe in arms, and recorded what he saw. How could I stand up in 1975, fifty years after his death and purport to contradict him? My answer is that as a sensible man I will not accept just any traveller's tales solely on the grounds that I have not made the journey myself. I will not trust the evidence even of a man's very eyes when I suspect them to be as jaundiced as Conrad's. And we also happen to know that Conrad was, in the words of his biographer, Bernard C. Meyer, "notoriously inaccurate in the rendering of his own history."[4]

But more important by far is the abundant testimony about Conrad's savages which we could gather if we were so inclined from other sources and which might lead us to think that these people must have had other occupations besides merging into the evil forest or materializing out of it simply to plague Marlow and his dispirited band. For as it happened, soon after Conrad had written his book an event of far greater consequence was taking place in the art world of Europe. This is how Frank Willett, a British art historian, describes it:

> Gauguin had gone to Tahiti, the most extravagant individual act of turning to a non-European culture in the decades immediately before and after 1900, when European artists were avid for new artistic experiences, but it was only about 1904–5 that African art began to make its distinctive impact. One piece

is still identifiable; it is a mask that had been given to Maurice Vlaminck in 1905. He records that Derain was "speechless" and "stunned" when he saw it, bought it from Vlaminck and in turn showed it to Picasso and Matisse, who were also greatly affected by it. Ambroise Vollard then borrowed it and had it cast in bronze . . . The revolution of twentieth century art was under way![5]

The mask in question was made by other savages living just north of Conrad's River Congo. They have a name, the Fang people, and are without a doubt among the world's greatest masters of the sculptured form. As you might have guessed, the event to which Frank Willett refers marked the beginning of cubism and the infusion of new life into European art that had run completely out of strength.

The point of all this is to suggest that Conrad's picture of the people of the Congo seems grossly inadequate even at the height of their subjection to the ravages of King Leopold's International Association for the Civilization of Central Africa. Travellers with closed minds can tell us little except about themselves. But even those not blinkered, like Conrad, with xenophobia, can be astonishingly blind.

Let me digress a little here. One of the greatest and most intrepid travellers of all time, Marco Polo, journeyed to the Far East from the Mediterranean in the thirteenth century and spent twenty years in the court of Kublai Khan in China. On his return to Venice he set down in his book entitled *Description of the World* his impressions of the peoples and places and customs he had seen. There are at least two extraordinary omissions in his account. He says nothing about the art of printing unknown as yet in Europe but in full flower in China. He either did not notice it at all or if he did, failed to see what use Europe could possibly have for it. Whatever reason, Europe had to wait another hundred years for Gutenberg. But even more spectacular was Marco Polo's omission of any reference to the Great Wall of China nearly 4000 miles long and already more than 1000 years old at the time of his visit. Again, he may not have seen it; but the Great Wall of China is the only structure built by man which is visible from the moon![6] Indeed, travellers can be blind.

As I said earlier, Conrad did not originate the image of Africa which we find in his book. It was and is the dominant image of Africa in the Western imagination and Conrad merely brought the peculiar gifts of his own mind to bear on it. For reasons which can certainly use close psychological inquiry, the West seems to suffer deep anxieties about the precariousness of its civilization and to have a need for constant reassurance by comparing itself to Africa. If Europe, advancing in civilization, could cast a backward glance periodically at Africa trapped in primordial barbarity, it could say with faith and feeling: There, but for the grace of God, go I. Africa is to Europe as the picture is to Dorian Gray—a carrier onto whom the master unloads his physical and moral deformities so that he may go forward, erect and immaculate. Consequently, Africa is something to be avoided just as the picture has to be hidden away to safeguard the man's jeopardous integrity. Keep away from Africa, or else! Mr. Kurtz of *Heart of*

Darkness should have heeded that warning and the prowling horror in his heart would have kept its place, chained to its lair. But he foolishly exposed himself to the wild irresistible allure of the jungle and lo! the darkness found him out.

In my original conception of this talk I had thought to conclude it nicely on an appropriately positive note in which I would suggest from my privileged position in African and Western culture some advantages the West might derive from Africa once it rid its mind of old prejudices and began to look at Africa not through a haze of distortions and cheap mystification but quite simply as a continent of people—not angels, but not rudimentary souls either—just people, often highly gifted people and often strikingly successful in their enterprise with life and society. But as I thought more about the stereotype image, about its grip and pervasiveness, about the willful tenacity with which the West holds it to its heart; when I thought of your television and the cinema and newspapers, about books read in schools and out of school, of churches preaching to empty pews about the need to send help to the heathen in Africa, I realized that no easy optimism was possible. And there is something totally wrong in offering bribes to the West in return for its good opinion of Africa. Ultimately, the abandonment of unwholesome thoughts must be its own and only reward. Although I have used the word *willful* a few times in this talk to characterize the West's view of Africa it may well be that what is happening at this stage is more akin to reflex action than calculated malice. Which does not make the situation more, but less, hopeful. Let me give you one last and really minor example of what I mean.

Last November the *Christian Science Monitor* carried an interesting article written by its education editor on the serious psychological and learning problems faced by little children who speak one language at home and then go to school where something else is spoken. It was a wide-ranging article taking in Spanish-speaking children in this country, the children of migrant Italian workers in Germany, the quadrilingual phenomenon in Malaysia and so on. And all this while the article speaks unequivocally about *language.* But then out of the blue sky comes this:

> In London there is an enormous immigration of children who speak Indian
> or Nigerian dialects, or some other native language.[7]

I believe that the introduction of *dialects,* which is technically erroneous in the context, is almost a reflex action caused by an instinctive desire of the writer to downgrade the discussion to the level of Africa and India. And this is quite comparable to Conrad's withholding of language from his rudimentary souls. Language is too grand for these chaps; let's give them dialects. In all this business a lot of violence is inevitably done to words and their meaning. Look at the phrase "native language" in the above excerpt. Surely the only native language possible in London is Cockney English. But our writer obviously means something else—something Indians and Africans speak.

Perhaps a change will come. Perhaps this is the time when it can begin, when the high optimism engendered by the breathtaking achievements of Western science and industry is giving way to doubt and even confusion. There is just the possibility that Western man may begin to look seriously at the achievements of other people. I read in the papers the other day a suggestion that what America needs at this time is somehow to bring back the extended family. And I saw in my mind's eye future African Peace Corps Volunteers coming to help you set up the system.

Seriously, although the work which needs to be done may appear too daunting, I believe that it is not one day too soon to begin. And where better than at a University?

Notes

1. Albert J. Guerard, Introduction to *Heart of Darkness* (New York: New American Library, 1950), p. 9.
2. Jonah Raskin, *The Mythology of Imperialism* (New York: Random House, 1971), p. 143.
3. Bernard C. Meyer, M.D., *Joseph Conrad: A Psychoanalytic Biography* (Princeton, N.J.: Princeton University Press, 1967), p. 30.
4. *Ibid.*, p. 30.
5. Frank Willett, *African Art* (New York: Praeger, 1971), pp. 35–36.
6. About the omission of the Great Wall of China I am indebted to *The Journey of Marco Polo* as re-created by artist Michael Foreman, published by *Pegasus* Magazine, 1974.
7. *Christian Science Monitor*, Nov. 25, 1974, p. 11.

Questions for Discussion and Writing

1. What conclusions does Achebe draw from the "trivial encounters" with which he begins the essay? On what grounds does he draw them, and why or why not are his arguments persuasive?
2. For what reasons does Achebe use Conrad's *Heart of Darkness* to illustrate his line of argument? Why does he blame Conrad as a writer for his racism?
3. In what ways does Achebe's argument here with Conrad involve serious questions of "artistic good faith" (p. 574)? In what ways is this essay about the power of language to define others? In support of your analysis use examples and brief passages from the essay.
4. In what ways does Achebe claim that Conrad stereotypes and falsifies the African continent?
5. Achebe imagines the "probable grounds" (p. 580) of those who might resist his argument. What are they, in what ways does he discount them, what is your analysis of their validity, and on what line of argument do you base it?
6. Why or why not do you think Achebe's lack of hope at the end of his essay is justified?

NORMAN MAILER

A Country, Not a Scenario

By his own account, Norman Mailer (born in 1923) has always been a public personality rather than a secluded artist. His adventures and misadventures are periodically recorded by what he calls that "Godawful Time Magazine *World." His most famous and acclaimed book,* The Naked and the Dead *(1948), was also his first in a long list of nonfiction, fiction, poetry, and several improvised films. In time out from his writing, Mailer ran unsuccessfully for mayor of New York in 1969, and credits his years as a marijuana smoker for the genesis of his existentialism. Mailer has described himself as "the onetime prophet of Hip."*

An exacting writer nevertheless, Mailer has said of his writing habits, "I try to go over my work in every conceivable mood. I edit on a spectrum which runs from the high clear manic impressions of a drunk which has made one electrically alert all the way down to the soberest reaches of depression where I can hardly bear my words."

In "A Country, Not a Scenario," published in Parade *in 1984, Mailer's tone is subdued—not the bold and shouting writer of his past.*

Before you read "A Country, Not a Scenario," write about a time in your life when you came face to face with a controversial reality that you'd only imagined for a long time. It could be a place foreign to you, as the Soviet Union is for Mailer, or a person who represents some category (religion or race perhaps) about which you had preconceived ideas. Describe your original ideas, how the experience with the place or person changed them, and what you learned from the experience.

H aving been in Russia recently for 15 days, I try to remember that I have spent my life deciding what I think about my own country. It is an uncommon day when I don't brood over whether America is better or worse than I believe it to be.

How then can I offer any perceptions of the USSR? I went there in the category of individual tourist. I had no guide and did not speak the language.

Obviously, I only offer modest conclusions. If, however, I thought they had no value, I would remain silent. Instead I tell myself that a child can have a good sense of the true emotions in the air when he enters a room full of adults. I can certify that going around Moscow and Leningrad and parts of Lithuania with about 100 words of Russian is next thing to being a child.

I say "100 words of Russian." It is an exaggeration. For two weeks, before I left New York, I studied by myself, but once I was there, I could only remember the wrong words. Ordering a meal, my vocabulary would bring up the terms for laundry. That has to carry you back to the year when you are learning to talk. New connections keep twisting your thoughts. In Russian, the word for "brave" sounds an awful lot like "smelly."

What a distance between Americans and Russians! You think about it all the time. In America, we tend to treat strangers as friends. Our first impulse is to say "yes." We feel more comfortable if we can call a man by his first name soon after we are introduced. Whereas, with Russians, it seems safe to say that only if you persist, do they begin to listen carefully. Should the Russian decide to agree, then you may be quickly promoted to family. It can prove a rude and emotional family. Russians address people they do not know with intimacy—they scold total strangers. On the other hand, their personal warmth is startling. The sudden love (I do not mean carnal love) that gleams in a Russian's eyes can be as warm and nourishing as marrow: to be accepted is to be treated with all the loving, jeering familiarity of family. One night in Leningrad, having dinner with a Russian friend who spoke English, I watched a middle-aged woman with glasses come up to me. She said in Russian (it was translated), "You do nothing tonight but feed your face. Why don't you dance with me?" On the floor, she moved stiffly like a good Soviet citizen. Still, we progressed a little over the length of two dances. Then she gave an embarrassed smile, and took off.

Yes, the perception of oneself as an American stays alive every hour of the day. It is as if you take on something of our presence as a nation. This sounds absurd, but you begin to feel a little responsible for our policy toward Russia. You walk the streets of Moscow thinking: Is the Soviet Union as we have painted it, or have we painted ourselves into a corner? After 40 years of reading newspaper accounts about Russia, the trouble is that the country is not quite the way one expected it to be. On the other hand, it is not wholly different. In this small gap, however, sits a large question.

Let me offer something we can understand. In Leningrad, at the Hotel Leningrad, a modern high-rise hotel not too unlike a high-rise Holiday Inn in such a place as Norman, Okla., breakfast was served cafeteria-style. You put hot cereal in a bowl and small sausages on your plate, plus pancakes, sweet rolls, and tea. If you wanted more, you could add salami, cheese, yogurt, hard-boiled eggs, some kind of rice dish, pickled cabbage, plus a couple of other items I have forgotten. The price was standard—one ruble, 20 kopeks—about $1.50 at the official Soviet rate of exchange when I was there. The buffet dinner (4 rubles, or $5) came with soup, appetizer, a roast, vegetables, and dessert.

On the other hand, one orange cost 2 rubles at a fruit stand. One is supping at the table of a curious economy.

Other contrasts were soon discovered. The headwaiter steered you to a table with strangers. The Soviet logic seemed to be that solitary diners use up too many tablecloths. Also, they tend to be full of gloom. On the other hand, long-married couples often have little to say to one another. So, put the solitaries and the married couples together. It can't make it any more gloomy, and it certainly saves tablecloths. Our American logic: Damn it, I'm alone, and I feel like eating alone—I'll pay a cover charge for the extra tablecloth—falls on ears that cannot hear. You are in a land where all, more or less, make do for all. If the hotel towels are rough on the skin, and the sheets on your bed feel no better than the towels, well, everyday needs cost little. Bread is almost free. Subway rides are less than 7 cents. Rent for a modest two-room apartment in a modern building (when your name, after years of waiting, finally comes to the head of the list) will be less than 15 rubles a month. Income tax is 13 percent. Higher education is free. Indeed college students are paid a stipend. Medical care is free. Of course, if you want a doctor who is much in demand and do not wish to wait two years for an appointment, you must have common acquaintances, or be able to offer a sumptuous gift, or both. Side by side with the inexpensive working economy is a secondary network of bribes, corruption, contacts, clout, and friends.

All the same, virtually everyone in the Soviet Union lives to some degree by the rules of the public economy, and their incomes and wage scales, by our standards, are odd in the extreme. For instance, a private in the Russian army is given about $6 a month as compared to American privates, who get $573 a month to start. Getting out of the army in Russia and going back to civilian life is like returning to a free economy.

With not too many exceptions, any male or female who is physically able and wants work has a job. The lowest pay, as any guide will inform you, goes to the old ladies who sweep the streets with brooms made of birch twigs. They receive 84 rubles a month. Yet doctors, teachers and lawyers receive no more from the government than 200 rubles a month. Workers in heavy-duty high-risk industry, 500 rubles. If two or three coal miners live in the same family, they can, after waiting half a decade for their turn, buy a small car for 10,000 rubles or more. All the same, there are more cars on the street than one anticipated.

Managers of factories make as much as 1000 rubles a month but often work 70 and 80 hour weeks. Even when they live well, they live modestly. Those notorious dachas we have read about that the Soviet bureaucracy goes to for weekends in the countryside are comparable for the most part to wooden cottages in Maine. Often the studs remain uncovered in the walls. Even the President and General Secretary of the Communist Party, Chernenko, as well as Andropov and Brezhnev before him, has each in his turn occupied the same apartment in Moscow. You can see it as you walk by on the street. You are looking at an apartment house put up probably before World War I. The edifice looks as shabby as any other on this avenue. One could be strolling past any row of large heavy old apartment houses on Eastern Parkway in Brooklyn, or Grand Concourse in the Bronx. Inside, it is rumored, the General Secretary has a duplex, and it is lavishly furnished, but from the street, every propriety that speaks of the equality of life in the Soviet Union is kept up. There will be no great and obvious differences of wealth to look upon. In Moscow, only one class is to be seen, and that is the middle class. The spectrum runs—by the measure of American eyes— from the lower middle class to a seedy, medium middle class. Nowhere does one encounter rich suburbs or slums.

Now, in private, other worlds will, of course, be found. The family of any plant manager making 1000 rubles a month doubtless has a good car, and if he is high enough in the hierarchy, he will have a chauffeur and enjoy other servants paid for by the state. His family will have access to special shops with luxury items and fine foods. The wives of such men are able to save many hundreds of hours a year by not having to wait on line to do their daily shopping. If this much knowledge of the Soviet Union had been acquired before I even went on my trip, it was fascinating all the same to see how much care is paid to concealing most of the evidence of inequality. One's possessions are simply not to be flaunted. The force of social hypocrisy is as intense on this point as the concealment, let us say, of sexual practices in small towns in the American Southwest. On Saturday night, the kids may be finding out a lot about each other in the backseats of automobiles, but one's town reputation is kept in reasonable maintenance by regular attendance Sunday at church. So it goes with the appearance of modest living in the USSR.

There are other small shocks to one's expectations. One has heard so much of Soviet lacks that one is prepared to greet a giant but wounded dinosaur. Instead, the country is not without a certain visible substance. Passing through the flat farmlands of Lithuania between the cities of Vilnius and Kaunas, one could be in Iowa. Already, in early spring, winter wheat is showing its first green, the silos rise frequently, and bizarre modern villages show concrete apartment houses on the plain that rise 10 or 15 stories. They are just as white, rectangular, cheap and ugly as their counterparts in America and, for that matter, all over the world. Trucks grind by at a great rate. Television transmission towers go up every 20 or 30 miles to spike the sky. The beautiful land is pocked by ugly sights—just as in America. Some of the newer factories have the same ongoing windowless walls that numb our American senses—just that little bit—as we pass them on our own highways. The world is getting uglier everywhere, and the newer parts of the USSR and America have the same flat prosperous nerve-deadening look. In America, so much of this new architecture looks humanly repellent, looks totalitarian. So does it look totalitarian in Russia as well. Of course, the Russians at least have justification: They were desperate for cheap housing after the vast depredations of World War II. They have been doing their best ever since to catch up. So their architectural monstrosities, while quite as ugly as ours, seem, all the same, a touch less offensive. Nonetheless, those panoramas of 15-story egg crates are as stupefying as a bruise on a bruise. Forget America and the Soviet Union. The mood of our world is being insulted equally from Calcutta to Vancouver.

But I avoid the near issue. For us, modern Russian architecture seems hardly the problem. Not yet. We worry instead about how much of a police state is the USSR. No other question is asked as often when you return. Yet how are you going to measure that? Talking to a seminar of journalists a couple of weeks after I came back, we all agreed that to the extent we invest in a particular scenario, we can always find the ongoing evidence to keep living with it. Decide that the Soviet Union is an evil force bent on war, aggrandizement and the totalitarian control of all humankind, and you will keep perceiving the country as such. But then, one difficulty with being a steady correspondent in Moscow is that your apartment will, of course, be bugged. The journalist lives in a ghetto with other journalists. The Soviets monitor his moves. How could he fail to be sensitive then to every nuance of a police state?

Yet, take an opposite scenario. Conceive of being the son of a high Soviet official stationed at the UN in New York. The boy likes to walk around the city. The father is full of Soviet horror tales about the streets of America. His fears are augmented by the knowledge that his apartment is bugged by American security forces. He is inclined to lecture the son at length about America's imperial desire for international conflict. "Look at all the evidence you find of that," he says, "in the violence on the streets." The son, however, tries to say, "The Americans I see on the streets don't seem to want war. I don't think they'll ever go to war happily here." And, of course, we know that the boy is right. The father is wrong. Americans do not have an imperial desire for international conflict. To the degree that one is unencumbered by a false scenario, one can see in a day what others will not perceive in 10 years. That is not superior perception nor intellect. It is simply the good fortune to have one's eyes saved from the tunnel vision of a scenario.

On the other hand, huge and powerful forces in America and the USSR are at work to keep old scenarios alive. A good many powerful people in both countries depend on keeping the relations between these two superpowers at the same ongoing abominable level. How much power will they lose if the people of both countries cease believing that the other nation is an evil force?

Let me tell you what I think. It is with true hesitation. Still, when friends ask me, "How big a police state do they have over there?" I respond, "Somewhat less than I thought."

Now, of course, I can hardly speak of the highest levels of Soviet life. All the same, it is safe, doubtless, to assume that the higher one rises in the bureaucracy or the Party and the more sensitive is one's work, the more complete will be the surveillance by the KGB. There is a large difference, however, between subtle and not so subtle methods of terror applied at the top, and the assumption that this is also true for all levels of society.

"Weren't you followed when you left your hotel?" people would ask after I came back to New York.

"No."

"Are you certain?"

"Well," I would answer, "I can't be certain. I just don't think so."

That must be a fair reply. There is a feeling to being followed: One has a sense of privacy or the lack of it—on the street and on one's telephone. "Every day," I answered my friends, "I would leave the hotel and walk around for miles. I would turn down streets and if they proved less interesting than I hoped. I would go back on my steps. I would walk into interesting courtyards and come out of them. My rambles were so purposeless that anyone assigned to follow me would have had a breakdown trying to figure out what I was up to."

"You're saying you could walk anywhere?"

"Yes. At least wherever I was—yes."

"You weren't scared?"

"Well, you don't feel much tension exploring those streets." And, to make a point, I would add, "Let me tell you my Leningrad story."

One night, I would explain, after going to the theater, I decided to walk back to my hotel. It was something more than two miles, but I wanted to see the canals of Leningrad at night. All went well until somewhere in the middle of this promenade. I had to pass through a park. It was perhaps a third of a mile in length and a few hundred yards in width, and it seemed deserted. Around a turn, however, I came on a sight that gave me a start. In the dark, perhaps a hundred yards off, someone was sitting on a bench. As I came nearer, I realized it was not one but two persons, and they had some large indefinable object between them. I was longing to take a detour, but there is a magnetism to the logic of these matters, so I kept walking. Then, I came nearer still, and saw a man and a woman on that bench with a baby carriage between them. Probably they were living in an overcrowded apartment and had come out to this park to put the baby to sleep.

"Then you're saying that there is little violence on the streets?"

"There's certainly not much in the air. Maybe all those people in America who keep screaming that we need safe streets ought to consider moving over to the Soviet Union. It's a very conservative place."

"You liked it?"

"I won't go that far. It's a sad place. I felt as if I were back on the Lower East Side of New York 100 years ago. I could have been watching my grandparents walking by."

Ah, those Moscow faces, bundled up against the last ravages of winter. Have you ever walked through the poor streets of Chicago on West Division Street (where almost everybody who goes by is Ukrainian or Polish)? Hardworking features surround you, full of worry, doubt, long-congealed anger, much concern for family, much dread at what life will bring next. The same faces were here, a generation willing to die in harness in order that their children have a little more. You could see this determination often in Russia: "I haven't gotten what I wanted," says the expression, "but maybe my kids will." It is moving. One feels sad. All these faces, worked by life, all the weather of each personal history carved into each nose and mouth. Since everyone who is of the same age has been churned through the same historical cataclysms, so to a degree did all these middle-aged and older Russians on the streets have the same expression—such an array of plain, hardworked faces—yes, life had come to them with a rock in each fist. These older Russians going by were as battered in their collective looks as old club fighters renowned for the dubious ability to take a tremendous punch. How many had been landed on each marked-up mug? The faces in American crowds are better-looking, but by comparison, innocent or smug.

It kept one thinking of what it meant to live in Russia over the last 70 years. Twenty million people were killed in the First World War and in the Bolshevik revolution and civil war that followed it. As many as 10 million may have perished in the early Thirties in the famine that followed the enforced collectivization of the farms under Stalin, and more than 20 million were slain by the Germans. Eight to 10 million died in the forced labor camps under Stalin. Then Khrushchev, coming to power after Stalin's death, eventually made public to the people of the USSR that Stalin had been not only a legend but a monster. Since the average Russian, reading his highly controlled press, had the reflex by now of believing that Stalin was an infallible leader, the shock was equal, let us say, to Americans being told that Dwight D. Eisenhower was a mass murderer of children.

Psychologically, the Russians never recovered. That is comprehensible. On a smaller scale, we have never been the same since the assassinations of JFK, Martin Luther King, and Bobby Kennedy. Of course, Khrushchev was soon deposed. The bearer of such ill tidings could hardly rule for long. By the late Sixties, after more than 50 years of slaughter, terror, and historic shock, of cumulative catastrophe where on average more than a million Soviet citizens were killed in war or perished in camps and prisons each year, the USSR now began to live with Brezhnev through two decades of sluggish, stagnant progress. Terror diminished, and rebuilding advanced to some degree. By huge emphasis on an armaments economy and a relative indifference to consumer goods, nuclear parity with the West was brought much closer. By now, however, the ideals of the Bolshevik revolution of 1917 had died ten times over. A vast social machine was still functioning, but the power of corruption had also swollen. The USSR was in metamorphosis from a stern, war-rationed economy, bulwarked by prodigious terror, to an immense welfare state drowning in cynicism, bribery, waste, shoddy products, and oppression.

"Why, then, do you say it's not a police state? It's still oppressive."

"Yes, but not nearly to the degree it used to be."

I thought of a dissident I had talked to. His face twisted with aristocratic contempt every time I asked about anyone who worked high in the Soviet establishment.

"What of the terror?" I asked.

The dissident shrugged. "Years ago, the secret police would come in the middle of the night. Nobody ever heard of you again. Now you're arrested and have a trial. You go to a camp, or you're exiled."

"Are the arrests frequent?"

"No. For every 20 they used to seize, now maybe they take one. The other 19 are left to worry."

One could hear the same all over. The situation was not good, in fact it was considerably worse than it had been just a few years ago, but, on the other hand, it was vastly improved from the time of Stalin. In those years, tens of millions had been arrested by his orders. Now one measured the political prisoners by the thousands. Helsinki Watch, which is not sympathetic to the USSR, gives as its best guess-estimate that over the past 15 years there have been 5000 political arrests and that the number of dissidents who are in prison this year might be 1000 individuals. Another estimate puts it at 10,000 prisoners. These are not happy figures but, in proportion to the Soviet Union's population, 270 million, we must recognize that one is speaking of a ratio of a single political prisoner for every 270,000 Soviet citizens, or, taking the highest estimate, one in every 27,000.

Sitting at a table in a Russian's home, discussing the regime, there is often a silence after a remark has been too critical. Someone will point to the ceiling as if to say, *"They* are listening." Of course, given the number of houses in which such conversations take place, the odds are considerable that this particular room is not being monitored at the moment. Maybe the KGB placed a working microphone here once, maybe they will put one in again, next month or next year, but the finger does not point to the ceiling in abject fear so much as with a wry, almost mocking respect. It underlines the sensibility of one's childhood: God is listening to my thoughts. Yet, as one soon learns, He does not strike for too little. Of course, it can take years before one gets brave enough to think: Maybe He is not listening at all. How, indeed, is one to know?

There is even a story so apocryphal that one hopes it is true. Dissidents tell it as a talisman. The dear friend—let us call him Glabikov—of a famous poetess was arrested for some minor act of dissidence. The poetess, in response to an old Russian tradition that esteemed artists have the right to petition the czar, now sent a letter to Andropov. At its conclusion she wrote, "If you do not release Glabikov, I do not know what I will do."

No answer came from the General Secretary. "Andropov is a gross man for not replying to me," said the poetess to her friends.

Then, one day, the KGB asked her to visit. One can picture the faces she encountered. In America, one can see the same faces on trade union leaders, corporate executives, Mafia godfathers, some Congressmen and—take a look—a couple of our President's close advisers.

If it helps the tale, you may also believe that the poetess was a beautiful woman, for indeed she was. Her voice was deep and sweet and mysterious and full of the awe that a good voice brings to the deep-rooted music of words.

"All right," said the KGB officer, "what is this last line in your letter? Why do you say that you do not know what you will do? What does this mean?"

"It means," said the poetess, "that I do not know what I will do if Glabikov is not released."

"No, what are you saying? Do you imply that you will commit suicide? Or that you will defect? Are you going to denounce us? What sort of scandal do you propose?"

"I mean," she repeated in lugubrious tones firm in their wonder at her own uncharted depths, "I mean that if you do not release Glabikov, I simply do not know what I will do."

Legend has it that Glabikov was released. How splendid if the story is true!

Of course, it is equal to a scenario. I offer it as a counterscenario to the other scenarios. Facets to contrast with other facets. It may be the only way to offer a portrait of Russia that is without scenario, to give, that is, a sketch of a huge and complex beast of a nation, a land difficult to live in, abrasive as steel wool, messed-up, by parts horrendous, but nonetheless a real country where people do not necessarily decide in advance that they are working for a doomed and evil machine, but instead grow up suffering and scheming, looking for better ways and means to live well and fornicate well, and even go bowling and play ball like thee and me.

Maybe, we are coming closer to the idea of what I wish to say. In Lithuania, in the city of Vilnius, I happened to wander into a Roman Catholic church around twilight. Mass was being celebrated, and the church was filled to capacity with old women, a few men, a few adolescents. The service was fervid. It was also beautiful. Beauty takes on the power of addiction in the gray antisensuous climate of March in the Soviet—indeed, pure beauty begins to feel as necessary as food. I do not know if I ever attended a Catholic service that was more intense. The point, however, is that my entrance into the church was casual, and the exit as easy. I was alone, and no policemen were outside, at least none that I could see. My own good simple tourist's reaction: "Holy cow, it's not that big a deal here anymore to go to church."

A trickier example. It may reveal more. An American who was born in Lithuania went back to visit her relatives, and they, bringing food, drove in to greet her at the hotel in Vilnius. They wanted her to come back to their village, 50 kilometers away. It's forbidden, don't you understand? she told them.

No, it's okay, they said. You can come with us.

As it turned out, the woman was right. It was an exceptional case, and her relatives had no understanding of exceptional cases. So soon as they started to drive her around town, they were followed by another car. This was startling to her relatives. They were farm people. Something like this had never happened before—*to them.*

If you were visited in your home in America by a relative who happened to be a Soviet official, your phone might be tapped by the FBI. If you discovered it, that would be unique to your experience. Of course, there is a difference between a visit by an average American tourist to her hometown in Lithuania and a Soviet on official business here, and in that separation may be measured the gap in the freedoms of the two countries. But my point is that these country people in Lithuania were less afraid of the authorities than was their visitor. They had not been living with our image of them. In fact, in this case, the American woman was right and the natives were wrong, but whatever else, her relatives were obviously not dwelling in prodigious daily fear.

Of course, Russia, by any measure, is a harsh country, so let me end with a harsh thought. It is sad but true that our American leaders accept fascism in other countries and do business with it. Our leaders can understand it. Fascism is an undemocratic form of government led by the rich and the military. Communism, however, terrifies the American system. After all, it is the tyranny of the poor when society breaks up altogether. So in America we are encouraged to abhor it in every form. We live with the scenario that Russia is an evil force. Now, the world is on the edge of destroying itself. Can we afford abhorrence any longer? It is significant that we have forgiven Nazi Germany for its concentration camps—and the 20 million people that the Nazis exterminated—we do great business with Germany—but we still do not exculpate the Russians for their gulags. We talk as if the slave labor camps are as hideous today as 30 or 40 years ago, and that, at least—let us look to thank the Lord for the real blessings—is not true any longer.

Estimates on Political Prisoners

Country†	Population	Prisoners
Turkey	46,312,000	13,000*
Uruguay	2,947,000	800
Cuba	9,706,000	1250**
El Salvador	4,813,000	400
Nicaragua	2,824,000	300
Argentina‡	28,438,000	1000***
USSR	270,000,000	1000***

Source: U.S. Helsinki Watch Committee.
†Listed in order of ratio between political prisoners and total population.
*Estimates reach 20,000.
**250 long-term plus 1000 serving short terms.
‡Before Falklands (1981).
***One estimate goes so high as 10,000.

We are a great nation. Can we take the step of assuming that we will be greater yet as we come to live with some more generous understanding of all our possibilities? Our world may be the most beautiful of all the planets, but the state of our international relations is more barren than the craters of the moon.

Questions for Discussion and Writing

1. Mailer questions at the beginning of his essay whether fifteen days as an "individual tourist" could provide a basis for offering any perceptions of the Soviet Union. In what ways, direct and indirect, does he answer this question?
2. What does Mailer mean by "scenario," and in what ways does his title reflect the changes he makes in his thinking as a result of his visit to the Soviet Union?
3. In what ways is Mailer's American background important in his perceptions of the Soviets? What parallels does he draw between the United States and the Soviet Union? What differences between the two countries strike him most forcefully? Why does he find the Soviet Union "a sad place"?
4. What is the significance of the story he tells about the woman who writes to the authorities pleading to release Glabikov? How does the story relate to the conclusions Mailer has drawn as a result of his experiences in the Soviet Union?
5. Mailer suggests a number of paradoxes in his essay. What are they, and how do they relate to his main ideas?

PREMCHAND

A Coward

Premchand, the pseudonym of Dhanpat Rai, was born in 1880 in a village near Benares, India. Although poor, Premchand's family was noted for producing men of letters; he studied Persian, Urdu, and Hindi, and wrote in both the Urdu and Hindi languages. A prolific writer in spite of his poor health, Premchand has the distinction of having created the genre of the serious short story in India. In both Urdu and Hindi, he transformed fiction from rambling romantic tales to realistic narratives comparable to the European fiction from which he gained his models—especially from Dickens, Tolstoy, Chekhov, and Gorky.

The village life that Premchand knew best became the richest subject for his work. Although life in the cities of India has changed dramatically over the years, the villages still operate within an ancient, rigid, and sometimes cruel social structure: an unyielding caste system, crushing poverty, the exploitation of the poor by landowners and moneylenders, and terror at the possibility of disgrace or loss of face. Premchand's stories re-create these pressures and take the reader to the heart of village culture.

"A Coward" explores the struggle between the power and control of the caste system and two young people attempting to choose their own relationship as students at a university. Although the caste system began among the Hindus with four major castes, each caste representing collective occupations, today there are reputed to be about five thousand subcastes of the original four. Brahman is still the highest caste—originally the caste of Hindu priests; Baniya, one caste down, is the class of merchants. When women marry in India, even now the arrangement usually of their parents, they move to the home of their in-laws, and there are subject to the dictates of their mother-in-laws, too often another cruel aspect of life, especially for women, in India.

Before you read "A Coward," write about a time in your life when you tried to defy a strict rule of your parents. Describe the situation and the rule, why your parents believed so strongly in it, the outcome of your defiance, and what you learned as a result of this experience.

The boy's name was Keshav, the girl's Prema. They went to the same college, they were in the same class. Keshav believed in new ways and was opposed to the old caste customs. Prema adhered to the old order and fully accepted the traditions. But all the same there was a strong attachment between them and the whole college was aware of it. Although he was a Brahman Keshav regarded marriage with this Baniya girl as the culmination of his life. He didn't care a straw about his father and mother. Caste traditions he considered a fraud. If anything embodied the truth for him it was Prema. But for Prema it was impossible to take one step in opposition to the dictates of caste and family.

One evening the two of them met in a secluded corner of Victoria Park and sat down on the grass facing one another. The strollers had gone off one by one but these two lingered on. They had got into a discussion it was impossible to end.

Keshav said angrily, "All it means is that you don't care about me."

Prema tried to calm him down. "You're being unjust to me, Keshav. It's only that I don't know how I can bring it up at home without upsetting them. They're devoted to the old traditions. If they hear anything about a matter like this from me can't you imagine how distressed they'll be?"

"And aren't you a slave of those old traditions too then?" Keshav asked her sharply.

"No, I'm not," Prema said, her eyes tender, "but what my mother and father want is more important to me than anything."

"And you yourself don't count at all?"

"If that's how you want to understand it."

"I used to think those old ways were just for silly hypocrites but now it seems that educated girls like you knuckle under to them too. Since I'm ready to give up everything for you I expect the same thing from you."

In silence Prema wondered what authority she had over her own life. She had no right to go in any way against the mother and father who had created her from their own blood and reared her with love. To Keshav she said humbly, "Can love be considered only in terms of husband and wife and not friendship? I think of love as an attachment of the soul."

"You'll drive me crazy with your rationalizations," Keshav said harshly. "Just understand this—if I'm disappointed I can't go on living. I'm a materialist and it's not possible for me to be satisfied with some intangible happiness in the world of the imagination."

He caught Prema's hand and tried to draw her toward him, but she broke away and said, "I told you I'm not free. Don't ask me to do something I have no right to do."

If she'd spoken harshly he would not have been so hurt. For an instant he restrained himself, then he stood up and said sadly, "Just as you wish," and slowly walked away. Prema, in tears, continued to sit there.

When after supper that night Prema lay down in her mother's room she could not sleep. Keshav had said things to her that shadowed her heart like reflections in unquiet waters, changing at every moment, and she could not calm them. How could she talk to her mother about such things? Embarrassment kept her silent. She thought, "If I don't marry Keshav what's left for me in life?" While she thought about it over and over again her mind was made up about just one thing—if she did not marry Keshav she would marry no one.

Her mother said, "Still not sleeping? I've told you so many times you ought to do a little work around the house. But you can never take any time off from your books. In a little while you'll be going to some strange house and who knows what sort of place it will be? If you don't get accustomed to doing housework, how are you going to manage?"

Naively Prema asked, "Why will I be going to a strange house?"

Smiling, her mother said, "For a girl it's the greatest calamity, daughter. After being sheltered at home, as soon as she's grown up off she goes to live with others. If she gets a good husband her days pass happily, otherwise she has to go through life weeping. It all depends on fate. But in our community there's no family that appeals to me. There's no proper regard for girls anywhere. But we have to stay within our caste. Who knows how long caste marriages are going to go on?"

Frightened Prema said, "But here and there they're beginning to have marriages outside the caste." She'd said it for the sake of talking but she trembled lest her mother might guess something.

Surprised, her mother asked, "You don't mean among Hindus?" Then she answered herself. "If this has happened in a few places, then what's come of it?"

Prema did not reply. She was afraid her mother had understood her meaning. She saw her future in that moment before her like a great dark tunnel opening its mouth to swallow her up. It was a long time before she could fall asleep.

When she got up early in the morning Prema was aware of a strange new courage. We all make important decisions on the spur of the moment as though some divine power impelled us toward them, and so it was with Prema. Until yesterday she'd considered her parents' ideas as unchallengeable, but facing the problem courage was born in her, much in the way a quiet breeze coming against a mountain sweeps over the summit in a violent gust. Prema thought, "Agreed, this body is my mother's and father's but whatever my own self, my soul, is to get must be got in this body. To hesitate now would not only be unfitting, it would be fatal. Why sacrifice your life for false principle? If a marriage isn't founded on love then it's just a business bargain with the body. Could you give yourself without love?" And she rebelled against the idea that she could be married off to somebody she had never seen.

After breakfast she had started to read when her father called her affectionately. "Yesterday I went to see your principal and he had a lot of praise for you."

"You're only saying that!"

"No, it's true." Then he opened a drawer of his desk and took out a picture set in a velvet frame. He showed it to her and said, "This boy came out first in the Civil Service examinations. You must have heard of him."

He had brought up the subject in such a way as not to give away his intention, but it was clear to Prema, she saw through it at once. Without looking at the picture she said, "No, I don't know who he is."

With feigned surprise her father said, "What? You haven't even heard his name? His picture and an article about him are in today's paper."

"Suppose they are?" Prema said. "The examinations don't mean anything to me. I always assumed that people who took those exams must be terribly conceited. After all, what do they aim for except to lord it over their wretched, penniless brothers?—And pile up a fortune doing it. That's no great career to aspire to."

The objection was spiteful, unjust. Her father had assumed that after his eulogy she would be interested. When he'd listened to her answer he said sharply, "You talk as though money and power mean nothing to you."

"That's right," she said, "they don't mean a thing to me. I look for self-sacrifice in a man. I know some boys who wouldn't accept that kind of position even if you tried to force it on them."

"Well, I've learned something new today!" he said sarcastically "And still I see people swarming around trying to get the meanest little jobs—I'd just like to see the face of one of these fellows capable of such self-sacrifice. If I did I'd get down on my knees to him."

Perhaps if she'd heard these words on another occasion Prema might have hung her head in shame. But this time, like a soldier with a dark tunnel behind him, there was no way for her to go except forward. Scarcely controlling her anger, her eyes full of indignation, she went to her room and from among several pictures of Keshav picked out the one she considered the worst and brought it back and set it down in front of her father. He wanted to give it no more than a casual glance, but at the first glimpse he was drawn to it. Keshav was tall and even though thin one recognized a strength and discipline about him; he was not particularly handsome but his face reflected such intelligence that one felt confidence in him.

While he looked at it her father said, "Who is he?"

Prema, bowing her head, said hesitantly, "He's in my class."

"Is he of our community?"

Prema's face clouded over: her destiny was to be decided on the answer. She realised that it was useless to have brought out the picture. The firmness she had had for an instant weakened before this simple question. In a low voice she said, "No, he's not, he's a Brahman." And even while she was saying it, agitated she left the room as though the atmosphere there were suffocating her, and on the other side of the wall she began to cry.

Her father's anger was so great at first that he wanted to call her out again and tell her plainly it was impossible. He got as far as the door, but seeing Prema crying his anger softened. He was aware of what Prema felt for this boy and he believed in education for women but he intended to maintain the family traditions. He would have sacrificed all his property for a suitable bridegroom of his own caste. But outside the limits of his community he could not conceive of any bridegroom worthy or noble enough; he could not imagine any disgrace greater than going beyond them.

"From today on you'll stop going to college," he said with a harsh tone. "If education teaches you to disregard our traditions, then education is wicked."

Timidly Prema said, "But it's almost time for the examinations."

"Forget about them."

Then he went into his room and pondered a long time.

◄►

One day six months later Prema's father came home and called Vriddha, his wife, for a private talk.

"As far as I know," he said, "Keshav's a well-brought-up and brilliant boy. I'm afraid that Prema's grieving to the point where she might take her life. You and I have tried to explain and so have others but nobody has had the slightest effect on her. What are we going to do about it?"

Anxiously his wife said, "Let her, but if she has her way how can you face the dishonour? How could I ever have borne a wicked girl like that?"

He frowned and said with a tone of reproach, "I've heard that a thousand times. But just how long can we moan about this caste tradition business? You're mistaken if you think the bird's going to stay hopping at home once it's spread its wings. I've thought about the problem objectively and I've come to the conclusion that we're obliged to face the emergency. I can't watch Prema die in the name of caste rules. Let people laugh but the time is not far off when all these old restrictions will be broken. Even today there have been hundreds of marriages outside the caste limitations. If the aim of marriage is a happy life for a man and a woman together we can't oppose Prema."

Vriddha was angry. "If that's your intention then why ask me?" she said. "But I say that I won't have anything to do with this marriage, and I'll never look at that girl's face again, I'll consider her as dead as our sons who died."

"Well then, what else can you suggest?"

"What if we do let her marry this boy? He'll take his civil service examinations in two years and with what he has to offer it will be a great deal if he becomes a clerk in some office."

"But what if Prema should kill herself?"

"Then let her—you've encouraged her, haven't you? If she doesn't care about us why should we blacken our name for her? Anyway, suicide's no game—it's only a threat. The heart's like a wild horse—until it's broken and bridled nobody can touch it. If her heart stays like that who's to say that she'll stick with Keshav for a whole life-time? The way she's in love with him today, well, she can be in love with somebody else just as much tomorrow. And because of this you're ready to be disgraced?"

Her husband gave her a questioning look. "And if tomorrow she should go and marry Keshav, then what will you do? Then how much of your honour will be left? Out of shyness or consideration for us she may not have done anything yet, but if she decides to be stubborn there's nothing you or I can do."

It had never occurred to Vriddha that the problem could have such a dreadful ending. His meaning struck her with the violence of a bullet. She sat silent for a moment as though the shock had scattered her wits. Then backing down, she said, "What wild ideas you have! Until today I've never heard of a decent girl marrying according to her own wish."

"You may not have heard of it but I have, I've seen it and it's entirely possible."

"The day it happens will be my last!"

"But if it has to be this way isn't it preferable that we make the proper arrangements? If we're to be disgraced we may as well be efficient about it. Send for Keshav tomorrow and see what he has to say."

◀━▼

Keshav's father lived off a government pension. By nature he was ill-tempered and miserly; he found satisfaction only in religious ostentation. He was totally without imagination and unable to respect the personal feelings of anybody else. At present he was still living in the same world in which he had passed his childhood and youth. The rising tide of progress he called ruination and hoped to save at least his own family from it by any means available to him. Therefore when one day Prema's father came to him and broached the prospect of her marrying Keshav, old Panditji could not control himself. Staring through eyes dim with anger he said, "Are you drunk? Whatever this relationship may be it's not marriage. It appears that you too have had your head turned by the new ideas."

"I don't like this sort of connection either," Prema's father said gently. "My ideas about it are just the same as yours. But the thing is that, being helpless, I had to come to see you. You're aware too of how willful today's youngsters have become. It's getting hard for us old-timers to defend our theories. I'm afraid that if these two become desperate they may take their lives."

Old Panditji brought his foot down with a bang and shouted, "What are you saying, Sir! Aren't you ashamed? We're Brahmans and even among Brahmans we're of high rank. No matter how low a Brahman may fall he can never be so degraded that he can countenance a marriage with a shop-keeping Baniya's daughter. The day noble Brahmans run out of daughters we can discuss the problem. I say you have a fantastic nerve even to bring this matter up with me."

He was every bit as furious as Prema's father was humble, and the latter, unable to bear the humiliation any longer, went off cursing his luck.

Just then Keshav returned from college. Panditji sent for him at once and said severely, "I've heard that you're betrothed to some Baniya girl. How far has this actually gone?"

Pretending ignorance, Keshav said, "Who told you this?"

"Somebody. I'm asking you, is it true or not? If it's true and you've decided to go against your caste, then there's no more room for you in this house. You won't get one pice of my money. Whatever is in this house I've earned, and it's my right to give it to whoever I want. If you're guilty of this wicked conduct, you won't be permitted to put your foot inside my house."

Keshav was familiar with his father's temper. He loved Prema and he intended to marry her in secret. His father wouldn't always be alive and he counted on his mother's affection; sustained by that love he felt that he was ready to suffer any hardship. But Keshav was like a faint-hearted soldier who loses his courage at the sight of a gun and turns back.

Like any average young fellow he would argue his theories with a passion and demonstrate his devotion with his tongue. But to suffer for them was beyond his capacity. If he persisted and his father refused to weaken he didn't know where he would turn, his life would be ruined.

In a low voice he said, "Whoever told you that is a complete liar and nothing else." Staring at him, Panditji said, "So my information is entirely wrong?"

"Yes, entirely wrong."

"Then you'll write a letter to that shopkeeper this very moment and remember that if there's any more of this gossip he can regard you as his greatest enemy. Enough, go."

Keshav could say no more. He walked away but it seemed to him that his legs were utterly numb.

The next day Prema sent this letter to Keshav.

Dearest Keshav,

I was terribly upset when I heard about the rude and callous way your father treated mine. Perhaps he's threatened you too, in which case I wait anxiously to hear what your decision is. I'm ready to undergo any kind of hardship with you. I'm aware of your father's wealth but all I need is your love to content me. Come tonight and have dinner with us. My mother and father are both eager to meet you.

I'm caught up in the dream of when the two of us will be joined by that bond that cannot be broken, that remains strong no matter how great the difficulties.

Your Prema

By evening there had been no reply to this letter. Prema's mother asked over and over again, "Isn't Keshav coming?" And her father kept his eyes glued on the door. By nine o'clock there was still no sign of Keshav nor any letter.

In Prema's mind all sorts of fears and hopes revolved. Perhaps Keshav had had no chance to write a letter, no chance to come today so that tomorrow he would surely come. She read over again the love letters he'd written her earlier. How steeped in love was every word, how much emotion, anxiety and acute desire! Then she remembered the words he'd said a hundred times and how often he'd wept before her. It was impossible to despair with so many proofs, but all the same throughout the night she was tormented by anxiety.

Early in the morning Keshav's answer came. Prema took the letter with trembling hands and read it. The letter fell from her hands. It seemed to her that her blood had ceased to flow. He had written:

I'm in a terrible quandary about how to answer you. I've been desperate trying to figure out what to do and I've come to the conclusion that for the present it would be impossible for me to go against my father's orders. Don't think I'm a coward. I'm not being selfish either. But I don't have the strength to overcome the obstacles facing me. Forget what I told you before. At that time I had no idea of how hard it was going to be.

Prema drew a long, painful breath, then she tore up the letter and threw it away. Her eyes filled with tears. She had never had the slightest expectation that the Keshav she had taken into her heart of hearts as her husband could be so cruel. It was as though until now she'd been watching a golden vision but on opening her eyes it had vanished completely. All her hope had disappeared and she was left in darkness.

"What did Keshav write?" her mother asked.

Prema looked at the floor and said, "He's not feeling well." What else was there to say? She could not have borne the shame of revealing Keshav's brutal disloyalty.

She spent the whole day working around the house, as though there was nothing wrong. She made dinner for everyone that evening and ate with them, then until quite late she played the harmonium and sang.

In the morning they found her lying dead in her room at a moment when the golden rays of dawn bestowed on her face the illusory splendour of life.

Translated by David Rubin

Questions for Discussion and Writing

1. In what ways does this story raise questions about who should have authority over a person's life? As the story begins, what is Keshav's answer to that question? What is Prema's answer? On what ideas do they base their answers?
2. What cultural assumptions do Prema's mother and father have about the person she will marry? What power does she have as their daughter, both in their eyes and hers, to assert herself? How and why do Prema's and her parents' assumptions change over the course of the story?
3. What are Keshav's and Prema's assumptions about love in this story? Why do they think they love each other? Why or why not do you think they do?
4. What aspects of this story do you find ironic? Who is the coward of the title?

TEWFIQ AL-HAKIM

Not a Thing Out of Place

Born in 1902 in Alexandria, Egypt, Tewfiq al-Hakim studied law in Cairo and Paris before winning his reputation as the Arab world's leading playwright.

Through more than fifty plays on social themes, al-Hakim introduced the theater of ideas to Egypt. Arab dramatists typically draw on two major sources as models: the tradition of satirical writing for puppet theater, related to the Karagöz *(the boastful, lowbrow characters of the shadow play) of Turkey, and the European models—especially for al-Hakim, Eugène Ionesco's theater of the absurd. "Not a Thing Out of Place" not only reflects this latter influence, but also helps us to approach in a playful frame of mind what appear to us to be cultural absurdities. It comes from a collection of al-Hakim's dramas entitled* The Fate of a Cockroach.

Before you read "Not a Thing Out of Place," write about a time in your life when you encountered a group of people whose behavior, though normal to them, appeared bizarre or crazy to you. Describe the situation and the people involved, their bizarre (at least in your terms) behaviors, and what happened when your world met theirs.

Characters

BARBER	Young Man
CUSTOMER	Young Lady
POSTMAN	Man in European Dress
	Villagers

A village square near the station. A barber has set up by a wall; he has a customer and is sharpening his razor.

BARBER (*Taking hold of the customer's bald head*): When there's a water-melon right there in front of you all nice and shiny, how can you find out whether it's red inside or unripe except by splitting it open with a knife?

CUSTOMER (*Disturbed*): What's the connection?

BARBER: Nothing at all, just that certain things remind one of others.

CUSTOMER: What things? What reminds you?

BARBER: Tell me, can you know what's inside this head of yours?

CUSTOMER: What are you getting at? Do you mean in the way of ideas?

BARBER: What ideas are you talking about, man? Who mentioned ideas? We're talking about water-melons.

CUSTOMER: I don't get it at all.

BARBER: Just let me explain. It's something that can be perfectly well understood. If you've got a water-melon in your hand, what do you do with it? Play football with it?

CUSTOMER: Of course not.

BARBER: Quite so. That's just what happened—my brother wasn't wrong then.

CUSTOMER: Your brother?

BARBER: Yes, my full brother. God bless him, he was a real fine barber like myself.

CUSTOMER: What about the water-melon?

BARBER: A customer's head—and not a wit better than that of your good self.

CUSTOMER (*With a cry of alarm*): Customer's head?

BARBER: And so what? Slice it.

CUSTOMER: What do you mean "so what"? Slice the customer's head?

BARBER: Isn't that the way to see whether it's red inside or unripe?

CUSTOMER (*Looking in fear at the razor*): With a razor?

BARBER: You see, at the time he happened to have the razor in his hand and the soap was on the customer's chin.

CUSTOMER (*Fearfully*): And what happened after that?

BARBER: I swear to you, they carted him off to hospital.

CUSTOMER: The customer?

BARBER: My brother.

CUSTOMER: Your brother? It was *he* they carted off? But why?

BARBER: What d'you think they said? They said he was mad. Can you believe it? Can you credit it?

CUSTOMER: I really can't. So they carted him off to the lunatic asylum?

BARBER: That's right, sir. Can you imagine such a thing?

CUSTOMER: And the customer?

BARBER: He was carted off by ambulance.

CUSTOMER: God Almighty! The good Lord preserve us!

BARBER (*Sharpening his razor on the palm of his hand*):   Just put yourself in my brother's place. In front of you there's a water-melon and you're holding a knife. What would you do?

CUSTOMER: And have you ever done it?

BARBER: God be my witness—up until now, no.

CUSTOMER: Any intention of doing so?

BARBER: Maybe. After all, is there anything wrong about slicing a water-melon with a razor?

CUSTOMER (*Tearing the towel from his neck*):   I'm off!

BARBER: Where to? There's still the other side to be done.

CUSTOMER: One side's quite enough. 'Bye. (*The customer makes his escape at a run.*)

A postman appears carrying a handful of letters.

POSTMAN: What's that customer of yours running off for with the soap still on his chin?

BARBER: Mad, God spare you.

POSTMAN (*Holding out the handful of letters*):   Take delivery of today's post.

BARBER: Just throw them down in the old basin as usual.

POSTMAN (*Hands him the letters*):   Take them and throw them in yourself, then come along and let's have a game.

BARBER(*Taking the letters and throwing them down into a nearby basin on the floor*):   What shall we play today?

A young man in European dress appears.

YOUNG MAN (*To the postman*):   Is there a letter for me? My name's . . .

POSTMAN (*Interrupting him*):   There are plenty of letters for you. Just choose yourself the letter you fancy.

YOUNG MAN: But I want a letter addressed to me.

POSTMAN: Are you new to the village?

YOUNG MAN: I arrived here only yesterday. I came for my cousin's wedding.

POSTMAN: You don't know how naïve you're being. In this village, son, we don't have the time to deliver letters to people. The whole postbag's in the basket . . .

BARBER: In the basin . . .

POSTMAN: In the master barber's basin—and what a blessed and auspicious basin it is! Everyone comes along and simply takes his pick—be it addressed to him, to someone else, it's no concern of ours. The great thing is to get rid of the post day by day.

YOUNG MAN: You mean you take a letter that doesn't belong to you?

POSTMAN: One letter, two—just as your fancy takes you.

YOUNG MAN: My fancy? What's my fancy to do with it? I want a letter that's mine.

POSTMAN: Every letter you have here is yours. Open any letter and you'll find it contains amusing things. Don't you want to be amused?

YOUNG MAN: Whatever are you saying? Is this how you're dealing with people's letters?

POSTMAN: Every day—and the people like it this way. In a couple of hours they've swiped the lot.

YOUNG MAN: But this is what's called chaos.

POSTMAN: Not at all. That chaos you're talking about is something altogether different.

BARBER: That sort of chaos doesn't happen here, my dear sir—thank God! Like me to give you a shave?

YOUNG MAN: No thanks. I've just shaved.

BARBER: I'll crop a bit of the fur off the water-melon?

YOUNG MAN: Water-melon?

POSTMAN: What he means, begging your pardon, is that he'll shave your head for you.

YOUNG MAN: No—thanks.

POSTMAN: Then grab yourself a couple of letters from the basin and take yourself off. The fact is we just haven't got the time.

YOUNG MAN (*Goes up to the basin and searches for a letter addressed to him*): No letters for me. 'Bye. (*He is about to depart.*)

POSTMAN (*Stopping him*): Going away empty-handed like that? Man, take yourself a letter from those in front of you. Like me to choose you one? (*He goes up to the basin and chooses a letter.*) Take this one—it's in a woman's handwriting. You'll enjoy it.

YOUNG MAN (*Hesitating*): Yes, but . . .

POSTMAN: But what? Don't say "but." Go on—don't embarrass me. Really, don't embarrass me.

BARBER: Go on and take it. Don't embarrass him. Put your trust in God and off you go. We just haven't got the time to attend to you.

YOUNG MAN (*Takes the letter from the postman*): Hope it's all right! What an extraordinary thing! (*He goes off with the letter.*)

POSTMAN: What were we talking about before that asinine young fellow came along?

BARBER: We were saying what would we play today.

POSTMAN: Yes, quite right—what shall we play? I'll tell you what—we'll play the game of the donkey and the philosopher.

BARBER: What's a philosopher?

POSTMAN: Someone with a big brain.

BARBER: That'll be me.

POSTMAN: No, you're the donkey.

BARBER: Why?

POSTMAN: Because a donkey's got a bigger brain.

BARBER: How's that?

POSTMAN: I'll tell you: Ever seen a donkey having a shave at a barber's?

BARBER: No.

POSTMAN: Is that clever of him or not?

BARBER: Yes.

POSTMAN: Right, then I'll be the donkey.

BARBER: Just now you said I'd be the donkey.

POSTMAN: I've changed my mind.

BARBER: What about me—who'll I be?

POSTMAN: You'll be the philosopher.

BARBER: No thanks, I don't want to be no philosopher.

POSTMAN: You silly man, a philosopher's more intelligent.

BARBER: Do you take me for a fool? Do you think I'm so gaga I don't know?

POSTMAN: Don't you believe me? All right, go and ask anyone: Is a donkey more intelligent than a philosopher? He'll tell you . . .

BARBER: I'll tell you myself. Ever seen a donkey going off to post a letter?

POSTMAN: No.

BARBER: Is that intelligent or not?

POSTMAN: Yes.

BARBER: Right, then I'll be the donkey.

POSTMAN: But, my dear fellow, I want to be the donkey.

BARBER: You be a donkey as well—then we'll both be donkeys. What's wrong with that?

POSTMAN: It's no good, one of us must be a philosopher. That's how the game's played.

BARBER: I'm no good for a philosopher—I've got a big brain.

POSTMAN: And I'm the empty-headed one?

BARBER: No, not at all, I just meant that. . . .

The young man reappears, the opened letter in his hand.

YOUNG MAN: This letter's from a girl to her fiancé. She tells him to meet her off the noon train.

POSTMAN: There's the noon train giving a whistle—it's inside the station.

YOUNG MAN: What's to be done now?

POSTMAN: Very simple—go and meet her at the station.

YOUNG MAN: Who shall I meet?

POSTMAN: Man, the girl who sent you the letter.

YOUNG MAN: She didn't send it to me.

POSTMAN: Isn't that it in your hand?

YOUNG MAN: But it isn't for me, it isn't mine.

POSTMAN: What did you open it for then?

YOUNG MAN: You handed it to me.

POSTMAN: And you took it and opened it and read it. It's therefore yours. Off you go and meet the lady at the station.

YOUNG MAN: And how shall I recognize her?

POSTMAN: You'll recognize her all right if she's pretty.

YOUNG MAN: Pretty?

POSTMAN: Pretty and on her own and getting off the train looking to right and left.

BARBER (*To the young man*):   Man, go and meet her. Don't be so gormless.*

YOUNG MAN: How extraordinary! Hope it's all right! (*He goes off in the direction of the station.*)

POSTMAN: Now take this young fellow: Is he a donkey or a philosopher?

BARBER: If he gets off with the lady he'll be a donkey.

POSTMAN: He'll be a philosopher, fool!

BARBER: How's that?

The customer, half his face in lather, reappears.

CUSTOMER: D'you like the idea of me walking around half shaved?

BARBER: Is that my fault?—it's you who ran off like a madman.

CUSTOMER: So it's I who's mad?

BARBER: Well, I then?

CUSTOMER: And what about your brother—you well know the one I mean?

BARBER: And what about my brother?

CUSTOMER: The water-melon . . .

BARBER: Man, have some sense—is this the season for water-melons?

CUSTOMER: Thanks be to God—you've put my mind at rest. So you had no intention . . .

*British slang for stupid.—Ed.

BARBER: To do what?

CUSTOMER: To slice the water-melon?

BARBER: Man, talk sense, can't you. Where's this water-melon you're talking of?

CUSTOMER: My head.

BARBER: This head of yours a water-melon?

CUSTOMER: You mean it's not a water-melon?

BARBER: You asking me?

CUSTOMER: Then what you said was a joke?

BARBER: What d'you mean "joke," man? Why should I joke with customers? All I say is dead serious.

CUSTOMER: You mean then that the story of the water-melon was serious?

BARBER: Of course it was serious.

CUSTOMER: Meaning that you were seriously intending to slice the water-melon?

BARBER: D'you think I was going to play football with it or just sit down and look at it?

CUSTOMER: Good God! 'Bye. (*He makes off hurriedly.*)

BARBER: Why's he run away again? What would you say about him too—a philosopher or a donkey?

POSTMAN: It seems there are a lot of philosophers around these days.

BARBER: Then why not ask him to play with us?

POSTMAN: A stranger wouldn't fit in with us.

BARBER (*Looking in the direction of the station*):   Good heavens! Just look—the young fellow's coming along with the lady.

POSTMAN: She must have turned out to be pretty!

The young man and the lady—a young and beautiful girl—approach. He is carrying her suitcase for her.

YOUNG LADY: But where is he? Why wasn't he waiting for me at the station?

YOUNG MAN: After all, *I* was waiting for you.

YOUNG LADY: But you're not he.

YOUNG MAN: Who am I then?

YOUNG LADY: How should I know who you might be?

YOUNG MAN: How don't you know—wasn't it you who wrote this letter and posted it to me? (*He shows her the letter.*)

YOUNG LADY: Yes, it was I who wrote and posted it, but . . .

YOUNG MAN: Fine, then I'm he.

YOUNG LADY: But you're not he.

YOUNG MAN: Was he old?

YOUNG LADY: No, young.

YOUNG MAN: And what am I—old or young?

YOUNG LADY: Young of course.

YOUNG MAN: That settles it—I'm he.

YOUNG LADY: How do you work that out?

YOUNG MAN: Don't you believe me? Come along and we'll ask some of the locals. (*He moves towards the postman and the barber.*) Please tell us, gentlemen: am I he or not?

POSTMAN: You are.

BARBER: The very same.

YOUNG MAN: You've heard for yourself.

YOUNG LADY: That's crazy talk.

POSTMAN: Tomorrow you'll come to your senses.

BARBER: In the same way as the gentleman has. (*He points at the young man.*)

YOUNG MAN (*To the young lady*): The most important people in the village have ruled that I am he—so I *am* he. Come on, let's go off to the registrar.

YOUNG LADY: Registrar?

YOUNG MAN: Of course. Aren't we engaged to be married? All that remains therefore is the registrar.

YOUNG LADY: But that's impossible.

YOUNG MAN: Why impossible? Everything's possible.

YOUNG LADY: Hey—and what about my fiancé?

YOUNG MAN: But, my dear lady, I'm your fiancé. It's I who received your letter and it was I who met you at the station. The villagers have borne witness to it.

YOUNG LADY: What an odd sort of village this is!

YOUNG MAN: What's wrong with this village? It's the very best; it's the one you arrived at to meet up with your fiancé and—Allah be praised—I've done just that.

YOUNG LADY: But that's absolutely impossible.

YOUNG MAN: Only too possible. Everything's possible here.

YOUNG LADY: But it's not reasonable.

YOUNG MAN: Everything's reasonable here. God be my witness—I am now absolutely convinced.

POSTMAN: Convinced that this village of ours is not chaotic?

YOUNG MAN: Absolutely so—in this place of yours not a thing is out of place.

BARBER: Put your trust in God then and off you go to the registrar's.

YOUNG MAN: And the village registrar, is he like your good selves, with never a thing out of place?

BARBER: Have no fear—put a summer water-melon in your stomach and relax!

POSTMAN: Let's do without the water-melon—this is not the place for it!

YOUNG MAN: What are you driving at?

POSTMAN: Relax—we're talking about some other water-melon.

YOUNG MAN: Then you're agreed about our being engaged and going off to the registrar's?

BARBER: Agreed.

POSTMAN: Absolutely agreed.

YOUNG LADY: But I'm not agreed.

YOUNG MAN: That's something to be said in front of the registrar—he'll deal with it.

YOUNG LADY: How'll he deal with it?

YOUNG MAN: Just as our good friend the postman dealt with matters—and he did so very soundly.

YOUNG LADY: It's extraordinary!

YOUNG MAN: I said that before you did. Come on, let's go off to the registrar's.

YOUNG LADY: Heaven knows how all this is going to end! (*The young man leads her away by the hand.*)

POSTMAN: The end will be like the beginning—all one and the same!

BARBER: And half a shave's like a whole one—all one and the same!

POSTMAN: And a letter of yours turns out not to be yours—all one and the same!

BARBER: And a head you think is a water-melon, and a water-melon you think is a head—all one and the same!

POSTMAN: And where the village registrar is concerned . . .

BARBER: All's one and the same.

POSTMAN: Let's give them a send-off.

BARBER: Bring the drum!

POSTMAN: Where's the flute?

BARBER: And let the village folk gather round—they're great ones for fun and gaiety.

POSTMAN: Yes, they never miss a chance for making merry. Go on, give them a call!

BARBER (*Together with the postman he calls out*):   Villagers! Villagers! Bring your drums and flutes! (*Some of the villagers begin to gather together.*)

A man in European dress with twirled moustaches appears.

MAN IN EUROPEAN DRESS: What's happening around here? Why are you calling to the villagers?

POSTMAN: What's it to you?

MAN IN EUROPEAN DRESS: What are you talking to me like that for?

BARBER: And who twirled your moustaches like that for you? What d'you reckon to have standing on them?

MAN IN EUROPEAN DRESS: And what are you being so rude for?

BARBER: And if I'm rude, who d'you think you are?

MAN IN EUROPEAN DRESS: And why would you be asking me that?

POSTMAN: In order to learn the reason for your honouring this place with your presence.

MAN IN EUROPEAN DRESS: And you still don't know why I'm here in this village?

POSTMAN: No, why?

MAN IN EUROPEAN DRESS: Why?

BARBER: Yes, why?

MAN IN EUROPEAN DRESS: I'm an Inspector . . .

POSTMAN (*In alarm*): Good God! We're in a real mess now! You're an Inspector? A Police Inspector?

MAN IN EUROPEAN DRESS: No . . .

BARBER: A Special Branch Inspector?

MAN IN EUROPEAN DRESS: An Inspector of Music in the band of the world-famous singer Nabawiya Santawiya, otherwise known far and wide as Naboubou!

BARBER: The Devil take you far and wide! You scared the life out of us.

POSTMAN: Yes, why didn't you say so right from the beginning? And what brought you here?

MAN IN EUROPEAN DRESS: We came for a wedding feast being held in the village.

BARBER: It must be the wedding of that fellow over there with the young lady.

POSTMAN: We were just about to give them a send-off.

MAN IN EUROPEAN DRESS: Why, are you two working in Madame Shakaa Bakaa's band?

BARBER: Shakaa Bakaa?

MAN IN EUROPEAN DRESS: That dead-beat singer who's competing with us wherever we go.

POSTMAN: No, sir, we don't work in any band.

MAN IN EUROPEAN DRESS: Amateurs?

BARBER: No, sir, we're respectable and sensible people. My honoured friend is the Grand Bey, Director of the District Post Office, while I myself am the owner of the hairdressing establishments in the district.

MAN IN EUROPEAN DRESS (*Looking at the corner of the barber's stall and the basinful of letters*): Just the place for them! Honoured to have made your acquaintance.

POSTMAN: Come on, let's give the young man and his lady a real send-off all the way up to the registrar's! Villagers! Villagers! Where are your drums? Where your flutes! Where the dancers among you?

The people of the village gather together with excited shouting, with singing and mad dancing, while chanting.

Dancing to sound of drum and flute
Into reverse the world we'll put—
And yet it's going right we'll find.
Whether sane or out of mind
It really matters not at all.
Come step it out now, one and all.

Curtain

Translated by Denys Johnson-Davies

Questions for Discussion and Writing

1. What observations can you make about the initial scene between the customer and the barber?
2. How does the arrival of the Postman and the Young Man in European Dress further confirm or change your observations? What is the significance of the Young Man's being described as wearing "European dress"?
3. What is the meaning of the play's title? In what ways is the title ironic or absurd? How could you argue that it is not ironic or absurd?
4. What are the sources of humor in the play—your humor and the characters' humor?
5. Would you describe the action of this play as an intercultural encounter or collision? Explain your position.

DEAN BARNLUND

Communication in a Global Village

Dean Barnlund has spent much of his life, both personal and profes-
sional, trying to understand others. His ongoing search for interper-
sonal understanding, however, is not confined to behavioral science.
He says his "real passions lie in the arts, principally architecture,
sculpture, music, and film." Travel occupies another significant facet
of his life: he's been around the world five times and to more than
eighty countries. "The unfamiliar and ambiguous intrigue me,"
Barnlund says.

During the time he is not traveling, writing, or researching, Barn-
lund is teaching interpersonal and intercultural communication at
San Francisco State University. His writing includes numerous theo-
retical and research papers published in journals of anthropology,
psychology, sociology, medicine, psychiatry, and communication.
He has also written several books, some of which are considered
classics in the fields of interpersonal and intercultural communica-
tion: Interpersonal Communication: Survey and Studies *(1968) and*
Public and Private Self in Japan and the United States *(1975), from*
which the essay "Communication in a Global Village" is taken.
*Barnlund's most recent book—*Communicative Styles of Japanese
and Americans—*continues his work with these comparative studies.*

Barnlund has never rested from his quest to develop his own inter-
personal and intercultural understanding—from the small details of
behavior to the big picture of what it means to be someone else, either
the person next door or across a culture.

Before you read "Communication in a Global Village," summarize the
insights you've gained as a result of your reading and writing about the
challenges of learning about other people and other cultures. In what ways
do we have to change ourselves, to what degree is communication possible
between people of the same background and of different backgrounds, and
for what reasons are you (or are you not) hopeful about these challenges?

Nearing Autumn's close.
My neighbor—
How does he live, I wonder?

BASHŌ

These lines, written by one of the most cherished of *haiku* poets, express a timeless and universal curiosity in one's fellow man. When they were written, nearly three hundred years ago, the word "neighbor" referred to people very much like one's self—similar in dress, in diet, in custom, in language—who happened to live next door. Today relatively few people are surrounded by neighbors who are cultural replicas of themselves. Tomorrow we can expect to spend most of our lives in the company of neighbors who will speak in a different tongue, seek different values, move at a different pace, and interact according to a different script. Within no longer than a decade or two the probability of spending part of one's life in a foreign culture will exceed the probability a hundred years ago of ever leaving the town in which one was born. As our world is transformed our neighbors increasingly will be people whose life styles contrast sharply with our own.

The technological feasibility of such a global village is no longer in doubt. Only the precise date of its attainment is uncertain. The means already exist: in telecommunication systems linking the world by satellite, in aircraft capable of moving people faster than the speed of sound, in computers which can disgorge facts more rapidly than men can formulate their questions. The methods for bringing people closer physically and electronically are clearly at hand. What is in doubt is whether the erosion of cultural boundaries through technology will bring the realization of a dream or a nightmare. Will a global village be a mere collection or a true community of men? Will its residents be neighbors capable of respecting and utilizing their differences, or clusters of strangers living in ghettos and united only in their antipathies for others?

Can we generate the new cultural attitudes required by our technological virtuosity? History is not very reassuring here. It has taken centuries to learn how to live harmoniously in the family, the tribe, the city state, and the nation. Each new stretching of human sensitivity and loyalty has taken generations to become firmly assimilated in the human psyche. And now we are forced into a quantum leap from the mutual suspicion and hostility that have marked the past relations between peoples into a world in which mutual respect and comprehension are requisite.

Even events of recent decades provide little basis for optimism. Increasing physical proximity has brought no millenium in human relations. If anything, it has appeared to intensify the divisions among people rather than to create a broader intimacy. Every new reduction in physical distance has made us more painfully aware of the psychic distance that divides people and has increased alarm over real or imagined differences. If today people occasionally choke on what seem to be indigestible differences between rich and poor, male and female, specialist and nonspecialist within cultures, what will happen tomorrow when people must assimilate and cope with still greater contrasts in life styles? Wider access to more people will be a doubtful victory if human beings find they have nothing to say to one another or cannot stand to listen to each other.

Time and space have long cushioned intercultural encounters, confining them to touristic exchanges. But this insulation is rapidly wearing thin. In the world of tomorrow we can expect to live—not merely vacation—in societies which seek different values and abide by different codes. There we will be surrounded by foreigners for long periods of time, working with others in the closest possible relationships. If people currently show little tolerance or talent for encounters with alien cultures, how can they learn to deal with constant and inescapable coexistence?

The temptation is to retreat to some pious hope or talismanic formula to carry us into the new age. "Meanwhile," as Edwin Reischauer reminds us, "we fail to do what we ourselves must do if 'one world' is ever to be achieved, and that is to develop the education, the skills and the attitudes that people must acquire if they are to build and maintain such a world. The time is short, and the needs are great. The task faces all human beings. But it is on the shoulders of people living in the strong countries of the world, such as Japan and the United States, that this burden falls with special weight and urgency."[1]

Anyone who has truly struggled to comprehend another person—even those closest and most like himself—will appreciate the immensity of the challenge of intercultural communication. A greater exchange of people between nations, needed as that may be, carries with it no guarantee of increased cultural empathy; experience in other lands often does little but aggravate existing prejudices. Studying guidebooks or memorizing polite phrases similarly fails to explain differences in cultural perspectives. Programs of cultural enrichment, while they contribute to curiosity about other ways of life, do not cultivate the skills to function effectively in the cultures studied. Even concentrated exposure to a foreign language, valuable as it is, provides access to only one of the many codes that regulate daily affairs; human understanding is by no means guaranteed because conversants share the same dictionary. (Within the United States, where people inhabit a common territory and possess a common language, mutuality of meaning among Mexican-Americans, White-Americans, Black-Americans, Indian-Americans—to say nothing of old and young, poor and rich, pro-establishment and anti-establishment cultures—is a sporadic and unreliable occurrence.) Useful as all these measures are for enlarging appreciation of diverse cultures, they fall short of what is needed for a global village to survive.

What seems most critical is to find ways of gaining entrance into the assumptive world of another culture, to identify the norms that govern face-to-face relations, and to equip people to function within a social system that is foreign but no longer incomprehensible. Without this kind of insight people are condemned to remain outsiders no matter how long they live in another country. Its institutions and its customs will be interpreted inevitably from the premises and through the medium of their own culture. Whether they notice something or overlook it, respect or ridicule it, express or conceal their reaction will be dictated by the logic of their own rather than the alien culture.

There are, of course, shelves and shelves of books on the cultures of the world. They cover the history, religion, political thought, music, sculpture, and industry of many nations. And they make fascinating and provocative reading. But only in the vaguest way do they suggest what it is that really distinguishes the behavior of a Samoan, a Congolese, a Japanese or an American. Rarely do the descriptions of a political structure or religious faith explain precisely when and why certain topics are avoided or why specific gestures carry such radically different meanings according to the context in which they appear.

When former President Nixon and former Premier Sato met to discuss a growing problem concerning trade in textiles between Japan and the United States, Premier Sato announced that since they were on such good terms with each other that the deliberations would be "three parts talk and seven parts 'haragei'."[2] Translated literally, "haragei" means to communicate through the belly, that is to feel out intuitively rather than verbally state the precise position of each person.

Subscribing to this strategy—one that governs many interpersonal exchanges in his culture—Premier Sato conveyed without verbal elaboration his comprehension of the plight of American textile firms threatened by accelerating exports of Japanese fabrics to the United States. President Nixon—similarly abiding by norms that govern interaction within his culture—took this comprehension of the American position to mean that new export quotas would be forthcoming shortly.

During the next few weeks both were shocked at the consequences of their meeting: Nixon was infuriated to learn that the new policies he expected were not forthcoming, and Sato was upset to find that he had unwittingly triggered a new wave of hostility toward his country. If prominent officials, surrounded by foreign advisers, can commit such grievous communicative blunders, the plight of the ordinary citizen may be suggested. Such intercultural collisions, forced upon the public consciousness by the grave consequences they carry and the extensive publicity they receive, only hint at the wider and more frequent confusions and hostilities that disrupt the negotiations of lesser officials, business executives, professionals and even visitors in foreign countries.

Every culture expresses its purposes and conducts its affairs through the medium of communication. Cultures exist primarily to create and preserve common systems of symbols by which their members can assign and exchange meanings. Unhappily, the distinctive rules that govern these symbol systems are far from obvious. About some of these codes, such as language, we have extensive knowledge. About others, such as gestures and facial codes, we have only rudimentary knowledge. On many others—rules governing topical appropriateness, customs regulating physical contact, time and space codes, strategies for the management of conflict—we have almost no systematic knowledge. To crash another culture with only the vaguest notion of its underlying dynamics reflects not only a provincial naïvete but a dangerous form of cultural arrogance.

It is differences in meaning, far more than mere differences in vocabulary, that isolate cultures, and that cause them to regard each other as strange or even barbaric. It is not too surprising that many cultures refer to themselves as "The People," relegating all other human beings to a subhuman form of life. To the person who drinks blood, the eating of meat is repulsive. Someone who conveys respect by standing is upset by someone who conveys it by sitting down; both may regard kneeling as absurd. Burying the dead may prompt tears in one society, smiles in another, and dancing in a third. If spitting on the street makes sense to some, it will appear bizarre that others carry their spit in their pocket; neither may quite appreciate someone who spits to express gratitude. The bullfight that constitutes an almost religious ritual for some seems a cruel and inhumane way of destroying a defenseless animal to others. Although staring is acceptable social behavior in some cultures, in others it is a thoughtless invasion of privacy. Privacy, itself, is without universal meaning.

Note that none of these acts involves an insurmountable linguistic challenge. The words that describe these acts—eating, spitting, showing respect, fighting, burying, and staring—are quite translatable into most languages. The issue is more conceptual than linguistic; each society places events in its own cultural frame and it is these frames that bestow the unique meaning and differentiated response they produce.

As we move or are driven toward a global village and increasingly frequent cultural contact, we need more than simply greater factual knowledge of each other. We need, more specifically, to identify what might be called the "rulebooks of meaning" that distinguish one culture from another. For to grasp the way in which other cultures perceive the world, and the assumptions and values that are the foundation of these perceptions, is to gain access to the experience of other human beings. Access to the world view and the communicative style of other cultures may not only enlarge our own way of experiencing the world but enable us to maintain constructive relationships with societies that operate according to a different logic than our own.

To survive, psychologically as well as physically, human beings must inhabit a world that is relatively free of ambiguity and reasonably predictable. Some sort of structure must be placed upon the endless profusion of incoming signals. The infant, born into a world of flashing, hissing, moving images soon learns to adapt by resolving this chaos into toys and tables, dogs and parents. Even adults who have had their vision or hearing restored through surgery describe the world as a frightening and sometimes unbearable experience; only after days of effort are they able to transform blurs and noises into meaningful and therefore manageable experiences.

It is commonplace to talk as if the world "has" meaning, to ask what "is" the meaning of a phrase, a gesture, a painting, a contract. Yet when thought about, it is clear that events are devoid of meaning until someone assigns it to them. There is no appropriate response to a bow or a handshake, a shout or a whisper, until it is interpreted. A drop of water and the color red have no meaning, they simply exist. The aim of human perception is to make the world intelligible so that it can be managed successfully; the attribution of meaning is a prerequisite to and preparation for action.[3]

People are never passive receivers, merely absorbing events of obvious significance, but are active in assigning meaning to sensation. What any event acquires in the way of meaning appears to reflect a transaction between what is there to be seen or heard, and what the interpreter brings to it in the way of past experience and prevailing motive. Thus the attribution of meaning is always a creative process by which the raw data of sensation are transformed to fit the aims of the observer.

The diversity of reactions that can be triggered by a single experience—meeting a stranger, negotiating a contract, attending a textile conference—is immense. Each observer is forced to see it through his or her own eyes, interpret it in the light of his or her own values, fit it to the requirements of his or her own circumstances. As a consequence, every object and message is seen by every observer from a somewhat different perspective. Each person will note some features and neglect others. Each will accept some relations among the facts and deny others. Each will arrive at some conclusion, tentative or certain, as the sounds and forms resolve into a "temple" or "barn," a "compliment" or "insult."

Provide a group of people with a set of photographs, even quite simple and ordinary photographs, and note how diverse are the meanings they provoke. Afterward they will recall and forget different pictures; they will also assign quite distinctive meanings to those they do remember. Some will recall the mood of a picture, others the actions; some the appearance and others the attitudes of persons portrayed. Often the observers cannot agree upon even the most "objective" details—the number of people, the precise location and identity of simple objects. A difference in frame of mind—fatigue, hunger, excitement, anger—will change dramatically what they report they have "seen."

It should not be surprising that people raised in different families, exposed to different events, praised and punished for different reasons, should come to view the world so differently. As George Kelly* has noted, people see the world through templates which force them to construe events in unique ways. These patterns or grids which we fit over the realities of the world are cut from our own experience and values, and they predispose us to certain interpretations. Industri-

---

*George Kelly is a psychiatrist and author of *The Theory of Personal Constructs,* (1955) from which this idea of templates comes.

alist and farmer do not see the "same" land; husband and wife do not plan for the "same" child; doctor and patient do not discuss the "same" disease; borrower and creditor do not negotiate the "same" mortgage; daughter and daughter-in-law do not react to the "same" mother.

The world each person creates for himself or herself is a distinctive world, not the same world others occupy. Each fashions from every incident whatever meanings fit his or her own private biases. These biases, taken together, constitute what has been called the "assumptive world of the individual." The world each person gets inside his or her head is the only world he or she knows. And it is this symbolic world, not the real world, that he or she talks about, argues about, laughs about, fights about.

Every communication, interpersonal or intercultural, is a transaction between these private worlds. As people talk they search for symbols that will enable them to share their experience and converge upon a common meaning. This process, often long and sometimes painful, makes it possible finally to reconcile apparent or real differences between them. Various words are used to describe this moment. When it involves an integration of facts or ideas, it is usually called an "agreement"; when it involves sharing a mood or feeling, it is referred to as "empathy" or "rapport." But "understanding" is a broad enough term to cover both possibilities; in either case it identifies the achievement of a common meaning.

It would be reasonable to expect that individuals who approach reality similarly might understand each other easily, and laboratory research confirms this conclusion: people with similar perceptual styles attract one another, understand each other better, work more efficiently together and with greater satisfaction than those whose perceptual orientations differ.

It must be emphasized, however, that perceptual orientations, systems of belief, and communicative styles do not exist or operate independently. They overlap and affect each other. They combine in complex ways to determine behavior. What a person says is influenced by what he or she believes and what he or she believes, in turn, by what he or she sees. His or her perceptions and beliefs are themselves partly a product of his or her manner of communicating with others.

People tend to avoid those who challenge their assumptions, who dismiss their beliefs, and who communicate in strange and unintelligible ways. When one reviews history, whether he or she examines crises within or between cultures, he or she finds people have consistently shielded themselves, segregated themselves, even fortified themselves, against wide differences in modes of perception or expression. (In many cases, indeed, have persecuted and conquered the infidel and afterwards substituted their own cultural ways for the offending ones.) Intercultural defensiveness appears to be only a counterpart of interpersonal defensiveness in the face of uncomprehended or incomprehensible differences.

Every culture attempts to create a "universe of discourse" for its members, a way in which people can interpret their experience and convey it to one another.

Without a common system of codifying sensations, life would be absurd and all efforts to share meanings doomed to failure. This universe of discourse—one of the most precious of all cultural legacies—is transmitted to each generation in part consciously and in part unconsciously. Parents and teachers give explicit instruction in it by praising or criticizing certain ways of dressing, of thinking, of gesturing, of responding to the acts of others. But the most significant aspects of any cultural code may be conveyed implicitly, not by rule or lesson but through modelling behavior. The child is surrounded by others who, through the mere consistency of their actions as males and females, mothers and fathers, salesclerks and policemen, display what is appropriate behavior. Thus the grammar of any culture is sent and received largely unconsciously, making one's own cultural assumptions and biases difficult to recognize. They seem so obviously right that they require no explanation.

It is when people nurtured in different psychological worlds meet that differences in cultural perspectives and communicative codes may sabotage efforts to understand one another. Repeated collisions between a foreigner and the members of a contrasting culture often produce what is called "culture shock." It is a feeling of helplessness, even of terror or anger, that accompanies working in an alien society. One feels trapped in an absurd and indecipherable nightmare.

It is as if some hostile leprechaun had gotten into the works and as a cosmic caper rewired the connections that hold society together. Not only do the actions of others no longer make sense, but it is impossible even to express one's own intentions clearly. "Yes" comes out meaning "No." A wave of the hand means "come," or it may mean "go." Formality may be regarded as childish, or as a devious form of flattery. Statements of fact may be heard as statements of conceit. Arriving early, or arriving late, embarrasses or impresses. "Suggestions" may be treated as "ultimatums," or precisely the opposite. Failure to stand at the proper moment, or failure to sit, may be insulting. The compliment intended to express gratitude instead conveys a sense of distance. A smile signifies disappointment rather than pleasure.

If the crises that follow such intercultural encounters are sufficiently dramatic or the communicants unusually sensitive, they may recognize the source of their trouble. If there is patience and constructive intention the confusion can sometimes be clarified. But more often the foreigner, without knowing it, leaves behind him or her a trail of frustration, mistrust, and even hatred *of which he or she is totally unaware.* Neither the foreigner nor his or her associates recognize that their difficulty springs from sources deep within the rhetoric of their own societies. Each sees himself or herself as acting in ways that are thoroughly sensible, honest and considerate. And—given the rules governing his own universe of discourse—each is. Unfortunately, there are few cultural universals, and the degree of overlap in communicative codes is always less than perfect. Experience can be transmitted with fidelity only when the unique properties of each code are recognized and respected, or where the motivation and means exist to bring them into some sort of alignment.

Cultural norms so completely surround people, so permeate thought and action, that few ever recognize the assumptions on which their lives and their sanity rest. As one observer put it, if birds were suddenly endowed with scientific curiosity they might examine many things, but the sky itself would be overlooked as a suitable subject; if fish were to become curious about the world, it would never occur to them to begin by investigating water. For birds and fish would take the sky and sea for granted, unaware of their profound influence because they comprise the medium for every act. Human beings, in a similar way, occupy a symbolic universe governed by codes that are unconsciously acquired and automatically employed. So much so that they rarely notice that the ways they interpret and talk about events are distinctively different from the ways people conduct their affairs in other cultures.

As long as people remain blind to the sources of their meanings, they are imprisoned within them. These cultural frames of reference are no less confining simply because they cannot be seen or touched. Whether it is an individual neurosis that keeps an individual out of contact with his [or her] neighbors, or a collective neurosis that separates neighbors of different cultures, both are forms of blindness that limit what can be experienced and what can be learned from others.

It would seem that everywhere people would desire to break out of the boundaries of their own experiential worlds. Their ability to react sensitively to a wider spectrum of events and peoples requires an overcoming of such cultural parochialism. But, in fact, few attain this broader vision. Some, of course, have little opportunity for wider cultural experience, though this condition should change as the movement of people accelerates. Others do not try to widen their experience because they prefer the old and familiar, seek from their affairs only further confirmation of the correctness of their own values. Still others recoil from such experiences because they feel it dangerous to probe too deeply into the personal or cultural unconscious. Exposure may reveal how tenuous and arbitrary many cultural norms are; such exposure might force people to acquire new bases for interpreting events. And even for the many who do seek actively to enlarge the variety of human beings with whom they are capable of communicating there are still difficulties.

Cultural myopia persists not merely because of inertia and habit, but chiefly because it is so difficult to overcome. One acquires a personality and a culture in childhood, long before one is capable of comprehending either of them. To survive, each person masters the perceptual orientations, cognitive biases, and communicative habits of his or her own culture. But once mastered, objective assessment of these same processes is awkward since the same mechanisms that are being evaluated must be used in making the evaluations. Once a child learns

Japanese or English or Navaho, the categories and grammar of each language predispose him or her to perceive and think in certain ways, and discourage him or her from doing so in other ways. When one attempts to discover why one sees or thinks as one does, one uses the same techniques one is trying to identify. Once one becomes an Indian, an Ibo, or a Frenchman—or even a priest or scientist—it is difficult to extricate oneself from that mooring long enough to find out what one truly is or wants.

Fortunately, there may be a way around this paradox. Or promise of a way around it. It is to expose the culturally distinctive ways various peoples construe events and seek to identify the conventions that connect what is seen with what is thought with what is said. Once this cultural grammar is assimilated and the rules that govern the exchange of meanings are known, they can be shared and learned by those who choose to work and live in alien cultures.

When people within a culture face an insurmountable problem, they turn to friends, neighbors, associates, for help. To them they explain their predicament, often in distinctive personal ways. Through talking it out, however, there often emerge new ways of looking at the problem, fresh incentive to attack it, and alternative solutions to it. This sort of interpersonal exploration is often successful within a culture for people share at least the same communicative style even if they do not agree completely in their perceptions or beliefs.

When people communicate between cultures, where communicative rules as well as the substance of experience differs, the problems multiply. But so, too, do the number of interpretations and alternatives. If it is true that the more people differ the harder it is for them to understand each other, it is equally true that the more they differ the more they have to teach and learn from each other. To do so, of course, there must be mutual respect and sufficient curiosity to overcome the frustrations that occur as they flounder from one misunderstanding to another. Yet the task of coming to grips with differences in communicative styles—between or within cultures—is prerequisite to all other types of mutuality. Without a serious and sustained effort to widen our universe of discourse, no global village can possibly survive.

References

1. Reischauer, Edwin. *Man and His Shrinking World*. Tokyo: Asahi Press, 1971, pp. 34–5.
2. Kunihiro, Masao, "U.S.–Japan Communications," in Henry Rosovsky (Ed.), *Discord in the Pacific*, Washington, D.C.: Columbia Books, 1972, p. 167.
3. For a fuller description of the process of assigning and communicating meaning, see Dean Barnlund, "A Transactional Model of Human Communication," in J. Akin and A. Goldberg (Eds.), *Language Behavior*, The Hague: Mouton, 1970.

Questions for Discussion and Writing

1. What does Barnlund mean by the term *global village*? What are the factors that will make it feasible?
2. What central questions does the author raise about the relationship be-

tween the concept of a global village and the ideas of community and culture?

3. What cultural attitudes must be generated if this village is to become a community rather than "clusters of strangers living in ghettos" (p. 616)? What are the elements in human relationships, reflected throughout history, that threaten the possibility of harmonious living in this village?

4. Barnlund argues that "differences in meaning, far more than differences in vocabulary" isolate cultures and "cause them to regard each other as strange or barbaric" (p. 619). Define what he means by "differences in meaning" here. Using examples from the essay and from your own life, discuss the kinds of consequences these differences have in people's communication.

5. In exploring the ways in which individuals assign and learn to assign meaning to events, Barnlund says that "people see the world through templates which force them to construe events in unique ways" (p. 620)— an idea he borrows from George Kelly. Explain what this idea means and its consequences for people who are trying to communicate.

6. Barnlund argues that "the grammar" of a culture is "sent and received largely unconsciously, making one's own cultural assumptions and biases difficult to recognize. They seem so obviously right they require no explanation" (p. 622). Paraphrase his meaning here and discuss its implications for the future of the global village.

RHETORICAL
TABLE OF CONTENTS

Please note: Wherever selections reflect more than one dominant mode, they have been listed twice.

NARRATION

W. P. Kinsella, *"The Moccasin Telegraph"*   3

Joanne Brown, *"Scoshi"*   11

Paul Bowles, *"You Have Left Your Lotus Pods on the Bus"*   36

H. Jathar Salij, *"A Weekend in Bandung"*   44

Sabine Ulibarrí, *"The Stuffing of the Lord"*   225

Raquel Puig Zaldívar, *"Nothing in Our Hands but Age"*   309

Yearn Hong Choi, *"Bloomington, Fall 1971"*   319

William E. Barrett, *"Señor Payroll"*   334

Juanita Platero and Siyowin Miller, *"Chee's Daughter"*   385

Ann Petry, *"Solo on the Drums"*   432

V. Goryushkin, *"Before Sunrise"*   437

Linda Hogan, *"Making Do"*   456

Doris Lessing, *"Sunrise on the Veld"*   471

Richard K. Nelson, *"Tingiivik Tatqiq: The Moon When Birds Fly South (September)"*   485

Massud Farzan, *"The Plane Reservation"*   530

DESCRIPTION

Zora Neale Hurston, *"How It Feels to Be Colored Me"* 61
William D. Montalbano, *"Latin America: A Quixotic Land Where the Bizarre Is Routine"* 107
Sabine Ulibarrí, *"The Stuffing of the Lord"* 225
Rimma Kazakova, *"America of the People"* 241
Gabriel García Márquez, *"Big Mama's Funeral"* 444
My Van Vu, *"The Village We Left Behind"* 467
N. Scott Momaday, *"Grandmother's Country"* 536

DEFINITION

Jawaharlal Nehru, *"What Is Culture?"* 66
Carlos Bulosan, *"Be American"* 274
Julio Cortázar, *"The Health of the Sick"* 396
Aharon Megged, *"The Name"* 409
Shelby Steele, *"I'm Black, You're White, Who's Innocent?"* 545
Richard Rive, *"The Bench"* 567
Norman Mailer, *"A Country, Not a Scenario"* 584
Premchand, *"A Coward"* 595
Tewfiq al-Hakim, *"Not a Thing Out of Place"* 604

PROCESS

Solon T. Kimball, *"Learning a New Culture"* 25
Ruth Prawer Jhabvala, *"Myself in India"* 53
Phyllis I. Lyons, *"Translating Cultures . . . Or, What's George Washington Doing in a Sushi Bar?"* 196
Carlos Bulosan, *"Be American"* 274
Spencer Sherman, *"The Hmong in America"* 291
Linda Hogan, *"Making Do"* 456
Richard K. Nelson, *"Tingiivik Tatqiq: The Moon When Birds Fly South (September)"* 485

CAUSE AND EFFECT

Spencer Sherman, *"The Hmong in America"* 291
William E. Barrett, *"Señor Payroll"* 334
Lawrence Stessin, *"Culture Shock and the American Businessman Overseas"* 339

David Halberstam, *"How Datsun Discovered America"*   365
Julio Cortázar, *"The Health of the Sick"*   396
Aharon Megged, *"The Name"*   409
Graham Sheil, *"The Picking Season"*   503
Milan Kundera, *"The Hitchhiking Game"*   515
Massud Farzan, *"The Plane Reservation"*   530

ILLUSTRATION

Jawaharlal Nehru, *"What Is Culture?"*   66
Robert Levine, with Ellen Wolff, *"Social Time: The Heartbeat of Culture"*   75
William D. Montalbano, *"Latin America: A Quixotic Land Where the Bizarre Is Routine"*   107
Edward T. Hall and Mildred Reed Hall, *"The Sounds of Silence"*   207
James R. Corey, *"Cultural Shock in Reverse"*   329

CLASSIFICATION

Gordon W. Allport, *"Linguistic Factors in Prejudice"*   161
Shirley Lauro, *"Open Admissions"*   185
Horace M. Miner, *"Body Ritual Among the Nacirema"*   235
Ishmael Reed, *"America: The Multinational Society"*   301
Milan Kundera, *"The Hitchhiking Game"*   515
Feng Jicai, *"The Tall Woman and Her Short Husband"*   558

COMPARISON/CONTRAST

Joanne Brown, *"Scoshi"*   11
H. Jathar Salij, *"A Weekend in Bandung"*   44
Janette Turner Hospital, *"Waiting"*   82
Richard Rodriguez, *"Memories of a Bilingual Childhood"*   171
Shirley Lauro, *"Open Admissions"*   185
Tahira Naqvi, *"Paths upon Water"*   246
Anne Tyler, *"Your Place Is Empty"*   257
Bharati Mukherjee, *"A Father"*   281
Similih M. Cordor, *"A Farewell to the Old Order"*   350
Jamaica Kincaid, *"Poor Visitor"*   479
Graham Sheil, *"The Picking Season"*   503

EXPOSITION

Paul Bowles, *"You Have Left Your Lotus Pods on the Bus"*   36
Robert Levine, with Ellen Wolff, *"Social Time: The Heartbeat
of Culture"*   75
Henry C. Binford, *"I Scream, You Scream . . . The Cultural
Significance of Ice Cream"*   91
Carol Simons, *"Kyoiku Mamas"*   99
Octavio Paz, *"The Day of the Dead"*   111
Nawal el-Saadawi, *"Love and Sex in the Life of the Arab"*   123
Peter Farb, *"Man at the Mercy of Language"*   145
Phyllis I. Lyons, *"Translating Cultures . . . Or, What's
George Washington Doing in a Sushi Bar?"*   196
Edward T. Hall and Mildred Reed Hall, *"The Sounds of
Silence"*   207
Gregory Bateson, *"Why Do Frenchmen?"*   219
Horace M. Miner, *"Body Ritual Among the Nacirema"*   235
Doris Lessing, *"Sunrise on the Veld"*   471

ARGUMENTATION

Zora Neale Hurston, *"How It Feels to Be Colored Me"*   61
Henry C. Binford, *"I Scream, You Scream . . . The Cultural
Significance of Ice Cream"*   91
Nawal el-Saadawi, *"Love and Sex in the Life of the Arab"*   123
Gordon W. Allport, *"Linguistic Factors in Prejudice"*   161
Richard Rodriguez, *"Memories of a Bilingual Childhood"*   171
Ishmael Reed, *"America: The Multinational Society"*   301
James R. Corey, *"Cultural Shock in Reverse"*   329
Lawrence Stessin, *"Culture Shock and the American
Businessman Overseas"*   339
Zhang Jie, *"Love Must Not Be Forgotten"*   421
Shelby Steele, *"I'm Black, You're White, Who's Innocent?"*   545
Chinua Achebe, *"An Image of Africa"*   572
Dean Barnlund, *"Communication in a Global Village"*   615

CREDITS

INDEX OF AUTHORS AND TITLES

Achebe, Chinua, "An Image of Africa," 572

Allport, Gordon W., "Linguistic Factors in Prejudice," 161

Barnlund, Dean, "Communication in a Global Village," 615

Barrett, William E., "Señor Payroll," 334

Bateson, Gregory, "Why Do Frenchmen?" 219

Binford, Henry C., "I Scream, You Scream . . . The Cultural Significance of Ice Cream," 91

Bowles, Paul, "You Have Left Your Lotus Pods on the Bus," 36

Brown, Joanne, "Scoshi," 11

Bulosan, Carlos, "Be American," 274

Choi, Yearn Hong, "Bloomington, Fall 1971," 319

Cordor, Similih M., "A Farewell to the Old Order," 350

Corey, James R., "Cultural Shock in Reverse," 329

Cortázar, Julio, "The Health of the Sick," 396

Farb, Peter, "Man at the Mercy of Language," 145

Farzan, Massud, "The Plane Reservation," 530

García Márquez, Gabriel, "Big Mama's Funeral," 444

Goryushkin, V., "Before Sunrise," 437

al-Hakim, Tewfiq, "Not a Thing Out of Place," 604

Halberstam, David, "How Datsun Discovered America," 365

Hall, Edward T., and Mildred Reed Hall, "The Sounds of Silence," 207

Hogan, Linda, "Making Do," 456

Hospital, Janette Turner, "Waiting," 82

Hurston, Zora Neale, "How It Feels to Be Colored Me," 61

Jhabvala, Ruth Prawer, "Myself in India," 53

Jicai, Feng, "The Tall Woman and Her Short Husband," 558

Jie, Zhang, "Love Must Not Be Forgotten," 421

Kazakova, Rimma, "America of the People," 241

Kimball, Solon T., "Learning a New Culture," 25

Kincaid, Jamaica, "Poor Visitor," 479

Kinsella, W. P., "The Moccasin Telegraph," 3

Kundera, Milan, "The Hitchhiking Game," 515

Lauro, Shirley, "Open Admissions," 185

Lessing, Doris, "Sunrise on the Veld," 471

Levine, Robert, with Ellen Wolff, "Social Time: The Heartbeat of Culture," 75

Lyons, Phyllis I., "Translating Cultures . . . Or, What's George Washington Doing in a Sushi Bar?" 196

637

Mailer, Norman, "A Country, Not a Scenario," 584

Megged, Aharon, "The Name," 409

Miner, Horace M., "Body Ritual Among the Nacirema," 235

Momaday, N. Scott, "Grandmother's Country," 536

Montalbano, William D., "Latin America: A Quixotic Land Where the Bizarre Is Routine," 107

Mukherjee, Bharati, "A Father," 281

Naqvi, Tahira, "Paths upon Water," 246

Nehru, Jawaharlal, "What Is Culture?" 66

Nelson, Richard K., "Tingiivik Tatqiq: The Moon When Birds Fly South (September)," 485

Paz, Octavio, "The Day of the Dead," 111

Petry, Ann, "Solo on the Drums," 432

Platero, Juanita, and Siyowin Miller, "Chee's Daughter," 385

Premchand, "A Coward," 595

Reed, Ishmael, "America: The Multinational Society," 301

Rive, Richard, "The Bench," 567

Rodriguez, Richard, "Memories of a Bilingual Childhood," 171

el-Saadawi, Nawal, "Love and Sex in the Life of the Arab," 123

Salij, H. Jathar, "A Weekend in Bandung," 44

Sheil, Graham, "The Picking Season," 503

Sherman, Spencer, "The Hmong in America," 291

Simons, Carol, "Kyoiku Mamas," 99

Steele, Shelby, "I'm Black, You're White, Who's Innocent?" 545

Stessin, Lawrence, "Culture Shock and the American Businessman Overseas," 339

Tyler, Anne, "Your Place Is Empty," 257

Ulibarrí, Sabine, "The Stuffing of the Lord," 225

Vu, My Van, "The Village We Left Behind," 467

Zaldívar, Raquel Puig, "Nothing in Our Hands but Age," 309

Instructor's Manual
to accompany

INTERCULTURAL
JOURNEYS THROUGH
READING AND
WRITING

Marilyn Smith Layton

NORTH SEATTLE COMMUNITY COLLEGE

HarperCollins*Publishers*

CONTENTS

Preface   I-1

1   STRATEGIES FOR READING AND WRITING   **I-3**

    1.   Reading Strategies   I-3
    2.   Writing Strategies: Discovery and Self-Discovery   I-5
    Writing or Peer Editing Groups   *I-7*
    Models of Response Statements for Student Writing Groups   *I-8*
    The Writer's Response   *I-9*

2   WRITING ASSIGNMENTS   **I-11**

    1.   Writing Sequences: Using the Reading Selections
       as Models   I-11
    Assignment #1   *I-11*
    Assignment #2   *I-12*
    Assignment #3   *I-13*
    Assignment #4   *I-14*
    Assignment #5   *I-15*
    Assignment #6   *I-16*
    Assignment #7   *I-16*
    Assignment #8   *I-17*
    2.   Writing Assignments on Sources Across the Book   I-18
    3.   Investigating Topics Beyond the Book   I-23
    4.   Collaborative Writing Assignments   I-25

**3   USING THE BOOK IN LITERATURE AND
    INTERCULTURAL CLASSES**   **I-31**

    1.   An Annotated Guide to Novels from Diverse
       Cultures   I-31

2. Sample Study Guides to Novels   I-37

Study Guide to The Good Conscience *I-37*
Study Guide to Yellow Raft on Blue Water *I-38*
Study Guide to The Beginning and the End *I-39*

4 ADDITIONAL BIBLIOGRAPHY FOR TEACHING AND EXPLORING CULTURE   **I-41**

PREFACE

How does one tell the story of a statistic? One man is a person, a thousand are a community, and a million are a statistic. . . . I decided finally to write something that wouldn't reinforce the statistics that make India's millions but would look instead for the faces behind the figures. As each face becomes a person, numbers cease being an abstraction. Written by one among the numbers, it is a story that has moved outward from a core that is integral and become an attempt to understand a condition that is shared.

ANEES JUNG, from her introduction to
UNVEILING INDIA, A WOMAN'S JOURNEY

In compiling the selections of this book, I have often felt overwhelmed by the choices of what to include and how to help students move from a core, their core, that is integral, toward understanding a condition that is shared. It is always the particular faces, the voices of the people themselves, that launch me into learning about the larger communities and statistics of which they form a part. In the beginning of my work on this book, I knew I wanted to create a book with a heart, but Anees Jung's explanation of her own battle with writing about the population of India helped me understand what I meant by heart.

Courses in our English departments—both in composition and literature—should be swamped with students waiting, on their own volition, to take them. The opportunity we have to draw on the most central issues and concerns of our lives—the making of meaning, the sorting out of feeling and thought through language, the vicarious identification and insights we gain from those great and small people in the books we read, the ways in which "English" involves history, philosophy, psychology, and a host of other studies in all the critical questions we face each day of our lives—such opportunity is the privilege and challenge of our profession.

And yet too often our classroom doors have no lines waiting. "English" is a service course, an adjunct if not to "content" courses, then to our students' lives, their have-to subject. As a profession, we sometimes work to sound like what we are not: scientists. We view the subject we teach critically, without heart. Perhaps more than we do, our students sense this paradox.

In my third decade of teaching composition, I still find the writing process a phenomenon. Students take the course requirements, the same hours together in the classroom, and weave them into their learning in ever surprising and unique combinations, some of which I do plan and conceive, and some of which I could never have imagined. Learning thus retains its mystery, mess, and magic.

As teachers, we help our students do more than read and write well: we help them learn to be comfortable with things temporarily out of control. Mess is part of the writing process, the confusion that results in working with ideas and language.

The certainty we can offer our students is our commitment to caring about them and their work. I hope the assignments and resources in this manual will motivate you, my colleagues, to try some of its ideas, to let me know which ones you find especially effective, to suggest changes for those that are not, and to enjoy the knowledge that comes from the discoveries we all make as we write.

We have made great progress in our profession these last two decades toward understanding the writing process. This book and this manual will use the elements of that knowledge in helping students to find pleasure in their learning—to leave class with new ideas about their lives and the lives of their fellow travelers, both close and far away.

Marilyn Smith Layton
Seattle, Washington

Chapter 1

STRATEGIES FOR READING AND WRITING

1. Reading Strategies

Reading is an intimate act, perhaps more intimate than any other human act. I say that because of the prolonged (or intense) exposure of one mind to another that is involved in it, and because it is the level of mind at which feelings and hopes are dealt in by consciousness and words.

Harold Brodkey,
READING, THE MOST DANGEROUS GAME

"It is not that we don't read," one older student in a class explained as the class was appreciating the insights of its collective analysis of something they had just read, "it's that for many of us, we're learning for the first time to run it through our lives and give it back."

A professor at a workshop on teaching composition left his conviction in my memory though not his name: "Reading is the stuff of writing," he said, "its base, its nourishment. If courses in composition only made students read, it would be enough to turn some of them into writers. Reading is what must go in. Writing is what comes out."

The opportunity to assign good reading to a class, and then to experience what a number of people have to say about the same piece, is one of the rewards of teaching. Many of our students have never experienced this end of reading—the sharing of insights and ideas, the idea that they too are full of such material if they can learn to tap it. In an age where so many forces have combined to distract our students from the habit and treasures of reading, we have the opportunity to help them discover its values.

Many students don't read because they never have been helped to believe that they are getting the right stuff from what they read. They've learned that only the smart students have access to the truths of reading. How can we help students to gain a sense of being in control as readers?

In this manual, I have chosen not to write about each selection in terms of what you can expect when you teach it (based upon what I've encountered when I've taught it) because I find that each time the same piece is read by a different class, results and responses change. Like books written on how to raise children, the truths apply most aptly to the writers of each book.

The "Before You Read" and "Questions for Discussion and Writing" sections that accompany each selection will help guide students through each source. Chapter Two in this manual offers many ways to help students understand their reading as they write about it.

In this section, I've included some general strategies that work for me in the teaching or guiding of reading:

Preview: Suggest that before students begin reading a selection, they read the introductory paragraph or paragraphs, the first line of every paragraph after that, and the last paragraph of the piece, emphasizing the value of speed in this process. Previewing helps students to know where they are going before they begin. If they read a selection following their writing on the "Before you read" suggestions, their comfort and confidence will further increase their motivation and curiosity.

Talk to the text: Like the question about whether noise exists from a tree's falling in the forest if no one is there to hear it, one can question the existence of a book independent of the life of the reader who, in bringing his or her own life to it, gives it life. Following the process of previewing, a reader creates a dialogue with a book: What jumps off the page for the reader? Underline it. What details seem worth remembering? Underline them. At which point do the writer's convictions begin to crystallize? Write in the margin.

Urge students to respond to the writer on the page. Their scratchings and notes are evidence of the ways in which they are beginning to absorb the material—the paths they're making through the forests of words.

Question: Students think that writers have the answers. They fail to perceive the questions the writer is trying to answer. If they are urged to write their own questions to the writer, they will begin to see what the selection answers and what it doesn't.

Have them review what they've underlined or noted in the course of their reading. Then have them write questions for which the answers would involve the facts or concepts in the material. Next to the questions they write, have them note which are questions of *fact* (the what questions) and which are questions of *concept* (the why and how questions), and which are questions of *synthesis* (the questions that help make connections within and beyond the selection). These fact, concept, and synthesis questions can be shared in small groups in which students compare their questions and responses.

Finally, they might write questions that ask for interpolations among ideas they've discussed in other selections and contexts, or write their own set of "Questions for Discussion and Writing."

Synthesize: Three questions become habits in reading effectively:

1. What does the text say? In answer to this question, students quote and paraphrase from the reading itself.
2. What does the writer mean? Here the direction is analytic, interpretative; students work with the connections they are making among the ideas.
3. What is your opinion of it, and why? When students have carefully probed the first two questions, their opinions have more depth, more validity. This last question is often the place where students wish to begin the discussion of a text, so it's important to help them learn to paraphrase main ideas, and to point to passages that support their interpretation of what the author means *before* they jump in with their opinions.

An alternate version of these questions is especially useful in helping students to avoid making judgments about other cultures until they have described and interpreted the behavior they've seen. In simple terms, the procedure here is to ask them to deal with their reading in the following format:

D. I. E.:

*D*escription: What I see.
*I*nterpretation: What I think.
*E*valuation: What I feel.

To help students practice these responses, choose a passage from the reading in which some unusual behavior or situation is occurring. Ask students to describe it, using no interpretive or evaluative words. Then ask them to move on to evaluating the behavior or situation, and finally to interpreting it. The chapter on "Encounters With American Patterns of Culture" will provide a number of examples that test and reflect the distinctions and importance among the acts of describing, interpreting, and evaluating.

2. Writing Strategies: Discovery and Self-Discovery

Your shelves are no doubt brimming with books written about the writing process. This section will not attempt to cover what has already been covered so well by so many. It will concentrate instead on writing strategies that help students in all classes that teach or require writing.

Many students have equated writing with drudgery, that impossible task that will lead them to frustration, failure, and video games. Our challenge is to show them that, although writing is indeed full of frustration—a punching bag that seems to swing at us on its own accord—writing, *their* writing, also has the power to unlock important knowledge for them. Writing is a way of discovering, a way to self-discovery.

We talk a lot in the classes I teach about the fears people have about writing. Mostly those fears represent past associations of being harshly judged as writers. (One writing teacher said that if we taught our children to speak the way we teach them to write, they'd all be stutterers.) In my years of teaching, I've rarely encountered this inclination of judgment, especially of student toward student, if I talk about a funny paradox we face as writers: If what we're writing about is not important to us, it won't be important—indeed, it can't be important—to others. Risk, therefore, is part of the writing process.

Readers read for that prose that matters to its writer. Excellent writing comes from this caring. Judgment on the part of the reader turns on when no evidence of caring or commitment is reflected in the writing. When the writer not only does not care but pretends to care, judgment begins. Human beings have a great immediate sense for detecting what is not genuine.

When we write, we are looking in a mirror at a part of ourselves; indeed it feels as if the mirror reflects our whole selves at the time. This mirror metaphor reflects the feelings and fears students have. I also give them another metaphor as they're shaking their heads in acknowledgment: the metaphor of writing as an emotional blotter, the world's cheapest psychiatrist.

When we write, we are giving light to the recesses of what we've known, what we've stored, even to what we are in the process of storing through what we read and live. In his autobiography *All the Strange Hours,* Loren Eiseley compared this retrieval process to the canvases that an artist might store in an attic, where the small beam of light from the attic window falls at the right time on different pictures. The reading and assignments in this book will work like those beams of light, evoking from students their stored knowledge and experience, in combination with their reading.

Writing means risk but it promises reward. Many of our students have never known its rewards. That's what our role involves: leading them through the process of writing enough times that they begin to believe in its possibilities, its rewards.

The "Before You Read" assignments preceding each selection provide an effective way of launching students into fast or free writing; it is often valuable to take class time for this kind of exercise. These assignments will help prepare them for the reading, and the natural connections between reading and writing will become evident to them.

The "Questions for Discussion and Writing" that follow each selection can also be used for quick writing, and to reinforce this reading and writing connection. One method is to number off the class according to the number of questions, having each person write on the question that corresponds to the number they call off. The best discussions in class occur for me after students have prepared their ideas and responses to the questions in writing that they then share in small groups. This process insures that every student has something to contribute to the large group because they've rehearsed these ideas and responses first in small groups.

For writing of papers that will be completed in two or more drafts, the use of writing or peer editing groups provides a number of excellent outcomes. These groups introduce students to the ways in which serious writers often work— through sharing their work with a small audience of colleagues or writers who provide them with information about the ways in which they are responding to the writing. This audience of the writing group not only creates evidence of the lessons we teach students about writing for an audience, but also allows students to gain some necessary distance from their work by seeing it through the eyes of others.

Writing or peer editing groups

The following is the format I use for writing or peer editing groups. Four people per group seem to work best, though variants of three or five will work too, depending on the amount of time available. (Small groups of three allow each writer to have only two people's responses.) For groups of four, I ask students to bring in five copies of their preliminary drafts (one for me) on days the class divides into writing groups.

Groups can be randomly formed by counting the number of students in class and dividing by four, having each person number off and then find classmates with that number. Instructors can also assign students to groups, balancing interests, backgrounds, sexes, and so forth.

With students A, B, C, and D ready with their papers, here's the process:

1. A reads; B, C, and D *listen only,* not reading their copies.
2. B, C, and D take time to *write down* their impressions of this first reading. The point is to hear the piece before responding to it in written form, to avoid the implications that written language mistakes can have for the person responding.

   Students are inclined to skip the written response to their classmates and to begin talking to each other immediately. It's a good idea to require that they write, because their writing appears to improve and increase the quality and depth of their response.
3. A reads the paper again, this time with B, C, and D reading along and noting the elements each person will want to respond to in the minutes following the reading, in which the three reader/responders will write fully on the paper, answering the following questions:

   What aspects of the paper did you find especially effective?

   What would you like to know more about?

What parts of it could be effectively cut or reorganized?

What suggestions do you have about its language and the ways in which language creates meaning?

4. I emphasize that A's job is to listen, not to feel defensive, to take all comments in, and to let them simmer in thought over a day or two before A decides what changes actually need to be made. In the sharing of their responses to the paper, B, C, and D take turns sharing all the comments they've written over the course of A's two readings.
5. B, C, and D have their turns at reading and receiving written and spoken critiques.

I spend time in class the day before the first writing group setting up the format, reassuring students that it will reward all of them to work together on each person's paper, and suggesting that they will gain practice and competence over the term not only in responding to others' writing but also in responding to people in other contexts. The challenge is to combine their honest responses with genuine tact and concern for their classmates.

Before the first writing group, I distribute the following page of phrases that can help them express themselves at the same time that these comments help elicit the intended responses and changes in the writer's thinking about problems in his or her paper.

The last hand-out of this section is a model of questions I ask students to complete before they hand in their final draft of their assignments.

Models of Response Statements for Student Writing Groups

1. I really got interested when you read the part about. . . .
2. I got lost when you started talking about. . . .
3. I don't know what you meant when you said. . . .
4. How did you get from . . . to . . . ?
5. You used a lot of strong descriptive words in the part about. . . .
6. What would happen if you took the part about . . . and made it the beginning?
7. What would happen if you moved the part about . . . ?
8. I couldn't tell whether the main point was . . . or. . . .
9. In the beginning you said . . . , but later you said—or I thought you said— . . ., and I thought there was a contradiction.
10. Do you mean here that . . . ?
11. Could you substitute this word . . . for . . . ?
12. When you tell me so much about . . . , it distracts me from what I think your main point is. (Good idea here to summarize the main point as you understand it.)
13. I wanted to know more about. . . .

14. When you wrote . . . , it just didn't work for me.
15. I didn't understand. . . .
16. . . . isn't too convincing without some stronger (or some more or just *some*) examples.

The Writer's Response to His or Her Own Paper

1. Circle your favorite line or lines of this paper, and explain here why they work well for you.
2. What were the problems you had in writing the paper?
   Which ones do you feel you've solved, and why?
   Which ones do you feel need more attention?
3. What help did your writing group give you with this paper?
   What help did you want but not receive? Be sure to list here the members of your group.
4. What kinds of help would you especially like to have from your instructor in responding to this paper?
5. What writing truths have you learned from writing this paper that you will apply to future papers?

Chapter 2

WRITING ASSIGNMENTS

1. Writing Sequences: Using the Reading Selections as Models

The assignments that follow are intended to be used during the course of a term to help students gain increasing control in their writing over increasingly complex and challenging ideas. The assignments also help students consider and make their own intercultural journeys through writing. The reading selections and class discussions will prepare students with examples of the ways in which other writers have used writing to explore meaning and ambiguity in their experiences.

Although the assignments are not so labeled, they move through and include the various rhetorical modes—from narration to description, to exposition, definition, and argument. Each assignment emphasizes a challenge in thinking, and the possibility of developing each paper by means of a number of strategies. The reason for avoiding labeling these papers by rhetorical strategy is that, except in the composition class, the rhetorical strategy never precedes our reasons for writing nor our assignments as writers. Subject determines development. Thus these assignments give the student the subject (and the questions) around which they will discover their papers and, at the same time, acquire experience with a number of different writing approaches, or modes.

Although this term-long sequence has progressive connections between and among the assignments, instructors should not feel limited to the order of the assignments as they appear.

Assignment #1

Selections to read in preparation: "Poor Visitor," by Jamaica Kincaid, and "Nothing in Our Hands But Age," by Raquel Puig Zaldívar.

The idea of culture is a concept we only learn as we grow older. When we are children, we think that the world we know is the world. Our first clues that life is different elsewhere happen in a number of ways—a night spent at a friend's house when we are very young, the loneliness that overtakes us suddenly at camp, the longing we have to take on the ways of a family we experience in a book, on television, at the neighbor's. We can remember our earliest lessons in learning that the habits and patterns of our lives did not coincide with the habits and patterns of others. Those early experiences jar and sometimes trouble our expectations.

In Kincaid's essay, we observe and feel her experience of homesickness on a first-time stay in another country, in another part of the world—homesickness turned into what we now call culture shock. In Zaldívar's story, we experience the strangeness of the new Cuban students in the class through the eyes of the teacher and a few of the classmates.

In preparation for the assignment, analyze the methods and techniques both writers use to make the experiences they explore vivid and effective for the reader. You might also consider other approaches they might have taken in their writing.

Assignment: Exploring a time in your life when you first encountered the feelings of culture shock, write this paper as a re-creation of that time. Here are some questions that might help you get started: What life had you left, if you had in fact gone somewhere? What were the most significant details you remember of the world you entered? In what ways did that new world surprise you? In what ways were you unprepared for the encounter? In what ways did the encounter change your attitudes about home or people? What did you learn as a result of this experience with another culture? (Note: This question of entering another culture need not involve travel to another country. As it does in Zaldívar's story, it can include any experience in which you participated in a new context of people and ideas. Even entering college can be a culture shock, depending on your life until that time.)

Assignment #2

Selections to read in preparation: "Scoshi," by Joanne Brown, and "The Stuffing of the Lord," by Sabine Ulibarrí.

In the first assignment, you were dealing with experiences of culture shock and the ways in which you suddenly found yourself having to deal with patterns and habits very different from your own. Patterns and habits condition us to have certain expectations in our relationships with people. When we are dealing with people from different cultural backgrounds, we are again challenged to examine the values and attitudes that underlie our expectations.

Relationships and friendships that connect us to people of different backgrounds and cultures teach us about ourselves. In examining them, we also create a portrait of the person involved, as Joanne Brown has done in her essay "Scoshi" and as Sabine Ulibarrí has done in his story/essay "The Stuffing of the Lord."

In preparation for the assignment, analyze the methods and techniques both writers use to make the experiences they explore vivid and effective for the reader. You might also consider other approaches they might have taken in their writing.

Assignment: Consider a relationship you've had with a person who has challenged, frustrated, confused, or changed you over a period of time (or even done all of those things.) Re-create the situation, but most important, re-create the person so that the reader might know him or her in the same close ways you do.

Here are some questions that might help you get started: What were your expectations in the beginning about this person and your relationship? What experiences in your own life had conditioned those expectations? What values and attitudes could you observe influencing that person, and in what ways were you able to learn of them (conversation, someone else's report, observations you made, and so forth)? What values and attitudes were influencing you, and why? What was the outcome of the experience, and what has it taught you about differences between people?

Assignment #3

Selections to read in preparation: "The Village We Left Behind," by My Van Vu, and "Latin America: A Quixotic Land Where the Bizarre Is Routine," by William D. Montalbano.

In the second assignment, you created a portrait of a person important to you in complex ways. For this paper, you'll be thinking about the relationship you have with a particular place. When we think about our own histories and the influences of the culture in which we grew up, we are often drawn back to a specific setting, in which its sounds, smells, and tastes are intimately bound with our visual memories. Our connections with place continue to flit through our thoughts over the years of our lives—the church where you were kicked out of Sunday school, the musty smell of your grandparents' home competing with special cookies sometimes waiting for you, the woods where you first discovered solitude (and other things), the country you left behind.

Through his essay, My Van Vu has not only re-created the village he left behind, but by extension, the Vietnam that was lost to war. Through the particular details of his home, we come to understand so much more, indirectly, about that war and its cost—a culture that is vanquished. In Montalbano's essay, we get a feeling, again through particular details, of his perceptions as a reporter of Latin America and its peculiarities—the concrete examples that underpin its "magical realism."

In preparation for the assignment, analyze the methods and techniques both writers use to make the experiences they explore vivid and effective for the reader. You might also consider other approaches they might have taken in their writing.

Assignment: Re-create a place important to you as a reflection of your life and, possibly, your cultural heritage. (It does not have to be a place you remember happily, of course.) It can be as small as a pantry in your home or as large as a country, but you'll need to re-create it concretely so that the reader can enter it, experience it, and understand it through your essay.

Here are some questions that might help you get started: In deciding the place you want to portray, what place would you remember as your favorite, and why? In what ways has this place contributed to your sense of continuity and belonging? What place would you never want to return to, and why? What happened in those places to make you feel the ways you do? What are the images you think of when you remember them? If you were going to deal with this assignment through photography rather than through words, on which details and angles would you focus your lens?

Assignment #4

In preparation for this assignment, read "Why Do Frenchmen?" by Gregory Bateson, and "Making Do," by Linda Hogan.

This assignment will give you an opportunity to consider a question or a problem that's been on your mind, one you've had about the reasons behind someone's action or behavior. You will not only be looking at this question from your own point of view, but from another person's perspective as well. You can choose the person whose perspective might be a good balance or foil to your own.

In both reading selections, the writer is probing questions of behavior. In "Why Do Frenchmen?" the writer uses a kind of script between naive daughter and knowing father to explore the ways in which people communicate differently with their bodies in different cultures, and the idea that "mere words" themselves do not exist. In "Making Do," we find again that the author has used two people's points of view to probe the loss not only of Roberta's children but of Indian culture, and the ways Roberta and others have coped with their grief over their losses, and find ways of "making do." Both selections thus deal with questions, and both attempt answers, although the answers themselves are ambiguous, evoking further questions on our part as readers.

In preparation for the assignment, analyze the methods and techniques both writers use to make the experiences they explore vivid and effective for the reader. You might also consider other approaches they might have taken in their writing.

Assignment: Recall a question you've been pondering or have pondered over a period of time about some matter important to you that you would like to figure out but haven't, and can't. Re-create that question for your reader in whatever format you choose, but consider it from at least two different people's points of view. Give at least one person the kind of distance that Roberta's sister has, for example, in "Making Do," or the father has in "Why Do Frenchmen?"

Here are some questions that might help you get started: What was the specific context or setting in which the question first came up for you? Who was involved? If you have ever probed this question with another person, what has been his or her response? Why has the response not been a satisfactory answer or explanation for you? What results could you imagine in your life if you were really to discover an answer to this question? What relevance would this question have to someone from another culture?

Assignment #5

In preparation for this assignment, read "Kyoiku Mamas," by Carol Simons, "The Day of the Dead," by Octavio Paz, and "I Scream, You Scream, . . . The Cultural Significance of Ice Cream," by Henry Binford.

The patterns and habits of a culture are always deeply tied to values and attitudes that reflect that culture's history, traditions, and means of survival. When we read about the influences that have created social patterns that we might find strange or irksome, we learn to accept them when we begin to understand them. Even a food as familiar to us as ice cream has its history and its reasons for prominence in our eating habits.

In "Kyoiku Mamas," Carol Simons reports on the grueling commitment of mothers to children in Japan, and examines the unseen forces that create their dedication. (Even the word "grueling" is a judgment across cultures.) In "The Day of the Dead," Octavio Paz explains the need in the Mexican people for fiestas that give them release even if that release threatens their lives. Henry Binford explains the complex cultural history of ice cream, none of which we realize as we stop by a store for a cone. All three essays explore the psychological and historical bases of behavior in the cultures they represent.

In preparation for the assignment, analyze the methods and techniques the writers use to make the experiences they explore vivid and effective for the reader. You might also consider other approaches they might have taken in their writing.

Assignment: Imagine a group of foreigners who want to be introduced to objects, ideas, or behaviors that are central symbols of American values. Select a symbol from one of these categories: McDonald's, a sweatshirt, a supermarket, or a shoe store, for example. (The list has no end as you can begin to imagine.) Introduce your object, idea, or behavior in a context that will show it off best, and then explain the ways in which you understand it to represent important American values. Consider in the development of your analysis whatever economic, political, historical elements you believe are relevant. The object of this analysis is to create understanding for those "foreigners" who are often ourselves. Feel free to play with ideas, to conjecture about meaning, to hypothesize, and to observe inconsistencies, ironies, and paradoxes in the subject you choose to explore.

Here is an example that might help you get started: a sequined sweatshirt. In what ways does it represent the cultural pride we take in informality? In what ways might it represent democratic values? In what ways might its expensive price, on the other hand, also reflect the paradoxes of our democratic values? Do Americans buy such sweatshirts in order to distinguish themselves from the masses, and if so, why?

Assignment #6

In preparation for this assignment, read "Be American," by Carlos Bulosan, "A Country, Not a Scenario," by Norman Mailer, and "America: The Multinational Society," by Ishmael Reed.

Although we use the words America and American every day of our lives assuming that we know what we mean and what defines their characteristics, all three reading selections show us the real differences through which people see the ideas those words represent.

Bulosan shows us the meaning of being American through the eyes of his cousin, an immigrant who arrives from the Philippines with his dreams. Mailer uses his experiences as a traveler to Russia to look at his own country in new ways. Reed looks at America through the evidence he sees everywhere of the many nations it represents.

In preparation for the assignment, analyze the methods and techniques the writers use to make the experiences they explore vivid and effective for the reader. You might also consider other approaches they might have taken in their writing.

Assignment: The object that you explored in Assignment #5 most likely helped you to consider the characteristics that made it peculiarly American, thus helping you to think about the values, patterns, and attitudes it represents. This assignment asks you what it means to call yourself an American, what it means to be American, and how you recognize others with the same characteristics.

Here are some questions to help you get started: When did you have your first clue about yourself as an "American"? Can someone who has come here from another country be American without formal citizenship? What can you find out from other family members concerning the meanings they attach to being American? If you or your classmates come from another country, what did being American mean to you and your family when you first arrived here? How have these meanings changed over time? What are the problems you encounter as you grapple with these questions and challenges of definition?

Don't be afraid of complexities as you prepare this paper. Your challenge is not to have The Answer, but to show the process and the problems through which you arrived at answers or, possibly, no answer.

Assignment #7

In preparation for this assignment, read "Man at the Mercy of Language," by Peter Farb, "How It Feels to Be Colored Me," by Zora Neale Hurston, and "I'm Black, You're White, Who's Innocent?" by Shelby Steele.

Language often lies at the center of critical moments between and among people. We cannot separate our perceptions of others from the categories we assign them through language. In "Man at the Mercy of Language," Peter Farb analyzes the relationships among language, perception, and culture that determine, often without our knowing, the ways we perceive the world around us. In "How It Feels to Be Colored Me," Zora Neale Hurston explains the stages she passed through in feeling the color of her skin, and the implications those experiences have had for her. In "I'm Black, You're White, Who's Innocent?" Shelby Steele uses an experience at a party he attended to examine each side's perceptions of race, power, and *presumed innocence,* and the ways in which language, feeling, and thought underpin those perceptions.

In preparation for the assignment, analyze the methods and techniques the writers use to make the experiences they explore vivid and effective for the reader. You might also consider other approaches they might have taken in their writing.

Assignment: Recall a time in your life when you suddenly found yourself pitted against a person or people different from you, a time when, quite by surprise, you felt yourself becoming angry and possibly turning to old perceptions that you thought you'd outgrown or forgotten. Re-create that time as vividly as you can, recalling the specific details of the encounter that will allow your reader to join you. Then analyze the ways in which language categories allowed you to channel your anger toward accusation and classification based on religion, culture, or race, perceptions based on your assuming your own innocence in the encounter.

Here are some questions to help you get started: What groups of people have you found yourself inclined to dismiss or reject based on characteristics that have irritated or even outraged you? In what ways did you presume your own differences from them? In what ways did you presume your innocence, and in what ways did your opponents presume theirs? What kinds of polite exchanges would you ordinarily use if you met them under unthreatening circumstances? What were the reasons behind your sudden turn against the person or people you want to write about?

Don't be afraid of encountering your own guilt or misgivings about the situation as you explore these questions of perception, prejudice, and presumed innocence. As you conclude your paper, you might want to say what both the experience and writing about the experience have helped you to learn.

Assignment #8

In preparation for this assignment, read "Your Place Is Empty," by Anne Tyler, "A Father," by Bharati Mukherjee, and "Communication in a Global Village," by Dean Barnlund.

The challenges of intercultural experience reflect themselves in every last reach of human affairs. The cultural inheritance of each individual is so complex and profound that grasping those complexities lies even beyond one's own reach. Communication between two people of similar cultural backgrounds often fails in spite of the assumptions they share. Families illustrate these challenges of interpersonal communication most fully because their members ostensibly share so many patterns, values, and attitudes. Coming to terms with living in another culture is the ultimate challenge for people who want to communicate clearly with each other.

In "Communication in a Global Village," Dean Barnlund analyzes the differences and challenges behind both interpersonal and intercultural communication. He gives us a conceptual, theoretical framework for analyzing and defining the failures in communication in situations such as we find in Tyler's "Your Place Is Empty" and Mukherjee's "A Father"—stories that reflect the gamut of communication intrapersonally, interpersonally, and interculturally.

In preparation for the assignment, analyze the methods and techniques the writers use to make the experiences they explore vivid and effective for the reader. You might also consider other approaches they might have taken in their writing.

Assignment: In reading both "Your Place Is Empty" and "A Father," you observe collisions of cultures within the families. As an expert now in intercultural communication, you are being asked to interpret the background of the people you know from the stories, the nature of the past and present conflicts both within and between characters, and what happened to bring the final scenes of the stories about.

Here are some questions to help you get started: What details in the stories reflect the characters' commitment to adjust to new values, attitudes, contexts, and meaning? What details in the stories reflect the confusion each person feels about his or her values and roles in facing the new culture? What values, attitudes, and practices does each person hold onto, and why? Which ones have they given up, at least temporarily?

What ideas from "Communication in a Global Village" have helped you to make this analysis? How are you going to use those ideas in your analysis? What are your conclusions about the state of the families at the end of the stories? What do these stories help you to learn about your own challenges with interpersonal and intercultural communication?

2. Writing Assignments on Sources Across the Book

The preceding section on writing sequences suggests ways to use selections from the book as models based upon which students explore and write about their own related experiences and insights. The assignments in this section suggest ways in which students can use two or more selections from the book in the process of learning to write from and about sources. My goal in creating these assignments has been to focus on elements of meaning within the reading that engage and challenge students. I remind students that figuring out how they will approach the assignment is always part of the assignment. Instructors will also discover their own connections among the readings, or expand on the ideas in the examples that follow.

In all these assignments, students will be exploring what each writer has to say about a particular topic, and the ways in which one writer's ideas and approach to a topic compare with and increase one's understanding of another writer's ideas and approach.

Students need to be encouraged, and taught if necessary, to use brief quoted passages from the readings in support of their analyses.

These assignments cover a wide spectrum of topics:

1. In preparation for this assignment, read "Learning a New Culture," by Solon Kimball, "Paths Upon Water," by Tahira Naqvi, and "Myself in India," by Ruth Prawer Jhabvala:

    Each person in these three selections is learning a new culture. What aspects of that new culture are they learning; in what ways are they becoming confused? Why and how does each person's struggle relate to and differ from the others'?

2. In preparation for this assignment, read "Man at the Mercy of Language," by Peter Farb, "Linguistic Factors in Prejudice," by Gordon Allport, and "Open Admissions," by Shirley Lauro:

    In what ways are Calvin and Alice in "Open Admissions" at the mercy of language? In what ways do linguistic factors in prejudice keep each character from seeing the other person as an individual with special needs? In what ways are the problems that Calvin and Alice are facing between them problems created by language?

3. In preparation for this assignment, read "What Is Culture?" by Jawaharlal Nehru, "Social Time: The Heartbeat of Culture," by Robert Levine with Ellen Wolff, and "Waiting," by Janette Turner Hospital:

    If Mr. Matthew Thomas were answering Nehru's question, what observations do you think he would make, based on your experiences of watching him in the airline office those two days? In what ways would Miss Jennifer Harper answer the same question?

    In what ways does Levine's analysis of social time as the heartbeat of culture help you to understand the different ways in which Thomas and Harper approach the same experience? Why are attitudes about social time so central to understanding what culture involves, and how cultures differ?

4. In preparation for this assignment, read "America of the People," by Rimma Kazakova, and "A Country, Not a Scenario," by Norman Mailer:

    Imagine that Kazakova and Mailer have met and are having a frank discussion about their impressions of the other's country. What would they say to each other, and how do you think each would respond, and why? Try to keep each person in character, according to the style and tone of their essays.

    (Because the relationship between the United States and the Soviet Union is changing in dramatic ways from the time these pieces were written, what would be different in their conversation if they were having it now rather than at the time each essay was written? You can choose the year in which their conversation is taking place.)

5. In preparation for this assignment, read "The Name," by Aharon Megged, "Love Must Not Be Forgotten," by Zhang Jie, and "Solo on the Drums," by Ann Petry:

   These selections all involve questions of forgetting and remembering. In each story, where do the conflicts lie for the characters over what should be remembered and what forgotten, and why? How does each of the main characters in the stories face the struggles of remembering and forgetting?

6. In preparation for this assignment, read "Culture Shock and the American Businessman Overseas," by Lawrence Stessin, and "How Datsun Discovered America," by David Halberstam:

   In what ways does Yutaka Katayama in "How Datsun Discovered America" reflect the validity of the ideas that Stessin presents about what the American needs to know in doing business overseas? How well prepared was Katayama to work for Nissan in California? In what ways do you think he might have avoided his end in the United States, and why? Where did Katayama fail, if you think he did, and why?

7. In preparation for this assignment, read "The Hmong in America," by Spencer Sherman, and "America: The Multinational Society," by Ishmael Reed:

   In what ways might the Hmong from Laos who have relocated in the United States have trouble agreeing with Reed's claim that America is multinational, and why? In what ways are the Hmong proof of Reed's argument, and why? What assumptions does Reed make that the Hmong might have difficulty understanding, and why?

8. In preparation for this assignment, read "Bloomington, Fall 1971," by Yearn Hong Choi, and "Culture Shock in Reverse," by James R. Corey:

   Although Choi's story does not involve his return to Korea, in what ways does his story reflect and support the ideas that Corey explains about the problems of re-entry for graduate students he knew returning from the United States to Saudi Arabia? What cultural patterns of values have come into conflict for Choi? How do his conflicts differ from those the Saudi students encounter when they return home? In what ways are the conflicts similar?

9. In preparation for this assignment, read "A Farewell to the Old Order," by Similih Cordor, and "Chee's Daughter," by Juanita Platero and Siyowin Miller:

   Dahn and Chee each encounter conflict with an old order, or the ways in which things have been done in their pasts. What are their conflicts, and what cultural traditions and patterns contributed to both the old and changing orders of their lives? In what ways would they each be better off with the new order of patterns and values? In what ways might the changes they are making in their lives represent a loss, and why?

10. In preparation for this assignment, read "The Health of the Sick," by Julio Cortazar, and "Before Sunrise," by V. Goryushkin:

In what ways do love and caring express themselves within each family? What parallels can you draw between these vastly different family settings? What differences do you observe? In what ways might you tie the differences to attitudes in each story about sickness and health, life and death?

11. In preparation for this assignment, read "Sunrise on the Veld," by Doris Lessing, and "The Picking Season," by Graham Sheil:

    The young men in these stories each make surprising discoveries about their place in the world through different encounters—in "Sunrise" with a dying buck, and in "Picking Season" with a German man named Alf. What are the insights each boy gains? In what ways might you compare their experiences? In what ways do the experiences differ? In what ways do you think these encounters will change the young men's lives, and why?

12. In preparation for this assignment, read "A Weekend in Bandung," by H. Jathar Salij, "The Hitchhiking Game," by Milan Kundera, and "The Coward," by Premchand:

    The couples in these stories are each engaged in trying to define themselves and to evaluate their relationship with each other. In what ways are their struggles similar, and why? In what ways do they differ, and why? What problems do they impose on their relationship because of their own needs, and what are those needs? What problems do their cultures impose on them? We know the outcome of the situation in "The Coward"; what do you project will be the outcome of the situations in "A Weekend in Bandung" and "The Hitchhiking Game"? Upon what observations and arguments do you build your predictions?

13. In preparation for this assignment, read "The Moccasin Telegraph," by W. P. Kinsella, and "Not a Thing Out of Place," by Tewfiq al-Hakim:

    Both this story and this play raise questions about the ways one perceives another culture, the expectations that the outsiders bring with them about the ways things will be. When patterns of other cultures do not square with the outsiders' observations, outsiders are likely to interpret the world they have entered in some peculiar way, finding that world absurd. As you explore the parallels of these two pieces, how would you define what is sane and normal in each world? What does each group of outsiders consider insane or abnormal? What cases can be made for not assuming that what seems crazy to the outsider actually *is* crazy? Explain the problems you encounter as you grapple with these questions.

14. In preparation for this assignment, read "Translating Cultures . . . or What's George Washington Doing in a Sushi Bar?" by Phyllis Lyons, and "You Have Left Your Lotus Pods on the Bus," by Paul Bowles:

    In "Translating Cultures . . . ," Phyllis Lyons explains the kind of historic, psychological, and aesthetic background information that the reader needs to know in order to understand a story like "The Garden." In Bowles's story, part of the meaning and the humor of the story rests with what the monks find incomprehensible about the Americans, and what the Americans find incomprehensible about the monks. What kinds of information would each group need to know about the other in order not to find their behavior confusing if not crazy? Create an imaginative explanation by each group that attempts to help the other group understand them. Can it be done? Why or why not? What would you imagine to be the problems in such an attempt?

15. In preparation for this assignment, read "Big Mama's Funeral," by Gabriel García Marquez, "Making Do," by Linda Hogan, and "Grandmother's Country," by N. Scott Momaday:

These three selections all undertake to memorialize people who have died, to deal with the loss to the family and community, and, indirectly, to trace the lives of the survivors. In what ways does each piece undertake these approaches? In each case, what is the relationship of the narrator to the story or essay? What similarities do you perceive in the ways each writer deals with the losses explored? What differences make each piece unique? If you were to extrapolate your own insights about death as a result of reading these three selections and writing about them, what would you say you learned, and why?

16. In preparation for this assignment, read "The Tall Woman with the Short Husband," by Feng Jicai, "The Bench," by Richard Rive, and "An Image of Africa," by Chinua Achebe:

These three selections explore the ways in which groups of people define each other, or fail to define each other—at least in ways that validate them. Each piece explores what Ralph Ellison calls invisibility (see Epigraph, Chapter 8). In what ways are people made invisible in each of these selections? What elements of language support the attempt of others to make or keep them invisible? How do the problems of invisibility compare and differ in each selection, and why?

17. In preparation for this assignment, read "Paths Upon Water," by Tahira Naqvi, "A Father," by Bharati Mukherjee, and "The Plane Reservation," by Massud Farzan:

These three stories reflect the difficulties parents have in facing changes in their children as a result of their being in a culture different from the one in which they (parents and/or children) were raised. What problems do you observe all four sets of parents encounter? In what ways do their problems differ? What is your prognosis for the future relationships of these four sets of parents and children, and upon what observations and ideas are you basing your predictions?

18. In preparation for this assignment, read "Body Ritual Among the Nacirema," by Horace M. Miner:

The Nacirema, as you know, name a strange and unique group of people. The essay parodies both a certain kind of reporting and language spoken by anthropologists and the group's behaviors themselves. Your assignment here is to write your own analysis and parody of the Nacirema, in the style of this article, but on another aspect of that group's culture. Every facet of their life is open to your pen. Have fun.

19. In preparation for this assignment, read "Memories of a Bilingual Child-hood," by Richard Rodriguez, and "Tingiivik Tatqiq, The Moon When Birds Fly South (September)," by Richard K. Nelson:

    In his essay, Rodriguez argues the case against bilingual education, based on the experience of his childhood education and entry into adulthood. In his story, Nelson recounts the influences of Kiluk's education in English as she returns to her Eskimo village. In what ways might Kiluk agree with Rodriguez's argument, and why? In what ways would her life suggest the difficulties of bilingual education? In what ways do Rodriguez's own experiences reflect the difficulties that education in a language different from one's family creates?

20. In preparation for this assignment, read "Your Place Is Empty," by Anne Tyler, and "Communication in a Global Village," by Dean Barnlund:

    In what ways does the story of Mrs. Ardavi's visit with her son Hassan and daughter Elizabeth illustrate the relationships that Barnlund defines between interpersonal and intercultural communication? In what ways does the story reflect the particular problems of the family? Why is an analysis of this kind difficult? What does it suggest to you about the differences between interpersonal, familial, and intercultural communication?

3. Investigating Topics Beyond the Book

For courses in which this anthology will be used in conjunction with writing research or investigative papers, this chapter offers examples and possibilities for using the book as a source of ideas and topics to investigate further. It also suggests ways in which the selections themselves can be used as models.

1. In "I Scream, You Scream . . . The Cultural Significance of Ice Cream," Henry Binford investigates the complex history that has made ice cream parlors a prominent fixture in American life. This assignment asks you to choose an object of your own to investigate, as Binford has done, not only for its history, but also for the ways in which that history is culturally significant. Examples of objects might include the following: blue jeans, sweatshirts, tennis shoes, vanity license plates, instant foods, kitchen machines, and thousands more. Your paper will reflect the object's history and your analysis of why it is more than just one more thing we use or enjoy—its embedded cultural values and meaning.

2. In "Man at the Mercy of Language," Peter Farb refers to the important work of Ludwig Wittgenstein of Cambridge University who said, "The limits of my language are the limits of my world." What contributions did Wittgenstein make to our understanding of the influences of language in our lives?

3. The titles of two essays in this anthology reflect the ways in which our expectations about language change over time. Both "Man at the Mercy of Language" by Peter Farb and "Culture Shock and the American Businessman Overseas" by Lawrence Stessin use what we would now call sexist language

not only in their titles but also throughout their essays. What have been the major influences in our changing perceptions about the use of the male pronoun or such words as man or mankind to signify both males and females? Why have the changes to non-sexist language been important to our views of ourselves? In what ways does Farb's essay itself suggest the importance of these changes?

4. In "Communication in a Global Village" by Dean Barnlund, Barnlund quotes Edwin Reischaer on his thoughts about preparing for this "one world." Reischaer played a critical role in the relationship between the United States and Japan following World War II. Who was Edwin Reischaer, and why was his work and his understanding of the concept of "one world" critical? (A film entitled "The Japanese" is narrated by Reischaer, and though it focuses on Japan, it also reflects a great deal about the man.)

5. Many selections within the anthology refer to special foods or traditions or rituals surrounding food. Two books will launch interested students on a variety of topics related to the relationships between food and culture: *The Sacred Cow and the Abominable Pig: Riddles of Food and Culture,* by Marvin Harris, and *Consuming Passions: The Anthropology of Eating,* by Peter Farb and George Armelagos. (Full bibliographic information can be found under the section entitled "Additional Bibliography for Teaching and Exploring Culture.")

6. In the story "A Coward" by Premchand, the caste system of India becomes an obstacle in the love between a young man and woman. What is the history of the origin of India's caste system? In what ways is this history related to Hinduism? What were the cultural and social intentions of early caste divisions? In what ways has the caste system become ever more complex? Why is the government of India today attempting to reduce its influence?

7. In the story "The Bench" by Richard Rive, Karlie gains a new sense of injustice; the result is his active response against a symbol of apartheid, the bench. How and why did this system of apartheid originate? What is its relationship to the beliefs of the Dutch Reform Church in South Africa, and how does the biblical story of Ham underpin the Afrikaners' sense of divine sanction in their laws?

8. Gabriel García Marquez says that for almost the first forty years of his life, "things did not work out for me." How did it happen then that he achieved recognition finally for his writing, and upon what achievements was his great honor the Nobel Prize for Literature (1982) granted? What forces finally created a broad appreciation for the "magical realism" that he refers to in his acceptance speech, from which William Montalbano quotes in "Latin America: A Quixotic Land Where the Bizarre Is Routine"?

9. The essay, "Love and Sex in the Life of an Arab" from a collection entitled *The Hidden Face of Eve,* by Egyptian psychiatrist Nawal el-Saadawi, traces present practices to the influences of Moslem beliefs and harsh desert life. What attitudes about sexuality does the Moslem religion teach? What are the

patterns of expectations for male and female sexual relationships? How accurately has el-Saadawi analyzed these influences in light of Moslem religious beliefs? Students interested in her analysis might also want to read relevant sections of *A Thousand and One Nights* to assess her claims about the myths it created for outsiders.

10. The essay, "I'm Black, You're White, Who's Innocent?" by Shelby Steele suggests the different perceptions blacks and whites have about the relationship among race, power, and innocence. A book entitled *Black and White Styles in Conflict* by Thomas Kochman explores the reasons behind these differences in depth. (Full bibliographic information can be found under the section entitled "Additional Bibliography for Teaching and Exploring Culture.") In what ways would Kochman explain what happened at the party between the black guests and the white? In what ways would his analysis support Steele's, and why? In what ways would it differ, and why? In the back of Kochman's book is a long reference section on related reading for students who want to extend their study of these issues.

11. In the play "Open Admissions" by Shirley Lauro, a black student named Calvin is demanding a kind of education from his teacher, Alice Miller, that she is unable to give him, unable even to grasp. The book of essays *Tapping Potential: English and Language Arts for the Black Learner,* edited by Charlotte K. Brooks, offers explanations and approaches that Miller might use. (Full bibliographic information can be found under the section entitled "Additional Bibliography for Teaching and Exploring Culture.") What suggestions and explanations in that book would help both Calvin and Miller understand what Calvin needs and how to give it to him in the classroom? What changes in her teaching style would Miller have to make, and why?

4. Collaborative Writing Assignments

The assignments that follow ask your class to work together in exploring topics related to their reading, and to discover the ideas and the core of their own papers through partnership or group exploration:

1. If your class has a variety of cultures represented (and it most likely does, even if your eye does not guess so at first), a term-long writing project can involve two culture-contrasting partners who get to know each other through shared experience, planned on a regular basis and written about in each person's journal. At the end of the term, a collaborative paper on their partnership can be written from the data and insights in their journals. In their papers, they will explore the partnership, the differences they encountered in each partner's perceptions of shared experience, and what they have learned from the extended experience.

2. Because the study of other cultures gives us the distance we need to look more closely at our own, the class may want to embark early in the term on

each person's writing a self-culture analysis. What have been the major influential cultural values, attitudes, and assumptions in each student's life, and why? In preparation create a long list of general categories of influences: family structure, religious background, international and intercultural heritage, disabilities—the categories are numerous. Interviews with each other may help each person recall important influences. Students ask if they'll be writing an autobiography in this assignment. Of course they will, but with the emphasis on cultural influences. They will learn from this assignment that one's culture cannot be separated from one's life.

A suggestion is to take at least one class period at the beginning of the term to write a first draft of this paper, for the instructor to keep these drafts, unread, for a number of weeks, and to return them for revision and further development when students have read and thought more fully about how they want to approach the analysis, and feel comfortable and safe within the class itself.

3. In small groups of men and women, students can discover some of the myths and beliefs by which they live. Suggest they empty their purses, wallets, and pockets on a table together to have a close look at the assembled objects. Some have practical significance; some symbolic significance. Have them describe the categories into which they fit, and then together begin to discuss the cultural significance of their meaning. Suggest they approach the objects as if they were learning about them as an outsider for the first time. What, for example, does something as common as their keys signify about attitudes toward privacy, honesty, and trust? What about the licenses they carry, the plastic cards, their memberships? After they've responded to their discoveries, have them write a report, either as a group or as individuals on what they've discovered about their cultural beliefs, values, and attitudes as a result.

4. This assignment asks the class to look at the home each person knew as a child as a source of further cultural insight.

Divide your class into pairs. Have each person take a large piece of paper and draw the floor plan of a house he or she lived in before the age of ten, then sketch in its furniture and as much as they can remember of its landscape. After drawing the details, each partner will take the other on a tour through their early life. How did the light come through the windows? How did the house smell? Was there a place that was theirs alone? What were the rules of the house? What were the significant memories they have of those years—personal, familial, and even on a larger scale, the influences of what was going on in the community and the world? In what ways, in other words, did the outside world enter that house? After both partners have completed this tour for the other, they might write a paper in which they re-create the home and life of their partner; the other option is to write a paper on the place each person has been thinking about as a result of this assignment. What have they learned about culture through thinking about the architectural space of a childhood home?

5. Following are the first two paragraphs from Ulibarri's story "The Stuffing of the Lord," in Spanish as he wrote it. The class assignment is for as many students as possible to either translate the paragraphs themselves into English or have someone fluent in Spanish translate them. When they return to class with their translations on the day assigned, have them come with copies of them for each small group that will be working together. In these small groups, students will read each translation in comparison with Thelma C. Nason's (the one in this anthology) and discover the differences between theirs and hers. Are they major or minor in meaning, and why? In what ways does the Spanish language seem to grasp the world differently than English? How do the translations differ among themselves? Based on their shared observations and translations, each group will write an analysis of this experience and present it to the class. You'll be fortunate as a class if there are Spanish speakers in the class to guide you.

   Here, then, is the Spanish:

   > El padre Benito casi casi me salvó el alma. Por cierto me puso en el camino de la salvación, produciéndoles a mis padres una espantosa sorpresa y exclamaciones de admiración a toda la población. Y allá donde Dios lo tenga el padre Benito me tendrá todavía por salvado.
   >
   > La verdad es que hasta la edad de doce años no había mostrado yo ni el menor olor de santidad ni mucho menos ninguna inclinación al sacerdocio o ningún otro docio, sácer o no. Al contrario, había dado muchas muestras de ir encaminado en opuesta dirección.

6. With the class in small groups, decide on a question they have about a nonverbal ritual or habit you would like to probe in the way that Bateson does with the script between father and daughter about the gestures she sees Frenchmen using. Each group will need to create two or three characters of their own to star in their script. Each group will share scripts with the class, with its members reading the roles.

7. "Body Ritual Among the Nacirema" satirizes the Nacirema. With the class in small groups, each group will discuss its own analysis of the Nacirema, based on other aspects of their life and culture, such as mating rituals, customs of educating their youth, modes of vehicular transportation— the list can entail any facet of that life and culture. Each person in the group can write an essay or the group can try it together. The essays will imitate the style of Miner's example, but their context and content will be original.

   The object is to write their analysis as if they, the anthropologists, are strangers/observers only, in a strange land. They will be recording what they see and infer *on their own*. Warn them against assuming anything about the whys behind what they know already.

8. In "The Day of the Dead," Octavio Paz helps readers understand the idea of this Mexican fiesta. Divide the class into small groups, with each group assigned a national occasion or holiday. Consider a diverse representation: Presidential Election Day, Martin Luther King Day, Christmas, New Year's

Eve, Labor Day, Thanksgiving, and July 4th just as starters. The object of each group will be to write an analysis of the day assigned, explaining 1) the ways in which the day is celebrated or observed, 2) the paradoxes an outsider would need to keep in mind in learning about it, and 3) the ways in which the day ties into or reflects cultural patterns and values. At an assigned time, each group will share its collaborative essay with the class.

9. As a class, tackle your own definition of American culture. What are its characteristics? How can students describe it so that a traveler, whom they'll need to define, coming to the United States for the first time will have a clear notion of what to look for and expect? At which city is the traveler entering this culture? What warnings do students have for the traveler? What are the elements they cannot explain, and why? As they attempt this definition, encourage them not to fear the obstacles they encounter. The obstacles may themselves prove to be invaluable warnings or tips to the traveler as well as to the writers.

10. Use your class as a laboratory for studying the current structures of the American family on a small scale. Divide the class into small groups. Have their members answer a number of questions you will ask about family: Who actually lives in the family home or apartment, how many siblings, who supports the family financially, who is home when, who makes the major decisions regarding the children, in what ways, if any, has divorce touched their families, and so forth? Each group will add their own questions to these samples.

    Have each group write an analysis of what their data suggest about the American family today. What patterns have they discovered, and what might these patterns have to do with our cultural values?

    At an assigned time, share these collaborative essays with the whole class, noting and discussing the significance of their differences and similarities.

11. Barnlund's essay begins with a quote from the poet Basho's *haiku* about his neighbor and Barnlund's own comments about our changing neighborhoods and their diversity. Each member of the class might be responsible for interviewing three or four of his or her neighbors and writing a paper on the differences and similarities discovered among them. On an assigned day, the class can meet in small groups that share their individual papers and then write a group paper, to be shared with the class, on conclusions that might be made about the neighborhoods that result when neighbors get presented in this way. From these experiences students might also discover some interesting profiles of their city or town.

12. Following Barnlund's example, have someone in the class provide a set of photographs, preferably slides, let everyone see the photographs for a set time, and then take class time for every person to write quickly about what the photographs contained and meant. Share these responses, and then write individual papers on the meaning this experience in class reflects about each person's perceptions of the same experience.

13. If your class has undertaken many of these and other collaborative efforts, a final project could involve writing about the value of collaboration. What values, attitudes, and expectations underlie the experience of collaborating, especially as writers? In what ways do those values, attitudes, and expectations differ from a "normal" classroom in which competition is often the underlying though unspoken basis of evaluation? What problems have students encountered as they collaborated with their classmates? In what ways did they solve them? Under what circumstances were they impossible to solve, and why? What rewards have they discovered in the process? What have they learned through collaboration that they might apply to other aspects of their lives?

Chapter 3

Using the Book in Literature and Intercultural Classes

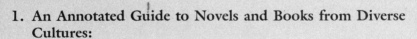

1. An Annotated Guide to Novels and Books from Diverse Cultures:

The getting and the giving of books is just as complicated a matter as the writing and the reading of them. That . . . is because there is so much that can be hidden in the cover and pages of a literary work. Always, to the messages already present, we can add our own. By liking and loving a book, we can supplement its story with a new story, the story of ourselves. And when we have done that, we can always hand it on, in the great book-lined circle of getting and giving that keeps the world, and the word, going round.

MALCOLM BRADBURY, from
THE COURTSHIP DANCE: ON GIVING AND GETTING BOOKS

What Bradbury says about books is true for shorter pieces—true, I hope, for many of the selections of this book. I've included this guide to novels and books in this manual for instructors who want to use this anthology as part of a course in literature that takes students through books to different cultures. Many selections in the anthology help students to understand the challenges and rewards of intercultural experience, thus making them more sensitive readers as they take their place in that great book-lined circle.

The annotated list of books to follow reflects an accumulation of books I've given and been given as a person who loves to read, most of all, in the shared context of a class. The story of my life that I bring to the reading of a book merges

in the classroom with the stories of students who are simultaneously supplement-
ing the life within a book. In that way, all teachers who teach books keep the
world and the word going round.

Following this list, you will find some sample study guides; I write them and
use them differently for each book. They provide a framework for the students
who find that kind of help useful to noticing certain aspects of the book as they
read. They also provide a way to have small groups discussing and exploring
important elements in their reading, and then to return to the larger group of
the class to share their insights. There are always one or two students in the class
who would prefer to throw these guides away, but most students find them
useful. The questions at least help us to begin focusing on certain dimensions of
the work, and stimulate students to begin writing and asking their own questions,
the major benefit, in my mind, of the idea.

Another suggestion is to use one of the guides as a model, and to have students
write their own guide to each book, collaboratively. (See notes under "Reading
Strategies" in the *Question* section.)

Here then are the books, in alphabetical order by author's name, tested over
a number of years in the course in contemporary world literature I teach. They've
all worked well in one way or another, and most in many ways. I have not
included books in which the translation lacks literary excellence. Like the selections in the anthology, these books come from diverse and often unfamiliar parts
of the world and the United States, and have been written following the second
world war.

Achebe, Chinua. *Things Fall Apart.* With its title taken from Yeats's poem "The
Second Coming," this book lands the reader in an Ibo village in Nigeria in which
its leader, Okonkwo, eventually leads the village in a fight against colonialism and
Christianity in a futile effort to preserve the tribal life and values that the first part
of the book establishes with such immediacy.

Amado, Jorge. *Gabriela, Clove and Cinnamon.* Gabriela, the compelling central
character of this book, is a woman who refuses to be obligated—to family, to
history, to constraints. She lives in the city and world of Ilheus, close to the
Brazilian cocoa plantations that have made so many of its occupants rich and
corrupt. Readers will learn much about the history and culture of Brazil, and
probably fall in love with Gabriela.

Anaya, Rudolfo. *Bless Me, Ultima.* Its story narrated by the young man Antonio,
this novel combines many insights not only into its predominant Hispanic, New
Mexican culture, but also in its exploration of a number of paths to faith—from
the beloved *curandera,* Ultima, to the Catholic church, to the young boys who
believe in the myth of the carp. It is a novel of Antonio's initiation into adulthood, and the profound love and hatred he encounters as he grows up—an
outstanding work that was over ten years in the writing.

Borland, Hal. *When the Legends Die.* For classes in which your students may have
limited vocabulary, this book combines a simple, always clear language with the

complex life of its main character Tom Black Bull, a Ute Indian from Colorado. Students of all ages and from many cultures identify with the struggles Tom faces in his life between the values he learned from the traditional Ute ways of his mother, and the often brutal world he encounters following her death. A story of initiation into adult life, the book also explores the power of one's past and its hold on the core of a person's life.

Coetzee, J. M. *Life and Times of Michael K.* Critic Cynthia Ozick, in commenting on this book from South Africa, wrote: "The literature of conscience is ultimately about the bewilderment of the naive." Michael K. is the mute son of a black servant in South Africa who wanders the country in spite of or perhaps because he cannot know the laws that would contain him. This is a story of his surviving, to be appreciated both for its literal surface and its symbolic underpinnings, that, whenever students wish to reach for them, are lurking everywhere.

————. *Waiting for the Barbarians.* A short novel whose setting at first appears to be South Africa (and written by an Afrikaner from that country), its magistrates from the Empire are poised at an outpost for an attack from the barbarians. The novel has its greatest impact not as a vision of South Africa but as a psychological exploration or parable of what constitutes civilization, justice, and the ways in which a nation's or a person's perceptions of the enemy can distort the lives not only of the barbarians but of themselves.

Desai, Anita. *Clear Light of Day.* One of the benefits of novels set far from our students' lives, this one in India, is that the distance provides time and comfort for students to discover the parallels with their own lives when they exist. This novel about a family living in Old Delhi, whose sister has just returned with her husband from foreign service in the United States, re-creates a family that we might tag "dysfunctional." The heat, dust, and decay of the setting and its effects on the family are alleviated in the clear light of day by the discovery of what family love means, and endures.

Doerr, Harriet. *Stones for Ibarra.* An American family from California gives up their luxurious life and returns to a small village in Mexico to resurrect the life and dream of their grandfather by reopening the Malaguena mine. A good novel for considering the intercultural encounters between this American family and the Mexican community they discover, as well as for considering the nature of their dream as they realize its reality.

Ellison, Ralph. *Invisible Man.* One of the great American novels, this is the story of a black man, never named, who lives in a cellar somewhere in New York City, his "home" a symbolic retreat from a life in which he has tried to make his mark, to gain visibility, only to be beaten each time by forces he could never overcome. "The most valuable resource available to the black author is his double vision," Ellison has said, "his simultaneous position *inside* and *outside* of our culture. These are positions . . . where values can be studied in action." This is a book of values in action.

Erdrich, Louise. *Love Medicine.* Through its large family of several narrators, this book lands its reader in Chippewa Indian life in North Dakota and Minnesota, and allows extraordinary insight into the mixing of Indian and white cultures, especially by means of the Catholic religion, and the "enduring verities of love and surviving."

Fuentes, Carlos. *The Good Conscience.* Set in Guanajuato, Mexico, this short novel is a big story about an extended family who raise a son named Jaime, a young man who works hard at creating his own values and relationship with God, in a struggle played out against the demands and hypocrisy of his family, society, and church. Once students get beyond the confusion of names and family history, they will find a story they may already understand in terms of their own lives, even as they will most likely regret Jaime's choices about having a good conscience at the end of the novel.

García Marquez, Gabriel. *Love in the Time of Cholera.* No novel I've taught has engaged students' awe more than this one. An encyclopedia of love, it traces a fifty-one year wait on the part of one Florentino Ariza for the woman he loves, Fermina Daza. It sometimes seems in the reading that García Marquez has kept us posted on what is happening to every person around Colombia in that half-century hiatus, but the insights (many of which we know already but have never seen in words) dazzle us all, even the younger students in the class who lack the perspective of years.

———. *One Hundred Years of Solitude.* A big book with big promises—mostly delivered—on learning about life in Colombia, major historical influences in Latin America, insight into the phrase "magical realism" as García Marquez captures it, and the one hundred years of the Buendia family in the author's imaginary town of Macondo, with all their family battles, wars, hopes, and revelations.

Gordimer, Nadine. *July's People.* Reflecting what Gordimer calls an "interregnum" in South Africa, this novel re-creates the world of their black servant, July, and his village, to which the Johannesburg family Smales have fled, following massive revolution in that city. The reader observes the disintegration of the white family separated from their systems of support, but the big question of the novel regards the ever-changing relationship of master and servant; the collisions between the two cultures also create good discussions and insights, especially about the life behind *apartheid.*

Hurston, Zora Neale. *Their Eyes Were Watching God.* A writer from the 1930s, Hurston has been rediscovered in the last two decades for her remarkable re-creation of southern black culture. The novel sets the reader firmly on the famous porch of the South from which Hurston claims she learned about life, and backtracks through its main character Janie's three marriages. Students love it for the world it creates, the love they feel vicariously, and the interesting issues of dialect and culture that the novel raises.

Kawabata, Yasunari. *Snow Country.* The most famous work of Japan's Nobel Laureate (1968), this book takes place in northern Japan, charting the relationship between a successful Japanese businessman, Shimamura, and a geisha, Komako, and his inability to love. Translated from the Japanese, the novel has been described as a series of linked *haiku,* a reflection of the richness and challenge of its intricate language and culture.

————. *The Sound of the Mountain.* This novel takes us into life with a Japanese family, focusing on the aging father, Shingo, as he listens to the sound of the mountain and his own approaching death. Through the story of this extended family and its generations, American readers will confront a number of questions regarding unfamiliar sexual mores and conventions. One young man in class gleefully said one day, "And now, as a result of reading this novel, I understand Uncle Delbert!"

Kogawa, Joy. *Obasan.* Balancing its narrative among history, memoir, and poetry, this novel tells the story of a Canadian Japanese family torn apart by Canada's World War II wholesale relocation of its Japanese citizens from the province of British Columbia to the harsh prairies of Alberta. Its language is often remarkable, especially as it fuses images from nature to the lives of its characters, pushing slowly on to the mysterious question of what happened to the mother of the first-person narrator, Naomi, following the mother's return to Japan in the midst of the tragic reshuffling of lives enforced by the government.

Konwicki, Tadeusz. *A Minor Apocalypse.* Written as a satire in 1979 when the Solidarity movement in Poland was growing in power, this novel appeared to be more prophetic than satiric with the imposition of martial law in 1981. A good choice for the study of writing that explores the surreal and the absurd, this novel can also be explored as a parable or as a way of creating history. Konwicki gives his main character his name; during the single day the novel recounts, he must decide whether to take his own life as a way of political protest against a totalitarian world in which he finds himself a slave.

Kundera, Milan. *The Unbearable Lightness of Being.* This book challenges its reader on many levels; it is full of allusions and themes that flow in and out of the narrative like a symphony. Set in Czechoslavakia, it is also full of sex, sensuous and explicit, a central theme in the life of one of its central characters, Tomas. Its story of Tomas and Tereza, Sabina and Franz, pulls on dream, biography, etymology, psychology, philosophy, and history in a dense and rich mix that explores the lives of its characters, and, by extension, allows us rare glimpses from oblique angles into our own.

Mahfouz, Nagib. *The Beginning and the End.* Set in Cairo around the time of World War II, this novel allows its readers to experience the bitterness of poverty in its war against the family's honor and reputation. Through a family stricken with the death of its father, students can relate to the novel effectively as its three brothers struggle against and with each other to make something of their lives. The novel also re-creates many facets of Egyptian culture. (Note: Mahfouz was the winner of the Nobel Prize for Literature, 1988.)

Mathabane, Mark. *Kaffir Boy.* An autobiography, this book works well on many levels. It educates readers about the intolerable conditions of South African ghettoes, or townships as they are called by the government, for their black or Bantu population. It also testifies to the power of education and of books in Mathabane's life, and to the accomplishments that the most deprived of human beings can realize. When Mathabane leaves South Africa to begin his education and tennis scholarship in the United States, he also leaves the reader with awe and incredulity.

Mishima, Yukio. *Death in Midsummer.* A riveting collection of six stories and one Noh play, the material was assembled in one book by the author himself. Each story introduces important facets of Japanese culture and values, including a story about some famous Kabuki actors who specialize in playing female roles. The Noh play is valuable for reading together as a class.

Morley, John David. *Pictures from the Water Trade.* A "novel" that is actually a thinly disguised autobiography, this book lets its readers experience Japan through the eyes of an Englishman who becomes completely fluent in the Japanese language and ultimately adopts the culture in so many unconscious ways that he has to leave Japan in order to retrieve his own past and culture. Morley takes on many intercultural challenges in this book, and the reward for the reader is accurate insights into Japanese culture, at least as assessed by students from Japan who have been in classes in which we've read this book.

Naipaul, V. S. *A Bend in the River.* An Indian merchant, Salim, sets up shop in a village on the bend of a river in east Africa; he and a group of friends face what it means to be in a culture but not of a culture, a result in part of the British Empire's leaving vast migrant populations on the move—physically displaced, homesick without ever having had a home, nostalgic for a nonexistent past. The novel also explores what happens to the country when one of its own citizens takes over its rule.

Narayan, R. K. *Malgudi Days.* A collection of stories compiled from three volumes of Narayan's work, this book is delightful for its humor, effective in its pathos, and a good introduction to the lives of a number of people in India, involved in a myriad of pursuits and moments of crises. Malgudi is Narayan's depiction of an Indian town or village, and although it was written near the end of colonial rule, it still validly reflects the villages of India today.

el-Saadawi, Nawal. *Two Women in One.* Written by a female Egyptian psychiatrist, this short novel, set in Egypt, portrays a young woman, Bahiah Shaheen, who fights against the tight codes of her parents, her religion, and her unusual role as a medical student in Cairo as she struggles to find herself. Students will recognize many aspects of their own struggles at the same time that they will be drawn into a culture vastly different from their own.

Tan, Amy. *The Joy Luck Club.* (Note: Though I have not yet taught this book because at the time of this writing it is only available in hardback, I will use it immediately once it's out in paper.) A remarkable book about mothers and daughters, life in China and the United States, and the poignant stories that its eight characters tell, this unusual novel takes its readers to the heart of intercultural experience, gain, and loss. Its characters are keenly developed, its language always engaging, its pages packed with the unexpected and yet familiar.

Walker, Alice. *Meridian.* This book re-creates the life of its central character, Meridian, an aging black woman who at the beginning of the novel appears a little crazy, a craziness that makes perfect sense as the reader eventually grasps the whole of her life and the struggle she has quietly lived against racism and sexism. The reader also gains many historic insights from her struggle to register southern blacks to vote during the 1960s.

Xianliang, Zhang. *Mimosa.* A collection of three novellas, this book helps its readers experience various aspects of the last four to five decades of life and struggle in China, from the Communist Revolution of 1949 through the Cultural Revolution of 1966–1976. Its stories show the influence of the West, and raise the question of the value of education and its threats in unexpected contexts.

Yehoshua, A. B. *The Lover.* A fascinating novel set in Israel, its narrative is developed through the monologues of six major characters and their perceptions. Although the question of who the lover is stimulates good discussion, the title is more important as a reflection of the novel's contrasts and ironies: youth and age, potency and impotence, Jew and Arab, sleeping and waking, redemption and destruction, comic and tragic moments, the familiar suddenly turned strange.

2. Sample Study Guides to Novels

Study Guide to The Good Conscience

1. What background and values does the first chapter establish about the place of Guanajuato and the families of the novel? What information there becomes important as you read the novel, and why?
2. Create a family tree out of the information you are given as you read, so that as the novel progresses, you will have an easy guide to who's who.
3. For what reasons does Jaime suffer as a young boy? What values does he perceive his father Rodolfo following? His Aunt Asunción? His Uncle Balcárcel?
4. What are Jaime's convictions as a young boy about the relationship between himself and God? In what ways does the Catholic Church influence him as he grows up? What values does Father Lanzagorta represent to Jaime? What values does Father Obregón represent?

5. What scenes or lines in the book made you laugh, and why? What scenes or lines made you cringe, and why? What values and attitudes of your own created your response?

6. As you read the book, keep track of the references in it to solitude. For what reasons do you think this condition is so frequently referred to? What does it have to do with the character of the town and the people in it?

7. What cultural values and attitudes guide the decisions and behavior of the people in this novel? In what ways do those values and attitudes parallel or differ from your own?

8. On page 103 of the book, the narrator asks, "Why has pain made him [Jaime] happy?" Why, in your opinion, has it?

9. On page 124, Jaime's father Rodolpho asks, "Why haven't we been like papa and mama? . . . Why haven't we been as happy as they were?" If you could answer Rodolpho, what would you say to him by way of analysis?

10. In what ways do Ezequiel Zuno and his mother Adelina influence Jaime's life? What relationship do they have to his dreams?

11. How do you perceive and feel about Jaime's choices at the end of the book, and what do you predict for his future?

12. What meanings do you interpret in the title? In the context of this story, what does having "the good conscience" mean?

Study Guide to Yellow Raft on Blue Water

1. For what reasons do you think the author used the image of the yellow raft in blue water as the title?

2. The novel is divided so that it has the feeling of being three autonomous novellas, connected by their characters' lives, setting, and history. What special effects does this choice of first-person narrations by the three main characters of the novel create for you?

3. As you read each section, what specific and general observations do you gain about each of the major characters? What changes in perceptions of each character occur for you as you move through each major narration? Why do you think Dorris ordered the narratives as he has?

4. Create a family tree through the generations. Be sure to include the parents of Aunt Ida. What do you learn about the families through this kind of exercise? In what ways does it help you to hold onto what you've read?

5. Create a timeline for the novel, clarifying what happens for whom, when. What ideas and insights do you gain from this timeline?

6. What are the responses and perceptions of each character that might teach the reader indirectly about cultural values and attitudes within the novel? Describe the behavior, and then explain the basis for your interpretation.

7. What is the role of religion, specifically Catholicism, in the world of this novel? What do you think it represents for the characters, and why?

Hurston, Zora Neale. *Dust Tracks on a Road: An Autobiography*. Urbana, Illinois: University of Illinois Press, 1984 (originally published 1942).

Hutchinson, William R., and Cynthia A. Poznanski, with Laura Todt-Stockman. *Living in Colombia: A Guide for Foreigners*. Yarmouth, Maine: Intercultural Press, Inc., 1987.

Jung, Anees. *Unveiling India, A Woman's Journey*. New Delhi, India: Penguin Books, 1987.

Kochman, Thomas. *Black and White Styles in Conflict*. Chicago: University of Chicago Press, 1981.

Kohls, L. Robert. *Developing Intercultural Awareness*. Washington, D.C.: SIE-TAR, 1981.

Lim, Shirley Geok-lin, Mayumi Tsutakawa, and Margarita Donnelly. *The Forbidden Stitch: An Asian American Women's Anthology*. Corvallis, Oregon: Calyx Books, 1989.

Memmi, Albert. *The Colonizer and the Colonized*. Boston: Beacon Press, 1965.

Milosz, Czeslaw. *The Captive Mind*. New York: Vintage Books, 1981.

Miller, Stuart. *Painted in Blood: Understanding Europeans*. New York: Atheneum, 1987.

Nydell, Margaret. *Understanding Arabs: A Guide for Westerners*. Yarmouth, Maine: Intercultural Press, Inc., 1987.

Patai, Raphael. *The Arab Mind*. Revised edition. New York: Charles Scribner's Sons, 1983.

Pickens, Judy E. *Without Bias: A Guidebook for Nondiscriminatory Communication*. 2nd edition. New York: John Wiley and Sons, 1982.

Roland, Alan. *In Search of Self in India and Japan: Towards a Cross-Cultural Psychology*. Princeton, New Jersey: Princeton University Press, 1988.

Romano, Dugan. *Intercultural Marriages: Promises and Pitfalls*. Yarmouth, Maine: Intercultural Press, Inc., 1988.

Seelye, H. Ned. *Teaching Culture: Strategies for Intercultural Communication*. Lincolnwood, Illinois: National Textbook Company, 1985.

Simonson, Rick, and Scott Walker. *Multicultural Literacy: Opening the American Mind*. St. Paul, Minnesota: Graywolf Press, 1988.

Smith, Elise C., and Louise Fiber Luce. *Toward Internationalism: Reading in Cross-Cultural Communication*. Rowley, Massachusetts: Newbury House, 1979.

Stewart, Edward C. *American Cultural Patterns: A Cross-Cultural Perspective*. Chicago: Intercultural Press, Inc., 1972.

Stonequist, Everett V. *The Marginal Man: A Study in Personality and Culture Conflict*. New York: Russell and Russell, 1961.

Storti, Craig. *The Art of Crossing Cultures*. Yarmouth, Maine: Intercultural Press, Inc., 1989.

Tanenbaum, Joe. *Male and Female Relationships: Understanding the Opposite Sex*. Yarmouth, Maine: Intercultural Press, Inc., 1990.

Win, David. *International Careers: Where to Find Them. How to Build Them.* Charlotte, Vermont: Williamson Publishing, 1987.

Wheeler, Thomas, ed. *The Immigrant Experience: The Anguish of Becoming American.* New York: Penguin Books, 1980.

Wurzel, Jaime S., ed. *Toward Multiculturalism: A Reader in Multicultural Education.* Yarmouth, Maine: Intercultural Press, Inc., 1988.

Chapter 4

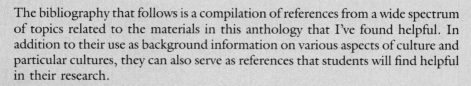

ADDITIONAL
BIBLIOGRAPHY FOR
TEACHING AND
EXPLORING CULTURE

The bibliography that follows is a compilation of references from a wide spectrum of topics related to the materials in this anthology that I've found helpful. In addition to their use as background information on various aspects of culture and particular cultures, they can also serve as references that students will find helpful in their research.

Acuna, Rodolfo. *Occupied America: A History of Chicanos.* 3rd edition. New York: Harper & Row, 1988.

Allen, Paula Gunn. *Spider Woman's Granddaughters.* Boston: Beacon Press, 1989.

——. *Studies in American Indian Literature.* New York: The Modern Language Association of America, 1983.

Austin, Clyde N. *Cross-Cultural Reentry: A Book of Readings.* Abilene, Texas: Abilene Christian University, 1986.

Banks, James A., and Cherry A. McGee Banks, eds. *Multicultural Education: Issues and Perspectives.* Boston: Allyn and Bacon, 1989.

Barnlund, Dean. *Communicative Styles of Japanese and Americans: Images and Realities.* Belmont, California: Wadsworth Publishing Company, 1989.

——. *Public and Private Self in Japan and the United States.* Tokyo, Japan: The Simul Press, 1975.

Batchelder, Donald, and Elizabeth G. Warner, eds. *Beyond Experience: The Experiential Approach to Cross-Cultural Education.* Brattleboro, Vermont: The Experiment Press, 1977.

Bellah, Robert N., et al. *Habits of the Heart: Individualism and Commitment in American Life.* Berkeley: University of California Press, 1985.

Benedict, Ruth. *The Chrysanthemum and the Sword: Patterns of Japanese Culture.* Tokyo, Japan: Charles E. Tuttle Company, 1980 (originally published 1946).

———. *Patterns of Culture.* Boston: Houghton Miflin Company, 1959.

Brooks, Charlotte K., et al., eds. *Tapping Potential: English and Language Arts for the Black Learner.* Urbana, Illinois: National Council of Teachers of English with the Black Caucus of the NCTE, 1985.

Campbell, Joseph. *Oriental Mythology: The Masks of God.* New York: Penguin Books, 1962.

Casse, Pierre. *Training for the Cross-Cultural Mind.* 2nd edition. Washington, D.C.: The Society of Intercultural Training, Education, and Research (SIETAR), 1981.

Chudacoff, Howard P. *How Old Are You? Age Consciousness in American Culture.* Princeton, New Jersey: Princeton University Press, 1989.

Copeland, Lennie, and Lewis Griggs. *Going International.* New York: Random House, 1985.

Davey, William G. *Intercultural Theory and Practice: A Case Method Approach.* Washington, D.C.: SIETAR, 1981.

Di Pietro, Robert, and Edward Ifkovic. *Ethnic Perspectives in American Literature.* New York: MLA, 1983.

Farb, Peter, and George Armelagos. *Consuming Passions: The Anthropology of Eating.* New York: Houghton Miflin Company, 1980.

Fieg, J. P., and J. G. Blair. *There IS a Difference: Seventeen Intercultural Perspectives.* Washington, D.C.: Meridian House International, 1975.

Fishlock, Trevor. *India File.* New Delhi, India: Rupa & Company, 1987.

Furnham, Adrian, and Stephen Bochner. *Culture Shock: Psychological Reactions to Unfamiliar Environments.* New York: Methuen, 1986.

Gandhi, Rajmohan. *Understanding the Muslim Mind.* Albany, New York: State University of New York Press, 1986.

Hall, Edward T. *Beyond Culture.* Garden City, New York: Anchor Books, 1977.

———. *The Silent Language.* Garden City, New York: Anchor Books, 1973.

Harris, Marvin. *The Sacred Cow and the Abominable Pig: Riddles of Food and Culture.* New York: Simon & Schuster, 1985.

Hirsch, E. D., Jr. *Cultural Literacy: What Every American Needs to Know.* New York: Vintage Books, 1988.

Hoopes, David S., and Paul Ventura, eds. *Intercultural Sourcebook.* Washington, D.C.: SIETAR, 1979.

Huizinga, Johan. *Homo Ludens: A Study of the Play Element in Culture.* Boston: The Beacon Press, 1950.

8. Underline phrases, lines, and passages that strike you as you read. How would you describe Dorris's writing style? How would you distinguish the voices of each narrator from the other?
9. What observations do you make here about family relationships? About values and attitudes pertaining to the family? Be specific: Describe particular situations you read as key, then explain the reasons for your analysis.
10. What insights have you gained from this novel—all three stories—as you complete the book?

Study Guide to The Beginning and the End

1. On page 101, Samira's commitment to the "sacred unity of the family" is articulated. In what ways do her children uphold this sacred unity, and in what ways do they seem to make a travesty of the idea?
2. In what ways is this novel the story of the three brothers? What observations and connections would you make about the order of their births and their resulting behavior and values? In what ways do you think your observations are influenced by your own cultural bias?
3. How would you characterize the roles of the women in this book? What parallels do you observe among them and their lives? Why or why not do you think that Nefisa is a central character?
4. What do you learn about the historical and political backgrounds out of which the life in this novel is created? On page 223, Hussein thinks that *"Egypt unmercifully devours its own offspring."* In what ways does the novel validate his observation? In what ways can you argue, as Ramses Awad does in the Introduction, that Mahfouz has devised a "narrative method that would imply criticism of the system without jeopardizing his interests or running the risk of antagonizing the authorities"?
5. The characters in this novel often must make choices influenced and pulled between fear and courage, survival and submission, desire and despair. In what ways does each person's convictions about his, her, or their reputations push them to choose, and why?
6. The past, his personal past, also becomes an immense force, especially for Hassanein, in the ways he responds to people and in the choices he makes. What do you learn about the force of the past from this novel, and why or why not do the truths about it in Hassanein's life apply to yours—in part, a question of cultural patterns again.
7. In concluding his Introduction, Ramses Awad claims that "a gleam of the hope for regeneration penetrates the almost overwhelming gloom of [this] novel," a novel that reflects Mahfouz's "powerfully tragic vision of life." Why or why not do you believe in gleams of hope as you finish the book? In what ways would you agree with Awad that the novel is a "masterpiece of human compassion"?
8. What meanings do you give to the title, and why? In what ways would you characterize Mahfouz's style, and why?